# Socioeconomic and Legal Implications of Electronic Intrusion

Dionysios Politis
*Aristotle University of Thessaloniki, Greece*

Phaedon Kozyris
*Aristotle University of Thessaloniki, Greece*

Ioannis Iglezakis
*Aristotle University of Thessaloniki, Greece*

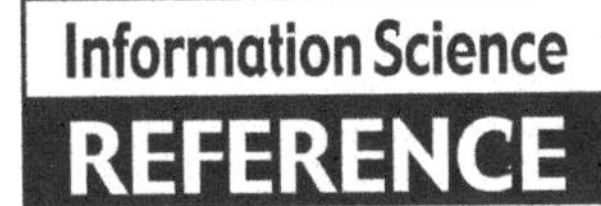


**INFORMATION SCIENCE REFERENCE**
Hershey · New York

Director of Editorial Content: Kristin Klinger
Senior Managing Editor: Jamie Snavely
Managing Editor: Jeff Ash
Assistant Managing Editor: Carole Coulson
Typesetter: Sean Woznicki
Cover Design: Lisa Tosheff
Printed at: Yurchak Printing Inc.

Published in the United States of America by
Information Science Reference (an imprint of IGI Global)
701 E. Chocolate Avenue,
Hershey PA 17033
Tel: 717-533-8845
Fax: 717-533-8661
E-mail: cust@igi-global.com
Web site: http://www.igi-global.com/reference

and in the United Kingdom by
Information Science Reference (an imprint of IGI Global)
3 Henrietta Street
Covent Garden
London WC2E 8LU
Tel: 44 20 7240 0856
Fax: 44 20 7379 0609
Web site: http://www.eurospanbookstore.com



Library of Congress Cataloging-in-Publication Data

Socioeconomic and legal implications of electronic intrusion / Dionysios Politis, Phaedon Kozyris and Ioannis Iglezakis, editors.
p. cm.

Includes bibliographical references and index.
Summary: "This book's goal is to define electronic SPAM and place its legal implications into context for the readers"--Provided by publisher.

ISBN 978-1-60566-204-6 (hardcover) -- ISBN 978-1-60566-205-3 (ebook) 1. Computer crimes--Social aspects. 2. Computer crimes--Law and legislation. 3. Computer networks--Security measures. 4. Consumer protection. 5. SPAM (Electronic mail)--Law and legislation. 6. Privacy, Right of. 7. Identity theft. I. Politis, Dionysios. II. Kozyris, Phaedon J. (Phaedon John) III. Iglezakis, Ioannis, 1965-
HV6773.S635 2009
364.16'8--dc22

2008043297

British Cataloguing in Publication Data
A Cataloguing in Publication record for this book is available from the British Library.

## Editorial Advisory Board



## List of Reviewers

# Table of Contents

# Detailed Table of Contents

**Preface** ............................................................ xiv

**Acknowledgment** ............................................................ xix

**Section I**
**The Social and Economic Dynamic for Electronic Crime**

**Chapter I**
The Socioeconomic Background of Electronic Crime ............................................................ 1
*Maria Karyda, University of the Aegean, Greece*

This chapter discusses current and emerging forms of network and computer-related illegality (electronic crime), its background, the motives driving individuals to such actions as well as strategies and techniques for controlling it. The chapter places emphasis on current and future trends and highlights the open issues that need to be addressed to tackle this phenomenon.

**Chapter II**
Intrusion in the Sphere of Personal Communications ............................................................ 25
*Judith Rauhofer, University of Central Lancashire, UK*

In this chapter the limits for the sphere of personal communications are set. Different understandings of the "right to be alone" or "the right to respect for private and family life" are provided. The significance of the information privacy is pointed out and the right to informational self-determinationis is deciphered. Having presented the substrate for personal data protection, a legal synopsis of the aforementioned subject is the concluding part of the chapter, with emphasis on data retention.

**Chapter III**
Criminal Sanctions Against Electronic Intrusion ............................................................ 47
*Irini E. Vassilaki, University of Goettingen, Germany*

The international dimension of intrusion is discussed in this chapter along with the different legislative approaches adopted by various countries leading to the development of computer specific-legislation concerning electronic intrusion in a rather homogeneous style approach. The integrity of information

and computer systems is presented and the misuse of devices, the illegal interception of data transfer and the illegal access to computer systems are bounded so to demonstrate the responsibility of providers or users.



In this chapter, a specific issue is addressed that concerns the protection of privacy vis-à-vis the efforts to combat identity theft and protect personal identifying information. There are, in particular, measures undertaken by legislators that involve penal sanctions and the introduction of new technological means for identity verification. Also, identity management schemes are introduced, which are utilized by service providers, mainly in the e-business sector, in order to support controlled access to resources. The solutions undertaken to protect identity are seen as measures enhancing privacy, which is endangered by identity theft. Personal information is largely available in the information society and its collection by identity fraudsters is also possible. Therefore, an effective protection of information protection should also include the protection of identity. The downside of the identity protection approach is that identity management actually presents risks to privacy, since the processing of personal data takes place in this context and it is argued that there are certain implications concerning the lawfulness of the processing. The use of electronic authentication through electronic cards or biometrics on passports and identity cards pose privacy issues, too. Subsequently, the legislation concerning identity theft and identity related crime is outlined. This is followed by specific analysis of privacy issues concerning identity management and identity verification methods, with particular reference to biometrics.



This chapter explores privacy issues posed by the use of RFID systems and applications. The existing legal framework for data protection is analyzed in order to discover how general privacy safeguarding principles could be applied in the case of RFIDs, with special focus on the main areas which are going to experience widespread use of such applications. The structure of the paper is based on a chronological order which follows the consecutive phases of contact and interaction between the individual and the RFID tag. The incorporation of a tag to a product or in the human body establishes the first point of contact of the individual with the RFID tag. This is the first part of the chapter. The symbiosis of the person with the tag is examined in the second part. Indeed, privacy concerns are equally significant during the phase of processing of personal information, even if processing is conducted lawfully, either based on the legal ground of the individual's consent or justified on another legal basis. Finally, the last part examines the legal regime of separation between the person and the tag.

A marketeer's point of view is presented in this chapter. Although legal restrictions safeguard processes and restrict annoying intrusive techniques, protecting customers, it can be argued that responsible privacy practices in the marketing profession will add value for consumers. As businesses compete with greater intensity to provide the customer with control over areas such as product offerings, services provided, and account management, privacy standards, being an important part of the customer-company relationship, formulate the grounds upon which businesses compete to provide greater customer control.



This chapter gives an interpretation of why the Internet seems to be an unfriendly place for privacy using terms of political science. The authors present the conflict between transparency of information and the protection of privacy. The technological texture poses old threats in new clothes, and overall, the loss of control over our personal information, the surveillance, and the disclosure of our private facts are disruptions and infringements upon our privacy in the new information age. Guaranteeing transparency and access to information are presuppositions of a democratic society; however, the threats that the Internet is posing to privacy are affecting the autonomy and freedom of the individual. The need for "reconceptualizing" privacy in the Internet, confirms the evolving, developing character of the right, whose substantial content is not given or static but is closely connected and constructed via societal change. The chapter explores the technological threats that the right to privacy confronts in the Internet, such as "cookies", "spam messages", the dangers they pose to the freedom and autonomy of the individual as well as the positive dimensions of the Internet, especially its role in democratic accountability and political dialog.



The ordinary and uncomplicated Spam menace is made possible by technological advances which enable the sender to dispatch millions if not billions of commercial messages without significant monetary cost and without wasting time. The present review will focus on fundamentals, exploring what has already been done and suggesting avenues of improvement. The chapter promotes basic approaches of handling Spam depending on the actions and choices of the receiver. The anti-Spam campaign needs effective enforcement powers and should be able to use all available technological know-how. As the vagaries of enforcement are presented, the role of the Internet Service Providers and advertisers is envisaged.

## Section II
## Electronic Intrusion: Technologies, Strategies and Methodologies



This chapter presents one of the most interesting and controversial legal developments in the United States having to do with the acceptance by some courts of a new modification to an old common law property interest. Under the theory of cyberproperty, the owners of computer chattels have been granted the right to prohibit non-damaging contact with their systems. Essentially, cyberproperty amounts to a right to "exclude others from network-connected resources." For a better comprehension, the right is analogized to the right to exclude others from real property.



Targeting information technology resources has marked a growing trend for all sorts of reasons that include, profit making, causing damage, carrying out espionage, exploiting human beings etc. Although information security is used to protect information assets, electronic crime remains firmly on the rise. Computer forensics is the analysis of data processing equipment such as a data carrier, a network and so forth, to determine whether that equipment has been used for illegal or unauthorised purposes. Establishing the chain of custody through appropriate policy frameworks can be used in order to assess the quality of the collected data. Policy for forensics may address the practices of forensics agents and labs in investigating cybercrime. This chapter concludes that full-scale harmonisation of policies on criminal law and legal processes is likely to only happen at regional level (e.g. the EU) rather than at a global scale. Along with the assumption that safe havens where criminals operate from are not likely to be suppressed any time soon, leads to the conclusion that cyber-crime is here to stay for the long run in spite of the good efforts made to trail digital suspects through digital forensics.



Enterprise Architecture has had a resurgence of interest in the IT community in the past ten year; in part because of a mandate for federal agencies of the United States government and in part because of the complexity of managing today's information systems environments. It has become a critical component of an overall IT governance program to provide structure and documentation to describe the business processes, information flows, technical infrastructure and organizational management of an information technology organization. Many different enterprise architecture frameworks have emerged over the past ten years. Two of the most widely used enterprise architecture frameworks (the Zachman Framework

In this chapter data-mining techniques are presented that can be used to create data-profiles of individuals from anonymous data that can be found freely and abundantly in open environments, such as the Internet. Although such information takes in most cases the form of an approximation and not of a factual and solid representation of concrete personal data, nevertheless it takes advantage of the vast increase in the amount of data recorded by database management systems as well as by a number of archiving applications and repositories of multimedia files.

**Chapter XV**
Surveillance of Employees' Electronic Communications in the Workplace: An Employers' Right to Spy or an Invasion to Privacy? ............................................................ 246
*Ioannis Iglezakis, Aristotle University of Thessaloniki, Greece*

The use of Information and Communication Technologies in the workplace is constantly increasing, but also the use of surveillance technology. Electronic monitoring of employees becomes an integral part of information systems in the workplace. The specific software which is used for monitoring electronic communications is, however, intrusive and infringes upon the employees' right to privacy. The issue of surveillance of employees' electronic communications is subject to different approaches in various jurisdictions. The most comprehensive protection to employees is afforded in the EU, however, there are still ambiguities concerning the balancing of interests between employers and employees.

**Section III**
**The Forensic Challenges for Intrusion**

**Chapter XVI**
Forensic Watermarking for Secure Multimedia Distribution ............................................................ 261
*Farook Sattar, Nanyang Technological University, Singapore*
*Dan Yu, Hewlett-Packard, Shanghai, China*

This chapter discusses on forensic tracking through digital watermarking for secure multimedia distribution. The existing watermarking schemes are elaborated and their assumptions as well as limitations for tracking are discussed. Especially, an Independent Component Analysis (ICA) based watermarking scheme is presented, which overcomes the problems of the existing watermarking schemes. Multiple watermarking techniques are used where one watermark is used for ownership verification and the other one is used to identify the legal user of the distributed content. In the absence of a priori information, i.e. the original data, original watermark, embedding locations as well as the strength, our ICA technique provides efficient watermark extraction scheme with the help of side information. The robustness against common signal processing attacks are presented. Lastly, the challenges in the forensic tracking through digital watermarking techniques are discussed.

**Chapter XVII**
Spam and Advertisement: Proposing a Model for Charging Intrusion ............................................................ 281
*Dionysios Politis, Aristotle University of Thessaloniki, Greece*

An issue factually challenging the peer-to-peer nature of the Internet is the increase of spam trafficking. Having reached record levels the last years, it raised consciousness that Internet communication was endangered by an erosive threat similar to the uncontrollable, massive free circulation of MP3s that devastated the musical industry. Recent combined advances in the software industry and in the legal front have reduced the phenomenon. The technical, social, financial and legal parameters of this campaign are examined in this chapter under the prism of a networked economy. A mathematical model is proposed for charging spam based on advertisement standards and weights.

**Chapter XVIII**
European E-Signatures Solutions on the Basis of PKI Authentication Technology .......................... 290
*Ioannis P. Chochliouros, Hellenic Telecommunications Organization S.A. (OTE), Greece*
*Anastasia S. Spiliopoulou, Athens Bar Association, Greece*
*Stergios P. Chochliouros, Independent Consultant, Greece*
*Konstantinos N. Voudouris, Technological Educational Institute of Athens, Greece*

This chapter presents systems of certification authorities and registration authorities and other supporting servers and agents that perform certificate management, archive management, key management, and token management functions. These activities that support security policy by monitoring and controlling security services, elements and mechanisms, distributing security information, and reporting security events are examined with the main focus on PKI authentication technology.

**Chapter XIX**
Security of Alternative Delivery Channels in Banking: Issues and Countermeasures ...................... 305
*Manish Gupta, State University of New York, USA*
*H. Raghav Rao, State University of New York, USA*
*Shambhu Upadhyaya, State University of New York, USA*

To sustain competitive advantages, financial institutions continuously strive to innovate and offer new banking channels to their customers as technology creates new dimensions to their banking systems. One of the most popular such diversification of channel is electronic banking (e-banking). Information assurance is a key component in e-banking services. This chapter investigates the information assurance issues and tenets of e-banking security that would be needed for design, development and assessment of an adequate electronic security infrastructure. The technology terminology and frameworks presented in the paper are with the view to equip the reader with a glimpse of the state-of-art technologies that may help towards learned and better decisions regarding electronic security.

**Compilation of References** ........................................................................................................ 328

**About the Contributors** ............................................................................................................ 357

**Index** ........................................................................................................................................ 364

# Preface

## INTRUSION INTO PRIVACY AND INTO INFORMATION SYSTEMS

In our network connected society, intrusion becomes a new form of trespassing, one which quite often leads to significant problems and poses great risks for the individual and for businesses, which are increasingly relying on modern information systems. The main appearances of intrusion, in the Information Society, are those concerning privacy intrusion and intrusion into information systems.

In particular, privacy intrusion is the act of intruding the personal sphere of the individual, which may involve the illicit collection and processing of personal data, the use of intrusive equipment, such as video cameras and key-loggers, but also of more sophisticated technologies, for example RFIDs. In the post 9/11 era, privacy poses as a negotiable good that can be compromised to preserve public security. Thus, surveillance poses as necessary measure in view of the threat of terrorism and organized crime.

Further, intrusion into a computer system can take many forms. We could note attempts at accessing and manipulating of information systems that can compromise the security and trust of such systems, which fall within the realm of e-crime. E-crime is undoubtedly one of the major challenges for the future of law enforcement. As information and communications technology (ICT) becomes more pervasive, the various kinds of electronic crime will be protagonists in all forms of criminal behavior.

The following means may be used for committing the act: electronic communications and transactions, spread of information via the Internet, falsification of physical characteristics and eventually ID theft.

The e-crime types may be categorized into four main groups (see Janczewski and Colaric, 2007):

- **Computer "threats", ranging from hacking to cracking:** Including viruses, worms, or spyware.
- **Offensive, intrusive or misleading material:** Communicated through a Web page, in e-mails, or over mobile phones.
- **Fraud:** Economic transactions via computer believed to have involved fraud.
- **Identity theft or personal data violation:** The use of credit cards for theft, and the use of confidential personal information.

The rapid growth of ICT over the last few decades has opened up new possibilities for governments and individuals. Governments are increasingly using Wide Area Networks, the Internet, and mobile computing in their daily interactions with citizens and businesses. E-government applications are facilitating interaction with businesses by centralizing information sources into topical gateways, using Web-based expert tools to help businesses access rules and regulations, and developing applications to allow electronic tax filings. For citizens, transactions, such as renewing licenses and certifications, paying taxes, and applying for benefits, have become less time consuming and easier to carry out.

Apart from government services, ICT has been also utilized in other sectors such as health, commerce, and of course, education. The increased use of ICT has actually been the motivating force for e-commerce.

E-technology allows organizations to deliver more services, more quickly, and directly. As a result, citizens do not interact with the government but also between them as peers promoting the e-commerce models they use (Papazoglou and Ribbers, 2006). These models may be P2P or B2B[1].

## THE TECHNOLOGICAL, SOCIAL AND ECONOMIC POTENTIAL OF INTRUSION

E-crimes are usually committed for personal financial interest, whether they be theft and misuse of ID numbers or other personal information and data, for their benefit in ways that cause damage to the real owners of the data. It can be done through counterfeiting credit cards and using information and credit cards to order goods through the Internet, or cheating others to send personal data to them. These practices are committed through e-mail to mislead receivers that the e-mail is from an office or a reputable organization, such as banks or financial institutions.

Using sophisticated computer hacking techniques, criminals can violate security systems and install programs that may gather enormous quantities of personal financial data. As a consequence, widespread losses are caused to banks, retailers, and consumers.

The new dimension in this socio-economic phenomenon is its global perspective. National legislation protecting our personal data seems ineffective since the Internet has no borders or limitations. In the end, the easy and largely anonymous access, the unique speed, the flow rate of the Internet, as well as its ability to process information over an infinitesimal amount of time, pose new challenges for the protection of our informational privacy, of our virtual goods, of our cyber property, and eventually, of our personality. Indeed, our legitimate use of the Internet leaves behind countless tracks and enables the miscreants to form and misuse our personal profile.

Since the emergence of Web 2.0, the new trend on the Internet invites users not as passive receivers of information, but as creators, or at least as gatherers and redistributors of media rich in content. User-created content is the core means of development for this new era and is expressed through blogs, Wikis, photo collections, music, and even videos online. Small, interconnected tools allow anyone to have his own place on the Web, through which one can demonstrate creative skills in writing, photography, film making and much more. Creating and sharing digital resources is becoming easier (Zeng et al., 2006). In synoptic terms, information has become a primary product of our society. As a result, a shared culture emerges throughout the Internet, based on co-ownership and co-management of collective knowledge – or at least of collective "taste".

An international culture of dealing online has been established. The creative and productive incorporation of new technologies across all frames and levels of our socio-economic environment constitutes indeed a promising frontier; however, up to now, it has not avoided multitudinous abuse.

## REGULATING THE BATTLEFIELD: THE LEGAL LIMITATIONS

Legal regulations of privacy seem necessary in order to protect informational privacy. As new risks for privacy are emerging with new technologies, specific provisions need to be addressed, in order to tackle with the new realities. However, law should not impose solutions that hinder innovative technologies, but rather reconcile the right to privacy with the rights of others and technological progress.

Furthermore, securing computers, networks and mobile devices against the increasing complexity or malware and cyber threats requires commitment, vigilance and uncompromising reliability. Technical measures ensuring the highest levels of permanent ICT security apply a defensive mechanism aiming to mitigate the risks from online threats and phishing attacks, which are constantly increasing in both volume and complexity. However, the attacks of a determined offender and available opportunities to act illegally (in other words, the presence of a suitable target), and the absence of a capable guardian or someone who might prevent the crime from being committed are phenomena seen in daily transactions with an alarming frequency. Although motivations for acting illegally may well have remained fairly constant over time, developments in computing and communications technologies have created many new opportunities for people to act illegally. At the same time, the computer security industry has increased its capacity as "electronic capable guardians".

Nevertheless, the globalization of the scene has given the opportunity to the world wide on-line community (estimated around the $1/5^{th}$ of this planet's population) to participate in cross-border transactions. There, the intentional commission of an act usually deemed socially harmful or dangerous is not always specifically defined or clearly excluded. This vulnerable situation where many things are not allowed but yet not specifically prohibited or punished, fuels, unfortunately, the boost of electronic criminality in its global perspective.

Crimes are classified by most legal systems for purposes such as determining which court has authority to deal with the case and what law to apply. In international law terms this is projected primarily as a jurisdictional issue. In addition, social changes often result in the adoption of new criminal laws and the obsolescence of older ones. The on-line community, at the same sense, explores prevailing theories of criminal activity, the conduct of all stages of criminal proceedings, and the various theories and practices for punishing electronic crime in its global manifestations.

The motivation, the formation and the impact of electronic crime on the social, economic and judicial sectors are presented in this book as a network of well connected factors. These factors that influence the roadmap to a homogenized confrontation of electronic crime are seen in Figure 1 (Politis et al, 2008).

## ORGANIZATION OF THE BOOK

This book is organized in 19 chapters clustered in 3 sections. A brief description of each of the 19 chapters can be found in the detailed table of contents.

Section I, titled "*The Social and Economic Dynamic for Eletronic Crime*" is comprised of eight chapters. In this section, background information is given about the factors that encourage and promote electronic crime.

Section II, titled "*Electronic Intrusion: Technologies, Strategies and Methodologies*" describes spearhead technologies that form the main context of the electronic crime literature. In this section, a more technical language is used to promote understanding of the scientific bias for illegal transactions.

*Figure 1. Primary and secondary factors influencing the social and economic background of electronic crime*

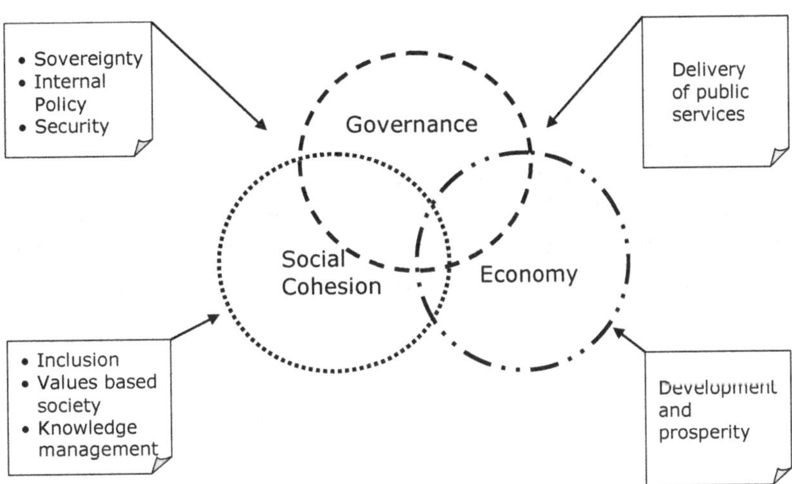


The legal texts of this section address the implications of electronic crime for commercial, contract and criminal law, with concerns for the homogeneity of law enforcement in cross border situations and other jurisdictional matters.

Section III is titled "*The Forensic Challenges for Intrusion*." Forensic engineering generally is defined as the investigation of questions, events and conditions having possible legal ramifications through the application of engineering principles and methodologies. Since litigation necessitates the use of expert testimony often involving highly technical issues, the expert is responsible for explaining highly technical subject matters in an understandable and sincere manner. Facts must be separated from speculation and the likely from the unlikely.

Comprising four highly technical chapters, it provides in-depth analysis of four distinct domains that are actively present in our everyday on-line habitat:

- Secure multimedia distribution
- Unsolicited electronic communication
- Electronic signature based authentication using public key infrastructures
- Security in e-banking transactions.

## REFERENCES

Janczewski, L. J., & Colaric A. M. (2007). *Cyber Warfare and Cyber Terrorism*. Hershey/New York: Information Science Reference.

Papazoglou, M. P., & Ribbers, P. (2006). *E-Business – organizational and technical foundations*. Chichester: Wiley.

Politis, D., Donos, G., Christou, G., Giannakopoulos, P., Papanagiotou-Leza, A. (2008). Implementing E-Justice on a National Scale: Coping with Balkanization and Socio-Economical Divergence. *Journal of Cases on Information Technology, 10*(2), 41-59.

Zeng, W., Yu, H., & Lin, C. Y. (2006). *Multimedia Security Technologies for Digital Rights Management*. Amsterdam: Academic Press.

## ENDNOTE

1 P2P stands for Peer to Peer, and collectively means any form of communication between two or more usual on-line users, in a globalized environment, in contradistinction to the centralized client-server transaction model. B2B signals the conceptual model for Business to Business communique, as an enhancement of the previous model for everyday e-Business transactions.

# Acknowledgment

This book would not be possible if the editors did not enjoy the entire support of the publisher, IGI Global. A chain of helpful consultants, whose last link was Ms. Julia Mosemann, walked with us the 18 month long bumpy way of forming the unstructured incoming material of interrelated articles to a reasonable thematic concatenation. For the history of the book, the first link was Dr. Mehdi Khosrow-Pour, whose enthusiasm and constructive suggestions formed the editing team and shaped the focus of the project.

Last, but not least, we would like to thank all the contributors of this book, who have contributed in our research focusing on privacy and information security.

In closing, we wish to express our deep appreciation to our families, to whom this book is devoted to, for providing us the needed inspirational resources to balance our careers and family trajectories.

*Dionysios Politis*
*Phaedon Kozyris*
*Ioannis Iglezakis*

*Thessaloniki, Greece*
*October 2008*

# Section I
# The Social and Economic Dynamic for Electronic Crime

# Chapter I
# The Socioeconomic Background of Electronic Crime

**Maria Karyda**
*University of the Aegean, Greece*

## ABSTRACT

*This chapter discusses current and emerging forms of network and computer-related illegality (electronic crime), its background, the motives driving individuals to such actions as well as strategies and techniques for controlling it. The chapter places emphasis on current and future trends and highlights the open issues that need to be addressed to tackle this phenomenon.*

## INTRODUCTION

The presence of Information and Communication Technologies (ICTs) in modern societies is pervasive and affects all aspects of the economic, social, political and private life of individuals. Commerce, financial functions (including banking, stock exchanges), air traffic control, communications, electric power management and energy distribution, communications, transportation, healthcare services, education and other critical activities are largely dependent on ICTs. Companies use information technology and networks for effective organization, in order to implement their business processes and to improve communication with business partners and consumers. In the United Kingdom, for instance, nearly all companies use the Internet; 97% of companies have an Internet connection, 81% have a Web site, with 89% of these being externally hosted. Moreover, their dependence on information and communication technologies is considered very high, since only one out of six small-sized UK companies could operate without use of information technology (DTI, 2006).

Governments and public authorities depend more and more on technology to improve the quality of public services provided to their citizens, to cut down on exceeding costs while achieving value for money for services provided, to improve the efficiency and effectiveness of public organizations, to reduce "red tape" and to align and better coordinate public administration, while individuals use technology in a wide range of their everyday lives for their professional (e.g. teleworking, collaborating, designing and manufacturing) and personal (e.g. education, entertainment, communication) lives.

Electronic crime (e-crime), or computer crime, or cyber crime refers to criminal activities where a computer or network is the source, tool, target, or place of a crime and is generally defined as a criminal activity involving an information technology infrastructure. Electronic crimes differ from traditional crimes, as we know them, mainly with regard to the location of the offender in relation to the scene of the crime: individuals now can commit an illegal act hundreds of miles away from their location, for instance hackers penetrating the computer system of a company in another country. Moreover, detection of electronic crime is often more difficult, since nothing may by physically missing as, for example, in cases of information theft or unauthorized access to computers and networks. E-crime affects all types of organizations (public, private etc.), as well as individuals, governments and public authorities with a wide range of consequences.

Generally, individuals' concerns about the security of information and communication infrastructures and the possibility to fall victims of some type of electronic crime are found to be very high. It is estimated, for example, that as high as 70% to 80% of European and US citizens have strong concerns over the privacy and security of their personal data. These concerns have a negative impact on the development of e-business and especially on client-oriented business functions (Business-to-Consumer). For instance, in a recent survey conducted for the European Commission about two thirds of the 11.832 individuals who participated, reported that they have been prevented from buying online or using on-line banking services because of security and privacy related concerns (Rand Europe, 2003). The same survey identified that a lack of trust and confidence in electronic services is a significant barrier to the development of e-Government. Businesses share, to some extent, the same concerns, since the protection of a company's information infrastructure is crucial for building customers' trust and for its overall operation and good reputation in general.

There are several aspects of electronic crime that remain underspecified; this chapter aims to provide an analysis of different aspects of electronic crimes and identify critical issues which are now rising as well as those that will evolve in the future. The first issue analyzed refers to the impact information and communication technologies have on crime. Then, the nature and different types of electronic crime are explored, by studying the different definitions, approaches and classifications found in the literature, in order to better understand and tackle it. Furthermore, the sources of electronic crime and different motives and characteristics of offenders are identified. We also discuss the impact electronic crime has on businesses and individuals and identify current and future trends. Finally, the chapter elaborates on the different approaches for controlling e-crimes.

## INFORMATION AND COMMUNICATION TECHNOLOGIES AND CRIME

### The Impact of ICTs: Old Crimes in New Bottles?

From the criminology point of view (Theoharidou et al, 2005) electronic crime can be understood as a matter of opportunities, based on the assumption that 'crime follows opportunity'. It is also widely acknowledged that the variety and volume of opportunities provided by information and communication technologies for electronic crime are proliferating. However, crimes usually need motivated offenders and a lack of adequate 'guardianship' to take place. Thus, to explore and comprehend the role of information and communication technologies with regard to crime, one must explore the opportunities provided by the technology, the motives and characteristics of individuals involved and the strategies and means used to control this threat.

To begin with, information technology has a 'democratic' nature, meaning that anyone can use it, as long as one possesses a minimum level of knowledge. The accessibility and user-friendliness of information and communication infrastructure provide users with a wide reach; despite the fact that the digital gap that is still present, worldwide penetration was estimated at about 21.1% for March 2008[1], access to Internet and ICTs is generally easy and costs relatively cheap. For instance, the Internet provides individuals seeking the widest possible visibility to promote their ideas (such as hactivists, vandals, or even terrorists) new opportunities to expand their reach. It has also been argued that the non-confrontational, impersonal and often anonymous nature of Internet communications has the potential to remove disincentives for committing offensive actions, such as cyber stalking.

Moreover, the exponential growth of connectivity creates more opportunities for prospective offenders and raises risks for prospective victims. A big part of business, financial, government and individual activities is now realized on-line, and great volumes of personal data records (including financial and other personal information) are also accessible online, thus providing new opportunities for prospective offenders to exploit them. Examples of areas of increased opportunities for criminals include the networking of financial and banking systems and the increased use of ICTs in business functions (both internally and at interorganization level, such as chain management and collaborative commerce information systems). It has been argued that it is especially white-collar crime that benefits from the advent of technology, since white collar offenders usually have both the technical knowledge and access to technical means (Savona & Mignone, 2004).

Prospective offenders exploit information and communication technologies not only by exploiting the new opportunities created, but also by using them for communicating and collecting information, for reducing the chances of being caught (e.g. by using cryptography and steganography techniques to communicate anonymously or via covert channels), for organizing their activities and for committing new types of crimes that wouldn't have been possible without technology. Offenders also make use of the possibility to stay anonymous or hide their trail, since a wide range of encryption techniques are available to users of ICTs, in order to protect the content of their communications, their identity as well as the fact that a communication is taking place. In other cases offenders use information and communication technologies and the Internet to communicate and facilitate the organization of illegal activities such as gambling, money laundering, child pornography, drug trafficking, weapons trade and so on (Grabosky, 2000).

Technology provides also the opportunity to reproduce and disseminate digital material (information, graphics, pictures, sound and any multimedia combination) without the need to possess sophisticated equipment, easily and at very low cost. This possibility makes copyright protected material easy to copy and redistribute by users. Moreover, networks and operating systems are becoming more complicated; malware developers seem to be following up with this trend and have been developing and trying out various components that, as they are combined, will create attacks that are more dangerous and more difficult to detect (CSI, 2007).

Due to its nature and the way it has been originally designed and implemented, the Internet is an intrinsically insecure network of networks. Linking now more than 300 million computers and an estimated number of 1,407,724,920 users worldwide (March 2008)[2], its architecture was designed to operate within an environment of trust and did not incorporate any security technologies. Ubiquitous connectivity has, on the one hand, generated new area activities for businesses and individuals, increased productivity, and provided new opportunities for communication, education, collaborative science and entertainment; on the other hand, however, it has created a large number of new vulnerabilities. For instance, the Computer Emergency Response Team Coordination Center (CERT/CC) at Carnegie Mellon University reports that 3,780 new electronic vulnerabilities were published in 2004, which is more than a 20-fold increase from the number of threats identified in 1995 (President's Information Technology Advisory Committee, 2005). For instance, in the first half of 2004, the average time between the public disclosure of a vulnerability and the release of an associated exploit was 5.8 days. This is a time period substantially reduced from the period of a few months estimated in prior years as published in the Symantec Security threat report[3]. It is also worth noting that electronic crime detection, investigation and prosecution processes are still at early stages of development; though digital forensics as a practice and discipline counts several years, its methods, practices and tools, as well as the necessary legal background are still evolving (Karyda & Mitrou, 2007).

Networking elevates the need for proximity (Brenner, 2004) and provides criminals with a potential of global reach without time constraints. Information and communication technologies make it possible for 'remote offenders' to be physically located in one place and cause damage to organizations and individuals located in distant places. Even worse, the global nature of networks and the Internet provides prospective offenders with the possibility to commit crimes that affect businesses and individuals in other countries, which raises significant constraints to the efforts of detecting, investigating and prosecuting offenders (Grabosky, 2000). Criminals exploit the lack of central management and the multi-jurisdiction on the Internet, for instance by locating their activities in countries with no relevant legal framework. This has also to do with the fact that it is not clear who is responsible for taking preventive measures to protect prospective victims. Since there is no central management or common legal framework, an individual user, for example, has to protect her personal data, which is stored on a computer or mobile device running commercial software, and that is connected to the Internet via an ISP provider, from offenders who are located in a country that has no computer-related legislation.

Conclusively, information and communication technologies have expanded the area of opportunities to commit a crime and, at the same time, they have formed a new environment where new types of behavior and activities can take place. Offenders exploit ICTs finding new ways to act, new possibilities (chances to exploit), and ways to avoid detection and not being caught. Under this perspective, technology can be the *object* of crime, when it forms the environment in which the crime is planned and committed (Savona & Mignone, 2004) or it can be the *subject* of crime, as for example, in cases where ICT is the target of crime, e.g. in case of denial of service attacks against a company's information and communication infrastructure. In other cases, technology serves as the *means* to commit a crime. In these cases networks and computers are used as tools to commit offences which are not new at all, as for example in the case of a person hacking into the computer system of a bank to transfer funds to his own accounts, or sending threatening emails (E-Crime Watch Survey, 2006). Finally, the use of ICTs in a criminal activity may also be *symbolic*, as for example, when they are used for intimidation or deception (Savona & Mignone, 2004).

Thus, it is not only "old crimes in new bottles" that need to be addressed, but also new types of what can be characterized as "illegal activities" in cyberspace. To address electronic crime in all its forms, technological systems, legal systems, law enforcement, and investigation procedures need to adapt accordingly, as will be discussed later in this chapter.

## Defining Electronic Crime

A broad definition commonly used, describes electronic crimes as illegal acts conducted using a computer or other form of electronic media (E-Crime Watch Survey, 2006). *Cybercrime* is another term commonly used in conjunction with electronic crime. According to the most common definition, a cyber crime is any crime committed over a computer network. For the European Union[4] the terms "computer crime," "computer-related crime," "high-tech crime" and "cybercrime" share the same meaning in that they describe: a) the use of information and communication networks that are free from geographical constraints and b) the circulation of intangible and volatile data.

The term *security incident* is often found in relative literature and is commonly used in surveys to describe events that involve security violations, such as the violation of security policies, laws, jurisdictions, etc. The main difference between electronic crimes and security incidents is that the latter may be caused on purpose or by accident, whereas committing an e-crime involves intention. Finally, *information warfare* is a term that is often related to cybercrime, since it refers to illicit activities using the same types of skills, knowledge and means that are used in electronic crimes. However, in the case of information warfare (or cyber warfare) these activities are war related and aim against the communications and computer infrastructure of governments or large organizations.

According to the approach adopted by the European Convention on Cybercrime (Council of Europe, 2001), which was signed in 2001, electronic crime or cybercrime are any actions that are *"directed against the confidentiality, integrity and availability of computer systems, networks and computer data as well as the misuse of such systems, networks and data by providing for the criminalization of such conduct*". More specifically, the European Convention classifies cybercrime into the following categories:

1. Offences against the confidentiality, integrity and availability of computer data and systems: This category includes action involving illegal access, illegal interception, data interference, system interference and misuse of devices.
2. Computer-related offences that includes computer-related forgery and fraud.
3. Content-related offences, referring to offences related to child pornography.
4. Offences related to infringements of copyright and related rights.

The European Convention on Cybercrime was enforced on 2004 and, apart from European Union member states it has also been signed by a number of states outside Europe, including the U.S., Canada and Japan. Besides providing a classification of cybercrime, the European Convention also contains provisions with regard to search and seizure of stored data, collection and interception of traffic data. Another important aspect of the European Convention on Cybercrime is that it places emphasis on the cooperation of law enforcement bodies in different countries, in cases where offenders are subject to different jurisdictions, by including provisions and principles on international co-operation and mutual assistance. It should be noted, however, that the Convention on Cybercrime does not cover all Internet-based criminal activities.

The U.S. Department of Justice, on the other hand, distinguishes cybercrime into two broad categories[5]:

a. **Computer and Internet related crime:** Including computer intrusion (hacking, for example), password trafficking, counterfeiting of currency, child pornography or exploitation, Internet fraud, spam, Internet harassment, Internet bomb threats and trafficking in explosive or incendiary devices or firearms over the Internet; and

b. **Intellectual Property crime:** Including copyright piracy, trademark counterfeiting and theft of trade secrets.

According to another classification (Carter, 1995), electronic crimes are categorized into crimes where 'the computer is the target', such as, for example, vandalism, trespassing, and information theft, crimes where the computer is 'the instrumentality of the crime' and offenders intervene with computer systems and processes to alter their primary licit use to something illicit. This type of crime refers to fraud and financial information theft (e.g. of credit card numbers). The third type of electronic crime in this classification refers to crimes where computers are 'incidental to other crimes', meaning that in these cases computers are used to facilitate the offender and that their use is not essential for committing the crime (e.g. money laundering). The last category refers to crimes which are directly 'associated with the prevalence of computers', including software piracy, copyright violation, and software and hardware counterfeiting.

According to the Communication of the Commission to the Council and the European Parliament for fighting against cybercrime, the main computer-related offences concern the following categories[6]:

1. **Privacy offences:** Illegal collection, storage, modification, disclosure or dissemination of personal data;
2. **Content-related offences:** The dissemination of pornography, in particular child pornography, racist statements and information inciting violence;
3. **Economic crimes, unauthorized access and sabotage:** Offences relating to unauthorized access to systems (e.g. hacking, computer sabotage and distribution of viruses, computer espionage, computer forgery, and computer fraud);
4. **Intellectual property offences:** Violations of the legal protection of computer programs and databases, copyright and related rights.

Finally, according to another approach[7], cybercrime legislation classifies related offences to the following categories: *illegal access* to the whole or any part of a computer system, *illegal interception* of non-public transmissions of computer data to, from or within a computer system performed by technical means, *data interference*, referring to the damaging, deletion, deterioration, alteration or suppression of computer data without right, *system interference*, referring to hindering without right of the functioning of a computer system by inputting, transmitting, damaging, deleting, deteriorating, altering or suppressing computer data, *misuse of devices*, *forgery* and *fraud*. To this list, child pornography and copyright infringements are usually added.

It is easy to conclude that there is no unified approach as to how an electronic crime is defined. Not only because different definitions are used by different jurisdictions, but also because the legal approach to defining cybercrime differs significantly from the technical perspective.

From a legal perspective, electronic crimes are commonly categorized using the traditional empirically-derived categories of 'crimes against persons', 'crimes against property', 'crimes against morality', 'crimes against the state' (Brenner, 2001), 'crimes against public interest and order' etc. and are more general in nature, so as to accommodate a wide range of possible offences (Savona & Mignone, 2004). The technical approach, on the other hand, focuses mainly on issues such as the techniques and tools used by offenders and the vulnerabilities exploited and the nature of offence committed, thus providing a wide range of types of electronic crimes, as will be described in the following of this chapter. This makes defining and reaching a common agreement with regard to evaluating and addressing electronic crime a difficult and complicated task.

## Types of Electronic Crime

Organizations, individuals and governments are facing a wide range of perspective electronic crimes, including, among others, hacking, denial of service attacks, sabotage, web site defacements, unauthorized access to computers, networks and information, dissemination of malicious code such as computer viruses, worms and Trojan horses, dissemination of offensive material, stalking, phishing, information forgery, financial fraud such as cyber-embezzlement, cyber fraud, electronic money laundering and tax evasion, identity theft, theft of confidential information, intellectual property infringement, electronic vandalism and terrorism and communications' interception, to name a few.

According to the survey conducted for the European Commission among businesses with online presence in seven European Union member states (Rand Europe, 2003), 27.5% of surveyed organizations were affected by security breaches, including unauthorized use and attacks to their information infrastructures. The vast majority of these companies (over 90%) named the infection by computer viruses as the most frequent type of security breach they suffered. Among other incidents reported, unauthorized access to their internal networks were less frequent (about 15%), identity theft (about 8%) and online fraud incidents were approximately 5%. The consequences of these incidents were reported as 'very' or 'rather' severe in 41% of the times.

For UK businesses virus infections comprise as much as 50% of the worst security incidents faced by them; 9% concerned unauthorized access to company's systems by outsiders, 2% concerned theft or unauthorized disclosure of confidential information, 2% of incidents were related to fraud or computer-related fraud, and 1% were identity theft incidents, while sabotage accounts for 11% of cases of system failure and data corruption incidents (DTI, 2006).

Similarly, respondents to the 2006 ISSA/UCD Irish Cybercrime Survey named infections from viruses and other malware (90%), misuse of information and communication systems (88%), theft of assets (63%), phishing and other customer-side attacks (56%) and leak of confidential information (46%) as the most common attacks their organizations had suffered (ISSA/UCD, 2006).

US companies participating in the 2007 Computer Crime & Security Survey named data protection and phishing attacks as the most critical issues, which they expect that they will face in the following two years (CSI, 2007). Identity management and access management were ranked next in priority, while companies named also: the need to convince upper management of the benefits of strong security; finding appropriate staff; awareness training; mobile device concerns; the insider threat; malicious code infections; phishing and web-related attacks as other issues of concern for the near future.

It should be noted that identity theft is one of the most rapidly increasing problem faced by Internet users; offenders commonly use a simple method of stealing a user's identity, known as '*phishing*', which involves the use of fake e-mail messages and fraudulent Web sites to trick recipients into revealing personal financial data. According to the US Consumers Union, as cited in (President's Information Technology Advisory Committee, 2005), 1% of U.S. households fell victim to such attacks at a cost of $400 million in the first half of 2004. Organizational Identity Theft, on the other hand, is a relatively recent type of e-crime against organizations and businesses. Nevertheless, 17% of respondents to the 2006 ISSA/USD Irish Cybercrime Survey reported that their organization had fallen victim to it (ISSA/UCD, 2006).

## Sources of Electronic Crime

### Motives and Characteristics

The multitude and the changing nature of electronic crime, which adapts to exploit the advent of technology and respond to advances in security controls and legislation, make it hard to identify a concrete profile of a person involved in such actions. However, some common characterizing features of these individuals can be identified so as to enhance understanding of this phenomenon and facilitate the effort to tackle it.

One can sketch a very wide spectrum of different profiles for individuals committing electronic crimes. At the one extreme, we can place enthusiastic teenagers equipped with a home computer with Internet access and plenty of time at their disposal. At the other end, however, organized groups of highly skilled individuals operating to serve various purposes are found. Between the two extremities there are many different types of individuals committing electronic offences. According to the profiles most commonly used in relevant literature, cyber criminals may fall into the categories of script kiddies, hackers, white-collar criminals, spies, terrorists, corporate riders, organized crime, professional criminals and vandals (Savona & Mignone, 2004; Nykodym, Taylor & Vilela, 2005).

Among the motives driving individuals to commit e-crimes we find all motives behind 'traditional' crimes, such as greed, lust, quest for power and/or money, revenge, adventure (Grabosky, 2000), endeavor to affirm one's ideas (political, social, religious, economic etc), intent to have fun or to prove oneself in the face of peers, aim to gain visibility and/or fame and so on. To this list, we can add other motives that are related to technology, such as hacking to highlight lack of security (Philippsohn, 2001). Another motive commonly driving young hackers is the ability to make an impact on large and allegedly well-secured systems, which can be considered an act of power. Moreover, many activities on the electronic frontier entail the exploration of the unknown, thus providing elements of adventure. For this reason, activities in cyberspace that are likely to invoke official condemnation attract individuals who are defiant, rebellious, or just curious. Finally, the intellectual challenge of mastering complex systems can also be regarded as motivation to individuals (Grabosky, 2000).

Hacking for political reasons, on the other hand, is often characterized as hactivism (Brenner, 2004). Recent examples include, for instance, coordinated attacks launched by Serb hackers against 50 websites, including that of Manchester United and Adidas, who had their sites stripped of content, and branded with the words "Kosovo is Serbia" (Philippsohn, 2001).

However, it is often not easy to differentiate between cyberwar, cyberterrorism and cybercrime. On April 2007, computer networks of numerous Estonian organizations, including the Estonian parliament, banks, ministries, newspapers and broadcasters, were the target of a co-ordinated denial of service attack realized by a rogue computer network (botnet). As a result, many of these networks were forced to shut down and the country suffered a serious disruption of activities. Since the attack occurred shortly after a diplomatic incident with Russia about the relocation of a Soviet World War II memorial, the government of Estonia attributed this attack to Russia, which denied any involvement. Although this was neither the first botnet originated attack nor the largest one, it was the first time ever that the basic electronic infrastructure of a country had been targeted; it was also the first time that a government had to defend itself at a cyberspace front[8]. This incident was at the time considered as one of the first major incidents of cyberwar; however there is still no evidence (more than a year later) that this attack was the work of the Russian government. It has been found, however, that young ethnic Russians were the major instigators of the attack, driven, possibly, by their objection to the relocation of the memorial[9].

As becomes evident from the case of the attacks against Estonia, sometimes it is difficult to identify the motives behind e-crimes. It is often the case that politically motivated computer crimes are disguised as fraud or other types of attacks; there are also cases where the real motive behind an attack is disguised as political. For example, in another recent case, Chinese hackers where attributed online identity thefts for political reasons, because the attacks appeared to originate in China and the software tools used were named in an anti-Korean style. However, further investigation of the event showed that the Chinese hackers ware actually 'hired' by Korean criminals who aimed to use stolen information for fraud in the Korean black market[10]. These, and other events, drive us to the conclusion that hackers, or other types of 'amateur' e-criminals may be used by professional criminals and organized crime for their purposes. It is also important to note that individuals or criminal groups with different motives often cooperate.

Another interesting observation with regard to the origins of cybercrime comes from the security company F-Secure[11] which, in a recent publication (2008) has predicted that in the following years there will be a significant increase in attacks originating from countries in Central America, Africa, China and India[12], whereas most of today's Internet related crime activities can be located in Russia, China and Southern America. According to F-Secure's security experts, cybercrime was characterized in the period from 1986 to 2003 from opportunistic 'hobbyists', usually at school age, who would experiment and learn their craft primarily by virus writing pursuing fame and/or fun; these 'script kiddies' were usually operating from areas in Europe, United States, Australia and India. Recently, within years 2003 to 2007, this trend has changed and young hobbyists have been replaced by professional criminals, often forming organized groups, who launch targeted attacks for financial benefits. Major areas of criminal activities are located in former Soviet countries, in China and in Brazil. In these places online crime presents a lucrative means to financial gains to people with sophisticated IT skills while the IT job market is very limited. According to the same report, in the future new e-criminal groups are expected to appear in places like Mexico and Africa, while e-crimes become more sophisticated. Finally, according to the information security expert M. Hypponen, the development of malware hotspots is connected to socio-economic factors, such as the lack of job opportunities in countries with high numbers of IT-skilled individuals[13].

Finally, as far as the identification of the motives driving illicit behavior with regard to the Internet and computer systems is concerned, it should be noted that it is often the case where people do not actually realize that their actions are illicit, or that they not fully apprehend the consequences of these actions. Novice computer and Internet users, for example, may share software or other digital content (music, pictures etc.) with friends and colleagues, not realizing that they are committing piracy and violating intellectual property rights.

## The Insider Threat

Offenders are usually categorized into insiders and outsiders (Theoharidou et al, 2005); insiders can be employees (current or former), contractors or consultants employed by an organization. They typically employ methods such as compromised accounts, backdoors, social engineering techniques, copying information to mobile devices (e.g. USB drives), password crackers and packet sniffers (E-Crime Watch Survey, 2006). Outsiders are individuals with no direct relationship with the organization that is the target of the e-crime (e.g. hackers penetrating a company's network).

Electronic crimes committed by insiders usually entail more damage (financial or other) for enterprises due to the fact that they have increased access rights, they can identify the assets of the company and are usually in place to hide their traces and thus prohibit or delay discovery. Among the hardest types of e-crimes to detect is those committed by collaborating insiders who span different levels in the company hierarchy. According to the Computer Crime and Intellectual Property Section of the US Department of Justice, 34% of the insiders committing cyber crime are between 20 and 29 years, 36% between 30 and 35 years, and 27% over 35 years (Nykodym, Taylor & Vilela, 2005 ). Although the majority of individuals accused were 30 and 35 years old, the most damage was done by persons over 35 years. It has also been found that insider attacks are targeted on their organization, aiming to proprietary information, customer and financial data, as well as intellectual property (E-Crime Watch Survey, 2006).

E-crimes committed by insiders often include unauthorized access and use of corporate, proprietary information and trade secrets that can be sold to market competitors, theft of intellectual property, fraud (e.g. credit card) and sabotage (alteration, deletion, access prevention) of computers, networks or data for revenge. On the other hand, outsiders are more commonly involved in offences involving virus, worms and other types of malicious code (e.g. Trojans, spyware), unauthorized access to information, systems and networks, the illegal generation of spam e-mails, denial of service attacks and phishing attacks (E-Crime Watch Survey, 2006).

Among the 671 security executives and law enforcement officials who participated in the fourth E-Crime Watch Survey (E-Crime Watch Survey, 2007) 34% attributed more damage caused to insiders, 37% to outsiders and 29% reported that the origin of the attack was unknown. Participants in the previous year's E-Crime Watch study (E-Crime Watch Survey, 2006) were significantly more concerned with intruders from outside their organization (58% of events were attributed to outsiders) than the insider threat (27% of incidents committed by insiders). Among the organizations that had experienced security events, 55% reported that at least one insider event had occurred within 2005. It seems, therefore, that the insider threat is getting worse.

Similarly, according to the ISBS 2006 survey (DTI, 2006) the source of the worst security breach incident suffered by UK companies was external at an average of 69%, and internal 32%. At the same time 21% of security incidents reported by companies participating in the study concern the misuse of information systems by company employees. For these businesses, illicit behavior by staff concerns, misuse of web access (17%), misuse of e-mail access (11%), unauthorized access to systems and data (4%), breaches of data protection laws and regulations (2%) and misuse of confidential information (e.g. intellectual property) (2%). It is important to note that breaches of data protection laws and regulations by employees occurred as often as once a month in 19% of respondents.

It is also often the case that the victims of computer-related crimes and attacks have their own beliefs with regard to the source of the attack and the motives of the attacker. These beliefs may be based upon factors such as past experience with similar events, the different sources of information which they have and many more. According to the DMS survey conducted for the European Commission among businesses of the European Union member states (Rand Europe, 2003), hackers were named as responsible for security breaches by about 40% of the respondents, about 38% of the attacks were attributed to internal users, while former employees were cited as sources of the attacks in only about 5% of the cases. Customers and suppliers/competitors were identified as responsible in 14% and 7% of the cases respectively. There were also a not negligible 21% of cases in which attackers were not identified or were referred to as 'others'. Another interesting finding of the same survey is that there seem to be differences on what organizations perceive to be the major source of attacks, depending on which country they are located. For example, in

Greece and France hackers were perceived as the major cause of breaches in about 60% of cases (58% and 65% respectively), in Italy customers were named responsible for breaches more frequently than insiders (although the difference is only 5%) and in Finland internal users surpass hackers by 10%.

## THE IMPACT OF ELECTRONIC CRIME

The impact of electronic crime can be traced at all different aspects of the use of information and communication technologies; with regard to companies and public authorities, e-crime adversely affects the growth of e-commerce and electronic government initiatives, as explained in the introduction of this chapter. With regard to individuals, offences like stalking and identity theft may prohibit users from taking part in digital social networks that are currently on the rise (Karyda & Kokolakis, 2007) and generally affect the development of trust relations in cyberspace.

For companies, in particular, the impact of electronic crimes includes not only financial losses, but also consequences like disruption to activities, damage to reputation, adverse media coverage, etc. It has been estimated, for instance, that the economic impact of e-crimes for businesses has increased from $265 million in 2000, to $378 million in 2001, to $450 million in 2002 (CSI, 2007). Relying on a single measurement, such as estimated financial losses, however, can lead to erroneous conclusions. For many organizations, the impact on their reputation may be more important than financial loss. Moreover, damage to a firm's reputation can last much longer than direct financial loss. Other indirect costs such as time spent investigating and reporting the incident, damage to reputation and loss of prospective customers need also to be considered.

According to the ISBS 2006 survey the biggest single impact of security breaches is business disruption. Responding to security breaches requires different amounts of staff time, depending on the situation, from less than a day (for 63% of malicious code infections up to a period of 11-50 days in 4% of systems failure cases, for example).

In financial terms, the range of the overall cost for the worst security incident suffered by large UK businesses within 2006, for instance, was estimated between £65,000 and £130,000, while the average cost was about £12,000 (up from £10,000 compared to 2004) (DTI, 2006).

With regard to the extent of this phenomenon, the majority of UK companies suffered a malicious computer-related attack within year 2005. According to the same survey there has been a decline of about 20% in the number of UK companies affected by security incidents from year 2004 to year 2006, while the average number of incidents suffered by the companies that were affected raised by 50% and the average cost per incident raised also by 50%. The average number of incidents faced by each of these companies was about 30. 17% of these incidents were attacks by outsiders (such as hackers), 8% concerned theft or computer-related fraud, and 29% involved systems failure and data corruption. At the same time, this survey shows also a steady rise in the percentage of companies that become victims of electronic offences: from 18% of companies that had suffered such an attack in 1999, to 44% in 2002, to 52% in 2005. It is also noteworthy that 63% of companies surveyed expect that they will face more security incidents in the near future and 59% expect that incidents will be harder to catch, compared to 13% that expect a decline in their number and 23% estimating that these will be less difficult to catch (DTI, 2006).

Among all types of security incidents reported by UK companies participating in the survey (namely: malicious code infection, information systems misuse by staff, breaches of confidentiality, attacks by outsiders, theft and computer-related fraud, physical theft of IT equipment and systems failure) the impact of computer fraud incidents was characterized as 'extremely serious' in 27%

of cases, whereas the consequences of malicious code infections, which was reported as the most common incident were 'not all serious' in 22% of cases and 'extremely serious' in only 3% of cases. Another important finding of this survey was that among security breaches suffered by these companies the most costly type was theft and computer-related fraud (DTI, 2006).

UK businesses spend on average between £1,000 and £2,000 recovering from their worst security breach incident. Interestingly, UK businesses that participated in the survey reported that they have increased their expenditures for implementing security controls by 43% in average; however 52% of companies had at least one malicious security event within 2005, compared to only 18% that had reported an attack six years before (year 1999). It is estimated that UK companies spend in average about 4-5% of their IT budget on securing their information and communication infrastructure (DTI, 2006).

At the same time, US companies participating in the 2007 Computer Crime & Security Survey estimate that in 2006 cybercrime cost them more than the year before. The average loss per US company, due to electronic crime and security violation events was estimated $345.000 for 2007. More specifically, financial losses as a result of computer-related financial fraud cost companies $21.124.750, system and network penetration by outsiders cost $6.875.000, losses from theft of confidential information was estimated at $5.685.000, sabotage of data or networks cost $1.056.000, the cost of web site defacements mounted $725.300, telecom fraud cost $651.000 and losses by blackmails were estimated at $160.000. 9% of US companies that participated in the survey reportedly spend over 10% of their overall IT budget on security controls, whereas almost half of companies spend between 1 to 5% of their IT budget. Compared to the results of the previous CSI Computer Crime Surveys, it is easy to reach the conclusion that security program budgets are rising (CSI, 2007).

It is worth noting, however, that although the impact (especially in terms of financial losses) of electronic crimes on business is severe and the number of incidents is rising, publicity around e-crimes is limited, because companies try to avoid negative publicity so as not to suffer more losses with regard to loss of confidence by their clients.

A European survey (Rand Europe, 2003) has indicated that the impact of electronic crime has also to do with location. According to the survey the severity of security incidents is greater in the south part of Europe (Mediterranean countries) than in the north part (lowest in Finland). The index used by this study to assess the severity of damages suffered in the seven participating countries (Finland, France, Germany, Greece, Italy, Spain and the United Kingdom), called the DSI (Damage Severity Index), is a compound indicator based on the seriousness of damages caused by different types of e-crimes, such as identity theft, on-line fraud etc.

The information and data presented above can only provide us with a partial picture of the extent of electronic crime. There are no reliable statistics concerning the full scale of this phenomenon. It is argued that published numbers and statistics are likely to under-represent the extent of the problem for a variety of reasons. In the first place, as already mentioned, many companies avoid reporting such incidents for fear of negative publicity and exposure to future attacks. Secondly, as respondents in most relevant surveys admit, reported incidents are only those that have been discovered. The number of incidents that remain undetected is not known, and depends on many issues, such as the competence and experience of administrators, user awareness, whether and which monitoring procedures and tools are used and so on. Finally, it is only recently that investigation and law enforcement authorities have started compiling data with regard to the use of computers and networks in illegal actions. Thus, it is expected that electronic crime cases are likely to grow, following the growth of use of computers and the Internet (Communication from the Commission, 2001).

## ELECTRONIC CRIME TRENDS

Electronic crimes and their consequences seem to be multiplying. According to the PITAC report published in 2005 (President's Information Technology Advisory Committee), the total number of e-crime attacks, including malicious code infections (viruses, worms), cyber fraud, and insider attacks in corporations, was rising by over 20 percent annually, with many types of attacks doubling in number. The 2006 E-Crime Watch Survey, on the other hand, estimates that e-crime incidents are declining, compared to previous years, yet their impact in terms of operational and financial losses is increasing (E-Crime Watch Survey, 2006). 63% of the interviewees (security executives and law enforcement personnel) reported operational losses, 40% reported financial losses and 23% reported that the reputation of their organization had suffered damage as a result of incidents of electronic crime. Moreover, 53% of information security professionals, members of the Information Systems Security Association (ISSA), who responded to the 2005 BSA/ISSA Information Security Survey (BSA-ISSA, 2005) estimate that a major cyber attack on their organization is likely to happen during the next 12 months.

However, the proliferation of technology and the increase of incidents also affect the way victims perceive these cases. According to the ISBS 2006 survey (DTI, 2006), the number of UK companies reporting attempts by outsiders to break into their networks has not risen for year 2006 compared with those reported in the previous two years but has actually dropped from roughly one incident per week to one a month, despite the fact that more companies have broadband connections, and evidence showing that an unprotected computer becomes target of hundreds of attacks as soon as it is connected to the Internet. This apparent controversy can be attributed to the changing perception of what constitutes a significant attempt to break into a network. Many businesses screen out incidents such as network vulnerability scans as relatively harmless attacks. 5% of companies suffer hundreds of such attacks daily, whereas 80% of companies reported only one incident of successful network penetration (within year 2005). It is also worth noting, that although 26% of businesses reported significant attempts in the same survey, 2% report actual penetration into their network by outsiders; 2% also report having suffered attacks on their Internet and telecommunications traffic (e.g. eavesdropping or interception), 5% reported denial of service attacks and 3% company impersonation events, such as phishing attacks (DTI, 2006).

### Targeted and Automated Attacks

32% of respondents to the 2007 SCI/Computer Crime and Security Survey (E-Crime Watch Survey, 2007) who reported that had suffered some type of security incident commented that they had fallen victims of a "targeted attack," meaning a malware attack aimed exclusively at their organization or at organizations within a small subset of the general population. 2% responded that they had suffered more than 10 such attacks within the previous year. Similarly, targeted attacks are also considered to be on the rise by security executives and law enforcement personnel responding to the 2006 E-Crime Watch Survey (E-Crime Watch Survey, 2006). 36% of respondents reported that their organizations were victims of attacks concerning theft of proprietary information, such as customer records, 33% reported system sabotage and 30% were victims of intellectual property theft. Targeted attacks are usually harder to detect than mass ones and cost more to enterprises.

Surveys also show that automated attacks like viruses, worms, and malicious code remain the most common form of e-crime. For instance, 72% of respondents to the 2006 E-Crime Survey reported having fallen victims of such an attack within last year (E-Crime Watch Survey, 2006). Another illustrative example refers to the fact that it has been estimated that, from January 2004 to June 2004, the rate at which new hosts joining the Internet were compromised and incorporated into "bot armies" rose from under 2,000 a day to more than 30,000 a day[14].

Finally, it is believed that there is a trend for growing network connections between hackers or small-time criminals and organized crime. This trend enables also offenders to act cross-nationally, thus impeding investigation and prosecution, and use sophisticated technology and computer expertise to realize and conceal their deeds (Grabosky, 2000).

## Financial Crime

As has been previously mentioned, up to now the greatest financial losses companies suffer were attributed to malicious code, end especially infections from viruses. Lately, however, financial fraud is identified as the source of the greatest financial losses (CSI, 2007) as organized crime groups use the Internet for major fraud and theft activities.

According to the 2006 ISSA/UCD Irish Cybercrime Survey, financial fraud and telecom fraud have affected 39% and 29% of organizations respectively (ISSA/UCD, 2006). Moreover, despite the fact that it is estimated that electronic crimes during year 2007 were at the same levels with those of the previous year, however it has been noticed that targeted, financially motivated attacks have risen (E-Crime Watch Survey, 2007).

Credit card fraud is one of the most common cases of financial e-crime; offenders hack into computer systems of business to steal customers' credit card details and use them for buying goods, make bids at online auctions, sell them and so on. Other types of financial electronic fraud include the artificial pumping of the shares of a company by generating artificial publicity (e.g. by publishing false take-over information) and then dumping the shares at the increased market value, misleading investors into buying high profit bonds that turn out to be fraud, joining pyramid schemes (Philippsohn, 2001) and diffusion of information that leads to the artificial inflation of stock prices.

The most common Internet-based financial fraud, however, concerns alluring bank customers to bogus web sites, where clients believing to be interacting with the real banking site provide their financial details, passwords etc. Other types of financial electronic crime include electronic money laundering (for instance through online auctions and gambling), to conceal the source of ill-gotten gains or conceal legitimate gains from tax authorities, the development of informal banking institutions and parallel banking systems that allow avoiding transaction reporting requirements where these exist, theft of confidential/business information to be sold to competitors and so on (Grabosky, 2000).

Finally, financial e-crimes can also take the form of extortion, where an enterprise has to pay offenders in order to avoid suffering damage, as in the case of Visa Corporation that was asked to pay 10 million pounds to hackers under the threat of crashing Visa's computer systems using stolen source code (Philippsohn, 2001).

# ADDRESSING CYBERCRIME

It becomes evident from the preceding analysis that electronic crime is a relatively new, multifaceted phenomenon that appears to change forms and follow the advents of technology. To address it, we need a combined approach of legislative, technical, procedural and other measures. Moreover a mix of proactive, as well as reactive methods are needed, in order for individuals, companies, organizations and states to be able to deter and prevent electronic crimes before they occur or mitigate the threat, detect them after they have been realized and take necessary measures to amend any damages caused. Despite the fact that expenditures on information technology security are rising and that most organizations employ technological solutions to protect themselves, security professionals have started to acknowledge that a combined approach is needed to address e-crime effectively. For instance, respondents to the 2006 Security Watch Survey acknowledge that organizations need to "...invest not only in technology solutions, but also in partnerships to assist in the development of policies and best practices that can help fight evolving cyber crime threats." (E-Crime Watch Survey, 2006)

According to the PITAC report, emphasis should be placed in the following areas in order to control cybercrime effectively: the development of authentication schemes, the design of secure fundamental protocols, secure software engineering and software assurance instead of common approaches to commercial software development, establishing holistic system security, monitoring and detection tools and techniques, the development and use of mitigation and recovery methodologies, the development of new techniques for cyber forensics, modeling and testing new technologies before these are put to use, the development of universally accepted security metrics, benchmarks, and best practices and finally addressing non-technological factors, such as psychological, societal, institutional, legal, and economic, that can compromise cyber security (President's Information Technology Advisory Committee, 2005).

Nearly four out of five of the UK companies that reported having experienced a security breach (DTI, 2006), took some type of action after the occurrence of the worst security incident. These measures included, among others, the deployment of additional security technology (by 30% of companies), changes to policies and procedures (26%), additional staff training (23%) and disciplinary actions (8%).

How ready are, however, companies to defend themselves against electronic crime attacks? Responding to the BSA/ISSA Information Security Survey (ISSA/UCD, 2006), 78% of security professionals interviewed said that their organization is prepared to against cyber attacks. Interestingly, however, only 19% of respondents believe that the employees of the organization are adequate in their information security duties and responsibilities.

## Legal Approach

To legally pursue e-criminals law enforcement officials need suitable legal tools; procedural rules with regard to the collection and handling of digital evidence need to be well-defined for prosecution (Karyda & Mitrou, 2007). Efforts are made towards this direction, including the adoption of new laws and the adaptation of existing ones, but the most important problem is that e-crimes are usually transnational, thus involving legal systems, jurisdictions and law enforcement authorities from different countries. There are countries with a lack of computer crime laws or with limited ones. For instance, the person identified as the author of one of the earliest computer viruses which caused massive problems to the computer systems of big enterprises as well as of individuals in more than 20 countries, known as the "Love Bug", could not be prosecuted, as no relevant legislation existed at the time in the Philippines, where he was located. Following this incident, the Philippines adopted relevant cyber crime laws. It thus become clear, that as far as the legal aspect of addressing electronic crime is concerned, countries must be able to face them both on an individual as well as on a collective level.

The latest advent in the direction of international cooperation against a specific type of e-crime (cyberwar) is the establishment of the Cooperative Cyber Defense (CCD) Centre of Excellence (COE) in Tallin, Estonia by NATO. The Centre, according to the NATO announcement will "conduct research and training on cyber warfare and include a staff of 30 persons, half of them specialists from the sponsoring countries, Estonia, Germany, Italy, Latvia, Lithuania, Slovakia and Spain."[15] This action comes in response to the cyber attacks launched against Estonia within 2007.

Complementary to legislative measures, there are also many provisions that can be adopted at national level. For instance, the European Union[16], aiming to protect the information society by improving the security of information infrastructures and combating computer-related crime proposes the following non-legislative measures:

- The establishment of specialized national units (law enforcement and judicial authorities).
- Specialized training for police and judicial authority staff.
- The creation of a harmonized set of rules for police and judicial record-keeping and appropriate tools for statistical analysis of computer crime.
- The establishment of a European forum to foster cooperation between the various players.
- Encouragement for direct action by industry against computer-related crime; and the funding of related research and technological development (RTD) projects.

Conclusively, international cooperation at the legal level is needed to effectively discover, investigate and prosecute electronic crimes. Furthermore, new legislation covering new types of electronic offences is needed, while current legislation should be reviewed and adapted, when necessary. 46% of respondents to the 2005 BSA/ISSA Information Security Survey believe that current cyber laws have made their organization more secure (compared to 33% in 2003), 53% have the opinion that more cyber laws will help even more; while only 30% think new laws will not help (BSA-ISSA, 2005).

## Information Sharing and Incident Reporting

It is also acknowledged that sharing information on e-crimes, particularly with regard to threats such as viruses, is critical for the success of protective measures, since both individual users and businesses can help prospective victims worldwide to take appropriated measures to shield themselves. According to the survey conducted for the European Commission (Rand Europe, 2003) more than 80% of regular Internet users are willing to report on-line violations to a third independent party, such as an ad hoc public agency. Businesses however, tend to handle the occurrence of e-crimes internally, avoiding to involve law enforcement (E-Crime Watch Survey, 2006). This can be attributed to issues such as the fear of negative publication for organizations that have suffered an attack, lack of evidence, inability to identify people responsible for the attack and the low level of damage caused (CSI, 2007; E-Crime Watch Survey, 2006). Similarly, only 15% of the respondents to the 2005 BSA/ISSA Information Security Survey (BSA-ISSA, 2005) said that their organization had reported a cyber incident or intrusion to law enforcement or other government organization during the past year, which is lower than the 19% of respondents who had answered positively in 2003. Of those who have reported an incident, 82% say their organization has assisted law enforcement in the investigation of the reported incident. Governments and public authorities, in particular, establish specialized task forces to defend themselves against organized attacks and also try to establish the necessary structures for prosecuting e-crimes.

Besides reporting incidents to authorities, companies have also the possibility to report security incidents and computer crimes to information sharing organizations, such as the Computer Emergency Response Teams (CERTs). About half of the companies participating in the 2007 CSI Computer Crime & Security Survey report that they belong to an information sharing organization (CSI, 2007). 30% of companies have reported incidents to law enforcement. Reasons named by companies for not reporting security incidents and computer related crimes to law enforcement include fear of negative publicity (reported by 26% of companies), belief that law enforcement could not help (22%), fear that competitors might take advantage of it (14%), the fact that they have sought civil remedy (7%), lack of awareness of law enforcement issue on the incident (5%), while 2% of companies named other issues. The fact that over 1 out of 5 companies attributed not reporting security incidents to the belief that law enforcement could not be of help needs further investigation and should be taken into consideration for adopting effective practice to fight e-crime. This could be attributed to reasons such as cynicism on law enforcement effectiveness or even realistic attitude towards the resources and abilities that authorities posses for addressing cybercrime.

However, according to the ISBS 2006 survey only 23% of UK companies are able to maintain evidence of a security breach to legal standard. Other measures employed by companies in order to respond to security breaches include the adoption of contingency plans for dealing with possible security breaches (by 50% of companies), logging (46%), while 23% have insurance policies that cover damage suffered from electronic crimes or viruses (DTI, 2006).

## Monitoring

Another approach adopted by many organizations in their effort to address the insider threat, involves monitoring their employees and running background checks on their current and potential staff. For instance, 59% of large UK businesses report that they always perform some sort of background checking, though the degree of checks can vary considerably (DTI, 2006). According to the same survey, 42% of UK businesses log and monitor their employees' access to web sites, while the vast majority of them employ also some type of filtering to scan their employees' e-mails for malicious code (viruses, spyware, trojans etc.). 15% of UK companies report to scan employees' outgoing e-mails for confidential information and 16% for inappropriate content. Moreover, in only 25% of companies employees can send encrypted messages to business partners.

Similarly, security professionals responding to the 2005 BSA/ISSA Information Security Survey responded that they use employee monitoring technologies at a wide range: 70% monitor web activity, 49% monitor internal emails, 36% monitor instant messaging and 50% monitor Internet emails. It should be mentioned that, with the advances in information and communication technologies which provide new opportunities for prospective offenders and create new vulnerabilities, business face the need to expand monitor and controls to include, for example instant messages (IM) (BSA-ISSA, 2006).

About one in ten UK companies log and monitor these messages, use monitoring tools to scan outgoing messages for inappropriate content while about 42% take no measures with regard to them (DTI, 2006). Other technological advances, such as, for example, Voice over IP (VoIP) telephony need also be assessed in terms of the opportunities they provide to offenders, so as to be appropriately managed. Employee monitoring, however, has raised concerns with regard to the right to privacy of employees as well as the psychological impact on them (Mitrou, & Karyda , 2006).

## Technical Controls

Information and communication technologies are employed both by individuals aiming to commit electronic crimes and by people pursuing to control these actions or investigate and legally prosecute them. Technologies commonly used to reduce the opportunities to commit an electronic crime include access control, authentication and authorization schemes (from simple password-based schemes to biometric devices), encryption, anonymization techniques, virus and malicious code detectors, blocking and filtering programs, etc, while to detect incidents monitoring tools are used, such as anomaly detection devices.

Nearly all UK businesses protect themselves from malicious code (98% have installed antivirus software and 74% use anti-spyware). Moreover, nine in ten very large organizations in UK reported that they have implemented intrusion detection or prevention software. These companies tend to report more virus infections than those that do not use this type of software; this brings in the foreground the issue of security incidents and electronic crimes that remain undetected and the importance of implementing detection and methods and tools (DTI, 2006).

Similarly, US companies use all types of available technology to protect their information and communication infrastructure by offenders. Almost all companies, among other, use antivirus software and firewalls (98% and 97% respectively), 80% use anti-spyware software, 69% use intrusion detection systems, 66% of companies encrypt their data in transit and 47% use encryption for data in storage, 40% apply some type of forensics tools, 44% use special software to manage their systems' logs and 18% use biometrics (CSI, 2007).

According to the 2006 E-Crime Watch the most effective technologies against e-crime include, in order of importance, firewalls, electronic access or control systems, password complexity, network-based anti-virus and encryption. The same study also shows that organizations spend an average $20 million on IT security and $19 million on physical security (Rand Europe, 2003). It is interesting to note that surveillance measures, commonly adopted especially by employers to thwart the insider threat are regarded among the least effective approaches protecting against e-crimes (E-Crime Watch Survey, 2006).

Most of the above mentioned technologies are supported by commercial software and hardware that is not only intended to be used by large enterprises and professional users, but also by home users and individuals with limited knowledge on computers and security. However, for companies to effectively protect themselves by e-crimes using the appropriate technology they need to employ qualified security professionals. It is estimated, however, that worldwide the number of professionals who are adequately qualified to handle such incidents is lower than the actual needs. In the UK, for example it is estimated that while rising, the number of qualified security professionals remains low compared to the total number of businesses (DTI, 2006). Thus, small businesses are very unlikely to have anyone qualified and are more likely to seek external guidance and expertise (e.g. external audits, IT service providers, consultants, security products vendors etc.), while large businesses are more likely to afford and be able to attract the specialist skills.

Security breaches suffered by European companies are mostly believed to originate from hackers (41%), internal users (29%), customers (14%), competitors (7%) or former employees (5%). It is also notable that most security managers become aware of the occurrence of security incidents by their own information security systems (62%) or by themselves (52%). Other priorities for European businesses in their effort to control security breaches include blocking unauthorised access to internal networks (over 90%), defining the security architecture (little less than 80%), expanding the budget for enhanced security (about 85%), while less than half on-line businesses name as 'high' or 'medium' information security priority the outsourcing of security management (Rand Europe, 2003).

It should be noted that, despite the plurality of measures employed by companies to protect themselves by security breaches and electronic crimes, companies seem to place the evaluation of their effectiveness low in their agenda; 35% of companies participating in the 2007 Computer Crime & Security Survey reported that they do not measure effectiveness at all, while the employees of 32% of companies have to undergo some mandatory test (written or digital), in 25% of companies staff compile reports on security incidents, 22% analyze the volume and type of security incidents and 13% check whether their employees can detect social engineering attacks. To evaluate security effectiveness most companies depend on employees to run internal audits (63%) and perform penetration testing (53%), while 53% of companies have also audits done by external organizations. Finally, 44% use software to monitor e-mails (CSI, 2007).

While organizations depend on their specialized employees (security officers, managers etc) to protect their information infrastructure against offenders, individuals have to depend mainly on their own efforts to protect themselves against electronic crime. Although technology provides a wide range of technical means that can be applied by home, and/or small office users, such as antivirus and antispyware software, network monitoring tools etc. security awareness among individual users remains an open issue.

With regard to developing new technological tools and techniques measures for fighting electronic crime, it is important to take into consideration that due to the nature of technology, as explained earlier in this chapter, these measures may be used by both offenders and defenders. In an effort to stop this 'dual use' of technology, several countries have adopted protective measures that prohibit the use of state of the art technology (placing for example constraints on the use of strong cryptography). This approach, however, has been criticized as controversial, as it poses also constraints to the ways legitimate users can protect themselves against offenders who would bypass such regulations and restrictions. Finally, it should be mentioned that offenders are usually one step ahead in the use of technology, creating novel attacks or exploiting existing vulnerabilities.

## Cyber Insurance

Cyber insurance is another approach employed by companies to mitigate this threat; for instance, 23% of companies in UK had a specialist insurance policy covering damage suffered from cybercrime or viruses (DTI, 2006). Among these companies, 20% report that they think they have full cover, 44% partial cover and 36% no cover. Moreover, a quarter of respondents reported that they were not aware of what their insurance cover actually includes. Contrary than what expected however, the market of cyber insurance is not growing very fast.

According to the 2007 SCI Computer Crime & Security Survey, 71% of US companies do not have an external insurance policy in order to minimize their risks with regard to computer crime and security (CSI, 2007). Similarly, only 9% of information security professionals who participated in the 2005 BSA/ISSA Information Security Survey Cyber reported that their organization had cyber liability insurance, while 46% said that they were not aware of whether there was one. Moreover, 57% said they would not consider carrying cyber liability insurance. It seems, therefore that liability insurance remains a little-used option for most organizations in their effort to combat cyber crime and protect their information infrastructure. It should be noted that this option does not apply in the cases of cyberwar where the computer and network infrastructure of an entire country are the target of electronic crime attacks.

## Education and User Awareness

To address electronic crime citizens need to be educated, so that when using the Internet, they maintain and update the security on their systems so that they cannot be compromised, for example, to fall victims themselves or to become agents in a DDoS attack. Businesses and organizations should also be aware and apply best practices for effective security management.

The importance of educating user and raising awareness with regard to computer crime and security issues is generally acknowledged for the effectiveness of any security program (DTI, 2006; CSI, 2007; E-Crime Watch Survey, 2007; BSA-ISSA, 2005). It seems, however, that neither companies nor governments invest on it, as a means to address cybercrime in a proactive way. For instance, 47% of US companies spend less than 1% of their IT budget on training and security awareness; only 6% of companies spend between 8 and 10% (CSI, 2007).

Interestingly however, 18% of US companies report that they do not apply any security awareness programs (CSI, 2007). Among those that do have security awareness programs in place, network security is identified as the most important topic (by 78% of companies), access control systems are rated as most important by 67% of companies and investigations and legal issues are the most important issue for 55%.

## CONCLUSION AND OPEN ISSUES

Electronic crime refers to the use of the information and communication technologies to commit 'traditional' offences by exploiting new opportunities, on the one hand and, on the other hand, it refers to the realization of completely 'new types' of criminal activities, which have been made possible by the advent of technology. However, a generally accepted definition and taxonomy of e-crimes is not available up to now. Despite significant attempts towards this direction (such as the Council of Europe's Convention on Cyber Crime), a common agreement that would promote international cooperation and thus facilitate the investigation and prosecution of e-crimes is still allusive.

The issue of electronic crime becomes a serious concern for more and more organizations, individuals and governments. The increasing proliferation of ICTs into all aspects of everyday life, including business and government functions and individual activities, especially as computers become embedded into most artefacts surrounding us, makes the need to address e-crime at all levels inevitable.

Analysis of current and future trends presented in this chapter has showed that future e-crime will be sophisticated and explicitly targeted, realized by high-skilled professional individuals who mainly pursue financial gains. These trends are empowered by specific socio-economic, as well as technical and legal factors, including:

- Delays of legal and regulatory systems to catch up with technical progress in information and communication technologies.
- The more political, financial and social activities move to the Internet, the more related electronic offences will appear (such as identity thefts, extortions, etc.).
- The proliferation of broadband connectivity and ubiquitous computing and the closing of the digital divide.
- The lack of job opportunities in developing countries with high ICT penetration.

Another serious concern which emerges is the issue of cyberwar, or information warfare, aiming critical infrastructures of states and governments.

Furthermore, the future of e-crime should be considered under the new evolving trends: the rise of social networking, the dissolving organizational boundaries (for instance virtual organizations and new forms of employment such as teleworking), and the advent of electronic government, electronic commerce and mobile commerce applications.

Another conclusion derived by the analysis is that electronic crime cannot be considered as a local phenomenon. International cooperation at the legal and technical level is needed, while major difficulties, such as bridging the differences between jurisdictions, deciding which law is applicable and enforcing it, extraditing offenders, carrying out the investigation etc. should be resolved. The Council of Europe's Convention on Cyber Crime (Council of Europe, 2001) has taken significant steps in the direction of creating a treaty intended to establish international standards for combating cyber crime. Moreover, the establishment of the Cooperative Cyber Defense Centre of Excellence by NATO is another effort towards this direction. However, a lot remains to be done in order to create global cooperation.

It is also important to note that electronic crime prevention is considered a common pretext for limiting access to technologies (for instance access to strong cryptography) or adopting measures with individual privacy implications (for example surveillance cameras and monitoring technologies commonly used to monitor employees in the workplace). It is evident that the quest for these two apparently opposite targets, security against cybercrime on one hand, and individual privacy protection on the other, will not be easily solved and many issues are still to arise (especially with regard to latest technological advents such as the use of RFIDs, biometric technology and so on. This constitutes one of the biggest challenges in the effort to control electronic crime: to find a balance between imperatives of law enforcement and the protection of the individuals' privacy, freedom of speech and cultural values (Grabosky, 2000; Mitrou & Karyda, 2006). It is also argued that, through over-regulation or premature regulatory intervention by governments, there is a risk of limiting investments and innovation which may impede receiving the benefits anticipated by the information and communication technologies (Grabosky, 2000).

Finally, the issue of liability is another challenge that needs to be addressed; there has been a long discussion as to whether hardware and software manufacturers and vendors should be hold liable for vulnerabilities or back doors in their products, which are exploited by offenders to commit their attacks. If manufactures were hold responsible, it is argued, they would be forced to produce more secure products and services and create updates to fix vulnerabilities as soon as these are discovered. Moreover, it is often argued whether Internet Service Providers should be held responsible if the services they provide have been exploited to commit an electronic crime (e.g. in the cases of defamatory material posted in blogs or newsgroups and music piracy).

Conclusively, the effective control of e-crime entails law enforcement, technological, procedural and market solutions. It is expected that the responsibility for controlling electronic crime will be shared among state authorities, individual users and businesses employing security specialists. It remains to be seen whether the emergence of "computer crime in a box", where software programs will perform "completed criminal actions" and then erase the related digital evidence, as has been hypothesized (Brenner, 2004), will become a reality.

## REFERENCES

Brenner, S. (2004). Cybercrime Metrics: Old Wine, New Bottles? *Virginia Journalof Law & Technology*, *9*(13), 3-52.

Brenner, S. (2001). *Cybercrime Investigation and Prosecution: the Role of Penal and Procedural Law*. Available at http://www.murdoch.edu.au

*BSA-ISSA Information Security Survey*. (2005). Available at http://www.issa.org

Communication from the Commission to the Council, the European Parliament, The Economic and Social Committee and the Committee of the Regions. (2001). *Creating a Safer Information Society by Improving the Security of Information Infrastructures and Combating Computer-related Crime*. Brussels, 26.1.2001. Available at http://europa.eu.int/ISPO/eif/InternetPoliciesSite/Crime/CrimeCommEN.html

Carter, D. (1995). *Computer Crime Categories: How Techno-criminals Operate*. Available at http://nsi.org/Library/Compsec/crimecom.html

Council of Europe, *Convention on Cybercrime*, Budapest 2001.

CSI. (2007). *The 12th Annual Computer Crime and Security Survey.*

Department of Trade and Industry (DTI). (2006). *Information Security Breaches Survey (ISBS)*, Technical Report. Available at http://www.dti.gov.uk/

*E-Crime Watch Survey*, 2006.

*E-Crime Watch Survey*, 2007.

Grabosky, P. (2000). Cyber Crime and Information Warfare. *Transnational Crime Conference*, Canberra, 9-10 March 2000.

ISSA/UCD Irish Cybercrime Survey. (2006). *The Impact of Cybercrime on Irish Organisations.* Available at http//www.issaireland.org

Karyda, M., & Kokolakis, S. (2007). Privacy Perceptions Among Members of Online Communities. Acquisti, A., De Capitani di Vimercati, S., Gritzalis, S., & Lambrinoudakis, C. (Eds.), *Digital Privacy: Theory, Technologies and Practices.* Auerbach Publications (Taylor and Francis Group)

Karyda, M., & Mitrou, E. (2007). Internet Forensics: Legal and Technical issues. Proceedings of the *2nd Annual Workshop on Digital Forensics and Incident Analysis* (WDFIA 2007), August 27, 2007, Samos-Greece.

Mitrou, E., & Karyda, M. (2006). Employees' Privacy vs. Employers' Security: Can they be balanced? *Telematics and Informatics Journal, 23*(3), 2006, 164 – 178.

Nykodym, N., Taylor, R., & Vilela, J. (2005). Criminal profiling and insider cyber crime. *Computer Law & Security Report, 21*, 408-414.

Philippsohn, S. (2001). Trends in Cybercrime: An Overview of Current Financial Crimes on the Internet. *Computers & Security, 20*, 2001, 53-69.

President's Information Technology Advisory Committee. (2005). *Report to the President, Cyber Security: A crisis of prioritization.* Washington, D.C. February 2005.

Rand Europe. (2003). *Benchmarking Security and Trust in the Information Society in Europe and the US, in the context of the IST-26276-SIBIS project* ("SIBIS Statistical Indicators Benchmarking the Information Society"). Available at http://www.sibis-eu.org

Savona, E. U., & Mignone, M. (2004). The Fox and the Hunters: How IC Technologies Change the Crime Race. *European Journal on Criminal Policy and Research, 10*, 3–26.

Theoharidou, M., Kokolakis, S., Karyda, M., & Kiountouzis, E. (2005). The insider threat to Information Systems and the effectiveness of ISO 17799. *Computers and Security Journal, 24*(6), 472-484.

## ADDITIONAL READING

Anderson, R. J. (2008). *Security Engineering: A Guide to Building Dependable Distributed Systems.* Wiley: Indianapolis.

Cashell, B., Jackson, W. D., Jickling, M., & Webel, B. (2004). *The economic impact of cyber-attacks.* CRS Report for Congress, Congressional Research Service, The Library of Congress. April 1, 2004.

Janczewski, L. J., & Colarik, A. M. (Eds.) (2007). *Cyber Warfare and Cyber Terrorism.* Hershey, PA: IGI Global

Kadrich, M. (2007). *Endpoint Security.* Indianapolis: Addison Wesley.

Lewis, J. A. (2003). Cyber terror: Missing in action. *Knowledge, Technology, & Policy, 16*(2), 34-41.

## KEY TERMS

**Cryptography:** Science of secret writing. It is a security safeguard to render information unintelligible if unauthorized individuals intercept the transmission. When the information is to be used, it can be decoded.

**Cyber Terrorism:** The premeditated use of disruptive activities, or the threat thereof, against computers and/or networks. Criminals attempt to disrupt, to cause harm or further social, ideological, religious, political turmoil to computer ot telecommunication services.

**Cybercrime:** The term embraces all criminal offences which are committed with the aid of communication devices in a network. This can be for example the Internet, the telephone line or the mobile network.

**Cyberwar:** With this neologism is conceived the use of computers and the Internet in conducting warfare in the community of networked coputers, worldwide. Parts of cyberwar are actions like gathering of data, equipment disruption, vandalism etc.

**Mobile Computational Devices:** Portable electronic devices that can be used for input, storage and processing of data and/or communications. May be able to capture, store and show multimedia formats and connect to networks. E.g. mobile telephones, Personal Digital Assistants (PDAs), portable computers, Tablet PCs.

**Phising:** In computing, phishing is an attempt to criminally and fraudulently acquire sensitive information, such as usernames, passwords and credit card details, by masquerading as a trustworthy entity in an electronic communication.

**Spyware:** It is computer software that is installed secretly on a personal computer to intercept or take partial control over the user's interaction with the computer, without the user's informed consent.

**Steganography:** In general, it is the process of hiding information. More specific, it is the branch of cryptography in which messages are hidden inside other messages; - used commonly for the process of hiding messages inside a computerized image file, as for example hiding the name and copyright notice of the owner of an image as protection against violation of the copyright.

**Trojans:** Also known as a trojan, is malware that appears to perform a desirable function but in fact performs undisclosed malicious functions. Therefore, a computer worm or virus may be a Trojan horse. The term is derived from the classical story of the Trojan Horse.

## ENDNOTES

1. http://www.internetworldstats.com/stats.htm
2. http://www.internetworldstats.com/stats.htm
3. http://enterprisesecurity.symantec.com/
4. Fight against Computer Crime, available at http://europa.eu/scadplus/leg/en/lvb/l33193b.htm
5. http://www.usdoj.gov/criminal/cybercrime/
6. http://europa.eu/scadplus/leg/en/lvb/l33193b.htm
7. http://www.cybercrimelaw.net
8. http://www.wired.com

9 http://www.schneier.com/crypto-gram-0805.html

10 http://english.chosun.com/w21data/html/news/200805/200805080022.html

11 http://www.f-secure.com/

12 http://www.f-secure.com/f-secure/pressroom/news/fsnews_20080117_1_eng.html

13 http://www.f-secure.com/f-secure/pressroom/news/fsnews_20080117_1_eng.html

14 Symantec Internet Security Threat Report available at http://enterprisesecurity.symantec.com

15 http://www.nato.int/docu/update/2008/05-may/e0514a.html

16 http://europa.eu/scadplus/leg/en/lvb/l33193b.htm

# Chapter II
# Intrusion in the Sphere of Personal Communications

**Judith Rauhofer**
*University of Central Lancashire, UK*

## ABSTRACT

*In this chapter the limits for the sphere of personal communications are set. Different understandings of the "right to be alone" or "the right to respect for private and family life" are provided. The significance of the information privacy is pointed out and the right to informational self-determination is deciphered. Having presented the substrate for personal data protection, a legal synopsis of the aforementioned subject is the concluding part of the chapter, with emphasis on data retention.*

## INTRODUCTION

Sophisticated information technology systems now permeate almost every aspect of modern life. At the same time, there is a threat – whether actual or perceived – that terrorism and organized crime pose to democratic systems of government. This has opened an area of tension between the fundamental right of individuals to respect for their private life and the interest of the state in the protection of its citizens from harm. Modern communications systems, in particular, are seen by many as both, a force for good and bad in the conflict between those who use those systems in the planning and commission of criminal offences and those whose role it is to investigate, prosecute and, ultimately, prevent the commission of such offences by gaining access to the information transmitted and generated by those systems. Historically, the efforts of law enforcement have concentrated on the interception (through wiretapping or otherwise) of communications by suspected individuals with a focus on the contents of those communications. Such surveillance measures were seen by the governments and courts of most democratic countries as restricting a number of basic human and civil rights, so that, consequently, their use was permitted only in limited circumstances and subject to judicial control and oversight.

With the increased use of electronic communication, however, the focus of law enforcement has shifted to information collateral to those communications, such as the time they where sent, the place from which they were sent and the person or persons to whom they were addressed. This data, which is generated as a matter of course by modern communications systems, not only allows the relevant agencies to track individual suspects but also, it is argued, to trace networks of criminals and to draw conclusions in relation to the methods they use and the level of organization they employ. Access to such collateral data is generally not seen as quite as intrusive as the interception of communications so that a lower threshold would apply when deciding whether or not such intrusions restrict individuals' fundamental rights. However, that data, where it is retained for a longer period of time, inevitably allows those with access to it to build a profile of the individuals to whom it relates, of their actions and their beliefs. Indeed, profiling is now seen as one of the most important weapons in the armory of public and private organizations. It is not only used for the purpose of criminal investigations, but also in the context of a range of other decision-making processes, including, among others, border controls, fraud prevention and financial risk assessment.

Its "human rights relevance" as well as its socioeconomic effect is therefore likely to be much higher than law enforcement agencies will have us believe, and it is both necessary and appropriate to examine these issues at a time when the increased storage and use of such collateral information is being introduced by governments the world over. This chapter will provide a brief historical overview of the legal protection of the right to privacy in Western jurisdictions with particular focus on the concept of "information privacy" and the development of specific data protection legislation in Europe. It will then examine recent legal developments at EU level, including the adoption of the Directive on the retention of data generated or processed in connection with the provision of publicly available electronic communications services or of public communications networks and amending Directive 2002/58/EC[1] (Data Retention Directive), which requires EU Member States to introduce legislation necessitating the blanket retention of communications data for specified periods. The chapter will look at the way the Directive has been implemented in Denmark, Germany and the UK and the level of harmonization that has so far been achieved. It will then provide an outlook of the consequences, some of them unintended, of blanket retention both in a human rights and in a socioeconomic context.

## PRIVACY

Although most Western jurisdictions now protect individuals' rights to control the use and disclosure of their personal information, those rules are based on different origins and, in many cases, different understandings of why such protection is necessary or justified.

### The "Right to be Let Alone"

In the US, the right to privacy can be traced back to the famous essay by Warren and Brandeis, which defined privacy as the "right to be let alone" (Warren and Brandeis 1890)[2]. This right, they argued, included the right to control the "communication of [the individual's] thoughts, sentiments, and emotions to others" (Warren and Brandeis, p.198), be they in expressed form (for example, a letter or a drawing) or a mere reproduction by a third party of words or sentiments expressed or actions carried out "in private". Warren and Brandeis claimed that the right to privacy could be based on legal concepts existing at the time, most notably the right to the protection of private property and the doctrines of contract and trust", but also on a notion which was only just developing: the right to the protection of an individual's personality.

To the extent that a right to privacy could be derived from a right to private property, it protected the unauthorized publication of an individual's personal information once he had "chosen to give them expression" (Warren and Brandeis, p.198). Unlike the doctrine of intellectual property rights, whose aim it was to secure to the creator of the work the profits arising from its publication, Warren and Brandeis argued that the common law right to private property enabled the individual "to control absolutely the act of publication and, in the exercise of his own discretion, to decide whether there [should] be any publication at all" (Warren and Brandeis, p.200).

In circumstances where a third party came into possession of the personal information as part of a contract or in the context of a trust or confidence, Warren and Brandeis further argued that the desired protection already had a basis in the doctrines of contract or trust (Warren and Brandeis, p.210). However, citing the case of *Pollard v. Photographic Co.*[3], where a photographer who had taken a lady's photograph was restrained from exhibiting it and from selling copies of it on the basis that this was a breach of confidence, they argued that this protection was insufficient to cope with emerging new technologies and should be adapted. They believed that while the narrower doctrines of contract and breach of confidence "may have satisfied the demands of a society at a time when the abuse to be guarded could rarely have arisen without violating a contract or a special confidence" (Warren and Brandeis, p.210) (for example because a picture could not be taken without the subject consciously "sitting" for it), once modern devices afforded "abundant opportunities for the perpetration of such wrongs without any participation by the injured party" (Warren and Brandeis, p.210) (for example, by taking pictures surreptitiously and without the subject being aware of it), the "protection granted by the law [had to] be based upon a broader foundation" (Warren and Brandeis, p.210). As a result, they set out to demonstrate that a right to privacy had to be recognized as a derivative of a more basic principle, namely that of "an inviolate personality" (Warren and Brandeis, p.205):

Although their essay achieved considerable renown, the constitutional relevance of the principles espoused in it - to the extent that they related to the regulation of state-sanctioned surveillance measures - were largely ignored by the US courts until the late 1960s[4]. This was despite numerous occasions where they could have been applied. Most notably, in the case of *Olmstead v. U.S.*[5] in 1928, where Brandeis himself acted as Associate Justice, the US Supreme Court was asked to review whether the use of wiretapped private telephone conversations, obtained by federal agents without judicial approval and subsequently used as evidence in the criminal courts, constituted a violation of the defendant's rights provided by, among others, the Fourth Amendment (protection against unreasonable searches and seizures). The Court came to the conclusion that wire tapping did not amount to a search or seizure within the meaning of that Amendment since "those who intercepted the projected voices were not in the house of either party to the conversation"[6]. The Court's understanding of state intrusions which would be prevented by the US Constitution was therefore firmly based on a concept of place (the home as protected space) rather than individual expectation of privacy (the individual's actions as protected activity). In his dissenting opinion, Brandeis raised the issue of privacy, arguing that the founders of the US Constitution "sought to protect Americans in their beliefs, their thoughts, their emotions and their sensations"[7]. However, it took nearly another 40 years until, in the similar case of *Katz v. United States*[8], the Court shifted its definition of what was included in the definition of "search and seizure". Although the Court denied that the Fourth Amendment could be translated into a general constitutional "right to privacy"[9], it concluded that the Government's activities in electronically listening to and recording the petitioner's words while using a public phone booth violated the privacy upon which he justifiably relied[10]. Thus, the Court moved away from a definition of privacy as one of a thing or a place[11] (for example, the phone booth) to the privacy of a person or a situation. In his concurring opinion, Justice Harlan further clarified this approach by formulating a two-part test for determining whether police activity constituted a search within the meaning of the Fourth Amendment. According to his test, something is a search if (1) the individual "has exhibited an actual (subjective) expectation of privacy," and (2) society is prepared to recognize that this expectation is (objectively) reasonable. Both, the individual's expectation and the public's recognition of that expectation could be assessed without reference to the question of whether the place where the intrusion occurred was a public or a private space. The right to privacy as a right against unwarranted state intrusion was therefore officially recognized.

## The Right to Respect for Private and Family Life

In Europe, Article 8(1) of the Convention for the Protection of Human Rights and Fundamental Freedoms, otherwise known as the European Convention on Human Rights (ECHR), protects an individual's right to "respect for his private and family life, his home and his correspondence". The ECHR was opened for signature in Rome on 4 November 1950 and entered into force in September 1953. It effectively requires Contracting States to adopt legislative and other measures to give effect to the Convention rights both in relation to interference by public authorities and (in a more limited way) by private organizations. Complaints under the ECHR can be brought against Contracting States either by other Contracting States or by individual applicants (individuals, groups of individuals or non-governmental organizations) resident in a Contracting State and affected by a violation by that State of a Convention right. The ECHR is ultimately interpreted and enforced by the European Court of Human Rights (ECtHR) in Strasbourg, although national courts of Contracting Member States may enforce it if it has been incorporated into domestic law[12].

Article 8(1) ECHR is not an absolute right. It is restricted by Article 8(2) ECHR which provides that no public authority must interfere with the exercise of this right unless such interference is "in accordance with the law" and is "necessary in a democratic society in the interests of national security, public safety or the economic well-being of the country, for the prevention of disorder or crime, for the protection of health or morals, or for the protection of the rights and freedoms of others".

The ECtHR's case law in relation to electronic intrusions was mainly developed in connection with a number of cases dealing with the interception by law enforcement agencies of telephone conversations. In Klass v. Germany in 1978, the ECtHR established that, although telephone conversations are not expressly mentioned in Article 8(1) ECHR, "such conversations were nonetheless covered by the notions of "private life" and "correspondence" referred to in that provision"[13]. In Malone v UK[14] it extended this definition to incorporate not only the content of such communications but also "metering data", that is records generated through the use of a device which registers the numbers dialed on a particular telephone and the time and duration of each call[15].

Although the Court accepted that Article 8(2) ECHR provided an exception to the privacy right set out in Article 8(1) ECHR and that the domestic legislature enjoyed a certain discretion concerning the fixing of the conditions under which a system of surveillance was to be operated, it insisted that the exception was to be narrowly interpreted:

*Powers of secret surveillance of citizens, characterizing as they do the police state, are tolerable under the Convention only in so far as strictly necessary for safeguarding the democratic institutions.*[16]

In order for the interference by the public authority not to infringe Article 8(1) ECHR, it must be "in accordance with the law". In this context, "law" is interpreted as covering not only written law but also unwritten law[17] including case law. However, the law in question must be "adequately accessible" to the citizen and must be formulated with sufficient precision to enable the citizen to "foresee, to a degree that is reasonable in the circumstances, the consequences which a given action may entail"[18]. In Malone, for example, where the police's activities where largely based on administrative procedures, the ECtHR found that this requirement had not been complied with.

The law must also at all times remain "within the boundaries of what is necessary in a democratic society"[19]. Whatever system of surveillance is adopted, the ECtHR's jurisprudence must be satisfied, that there "exist adequate and effective guarantees against abuse"[20].

Despite the fact that it does not explicitly appear within the text of the ECHR itself, the principle of proportionality is also a "vital factor"[21] in the ECtHR's jurisprudence. It attempts" to find a balance between the interests of the individual and the interest of the wider community" by looking at the interference complained of [...] in order to determine "whether the reasons adduced by the national authorities to justify it are relevant and sufficient and whether the means employed were proportionate to the legitimate aim pursued"[22]. The ECtHR will also consider if there is a less restrictive alternative to the measure employed. For example, in Cambell v. United Kingdom, the ECtHR found that a blanket rule on the opening of prisoners' mail was a disproportionate response to the problem of ensuring that prohibited material was not contained in the mail[23]. The Court found that the same objective could have been met by opening the mail in the presence of the prisoner without actually reading it.

Finally, any interference with a Convention right must be subject to an effective control. In Klass v. Germany the ECtHR states that "it is in principle desirable to entrust supervisory control to a judge"[24] although it has not so far taken issue with the system established in the UK through the Interception of Communications Act 1985 and the Regulation of Investigatory Powers Act 2000 (RIPA) whereby supervision is carried out by a judicially qualified "Commissioner".

## Information Privacy and the Right to Informational Self-Determination

In the intervening years since the publication of Warren and Brandeis' essay the concept of privacy was the subject of much scholarly focus. In his excellent account of the historical origins of privacy, Gormley (1992) distinguishes between four "clusters" of scholarship that have classified the right to privacy alternatively as:

- "An expression of one's personality or personhood"[25].
- A consequence of an individual's personal autonomy, that is the "moral freedom of the individual to engage in his or her own thoughts, actions and decisions"[26].
- Citizens' ability to regulate information about themselves, and thus control their relationships with other human beings[27].
- A "mix-and-match" approach, breaking down privacy into two or three essential components[28].

Most relevant in the context of this chapter is the concept of "information privacy" put forward by Westin and Fried. Westin defined this concept as "[t]he claim of individuals, groups, or institutions to determine for themselves how, when, and to what extent information about them is communicated to others" (Westin 1967, pp.324-325). Westin returned to the approach, already considered by Warren and Brandeis, whereby information privacy should be understood in the context of property rights:

*Personal information, thought of as the right of decision over one's private personality, should be defined as a property right, with all the restraints on interference by public or private authorities and due-process guarantees that our law of property has been so skillful in devising. Along with this concept should go the idea that circulation of personal information by someone other than the owner or his trusted agent is handling a dangerous commodity in interstate commerce, and creates special duties and liabilities on the information utility or government system handling it.*[29]

Westin's definition was later mirrored in a decision by the German Constitutional Court on the constitutionality of a proposed compulsory national census[30]. However, the Court reasoned that the right to privacy did not derived, as Westin had put forward, on individuals' property rights, but – in a return to Warren and Brandeis's original suggestion – from their personality rights. The Census Act 1983[31], which had been adopted unanimously by both houses of the German Parliament, provided for a comprehensive collection of personal data relating to German citizens. The Court held that Art. 2 I in connection with Art. 1 I of the German Constitution (Grundgesetz – GG), which protect individuals' right to the free and unhindered development of their personality, also guaranteed individuals' right to control both the disclosure of their personal data and the purposes for which that data was used. It confirmed that from the constitutionally guaranteed personality right followed the basic right of the individual "to decide himself when and within which limits details of his personal live should be disclosed"[32]. In the context of modern data processing procedures this "right to informational self-determination" required the protection of the individual against the unlimited collection, storage, use and disclosure of his personal data[33].

Like the ECtHR, the Constitutional Court acknowledged that the right to informational self-determination was not an absolute right which granted the individual unlimited control of "his" data. Instead, it held that this right was subject to restrictions on the basis that each individual's personality developed within his social community and was dependent on communication with other members of that community. The individual therefore had to accept restrictions of this right where such restrictions overwhelmingly served "the common good"[34].

## DATA PROTECTION

It could be argued that the development of the concepts of information privacy and informational self-determination brought recognition to and supported the fledgling area of data protection law that had slowly developed in many Western European countries in response to the increased use of automated data processing systems by public authorities.

Hessian was the first German federal state to introduce such provisions when it adopted the State Data Protection Act of 1970[35]. The Act was seen as pioneering in the area of data protection, not just in Germany, but globally. It was followed by the *Datalagen* in Sweden in 1973, the first German Federal Data Protection Act (*Bundesdatenschutzgesetz*) in 1977[36], as well as other national laws in France[37], Denmark[38], Norway[39] and Austria[40] in 1978, and Luxembourg[41] in 1979. By 1981, there was therefore a core group of European states which had "moved to introduce data protection law at the national level without waiting for an international consensus" (Cannataci & Mifsud-Bonnici 2005).

The absence of such a consensus led to a number of international initiatives designed not only to achieve a basic level of protection of individual information privacy rights but also to avoid the establishment of so-called "data havens" in countries with no data protection legislation (Savage & Edwards 1986).

## OECD Guidelines

To this end the Organisation for Economic Co-operation and Development (OECD) introduced non-binding "Guidelines on the Protection of Privacy and Transborder Flows of Personal Data" (OECD Guideline 1980) which outlined a number of basic concepts to be adopted by member states in order to protect citizens against the misuse of their personal information by public and private organizations. The Guidelines exhibit four basic themes – the need to guarantee basic rights of privacy, the need to ensure free flow of information, the avoidance of unjustified national restrictions on transborder data flow and the need to harmonize the provisions of the various national laws (Moakes 1986). On 11 April 1985, the Governments of OECD member states adopted a "Declaration on transborder data flows" (OECD Declaration 1985) designed to act "as a benchmark against which national laws [...] may be judged" (Moakes 1986, p. 80).

## Council of Europe Convention

Around the same time as the OECD Guidelines, the Council of Europe adopted a "Convention for the Protection of Individuals with Regard to Automatic Processing of Personal Data" (Council of Europe Convention 1981). In contrast to the OECD Guidelines, the Convention was an international treaty designed to establish legally binding "parameters within which a person enjoyed a right to protection of his personal data" (Cannataci & Mifsud-Bonnici 2005, p.6). It was opened for signature in January 1981 and came into force, in accordance with its commencement provisions, in March 1985 when the Federal Republic of Germany became the fifth State to ratify it.

Some commentators (Savage & Edwards 1986, p.711; Moakes 1986, p. 81) have argued that the Convention was the result of a need to address two fundamental concerns. First, the temptation of organizations based in countries with privacy and data protection controls to relocate their operations to "data havens" with no protective legislation. Such relocation by a sufficient number of organizations could frustrate the legislative policy of the respective states to grant basic protection to information privacy rights. Secondly, the existence of protective legislation might lead countries providing such protection to adopt measures (for example, export licenses) controlling and ultimately limiting the transfer of data to countries which did not provide such protection. This would have had the potential to impede the free flow of information on which the global economy had come to rely.

Indeed, many countries without data protection laws – including in particular the United States with its dominance in the information and information technology industry - regarded the development of laws restricting transborder data flows as "unduly restrictive and blatantly protectionist" (Moakes 1986, p.82). The Convention provided that no Signatory State should prohibit or impede the free flow of data to other Signatory States[42]. Although the Convention does not explicitly prohibit the transfer of data to non-signatory countries, in many cases such restriction would be included in the national data protection laws then in force or adopted by signatory states as a result of the Convention.

Consequently, while the Convention undoubtedly represents a defining moment in the establishment of international data protection standards, it should be borne in mind that its adoption is owed not only to a desire to protect fundamental rights and freedoms of individuals but also to a desire to establish and maintain a "common market" for personal information. Moakes (1986) argued at the time that "the real reasons for the enactment of data protection laws are [...] clearly economic and not political. No state wishes to be out of line and risk its trading position" (p.83).

## The EU Data Protection Directives

The dual purpose on which much of the 1981 Convention was based was also recognized in EC Directive 95/46/EC on the protection of individuals with regard to the processing of personal data and on the free movement of such data (Data Protection Directive)[43] which as adopted by the European Parliament and the Council in October 1995. It introduced an extensive data protection regime by imposing broad obligations on those who collect personal data, as well as conferring broad rights on individuals about whom data is collected. It specifically refers to the 1981 Convention as well as the Human Rights Convention as its "point of departure" (Cannataci & Mifsud-Bonnici 2005, p. 7) and cites both the respect for the fundamental rights and freedoms of individuals, notably the right to privacy, and the need for economic and social progress, trade expansion and the well-being of individuals as its *raison d'être*.

The EC later supplemented the Data Protection Directive with two additional directives regulating data protection issues in specific sectors. In 1997, it adopted EC Directive 97/66/EC concerning the processing of personal data and the protection of privacy in the telecommunications sector (Telecommunications Privacy Directive)[44] which dealt specifically with the protection of data generated in the course of the use of telecommunication services. In 2002, following the "dot-com boom", it adopted EC Directive 2002/58/EC concerning the processing of personal data and the protection of privacy in the electronic communications sector (E-Privacy Directive)[45] in an attempt to introduce more "technology neutral" provisions to ensure that "consumers and users [...] get the same level of protection regardless of the technology by which a particular service is delivered"[46].

## The European Union Charter of Fundamental Rights

With the secondary legal framework in place, the EU began to concentrate on establishing constitutional protection for fundamental rights including the protection of personal data. In 1999, the European Council during its meeting in Cologne took the decision to draw up a Charter of fundamental rights designed to enshrine the fundamental rights and freedoms as well as basic procedural rights guaranteed by the ECHR and derived from the constitutional traditions of the Member States as general principles of Community law. The European Parliament approved the Charter in November 2000 and the Presidents of the European Parliament, the Council and the Commission signed and proclaimed the Charter on behalf of their institutions on 7 December 2000 in Nice[47].

Article 8(1) of the Charter includes a right of every EU citizen "to the protection of personal data concerning him or her". Article 8(2) provides that "such data must be processed fairly for specific purposes and on the basis of consent of the person concerned or some other legitimate basis laid down by law". It also grants a right of access to the individual to data which has been collected concerning him or her, and a right to have such data rectified. The provisions echo those contained in the Data Protection Directive and, indeed, the "explanation" with regard to which the individual Charter rights must be interpreted and applied[48] state that the right is based on that Directive as well as Article 8 ECHR and the provisions of the 1981 Council of Europe Convention.

The Charter was originally supposed to be included as Part Two of the Treaty establishing a Constitution for Europe. However, following the "no" votes in referenda on the Treaty in France and the Netherlands, the ratification process was put on hold. The Charter is now included (with minor amendments) in Article 6 of the Treaty on European Union as revised by Article 1(8) of the Treaty of Lisbon. The latter, which replaced the Constitutional Treaty, was signed on 13 December 2007 It is intended that it will come into force in 2009 subject to its successful ratification by all EU member states. This would give legal force to the provisions of the Charter including its Article 8. However, one EU Member State, Ireland, rejected ratification of the Treaty through a public referendum in 2008. As a result, it is currently unclear whether this deadline will be met.

## ELECTRONIC INTRUSION AND DATA RETENTION

It is widely held that as information technology and electronic business models evolve, the use of that technology for less salubrious purposes also increases. If information technology opens up new avenues of communication, it also opens up new avenues of committing crime, both against the individual and against the state.

As a result, the use of data generated in the course of an individual's use of such technology (communications or traffic data) has become a contentious issue between those who want to protect the private sphere of individuals by restricting the disclosure of that data and those who feel that limited electronic intrusion by law enforcement authorities (LEAs) is justifiable for the purpose of national security and crime prevention.

### Communications Data

Communications data does not include the contents of any telephone calls made, electronic messages sent or online purchases made. Instead, the term refers to information collateral to those activities. In the case of e-mail, the data may include the time the e-mail was sent, the addressee and the size of the file. In the case of telephone calls, it contains the number called and the number from which the call was made as well as the length of the call. Telecommunications providers can track the geographical coordinates of a mobile phone to within a few hundred meters (location data). ISPs providing access to the Internet can keep a log of the time access was initiated and terminated[49] and, in the case of access to the World Wide Web, the URLs of websites visited and the order in which they were accessed. Communications data can therefore constitute "a near complete map" (Bowden 2002, p.6) of an individual's private life: who they talk to, where they go and what they read online.

The subscriber data communication service providers (CSPs) hold on their customers (including name, billing address, etc.) means that communications data linked to a specific individual's account must be classified as "personal data". Like telephone metering data before it, it is therefore covered by the definition of private life contained in Article 8 ECHR, the Data Protection Directive and the various national data protection laws.

### Retention of Communications Data before 9/11

The Data Protection Directive requires Member States to ensure that data controllers only collect personal data for specified, explicit and legitimate purposes and not further process them in a way incompatible with those purposes[50]. Under Article 6(1)(d) data controllers must also take every reasonable step to ensure that data which is inaccurate or incomplete is erased or rectified.

The Telecommunications Privacy Directive required Member States to ensure the confidentiality of communications by means of public telecommunications networks and publicly available telecommunications services[51]. It also stipulated that telecommunications service providers had to erase or make anonymous any traffic or billing data they generate upon termination of the call unless they required such data for their own billing or marketing purposes (the latter use being subject to the subscriber's consent)[52]. Article 14(1) of the Telecommunications Privacy Directive only permitted derogation from that principle in very limited circumstances "when such restriction constitutes a necessary measure to safeguard national security, defense, public security, the prevention, investigation, detection and prosecution of criminal offences or of unauthorized use of telecommunication systems". There was substantial doubt about the question whether this would permit a Member State to require the blanket retention of communications data. As a result, most CSPs did not retain such data once it was no longer required for the CSPs' own business purposes. CSPs which continued to retain communications data beyond the requisite period were likely to face civil and criminal liability.

Early drafts of the E-Privacy Directive mirrored almost exactly the data protection regime set out in Articles 6 and 14(1) of the Telecommunications Privacy Directive. It is maybe unsurprising that this situation was felt, by many LEAs, to unfairly advantage criminals or criminal organizations which increasingly made use of telecommunication and other new methods of communication such as electronic mail and mobile telephony in the commission of, sometime serious, crime. LEAs claimed that the CSPs' obligation to delete communications data meant that the pool of data which might prove useful for the purpose of law enforcement was reduced unnecessarily and too early in the proceedings. In order to re-balance the situation, LEAs argued that legislation was required which made the retention of such data mandatory.

As a result of intensive lobbying by the UK, among others, Article 15(1) of the E-Privacy Directive in the form eventually adopted extended the scope of the public interests previously contained in Article 14(1) of the Telecommunications Privacy Directive. Member States now have the right to suspend the CSPs' obligation to erase communications data as long as this constitutes a necessary, appropriate and proportionate measure within a democratic society to safeguard, among other things, the prevention, investigation, detection and prosecution of criminal offences. Article 15(1) furthermore explicitly allows member states to adopt legislative measures providing for the retention of data for a limited period, provided that this is justified on the grounds laid down in Article 15(1).

## The Mandatory Retention of Communications Data

The paradigm shift that was brought about through the extension of the scope of Article 15(1) of the E-Privacy Directive prepared the ground for far reaching reform proposal concerning the mandatory retention of communications data. In April 2004, the governments of the UK, France, Ireland and Sweden submitted a joint proposal for a draft Framework Decision which was intended to put in place a pan-European framework. The proposal as drafted would have required the retention, for a minimum of 12 months and a maximum of 36 months, of all communications data generated by CSPs within the EU.

In May 2005, the European Parliament released a report in which it criticized the draft Framework Decision on three grounds: the Council's incorrect choice of legal basis[53], the disproportionality of the measures and the possible contravention of Article 8 of the European Convention on Human Right[54]. As a result, the European Commission adopted a proposal for a Directive on the retention of telecommunications data in September 2005[55] which was eventually adopted by the European Parliament and the Council less than 3 months later after one of the shortest legislative procedures in the history of the EU[56]. It came into force on 3 May 2006.

The Data Retention Directive provides for a retention period of six months to 24 months[57], with an option for individual member states to introduce longer periods where they face "particular circumstances warranting an extension for a limited period"[58]. Retained data will be available for the purposes of the investigation, detection and prosecution of serious crime[59]. The definition of "serious crime" is left to the national law of the Member States.

Member States must require CSPs to retain a wide range of data, including:

- Data necessary to trace and identify the source of a communication (telephone number, name and address of subscriber, sender's IP address, etc.).
- Data necessary to identify the recipient of a communication (number dialed, name and address of recipient, IP address of recipient, etc.).
- Data necessary to identify the date, time and duration of a communication (date of the communication, start and end time of a telephone conversation, logo-on and log-off time of Internet access service).
- Data necessary to identify the type of communication.
- Data necessary to identify users' communication equipment or what purports to be their equipment.
- Cell site data necessary to identify the location of mobile communication equipment.[60]

Data relating to unsuccessful call attempts need only be retained if this is already done by the provider for its own business purposes[61].

The Data Retention Directive does not include any obligation on member states to reimburse CSPs for the costs of retention. Instead, member states are free to decide whether or not they will compensate providers.

The Data Retention Directive also does not regulate the gaining of access to, and use of, the retained data by public authorities and law enforcement authorities of the member states. Member states have the right to regulate access under their national laws (subject to their international legal obligations).

## Transposition of the Directive by EU Member States

Member states had until 15 September 2007 to implement the Directive in relation to data generated in the course of the provision of fixed-line and mobile telephony services[62] although they have the option to notify the Council and the Commission by way of a declaration under article 15(3) that they wish to postpone its application to the retention of communications data relating to internet access, internet telephony and internet e-mail until no later than 15 March 2009[63].

Denmark was the first member state to implement the Directive through an Administrative Order based on section 786 of the Administration of Justice Act. This section had been extended in June 2002 through the "Law Concerning the Change of Criminal Code, Administration of Justice Act, Law of Competition and Consumer Regulation of the Telecommunications Market, Law of Small Arms, Law of Extradition and Law of Extradition of Criminals to Finland, Iceland, Norway And Sweden" (No. 378, June 6, 2002), an "anti-terrorism package" that had been introduced after the 9/11 attacks. Companies that provide "publicly available electronic communications services or public communications networks" must retain communications data for twelve months for the purpose of detecting, investigating and prosecuting serious crimes and will risk fines for non-compliance. The order applies only to electronic communications services that are "commercial" in nature. In general, a service is considered commercial when the purpose of offering it is to generate a profit, but the evaluation is carried out on a case-by-case basis. As examples of such noncommercial services the Memorandum that accompanies the order mentions library networks, university networks, hospital networks, and workplace networks. Thus, employers providing e-mail and Internet to their employees would not be required to retain communications data in Denmark. Although CSPs are not reimbursed for costs incurred in setting up retention facilities, the Administrative Order does not include any obligation to make additional investments. Public authorities are expected to reimburse providers for each individual request for retained data[64].

The UK implemented the Directive through the Data Retention (EC Directive) Regulations 2007 (2007 Regulations)[65] which were adopted on 26 July 2007 and came into force on 1 October 2007. In recognition of the fact that the retention of communications data relating to the internet constituted "a more complex issue, involving much larger volumes of data and a considerably broader set of stakeholders within the industry" (Home Office Consultation Paper 2007, p.5), the UK Government decided to make a declaration in accordance with Article 15(3) of the Directive thereby postponing its application to the retention of communications data relating to internet access, internet telephony and internet e-mail to 15 March 2009. Accordingly, the Regulations only concern providers of fixed-line and mobile telephony services[66]. The Regulations apply to all public communications providers, that is, all providers of a public electronic communications network or of public electronic communications services[67]. In order to avoid duplication of storage[68] and associated costs, Regulation 3(3) provides that the Regulations do not apply to providers, whose data is retained in the UK, in whole or in part, by another public communications provider. Providers, or categories of providers, must be given a written notice specifying the extent to which and the date from which the Regulations are to apply to them[69]. In practice, this is likely to lead to a situation where data is retained by "upstream" rather than "downstream" providers, so that, for instance, there may be no need for resellers of communications services to retain communications data provided they have assurances that the data is being retained by their suppliers. Some providers feared that this could lead to a situation where individual public communications providers might not be able to interpret whether and how the Regulations apply to their business (Home Office Working Document 2007). This issue was also discussed in a meeting of the UK Internet Service Providers' Association (ISPA) on 25 April 2007. In response to the concerns expressed by some ISPA members that they might inadvertently fall foul of the provisions of the Regulations because they had wrongly assumed that, absent a notice from the government under regulation 3(4), they would not have to retain the relevant data, Simon Watkin, a Home Office representative, reassured them that the government would not seek to enforce the Regulation against such providers. However, some providers questioned whether such reassurance would provide their advisors with the necessary legal certainty as, in this case, it seemed to be up to the discretion of the relevant government department whether or not their non-compliance with the Regulations would be deemed lawful or not. Consequently, some respondents to the consultation suggested that there should be "a more rigid regime" whereby the responsibility to ensure communications data is retained lies either with the public communications provider with a direct subscriber relationship or with the "upstream" provider. This would also provide for a more predictable way in which to determine the application of the Regulations to individual providers. However, the government rejected the inclusion of more specific provisions in the Regulations. It argued that because business practice differed between public communications providers, a more flexible approach was required to ensure appropriate expenditure of public money. As all reimbursement of costs must be agreed in advance (see below), the government believes that through the reduction in the overall number of providers required to comply with the Regulations which results from this approach, unnecessary expenditure can be avoided and duplication can be minimized.

Providers must retain communications data[70] for a period of 12 months. Reimbursement of any expenses incurred by CSPs in complying with the regulations may be reimbursed at the discretion of the Home Secretary[71]. However, such reimbursement will be conditional on the expenses having been notified to the Home Secretary and agreed in advance. The Home Secretary may also require providers to comply with any audit that may be reasonably required to monitor any claim for reimbursement.

In August 2008, the Home Office launched a consultation on draft regulations (Draft Regulations) that will enable the transposition of the Data Retention Directive with respect to internet-related data (Home Office Consultation Paper 2008). The Draft Regulations are intended to replace the 2007 Regulations. Responses on the consultation were requested by 31 October 2008. At the time of writing, it is assumed that the Draft Regulation will be adopted with effect from March 2009 in order to comply with implementation deadline set out in Article 15 of the Data Retention Directive.

In Germany, the *Act for the Regulation of Telecommunications Surveillance and other Covert Surveillance Measures and the Transposition of Directive 2006/24/EC*72 was adopted by Parliament on 10 November 2007 came into force on 1 January 2008. It inserts new sections 113a and 113b into the Telecommunications Act of 2004, which require providers of publicly available telecommunications services to retain communications data for a period of six months. The new provisions apply to providers of telephony services as well as to electronic and Internet communications providers. Providers that fail to comply with the retention requirements commit an offence and are liable to a fine of up to €500000. The Act does not include provisions for the reimbursement of providers of the costs incurred by them in the course of retaining the data. It seems clear that the German authorities see that cost as part of the "cost of doing business".

## Issues Arising in the Course of Implementation

It has been said that the Directive constitutes a victory of "subsidiarity" over "harmonization". Too many contentious issues had to be left for determination by the Member States in order to achieve a compromise and the consequences of differences in the implementation of the Directive will have to be assessed once all member states have completed transposition. However, it is likely that because of those differences the adoption of the Directive may have unintended consequences both of an economic and a legal nature.

For example, it has already become clear that the right of Member States to define what constitutes "serious crime" for which data can be retained will lead to an uneven application of the Directive in different Member States. In the UK, section 81(2) and (3) RIPA define "serious crime" as any offence for which a person without any previous convictions could reasonably be expected to be sentenced to imprisonment for a term of three years or more or which "involves the use of violence, results in substantial financial gain or is conduct by a large number of persons in pursuit of a common purpose". The German Telecommunications Act, on the other hand, dispenses with the requirement of "seriousness" altogether and allows providers to disclose retained communications data to LEAs where this is necessary for the prosecution of any criminal offence[73]. This could result in a situation where CSPs in Member States with a wider definition of "serious crime" will have to comply with a higher number of requests than those in States with a more restrictive definition. Interestingly, in the case of *Promusicae v Telefónica de España SAU*[74], the ECJ recently declared that the member states are not under an obligation to enact provisions allowing the use of personal data for civil procedure purposes. It did not, however, specifically prohibit the enactment of such legislation. It therefore remains conceivable that individual member states may go down that route.

Member States' freedom to legislate in this area also leaves them open to lobbying by various industries. For example, the UK Creative and Business Media Association (CMBA), an organization representing the interests of major players in the digital content industry, has already demanded that access to retained data should be granted for the purpose of investigating other crimes, such as intellectual property infringement. This could lead to a situation where an instrument which was brought in as an anti-terrorist measure may in the future be used to prosecute illegal file-sharers.

The number of authorities that have access to the retained data and the number of purposes for which those authorities can access that data will also influence the number of requests and thereby the cost, both financial and in terms of loss of human rights, of the scheme. For example, in the UK, a "public authority" which may access retained data under RIPA includes any body or office which is listed in section 25 (1) RIPA. Initially, the relevant public authorities specified by RIPA included the police, the National Criminal Intelligence Services, the National Crime Squad, Customs and Excise, the Inland Revenue and the intelligence services[75]. RIPA provides that individuals within these organizations permitted to access communications data will be authorized ("designated") by order (section 25(2), RIPA).

However, RIPA also allows the government to specify further public authorities which may be entitled to obtain communications data under these provisions. The first Order of this kind came into force on 5 January 2004[76]. It specifies a number of additional public authorities including, among others, the Financial Services Authority, the Department for Trade and Industry, the National Health Service, the Department of Health, the Home Office, Local Authorities, the Charity Commission and the Gaming Board for Great Britain. Restricted access is provided to certain individuals working for, among others, the Foods Standards Agency, the Environment Agency and the Health and Safety Executive. The list was further extended in July 2006[77].

RIPA also lists a number of purposes (RIPA purposes) for which those designated under the Act may obtain access to communications data held by CSPs[78]. Originally, access could be obtained:

- In the interests of national security.
- For the purpose of preventing or detecting crime or of preventing disorder.
- In the interests of the economic well-being of the UK.
- In the interests of public safety for the purpose of protecting public health.
- For the purpose of assessing or collecting any tax, duty or levy.
- For the purpose, in an emergency, of preventing death or of preventing or mitigating injury or damage to a person's physical or mental health.

However, additional purposes were added in July 2006 permitting access to retained data for the purpose of:

- Assisting in identifying any person who has died otherwise than as a result of crime or who is unable to identify himself because of a physical or mental condition, other than one resulting from crime.
- Obtaining information about the next of kin or other connected persons of such a person or about the reason for his death or condition[79].

Despite the fact that the Directive only allows the retention of communications data "in order to ensure that [they] are available for the purpose of the investigation, detection and prosecution of serious crime" it becomes clear that, once retained, such a pool of data is likely to create "unwholesome desires". Within a short period of time the mere existence of that pool will inspire – and, as has been shown above, already has inspired - calls for their use for other purposes and by authorities outside law enforcement.

There is also a lack of harmonization in relation to cost reimbursement by the Member States. Although the European Commission confirmed that it does not view compensation of providers as illegal state aid[80], it is clear that the reimbursement of providers in some Member States, but not others, creates inequalities and possible competitive advantages or disadvantages. This may ultimately lead to a migration of providers to those Member States where authorities are obliged to reimburse costs which has to run counter to the European Union's objective of creating a common internal market for goods and services.

Finally, in view of the fact that the retention of communications data clearly engages the fundamental rights to privacy and data protection protected by the ECHR, the Charter of Fundamental Rights and the Constitutions of many of the Member States, differences in the type of data to be retained, the type of provider obliged to retain the data and the length of the retention period will affect the extent to which that right to privacy is being restricted.

## Legal Challenges to Data Retention

Already, the Directive has come under fire from both supporters and opponents of data retention. In September 2006, the Government of Ireland brought an action before the ECJ against the Council and the European Parliament for the annulment of the Directive on the grounds that that the choice of Article 95 TEC as the legal basis for the Directive "is fundamentally flawed"[81]. It submitted that, as the "sole or, alternatively, the main or predominant purpose of the Directive is to facilitate the investigation, detection and prosecution of serious crime, including terrorism", the only permissible legal base for the measures contained in the Directive was Title VI TEU, in particular Articles 30, 31(1)(c) and 34(2)(b). It argues that measures adopted under Article 95 TEC must have as their "centre of gravity" the approximation of the laws of the member states. The Directive, however, was concerned with combating serious crime and was not intended to address any defects in the internal market. In view of the lack of harmonization brought about by the Directive, it is difficult to argue with this point of view. However, the question must be asked whether a failure to achieve harmonization in the execution of the Directive can reasonably be used to argue against the legal basis on which it was adopted. In October 2008, the Advocate General, in his opinion[82], found that the Directive did not contain any provisions liable to come within the notion of "police and judicial co-operation in criminal matters". At the same time, he notes that the national provisions adopted by individual member states before the Directive was adopted had varied substantially. At the time of writing, the case is still being considered by the ECJ.

In Germany, a writ for judicial review of the German Act implementing the Directive was filed before the German Constitutional Court in January 2008. It is in the form of a class action backed by more than 30000 complainants[83] who claim that the blanket retention of communications data of all citizens violates the right to the secrecy of telecommunications protected by Article 10 (1), third indent GG as well as the right to informational self-determination protected by Article 2(1) in conjunction with Article 1(1) GG. In particular, the complainants argue that the blanket retention of communications data is disproportionate to the purpose it seeks to achieve and that similar results could be achieved through the adoption of less intrusive measures.

In a preliminary decision in March 2008[84], the Court restricted the use of data retention by German LEAs initially until September 2008. Notably, it criticized that the Act in question for currently permitting access to the retained data for all crimes and not just 'serious crimes' as specified in the Directive. Accordingly, where German LEAs seek to access retained data for less serious crimes, the Court stipulated that such access should only be granted where there is real evidence that the data subject in question was involved in the crime being investigated. It extended the restriction for an additional six months in September 2008.

The Court also imposed a number of strict procedural rules on the granting of access to LEAs and ordered the German Government to provide it with information, by September of 2008, on the extent to which LEAs make use of their right to access retained communications data. While the preliminary decision does not necessarily mean that the Court will eventually reject the provisions of the Data Retention Directive as unconstitutional, it gives the strongest indication yet, that it is at least prepared to rule in this matter rather than defer to the decision of the ECJ in the Ireland challenge.

## CONCLUSION

The blanket retention of communications data generated by all citizens is representative of a paradigm shift in the role of LEAs from "patrolling preventative" to patrolling investigative" to "directed patrolling, proactive and reactive investigative". Rather than investigating and prosecuting crimes that have already been committed, LEAs in their new role focus, rather in the way depicted in the movie "Minority Report"[85], on the prevention of crimes that may be committed in the future. This role, which can only be fulfilled through access to information about all citizens (rather than just suspects in a particular case) and through detailed profiling of those citizens on the basis of that information, can ultimately lead to a presumption of "guilty until proven innocent". Any morphing of a reactive force into a proactive, intelligence-based force must therefore be accompanied by stringent safeguards and oversight of that force to avoid the sacrifice of this fundamental tenet, the presumption of innocence, which underpins every democratic system that is based on the rule of law.

At the time of writing, many Member States have yet fully to transpose the Directive even though the implementation period[86] for telephony data expired on 15 September 2007. In view of the pending cases before the ECJ and the German Constitutional Court, both CSPs and privacy campaigners will hope that implementation may, in the end, not be necessary. However, it is at least possible that by the time the legal issues have finally been resolved, the technical infrastructure required to facilitate both data retention and access to retained data will be firmly in place. Regardless of the outcome of the specific legal challenges currently being decided, it is therefore likely that governments will find a way to make use of that infrastructure in the medium to long term unless their constituents find a way to stage their protests more effectively. It is not in doubt that the fight against crime and terrorism would be aided by permitting a limited number of law enforcement agencies restrictive access to communications data for clearly specified purposes only. However, no business case had yet been made that electronic intrusion on the scale envisaged by the Data Retention Directive is necessary for that purpose. Even a study commissioned in 2005 by the UK EU Presidency (UK Presidency Paper 2005) one of the strongest supporters of blanket data retention, found that the majority of the data requested by LEAs where generated less than three months prior to the request. The mandatory retention in excess of that three-month period therefore seems neither appropriate nor proportionate to achieve the stated objective. The extension of possible uses to which retained data may be put and the number of agencies which are permitted to use it constitute a real threat to the fundamental rights of individuals and the democratic order.

In its Census Decision, the German Constitutional Court described informational self-determination as an essential condition for the functioning of a democratic society. According to Simitis (1984), this means that a loss of informational self-determination will also always constitute a loss of "democratic sub-stance" (p.399). As Ganley (2002) argues, "protection is not simply needed to guard against unwanted observation, but to guard against the possibility of observation itself". A person who is uncertain whether or not and when they are being watched is likely to behave as if they were being watched constantly. The German Constitutional Court acknowledged that this permanent threat of being observed is a powerful tool of social control in the hands of the observer. The unchecked use of personal data by public authorities is likely to have negative effects on social trust and social coherence. Allowing public authorities, particularly in the area of law enforcement and national security, to create data images of ordinary citizens for the purpose of profiling, may lead to a form of "social categorizing" which may privilege some citizens and disadvantage others by including them in "suspected categories" in advance of any crime committed by them. Members of such "suspected" categories (for example, members of Muslim communities) may internalize that suspicion resulting in a perception of "unwanted observation" and an avoidance of activities and associations that might be misconstrued. This may lead to a loss of political participation by specific minority groups, which is likely to damage the political fabric of any democratic society.

One could argue that citizens of informational societies substitute trust in the state for trust in each other when they agree to a trade their right to privacy for a perception of security. However, measures that undermine social trust also undermine, through their emphasis on individual behavior, social solidarity. Where we trust an all-seeing, all knowing state (however benevolent it may be in its intentions) more than we trust our fellow citizen, the state's panoptic may also have succeeded in damaging the "social fabric" of a society.

## REFERENCES

Bowden, C. (2002). Closed circuit television for inside your head: blanket traffic data retention and the emergency anti-terrorism legislation. *Duke Law & Technology Review, 5.*

Cannataci, J. A., & Mifsud-Bonnici, J. P. (2005). Data Protection Comes of Age: The Data Protection Clauses in the European Constitutional Treaty. *Information & Communications Technology Law, 14*(1), 5-15.

Cooley T. M. (1888). *Law of Torts*, 2d ed. Chicago: Callaghan.

*Council of Europe Convention for the Protection of Individuals with Regard to Automatic Processing of Personal Data* (1981). Retrieved on November 23, 2008 from http://conventions.coe.int/Treaty/en/Treaties/Html/108.htm

Fried, C. (1968). Privacy. *Yale Law Review, 77,* 475-493.

Ganley, P. (2002). Access to the Individual: Digital Rights Management Systems and the Intersection of Informational and Decisional Privacy Interests. *International Journal of Law and Information Technology*, (pp. 241-293).

Gavison, R. (1980). Privacy. *Yale Law Journal, 89,* 421-471.

Gormley, K. (1992). One Hundred Years of Privacy. *Wisconsin Law Review*, (pp. 1335-1441).

Home Office Working Document (2007). *The Initial Transposition of Directive 2006/24/EC: Government Responses to the Consultation*, June 2007. Retrieved on November 23, 2008 from http://www.homeoffice.gov.uk/documents/euro-directive-retention-data/cons-responses-07--euro-directive?view=Binary

Henkin, L. (1974). Privacy and Autonomy. *Columbia Law Review, 74,* 1410-25.

Home Office Consultation Paper (2007). *The initial transposition of Directive 2006/24/EC on the retention of data generated or processed in connection with the provision of publicly available electronic communications services or of public communications networks and amending Directive 2002/58/EC*, 27 March 2007. Retrieved on November 23, 2008 from http://www.homeoffice.gov.uk/documents/euro-directive-retention-data/cons-eur-dir-comm.pdf?view=Binary

Home Office Consultation Paper (2008). *Transposition of Directive 2006/24/EC.* August 2008. Retrieved on November 23, 2008 from http://www.homeoffice.gov.uk/documents/cons-2008-transposition?view=Binary

Moakes, J. (1986). Data protection in Europe – Part 1, *Journal of International Banking Law, 1*(2), 77-86.

*OECD Declaration on Transborder Data Flows* (1985). Retrieved on November 23, 2008 from http://www.oecd.org/document/32/0,3343,en_2649_34255_1888153_1_1_1_1,00.html.

*OECD Guidelines on the Protection of Privacy and Transborder Flows of Personal Data of 23 September 1980.* Retrieved November 23, 2008 from http://www.oecd.org/document/0,2340,en_2649_34255_1815186_1_1_1_1,00.html.

Pound, R. (1915). Interests in Personality. *Harvard Law Review, 28*, 343-365

Prosser, W. (1960). Privacy. *California Law Review, 48*, 383-423.

Rauhofer, J. (2006a). History does not matter to them – Moves towards the adoption of mandatory communications data retention in the European Union. In P. Sint & E. Schweighofer (Eds.), *Knowledge Rights – Legal, Societal and Related Technological Aspects: Proceedings of an International Conference, Vienna, 16th – 17th February 2006* (pp. 203-215) Vienna: Austrian Computer Society Series, Volume 202.

Rauhofer, J. (2006b). Just because you're paranoid, doesn't mean they're not after you: Legislative developments in relation to the mandatory retention of communications data in the European Union, (2006) *SCRIPTed* 3:4, 322. Retrieved on November 23, 2008 from http://www.law.ed.ac.uk/ahrc/script-ed/vol3-4/rauhofer.asp.

Savage, N., & Edwards, C. (1986). Transborder Data Flows: The European Convention and United Kingdom Legislation. *The International and Comparative Law Quarterly, 35*(3), 710-717.

Simitis, S. (1984) Die informationelle Selbstbestimmung – Grundbedingung einer verfassungskonformen Informationsordnung, *Neue Juristische Wochenschrift*, (pp. 394-405).

Taylor, N. (2003). Policing, privacy and proportionality, *European Human Rights Law Review*, Supp (Special issue: privacy 2003), (pp. 86-100).

UK Presidency Paper (2005). *Liberty and Security – Striking the right balance*, Paper by the UK Presidency of the European Union. Retrieved on November 23, 2008 from http://www.edri.org/docs/UKpresidencypaper.pdf.

Warren, S. D. & Brandeis, L. D. (1890). The right to privacy. *Harvard Law Review*, 4, 193-220.

Westin, A. F. (1967). *Privacy and Freedom.* New York: Atheneum.

## ADDITIONAL READING

Flegel, U. (2007). Privacy-Respecting Intrusion Detection. *Series: Advances in Information Security, 35.* Springer: New York.

Meikle, G. (2002). *Future active: Media activism and the Internet.* Routledge.

Vacca, J. R. (2005). *Computer Forensics: Computer Crime Scene Investigation.* Massachusetts: Charles River Media.

Von Neumann, J. (1958). *The Computer and the Brain*. Yale University.

Warrer, M. J. (2003). The impact of hackers. In *Proceedings of the Second European Conference on Information Warfare and Security*, University of Reading, United Kingdom, June 30 - 1 July 2003.

Wilkinson, P. (1975). *Political Terrorismn*. ew York: Halstead Press.

## KEY TERMS

**Computer Fraud:** A fraud committed with the aid of, or directly involving, a data processing system or a computer network.

**Computer Virus:** A computer program that can copy itself and infect a computer without permission or knowledge of the user. The term "virus" is also commonly used, albeit erroneously, to refer to many different types of malware and adware programs. The original virus may modify the copies, or the copies may modify themselves, as occurs in a metamorphic virus. A virus can only spread from one computer to another when its host is taken to the uninfected computer, for instance by a user sending it over a network or the Internet, or by carrying it on a removable medium such as a floppy disk, CD, or USB drive...

**Cyber Crime:** The term contains all criminal offences which are committed with the aid of communication devices in a network. This can be for example the Internet, the telephone line or the mobile network.

**Data Retention:** In more simple words data preservation. It generally refers to storing data for backup and historical purposes. Relevant terms are backup program, archive, disaster recovery and litigation hold. These actions are committed by governments and commercial organisations.

**Infringement:** A violation, as of a law, regulation, or agreement. In the computer world it may mean a violation of the Copyright legislation or Copyright Infringement of Computer Software etc.

**Internet Service Provider (ISP):** An ISP is a company or Institution, Organization etc that provides individuals and other companies access to the Internet and other related services such as Web site building and virtual hosting. An ISP has the equipment and the telecommunication line access required to have a point-of-presence on the Internet for the geographic area served. The larger ISPs have their own high-speed leased lines so that they are less dependent on the telecommunication providers and can provide better service to their customers.

**IT Crime:** Another term, somewhat broader, for Computer Crime.

## ENDNOTES

1. 2006/24/EC, OJ L 105/54.
2. In fact, the phrase „right to be let alone" had been coined by Judge Cooley several years earlier (Cooley 1888 p.29).
3. 40 Ch.Div. 345 [1888].
4. Although during that time privacy torts developed that protected individuals from privacy intrusions by private parties, see Prosser (1960).
5. 277 U.S. 438 (1928).
6. Ibid.
7. Ibid.
8. 389 U.S. 347 (1967).
9. It argued that such a general right – a person's right to be let alone – was left largely to the law of the individual States as shown, for example in Time, Inc. v. Hill, 385 U.S. 374 and Kovcs v. Cooper 336 U.S. 77.
10. Katz v. United States, 389 U.S. 347 (1967).

11 As was the case in *Olmstead* where the Court had still relied on a doctrine of trespass.

12 For example, the UK incorporated the ECHR into domestic law in 1998 through the Human Rights ct 1998.

13 (1978) 2 E.H.R.R. 214. See also Amann v. Switzerland (2000), 30 E.H.R.R. 843.

14 (1984) 7 E.H.R.R. 14.

15 Although, in PG and JH v. United Kingdom [2002] Crim LR 308, the Court found that the collection and use of such information was "necessary in a democratic society" where it was obtained and used in the context of a specific investigation into, and trial of, a suspected conspiracy to commit armed robberies.

16 Klass v Germany, see note xix.

17 Malone v. UK, see note xx.

18 Sunday Times v United Kingdom (1983), 2 E.H.R.R. 245.

19 Klass v Germany, see note xix.

20 Ibid.

21 So for example Taylor (2003).

22 Jersild v. Denmark (1995) 19 E.H.R.R. 1.

23 (1993), 15 E.H.R.R. 137.

24 Klass v Germany, see note xix.

25 See, for example, Pound (1915, p.357) who follows Warren and Brandeis' line of argument and who traces back the notion of a possible injury of an individual's personality rights to the Greek concept of *contumelia,* where the injury to honor is the essential point, not the injury to the body, and the Roman law concept of *iniuria*, which, he argues has come to include "any willful disregard of another's personality".

26 See for example, Henkin (1974, p.1425).

27 See, for example, Westin (1967, pp.7-13) and Fried (1968, pp.477-478).

28 See, for example, Ruth Gavison's (1980, p.433) definition of privacy as guaranteeing "secrecy, anonymity and solitude.

29 Ibid.

30 BVerfGE 65, 1

31 Volkszählungsgesetz vom 25. März 1982 (VZG), BGBl. I, p.369

32 BVerfGE 65, 1, pp.41-42 (translation by the author)

33 Ibid.

34 Ibid.

35 „Datenschutzgesetz“ of 7 October 1970 (HDSG), GVBl. I, p. 625

36 „Gesetz zum Schutz vor Missbrauch personenbezogener Daten bei der Datenverarbeitung, Bundesdatenschutzgesetz“ (BDSG 1977), BGBl. I, p. 201

37 Loi n° 78-17 du 6 Janvier 1978 relative à l'informatique, aux fichiers et aux libertés

38 Lov nr 294 af 8 juni 1978 om offentlige myndigheders registre

39 Lov om personregistre mm av 9 juni 1978 nr 48

40 Bundesgesetz über den Schutz personenbezogener Daten BGBl. 565/1978

41 Loi du 31 mars 1979 réglementant l'utilisation des données nominatives dans les traitements informatiques

42 Article 12 of the Convention

43 OJ L 281/31.

44 OJ L24/1, 30 January 1998

45 OJ L201/37, 31 July 2002

46 See Proposal for a Directive of the European Parliament and of the Council concerning the processing of personal data and the protection of privacy in the electronic communications sector, COM (2000) 385 FINAL, Explanatory Memorandum, para. 2.

47 OJ C 303/2.

48 Article 1 (8) of the Treaty of Lisbon amending the Treaty on European Union and the Treaty establishing the European Community (2007) OJ C 306/01 (Treaty of Lisbon).

49 However, in the age of "always-on" broadband access, the time between log-in and log-off can now be several months, so that this data is likely to have lost much of its usefulness for law enforcement authorities.

50 Article 6(1)(a) Data Protection Directive
51 Article 5(1) Telecommunications Privacy Directive
52 Article 6 Telecommunications Privacy Directive
53 The Council intended to introduce the proposal on the basis of Article 31(1) (c) and Article 34(2)(b) of the Treaty on the European Union (TEU) as a third pillar measure. However, the other parties argued that it should be taken on the basis of Article 95 of the Treaties establishing the European Communities (TEC) as a first pillar measure by following the co-decision procedure which would permit the Parliament to be involved in the adoption of any proposal.
54 See European Parliament Report, A6-1074/2005, 31 May 2005.
55 COM/2005/438/FINAL
56 For a detailed description of the legislative process, see Rauhofer (2006a and 2006b).
57 Article 6 Data Retention Directive
58 Article 12(1) Data Retention Directive
59 Article 1(1) Data Retention Directive
60 Article 5 Data Retention Directive
61 Article 3(2) Data Retention Directive
62 Article 15(1) Data Retention Directive
63 It has been reported that such declarations have been submitted by Austria, Belgium, Cyprus, Czech Republic, Estonia, Finland, Germany, Greece, Latvia, Lithuania, Luxembourg, The Netherlands, Poland, Slovenia, Sweden, and the United Kingdom, also exact reports in this respect are difficult to come by. On 22 January 2008, MEPs Alexander Alvaro and Marco Cappato have submitted a written question to the European Commission regarding the status of implementation of the Directive by the member states and the identity of the states which have entered a derogation under Article 15(3), Written Question by Alexander Alvaro (ALDE) and Marco Cappato (ALDE) to the Commission of 22 January 2008, E-0125/08.
64 See Summary Report of a Meeting on Implementation issues surrounding the Data Retention Directive of 14 March 2007, JLS DI/NK/D (2007) 4654.
65 SI 2007/2199
66 Regulation 4(5) of the 2007 Regulations.
67 Regulation 3(1) of the 2007 Regulations.
68 See Recital 13 of the Data Retention Directive.
69 Regulation 3(4) of the 2007 Regulations.
70 Specified in Regulation 5 of the 2007 Regulations.
71 Regulation 10 of the 2007 Regulations.
72 BGBl. I 2007/3198
73 §113b Nr. 1 Telecommunications Act 2004
74 Judgment of the Court (Grand Chamber) of 29 January 2008 (Reference for a preliminary ruling from the Juzgado de lo Mercantil No 5 de Madrid — Spain) — Productores de Música de España (Promusicae) v Telefónica de España SAU, C-275/06, OJ C 64/9.
75 Section 25(1)(g), RIPA
76 Regulation of Investigatory Powers (Communications Data) Order 2003 (SI 2003/3172)
77 Regulation of Investigatory Powers (Communications Data) (Additional Functions and Amendment) Order 2006 (SI 2006/1878)
78 Section 22(2) RIPA
79 Regulation of Investigatory Powers (Communications Data) (Additional Functions and Amendment) Order 2006 (SI 2006/1878)
80 Note from Vice-President Franco Frattini to the Commission, Proposal for the Directive on data retention, 7 December 2005, SP (2005) 4782/2
81 Action brought on 6 July 2006 — Ireland v Council of the European Union, European Parliament (Case C-301/06), OJ C 237/5
82 Opinion of Advocate General, Ireland v European Parliament and Council of the European Union, Case C-301/06, 14 October 2008.
83 The German language version of the writ is available at http://wiki.vorratsdatens-

peicherung.de/images/Verfassungsbeschwerde_Vorratsdatenspeicherung.pdf, last accessed on 18 February 2008.

84 Interim decision of the German Constitutional Court of 20 March 2008, 1 BvR 256/08.

85 Steven Spielberg, 2002.

86 The German news agency dpa reported in January 2008 that the EU Commission sent official letters of complaint to 19 member states because they have not yet transposed the Data Retention directive. See, for example, http://www.heise.de/newsticker/meldung/101268 , last accessed 18 February 2008.

# Chapter III
# Criminal Sanctions Against Electronic Intrusion

**Irini E. Vassilaki**
*University of Goettingen, Germany*

## ABSTRACT

*The international dimension of intrusion is discussed in this chapter along with the different legislative approaches adopted by various countries leading to the development of computer specific-legislation concerning electronic intrusion in a rather homogeneous style approach. The integrity of information and computer systems is presented and the misuse of devices, the illegal interception of data transfer and the illegal access to computer systems are bounded so to demonstrate the responsibility of providers or users.*

## INTRODUCTION

A legal comparative review of the criminal provisions concerning the punishment of the electronic intrusion is a complex operation that is impeded by the following factors:

- Electronic intrusion is - like the most forms of IT-Crime – an **international phenomenon.** In the most of the cases the perpetrators act within the boarders of one country whether the consequences of their activities appear in another one. That means that in a lot of cases is unclear, which is the applicable national criminal law.
- The national criminal systems have **different approaches**. Some countries face the new challenge with the application of the traditional criminal provisions. In the most of the cases these countries amend alternatives that enable the criminalization of the corresponding behaviors. Other countries however, prefer to create specific criminal provisions that cover specific forms of electronic intrusion.

- This form of IT-Crime is direct **depending on technique**. The revision of criminal provisions either as alternatives to existing articles or as new sections generates the following problem: the techniques that are the modus operandi of electronic intrusion change rapidly. However, criminal law has to provide legal certainty. This means that frequent change of the formulation of criminal provisions is neither desirable nor possible. The consequence is that the criminal provisions can either have general terms, which may not cover some of the techniques of electronic intrusion or to include technical terms. Through the last approach, however, the criminal provision will be useless, when the related technical terms become obsolete.

For these reasons, there are no uniform solutions in combating electronic intrusion. The following analysis will concentrate on some of the phenomena of electronic intrusion and will present the main principles that the national legal orders follow in order to criminalize such illegal behavior.

## DEVELOPMENT OF COMPUTER SPECIFIC-LEGISLATION CONCERNING ELECTRONIC INTRUSION

Many countries enacted computer specific-legislation at the beginning of the 1980s as a reaction to computer economic crime. The amendments became necessary because new forms of criminality threatened intangible goods (e.g. bank deposits or computer programs) and could not be covered by the traditional criminal provisions. In most of the cases, the national legislator amended existing laws to punish computer specific crime, e.g. computer fraud, and created new provisions to fight the unauthorized access to computer systems.[1]

During the1980s the legislation mainly covered four offences: computer-related fraud, computer sabotage, computer espionage and illegal access to computer. Significant was the amendment of the "hacking" provisions in the national legislation that punished the mere illegal access to computer systems committed via telecommunication systems. Hacking became therefore the "basic offence" of the computer criminal law that protected the "formal sphere of secrecy" against illegal access to computer-stored data and computer communication.

Beginning with the 1990s,"hacking" as form of electronic intrusion increased. Cases such as that of the "German hackers" who, using international data networks, gained access - among others - to the Pentagon in order to sell the collected data to the KGB (Ammann, Lehnhard , Meißner , Stahl, 1989; Hafner, Markoff, 1991; Stoll, 1989) made obvious the dangerousness of such behaviors. During the same period, the press published amazing cases about the exploitation of viruses and worms that made the vulnerability of the computer systems obvious (Hafner, Markoff, 1991; Weihrauch 1988).[2] In the decade of the 1990s, electronic intrusion combined the distribution of illegal contents on the Internet with a broad wave of criminal activities e.g. program piracy, indicating that many perpetrators of such offenses belong to groups of organized crime (International AntiCounterfeiting Coalition, 2003; Union de Fabricants, 2003).[3]

During the decades of 1990 and at the beginning of 2000s, the evaluation of illegal intrusion on computer systems e.g. computer-related crime, became more complicated. This fact is the result of two factors:

- There is **no homogenous pattern** concerning the infringed legal interests. Computer hacking, sabotage or illegal intrusion served different interests such as terrorism, financial gain or Nazi-propaganda. The modus operandi of the perpetrators became more sophisticated and used all the possibilities of the Internet. Therefore, criminological research became difficult and no international statistic elaborated by criminologists (Sieber, 1987) could provide reliable corresponding information and data.

- The **lack of statistical progress** constitutes an additional factor that impedes the development of international principles and/or rules regarding the punishment of illegal intrusion.

Nevertheless, national legislation covered through criminal provisions the following main criminal activities in connection with illegal intrusion: illegal access to computer systems, espionage of computer system and data interference. For the preparation or amendment of their laws, many states took under consideration the corresponding provisions of the Convention of Council of Europe on Cybercrime.[4] The approaches in the new laws vary. As will be discussed below:

Some countries, such as Cyprus, Portugal and United Kingdom, have adopted **specific legislation** to combat computer crime. The corresponding criminal provisions can also be contained in legislation that punishes other forms of criminality. This is for instance the case in Romania, where the offences concerning computer crime are included in Anticorruption Law No 161/2003.

The majority of countries, e.g. Albania, Austria, Bulgaria, Denmark, Estonia, Finland, France, Germany, Greece, Italy, Latvia, Lithuania, Netherlands, Norway, Republic of Serbia, Slovak Republic, FYROM, Spain, Switzerland, Turkey, and Ukraine, have added **new provisions in their Penal Codes**. In this way, the infractions are distributed in diverse chapters protecting the diverse legal interests. However, the systematic approaches are different. One group of countries created the new statutes besides the traditional criminal provisions. The interception of computer systems for instance follows the traditional wiretap statutes and the hacking provisions are set up after the provisions concerning the secrecy of correspondence. Another group placed the new provisions in new paragraphs, namely as qualified forms of the traditional offense.

A third group of countries, e.g. Belgium, Luxemburg, Malta, created an **autonomous chapter of Computer Crime-provisions**. In this way, they made a clear decision which forms of computer crime should be punished and avoided the division of the criminal provisions in different chapters of Penal Code.

## Illegal Access to Computer Systems and/or Hacking

The illegal access or the so called hacking constitutes a dangerous threat against the security, confidentiality, integrity and availability of computer system and data. On similar occasions, the traditional criminal provisions protect the secrecy of correspondence, telephone communication and material within the scope of professional secrecy. The need to protect data that are transmitted through or stored in computer systems required the development of a "formal sphere of secrecy" as far as it concerns certain types of data. The legal protection of such "formal sphere of secrecy" can be regarded as analogical, in the information society, to the traditional forms of secrecy.

When the first cases of hacking were publicized, the prosecutors realized that the "formal sphere of secrecy" which was infringed by the hackers could not be guaranteed by the traditional criminal provisions. The traditional wiretap statutes of most legal systems referred only to the interception of oral communication (Criminal Code, 2008a; Codice Penale, 1999c; Title 18, 2007; Title 47, 2006; C-46 Criminal Code, 1985). Similarly, the provisions on trespassing and forgery could not be used (R v. Gold and Shifreen, 1988). The applicability of penal provisions was even more difficult with respect to unauthorized access to data processing and storage systems.

In response to the new cases of "hacking", many states adopted new statutes protecting a "formal sphere of secrecy" for computer data by criminalizing the illegal access to or use of a third person's computer or computer data. Many states modified their legislation in order to implement the corresponding provisions contained in the Convention on Cybercrime of the Council of Europe. However, the national statutes differed considerably.

Many countries punish the **mere illegal access** to computer systems. However, their approach is diverse. First, different are the systematic approaches. Some countries locate the hacking-provision within specific laws alongside the Penal Code (Anti-Corruption, 2003a) when others prefer the traditional solution, namely the amendment of the hacking provision in the Penal Code either as a new provision (Codice Penale, 1999a; Computer Misuse Act, 1990) or as a qualified form of an existing offence (General Penal Code, 1994a; General Penal Code 1998). These differences are obvious also from the perspective of the legal interests that are protected by the criminalization of the illegal access. Instead of protecting a "formal sphere of secrecy", a number of countries consider hacking as a "breach of computer peace" (Statute book of criminal law, 1997a) or "breach of data secrecy" (The Penal Code, 1998). Variable is also the way of the perpetration of the illegal access. For some countries, it is adequate that the operation takes place "unlawfully" (Criminal Code, 2004a) when others require "fraudulent" (Code Penal, 2002a; Code Penal, 1993a) acts.

Most of the countries punish the access to computer systems when the accessed data are **protected by security measures**. Some of them require a "specific secured computer system"(Penal Code, 2004; Criminal Code, 1998; Swiss Penal Code, 2004a) when for other legal systems sufficient is the break of "protection of security measures" (Criminal Code, 2003a; The Penal Code of Finland, 1995b; Act IV, 2005a; Criminal Code, 2006d)[5]. Both cases involve lack of clarity. The question that arises is: How high should be the level of the infringed security measures? Is any kind of safety precaution, e.g. password, sufficient? If the answer is affirmative, how complicated should be the password? If the law requires complicated safety measures, who should be considered to infringe them? Is technical knowledge necessary or can the perpetrator be everybody who has the possibility to violate any kind of safety precautions? The national cases does note provide us with standardized solutions. In general, the middle solution prevails. High level of technical expertise is not demanded. However, the commission of hacking presupposes a minimum level of computer protection. That has as consequence that the perpetrator need not have specific technical knowledge. Sufficient is the factual possibility of breaking the secured information system.

The punishment of illegal access is dependent in some countries on the possibility of **obtaining information** (Penal Code, 1997a) **or the disturbing** of the work of the computer system (The Criminal Code of the Russian Federation; 1996a).

Some countries punish illegal access if the perpetrator has a **harmful intention**. The corresponding provisions vary. Some of them demand intention of the perpetrator to obtain unlawful gain (Diary of the Republic, 1991) when for others material or other gain suffices (Criminal Code, 2004c). Other national legislations require that the offender intend to cause a disadvantage for an other person (Penal Code, 2004b).

Some national legislation punishes **specific circumstances** under which illegal access takes place, namely the position that the offender holds. There are three different concepts that concern the characteristics of the perpetrators. Some countries provide severe sanctions when hacking is committed by a public official or by an officer of a judicial service (Criminal Code, 2003d; Codice Penale, 1999a). For others, significant is that the offender violates his secret duty or his responsibilities that result from his position (The Penal Code of Finland, 1995a; The Criminal Law, 2006d). Other statutes underline the intent of the participants to act as an association for the commitment of illegal access to the computer systems (Code Penal, 2002d; Code Penal, 1993c).

Besides the main offense of hacking, many countries punish as **qualification** activities that cause specific results. According some legislation, the severe penalties will be imposed, if illegal access has **minimum damage** as consequence. This could be damage on money (Penal Code, 2004a; Code Penal, 1993b; Criminal Code, 2004d; Criminal Code, 2004b), damage to operation of the government or other state authority (General Penal Code, 1994c; Chapter 9, 2004c) or hindering of the computer system (State book of criminal law, 1997b; Code Penal, 1993a; Criminal Code, 2006e; Anti-Corruption, 2003c). Another group of provisions treat as qualification for the illegal activities, if they have as result the **obtaining, modification or damage of information** (Code Penal, 2002a; Codice Penale, 1999a; The Criminal Law, 2006a; Penal Code, 1997b; Criminal Code, 2006b; The Criminal Code, 2000b).

Some other countries construct provisions involving a **combination of hacking as basic offence and qualified forms** of illegal access (Code Penal, 2002a; Penal Code, 2002b; Straffeloven, 2005).

Many countries additionally punish the **preparatory acts** of hacking, criminalizing the misuse of devices that aim at the realization of the illegal access to a computer system (Criminal Code, 2003e; The Penal Code of Finland, 1999; Criminal Code, 2008b' Codice Penale, 1999b; General Penal Code, 1994b; The Criminal Code of the Russian Federation, 1996b; Criminal Code, 2006c; Criminal Code, 2005a; The Criminal Code, 2000b; Anti-Corruption, 2003d; Anti-Corruption, 2003d).[6]

The above analysis provides us with the following results. The majority of national laws, in so far as it concerns the punishment of hacking:

- They recognize the formal sphere of secrecy as new protected legal interest.
- For the illegal access to computer system, they require the infringement of security measures.
- If the hacking takes place under particular circumstances, it will be punished as aggravated qualification.
- Specific preparatory acts of hacking are classified as criminal offense.

## Integrity of Information and Computer Systems

Besides the protection of the "formal sphere of secrecy" for computer data, most countries protect the integrity of the information and the computer system that transmit and process data. Traditionally, the integrity is guaranteed by criminal statutes that protect the corporeal property, where such damage takes place. Until the beginning of 1980s, in most legal systems the integrity of computer-stored data was covered by general provisions for damage to property, vandalism or mischief. However, these provisions were developed to protect tangible objects, so that their application in the information sphere posed new questions. Therefore, most countries began to enact new provisions that would be able to face the new challenges. The countries, however, follow different approaches.

Some of them enacted the corresponding provisions as a **specific provision after the hacking** criminal statute (Criminal Code, 2003b; The Penal Code of Finland, 1990; Act IV, 2005b; Criminal Code, 2004c; Criminal Code, 2006f). The national legislator provides a "formal sphere of integrity" as a specific case of the above-mentioned "formal sphere of secrecy".

The majority of the legal statutes created however specific provisions concerning the integrity of the information and the computer systems. Nevertheless, the differentiations within the national approaches are significant. Some of the countries enacted one provision that criminalizes **both data and system interference** (Criminal Code of the Republic of Albania; 2001b; Code Penal, 2002b; The Criminal Law, 2006b; Statue book of criminal law, 1997b; Code Penal, 2007). Article 4 of the Convention on Cybercrime of the Council of Europe, covers the damaging, deletion, deterioration, alteration or suppression of computer data. System interference is on the other hand - according Article 5 of the Convention on Cybercrime - the hindering of the functioning of a computer system by inputting, transmitting, damaging, deleting, deteriorating, altering or suppressing computer data. Other legal statutes **differentiate** between data interference and system interference. Some of them criminalize mainly the damage to computer equipment or information carrier (Penal Code, 2002c; Chapter 9, 2004b; Penal Code, 1997d). Other countries criminalize the **mere data interference**. In these legal orders the damage caused by the suppression or modification is not an element of the offence (Chapter 9, 2004a; Penal Code, 1997c; Criminal Code, 2006a; Swiss Penal Code, 2004b; Penal Code, 2007a; Criminal Code, 2005b). Some countries punish, however, the attack only in case that a **substantial harm** or a disturbance takes place (Criminal Code, 2008d; General Penal Code, 1994d; Penal Code, 1997d; The Penal Code, 2003; Criminal Code, 2005c).[7] Such provisions punish directly phenomena such as spam or attacks involving "denial of services". A few countries require that the serious damage should hinder the function of a computer system having **particular significance for state affairs,** such as the national defense, transport safety, the operation of the government etc (General Penal Code, 1994d; Penal Code, 1997d; Criminal Code, 2006b; Criminal Code, 2005b).

Taking under consideration the dangerousness of the exploitation of viruses some states have passed criminal provisions which specifically address the virus problem. Most of them, besides the criminal provision that punishes the **dissemination of a computer virus,** have added a **qualification** when the virus caused considerable damage to a computer system (Penal Code, 2002d; Penal Code, 2007b; Criminal Code, 2004f; The Criminal Law, 2006c). Other national statutes provide broader criminalization and penalize already the **creation of viruses** and the providing of instructions for the creation of such malicious programs (Criminal Code, 2006c; Swiss Penal Code, 2004b; The Criminal Code, 2000b).

Differentiated is the legal situation so far as it concerns the **intention** of the perpetrators to violate the integrity of information. The degree of the intention within the legal systems varies. Some countries punish the unlawful, unauthorized or "without right" infringement (Criminal Code, 2008c; Act IV, 2005a; Penal Code, 1997c; Anti-Corruption, 2003b; Anti-Corruption, 2003c).[8] Other legal systems demand purpose for damaging or destroying information or hindering the functionality of a computer system (The Criminal Law, 2006b; Criminal Code, 2005c). Nevertheless there are statutes that punish even the unintentional or negligent violation of data or computer system (General Penal Code, 1994d; Code Penal, 2007). Apparently, the degree of the intent is related to level of the dangerousness of the corresponding criminal behavior.

Some legal systems provide an even further protection of the "formal sphere of integrity", because they punish even the **attempted violation** (Criminal Code, 2004f; Criminal Code, 2008c).

For a wider punishment, some statutes provide "expressis verbis" for the **liability of legal persons** in so far as it concerns the data and system interference. It is obvious that in such cases against a legal person administrative sanctions can be ordered (The Criminal Code, 2000a).

Consequently:

- Most of the legal systems protect a "formal sphere of secrecy" and criminalize data and/or system interference.
- Many countries provide for specific criminal offences that punish the dissemination of computer viruses.

- The perpetrators should act "unlawful", "unauthorized" or "without right".

## Illegal Interception of Electronic Data Transfer

Traditionally, the criminal law protects the right to privacy of communications from tapping and recording of oral telephone conversations between persons. The right to privacy of correspondence is guaranteed by Article 8 of the European Convention on Human Rights. The new information technologies that enable the communication or rather the exchange of data between persons and computers or between computers, made clear that the existing criminal provisions were not able to defend the new forms of communications from violations. Therefore, many national legal orders modified their criminal laws in order to protect all forms of electronic data transfer, whether by telephone, fax, e-mail or file transfer. Punishable is each form of interception by technical means, namely listening to, monitoring or surveillance of the content of communications. Prohibited in this content is the use of technical devices to collect and record wireless communications and the use of software, passwords and codes. Common element of the modified provisions is that the protection applies to "non-public" transmission of data. The private nature is related to the nature of the communication process and not to the nature of the data transmitted.

Some legal systems added, in the **traditional provision** that punishes taping and recording of oral conversation between persons, a sentence or section that covers the cases of the illegal interception of electronic data transfer.[9]

Other countries amended **specific statutes** that cover this issue, in order to endow the provision with the precise elements needed for its adequate application.[10]

According to most statutes, the perpetrator should act **intentionally**, without authority and, in some cases, in order to procure economic gain (Criminal Code of the Republic of Albania, 2001a; Penal Code, 2004c; Criminal Code, 2005d).[11]

Similar to the punishment of computer sabotage, some countries penalize the **preparatory acts** of the illegal interception, namely the use of technical devices that facilitate the taping and recording of data transfer (Penal Code, 2002a). Other countries add a **qualification,** if the interception is committees in connection with a computer system of a governmental body or an institution of special public interest or if significant damage is caused (Criminal Code, 2003c). Additionally, some statutes provide "expressis verbis" for the **liability of legal persons** in so far as it concerns the data and system interference. Also in this case it is obvious that, against the legal person administrative sanctions can be also imposed (The Criminal Code, 2000c).

Consequently:

- Most legal systems penalize the illegal interception of electronic data transfer beside the right to privacy of communications.
- In order to be punished, the perpetrators should act intentionally.

## Misuse of Devices

It is obvious that the realization of electronic intrusion often requires the possession of means of access ("hacker tools") or other tools. In order to punish such activities efficiently, many legal systems adopted provisions that punish the creation and distribution of such devices.[12]

In the most cases, the provisions penalize the production, sale, import, distribution or in another way making available devices or computer programs that are designed or adapted for the purpose of committing such criminal offenses. The comparative analysis of such statutes illustrates the common problems of these provisions:

- It is not easy to prove which devices are designed to commit a computer related crime. The differentiation between them and the so-called **"dual use" devices,** that can be used also for legal purposes is difficult. An "objective" element that could exclude such devices is not available. Therefore, the interpretation is based simply on the subjective element of the intent of committing a computer offense. It is apparent that it will be complicated to collect the corresponding evidence that will lead to punishment.

- The **development of new software and computer-tools** can be placed at risk. As the statutes do not contain exceptions from punishment, in cases that the development of such devices serve research or test of the IT-Security, the scientific work will became difficult. To overcome such complications, some computer firms change their registered offices toward countries that do not penalize the misuse of devices.

To avoid the overcriminalization, some countries require that the misuse should be committed **intentionally and without right,** e.g. to attack computer systems and for illegitimate reasons (Code Penal, 2002c; Criminal Code, 2004e; Anti-Corruption, 2003d). By this way they want to cover devices that were developed for test reasons and network analysis devices designed to control the reliability of the information technology products.

Other countries face this problem by **abolishing the punishment where** the offenders confess to the authorities their involvement in the creation of such devices or assist to identify the persons involved (Act IV, 2005c).

Consequently:

- The criminalization of the abuse of devices is very difficult in so far as it concerns the collection of evidence that enable the punishment of this activity.
- The legal systems require intentional commitment of the misuse to enable the implementation of the corresponding criminal provision.

## Responsibility of Internet Service Provider

Besides the criminal liability of the direct offenders of the electronic intrusion-cases, the question remains whether there is an additional liability for internet service and access providers that "assist" the activities of the offenders. In general, the issue of co-liability of ISPs has been controversial. The differentiations are based on two main topics:

- The national laws are often based on a different understanding of the technical issues involved. Often it is not decided which functions performed by ISPs are to be regulated. The result is that a general provision is not capable of providing adequate solutions.
- The national laws have different positions with respect to the value of the freedom of information that supports the exploitation of Internet. Mainly in some Asian countries, this fundamental right seems to be of less importance or is even considered being dangerous to the safety and integrity of computer systems. In such cases one notices an extension of the criminal liability to ISPs.

On the international level, most statutes do not in general include specific criminal provisions on the criminal liability of the ISPs. The corresponding questions usually are answered by the application of traditional legal concepts. The ISPs can be punished as accomplices of the main offender. This has as consequence, that the criminal liability of the ISPs depends on the following questions:

- Do the ISPs have the actual knowledge about a specific illegal action e.g. electronic intrusion?

- Taking under consideration the technical possibilities,– can it be practicable for the ISPs to prevent the corresponding computer crime or to reduce its consequences?

Therefore, the mere access and networks providers cannot be held criminally liable automatically for the information e.g. programs that they provide access to and transport via their computer systems. The technical and legal circumstances do not allow them to perform the necessary actions of supervision and control over such activities. This approach is e.g. reflected in Art. 12-15 of the Electronic Commerce Directive of 8th June 2000 of the European Community. In general, the question of co-liability of ISPs has considerable uncertainties and differences. The factors that differentiate the question of criminal liability are – among others:

- The degree of knowledge of the illegal activities.
- The ability of the ISPs to exercise control.
- The longevity of the incriminated information and the illegal activity.

## CONCLUSION

Almost all legal systems of the world recognize the necessity of the criminal protection against electronic intrusion. In most of the national criminal systems the main forms of electronic intrusion, namely hacking, computer sabotage and interception of electronic data transfer as well as the misuse of electronic devices is prohibited. The differences, however, among the national legal systems create uncertainties and difficulties in so far as it concerns the implementation of the criminal sanctions.

Nevertheless, the fact that most of the criminal provisions follow the legal framework supplied by the "Cybercrime Convention" of the Council of Europe provides some common legal principles that guarantee the punishment of this phenomenon and can assist in the further development of the international Criminal Information Law.

## REFERENCES

Act IV of 1978 on the Criminal Code, Chapter XVII, Title I, Section 300/C, Criminal code of the Republic of Hungary, Section 300/C (2005a).

Act IV of 1978 on the Criminal Code, Chapter XVII, Title I, Section 300/C, Paragraph 2a, Criminal code of the Republic of Hungary, Section 300/C, Paragraph 2a (2005b).

Act IV of 1978 on the Criminal Code, Chapter XVII, Title I, Section 300/C, Criminal code of the Republic of Hungary, Section 300/E (2005c).

Ammann, T., Lehnhard, M., Meißner, G., Stahl, S. (1989). Hacker für Moskau. Reinbek: Wunderlich Verlag.

Anti-Corruption Law 161/2003, Chapter III, Section 1, Article 42-1 Romanian Anti-Corruption Law 161/2003, Article 42-1 (2003a).

Anti-Corruption Law 161/2003, Chapter III, Section 1, Article 44-1 Romanian Anti-Corruption Law 161/2003, Article 44-1 (2003b).

Anti-Corruption Law 161/2003, Chapter III, Section 1, Article 45 Romanian Anti-Corruption Law 161/2003, Article 45 (2003c).

Anti-Corruption Law 161/2003, Chapter III, Section 1, Article 46 Romanian Anti-Corruption Law 161/2003, Article 46 (2003d).

C-46, Criminal Code, Invasions of Privacy, Section 183, Canadian Criminal Code, Section 183 et seq. (1985).

Chapter 9, Criminal Code, Book First, Part II, Title IX, Section 337C, Paragraph 1, Criminal Code of the Republic of Malta, Section 337C (2004a).

Chapter 9, Criminal Code, Book First, Part II, Title IX, Section 337D (a), Criminal Code of the Republic of Malta, Section 337D (a) (2004a).

Chapter 9, Criminal Code, Book First, Part II, Title IX, Section 337F, Paragraph 2, Criminal Code of the Republic of Malta, Section 337F (2004b).

Code Penal, Book II, Title IX, Chapter II, Section VII, Article 509-1. Penal Code of the Grand Duche of Luxembourg, Article 509-1 (1993a).

Code Penal, Book II, Title IX, Chapter II, Section VII, Article 509-4. Penal Code of the Grand Duche of Luxembourg, Article 509-4 (1993b).

Code Penal, Book II, Title IX, Chapter II, Section VII, Article 509-7. Penal Code of the Grand Duche of Luxembourg, Article 509-7 (1993c).

Code Penal, Book III, Title II, Chapter III, Article 323-1, Criminal Code of the French Republic, Article 323-1 (2002a).

Code Penal, Book III, Title II, Chapter III, Article 323-2, Criminal Code of the French Republic, Article 323-2 (2002b).

Code Penal, Book III, Title II, Chapter III, Article 323-3-1, Criminal Code of the French Republic, Article 323-3-1 (2002b).

Code Penal, Book III, Title II, Chapter III, Article 323-4, Criminal Code of the French Republic, Article 323-4 (2002c).

Code Penal, Book II, Title IXbis, Article 550bis, Belgian Penal Code, Article 550bis (2007).

Codice Penale, Libro II, Titolo XII, Capo III, Sezione IV, Artt 615 ter, Italian Penal Code, Artt 615 ter (1999a).

Codice Penale, Libro II, Titolo XII, Capo II, Sezione IV, Artt 615 quinquis, Italian Penal Code, Arti 615 quinquies (1999b).

Codice Penale, Libro II, Titolo XII, Capo III, Sezione V, Artt 617 bis and 623 bis, Italian Penal Code, Artt 617 bis and 623 bis (1999b).

Computer Misuse Act 1990, Chapter 18, Article 1, Section 1a (1990).

Criminal Code, Title 4, Chapter 15, Section 202a, German Criminal Code, Section 202a (1998).

Criminal Code, Special Part, Chapter 17, Section 223-1, Croatian Criminal Code, Section 223-1 (2003a).

Criminal Code, Special Part, Chapter 17, Section 223-3, Croatian Criminal Code, Section 223-3 (2003b).

Criminal Code, Special Part, Chapter 17, Section 223-4, Croatian Criminal Code, Section 223-4 (2003c).

Criminal Code, Special Part, Chapter 17, Section 223-5, Croatian Criminal Code, Section 223-5 (2003d).

Criminal Code, Special Part, Chapter 17, Section 223-6,7, Croatian Criminal Code, Section 223-6,7 (2003e).

Criminal Code, Second Volume, Third Chapter, Tenth Section, Article 243, Paragraph 1, Criminal Code of the Republic of Turkey, Article 243 (2004a).

Criminal Code, Second Volume, Third Chapter, Tenth Section, Article 244, Paragraph 4, Criminal Code of the Republic of Turkey, Article 244 (2004b).

Criminal Code, Special Part, Chapter 23, Section 251-1, Criminal code of the former Yugoslav Republic of Macedonia, Section 251-1 (2004c).

Criminal Code, Special Part, Chapter 23, Section 251-3 to 251-5, Criminal code of the former Yugoslav Republic of Macedonia, Section 251-3 to 251-5 (2004d).

Criminal Code, Special Part, Chapter 23, Section 251-6, Criminal code of the former Yugoslav Republic of Macedonia, Section 251-6 (2004e).

Criminal Code, Special Part, Chapter 23, Section 251a-1,3, Criminal code of the former Yugoslav Republic of Macedonia, Section 251a-1,3 (2004f).

Criminal Code, Part 2, Special Section, Title 4, Section 246, Criminal Code of the Slovak Republic, Section 246 (2005a).

Criminal Code, Part 2, Special Section, Title 4, Section 247, Paragraph 1b, Criminal Code of the Slovak Republic, Section 247, Paragraph 1b (2005b).

Criminal Code, Part 2, Special Section, Title 4, Section 247, Paragraph 1c-d, Criminal Code of the Slovak Republic, Section 247, Paragraph 1c-d (2005c).

Criminal Code, Part 2, Special Section, Title 4, Section 247, Paragraph 2a, Criminal Code of the Slovak Republic, Section 247, Paragraph 2a (2005d).

Criminal Code, Chapter 27, Article 298, Criminal Code of the Republic of Serbia, Article 298 (2006a).

Criminal Code, Chapter 27, Article 299, Criminal Code of the Republic of Serbia, Article 299 (2006b).

Criminal Code, Chapter 27, Article 300, Criminal Code of the Republic of Serbia, Article 300 (2006c).

Criminal Code, Chapter 27, Article 302, Paragraph 1, Criminal Code of the Republic of Serbia, Article 302, Paragraph 1 (2006d).

Criminal Code, Chapter 27, Article 302, Paragraph 3, Criminal Code of the Republic of Serbia, Article 302, Paragraph 3 (2006e).

Criminal Code, Part 2, Special Section, Title 9, Section 257, Criminal Code of the Czech Republic, Section 257 (2006f).

Criminal Code, Title 4, Chapter 15, Section 201, German Criminal Code, Section 201 (2008a).

Criminal Code, Title 4, Chapter 15, Section 202c, German Criminal Code, Section 202c (2008b).

Criminal Code, Title 4, Chapter 27, Section 303a, German Criminal Code, Section 303a (2008c).

Criminal Code, Title 4, Chapter 27, Section 303b, German Criminal Code, Section 303b (2008d).

Criminal Code of the Republic of Albania, Special Part, Chapter II, Section VIII, Article 122, Criminal Code of the Republic of Albania, Article 122 (2001a).

Criminal Code of the Republic of Albania, Special Part, Chapter III, Section VII, Article 192/b, Criminal Code of the Republic of Albania, Article 192/b (2001b).

Diary of the Republic, Series 1, Law 109/91, Chapter 2, Article 7, Paragraph 1, Portuguese Criminal Law, Article 7, Paragraph 1 (1991).

General Penal Code, Chapter 13 Felonies against the general order and peace, Article 145, Paragraph 1, Criminal Code of the Kingdom of Norway, Article 145 (1994a).

General Penal Code, Chapter 13 Felonies against the general order and peace, Article 145b, Paragraph 1, Criminal Code of the Kingdom of Norway, Article 145b (1994b).

General Penal Code, Chapter 14 Felonies against public safety, Article 151a, Criminal Code of the Kingdom of Norway, Article 151a (1994c).

General Penal Code, Chapter 14 Felonies against public safety, Article 151b, Criminal Code of the Kingdom of Norway, Article 151b (1994d).

General Penal Code No. 19, Chapter XXIV Offenses against personal freedom, Article 228, Paragraph 1, Icelandic General Penal Code, Article 228 (1998).

Hafner, K., Markoff, J. (1991). CYBERPUNK: Outlaws and hackers on the computer frontier. Simon & Schuster.

International AntiCounterfeiting Coalition (IACC). (2003). Facts on Fakes. Retrieved from: http://www.iacc.org/resources/Facts_on_fakes.pdf

Penal Code, Particular Part, Chapter XXXIII, Article 267, Section 1, Criminal Code of the Republic of Poland, Article 267, Section 1 (1997a).

Penal Code, Particular Part, Chapter XXXIII, Article 267, Section 2, Criminal Code of the Republic of Poland, Article 267, Section 2 (1997b).

Penal Code, Particular Part, Chapter XXXIII, Article 268, Criminal Code of the Republic of Poland, Article 268 (1997c).

Penal Code, Particular Part, Chapter XXXIII, Article 269, Section 1, Criminal Code of the Republic of Poland, Article 269, Section 1 (1997d).

Penal Code, Special part, Chapter 3, Section V, Article 171-3, Criminal code of the Republic of Bulgaria, Article 171-3 (2002a).

Penal Code, Special Part, Chapter IX, Section 319, Criminal code of the Republic of Bulgaria, Section 319 (2002b).

Penal Code, Special Part, Chapter IX "A", Section 319b, Criminal code of the Republic of Bulgaria, Section 319b (2002c).

Penal Code, Special Part, Chapter IX "A", Section 319d, Criminal code of the Republic of Bulgaria, Section 319d (2002d).

Penal Code, Special Part, Fifth Section, Article 118, Paragraph 1, Austrian Penal Code, Article 118, Paragraph 1 (2004a).

Penal Code, Special Part, Fifth Section, Article 118a, Austrian Penal Code, Article 118a (2004b).

Penal Code, Special Part, Fifth Section, Article 119a, Austrian Penal Code, Article 119a (2004c).

Penal Code, Special Part, Chapter 13, Division 1, Subdivision 2, Section 206, Paragraph 1, Criminal Code of the Republic of Estonia, Section 206, Paragraph 1 (2007a).

Penal Code, Special Part, Chapter 13, Division 1, Subdivision 2, Section 208, Criminal Code of the Republic of Estonia, Section 208 (2007b).

R v. Gold and Shifreen. 2 Weekly Law Reports AC 984 (House of Lords 1988).

Sieber, U. (1987). The International Handbook on Computer Crime. John Wiley & Sons, Inc.

Statute book of criminal law, Second book indictable offenses, Title V Indictable offenses against the public safety, Article 138a, Dutch statute book of criminal law, Article 138a (1997a).

Statute book of criminal law, Second book indictable offenses, Title V Indictable offenses against the public safety, Article 138b, Dutch statute book of criminal law, Article 138b (1997b).

Stoll, C. (1989). The cuckoo's egg: Tracking a spy through the maze of computer espionage. Pocket Books.

Straffeloven, Special Part, Chapter 27, Section 263, The Danish Penal Code, Section 263 (2005).

Swiss Penal Code, Book 2, Chapter 2, Article 143 bis, Criminal Code of the Swiss Confederation, Article 143 bis (2004a).

Swiss Penal Code, Book 2, Chapter 2, Article 144 bis, Criminal Code of the Swiss Confederation, Article 144 bis (2004b).

The Criminal Code, Special Part, Chapter 30, Article 196 to 197, Lithuanian Criminal Code, Article 196 to 197 (2000a).

The Criminal Code, Special Part, Chapter 30, Article 198-2, Lithuanian Criminal Code, Article 198-2 (2000b).

The Criminal Code, Special Part, Chapter 30, Article 198-3, Lithuanian Criminal Code, Article 198-3 (2000c).

The Criminal Code of the Russian Federation, Special Part, Section IX, Chapter 28, Section 272, Paragraph 1, Criminal Code of the Russian Federation, Section 272 (1996a).

The Criminal Code of the Russian Federation, Special Part, Section IX, Chapter 28, Section 273, Paragraph 1, Criminal Code of the Russian Federation, Section 273 (1996b).

The Criminal Law, Special Part, Chapter XX, Section 241, Criminal Code of the Republic of Latvia, Section 241 (2006a).

The Criminal Law, Special Part, Chapter XX, Section 243, Criminal Code of the Republic of Latvia, Section 243 (2006b).

The Criminal Law, Special Part, Chapter XX, Section 244, Criminal Code of the Republic of Latvia, Section 244 (2006c).

The Criminal Law, Special Part, Chapter XX, Section 245, Criminal Code of the Republic of Latvia, Section 245 (2006d).

The Penal Code, Part 2 On crimes, Chapter 4 On crimes against liberty and peace, Section 9c, The Penal Code of the Kingdom of Sweden, Section 9c (1998).

The Penal Code, Book II, Title, XII, Chapter VI, Section III, Article 256, The Spanish Penal Code, Article 256 (2003).

The Penal Code of Finland, Chapter 35, Sections 1-3, Finnish Penal Code, Sections 1-3 (1990).

The Penal Code of Finland, Chapter 38, Section 1, Finnish Penal Code, Section 1 (1995a).

The Penal Code of Finland, Chapter 38, Section 8, Finnish Penal Code, Section 8 (1995b).

The Penal Code of Finland, Chapter 34, Section 9a, Finnish Penal Code, Section 9a (1999).

Title 18 Crimes and Criminal Procedure § 2510-2521, U.S.C. § 2510-2521 (2007).

Title 47 Telegraphs, Telephones, and Radiotelegraphs § 605, U.S.C. § 605 (2006).

Union de Fabricants (2003). *Counterfeiting & organized crime*. Retrieved from: http://www.interpol.int/public/financialcrime/intellectualproperty/publications/UDFCounterfeiting.pdf

Weihrauch. (1988). Der Morris-Wurm im Internet. *Datenschutz-Berater*, 12, 1 et seq.

## ADDITIONAL READING

Carrier, B. (2003). Defining Digital Forensic Examination and Analysis Tools Using Abstraction Layers. *International Journal of Digital Evidence*, Winter 2003a. http://www.ijde.org.

Jones, K., Bejtlich, R., & Rose, C. (2005). *Real Digital Forensics: Computer Security and Incident Response*. London: Addison-Wesley Professional.

Parker, D.B. (1998). *Fighting Computer Crime: A New Framework for Protecting Information*. New York: Wiley.

Politis, D., Papasteriadou, N., & Gallardo, M.A. (2003). The Impact of New Technologies on Forensic Engineering and Expert Witnessing in Courts of Law. In Politis, D., & Papasteriadou, N. (Eds.) *Recent Advances in Court Computerisation and Legal Databases – First steps towards e-Justice*. Athens: Ant. N. Sakkoulas Publishers.

Sterling, B. (1993). *The Hacker Crackdown: Law and Disorder on the Electronic Frontier*. New York: Bantam Books.

Schwartau, W. (Ed.). (1996). *Information warfare: Cyberterrorism: Protecting your personal security in the information age* (2nd ed.). New York: Thunder's Mouth Press.

## KEY TERMS

**Electronic Surveillance:** Activity involving the use of electronic equipment to track an individual's activities.

**Information Warfare:** The actions intended to protect, exploit, corrupt, deny, or destroy information or information resources in order to achieve a significant advantage, objective, or victory over an adversary.

**Internet Service Provider (ISP):** It is the company that sits in between the Internet and someone that wants to use the Internet. These companies are usually the telephone or cable companies themselves, but sometimes they are independent providers of Internet access. In the latter case, they still need to work with the phone and cable companies since they are the ones that provide the communications infrastructure.

**IT-Crime:** Information security violation and generally speaking criminal activity and technology crime investigation focused on advanced technologies like Wireless Technologies, 3G Mobile Telephony, Multimedia Messaging, Virtual Money and Archives of Personal Data.

**Security:** Something that gives or assures safety, as: (a) Measures adopted by local authorities or governments to prevent espionage, attack, or sabotage; (b) Measures adopted to prevent criminal activities.

## ENDNOTES

1 See, for Austria, the Criminal Code Amendment Act of 1987 (Bundesgesetzblatt 1987/605); for Australia, Section 408e of the Queensland Criminal Code as amended in 1979, Sections 222, 276 of the Northern Territory Criminal Code as amended in 1983, Section 115 of the New South Wales Crimes Act 1900 in its application to the Australian Capital Territory, as amended in 1985, the Crimes (Computers) Act No. 36 of 1988 of Victoria, as well as additional legislation passed in the Australian Capital Territory, the Commonwealth, New South Wales, the Northern Territory, South Australia and Victoria; for Canada, The Criminal Law Amendment Act 1985 (S.C. 1985, c. 19); for Denmark, the Penal Code Amendment Act of 6 June 1985 on Data Criminality; for Germany, the Second Law for the Suppression of Economic Crime of 15 May 1986 (Bundesgesetzblatt I, 1986, p. 721); for Finland, the Laws Amending the Criminal Code No. 769/1990 of 24 August 1990 (first phase of the total reform of the Criminal Code), and No. 578/1995 of 28 April 1995 (second phase of the total reform of the Criminal Code); for France, the Law on Infringements in the Field of Informatics of 5 January 1988; for Greece, Law No. 1805/88 of 30 August 1988; for Italy the Amendment of 1978 to Section 420 Penal Code (concerning attacks to public utility plants and research or data processing facilities); for Luxembourg, Law of 15 July 1993 Aiming to Reinforce the Fight Against Economic Crime and Computer Fraud; for Malaysia, Computer Crime Law of 1997; for the Netherlands, Dutch Computer Crime Act of 23 December 1992, as amended in 1994 and 1995; for Japan, the Penal Code Amendment Act of 1987; for Norway, the Criminal Code Amendment Act of 12 June 1987; for Spain, Criminal Code 1995 (Law No. 10/1995 of 23 November 1995), especially Articles 248.2, 256, 264.2, 278 et seq.; for Sweden, Section 21 Data Protection Act of 4 April 1973, and the

Criminal Code Amendment Act of July 1986 (Law No. 123); for Switzerland, 1994 Revision of Property Crime Provisions; for the United Kingdom, the Forgery and Counterfeiting Act of 1981, and the Computer Misuse Act 1990 of 29 June 1990, draft for a new Section 15a Theft Act 1968; for the United States of America, the Credit Card Fraud Act of 1984 (Publ. L. 98-473) and the Counterfeit Access Device and Computer Fraud and Abuse Act of 1984 and the Computer Fraud and Abuse Act of 1986 (both codified as amended at 18 U.S.C. §§ 1029-1030) as well as State legislation in every state but Vermont. For a comparative analysis of the various laws see *Sieber*, The International Handbook on Computer Crime, 1986, pp. 42 et seq.

2 So was for instance the case of the "Internet-worm" created by an American student affected and closed down about 6,000 computer systems within the "Internet"-network in only a couple of days.

3 For the connection between piracy and organized crime see also: www.fbi.gov/hq/cid/orgcrime/lcn/ioc.htm; *FPI*, Music Piracy Organized Crime and Terrorism, 3td Ed. 2002, p.7.

4 The text and explanatory report of the Convention see under: http://conventions.coe.int/Treaty/Commun/QueVoulezVous.asp?NT=185&CM=8&DF=&CL=ENG

5 See e.g. for Cyprus Article 4 Law No 22 (III) 04,

6 For Detailed on misuse of devices see below B.4.

7 See e.g. for Cyprus Art. 7 Cyprus Law No 22 (III) 04.

8 See e.g. for Cyprus, Article 6, 7 Cyprus Law No 22 (III) 04.

9 See e.g. for Albania, Article 122 Criminal Code; For Denmark, Section 193 Penal Code; for Finland, Chapter 38, Section 3 par. 1 Nr. 2 Penal Code; for France, Article 226-15 par. 2 Penal Code; for Republic of Serbia, Article 298 par. 1 Criminal Code; for Sweden, Section 9b, Law 1075:239; for Turkey, Article 243 par. 1 Criminal Code; for Ukraine, Article 163 Criminal Code.

10 See e.g. for Austria, Section 119 (1) Penal Code; for Bulgaria, Article 173, par. 3 Penal Code; for Republic of Croatia, Article 223 par. 4 Criminal Code; for Cyprus, Article 5, Cyprus Law No 22 (III) 04; for Estonia, Section 207 Penal Code; for Germany, Section 202b Criminal Code; for Lithuania, Article 198, par. 1 Criminal Code; for Portugal, Article 8, Law Nr. 109/91; for Romania, Article 43, par. 1 Romanian Law no 161/2003; for Slovak Republic, Section 247, par. 2a Criminal Code.

11 See e.g. for Cyprus, Article 5, Cyprus Law No 22 (III) 04.

12 See e.g. for Albania, Article 286/a Criminal Code; for Austria, Section 126c Criminal Code; for Belgium, Article 550bis 4 Criminal Code; for Republic of Croatia, Article 223, 6, 7 Criminal Code; for Finland, Chapter 34, Section 9a Penal Code; for France, Article, 323-3-1 Penal Code; for FYROM, Article 251 (6) Criminal Code; for Germany, Section 202c Criminal Code; for Hungary, Article, 300/E par. 3 Criminal Code; for Latvia, Section 193, par. 2 Criminal Code; for Lithuania, Article 198-2 Criminal Code; for Luxembourg, Article, 509-7 Criminal Code; for Malta, Article 337F par. 4 Criminal Code; for Norway, Section 145b Penal Code; for Romania, Article 46, Romanian Law no 161/2003; for Switzerland, Article 144bis par. 2 Penal Code; for UK, Section 37, Computer Misuse Act.

# Chapter IV
# Protecting Identity without Comprising Privacy:
## Privacy Implications of Identity Protection

**Ioannis Iglezakis**
*Aristotle University of Thessaloniki, Greece*

## ABSTRACT

*In this chapter, a specific issue is addressed that concerns the protection of privacy vis-à-vis the efforts to combat identity theft and protect personal identifying information. There are, in particular, measures undertaken by legislators that involve penal sanctions and the introduction of new technological means for identity verification. Also, identity management schemes are introduced, which are utilized by service providers, mainly in the e-business sector, in order to support controlled access to resources. The solutions undertaken to protect identity are seen as measures enhancing privacy, which is endangered by identity theft. Personal information is largely available in the information society and its collection by identity fraudsters is also possible. Therefore, an effective protection of information protection should also include the protection of identity. The downside of the identity protection approach is that identity management actually presents risks to privacy, since the processing of personal data takes place in this context and it is argued that there are certain implications concerning the lawfulness of the processing. The use of electronic authentication through electronic cards or biometrics on passports and identity cards pose privacy issues, too. Subsequently, the legislation concerning identity theft and identity related crime is outlined. This is followed by specific analysis of privacy issues concerning identity management and identity verification methods, with particular reference to biometrics.*

## INTRODUCTION

The protection of identity is considered essential today for the reason that identity theft is becoming a serious issue in modern society. As this problem reaches the level of alarm, studies are being carried out which focus on the motives and methods of Internet based identity theft (Marshall & Tompsett, 2005), on the typology of identity related crime (Koops & Leens, 2006) and, what is more important, on the feasibility of measures aiming at combating identity related crime (Halpern, 2006). The said studies stress out expressly that identity theft and identity fraud, which is a broader term, are seen as forthcoming threats, which can jeopardize the interests of users of Internet.

The issue of identity theft is arising due to the availability of information from various online sources. There is a diversity of offered personal information on the Internet, varying from harmless data to more sensitive one, and the collection of information from multiple sources can be used by cybercriminals in order to identity themselves as another person with the intention to commit a financial crime (Marshall & Tompsett, 2005). So, for example, the European Network and Information Security Agency (ENISA) presented recently a Position Paper on Security Issues and Recommendations for Online Social Networks at the e-challenges conference in Hague, in which it outlined the threats to users and providers of such services, e.g. digital dossier aggregation (creation of digital dossiers of personal data), secondary data collection (collection of traffic data), face recognition (user images being used to enable linking to apparently anonymous profiles) etc.[1]

By and large, it seems that the Internet can be used as a medium for the exploitation of identity information, which is available in a wide variety and its acquisition is an easy task, while it is difficult for law enforcement authorities to seek and capture illegal activities. Information and Communication Technologies (ICTs) and the Internet make it possible for anyone to collect personal information through the access of public records. Identity thieves have been able to take on the identity of a victim or even work anonymously in order to access web resources in order to commit fraud (Chawki & Wahab, 2006).

The Internet is, of course, not the only source for obtaining personal information that can lead to identity fraud. Fraudsters seem to be able to find any piece of information relating to an individual and may use various tactics to get it. A recent example is the theft of a laptop in UK, which contained unencrypted information about 600,000 people.[2] Similar incidents have also taken place with regard financial information and the competent authorities have sanctioned financial organizations for their failure to take appropriate measures. The methods of obtaining identity information are either technical or non-technical. The former methods include key logging, (e.g., via malware on user's system), hacking into a legitimate database and collection of data by a counterfeit website (preceded by phishing attacks), whereas the latter include the retrieval of materials from waste bins, social engineering and mail or data theft (Furnell, 2007a, p. 6).

Identity theft is committed by offenders in order to perpetrate fraud, usually by obtaining a financial benefit in someone else's name[3]. In more particular, it has as its object the personal identifying information of another individual, including inter alia name, address, date of birth, phone numbers, utility bills, passport, driving license, birth certificate, bank details and credit card information, employment information, social security number, e-mail address, passwords, etc., and it purports to opening or taking over of credit card accounts, applying for loans, etc (Chawki & Wahab, 2006, p. 3). However, the appropriation of an identity itself will not give rise to criminal offense, unless it is performed with the intention to commit an illicit activity (Savirimuthu & Savirimuthu, 2007, p. 439). Identity fraud is generally related to threats such as phishing and pharming, which are emerging as new forms of fraud committed electronically.

The protection of the online identity is, therefore, a serious issue, for it is essential particularly in the context of electronic communication to allow secure user authentication and protect the right of identity (Borges & Schwenk). Also important is the protection of the offline identity as well. Identity fraud challenges identity verification policies and is not restricted to online activities, but also refers to document fraud, i.e. the use of counterfeited legal identity documents, which makes the protection of the offline identity also significant (Grijpink, 2004, p. 29). This aspect of identity fraud is becoming increasingly important particularly after the events of 11 September 2001. Therefore, it becomes evident that a new approach to identity policy is required, one that would combat effectively identity fraud and identity related crime.

## THE CONCEPT OF IDENTITY AND ITS THREATS

### A Short Introduction to Identity

Identity can be conceptualized in many ways (Meints, 2006, p. 576). This is due to the multiplicity of aspects of a person's life, ranging from private and family life to social and work life and, also to citizen and customer life (FIDIS, D 2.1, p. 27). As a result, identity may refer to any particular facet and specific accreditation of a person, such as profession, marital or employment status, membership in a group or other characteristic, e.g. nationality, etc. All these identity aspects underlie the problematic of identity and of a person's identification (Nabeth, 2006).

In particular, identity is defined as 'the subset of attributes of an individual person which sufficiently identifies this individual person within any set of persons' or, in other words, 'which sufficiently distinguishes this individual person from all other persons within any set of persons' (Pfitzmann & Hansen, 2008, p. 29). Such a definition underlines that there is not one single identity, but several identities, depending on the attributes assigned (see Fig. 1) (FIDIS, D2.3, pp. 21, 25).

A specific issue concerns the rights attached to a person due to his competences or membership in a social, ethnic group or business or professional entity. The evidence of an accreditation or affiliation by a person is offered by an identity document (identity card, passport) or by a token (e.g. an e-mail address, access code or a key providing access to an infrastructure). And also important is the issue of management of identity, that is, the management of access to identity information and of control of such information. The disclosure of such information can have negative consequences, since it may have an impact on freedom to act[4], or lead to exploitation of such information, such as in case of spamming (FIDIS, D.2.3).

Since there is no consensus as to the precise content of identity, it seems appropriate to distinguish between three broad defined levels of identity, i.e. personal identity, social identity and economic identity.[5] The first level includes information closely connected with the physical existence of a person, such as name, date and location of birth, permanent or instant location (mobile phone), and the biological, health and

*Figure 1. Examples of attributes*

- Name
  - o First name or given name
  - o Last name
  - o Married name
  - o Maiden name
  - o Nick name
  - o Pseudonym
    - Stage name
- Identifier
  - o ssn (social security number)
  - o Login
  - o used as identifiers (identifier is only a secondary function)
    - Biometric attributes, etc.

psychological characteristics. The second level refers to affiliation to a family or a group (including citizenship) and the liaisons of a person to other persons (friends, etc.) and its interests. Finally, the third level concerns the employee or business identity and customer or client identity (FIDIS, D 2.3).

In the online environment identity represents a specific aspect of real-world identity or a transaction between different persons or entities who communicate using an online identity token, such as an e-mail address or an electronic signature. Thus, an online identity is an artificial representation of a person's identity or, more precisely, of a partial identity (Marshall & B.C. Tompsett, 2005, p. 129). On the Internet, however, validation of identity is particularly important, due to the nature of the Internet as an open network, allowing anonymous communication between users, which presents various risks (Mason, 2004, p. 165). Identification may pose problems where identity information is stolen or forged and as a result, incorrect identification takes place, which relates to identity theft and identity fraud.

## Identity Theft and Identity Related Crime

Identity theft is concerning an increasingly rising number of people who become victims of fraudsters. The level of identity theft rises constantly in United States, where it represents the number one complaint received by the U.S. Federal Trade Commission (FTC), accounting for 32% of public complaints in 2007, with credit card fraud being the most common form of identity theft.[6] Europe is also affected, as identity theft is one of the fastest growing crimes both on- and offline[7], and this problem will gain more importance in the future particularly due to the growing penetration of Internet technology.

The concepts of identity fraud and identity theft are ill-defined and used interchangeable, although they differ in their details. In particular, identity fraud is defined in a study by the UK Cabinet Office as follows:

*ID fraud arises when someone takes over a totally fictitious name or adopts the name of another person with or without their consent.*

Another author adopts a broader definition, defining identity fraud as meaning:

*that somebody with dishonest intentions deliberately passes himself off under an identity that does not belong to him by using the identity of another existing or fictitious person.* (Grijpink, 2004, p. 29)

In contrast, identity theft is defined as a subset of identity fraud. A definition of identity theft is given in the US Identity Theft and Assumption Deterrence Act defines identity theft as:

*the knowing transfer or use, without lawful authority, of a means of identification of another person with the intent to commit, or to aid or abet, any unlawful activity that constitutes a violation of Federal law, or that constitutes a felony under any applicable State or local law.*

This definition places importance on the subsidiary aspect of identity theft, indicating that an identity is abused to commit another crime. Essentially, identity theft means fraud or generally an illegal activity where the identity of an existing person is used as a target or as a tool without that person's consent (Koops & Leenes, 2006, p. 556).

Identity-related crime is an even broader term than identity fraud, which concerns all illegal activities that have identity as a target or principal tool (Koops & Leenes, 2006, op. cit.). This term comprises new types of fraud such as phishing[8], sniffing[9] and farming[10], which target identity information as a valuable asset in the information society. Phishing and pharming have as primary target clients of online banking services (Gajek, Schwenk & Wegener, 2005), whilst security threats endanger electronic transactions in general and primarily, e-commerce and e-government (Wimmer & B. v. Bredow, 2002).

### The Socioeconomic Background of Identity Theft

The volume of attacks on identity information is constantly rising, particularly in the online environment, making identity fraud a significant problem. In the U.S., the total number of victims of identity theft was 8,3 million in 2006 and the damage amounted $ 15,6 billion (FTC, 2006, p. 3). Since stolen identity information is used to commit financial crimes, the impact on losses resulting from identity fraud is substantial. In the UK it is estimated that identity fraud costs the economy £1.7 billion (Savirimuthu & J. Savirimuthu, 2007, p. 438) and also that it accounts for a criminal cash flow of £10 million per day.[11] Certainly, these figures may not be accurate, since there are economic losses which have not been reported to authorities and others which were not discovered by injured parties.

For individuals, identity theft has very negative effects, since many individuals suffer damages ranging between $100 and $499 (FTC, 2006, p. 8). But even when no expenses are incurred, victims have to spend many hours resolving various problems (FTC, 2006, p. 5) concerning the impairment of their identity (Furnell, 2007a, pp. 6-11). Victims may also face damage in their reputation, e.g. loss in creditworthiness and in extreme cases, wrongful arrests and prosecution (Meints, Rost, Zuccato, Delaitre & Maghiros, 2006, p. 66 et seq.). A crucial factor is the time taken to discover the crime. The damage to a victim is significant smaller if the misuse is discovered quickly. The longer it takes for victims to discover the theft, the greater is the victim's loss and suffering (FTC, 2003, p. 8). Additionally, it is worth mentioning that financial status and education plays a role in discovering incidents of identity theft. Low-income, less-educated victims take longer to discover or report the crime and this results in greater suffering.

As regards the identity of identity thieves, an investigation from the US Secret Service points out that they are mostly young males who were not engaged before in criminal activities.[12] One third of such crimes were committed by insiders, whereas 60% of the offenders did not know their victims. Nearly all of them worked alone and 42,5 % were aged from 25 to 34 years, while 18,5% were aged from 18 to 24. The motives of identity thieves were mostly economic: 45,3% committed identity thief to obtain and use credit, 33% to procure cash, 20,9% to apply for loans to buy vehicles, 7,7% to manufacture and sell fraudulent IDs, 4,6% to obtain cell phones and services, 3,8% to gain government benefits, while 22,7% did it to conceal actual identity and 2,2 % to procure drugs. Another interesting finding is that the average loss caused by each crime was US $ 31000, while one case involved a loss of US $ 13 million. Regarding the enforced penalties on identity thieves it is mentioned in the case files of the Secret Service that 56% of the defendants served a sentence of 24 months or less and about 29% served less than a year.

Other negative aspects of identity theft are those concerning the damage to consumer trust in online transactions (de Bruin, 2002), which results in the loss of revenues for providers of online services. Finally, one could also note the cost of discovery and investigation of crime and the cost of resolving the problems created by theft or fraud (Meints, 2006, p. 77).

## LEGISLATION ON IDENTITY THEFT

### Criminal Legislation Pertaining to Identity Related Crime

The protection of identity through legal means includes primarily the provision of criminal sanctions for identity theft and/or identity fraud. However, provisions on such crimes are only foreseen in the United States, while in Europe – with the exception of the UK – there is no specific legislation. In particular, the U.S. Identity Theft and Assumption Deterrence Act of 1998 was passed in 1998, which amended 18 U.S.C.[13] This act refers to fraud and related activity in connection with identification documents and information. It was adopted in order to fill the gap that existed under previous legislation and in particular, because 18 U.S.C. § 1028 covered only the fraudulent creation, use, or transfer of identification documents and not the theft or criminal use of the underlying personal information (Chawki & M. S. Wahab, 2006, p. 26).

The Identity Theft Act added Section § 1028(a)(7) which provides that it is a federal crime when anyone 'knowingly transfers or uses, without lawful authority, a means of identification of another person with the intent to commit, or to aid or abet, any unlawful activity that constitutes a violation of Federal law, or that constitutes a felony under any applicable State or local law'.

Furthermore, it amended several provisions of the same statute. Accordingly, the provisions of § 1028(b) were extended to identity theft; section § 1028(b)(1)(D) provides that the punishment for an offense under § 1028(a)(7) is a fine or imprisonment for not more than 15 years, or both, if the offense is an offense that involves the transfer, possession or use of one or more means of identification if, as a result of the offense, anything of value aggregating $1,000 or more during any one-year period. In any other case, a fine or imprisonment for not more than five years or both is provided under § 1028(b)(2)(B). Section § 1028(f) provides that attempts or conspiracies to commit offenses such as identity theft are subject to the same penalties as those prescribed for the offense of which was the object of the attempt or conspiracy. If the offence is committed to facilitate a drug trafficking crime, or in connection with a crime of violence, or after a prior conviction for identity theft, a fine or imprisonment for not more than 20 years is imposed (Section § 1028(b)(3)). Also, section § 1028(b)(5) provides for the forfeiture to the U.S. of any personal property used or intended to be used to commit the offense.

In the UK the Fraud Act 2006 provides for criminal provisions that can be applied to identity related crime. This act regulates the general offence of fraud that can be committed: a) by false representation, b) by failing to disclose information and c) by abuse of position. False representation is further defined in section2, which states that a person is in breach of this section if he: a) dishonestly makes a false representation, and b) intends, by making the representation, i) to make a gain for himself or another, or ii) to cause loss to another or to expose another to a risk of loss. This Act covers identity fraud and particularly phishing and similar identity related crimes (Savirimuthu & J. Savirimuthu, 2006, p. 441).

In the other European countries there are specific provisions concerning the forgery of official identity documents or impersonation and also the use of false identity is penalized as an attempt to defraud, but the theft of an identity to commit fraud is generally not sanctioned (Koops, 2005, p. 10).

Similarly, the Cybercrime Treaty does not penalize identity theft and fraud as such, but includes provisions on computer crimes, which are related to identity related crimes. In Article 2 illegal access is defined as intentionally accessing a computer system without right; this is the case where an offender hacks into a computer system with the intention to steal personal information. Illegal interception is defined in Article 3 as intentionally intercepting without right, made by technical means, of non-public computer transmissions of computer data (e.g. network traffic analysis).

Further, Article 7 defines computer-related forgery as 'intentionally introducing, altering or deleting data in a computer system without right and with the intent that is be considered or acted upon for legal purposes as if it were authentic'. And finally, Article 8 defines computer-related fraud as 'intentionally and without right, causing of a loss of property to another person by any input, alteration, deletion or suppression of computer data, any interference with the functioning of a computer system, with fraudulent or dishonest intent of procuring, without right, an economic benefit for oneself or for another person. These two provisions are the ones addressing primarily identity fraud, as it include cases in which stolen identity information is used to obtain an economic benefit.

## Protection of Identity as a Means of Protecting Privacy

Protection of personal identity, i.e. protection of the attributes assigned to a person, purports to protection of personal information and to protection of the financial interests of the individual. Regarding privacy protection, the legislative framework in most European countries follows the prerogatives of the European Directive on Data Protection (Directive 95/46/EEC of 24 October 1995 on the protection of individuals with regard to the processing of personal data and on the free movement of such data "the Directive").[14] Non-EU countries, such as the United States follow a different approach to protection of privacy as they lack a comprehensive privacy law for the private sector where sector-specific laws apply instead, focusing on financial privacy (Fair Credit Reporting Act, etc.), children online privacy (Children's Online Privacy Act of 1998), etc (Manny, 2003).

The US Privacy Act of 1974 includes principles of Fair Information Practices, which were first formulated by the U.S. Department of Health, Education and Welfare in 1973 (Smith, 1993, pp. 50-51), are the following: (1) collection limitation: no secret system for collecting personal data may exist, (2) disclosure: a person must have the possibility to look at the profile generated on him and its use, (3) secondary usage: it must be possible for a person to prevent the use of his profile for other purposes if he does not agree with the intended use, (4) record correction: it must be possible for a person to correct or add to a profile with personal data generated about him, (5) security: an organization that generates, maintains, uses or spreads personal data must, on the one hand, ensure that this data is used for the intended purpose and, on the other hand, take precautionary measures to avoid an abuse of the data. These principles were further elaborated into the principles for the protection of privacy issued by the OECD[15] and represent Fair Information Practice Principles that have been widely accepted as a basis for privacy legislation in the U.S., Canada, and Europe, as well as in other countries. These are the principles of openness[16], collection limitation[17], purpose specification[18], use limitation[19], data quality[20], individual participation[21], security safeguards[22] and accountability[23].

On the basis of the EU Directive, identity data are qualified as personal information according to Article 2a of the Directive, which defines as personal data any information relating to an identified natural person.[24] This is so, because these data are related to a natural person and their protection from identity thieves contributes to the protection of its privacy. Furthermore, the collection, storage and further use of this information constitute processing of personal data under Article 2b of the Directive and it falls within the field of application of the Directive if processing takes place by automatic means, and this is the cases where personal information is obtained by technical means. This would also be the case if no automatic means are used and information is obtained by non-technical means, but the data form part of a filing system. If no such system is used for the filing of information, the Data Protection Directive and the national laws that have implemented it would not apply.

This privacy approach does not cover other types of identity, such as the online (or offline) corporate identity, which includes information identifying a corporation or business, e.g., a website, a physical or e-mail address, etc (Marshall et al, 2005, p. 129). Information relating to a legal person does not constitute personal data and is excluded from the field of application of data protection laws. A single exception is established by the e-Communications Directive (Directive 2002/58/EC of 12 July 2002 concerning the processing of personal data and the protection of privacy in the electronic communications sector[25]), which extends the protection of its provisions to the legitimate interests of subscribers who are legal persons.[26]

Nevertheless, the protection of a network identity, which includes the devices that persons are using in order to communicate (Marshall et al, 2005, 130), is prone to the aforementioned privacy approach. Although traffic data, such as the IP address have a technical character, they constitute personal data, since they refer to a natural person, as this has been established by the European Court of Justice in the case Productores de Música de España (Promusicae) v Telefónica de España SAU[27]. The protection of traffic data is provided for in Articles 5 and 6 of Directive 2002/58/EC. Particularly the former provision provides a safeguard of confidentiality of such data, prohibiting any interception or surveillance etc.

Identity theft consisting in the acquisition ("harvesting") of identity information related to an online or an offline identity and concerning a natural person and the storage, manipulation and disclosure of such data are operations, which can be regarded as processing of personal data. In order for this type of processing to be lawful it has to comply with the rules of the Data Protection Directive concerning the legitimacy of processing.

Under Article 7, personal data may only be processed if: (a) the data subject has unambiguously given his consent; or (b) processing is necessary for the performance of a contract to which the data subject is party or in order to take steps at the request of the data subject prior to entering into a contract; or (c) processing is necessary for compliance with a legal obligation to which the controller is subject; or (d) processing is necessary in order to protect the vital interests of the data subject; or (e) processing is necessary for the performance of a task carried out in the public interest or in the exercise of official authority vested in the controller or in a third party to whom the data are disclosed; or (f) processing is necessary for the purposes of the legitimate interests pursued by the controller or by the third party or parties to whom the data are disclosed, except where such interests are overridden by the interests for fundamental rights and freedoms of the data subject.

It is evident that none of the aforementioned provisions is met. In particular, nobody would consent to the collection and fraudulent use of his identity data, and no other requirement is fulfilled, not even the one mentioned in lit. f., since the interests pursued by the controller, i.e. the "identity thief", are not legitimate, since the identity thief aims to use such information in order to commit fraud or another criminal act (Dammann, 1997, p. 153). This practice contravenes also the collection limitation principle, as the personal data are not obtained by lawful and fair means.

Furthermore, some categories of personal information that are collected by identity thieves constitute sensitive information as defined in Article 8 of the Data Protection Directive. This is the case, e.g., where the name and/or the nationality reveal the racial or ethnic origin, or where biometric information is stolen which is concerning health. Health information may also be directly concerned in case information from an electronic card or from an electronic patient file is stolen. Identity information concerning membership in a political party or group, etc., would reveal political and other beliefs which are also sensitive data.

The infringements of data protection laws include, besides the violation of substantive privacy rights, the violation of formal requirements, such as the notification of the processing to the supervisory authority, etc., and the violation of the rights of the data subject. European data protection laws provide for remedies in case of infringements and many provide also impose criminal sanctions.

Occasionally, the acquisition of identity information is carried out by spyware, i.e. software which is installed on computers of Internet users without their consent and knowledge. This software collects data on the specific application of the user and his surfing habits, while some spyware programs collect personal information of the Internet user such as bank account and credit card numbers and other confidential information (De Schrijver & Schraeyen, 2005, p. 17). Hence, the use of such software can be seen as a violation of the confidentiality of electronic communication. This is made clear in the e-Privacy Directive (Directive 2002/58/EC)[28], which provides in Article 5 (3) that Member States are obliged to ensure that the use of electronic communications networks to store information or to gain access to information stored in the terminal equipment of a subscriber or user is only allowed on condition that the subscriber or user concerned is provided with clear and comprehensive information in accordance with Directive 95/46/EC, inter alia about the purposes of the processing, and is offered the right to refuse such processing by the data controller.

It derives from the aforementioned provision that the storage and use of spyware is only permitted where the information requirements are complied with and also, that the person concerned can refuse this. Evidently, these requirements cannot be met by spyware, which is used to 'steal' identity information, and therefore, the use of such spyware is to be regarded as an infringement of the confidentiality of communications.

In the United States, where problems concerning spyware have been felt more acute, there are already a number of court cases dealing with this problem. Although there is specific spyware legislation in some states such as Utah and California, there is still no such law on federal level. A noteworthy proposal was the so-called 'Spy Act' ('Securely Protect Yourself Against Cyber Trespass Act'), sponsored by May Bono, which was approved by the House of Representatives[29], but never became law[30]. This law would prohibit the use of computer software known as spyware to collect personal information and to monitor the behavior of computer users without a user's consent. The Federal Trade Commission (FTC) would be directed to enforce this bill's provisions relating to spyware, including assessing and collecting civil penalties for unfair or deceptive business practices.

It is pointed out that there are also other legislative grounds in US law that can be evoked to fight against spyware, such as the Electronic Communications Privacy Act (ECPA) and other acts (De Schrijver & J. Schraeyen, 2005, p. 18). Particularly, the ECPA prohibits the interception of communication and its objective is analogous to the e-Privacy Directive. Section 2511 of the ECPA prohibits the use of web-monitoring applications such as spyware; however, most actions were unsuccessful mainly due to the consent exception provided for in this section. In the case *Pharmatrak II* it was provided that such occurrences require the complete consent of the parties concerned.

## Conclusion

Identity theft can be seen as a violation of privacy, since it consists in the unlawful acquisition of an individual's personal information. Rules sanctioning identity theft are therefore enhancing privacy and those are in particular the rules established by legislation such as the U.S. Identity Theft and Assumption Deterrence Act and the rules of the Cybercrime Convention, which are related to identity theft and identity fraud. The main objective of criminal law provisions, however, is to safeguard the economic interests of the individual, which will be breached when identity information is used to commit fraud or other illegal activity.

In absence of clear rules concerning identity theft in most countries with the exception of US, it seems that there is a regulative gap. In order to fill this gap, legislators could use the example of the US law as a source of inspiration in order to improve the existing situation. The improvement of the regulative framework would thus be proved to be privacy enhancing and safeguarding the legitimate interests of individuals.

In Europe, the data protection legislations play also an important role for the prosecution of identity theft and identity related crime, as they provide rules concerning the collection and processing of personal information, which are modeled on the basis of the Data Protection Directive and the Directive on Data Protection on electronic communications. Additionally, intellectual property regulations could be applied insofar as the name or trademark of a corporation or organization is abused for criminal purposes, particularly in the case of phishing (Leenes, 2006, p. 21).

However, although criminal law provisions are necessary, they are not sufficient to tackle identity theft in practice (Savirimuthu & J. Savirimuthu, 2007, p. 442). Other countermeasures to combat identity fraud include the introduction of improved information security measures, the management of digital identities and the introduction of new identity verification methods, including inter alia of use of biometrics, etc. However, online authentication systems pose privacy problems, since they seem to infringe data protection rules[31], and also, new technologies such biometrics, which are used for identity verification, are regarded by some authors as invading privacy (Hilley, 2007, pp. 6-7).

## PRIVACY ISSUES IN ONLINE IDENTITY MANAGEMENT

### Digital Identities and Authentication

A digital identity is a collection of information that belongs to an individual or an organization, which is characterized through specific attributes and which has at least one identifier (Hansen & Meints, 2006). Most frequently, a digital identity is a representation of a specific aspect of a person's identity, although the connection to a person is not always apparent. Particularly if the identifier used does not reveal the actual name of a person, it effectively corresponds to a pseudonym (Hansen & Meints, 2006, p. 543).

Digital identities are used to authenticate users of online services. During the process of identity authentication, which is intended to provide to a person access to restricted resources or areas, identity information are disclosed concerning a person's characteristics or profile. This, however, entails the risk of infringing privacy and endangers important principles of the state of law such as self determination and personal autonomy, in case e.g. profiling of users is used to manipulate people behavior in a massive scale (Hildebrandt, 2006; Hildebrandt, Gutwirth & Hert, 2005). To address this issue, identity management is examined in the next sections.

### The Expansion of Online Authentication Services

Online authentication becomes increasingly important on the Internet, as many websites require users to authenticate themselves in order to be able to enjoy access to the services they offer, which are confidential, or because such services are offered at remuneration etc. Users are thus required to provide identification information such as an e-mail address or a user name and verification, i.e. a password (Furnell, 2007b). This procedure has, however, many drawbacks, since it is burdensome for most users, as it has as a consequence user dissatisfaction (so-called "password fatigue") and it presents security risks, in case the same identity credentials are used for identification (Olsen & Mahler, 2007a, p. 342).

To solve this problem, technical measures are introduced, which include the management of passwords by the Internet browser or the use of a proxy-server registering passwords concerning a number of web sites, in which a user has to log in and which can be accessible by different pc's. A more sophisticated solution is the development of identity managements systems, which allow electronic authentication in various web sites. In more particular, authentication is provided to users by a third party that employs a specific authentication protocol. The end-user has to be verified by the authentication provider before entering a site of a service provider and the service provider has to trust the authentication provider and accept the introduction of user (WP 68, 2003, pp. 2 et seq.). Accordingly, an identity management system consists in the technology-based administration of identity attributes including the development and choice of the partial identity and pseudonym to be used and/or reused in a specific context or role (Pfitzmann & Hansen, 2008, p. 31). Many identity management systems provide users a seamless user-experience in that they enable them to access multiple Internet resources after being authenticated once (single sign-on – Figure 2 [Pfitzmann, 2003]).

## The Context of Identity Management

The Internet today presents many opportunities for users and businesses as a platform for e-commerce. Consumers increasingly use the web to complete daily transactions, such as shopping and banking, while companies also collaborate in e-business channels, in which the borders between the Internet itself and corporate Intranets disappear (Buchholz, 2002, p. 527). The Internet, however, is an open network that is targeted by identity thieves and fraudsters, as it has already been mentioned. The reason that identity protection on the Internet poses such problems is that Internet was designed as an open and decentralized network, without a system of digital identity.[32]

A single digital identity system could not be adopted for online identification as a solution to the identity problem, as this would be the end of anonymous communication on the Internet, jeopardizing its open character and would pose significant privacy problems. Instead, an identity management system that would connect various identity management systems in a collaborative manner seems more appropriate. In more particular, a special authentication protocol is used, which has a tripartite architecture, i.e. one connecting an end-user, a service provider and an authentication provider. The end-user should have his identity verified before being served by the service provider, who, in turn, trusts the authentication provider and accepts the introduction of a user (WP 68, 2003, p. 3).

Identity management systems in essence delegate authentication of users to an identity provider in order to provide those users access to

*Figure 2. Single sign-on*

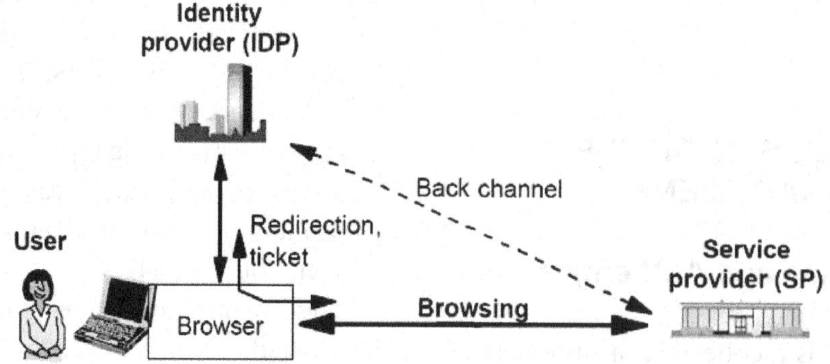

web sites and other resources (Olsen & Mahler, 2007a, p. 344). Users have the benefit of a more seamless user-experience, since they have to be authenticated only once and may then access different web site and resources.

A comprehensive identity management system was .NET Passport, which was developed in 1999 by Microsoft that was created to provide access to multiple Internet resources. In this system, a single authentication server was used, operated by Microsoft, which provided users access to multiple participating websites after a single authentication procedure (single sign-on) (Olsen & T. Mahler, 2007a, p. 346). .NET Passport was quite successful, as it registered over 250 million accounts and allowed access to 69 external websites worldwide (WP 69, p. 5). It collected three categories of data, i) minimal information (e-mail address and password), ii) credentials (secret question and answer, etc.), iii) maximal profile information (above-mentioned data plus first name, last name, time zone, gender, date of birth, occupation and accessibility).

Another system of identity management is the federated identity management by Liberty Alliance. This project was established in 2001 as a response to Microsoft's identity management system. In this system, a federated model is used, i.e. authentication is undertaken by a contract party within a 'circle of trust'. In particular, a Circle of Trust (CoT) is defined by the Liberty Alliance as a federation of service providers and identity providers that have business relationships based on Liberty architecture and operational agreements and with whom users can transact business in a secure and apparently seamless environment.[33] After single sign-on of the user with an identity provider, the user can then navigate to various service providers within a trust domain. This type of identity management presupposes that identity credentials of users are shared between many parties belonging to the aforementioned circle of trust, while users are in control of the use of their identity information (WP 68, Olsen & Mahler, 2007a, p. 346).

The differences between these systems of identity management are evident: while .NET Passport is based on one single centralized identity provider, the specifications of Liberty Alliance provide for multiple identity providers. Further, the first model uses a single identifier for each user, the Passport Unique Identifier (PUID), which was not linked to any user information, whereas Liberty does not use a single identifier, but a unique handle for a user and a federated pair of websites, which is not used to link the user to any other partial identifiers. The type of contractual relationships also presents differences, ranging from the centralized model of Microsoft's, which enters into contracts with service providers and the Liberty Alliance specifications, which is implementation dependent and where a contract between every site in a circle of trust is entered into or a contract is concluded between participating service providers and one party that organizes and administrates the circle of trust (Olsen & Mahler, 2007a, p. 350).

Another method for online verification of identity is Public Key Infrastructure (PKI), which consists in the use of digital signatures and digital certificates in electronic communication. Such signatures are electronic signatures based on public key cryptography, that is, they are created and verified by asymmetric cryptographic techniques, employing a pair of two keys, a private and a public key.[34] Key management is essential in PKI, for it is a guarantee for secure signature creation and minimizes the risks of identity theft.[35] It is also notable that PKI applications contribute to enhanced privacy protection, as this method of authentication makes the provision of identity information redundant (Dumortier & Goemans, 2004, p. 201).

## Data Protection Issues in Identity Management Systems

Disclosure of personal information which takes place beyond the control of the data subject may put his/her privacy at risk, thus infringing the subject's right to control the processing of his/her personal data, which is referred to as the right to informational self-determination.[36] This is the case where identity information flows without restraint between organizations participating in a circle of trust, which have access to such data and can exploit them without the consent of the user (Olsen & Mahler, 2007a, p. 349). Identity management systems, in a certain aspect, limit the risks to privacy, as they allow single sign-on, and prevent, therefore, undesired data collection and linking of the collected data, which might result if users had to authenticate themselves towards many service providers. However, identity management systems also pose problems concerning protection of users' personal data.

The Working Party established by Article 29 of the Directive 95/46/EC (hereinafter 'Working Party') identified a number of data protection issues concerning on-line authentication systems, concerning mainly the .NET Passport initiative (WP 68). It noted at first the lack of clear and transparent information about this system, as it failed to provide information about key aspects of the processing such as the identity of the controller, the purpose of the processing, the rights of the data subject, and the recipients of the data. It also did not inform users about the transfer of personal data to a third country and about the link between Hotmail and Passport. The Working Party underlined, further, that consent given by users was not sufficiently informed, freely given and specific. It also expressed its concern about the amount of data collected, for personal data were transmitted to all participating sites the data subject visits and sings in to, regardless whether it was necessary, and this contravened the principle of proportionality. The level of protection afforded by participating sites was not clear enough, as Microsoft did not control the data protection practices of participating sites.

A particular concerning point was the use of the PUID, which was generated at registration and endured for the life of the account. This would enable participating sites to disseminate to each other information about .NET Passport users and build user profiles. Users, on the other hand, had no access to their PUID. Other problems concerned the difficulties in unsubscribing from Passport and the possible security risks associated with the concentration of data in two big databases, which could be targeted by hackers.

Following the recommendations of the Working Party, Microsoft agreed to comply with them, however, in 2003 it ceased the use of .NET Passport for external sites and the latter changed into a single-organization single sign-on identity management system. Soon after that .NET Passport was renamed into Live ID (Olsen & Mahler, 2007a, p. 346). In contrast, the specifications of the Liberty Alliance continue to exist and influence organizations.[37] There are other systems also, such as the Security Assertion Markup Language (SAML)[38], the Shibboleth system[39] and specific systems developed by researchers focusing mainly at privacy (Camisch et al., 2007, p. 47).

Certain privacy issues are common to all identity management systems and should be dealt with. To start with, defining roles and responsibilities is necessary in such situations where personal data are processed in cooperation between participants in an identity management system. In international data protection regulations responsibility falls to the controller, i.e. the natural or legal person, public authority, agency or any other body which alone or jointly with others determines the purposes and means of the processing of personal data, pursuant to the definition of Article 2 (d) of the Data Protection Directive, which is similar with the one given in Article 1 (a) of the OECD Guidelines and in Article 2 (d) of the Convention No 108 of the Council of Europe. The Directive makes the distinction between the controller and the processor, and defines the latter as 'a natural or legal person, public authority, agency or any other body which processes personal data on behalf of the controller'. The former, however, is under the obligation to comply with the requirements of data protection legislation transposing the provisions of the Directive.

Accordingly, it is crucial to determine which role the participants in identity management schemes play and whether they could be regarded as processors or controllers (Olsen & Mahler, 2007b, p. 417 et seq.). The Working Party suggested to consider all participating sites in an identity management scheme as controllers in respect of their own processing operations (WP 68, p. 9, 12). In particular, this means that any service provider in a 'circle of trust', i.e. in identity management systems that follow the Liberty Alliance specifications, will be the controller of the personal data concerning its customers and/or employees and thus responsible for complying with data protection rules. Moreover, it is not crucial which role Liberty assigns to a participant, since one may be classified as a controller (or joint controller) depending on the role it actually performs in practice within a circle of trust (Liberty Alliance, 2005, p. 15).

In case there are multiple collaborating organizations within a circle of trust, it is certainly difficult to identify the controller. But in order to do so, it has to be determined who has actual control over the data and, in particular, determines how and for what purposes the data are processed. And therefore, if the data controller's responsibility has been delegated to another organization, the delegating organization would continue to be the data controller if it actually has control over the means and purposes of the processing (Olsen & Mahler, 2007b, p. 420).

However, no responsibility can be placed on the designers of online authentication systems, since these are not controllers and obviously not processors. The Article 29 Working Party expressed a different approach in this issue (WP 68, pp. 14-15), but there is no legal ground on which this could be based. On the contrary, it is the provider who implements an identity management system, regardless how it is designed, who bears the burden of complying with the law.

Further, the stipulation in a contract of duties and responsibilities between controllers is foreseen by the Article 29 Working Party as advisable.[40] This is particularly important for the allocation of responsibility, although it is not mandatory by law. In particular, the Directive only imposes an obligation to conclude a contract between the controller and the processor in Article 17 (3)[41] and does not impose such an obligation to joint controllers or to collaborating single controllers. However, a contract regulating the relationships between participants in an identity management scheme is essential to ensure compliance with privacy rules, and this is also recognized by the Liberty Alliance. The formation of the contractual framework will depend on the nature and scope of the circle of trust. Thus, a relatively light framework may be enough for a small number of relatively static business partners, whereas in larger and more dynamic circles of trust it may be necessary to establish federation-wide rules and common operating procedures and processes that would minimize the problems of bi-lateral negotiations and multiple contracts with many interdependencies (Liberty Alliance, p. 6).

In the relationship between controller and processor, it is clear that full responsibility lies with the controller. The processor is only bound to carry out the controller's instructions. Pursuant to the Data Protection Directive, the controller must choose a processor providing sufficient guarantees in respect of the technical security measures and organizational measures governing the processing to be carried out (Article 17 (2) of Directive 95/46). The processor must, further, ensure compliance with those measures and this means that the controller should supervise the processor. And finally, it is provided that the carrying out of processing by way of a processor must be governed by a contract or legal act binding the processor to the controller, which should stipulate that the processor shall only act on instructions from the controller and that the processor must implement appropriate technical and organizational measures to protect personal data (Article 17 (3) of Directive 95/46).

Security is a fundamental requirement in any processing of personal data and also in identity management systems. Both the controller and the processor are obliged under the Data Protection Directive to take appropriate technical and organizational measures for the protection of personal data (Article 17 (1) and (3) of Directive 95/46).[42] This obligation refers to particular risks such as accidental or unlawful destruction or accidental loss, alteration, unauthorized disclosure or access. Particularly, in the case of identity management systems secure transmission of identity and attribute data over networks should be observed and this in addition to the security obligations applying with regard to electronic communications services (Liberty Alliance, p. 28). Pursuant to Article 4 (1) of Directive 2002/58/EC, the provider of electronic communications services are under the legal obligation to ensure security of its services and where this appropriate to cooperate with the network provider as far as network security is concerned. The determination of an appropriate level of security is not particularly defined in the EU Directives, but that depends on the risk that the processing presents and on the nature of the data.[43]

In accordance with the recommendations of the Article 29 Working Party, it should be allowed anonymous or pseudonymous use of online authentication systems and only where this inhibits full functionality, the system should be built so that it would require minimal information for the authentication of the user and enable him/her to decide about providing additional information, such as profile data (WP 68, p. 15). This form of identity management in which the user manages his presentation before other communication partners facilitates the protection of the user's personal data. However, in certain areas particularly in public law, anonymous or pseudonymous communication is not permitted (Krasemann, 2006).

An essential requirement for identity managements systems is to ensure that users are informed about the privacy implications of using such systems. This was expressed by the Article 29 Working Party in relation to .NET Passport. The Working Party considered that users should be provided with clear information about the controller identity, the purposes of processing, data collected, recipients, etc. and that they should be given clear alternatives and control over the disclosure of information to participating sites (WP 68, pp. 6-8. 15). This is a prerequisite for lawful and fair processing of personal data, which derives from Articles 10 and 11 of the Data Protection Directive and the openness and individual participation principles of fair information practice.

However, this requirement could hinder the deployment of single sign-on services, as the provision of extensive information may be a burden for the user who is required to process this information and assess its relevance (Olsen & Mahler, 2007b, p. 421). A particular problem is that online notices are long and contain legal terms and industry jargon, and therefore, their value has been questioned.[44]

An appropriate solution of this problem is to provide multi-layered information notices, in accordance with the proposal of the Article 29 Working Party (WP 100, 2004). Accordingly, there could be three layers of information: i) the short notice, which must offer the core information (identity of the controller and purposes of processing) and any additional information which in view of the particular circumstances of the case must be provided beforehand to ensure a fair processing, ii) the condensed notice, which provides all relevant information required under the Data Protection Directive and iii) the full notice, which includes all national legal requirements and specificities. It is, therefore, sufficient for controllers to include a simplified short notice in the user-interface, insofar as this is integrated in a multi-layered information structure, in which more information is available (Olsen & Mahler,

2007b, p. 422).

A similar issue is concerning the process of obtaining consent, which would legitimize the processing of personal data under the Data Protection Directive (Article 7 a) and the Fair Information Practice Principles, particularly the collection and use limitation principles. In the online environment it is not possible to obtain written confirmation of consent from the data subject and, therefore, other alternatives have to be considered. The Liberty Alliance framework incorporates various mechanisms, such as usage directives, consent attributes and consent headers (Liberty Alliance, p. 19). Particularly, usage directives enable principals to communicate their privacy preferences, and service providers to communicate their requirements, with regard to the use of a principal's personal information. They allow for the use of any privacy preferences expression language (PPEL), such as the Platform for Privacy Preferences (P3P), which enables Websites to express their privacy practices in a standard format that can be retrieved automatically and interpreted easily by user agents.[45]

The application of usage directives for the declaration of consent would be valid, particularly since the Data Protection Directive only requires that the consent is unambiguously and does not provide any formal requirements. However, it has be ensured that the content of the liberty specifications fulfils the requirements for lawful processing and that the specific conditions, i.e. the purpose of processing, the recipients of the data, the storage period, etc., are complied with (Olsen & Mahler, 2007b, p. 423-425).

It is also notable that the Data Protection Directive provides specific rules for the transfer of personal data from an EU Member State to a third country. Pursuant to Article 25 (1), the transfer can only place if the third country in question ensures an adequate level of protection. The adequacy is determined on a case-by-case basis by the EU Commission, according to Article 25 (6) of the Directive. However, the Directive provides derogations from this principle in Article 26, such as when the data subject has given his consent unambiguously to the proposed transfer or the transfer is contractually necessary etc., and also if the controller adduces adequate safeguards with respect to the data protection. The latter applies, for instance, to companies complying with the safe harbor privacy principles.[46] The Article 29 Working Party recommends that in case of a transfer of personal data to a third country authentication providers should work with service providers who take all necessary steps to provide adequate protection or that put in place sufficient safeguards to ensure the protection of the personal data of the users of the system, by using contracts or binding corporate rules. It also stresses that if consent is used as a basis for the transfer, sufficient information and choice should be given to the user (WP 68, p. 15).

In order to overcome the issue of complying with the provisions on transborder transfer, it is possible for a circle of trust to implement a mechanism for participants to share data with other participants in destination countries, which have been approved by the EU Commission. In case the country of destination does not provide an adequate level of protection, it is possible to enter into a contractual agreement that would legitimate the transfer. In particular, bi-lateral contractual agreements are workable for many closely defined and relatively static circles of trust. This solution is not appropriate for dynamic schemes, however, in which there are a large number of participants or where new participants join or leave frequently (Liberty Alliance, p. 31).

## Data Protection Issues in Relation to Identity Management by Means of PKI

The employment of PKI as a means for online identification of individual and corporate users may also pose significant privacy risks. In particular, for the issuing of a digital certificate it is necessary to provide evidence of identity. The disclosure of personal data during this process may have negative results for privacy in case the level of identification is excessive in relation to the specific application (Dumortier & Goemanns, 2004, p. 10). Also, the possible extent of personal information contained in digital certificates, which are publicly available, raises concerns, as this may facilitate possible tracking of an individual's transactions and lead to profiling of the individual (Federal Privacy Commissioner, 2001a, p. 10). The same considerations have been expressed in relation to the possibility of browsing of public key directories and downloading of data to be used for profiling or other uses that may infringe the right to privacy (Federal Privacy Commissioner, 2001a, Dumortier, & Goemanns, 2004).

Other issues are related to proliferation of PKI technology. It is probable that the use of PKI could become a de facto unique identifier system and that additional uses for certificates or associated information could be introduced (International Working Group on Data Protection in Telecommunications, 2001, p. 3). And also, some PKI application could require a higher risk of identification than other. In such cases serious privacy risks are raised.

In order to deal with these issues, privacy organization and groups published recommendations and guidelines (Federal Privacy Commissioner, 2001b). The EU legislator has reacted and included appropriate solutions in Directive 1999/93/EC on a Community framework for electronic signatures.[47] It is notable that there are no equivalent provisions neither in international legislation such as the UNCITRAL Model law on Electronic Commerce of 1996 nor in the US Electronic Signatures in Global and National Commerce Act (E-Sign Act) of 2000.

The E-Signatures Directive allows the use of pseudonymous certificates, which are preferable to identity certificates in cases where identification of the certificate holder is not required. In particular, Article 8 (3) of the Directive states that "without prejudice to the legal effect given to pseudonyms under national law, Member States shall not prevent certification service providers from indicating in the certificate a pseudonym instead of the signatory's name".

Further, the Directive includes a general provision stating that Member States shall ensure that certification-service-providers and national bodies responsible for accreditation or supervision comply with the requirements laid down in the Data Protection Directive (Article 8 (1)). In particular, it establishes that a certification-service-provider which issues certificates to the public may collect personal data only directly from the data subject, or after the explicit consent of the data subject, and only insofar as it is necessary for the purposes of issuing and maintaining the certificate. The data may not be collected or processed for any other purposes without the explicit consent of the data subject (Article 8 (2) of Directive 1999/93). These provisions make certain that unnecessary information collection does not take place, which may be excessive and could thus represent an intrusion to privacy.

There are, however, no provisions relating to public certificate directories in the e-Signatures or the Data Protection Directives. The provisions concerning data minimization and use of pseudonyms could, therefore, be applied in order to diminish privacy risks. Still, certificate holders should have the right recognized not to be included in such directories and carry out private dissemination of their public certificate.

## Conclusion

The proliferation of identity management schemes will continue and relevant initiatives will gain even more significance in the future. It certainly is a fact that identity management finds application in many different areas, besides online authentication, such as location based services (Kosta et al. 2008), ubiquitous services (Delaitre, 2005, p. 31), etc., and this means that this concept can be adapted to many environments. It is also notable that there are many research projects focusing on identity management, which will also contribute to its further progress.[48]

Privacy considerations should also be taken into account by designers of identity management systems, which have to incorporate data protection measures into the architecture of such systems. This seems essential in view of the fact that protection of informational privacy would increase user trust in the said systems and thus, promote their acceptability by users of online services (Olsen & Mahler, 2007b 425-426). Furthermore, the protection of personal data is an imperative that has to be respected because it purports to protection of a fundamental right. It is, therefore, evident that identity management systems need fully respect the data protection rules and principles.

## PRIVACY ISSUES IN RELATION TO IDENTITY VERIFICATION IN THE EXAMPLES OF BIOMETRICS AND ELECTRONIC IDENTITY CARDS

### Identity Crisis

Legislators worldwide have realized that a new approach is required for the fight against the fraudulent use of identities and this is one that makes use of new – and promising – technologies, such as biometrics. Particularly, in the upshot of terrorist attacks in the U.S.A. and in Europe, specific programs have been introduced involving the introduction of biometrics in passports. Such initiatives concentrate on identity documents and in more particular, on passports and identity cards, as well, in order to ensure the effectiveness of border controls and enhance security.

Identity authentication in the electronic environment also poses risks that need to be tackled with secure technologies and verification policies (Mason, 2004, p. 164). These risks have been elucidated in the introduction and they are hindering the full exploitation of the information society by governments and businesses, introducing e-government and e-commerce services, respectively. One would thus welcome the employment of secure technologies for online authentication and verification of identity, e.g. in electronic identity cards (Reisen, 2008).

However, biometrics raises serious privacy concerns (Cavoukian, 1999). This is due to the fact that biometric information is of a sensitive nature. So, e.g., the fingerprint is associated with criminality and its storing signifies a loss of dignity and privacy, while it would also be possible for third parties to access this data and use it without consent of the individual concerned. Another concern is that the biometric data are used for secondary purposes not compatible with the purposes for which they were collected ('function creep'). Moreover, biometric data are centrally stored and accessed by various governmental bodies. This feature of biometric technology enhances the possibilities of surveillance, raising thus fears of a possible implementation of a "Big Brother". In addition, there are also other risks associated with the use of biometrics, such as that the data quality may be poor, etc.(Kindt, 2007, p. 168).

In the following section attention will be drawn to practical issues and the implementation of data protection legislation upon authentication and identification technologies such as biometrics.

### Legal Review of Biometric Applications

In an early review of the data protection implications of biometric technology, the Working Party adopted an opinion on 1 August 2003 (WP 80, 2003).The Working Party focused primarily on verification technologies (i.e. identification on the basis of particular characteristics) and not on identification (i.e. comparison of a biometric characteristic with data held in central databases), as biometric techniques for identification were not fully developed at that time (Kindt, 2007, p. 167).

The Working Party underlines that the principle of purpose specification should be applied, which implies firstly that the purpose for which the biometric data are collected and processed should be clearly determined, and furthermore, that the principle of proportionality and legitimacy should be respected. In particular, it stressed out that for access control purposes biometric systems are preferable, which are related to physical characteristics that do not leave traces (e.g. shape of the hand but not fingerprints) or systems that leave traces but do not rely on the memorization of data in the possession of someone else than the individual concerned (WP 80, 2003, p. 6). In extreme cases, however, where such systems are implemented, e.g. in high security installations, processing may need to be submitted to prior checking by data protection authorities. Furthermore, the application of the principle of proportionality implies a strict assessment of the necessity and proportionality of the processed data. The Working Party quotes a decision of the French CNIL, in which the CNIL has refused the use of fingerprints in the case of access by children to a school restaurant, but accepted the use of the outline of the hand pattern, for the same purpose.

In this opinion, other principles and rules of data protection law are also addressed. The Working Party mentions the principle of fair collection and the right to information of the data subject, the criteria for making data processing legitimate, in accordance with Article 7 of the Data Protection Directive, the need for establishing security measures, the need to respect sensitive data by applying Article 8 of the Directive. It notes that the processing of biometric data as unique identifiers poses specific risks that have to be addressed and underlines the importance of Privacy Enhancing Technologies and of codes of conduct.

The use of biometric technology for identification of an individual poses more complicated problems. Currently, a great number of states have started to implement biometrics in passports and identity cards (Hornung, 2004). On EU level, a Regulation on standards for security features and biometrics in passports and travel documents issued by Member States was adopted on December 13, 2004.[49] The Regulation establishes the obligation of EU Member States to include biometric features in passports and travel documents. Under Article 6, facial images had to be included at the latest 18 months and fingerprints at the latest 36 moths after the establishment of technical standards that took place in February 2005. This data should be stored on RFID passive chips and with an intended read range of about ten centimeters.

The adoption of this Regulation proved to be a highly controversial issue from a legal, ethical, political and technical point of view. The Chairman of the Working Party on August 18 2004 addressed a letter in which it pointed out certain concerns.[50] In this letter, it emphasized the opposition of the Working Party to the storage of all EU passport holders′ biometric and other data in a centralized data base of European passports and travel documents. It included also various proposals concerning the purpose of introducing biometric features that had to be explicit, appropriate, proportionate and clear. And further, it addressed security issues and questioned who would have access to the storage medium and for which purposes. Subsequently, the Working Party adopted on 30 September 2005 an opinion, in which it reiterated its concern for the problematic aspects of the introduction of biometrics in passports and travel documents and made other proposals (WP 112, 2004). The European Parliament also opposed the storage of fingerprint data and required changes of the initial proposal of the EU Passport Regulation.

Besides the EU, there are also other countries implementing biometric passports (Hornung, 2007, p. 253). The USA plays a role in this development, since it requires from the governments of countries that wish to participate in the visa waiver program to issue passports that comply with biometric and document identifying standards established by the ICAO.[51] It seems thus that the use of passports with biometric identifiers would be the general rule in the future, while their implementation in electronic identity cards is also a possibility. And this raises certainly quite a few data protection issues.

To start with, a leading principle in the review of biometrics is the purpose specification and proportionality principle, as stated by the Working Party (WP 80, 2003). A certain difficulty concerns the interpretation of 'fair and lawful processing' of biometric data in specific cases (Kindt, 2007, p. 169). In order for the processing to be fair, on the one hand, it has to respect the individual's privacy and autonomy, and further, be transparent, i.e. respect the principle of openness.[52] Lawfulness, on the other hand, means that the processing should be based upon a specific legal base and not conflict with other legislation.

Depending on the legal basis of the processing, which defines the purposes of the data processing, the latter should be restricted to those purposes. The EU Regulation follows this requirement, as it lays down in Article 4 (2) that 'no information in machine-readable form shall be included in a passport or travel document unless provided for in this Regulation, or its Annex, unless it is mentioned in the passport or travel document by the issuing Member State in accordance with its national legislation'. The purposes of the biometric features included in passports are enshrined in Article 4 (3), which provides that 'for the purpose of this Regulation, the biometric features in passports and travel documents shall only be used for verifying (a) the authenticity of the document; (b) the identity of the holder'.

According to the principle of data quality, established in Article 6 (1) (d) of the Data Protection Directive, personal data must be accurate, and, where necessary, kept up to date. And further, every reasonable step must be taken to ensure that data which are inaccurate or incomplete, having regard to the purposes for which they were collected or for which they are further processed, are erased or rectified.

The principle of proportionality and the principle of data quality lead us to the issue of the choice of the biometric identifier. Such an identifier must be suitable for the purpose of processing, i.e. secure identification of the holder of a passport or a travel document or identity card. In more particular, the biometric should be universal present, unique to the individual, stable over time and easily measurable (UK Parliamentary Office, 2001). Further, the biometric system must operate with low failure rates, which means that false acceptance rate and false recognition rate should be less than 1% (Hornung 2004, p. 50). It is notable that the principle of proportionality does not imply a preference of one biometric feature over the other, since each type of biometric data has its particular risks (Hornung 2004, p. 51). This certainly differentiates biometrics employed in identification documents from biometrics used in access control systems, which could be subjected to a categorization concerning their intrusiveness (WP 80, 2003, p. 6).

Most biometric systems use biometric templates, which include certain extracted feature from the raw data. The reason for this is that templates require less storage space. Templates are said to be preferable from the aspect of data protection law, because they are constructed so as to exclude additional raw data, which is sensitive, or as that it is impossible to deduce the identity of the person from the template itself and also to reconstruct the original raw data, and so they contribute to data minimization (Hornung 2004, p. 53). A drawback of the storing of biometric templates is that for each matching raw data is still required.

The EU Passport Regulation does not provide for the storage of data, whereas most countries use or plan to use central biometric databases. The objective of establishing of central databases is to prevent citizens from establishing more than one identity by obtaining several identity cards with different names, especially in those countries not possessing a general register of residents (Hornung 2007, p. 256). The use of central biometric databases poses privacy concerns, but these could be eliminated if access is provided restrictively to public authorities (WP 112, 2004, p. 8).

Furthermore, it is recommended to install back-up procedures that would face the problem that a portion of the population will be unable to present a biometric feature. False rejection is thus a possibility for an unidentified number of people and to face this problem, back-up procedures are required which would ensure secure identification and avoid discrimination of those unable to enroll in the system (Hornung 2007, p. 257).

Ensuring data security is an essential requirement for biometrics. In particular, public key cryptography can provide security safeguards and, therefore, its use is recommended. In biometric passports of the first generation a basis access control system (BAC) is used, in which the electronic data is encrypted with an individual key depending on the characters of the machine-readable zone (MRZ) of the passport. While this system has been criticized over the level of security it provided, the second generation of passports will be equipped with an extended access control system (EAC), including additional security features (Hornung 2007, p. 258).

## Conclusion

The risks for the protection of personal data which are posed by the applications of biometrics are significant and varied. Particularly, as far as their implementation in passports and national identity cards is concerned, there are technical, ethnical, policy and legal issues that have to be tackled. The legal review of specific projects will depend upon national legislation, which establishes constitutional rights to individuals and provides specific provisions in the field of data protection.

## REFERENCES

Borges, G., & Schwenk, J. (2007). *Identitätsschutz: eine zentrale Herausforderung für IT und E-Commerce.* Available online at: https://www.a-i3.org/images/stories/recht/itgipfel_paper061218.pdf

Bruin, R. de (2002). *Consumer Trust in Electronic Commerce: Time for Best Practice.* Kluwer Law.

Buchholz, C. (2002). Digital Identities and Federations. *Datenschutz und Datensicherheit* (9), 527.

Camisch, J., Hohenberger, S., Karjoth, G., Meints, M., & Wohlgemuth, S. (2007). Privacy-aware Business Process Design and Identity Management. In *FIDIS Deliverable, D13.2: Study on Privacy in Business Processes by Identity Management*, online available at: www.fidis.net

Cavoukian, A. (1999). *Privacy and Biometrics.* online available at: http://www.pcpd.org.hk/english/infocentre/files/cakoukian-paper.doc

Chawki, M., & Wahab, M. S. (2006). Identity Theft in Cyberspace: Issues and Solutions. *Lex Electronica, 11*(1), available online at: http://www.lex-electronica.org/articles/v11-1/chawki_abdelwahab.htm

Delaitre, S. (2005). Identity schemas in ubiquitous (and mobile computing). In: *FIDIS, D2.3: Models.*

Dumortier, J., & Goemans, C. (2004). Legal Challenges for Privacy Protection and Identity Management. In *Proceedings of the NATO/NASTEC Workshop on Advanced Security Technologies in Networking,* Bled (Slovenia) 15-18 September 2003, pp. 191-212.

Federal Privacy Commissioner (Australia), (2001a). *Privacy Issues in the Use of Public Key Infrastructure for Individuals and Possible Guide-*

*lines for Handling Privacy Issues in the Use of PKI for Individuals by Commonwealth agencies*, online available at: http://www.privacy.org.au/Papers/PCPKIGs0107.doc.

Federal Privacy Commissioner (Australia) (2001b). *Privacy and Public Key Infrastructure: Guidelines for Agencies using PKI to communicate or transact with individuals*, online available at: http://www.privacy.gov.au/government/guidelines/#a

Federal Trade Commission (2003). *Identity Theft Survey Report*, online available at: http://www.ftc.gov/os/2003/09/synovatereport.pdf

Federal Trade Commission (2006). *Identity Theft Survey Report*, available at: http://www.ftc.gov/os/2007/11/SynovateFinalReportIDTheft2006.pdf

*FIDIS Deliverable D2.3: 'Models'*; available online at: http://www.fidis.net/resources/deliverables/identity-of-identity/int-d2300/

*FIDIS, 'D 2.1: Inventory of topics and cluster'*, p. 27 et seq., available online at: http://www.fidis.net

Furnell, S. (2007a). Identity impairment: The problems facing victims of identity fraud. *Computer Fraud & Security*, (12), 6-11.

Furnell, S. (2007b). An Assessment of website password practices. *Computer Law & Security Report* (7-8), 445-451.

Gajek, S., Schwenk, J., & Wegener, C. (2005) Identitätsmissbrauch im Onlinebanking. *Datenschutz und Datensicherheit,* (11), 639-642.

Grijpink, J. (2004). Identity fraud as a challenge to the constitutional state. *Computer Law & Security Report,* (1), 29.

Halperin, R. (2006). Identity as an Emerging Field of Study. *Datenschutz und Datensicherheit,* (9), 533-537.

Hansen, M., & Meints, M. (2006). Digitale Identitäten – Überblick und aktuelle Trends. *Datenschutz und Datensicherheit,* (9), 543-547.

Hildebrandt, M. (2006). Privacy and Identity. In E. Claes, A. Duff, & S. Gutwirth (Eds.), *Privacy and the criminal law,* (pp. 43-57).

Hildebrandt, M., Gutwirth, S., & Hert, P. De (2005). *Implications of profiling on democracy and the rule of law, FIDIS (Deliverable 7.4),* available online at: http://www.fidis.net/resources/deliverables/profiling/int-d74000/

Hilley, S. (2007). Biometrics: the right to identity or privacy invasion? *Computer Fraud and Security,* (1), 6-7.

Hornung, G. (2004). Biometric Identity Cards: Technical, Legal, and Policy Issues. In S. Paulus, N. Pohlman, & H. Reiner (Eds.), *Securing Electronic Business Processes,* (pp. 47-57).

Hornung, G. (2007). The European Regulation on Biometric Passports: Legislative Procedures, Political Interactions, Legal Framework and Technical Safeguards. *Script-ed* (3), 246- 262.

International Working Group on Data Protection in Telecommunications (2001). *Working Paper on Data protection aspects of digital certificates and public-key infrastructures.*

Kindt, E. (2007). Biometric applications and the data protection legislation. *Datenschutz und Datensicherheit,* (3), 166-170.

Koops, B. J. (2005). *A survey on legislation on ID theft in the EU and a number of other countries* (Fidis Deliverable, D. 5.1).

Koops, B.-J., & Leenes, R. (2006). Identity Theft, Identity Fraud and/or Identity-related Crime. *Datenschutz und Datensicherheit,* (9), 553-556.

Kosta, E., Zibuschka, J., Scherner, T., & Dumortier, J. (2008). Legal considerations on privacy-enhancing Location Based Services using PRIME technology. *Computer Law & Security Report 2008*(2), 139-146.

Krasemann, H. (2006). Selbstgesteuertes Identitätsmanagement. *Datenschutz und Datensicherheit,* (4), 211-214.

Leenes, R. (n.nd). Introduction. In *FIDIS, ID-related Crime: Towards a Common Ground for Interdisciplinary Research* (Fidis Deliverable, D 5.2b).

Liberty Alliance Project (2005). *Circles of Trust: The Implications of EU Data Protection and Privacy Law for Establishing a Legal Framework for Identity Federation.*

Manny, C. H. (2003). Personal privacy – transatlantic perspectives. *Computer Law & Security Report,* (1), 4-10.

Marshall, A. M., & Tompsett, B.C. (2005). Identity theft in an online world. *Computer Law & Security Report,* (2), 128-137.

Mason, S. (2004). Validating Identity for the electronic environment. *Computer Law & Security Report,* (3), 164-170.

Meints, M. (2006). Identität. *Datenschutz und Datensicherheit,* (9), 576.

Meints, M., Rost, M., Zuccato, A., Delaitre, S., & Maghiros, I. (2006). Socio-Economic aspects. In *FIDIS, ID-related Crime: Towards a Common Ground for Interdisciplinary Research,* (p. 66). et seq., available online at: www.fidis.net.

Nabeth, T. (2006). Identity of Identity: Building a Shared Understanding of the Concept of Identity in the FIDIS Network of Excellence. *Datenschutz und Datensicherheit,* (9), 538-542.

Olsen, T., & Mahler, T. (2007a). Risk, responsibility and compliance in 'Circles of trust' – Part I. *Computer Law & Security Report,* (4), 342-351.

Olsen. T., & Mahler, T. (2007b). Risk, responsibility and compliance in 'Circles of trust' – Part II. *Computer Law & Security Report,* (5), 415-426.

Pfitzmann, A., & Hansen, M. (2008). Anonymity. *Undetectability, Unobservability, Pseudonymity, and Identity Management – A Consolidated Proposal for Terminology.* Available online at: http://dud.inf.tu-dresden.de/Anon_Terminology.shtml

Pfitzmann, B. (2003). Privacy in Enterprise Identity Federation: Policies for Liberty Single Signon. *Proc. Workshop on Privacy Enhancing Technologies,* Springer Verlag.

Reisen, A. (2008). Digitale Identität im Scheckkartenformat. *Datenschutz und Datensicherheit,* (3), 164-167.

Savirimuthu, A., & Savirimuthu, J. (2007). Identity Theft and Systems Theory: The Fraud Act 2006 in Perspective. *SCRIPT-ed* (4), p. 439, available online at: http://www.law.ed.ac.uk/ahrc/script-ed/vol4-4/savirimuthu.asp

Schrijver, S. De, & Schraeyen, J. (2005). Spyware: Innocent espionage in cyberspace? *Communications Law,* (1), 17-24.

Smith, R. E. (1993). The law of privacy in a nutshell. *Privacy Journal,* (6), 50-51.

UK Parliamentary Office of Science and technology (2001, November). *Biometrics & Security, 165.*

Wimmer, M., & Bredow, B. v. (2002). Sicherheitskonzepte fur e-Government. *Datenschutz und Datensicherheit,* (9), 536-541.

WP 100 (2004). Article 29 Working Party. *Opinion on More Harmonised Information Provisions.* November, 25, 2004.

WP 112 (2004). *Article 29 Working Party, Opinion on Implementing the Council Regulation (EC) No 2252/2004 of 13 December 2004 on standards for security features and biometrics in passports and travel documents issued by Member States.*

WP 68 (2003). *Article 29 Working Party, Working Document on on-line authentication services, adopted on 29 January 2003.*

WP 80 (2003). *Article 29 Data Protection Working Party, Working Document on biometrics, adopted on 1 August 2003.*

## ADDITIONAL READING

Azari, R. (2003). *Current Security Management & Ethical Issues of Information Technology.* Hershey, PA: IRM Press.

Collins, J. M. (2006). *Investigating Identity Theft: A Guide for Businesses, Law Enforcement, and Victims.* New Jersey: Wiley.

Firesmith, D. G. (2003). Engineering security requirements. *Journal of Object Technology, 2*(1), 53-68.

Lalopoulos, G. K., Chochliouros, I. P., & Spiliopoulou, A. S. (2005). Challenges and perspectives for Web-based applications in organizations. In M. Pagani (Ed.), *Encyclopedia of Multimedia Technology And Networking.* Hershey, PA: Idea Group Publishing.

Moukiou, Ch. (2003). The European Legal Frame and its Effectiveness in Greek Reality – The Special Issue of Digital Signature. In D. Politis & N. Papasteriadou (Eds.), *Recent Advances in Court Computerisation and Legal Databases – First Steps towards e-Justice.* Athens: A.N. Sakkoulas Publications.

## KEY TERMS

**Authentication:** The process of verifying an identity declared by or for a system entity, in order to decide whether a subject (as defined in the literature) is allowed to access certain information. Usually Internet business and many other transactions require a stringent authentication process. The use of digital certificates issued and verified by a Certification Authority as part of a public key infrastructure is considered likely to become the standard way to perform authentication on the Internet.

**Biometrics:** The automated methods used to recognize a person. They are based on any one or more physiological or behavioral characteristics using features like face, fingerprints, hand geometry, handwriting, iris, retina, vein, voice etc.

**Certification:** The process in which a Certification Authority issues a digital certificate to secure everything from corporate network access to monetary electronic transactions to physical access of secured facilities. Trusting an invalid certificate can expose an organization to potential fraud, theft, and compromise.

**Certificate, Public Key:** A specially formatted block of data serving as an identity certificate. It incorporates a digital signature to bind together a public key with identity information (the name of a person or an organization, their address, etc.) Therefore, the certificate carries the digital signature of a Certification Authority to verify that a public key belongs to a certain individual.

**Public-Key Infrastructure (PKI):** A system of certification authorities (and, optionally, registration authorities and other supporting servers and agents) that enables computer users without prior contact to be authenticated to each other, and to use the public key information in their public key certificates to encrypt messages to each other. In practice, a PKI consists of client software, server software, hardware (e.g., smart cards), legal contracts and assurances, and operational procedures.

**.NET Passport:** It is a personal authentication service, promoted by Microsoft since 1999, aiming to provide to Internet based transactions increased speed and security when making purchases online.

## ENDNOTES

1 See http://www.enisa.europa.eu/doc/pdf/deliverables/enisa_pp_social_networks.pdf; Social networking sites are being criticized for infringing privacy by making personal information available to many people and not just to users' friends. It is notable that the US Federal Trade Commission has fined a social networking site for collecting information on thousands of young people aged under 13 without their parents' permission, see 'FTC fines child social networking site for privacy violations', *Computer Fraud & Security* 2008 (3), p. 3. Social networking sites are also target of phishing attacks by identity thieves; see J. Kirk, 'Phishing Scam takes Aim at MySpace.com', online available at: http://www.pcworld.com/article/id,125956-page,1/article.html?RSS=RSS

2 'UK Ministry of Defence cracks down on IT security after laptop theft', *Computer Fraud & Security* 2008 (3), p. 2.

3 See Oxford English dictionary, http://dictionary.oed.com

4 It is notable that the Greek Data Protection Authority held in its decision 510/2000 that data related to religious beliefs should not be included in identity cards, since religion refers to the inner world of the individual and its is neither appropriate nor necessary in order prove one's identity. Also other information which was included in identity cards, such as fingerprint, spouse's name, maiden name, profession, home address and citizenship, was considered as not necessary for the purpose of identification of an individual; see I. Iglezakis, 'Regulation of Personal Data Processing', *Cyber law (Hellas)*, 2003, p. 237.

5 Durand proposed a similar distinction; see A. Durand 'Three Levels of Identity', *Digital Identity World*, March 16, 2002.

6 See 'ID theft levels rise unabated', *computer Fraud & Security* 2008 (3), p. 1.

7 See http://www.bbc.co.uk/chatguide/glossary/idtheft.shtm; see also http://www.heise.de/newsticker/BKA-Internet-Taeter-spaehen-umfassend-private-Daten-aus--/meldung/105675

8 According to Chawki & Wahab, phising "is the act of sending an e-mail to a user falsely claiming to be an established legitimate enterprise in an attempt to scam the user into surrendering private information that will be used for identity theft. The e-mail directs the user to visit a Web site where they are asked to update personal information, such as passwords and credit card, social security, and bank account numbers, that the legitimate organization already has. The Web site, however, is bogus and set up only to steal the user's information. Thus, phising is essentially a method of committing credit card fraud, identity theft and/o generic theft." See M. Chawki & M. S. Wahab, op. cit., p. 15 et seq.

9 Sniffing is the act of using a "sniffer" program to capture network traffic for analysis, which will reveal information such as username and passwords that could be used for identity fraud.

10 Pharming is an attack aiming to redirect a website's traffic to another, bogus website, so that hackers can obtain personal information predominantly of a financial nature.

11 See CIFAS, 'Is Identity Theft Serious?', online available at: http://www.cifas.org.uk/default.asp?edit_id=561-56#Is_Identity_Theft_Serious_

12 'Identity thieves – young, male and new to criminal activity', *Computer Fraud & Security* 2007 (1), p. 1.

13 See http://straylight.law.cornell.edu/uscode/18/1028.html

14 OJ L 281/31, 23.11.1995.

15 "OECD Guidelines on the Protection of Privacy and Transborder Flows of Personal Data," OECD, 1980.

16 There should be a general policy of openness about developments, practices and policies with respect to personal data. Means should be readily available of establishing the existence and nature of personal data, and the main purposes of their use, as well as the identity and usual residence of the data controller.

17 Collection Limitation Principle: There should be limits to the collection of personal data and any such data should be obtained by lawful and fair means and, where appropriate, with the knowledge or consent of the data subject.

18 The purposes for which personal data are collected should be specified not later than at the time of data collection and the subsequent use limited to the fulfillment of those purposes or such others as are not incompatible with those purposes and as are specified on each occasion of change of purpose.

19 Personal data should not be disclosed, made available or otherwise used for purposes other than those specified in accordance with Paragraph 9 except: a) with the consent of the data subject; or b) by the authority of law.

20 Personal data should be relevant to the purposes for which they are to be used, and, to the extent necessary for those purposes, should be accurate, complete and kept up-to-date.

21 An individual should have the right: a) to obtain from a data controller, or otherwise, confirmation of whether or not the data controller has data relating to him; b) to have communicated to him, data relating to him within a reasonable time; at a charge, if any, that is not excessive; in a reasonable manner; and in a form that is readily intelligible to him; c) to be given reasons if a request made under subparagraphs(a) and (b) is denied, and to be able to challenge such denial; and d) to challenge data relating to him and, if the challenge is successful to have the data erased, rectified, completed or amended.

22 Personal data should be protected by reasonable security safeguards against such risks as loss or unauthorised access, destruction, use, modification or disclosure of data.

23 A data controller should be accountable for complying with measures which give effect to the principles stated above.

24 A similar definition is included in the OECD Guidelines (Art. 1b).

25 OJ L 201/37, 31.7.2002.

26 See Recital Nr. 12 of the Directive.

27 C-275/06.

28 See Recital 24 of the Directive: 'Terminal equipment of users of electronic communications networks and any information stored on such equipment are part of the private sphere of the users requiring protection under the European Convention for the Protection of Human Rights and Fundamental Freedoms. So-called spyware, web bugs, hidden identifiers and other similar devices can enter the user's terminal without their knowledge in order to gain access to information, to store hidden information or to trace the activities of the user and may seriously intrude upon the privacy of these users. The use of such devices should be allowed only for legitimate purposes, with the knowledge of the users concerned'.

29 See http://www.wired.com/politics/law/news/2005/03/66848

30 See http://www.govtrack.us/congress/bill.xpd?bill=h109-29

31 The Article 29 Working Party has addressed privacy issues raised by online authentication systems already in 2002; see Working

Document First orientations of the Article 29 Working Party concerning on-line authentication services, adopted on 2 July 2002.

32 See 'Microsoft's Vision for an identity Metasystem', online available at: http://www.identityblog.com/?p=355

33 See the Liberty Glossary at: www.projectliberty.org/liberty/content/download/868/6180/file/liberty-glossary-v2.0.pdf

34 See EC Commission, Towards a European Framework for Digital Signatures And Encryption, COM(97) 503, p. 3.

35 See EC Commission, op. cit., pp. 4-5.

36 See the census decision of the German Constitutional Court, BVerfGE 65, 1.

37 See http://www.projectliberty.org/

38 See http://xml.coverpages.org/saml.html

39 See http://shibboleth.internet2.edu/

40 See WP 68, op. cit., where it is noted that: "...it is advisable for the different players to have clear contractual agreements between them where the obligations of each party are made explicit".

41 "The carrying out of processing by way of a processor must be governed by a contract or legal act binding the processor to the controller and stipulating in particular that: 1) the processor shall act only on instructions from the controller, and 2) the obligations set out in paragraph 1, as defined by the law of the Member State in which the processor is established, shall also be incumbent on the processor".

42 This requirement is also expressed in the Fair Information Practice Principles (security safeguards).

43 See Article 4 (1) b of Directive 2002/58/EC; Liberty Alliance, op. cit., p. 27-28.

44 See Consumer International, Privacy@net, An international comparative study of consumer privacy on the internet, 2001, online available at: http://www.consumersinternational.org/Shared_ASP_Files/UploadedFiles/80732215-7329-4A22-A02A-9A8062C65BC7_Doc30.pdf

45 See http://www.w3.org/P3P/

46 See Commission Decision 2000/520/EC, OJ L 215/7, 25.8.2000. The list of companies and organizations that participate in this scheme is available at http://www.export.gov/safeharbor/.

47 OJ L 013/12, 19/1/2000.

48 These are European projects: FIDIS (Future of Identity in the Information Sosiety), http://www.fidis.net; PRIME (Privacy and Identity Management for Europe), https://www.prime-projects.eu: and GUIDE (Government User Identity for Europe), http://istrg.som.surrey.ac.uk/projects/guide

49 Council Regulation No 2252/2004 of 13 December 2004 on standards for security features and biometrics in passports and travel documents issued by Member States, OJ L 385/1, 29.12.2004.

50 Letter of the Chairman of the Art. 29 Working Party to the President of the European Parliament, the President of the LIBE Committee, the Secretary General of the Council of the European Union, the President of the European Commission, the Director General of DG Enterprise and the Director General of DG Justice and Home Affairs, dated the 18 August 2004 (not published).

51 Section 303 of the Enhanced Border Security and Visa Entry Reform Act.

52 See Recital Nr. 38 of Directive 95/46/EC.

# Chapter V
# RFID Technology and its Impact on Privacy:
## Is Society One Step before the Disappearance of Personal Data Protection?

**Tatiana-Eleni Sinodinou**
*Bar Office of Thessaloniki, Greece*

## ABSTRACT

*The present chapter explores privacy issues posed by the use of RFID systems and applications. The existing legal framework for data protection is analyzed in order to discover how general privacy safeguarding principles should be applied in the case of RFIDs, with special focus on the main areas which are going to experience widespread use of such applications. The structure of the chapter is based on a chronological order which follows the consecutive phases of contact and interaction between the individual and the RFID tag. The implementation of a tag to a product or in the human body establishes the first point of contact of the individual with the RFID tag. This stage of data processing is examined in the first part of the chapter. In more particular, this part deals with the application of general principles of fair processing, such as information transparency, the debate about the necessity to require the prior consent of the individual (possible opt-in and opt-out solutions) and the precondition of a clearly defined purpose of the data processing. The symbiosis of the person with the tag is examined in the second part. Indeed, privacy concerns are equally significant during the phase of processing of personal information, even if processing is conducted lawfully, either based on the legal ground of the individual's consent or justified on another legal basis. The requirement of data quality and the obligation to secure the RFID system against unauthorized interceptions or alterations of data by third parties constitute essential guarantees of fair data processing. Privacy protection in the activation phase of the tag is also ensured by the obligation to inform the tagged individual every time a reading takes place and by the right to verify the accuracy of the tag data, whether stored from the beginning or added at a later date. Finally, the last part of the chapter examines the legal regime of separation between the person and the tag. This phase refers to the termination of the processing either by act of the data subject or by act of the RFID system controller. The focus is given to the exercise of the right to object to the processing of personal data through RFID devices. In this context practical solutions, such as the "tag kill" or "tag sleep" command should be taken into consideration in order to the make the exercise of the right to object feasible.*

## INTRODUCTION

New technologies have introduced a dynamic dimension in the exercise of individual liberties. However, they constitute at the same time a possible source of dominance, injustice, control and manipulation of the individual (Fraussinet in: Lucas, Deveze & Fraussinet, 2001, p.1). Technological evolution leads to complex pervasive technological realities which demand a strong protection of privacy. One of the most pertinent examples of new quasi-invisible forms of intrusion to privacy is the extended use of RFID systems.

RFID technology is based on the use of smart tags[1] which store and emit data through radiofrequencies by the means of miniscule antennas. The data and other information stored on the tag are received by a transceiver (reader)[2], which is also equipped with an antenna. Antennas are the conduits between the tag and the reader, which controls the system's data collection and communication (Flint, 2006). The salient features of this technology are that they permit the attachment of a unique identifier and other information – using a micro-chip – to any object, animal or even a person, and the reading of this information through a wireless device ("Radio Frequency Identification (RFID) in Europe: steps towards a policy framework", 2007).

The central idea is to give a unique identity to every "object", one which contains a smart tag, which can be transmitted to the reader ("Working document on data protection issues related to RFID technology", 2005).

This technology was first used on a large scale by the Royal Air Force during World War II to track enemy aircraft (*Identify Friend or Foe System*) (Lemoine, 2003). Nowadays, the commercial and social applications of RFID smart devices are limitless (Reid, 2007). The use of RFID technology can facilitate various activities in many sectors, such as in transports, in product distribution, in the retail sector, in the pharmaceutical industry, in healthcare services[3], logistics, the fight against counterfeiting[4], in aviation, in the automobile industry or in general every time it is necessary to control access ("Working document on data protection issues related to RFID technology", 2005).

From a technological point of view, there are two types of RFID tags: the passive and the active tags. Passive tags do not have an internal battery and cannot transmit data unless a reader activates them. On the contrary, active tags have an internal battery which permits the tag to emit the stored data but also to be rewritten and to store new data. Active tags offer more possibilities of data processing and are considered to be more privacy intrusive than passive tags.

RFID systems raise privacy and consumer protection concerns if they permit the identification of individuals. While the person's name is the most common feature of identification, identification can take place by use of other elements, such as the person's address, the date and place of birth and biometric data (photos, fingerprints, DNA) (Kotschy, 2006, p. 31). Moreover, privacy intrusion does not always require full identification of the person. Information related to an identifiable person could also qualify as personal data. Information not containing the usual identification features can be personal data if the controller could identify a person by means likely reasonable to be used (Directive 95/46/EC, Recital 26). Information can be qualified as personal data without necessarily having a direct link to an individual. Even information indirectly linked to a person whose identity can be indirectly recognized can be personal data. For example, the IP address is directly linked to a computer and does not directly refer to a natural person. However, if it is combined with other information, such as the name of the subscriber of the Internet account, it could determine the identity of the person who was attributed the IP address (Fraussinet in: Lucas, Deveze & Fraussinet, 2001, p.78).

From a personal data protection point of view, we could distinguish cases of direct or indirect identification of the individual in both types of RFID tags.

First of all, identification can be direct. A first example is when personal data, such as the name of a person, the credit card number, the identity card number, etc. are directly stored on the tag. In this case, direct recognition of the person occurs. A typical example is when a person uses a smart travel card which contains the name of the card holder, his address and other personal data. Smart travel cards permit the private or state entity who published them and controls their use to know exactly when the card holder uses the card and by consequence where he or she is at a specific moment.

A second example of direct identification is when the information stored in the tag is not personal data, but could directly identify a person if it is correlated with personal data. This could happen if the RFID tag number of a product is linked to the record of the customer who bought it. For example, a store could tag its products with unique product codes which the retailer systematically combines with customer names collected upon payment with credit cards and later on linked with the retailer customer database. Another example could be the case where a supermarket implements tags in loyalty cards which identify individuals by their names to learn and record consumer habits while consumers are in the store, including the time spent in a given section of the supermarket, the number of times the consumer visits the supermarket without buying, etc.("Working document on data protection issues related to RFID technology", 2005, p. 5)

In both cases, identification could possibly lead to automated decision taking. After learning a person's identity via RFID, people or devices associated with the reader network can take actions regarding that person (ranging from further surveillance and arrest on the one hand, to displaying targeted ads on the other) based on their knowledge of who he/she is and what he/she is like (Weinberg, 2007).

Identification of the individual can also be indirect. In case of indirect identification, it is even possible to create the profile of the individual without usual identification features, such as his name. Indeed, even if the individual is not immediately and directly identified at the item information level, he/she can be identified at an associative level because of the possibility of identifying him or her without difficulty via the large mass of information surrounding or stored about the individual. For example, one could consider the case of an individual using a smart shopping card which has been anonymously distributed by the supermarket. The supermarket could set up a file using the identification number stored in the shopping cards and could monitor which products an individual (identified by the shopping card) purchases, how often such products are purchased by him/her and by consequence his/her consumer habits ("Working document on data protection issues related to RFID technology", 2005, p. 6).

This study is divided in three parts. We are going to describe and analyse in a chronological order the relationship between the person – referred to as the data subject - and the RFID tag. Firstly, the beginning of this relationship and more precisely the legal regime of implementation of the RFID tag. Secondly, the rules applying to the symbiosis of the person and the tag. And finally, the end of this turbulent affair, the legal rules governing the termination of the data processing.

## THE FIRST CONTACT BETWEEN THE PERSON AND THE TAG: A COMPULSORY UNION?

With miniature tags and silent invisible radio-based transfers, the RFID technology is a passionate subject of discussion among consumer organizations and defenders of civic freedoms. However, it could be unfair to qualify these reactions to the recent use of RFID as irrational: if the existing legal framework clearly implies the consent or at least the notification of the individual, the enforcement of the general principles of privacy protection is in practice being outstripped by the exponential RFID application growth.

### Privacy Safeguarding Principles Applied to the Implementation of RFID tags

#### The Right of Information

RFID technology uses the basic structure of every communication process: the emission of information (of "the message") by the emitter and its reception by the receiver. However, while in normal communication processes the emitter and the receiver are equal actors who act in free will, RFID infrastructures could disturb this balance. First of all, this happens because the transmission of the message takes place automatically in an opaque way without the active participation of the individual. Where active tags are used, this process is even more incomprehensible to the individual. In this context, the individual can lose control of the communication of his personal information. If the individual did not have the right to be informed about the implementation and use of RFID tags, he/she would no longer be an active subject of the free communication process and he could be demoted to a simple passive emitter of information.

The notification of the individual in a clear and comprehensible manner about the presence of the RFID tag and the presence of readers is crucial. The right to be informed of the processing of personal data is an indispensable prerequisite for the fair and lawful processing of personal data in the European personal data protection legal tradition. According to article 10 of the Directive 95/46/EC the controller must provide the data subject with basic information, such as the identity of the controller and the purposes of the processing for which the data is intended; depending on the circumstances of the processing it may be necessary to provide further information. Besides, prior notification of the individual is a precondition for the validity of his/her consent to the processing of personal data[5].

The notification requirement is also established in Directive 2002/58/EC, which defines certain personal data protection principles in the electronic communications sector ("Directive 2002/58/EC"). Article 9 of the Directive states that the processing of location data relating to users or subscribers of public communications networks or publicly available electronic communications services can take place only if it is anonymized, or with the consent of the users or subscribers to the extent and for the duration necessary for the provision of a value added service. Prior to obtaining their consent, the service provider must inform the users or subscribers of the type of location data other than traffic data which will be processed, of the purposes and duration of the processing and whether the data will be transmitted to a third party for the purpose of providing the value added service.

These two directives could be applied in case of the processing of personal data through RFID infrastructures. Directive 2002/58/CE complements the general Data Protection Directive and could be applied when RFID systems process location data, but it is not certain that it can cover all RFID applications, because it is limited to the processing of personal data in connection with the provision of publicly available electronic communications services in public communications networks[6].

The notification requirement concerning the processing of personal data is also recognized as a requirement of fair processing in U.S.A. There is no universal law in U.S.A. recognizing personal data protection or privacy protection. Nevertheless, although the term "privacy" does not appear in the U.S. Constitution or the Bill of Rights, the U.S. Supreme Court has ruled in favor of various privacy interests (J. Slemmons Stratford & J.Stratford, 1998). In addition, there have been a number of laws dealing specifically with the concept of data protection such as the Privacy Act of 1974[7]. The U.S. Privacy Act of 1974 establishes some principles of fair information practices, including an obligation to notify the individual[8]. Moreover, in U.S.A. the principles of privacy protection apply which were elaborated by the OECD, such as collection limitation, openness, purpose specification, use limitation, data quality, individual participation, security safeguards and accountability ("OECD Guidelines on the Protection of Privacy and Transborder Flows of Personal Data", 1980).

Furthermore, proper notification of the individual about the presence of RFID infrastructure and the purposes of the processing is often stated as a condition of fair processing in "best practice" principles and guidelines addressed to organizations, institutions and businesses which operate information systems involving the use of RFID technology. For example, the notification of the consumer is an essential precondition of the general principle of transparency established by the Privacy Best Practices for Deployment of RFID Technology of the Center for Democracy and Technology (CDT) working group on RFID ("CDT Working Group on RFID: Best Practices for Deployment of RFID Technology of the Center for Democracy and Technology", 2006).

In this early stage, the right of notification requires that the individual is clearly and fully informed about the presence of the tag and its usage, about what information is stored on the tag and – in case of re-writable tags – what information could be added, about the identity of the data controller, the purpose of the processing and the duration of the processing and whether the RFID tag can be deactivated or not. This could be done by the use of special logos or notices or when the use of the tag is linked to the provision of services or to employment contracts with specific contractual terms.

The condition of proper notification of the individual should not be considered as fulfilled if the information is incomprehensible, such as if its understanding demands special technical skills. The right of notification of the individual is linked to an obligation of notification for the RFID system controller. In case of contest, the latter has to prove that information was provided in an appropriate, concise and clear way. Additionally, even if the obligation of notification is imposed only on the data controller, best practices and good faith could also imply an obligation of notification to companies incorporating RFID tags in their products.

## The Debate: Opt-In or Opt-Out Principle?

Undeniably, as has already been highlighted, the right of notification is crucial, because it implies the idea of choice: if the consumer is informed before the purchase that the product has an RFID tag, he can choose not to buy it and opt for another product. Nevertheless, this is unfortunately not always the case. In fact, in many situations, the person does not have a real option, either because the tag is linked to the use of a monopoly service, or because all services in the sector use RFID tags; or even because the person has no other choice but to buy the product. A crucial question in these cases is whether the individual has the right to ask that the tag be deactivated. In other words, does the person have the right to oppose the activation of the tag?

Usually, doctrine makes a distinction between two systems: the opt-in system presupposes the prior approval of the person each time a collection of data is realized; the opt-out system presumes that the person has agreed to the collection if he hasn't expressly declared the contrary. Personal data protection legislations often switch between these two concepts, depending on the technology concerned.

Both approaches require the proper notification of the individual of the existence and the activation of the tag. In the opt-in system, the individual has to be informed of the presence of the tag prior to its activation (which takes place lawfully only after his consent), while in the opt-out system the individual is informed after the activation and is given the right to deactivate the tag. In both systems, it must be guaranteed that the possibility of deactivation is real, user friendly and efficient.

Although both options give the individual the possibility of deactivating the tag, the opt-in approach is more protective for privacy. The application of the opt-in principle is proposed by the European Data Protection Supervisor as a precondition of the lawful use of RFID infrastructures. According to the opinion of the European Data Protection Supervisor, all RFID applications solutions should respect and implement as a prerequisite an opt-in principle at the point of sale. Enabling the RFID tags to continue transmitting information after the point of sale would be unlawful unless the data controller had appropriate legal grounds, such as the consent of the data subject or if such disclosure was necessary in order to deliver a service. In these cases, both legal approaches would then qualify as 'opt in'. Tags should be deactivated at the point of sale unless the individual who bought the product to which the tag is attached wanted to leave it active. By exercising the right to leave it active, the individual would be consenting to the further processing of his or her data, such as to the transmission of the data to the reader at his or her next visit to the data controller. As it is stated to the Opinion, there are many options to implement the opt-in principle. For example, as an alternative to the removal of the tag, it could be envisaged that the tag would be blocked, temporarily disabled or following a security policy model called resurrecting duckling model, locked to a specific user. In the case of tag with a short life cycle, the address of the tag which pinpoints to information stored in a database could also be erased from the reference database avoiding further processing of additional data collected by the tag (Opinion of the European Data Protection Supervisor, 2007).

In the U.S., prior consent of the individual is also considered as a legal ground of lawful interception under the Electronic Communications Privacy Act[9] which outlaws wiretapping and other forms of electronic eavesdropping. According to Reuven R. Levary et al.(Reuven R. Levary et al., 2005), RFID is incredibly similar to wiretapping in its use and could be classified as electronic communication. Therefore, it would be reasonable to assume that it cannot be employed to obtain and use information legally unless consent is given.

In practice, for the moment, companies using RFID rarely provide the option of deactivation and thus do not even consider the possibility of a refusal. One of the main arguments against the application of the opt-in principle is that it does not take into consideration the technical features of the tags and readers and cannot fit in all RFID applications. For example, according to Natsui, it is impossible to develop such an RFID reader/writer that has a function of getting consent, informing purpose or removing data and so on. Usually, an RFID reader/writer only has the ability to process radio waves, and does not have any function to notify the existence of such a reader/writer or get prior consent from anyone who has or wears some RFID tags (Natsui, 2004).

While the application of the opt-in principle is not problematic in the case of retail purchase of goods, in other areas such as in security controls or in transports it could cause some problems. Even if nowadays RFID applications are still scarce, in a future world where every item has its own identity attributed by the RFID tag, it won't be possible to ask for prior consent of the individual in each step of everyday human activities. Therefore, at least in some specific cases the alternative solution could be the application of the opt-out principle. Thus:

*it does not seem practical to conduct an opt-in regime where the consumer would have to ask for the installation of an RFID tag into its product at the point of sale. Theoretically, a feasible opt-in regime would be one where all RFID tags are deactivated at the checkout counter, unless the consumer requires the contrary; but it will be very costly and inefficient.* (Eschet, 2004, p. 44)

As it is stated in the Electronic Privacy Information Center's (EPIC) survey about RFID, many RFID applications do not include this choice at all and, when it is included, the actual mechanism for disabling the tag varies widely. Further, it is clear that several applications are being developed which read RFID tags on an individual's person without their explicit knowledge and consent (EPIC questions to RFID industry, Summary of Manufacturers and Retailers' Answers, 2004). We can expect that this behaviour will in the near future lead to some first jurisprudence on the matter. If a retailer leaves the tag activated after the point of sale, some interesting hypothetical scenarios could arise. For example, could the individual take legal action against the retailer for essentially stalking his physical movements? Or could an individual bring a tort action for intentional infliction or emotional distress or invasion of privacy on the basis of being under constant surveillance (Ayoade, 2007, p. 557)?

Special consideration should be given to the case of RFID tag usage by an employer. RFID tags could provide simple and efficient checks of employees' obligations, such as the calculation of labor time and the surveillance of employees' movement, and therefore could be very useful for companies. Could an employee expressly deny the use of the tag? In employment contracts, the consent of the employee to be tracked and controlled through RFID devices may be considered as a normal part of the employment relationship. This is a highly controversial issue and from a legal point of view it is advisable that the consent of employees to the processing of their personal data through RFID tags is given by express specific terms in employment contracts.

## The Specific Purpose of the Implementation of the Tag

The use limitation principle (the purpose principle) is one of the fundamental principles of the lawful processing of personal data. The data controller must clearly define the concrete purpose which justifies the processing of personal data. This is expressly stated in Directive 95/46/EC[10]. The processing of personal data is lawful only if it is conducted for a specific and legitimate purpose which defines the form and the extent of the processing. The data subject must be plainly informed about the purpose of the processing. The purpose cannot be modified later or further extended.

Proper informing of the person as to the principal purpose or purposes for which the information is intended to be used is one of the obligations of the data controller set by the U.S. Privacy Act of 1974. The necessity of a clear and specific purpose is also recognized as a precondition of lawful processing by the OECD Guidelines on the Protection of Privacy ("OECD Guidelines on the Protection of Privacy and Transborder Flows of Personal Data", 1980).

The data subject must be fully informed about the purpose of the processing. If the data subject has given his informed consent about a specific purpose of processing through RFID systems, the private or state entity employing the RFID cannot change this purpose. For example, if the consumer has authorized the processing through RFID in order to be able to use the loyalty card of a specific grocery store, the identification of the products he/she buys may not be combined with his personal data and further communicated to third parties for marketing purposes.

## Main Areas of RFID Applications

### RFID in the Healthcare Sector

Use of the radio identification technology has become a great concern in the health sector. The possibilities are countless: at first, we can imagine the induction of RFID on drugs, with data about the product's structure, the expiration date, the patient's name; RFID could also be used to organize equipment tracking. Mainly, however, a huge concern is the direct implementation of RFID tags in the body. For pets, a global system of identification already exists in many countries. This consists of the implementation of an RFID tag under the skin. The tag includes information such as the name of the pet, the race, the name and the address of the owner of the pet, etc. For humans, similar chips have already been designed. In that case, the technology is ready for use but, as can easily be understood, the use of RFID tags conflicts seriously with universal philosophical, political and legal values. A tag could contain information about blood type, illnesses and allergies of the patient, about his medication, perhaps even his medical history (Jervis, 2005)[11]. In an emergency situation, when the patient is unconscious, this information may be life-saving.

The general principle which applies in the use of RFID systems in the health sector is that the patient must decide if he wants to use this technology. Nevertheless, there are some exceptions. Thus, in many countries personal data protection legislations could permit the use of the tag even without the patient's consent, such as in case of health emergencies[12] or in the domain of medical research. However, these exceptions should be interpreted strictly.

### RFID Use for Security Purposes

Governments are already big consumers of RFIDs. Widespread RFID use by governments causes fears of possible unlimited control of citizens by governments and police authorities. Science fiction scenarios often portray the future as a world in which every individual has been tagged with a microchip and can be easily traced by state agencies at any time. These scenarios are very close to the historical and sociopolitical background which lead to the adoption of the personal data protection; at first, in most countries, the legal protection of personal data was achieved as a response to the specter of Big Brother: the government knowing everything about the habits, desires, political opinions, private occupations of the citizens (Bennett, 1992, p. 46). Personal data protection legislations had to be adapted when it became apparent that industries and multinational companies, surfing on the digital revolution, were making huge data mines of consumer profiles. And now the threat of government interference in citizens' privacy rises again in the context of the globalization of RFID uses. RFID tags can be found on ID tags, on official papers, passports[13], even on currency. In this context, it is obvious that the governmental use of RFID systems is an issue of higher importance for personal data protection authorities. For example, according to the Dutch Data Protection Authority:

*Governments are always interested in places where a lot of data about persons is gathered. Other parties have a similar interest. However, the government is able to influence the boundaries of what is (legally) permissible. The government must not aim to boost the use of RFID in order to be able to have increasing amounts of data. Society must be able to rely on the fact that what is permissible corresponds with what is socially desirable.* (Beugelsdijk, 2006)

Processing of data for security purposes is one of the most delicate privacy issues[14]. The crucial question in a post-September 11th world is to define the limits of processing operations concerning public security and national defense. For example, are there any limits to the nature of data which is collected for security purposes? It must be clearly understood that security matters cannot excuse every intrusion of privacy. Thus, in California, for example, the government recently decided to limit the use of RFID and more precisely to prohibit RFID use in public schools (McKenna Long & Aldridge, April 20, 2007). In the near future governments will have to pass legislation on the legitimacy of RFID data as evidence in court. According to Reuven Revary et al. (2005), "*RFID technology will likely affect law enforcement's ability to gather evidence to prosecute crimes.*"

## RFID in the Transport Area

RFID is very often used in the transport domain: embedded on the metro ticket, on the free city bike, on the bus. Tags can also be inserted in driver's licenses[15]. By definition, the tag offers the possibility of determining its exact position and by consequence, the exact position of the person wearing the tag or traveling with the tag. The tags used in the transport domain may contain some supplementary information and the readers are thus able to determine with precision the time of the beginning and of the end of travel. In the case of travel cards, the tags sometimes store additional information such as how often a person travels, the duration of each journey and/or the most preferred destinations. Thus, it is not exaggerated to characterize this use of RFID as very risky and potentially very dangerous and threatening for the human fundamental right to privacy but also the right of freedom of movement and the right to travel anonymously.

## RFID in Usual Consumer Goods

The use of RFID in the chain of production was the first purpose of the technology, far before other applications were found. One would even claim that a link of causality could be established between the decision of the Wal-Mart Company in 1993 to use RFID in its distribution chains and the actual boom of RFID in post-industrial societies(Chia Cheng Chao, Jiann-Min Yang & Wen-Yang Jen, 2007).

The concept there is to follow the product from the early stage of production to the retailer. In this context, tags are not involved in privacy matters. But at the moment the tag is installed on the product, it could be easily used after sale in order to profile the consumers. For example, a jacket may have a RFID tag which includes data about the store, the price and the year of manufacture of the product. This is basic product data, which is apparently privacy harmless. However, the moment the individual wears the jacket, this could become indirect personal data, because somebody who can access the data through an appropriate reader is able to determine the consumer habits of the individual. The scope of use of RFID covers a lot of sectors of the economy and may lead to the creation of crossed data mining for profiling purposes. While barcodes offer to retailers the possibility of monitoring which products are purchased, RFID tags go much further. RFID permits the monitoring of the consumer's activity inside the store and outside the store, after sale (Ayoade, p. 558). National authorities and personal data protection bodies are concerned by this phenomenon. Provided that the practical development of RFID remains at the moment at an early stage, there is still time to analyze case by case the use of RFID technology in different sectors, including its use in supply chains and consumer products: "A close examination of the cost and benefits of specific security and privacy-related risks prior to the selection of RFID systems and the deployment of RFID applications is needed"("Radio Frequency Identification (RFID) in Europe: steps towards a policy framework", 2007, p. 6).

## THE SYMBIOSIS: THE TAG, AN INDISCREET COMPANION?

The relation between the individual and the tag starts with the act of implementation of the tag into the product, the pet or even the human body. Even if the individual has given his/her consent to the use of RFID infrastructure for a specific purpose, the processing of personal data is not lawful if the data controller does not respect a series of basic universally accepted privacy protection principles. In other words, like in most of human relations, even if the beginning seems idyllic, things could very easily turn out bad during the cohabitation of the person with the tag.

### Principles of Fair Processing of the Data Collected Through RFID

As has been already discussed in previous paragraphs, fair processing of personal data is subject to specific requirements established by legislation, jurisprudence or codes of conduct. The implementation of the tag is only the first step of the process. The data controller has to fulfill a number of obligations during the further phases of processing such as data quality and the guarantee of the security of the tag in order to avoid the disclosure of the collected information to third parties.

### Data Quality

Principles relating to data quality constitute the essence of the right to data privacy. (Kotschy., 2006, p. 43) According to the principles of OECD about data quality, personal data should be relevant to the purposes for which they are to be used, and, to the extent necessary for those purposes, should be accurate, complete and kept up-to-date. This fundamental principle of data quality was originally formulated in the OECD Privacy Guidelines and later incorporated in the Directive 95/46/EC[16].

The principle of data quality is inextricably linked to the principle of the defined purpose of the processing, which has been analyzed in the previous sections. The specific purpose of the processing defines the nature and the volume of the personal data which need to be processed. Only data which is relevant to the purpose of processing may be stored or collected by the tag. The personal data which is stored or linked to the tag should be limited to the minimum needed to accomplish the strictly defined purpose of the processing. The requirements of data "relevance" and of data-minimization constitute a specific expression of the general principle of proportionality in personal data protection legal frameworks. For example, travel smart cards should not contain information irrelevant to the purpose of the processing or more information than is needed in order to pass the tolls, such as health data or race data of the card holder.

Two other data quality key principles are the accuracy of the data and the duration of the processing. The obligation of accuracy implies that the data controller should process only accurate data and if necessary proceed to rectifications. This is essential in RFID systems, because data processed in some RFID applications could be used in order to make decisions which affect the individual. The time limit principle entails that the processing of data is not perpetual but limited in time and that stored data should be deleted if their processing is no longer necessary for the fulfillment of the purpose of processing.

## Safeguarding the Security of the RFID System

As we have seen above, whether the tag is used in the healthcare or the in retail sector, one of the biggest concerns lies in the possibility for a third party to clandestinely access the data which is stored on the tag (Lockton, Rosenberg, 2005, p. 221). In the near future, it may not be strange to wear five or seven tags at the same time: on the passport, the driver license, the credit card, the work badge, some of our clothes, the transit card and even under the skin. The sum of this information reveals quite a lot about the personality of the individual and the moment the person accepts the tags, the only protection he or she could rely on against third-party intrusion consists of the encryption of the data. A weak or nonexistent encryption leads to an increased risk of the data being hacked[17]. Personal data linked to RFID tags should be protected against unauthorized interception, access, disclosure, copying, use, modification, or linkage.

The legal aspects of the data security issue present two faces: companies using non-safe radio frequencies or obsolete encryption programs should be held liable[18]; also, the governments must take appropriate legal measures against RFID hacking in order to discourage RFID hack attempts[19]. The responsibility of the entity organizing the collection of data through RFID is in risk of turning into a field of legal conflict, since normally this kind of responsibility must be assesssed *in concreto,* according to the state of the art, but in the case of RFID the assessment of the responsibility could be stricter because even the slightest security flaw on a public tag will lead to major leak of personal data.

Another issue is the determining the person responsible for the security of RFID systems. While in general the obligation lies with the data controller – the person who is competent to decide about the processing or has ordered the processing – it should be taken into consideration that RFID infrastructures usually involve many different actors, such as the manufacturer of the tag and the reader, the entity employing the tag, the EPC database[20], etc. Therefore, a crucial question is whether the obligation of security should be extended to all these actors or not (Lemarteleur, 2004, p. 27).

The crucial role of manufacturers of RFID devices is underlined by the Working Party on the protection of individuals with regard to the processing of personal data of article 29. In the working document on data protection issues related to RFID, it is emphasized that while the users of RFID applications are ultimately responsible for the personal data gathered through the application in question, manufacturers of RFID technology and standardization bodies are responsible for ensuring that data protection/privacy compliant RFID technology is available for those who employ the technology. For example, the design of RFID tags, RFID readers as well as RFID applications may have a great impact in preventing any unlawful forms of processing by making it technically impossible for unauthorized persons to access personal data (Working document on data protection issues related to RFID technology, p. 12).

## The Rights of the Person During the Processing of Data

### The Right to be Informed that the Processing (Reading) Takes Place

Normally, there is no need to make a distinction between the right of notification of the individual when his personal data are about to be processed into a database and the right of notification at the moment the data is collected: the two acts are in practice the same. But in RFID applications, even if the person has been notified of the existence of the RFID tag, this does not mean that he knows when the tag is communicating with the reader. Even if the simple random transfer of data from the tag to the reader, corresponding to the need periodically to measure the level of the battery, is obviously not concerned by the right of information, things could be different when an effective transfer of personal data takes place.

For example, if we consider an active tag embedded on a transport ticket, tracing the route and the time passed on the public transport by the user, he has to be informed not only that the ticket is linked to RFID but also whenever he enters a "control" area. This should of course not be a problem with short range frequencies used for credit cards, but for others frequencies, the range of the reader makes it practically invisible. With modern cheap long-ranged tags, it is not possible for the user to determine the exact instant the tag is being read, but the right of notification implies that a kind of notice must explain if a tag reader is in service in the area.

In other words, hidden checkpoints should be considered illegal regarding fundamental principles of privacy protection. This second aspect of the right of notification could also be linked to the general principle of lawfulness of the collection of data or the OCDE general principle of notice:

*the standard of notice basically aims at having no secret data systems. Consequently, in the context of RFID technology (in light of the continuing exposure and implications after living the retail environment), a practice of merely notifying the consumer of the existence of the technology in the retail environment is a must, but will not suffice on its own. The consumer ought to be alerted to the presence of an RFID tag in every specific product that he considers purchasing and should also be alerted to every environment that is under surveillance by RFID readers.* (Eschet, 2004, p. 43)

### The Right of Verification of the Accuracy of the Data

The right of the individual to access the personal data and verify its accuracy is one of the classical principles of the personal data legal framework. However, this principle will be difficult to adapt to the RFID environment, because as it has been suggested, the data needs to be encrypted to ensure access security. The principle of access to the data incorporated in the tag or/and stored in the RFID-user's database can not be bypassed, even if technological barriers occur, because the right of access is a precondition for the enforcement of other data protection principles, such as the principle of data quality.

In practice, it falls to the group or entity centralizing data from tags and running the database to give the individual access to to the specific data related to him- or herself. If it appears that some data is irrelevant or false inside the tag itself, the company has the responsibility to destroy it in case of a passive tag or to update it, if possible, with accurate information.

## THE SEPARATION: THE END OF PERSONAL DATA PROCESSING

The active RFID tag embedded with a battery can last for more than 10 years, while the passive tags which take energy directly from the transmitter possess a longer lifetime. We can characterize this as the "natural end" of the process, but in fact the collection of data through RFID has every reason to be stopped prematurely, either by the individual or by the company handling the tag management.

### The Termination of the Processing by the User: The Right to Deactivate the Tag

According to fair information practices, the individual does not only have the right to be informed and to have access to the data, but also to terminate the processing of his personal data. The right of opposition is not indeed limited to the moment of the collection of data but can also be exercised later. It should also be possible to exercise it without any cost. A direct link obviously exists between the right to object to the processing and the obligation of the data controller to ask for the consent of the individual when it is required. The free withdrawal of the data subject's consent at any moment is one of the basic principles of personal data protection, while at the same time national legislations widely recognize either a general or less extended specific right to object (Millard Ch. & Church P., 2006, p. 73).

If the legal ground of the processing is the informed consent[21], the individual could normally withdraw its consent and thus have the right to deactivate the tag without any penalties. In case of data processing on the basis of contractual obligations, the individual could freely and without any legal repercussions deactivate the tag from the moment the data stored in the tag is not necessary to the performance of the contract. For example, he can deactivate the tag on the transport ticket after he left the bus or the train. On the contrary, the user does not have the right to disable the tag, while he is still traveling. If he does so without legitimate legal grounds, this will probably be a breach of contract.

Thus, the issue is how the right to oppose to the transfer can be exercised. The response comes from the technological sector, discussing the possibilities of a so-called "tag sleep" or "tag kill":

*There are two methods to do this: Either you set a flag inside the RFID chip telling it not to respond anymore, or you simply destroy it, for instance blowing it by applying too much power. In the first case you can never be sure that the chip is not later re-activated without your knowledge. For this reason the latter of the two alternatives is probably the most acceptable for the common consumer.* (Hjorth, 2004, p. 25)

However, even if the simple brutal approach of destroying the tag looks more suitable for the consumer, there is still a long debate about the advantages and disadvantages of this way of permanent deactivation of the tag:

*Killing or discarding tags enforces consumer privacy effectively, but it eliminates all of the post-purchase benefits of RFID for the consumer. The receiptless item returns, smart appliances, aids for the elderly, and other beneficial (...) will not work with deactivated tags. And in some cases, such as libraries and rental shops, RFID tags cannot be killed because they must survive over the lifetime of the objects they track. For these reasons, it is imperative to look beyond killing for more balanced approaches.* (Juels, 2006).

This could be realized by the virtual deactivation.

## The Termination of the Processing by the Tag Controller

The question of the termination of processing by the company which manages RFID systems seems at first sight curious. The tag controller has in fact every interest to continue the processing as long as the data collected can be a source of useful information. However, as has already been analyzed, data collection should be linked to a legitimate purpose. From the moment this purpose is no more legitimate, or when it is accomplished, data collection must stop. This is one of the data quality principles set by OECD and the EU Directive 95/46/EC. It is also illustrated by the Guidelines for regulation of Computerized Personal Data Files (U.N. Resolution 45/95 of 14 December 1990), in article 3 c: "The period for which the personal data are kept does not exceed that which would enable the achievement of the purposes so specified".

For example, let's consider an RFID tag embedded on a work badge. The purpose of the processing of data for the employer is to monitor the employee's activities. So no collection of data can take place outside the working time, because the purpose of the collection would not be fair. To ensure that no one will have access to the tag outside the office, the company should install checkpoints at the exit of the building where the tag could be temporally deactivated by a kill command.

In the RFID area, the focus is usually given to collection of data (data stored or data re-written on the tag) and to the possibilities of deactivation of the tag. However, one should never forget that there is a database linked to the tag. The right to "kill the tag" implies also a kind of "right to oblivion" (Warner, 2005, p. 75) in the database. In other words, the tag and the database manager have the legal obligation to delete the data when their conservation is no more necessary for the accomplishment of the purpose of data processing.

It is difficult to determine in practice the length of fair conservation time of the data: "Not only were data retention rules to depend on the purposes of the processing in question, but also any fixed retention periods established following these rules would need to depend on the particular type of data in question" (Warner, 2005, p. 87). The duration of the retention is inextricably linked to the purpose of the processing and it must be evaluated on the basis of the principle of proportionality. For example, a person has the habit of buying shoes in a specific store. Each year, as he/she enters the store a reader takes the entire consumer's purchase record from the smart tag in his/her old shoes and writes this data on the tag of the new shoes he/she just bought or copies this information into an internal company database. The years passing, the company obtains a full picture of the consumer's habits: preferences, price range, etc. For how long may the retailer continue to gather, update and assemble the personal data of the consumer? At first we should define the purpose of data collection. If we agree to define it as the company's will to understand and evaluate the habits of its clients in order to improve products and services, a retention span of a few years seems to be the maximal possible duration of retention of the client's data.

## CONCLUSION

The exponential growth of RFID applications has been acknowledged by scholars, governments and civil rights organizations[22]. Like a lot of new technologies which appeared in the digital era, the RFID shows several positive and negative aspects. For the moment, in order to better determine the impact of RFID on privacy, governments decided to wait for this technology to be mature. It is undeniable that a lot of problems of privacy intrusion should find a solution in technological ways, such as "security and privacy- by- design"[23], better encryption or standardization of a "kill command" to deactivate the tag. Existing data protection legal framework could provide a satisfactory base-line against privacy intrusions through RFID devices. However, it is equally obvious that the application of fair information practices to RFID systems causes a series of critical legal issues and calls for tailored made solutions and specific regulation (Eschet, 2004, p. 43): provisions about the imposition of an RFID-logo, clear choice for an opt-in or an opt-out regime, etc. These regulations should not replace the actual legal framework but complete it by providing some useful clarification. This data protection legislative policy combined with self-regulatory industry initiatives would benefit not only consumers but also industries, which actually need a secure and balanced legal framework in order to further develop this technology and to generate more consumer trust and confidence (Reid, 2007, p. 58).

## REFERENCES


Ayoade J. (2007). Roadmap to solving security and privacy concerns in RFID systems. *Computer Law & Security Report, 23*(2007), p. 557.

Bennett, C. (1992). *Regulating Privacy, Data protection and Public Policy in Europe and the United States.* Ithaca, New York: Cornell University Press, 1992.

Beugelsdijk R. (2006). RFID, Promising or irresponsible? Contribution to the social debate about RFID. *College bescherming persoonsgegevens.* The Hague, October 2006.

Brito J. (2004). Relax Don't Do It: Why Rfid Privacy Concerns are Exaggerated and Legislation is Premature., *UCLA Journal of Law and Technology*, (5), 2.

CDT Working Group on RFID (2006). *Best Practices for Deployment of RFID Technology of the Center for Democracy and Technology*, Interim Draft, May 1, 2006. Retrieved from http://www.cdt.org/privacy/20060501rfid-best-practices.php

Chia, C. C., Jiann-Min, Y., & W.-Y., Jen (2007). Determining technology and forecasts of RFID by a historical review and bibliometric analysis from 1991 to 2005. *Technovation*, Vol. 27, Issue 5, May 2007, p.p. 268-279.

Commission nationale de l'informatique et des libertés. Séance du 30 octobre 2003. Communication de M. Philippe Lemoine relative à la Radio-Identification (Radio-Tags ou RFIDs), p. 1. Retrieved from http://www.cnil.fr

Directive 2002/58/EC of the European Parliament and of the Council of 12 July 2002 concerning the processing of personal data and the protection of privacy in the electronic communications sector (Directive on privacy and electronic communications), *Official Journal of the European Communities*, 31.7.2002, L 201/37.

Directive 95/46/EC of the European Parliament and of the Council of 24 October 1995 on the protection of individuals with regard to the processing of personal data and on the free movement of such data, *Official journal of the European Communities*, 23. 11. 95, n. L 281/31.

ECPA Pub. L. 99-508, Oct. 21, 1986, 100 Stat. 1848, 18 U.S.C. § 2510.

EPIC, Electronic Privacy Information Center (2004). *EPIC questions to RFID industry, Summary of Manufacturers and Retailers' Answers.* Retrieved from http://www.epic.org/privacy/rfid/survey.html

Eschet, G. (2004). FIPs and PETs for RFID: protecting privacy on the web of radio frequency identification. *Jurimetrics, The Journal of Law, Science and Technology, 45*, 44.

Flint, D. (2006). RFID tags, security and the individual. *Computer Law & Security Report* (22 ), 165-168.

Frayssinet J. (2001). La protection des données personnelles. In Lucas, Deveze & Fraussinet, *Droit de l'informatique et de l'Internet,* Thémis, Droit privé, PUF, Paris, 2001, p. 1.

Hjorth, Th. (2004). *Supporting privacy in RFID systems.* IMM, DTU, Lyngby, Denmark, December 14, 2004.

Jervis, C. (2005). Chips with everything: Is RFID ready for healthcare? *British Journal of Healthcare Computing and Information Management, 22*(2). Retrieved from http://www.kineticconsulting.co.uk/

Juels, A. (2006). RFID Security and Privacy: A Research Survey. *IEEE Journal on selected areas in communications, 24*(2), February 2006, p. 381-394.

Kotschy, W (2006). Directive 95/46/EC. In Bullesbach, Poullet & Prins (ed.), *Concise European IT Law.* Kluwer Law International, the Netherlands.

Lemarteleur, X. (2004). *Traçabilité contre vie privée: les RFIDs ou l'immixtion de technologie dans la sphère personnelle.* Mémoire, DESS droit du multimédia et de l'informatique, Université Paris II, Panthéon /Assas, octobre 2004. Retrieved from Juriscom.net, 22 octobre 2004, http://www.juriscom.net

Lockton, V., & Rosenberg, R. (2005). RFID: the next serious Threat to Privacy. *Ethics and Information Technology,* 7(4), 221.

Mc Kenna, L. (2007). *Aldridge's Blog. California Senate fights required RFID in schools.* (April 20, 2007). Retrieved from http://rfidlawblog.mckennalong.com/archives/state-legislation-california-senate-fights-required-rfid-in-schools.html

Millard, Ch., & Church, P. (2006). Directive 95/46/EC, article 14 (2006). In Bullesbach, Poullet & Prins (Ed.), *Concise European IT Law.* The Netherlands: Kluwer Law Internatinal.

Natsui, T. (2004). *Traceability system using RFID and legal issues.* Retrieved from www.sics.se/privacy/wholes2004/papers/takato.pdf

OECD (1980). *OECD Guidelines on the Protection of Privacy and Transborder Flows of Personal Data.*

Opinion of the European Data Protection Supervisor on the communication from the Commission to the European Parliament, the Council, the European Economic and Social Committee and the Committee of the Regions on 'Radio Frequency Identification (RFID) in Europe: Steps towards a policy framework', COM(2007) 96, *Official Journal of the European Union*, 23.4.2008, C101/7.

Radio Frequency Identification (RFID) in Europe: steps towards a policy framework (2007). *Communication from the Commission to the European Parliament, the Council, the European Economic and Social Committee and the Committee of the Regions.* COM(2007)96 final.

Reid A. (2007). Is society smart enough to deal with smart cards. *Computer Law & Security Report,* (23), 53-61.

Reuven, R., Levary, et al (2005). Radio Frequency Identification: Legal Aspects. 12 *RICH. J.L. & TECH.* 6 (2005), p. 12. Retrieved from http://law.richmond.edu/ jolt/v12i2/article6.pdf

Slemmons, S. J., & Stratford, J. (1998). *Data Protection and Privacy in the United States and Europe.* Retrieved from atalib.library.ualberta.ca/publications/iq/ iq22/iqvol223stratford.pdf

*The Privacy Act of 1974*, 5 U.S.C. § 552a. Available on line: http://www.usdoj.gov/

*U.N. Resolution 45/95* of 14 December 1990.

Warner, J. (2005). The right to oblivion: Data retention from Canada to Europe in Three backward Steps. *University of Ottawa law & technology journal, 2.*

Weinberg, J. (2007). *Tracking RFID.* Retrieved from http: //www.law.wayne.edu.

*Working document on data protection issues related to RFID technology*, January 19, 2005. Article 29 Data Protection Working Party on the protection of individuals regarding to the processing of personal data. Retrieved from http://www.europa .eu.int./comm/privacy

## ENDNOTES

1 In practice we could distinguish at least three different RFID devices: the *smart labels*, the *smart cards* and the *smart tags*. See M. Rivas, "RFID Privacy Workshop", MIT, http://www.find.org. From now on, we are going to use the term *smart tags* to describe all these devices. These micro chips are almost invisible as they can be such miniscule as the half of a grain of sand: J. Brito, "Relax Don't Do It: Why RFID Privacy

Concerns are Exaggerated and Legislation is Premature", *UCLA Journal of Law and Technology*, 2004 (5), p. 2.

2 The transceiver (TRANSmitter/reCEIVER) is the reader. The RFIds are also called transponder (TRANSmitter/resPONDER). Commission nationale de l'informatique et des libertés. Séance du 30 octobre 2003. Communication de M. Philippe Lemoine relative à la Radio-Identification (Radio-Tags ou RFIds), p. 1, http://www.cnil.fr.

3 In the U.S.A., the 20th of October 2004 the Food and Drugs Administration (FDA) approved the use of RFID infrastructures in healthcare services. See: http://www.fda.gov/oc/speeches/ 2004/cleveland1020.htm.

4 The Central European Bank announced that euros will contain smart RFID tags in order to fight against counterfeiting and fraud. See: 25ème Conférence Internationale des Commissaires à la protection des données et à la vie privée, Sydney, 12 September, 2003. Résolution sur la Radio-Identification. Final version, 20 November, 2003, p. 2-3. Retrieved from http://www.privacyconference2003.org.

5 According to article 2 h) of the Directive 95/46/EC, consent is valid only if the person has been informed ("informed consent").

6 The Proposal for a directive of the European Parliament and of the Council amending Directive 2002/22/EC on universal service and users' rights relating to electronic communications networks, Directive 2002/58/EC concerning the processing of personal data and the protection of privacy in the electronic communications sector and Regulation (EC) No 2006/2004 on consumer protection cooperation, (COM(2007)0698 – C6-0420/2007 – 2007/0248(COD) includes specific reference about the application of the Directive 2002/58/EC by RFID devices in order to dissipate any doubt. The proposed amendment of recital 28 of the Directive 2002/58/EC states as following: "When such devices are connected to publicly available electronic communications networks or make use of electronic communications services as a basic infrastructure, the relevant provisions of Directive 2002/58/EC, including those on security, traffic and location data and on confidentiality, should apply".

7 The Privacy Act of 1974, 5 U.S.C. § 552a , available on line: http://www.usdoj.gov/.

8 Section (e) "Agency requirements" states that "Each agency that maintains a system of records shall-- (3) inform each individual whom it asks to supply information, on the form which it uses to collect the information or on a separate form that can be retained by the individual (A) the authority (whether granted by statute, or by Executive order of the President) which authorizes the solicitation of the information and whether disclosure of such information is mandatory or voluntary; (B) the principal purpose or purposes for which the information is intended to be used;(C) the routine uses which may be made of the information, as published pursuant to paragraph (4) (D) of this subsection; and (D) the effects on him, if any, of not providing all or any part of the requested information;"

9 ECPA Pub. L. 99-508, Oct. 21, 1986, 100 Stat. 1848, 18 U.S.C. § 2510.

10 Article 6 par. 1 (b) states that "Member states should provide that personal data must be: b) collected for specified, explicit and legitimate purposes and not further processed in a way incompatible with those purposes".

11 The article gives some concrete examples of application of RFID tags in the health service's sector. For example, in England, in the Wirral Hospital NHS Trust emergency department uses RFID tags to prevent new borns or others vulnerable patients to be removed without authority; in US, in the

Massachusetts General Hospital RFID devices are used to prevent blood transfusion errors.

12 In the U. S., the Food and Drug Administration authorized an application based on the setting under human being skin of a RFID tag giving the medical file index of a patient usable in emergency cases: cited in Article 29 Data Protection Working Party, Working document on data protection issues related to RFID technology, op. cit., p. 4. In Europe, article 7 of the Directive 95/46/EC provides that processing of personal data can be done without the consent of the person if it is necessary in order to protect the vital interests of the person. According to the Working Document on data protection issues related to RFID technology of the Article 29 Data Protection Working Party, a hospital that uses RFID in surgical instruments to eliminate the risk of leaving an item inside of a patient at the conclusion of an operation may not need the patient's consent on the basis of this provision. See: Working document, p. 10.

13 RFID passports have been developed in many countries since the past ten years, including the US passports. See: Radio Frequency Identification (RFID) chips in passports and visas (2006). Retrieved from http://www.workpermit.com/news/2006_11_10/global/rfid_tags_travel_documents.htm.

14 Directive 95/46/EC does not apply in case of processing operations concerning public security, defence, State security and the activities of the State in the area of criminal law (article 3 par. 2). Furthermore, article 8 par. 4 provides the possibility of Member States to lay down more exceptions to the processing of the so called "sensitive" personal data for reasons of substantial public interest, in addition to those provided by article 8 par. 2.

15 This system exists already on the Vermont for example. See: http://epic.org/privacy/surveillance/spotlight/ 0907/default.html. In Pakistan, driving licenses contain even some information about traffic violations and outstanding penalties. For more information, see the Web page of the national authority about RFID-based driver license: http://www.nadra.gov.pk/site/395/default.aspx.

16 Article 6 states that: "Member States shall provide that personal data must be: (a)...; (b)...; (c) adequate, relevant and not excessive in relation to the purposes for which they are collected and/or further processed; (d) accurate and, where necessary, kept up to date; every reasonable step must be taken to ensure that data which are inaccurate or incomplete, having regard to the purposes for which they were collected or for which they are further processed, are erased or rectified; (e) kept in a form which permits identification of data subjects for no longer than is necessary for the purposes for which the data were collected or for which they are further processed. Member States shall lay down appropriate safeguards for personal data stored for longer periods for historical, statistical or scientific use".

17 For example, recently, a Dutch RFID-base card security has been seriously compromised. See: G. Hulme, Students Successfully Hack RFID Crypto. 3-11 2008, The information week (available on line: http://www.informationweek.com/blog/main/archives/2008/03/ students_succes.html).

18 In Europe for example, this matter is settled by articles 16 and 17 of the EU Directive 95/46/EC. OECD Guidelines on the Protection of Privacy and Transborder Flows of Personal Data state that personal data should be protected by reasonable security safeguards against such risks as loss or unauthorised access, destruction, use, modification or disclosure of data.

19 For example in US, the Wiretap Act, 18 U.S.C. §§2510-2522, determines that it's illegal to intercept wire or electronic communication, even if it is easy to do so.

20 The Electronic Product Code (EPC) is the next generation of product identification similar to the UPC (Universal Product Code) or barcode. EPC Global Inc. manages in an international level the Electronic Product Codes. Each product has its own identification number. The reader searches through Internet the number of the product in a database managed by EPC global. This database contains all the EPC numbers. More information about EPC can be found at : http://www.epcglobal.org.

21 The processing of personal data through use of RFID devices can be based on different legal grounds, such as the consent of the individual, the carrying out of a contract, an obligation imposed by law, etc.

22 In USA, for example, the CASPIAN organization introduced in 2003 a model act designed to regulate RFID (The RFID Right to Know Act) and claims to have already influenced RFID legislation on Utah (H. B. 251, Radio Frequency Identification - Right to Know Act) and California. For more information, see their website: http://www.nocards.org/.

23 Privacy protective RFID design is being promoted by the EU. In particular, the Communication of the European Commission about RFID states that "*As end users typically are not involved at the technology design stage, the Commission will support the development of a set of application-specific guidelines (code of conduct, good practices) by a core group of experts representing all parties*". See: Communication from the Commission to the European Parliament, the Council, the European Economic and Social Committee and the Committee of the Regions, Radio Frequency Identification (RFID) in Europe: steps towards a policy framework, op. cit. p. 9.

# Chapter VI
# How Much is Too Much?
## How Marketing Professionals can Avoid Violating Privacy Laws by Understanding the Privacy Principles

**Nicholas P. Robinson**
*McGill University, Canada*

**Prescott C. Ensign**
*Telfer School of Management, University of Ottawa, Canada*

## ABSTRACT

*A marketeer's point of view is presented in this chapter. Although legal restrictions safeguard processes and restrict annoying intrusive techniques, protecting customers, it can be argued that responsible privacy practices in the marketing profession will add value for consumers. As businesses compete with greater intensity to provide the customer with control over areas such as product offerings, services provided, and account management, privacy standards, being an important part of the customer-company relationship, formulate the grounds upon which businesses compete to provide greater customer control.*

## INTRODUCTION

The numbers were staggering. Over "45 million credit and debit cards, from transactions going back as long ago as 2002" were captured by criminals who had used complex technology to hack into the computer system of Winners – a North American department store chain with numerous outlets in Canada and the United States (Roseman, 2007). The effect, according to a report released by the privacy commissioners of Canada and the province of Alberta was that hundreds of thousands of Canadian and American consumers had their personal data misappropriated and were at risk of identity theft and other related problems (Office of the Privacy Commissioner, 2007).

More worrisomely, the store had not exercised the restraint required by Canada's comprehensive privacy law, the Personal Information Protection and Electronic Documents Act (or "PIPEDA" or the "PIPED Act"), and had unwittingly exacerbated the situation. The company had "collected too much personal information from customers, kept it for too long and relied on weak technology to protect it, according to a joint probe" released by the privacy commissioners (Office of the Privacy Commissioner, 2007). Given events such as the breach at Winners, one can understand the reasons for increased interest in consumer privacy in Canada.

The advent of new technology has made personal data globally mobile and made remote access possible for thieves and fraudsters internationally. In this light, Canada and numerous other nations have enacted privacy legislation to combat the threat of privacy breaches like the one at Winners. The PIPED Act came to force for the public sector in 2001 but has been in force for the private sector since 2004 (PIPEDA, 2000). The legislation, compelled by pressures from the European Union to develop more comprehensive privacy laws, elaborates on a number of principles that private sector businesses must follow and has created methods for recourse by individuals who feel their privacy, known as data protection in Europe, has been violated (European Directive 95/46/EC). The legal implications of electronic intrusion and new privacy laws can be understood as both a threat and an opportunity, as it has increased the cost of acquiring and managing personal information while spurring the creation of marketing practices that are more respectful of consumers' privacy concerns (Robinson & Large, 2004, p. 49).

In fact, it can be argued that responsible privacy practices in the marketing profession will add value for consumers while helping to avoid future breaches, like the one at Winners. The privacy principles elaborated in PIPEDA will both help to protect vulnerable consumers from the threat of electronic intrusion while having a mixed impact on the marketing profession. By examining the three years' worth of available case law, one can understand the costs and benefits of privacy laws and the necessity of privacy legislation in light of electronic threats. Indeed, privacy will be one of the defining human rights issues of the 21st century given that technological advances and the increased disclosure of personal information will make those who control personal information, namely businesses and governments, increasingly powerful. The marketing profession will play a pivotal role in democratizing privacy rights and discouraging electronic intrusion by actively supporting privacy legislation and other government endeavours to protect the citizen's privacy interests (NB: An implied right to privacy exists in Canada and many other countries (Canadian Charter of Rights, 1982, s.7)).

## BACKGROUND: THE PRIVACY PRINCIPLES IN ACTION

The privacy principles elaborated in PIPEDA serve as a guide to businesses and others who are subject to the Act. The privacy principles apply to all personal information that is "collected, used, or disclosed by an organization in the private sector" (Tacit, 2003, p.1). Personal information, according to the Canadian Act, includes information about any "identifiable individual, other than an individual's name, title, business address or telephone number as an employee of an organization" (Tacit, 2003, p.1). Exceptions are included for artistic and journalistic pursuits, and other areas of public interest where privacy law could be prohibitive to a socially beneficial activity (Tacit, 2003, p.3).

Those who are subject to PIPEDA must therefore attempt to develop business practices that are consistent with the Act's spirit. The privacy principles, developed by the Canadian Standards Association and inspired by a similar set of OECD principles, include: (1) limiting collection,

(2) accuracy and completeness, (3) identifying purposes, (4) consent, (5) limiting use retention and disclosure, (6) safeguards, (7) openness, (8) challenging compliance, (9) access, and (10) accountability (PIPEDA, 2000, Schedule 1 s. 5). These principles are designed to be interpreted according to the particular scenario and cannot be uniformly applied given the particularities of the uses of personal data, the subject of the data, and the overall scenario.

The first of the ten privacy principles, accountability, requires that all organizations that are subject to the law, large and small, designate someone who is "accountable for the organization's compliance with the ...principles" (PIPEDA, 2000, s. 5 (4.1)). Though the management of personal information may be delegated to others, the designated individual must ensure that the organization has the policies and practices necessary to ensure compliance. All "personal information in its possession or custody, including information that has been transferred to a third party for processing" is covered by this definition (PIPEDA, 2000, s.5 (4.1.3)). The principle of accountability, as with all other principles, is interdependent and supports an individual claimant's ability to challenge the organization's compliance. From a marketing standpoint, this implies that marketing professionals will have to give deference to privacy concerns, and give deference to the designated individual, in order to ensure campaigns are compliant. This is of special importance when personal data is transmitted and shared in order to produce an effective marketing campaign. The designated compliance officer in charge of ensuring accountability would oversee activities involving sales lists and customer data.

Marketers are also required to identify the purposes of the information being collected "at or before" it is collected (PIPEDA, 2000, s.5 (4.2)). This adds an additional layer of administration when surveys and other market research activities are being undertaken, as participants must be informed of the reasons for the collection of information and its uses. Further, the information being collected must have a logical nexus with the purpose identified—in other words, it must be "necessary" to achieve the identified purpose (PIPEDA, 2000, s. 5 (4.2.2)). In the case Eastmond v. Canadian Pacific Railway, where a video camera was installed in a rail yard, the court deemed the purpose of encouraging workplace safety and protecting company machinery from vandalism and theft acceptable (Eastmond v. CPR, 2004, para. 178). The court went even further by stating that every purpose must be "analysed in a contextual manner" giving weight to the "particular circumstances" and suggested that the purpose of collecting the information, and the purpose of disclosing the information need not be identical (Eastmond v. CPR, 2004, para. 131). This principle implies that marketers can no longer arbitrarily use information collected for one purpose and then for another purpose later on, unless the original participants are informed of the new purpose (Eastmond v. CPR, 2004, para. 178). Further, the flexibility that market researchers once had in using information to for new purposes is compromised and collecting information that has no immediate nexus with the proposed purpose is forbidden.

The purposes identified by the organization must be consented to along with the particular uses named and any disclosures of the personal information to other parties. Consent, the third privacy principle, is "required for the collection of personal information and the subsequent use or disclosure of this information" (PIPEDA, 2000, s.5 (4.3.1)). Consent can be obtained orally, implicitly through one's use of a product or service, and through written documents, such as an application form or a check-off box. In jurisprudence, application forms describing the reason for obtaining biometric data (opt-in consent) and signs indicating the presence of video surveillance systems (opt-out consent) have been considered valid forms of consent (Turner v. Telus Communications, 2005; Eastmond v. CPR, 2004).

Further, in instances where consent would make the achievement of the purpose impossible or difficult, explicit consent may not have to be sought (Eastmond v. CPR, 2004, p. 186). In Turner v. Telus, an application form to collect biometric data (including a voice imprint) was considered sufficient consent (Turner v. Telus, 2005, para. 58). A minority of employees refused consent in this case, without any repercussions from Telus, making this case an example of how privacy laws empower individual citizens to protect their privacy interests. For the marketing profession, being unable to obtain consent may stand as a barrier to certain research projects.

However, the barrier posed by the consent requirement advances several other goals that all pieces of privacy legislation aim to achieve. For instance, limiting the collection of information and empowering the consumer to take control over his or her personal data. All privacy laws aim to limit the collection of information by organizations in order to lessen the chances of abusive use of personal information and privacy breaches, as in the Winners case. Limiting collection, the fourth privacy principle, is interdependent with many of the other principles. For instance, collection can be limited on the basis that information may only be collected for a particular purpose, and likewise, with the consent of the individual. The information collected should be "limited to that which is necessary for the purposes identified by the organization", both in terms of the "type and the amount" of information collected (PIPEDA, 2000, s. 5 (4.4)). Further, the Act states that information should not be collected "indiscriminately" (PIPEDA, 2000, s. 5 (4.4.1)). The electronic disclosure of personal information by the Bank of Nova Scotia to the Royal Bank of Canada for a purpose other than the purpose the individual customer consented to at the time of collection has been deemed to be inconsistent with PIPEDA (B.M.P. Global Distribution v. Bank of Nova Scotia, 2005). When information is collected, it can only be disclosed for the purposes specified and consented to by the individual in question, with some exceptions for certain groups like investigative bodies. Likewise, cameras geared to observe only those entering and leaving CPR company facilities were deemed to have been consistent with the principle of limiting collection (Eastmond v. CPR, 2004, para. 178). Data mining activities that arbitrarily (and indiscriminately) collect consumer information, as with cookies and other electronic tools used to gather information on target customers, likely would not meet the standards of limiting collection. Thus, it can be said that the principle of limiting collection restricts many marketing practices.

Limiting collection is also related to the fifth principle, limiting use, retention and disclosure. This principles states that personal information should be "retained only as long as necessary for the fulfilment of those purposes" and can only be used or disclosed in a manner that is consistent with the purpose identified and consented to (PIPEDA, 2000, s. 5 (4.5)). Further, to discourage the propagation of personal information subject to privacy concerns, the principle of limiting use, retention and disclosure requires that information that is no longer necessary to serve the original purpose be "destroyed, erased, or made anonymous" (PIPEDA, 2000, s. 5 (4.5.3)). In the case Eastmond v. CPR, the court ruled that CPR had implemented practices that were consistent with limiting retention and disclosure. The company kept video captured by cameras for 92-hour periods and the video was only viewed if a "trigger" incident, such as a theft or another incident, occurred (Eastmond v. CPR, 2004, para. 138). Further, the video was kept under lock and key and disclosure was only made available to company officials and police (Eastmond v. CPR, 2004, para. 178). Conversely, the Bank of Nova Scotia's disclosure of information about a counterfeit cheque to the Royal Bank was deemed to run counter to the principle of limiting disclosure as the disclosure was not consented to by the customer and not captured under any of the Acts exceptions for disclosure without consent. The privacy principles therefore limit subsequent uses of private information, even for compelling business purposes, and curtail the marketer's ability to freely manage and use data.

The sixth privacy principle, accuracy, states that information should be "accurate, complete, and up-to-date as is necessary for the purposes for which it is to be used" (PIPEDA, 2000, s. 5 (4.6)). The individual's right to access the information and request that errors and omissions be corrected supports this obligation. In fact, courts have interpreted the accuracy principle as meaning that the customer can compel the organization to correct information, not that the organization is responsible for ensuring "that records kept by private organizations be inalterable or that their integrity be guaranteed" (PIPEDA, 2000, s. 5 (4.6)). In the case Vandebeke v. Royal Bank of Canada, a client's incomplete and supposedly inaccurate bank records caused a prejudice (Vandebeke v. RBC, 2006). The court stated that the bank's responsibility was limited to ensuring that the customer could rectify problems with his information (Vandebeke v. RBC, 2006, para. 22). From the perspective of a marketing professional, securely maintaining information is an onerous task in itself. It would be difficult to assure the complete accuracy of information, especially when an organization is not at fault for the inaccuracy or incompleteness of information. Privacy laws therefore strikes a balance between the rights of the individual and the abilities of the organization and establishes an effective regime for the self-monitoring of an individual's data.

The seventh privacy principle, security safeguards, is interdependent with the sixth principle, as safeguards are needed to ensure accuracy and protect data from tampering. In order to ensure accuracy, "security safeguards appropriate to the sensitivity of the information" must be taken using physical, organizational and technological measures to protect the data (PIPEDA, 2000, s. 5 (4.7)). This means that the level of protection provided should be commensurate with the nature and amount of information stored. The safeguards employed by Winners, for instance, were deemed to have been incommensurate with the sensitivity of the credit card information that was stolen (Roseman, 2007). In Turner v. Telus, the court stated that a proactive approach to protecting personal data is necessary to ensure that safeguards are in place (Turner v. Telus, 2005, para. 22). The company's use of biometric employee data, though potentially harmful to the employee's privacy, was deemed important to protecting the customer's privacy. Safeguards are important in ensuring that the information used is of good quality, and therefore mutually benefit both the individual and the marketing professional applying the information.

Openness is also necessary to encourage self-enforcement by individual consumers and others. Openness, the eighth principle, means that the organization should make "readily available to individuals specific information about its policies and practices relating to the management of personal information" (PIPEDA, 2000, s. 5 (4.8)). Information on policies, practices, and those designated as accountable for the company's compliance facilitates access to information makes it easier for individuals to challenge compliance. Being open with regards to the management of information by a company complicates the role of the marketing professional, as one must ensure that they comply with internal policies while communicating how the information in question is being managed. The openness principle increases the burden of responsibility on the marketing professional and therefore encourages practices that are respectful of an individual's privacy rights. For precisely this reason, in the case Thomas v. Robinson the company sought a declaration that the databases it managed were excluded under privacy legislation in the province of Ontario (Thomas v. Robinson, 2001). Openness runs counter to protecting sensitive information and represents a cost when a company wishes to conceal its operations from the public—especially considering the burden that may be posed by outside interference in marketing activities. This being said, openness is also essential to ensuring the consumer's right to privacy is protected.

The ninth principle, access, requires that an organization inform an individual "of the existence, use, and disclosure of his or her personal information and shall be given access to that information" upon request (PIPEDA, 2000, s. 5 (4.9)). Further, the individual has a right to request that the information be complete and accurate and have necessary corrections made. The information must be furnished to the individual within a "reasonable time" and may often be subject to a fee, in order to cover the costs of furnishing the information (PIPEDA, 2000, s. 5 (4.9)). In the case Rousseau v. Wyndowe, the court ruled that an individual had no right to access original notes made by a medical professional where the exact same material could be accessed through electronic records (Rousseau v. Wyndowe, 2006). Providing access through an electronic database was deemed to be sufficient where paper copies had been destroyed. In some circumstances, the Act states that outright denying access to documentation of personal information is permitted.

The last privacy principle, challenging compliance, states that an individual should be able to "address a challenge concerning compliance with the above principles to the designated individual" accountable for an organization's compliance (PIPEDA, 2000, s. 5 (4.10)). In other words, the organization has a responsibility to facilitate the individual's complaint by "informing individuals" of the relevant procedures and options they have to pursue the complaint (PIPEDA, 2000, s. 5 (4.10)). The principle of challenging compliance is closely related with the principles of access and openness and can only function where these other two principles exist. Further, compliance with the law can be challenged through complaints to government appointed privacy officers who are responsible for administering complaints and inquiries regarding each jurisdiction's respective legislation. Many jurisdictions in Europe and elsewhere have privacy commissioners who facilitate complaints and monitor compliance. The ability of the individual to challenge compliance adds impetus for marketing professionals to follow the privacy principles given that the repercussions of non-compliance can be costly.

Though this ordering of the privacy principles is Canadian by definition, other organizations (particularly in Europe) have produced their own principles that are nearly identical to the Canadian principles. For instance, the OECD principles include use limitation, collection limitation, data quality, purpose specification, security safeguards, openness, individual participation, and accountability (OECD, 2007). These principles are also reflected in several EU directives, some of which have had the practical effect of forcing third party data users in countries like Canada to comply with European privacy standards. In this light, PIPEDA and other schemes such as the US Safe Harbor Agreement are responses to the EU directive and are "substantially similar" to the European standards (EC Directive 95/46/EC, 1995). In fact, the Canadian privacy principles and PIPEDA itself are mirror reflections of the EU standards and the OECD principles. This being said, unlike Canada, the United States opted to find a non-legislative solution to meeting the EU's demands that European data transferred abroad be treated in a manner that adequately meets EU privacy standards, something that has been advocated by business groups in the United States (Kutais, 2007, p. 60). The end product, the US Safe Harbor agreement is an opt-in program for US companies that transfer data between Europe and the United States and requires participating companies to comply with fixed privacy standards (Government of the United States, 2007). In addition to any guarantees created by the US Safe Harbor agreement, European nationals and others have access to judicial recourse against US companies that abusively violate a consumer's privacy through conventional court actions. US companies may be held liable for injuries caused by privacy violations through tort law and are subject to numerous other pieces of legislation that limits their use of personal information.

## MAIN THRUST: ELECTRONIC INTRUSION AND PROTECTING THE CONSUMER

### Issues

*We know that one of the great conundrums of e-business is that it gives enterprises a powerful new capability to capture and analyze massive amounts of customer information so they can serve individuals more effectively. Yet this very capability troubles some people, who see it as a means to disclose or exploit their personal information. These are legitimate concerns, and they must be addressed if the world of e-business is to reach its full potential. At its core, privacy is not a technology issue; it is a policy issue. And the policy framework that's needed here must involve the technology industry, the private sector in general, and public officials.* November 2001, IBM Chairman, Louis Gerstner, Jr. (Privacy Guru Joins IBM, 2001, p. 1).

IBM Chairman Louis Gerstner Jr., like many other business leaders, recognizes the enormous potential and threat that new technology poses. The rise of countless new ICTs ("information communications technologies") has meant that marketers can better serve consumers and marketers have greater power to use, and even abuse, private information. Electronic tracking systems, cookies, spy ware, and spam are all realities of the modern Internet age. They are also examples of how the Internet has opened up new avenues to sell products and collect data. This being said, privacy law serves the important purpose of curbing the negative impact of some of these intrusive techniques and delineating when their use is acceptable.

Some of these intrusive techniques are, by definition, nuisances to consumers. Spam, which can be defined as "unsolicited commercial email (UCE) or junk mail", is a commonly cited problem for many Internet users who find their private information being collected and sourced to companies interested in promoting their wares (Kutais, 2007, p. 60). Sophos Research has found that the United States is the world's biggest spam producer (at 56.7%), followed by other members of the so called "dirty dozen" including Canada at 6.8%, China at 6.2%, Brazil at 2%, and France, Germany, Spain, and the UK at between 1% and 2% (Sophos Research, 2007). Though there may be civil and even criminal liability for mass spam operations, several other forms of electronic intrusion have traditionally posed a greater threat to consumer privacy and business interests. In the United States and many other countries, for example, actions that violate the privacy principles may be criminally punishable. For instance, the US Computer Fraud and Abuse Act (CFAA), 18 USC ss. 1030 states that data manipulation, which involves corrupting existing information, is a criminal offence (US Computer Fraud and Abuse Act). Data manipulation relates directly to the principle of data accuracy in privacy law, which stresses the consumer's right to have their personal data corrected for accuracy. Further, it places the onus on private sector organizations and marketers to ensure data is safely protected, as intruders can manipulate customer data leaving the company liable.

Perhaps the most troubling form of electronic intrusion involves the use of spy ware and other electronic tools to collect private information. As in Winners, hackers will often integrate electronic tools into existing computer systems in order to expropriate personal data such as credit card information. In the United States, several pieces of existing and proposed legislation attempt to address the overwhelming problem of unauthorized electronic collection of personal data. The Children's Online Privacy Protection Act sets rules for the collection of information concerning children under the age of 13 via websites, most notably by requiring parental consent to obtain information (Kutais, 2007, p. 59 & 63).

Further, legislation has been proposed by the 108th US Congress to impose sweeping provisions regulating consumer privacy for all US citizens (Kutais, 2007). The Consumer Privacy Protection Act is a comprehensive piece of legislation that is remarkably similar to Canadian and European privacy laws, and substantially embraces the same principles, though still employing a self-regulatory framework (Kutais, 2007, p. 63). In addition, four bills that deal specifically with the issue of Internet spy ware are pending approval (Kutais, 2007, p. 72). The SPY ACT, an acronym for Securely Protect Yourself Against Cyber Trespass, would make it unlawful for anyone to "collect personally identifiable information through key logging" and other means, and would prohibit the collection of certain types of information without consent (Kutais, 2007, p. 72). The Spy Act also contains numerous provisions related to tampering with elements of a computer's software for the purpose of collecting information, such as the installation of a spy ware device or the modification of computer settings (Kutais, 2007, p. 72-73). Opponents to this legislation and other pieces of legislation have argued "not to preclude the evolution of tools and marketplace solutions to the problem" of electronic intrusion and spy ware (Kutais, 2007, p. 75). This argument is a valid one, and, at that, one that has been made in a number of different contexts. For instance, in a similar vein, while the United States was negotiating the Safe Harbour Agreement with the EU a US lobbyist made the argument that had a legislative solution been implemented to protect consumer privacy 100 years earlier modern credit reporting may never have evolved (Robinson & Large, 2004, p. 10). Freedom of information is paradoxically as important as protecting privacy, given that information enables debate and dynamism—both of which capitalism needs to thrive.

The American approach to privacy can therefore be viewed as far less paternalistic than the Canadian or European approaches that aim to protect unsophisticated and vulnerable individuals from privacy breaches (Politis, 2001, pp. 258-267). Though non-legislative solutions may work for savvy internet users who wish to be able to "have control over whom they shared that information with" (in the words of FaceBook founder Mark Zuckerberg), failing legislation many individuals may be uncertain about their rights and fall prey to intrusive data collection practices (Stinchcombe, 2006). In this sense, it can be argued that privacy law should empower the consumer to have control while protecting those who are potentially vulnerable. Discounting explicit breaches of consumer privacy, such as the one at Winners, statistics indicate that in the United States alone "one in four credit reports contain errors serious enough to disqualify consumers from buying a home, opening a bank account, or getting a job" (The Direct Marketing Association, 2007).

Arguably, facts like this should be troubling enough to spur on greater powers for consumers who wish to guard their privacy. Marketers as well have argued that healthy privacy practices are beneficial to consumer relations and can have a positive business impact, despite the administrative overhead. Satisfied customers, it is argued, "return to the organization that has treated them well in the past" and will appreciate privacy practices that meet the consumer's expectations (Gilbert, 2002, p. 6 as cited in Robinson & Large, 2004, p.3). This being said, the consumer's desire for privacy and desire for "customized" or individual treatment are "inherently contradictory" (Trott & Jones, 2001, p. 1 & 12). Weak privacy standards make the indiscriminate collection of information possible and allow companies to deliver better solutions, both in marketing and in sales, to customers (Trott & Jones, 2001, p. 1 & 12). This means that respecting the privacy principles by employing ethical consumer-driven uses of technology can both improve customer relations and make it more difficult for a firm to devise novel solutions to consumer needs.

## Solutions

According to numerous scholars, the customer's faith in the company and its privacy practices will dictate whether the customer chooses to engage in further transactions with the business. One scholar states that online trust is "a key differentiator that determines the success or failure of many companies conducting their business over the Internet" (Lauer & Deng, 2007, p. 323). Similarly, others note that customer and employee demands cannot be "realized without suitable privacy, security, and trust technologies to ensure that business data is appropriately protected and business partners can inter-work with confidence" (Knight, Buffet, & Hung, 2007, p. 285). Moreover, privacy is identified as just one of the many ways that a company can enhance trust (Lauer & Deng, 2007, p. 323). Trust can be "enhanced through two complementary approaches: secured information technology and trusted business practices" (Lauer & Deng, 2007, p. 323). Privacy practices are therefore critical to the firm's long-term relationship with clients and even employees and respecting privacy laws and the consumer's privacy interests should be at the forefront of every CEO's mind (Lauer & Deng, 2007, p. 323). One scholar's research has concluded that a stronger privacy policy means "higher perceived trust-worthiness" and "higher perceived trustworthiness leads to greater trust" (Lauer & Deng, 2007, p. 329). In turn, "greater customer trust results in a higher level of customer truthfulness" as well as "greater customer loyalty" (Lauer & Deng, 2007, p. 329). According to Lauer and Deng (2007, p. 329) the perceived integrity, benevolence and ability of the business is determinative of the extent to which the consumer trusts the business with his or her personal information, and the level of vulnerability the customer is willing to accept. According to the model espoused, "to trust another party, a trustor must perceive that the trustee has the ability to do good to the trustor in the relationship, and adheres to a set of principles that the trustor finds acceptable" (Lauer & Deng, 2007, p. 325). This idea has been corroborated by Ensign (2002, p. 136), who found that reputation, based both on past history and expectations for future actions, is influential in determining whether an individual would share knowledge in an office environment.

With regards to consumer-business relations, trust is a critical factor that has both costs and benefits. Many companies have enacted "fair information practices" on the basis of "ethical imperatives or on faith that an ethical stance will lead to business benefits down the road" while accepting that this action may also mean foregoing practices that have short-term pecuniary benefits and are less respectful of consumer privacy (Lauer & Deng, 2007, p. 330). The example of the sale of customer data, which would be in clear violation of the disclosure principle if not undertaken with the consent of the individual concerned, is given (Lauer & Deng, 2007, p. 330). These authors also note "the most desirable customers, those with discretionary income and higher levels of education, are often the most privacy aware" (Lauer & Deng, 2007, p. 330). Further, a solid privacy policy can protect a firm from the embarrassment faced by companies such as Winners that had weak practices in place. A "strong privacy policy can serve as insurance against privacy disasters where customer data is exposed and a company may experience loss of reputation and a decline in stock value" (Lauer & Deng, 2007, p. 330). For this reason, it is critical that companies design privacy policies that embrace the privacy principles and then act on these policies by implementing technological and procedural controls that are sufficient to achieve the standards set by the policy.

An adequate privacy policy should include provisions that address all the privacy principles—namely, collection limitation, accuracy and completeness, identifying purposes, consent, limiting disclosure/use/retention, safeguards, openness, challenging compliance, accountability and access. Further, by obtaining the certification of a recognized independent Internet privacy watchdog, such as TrustE (www.truste.org). These organizations are act as non-governmental watchdogs and are especially popular in the United State where privacy laws are more of a patchwork than other countries, like Canada or Europe. In order to qualify for the certification, the company must have policies and practices in place that meet TrustE's standards. For instance, Microsoft's online privacy statement provides a good example of how the privacy principles can be put into action. In fact, a privacy policy itself exemplifies the principle of openness by creating a dialogue between consumers and the company.

Microsoft's privacy policy identifies and defines the range of information that the company collects online—"We may also collect demographic information, such as your ZIP code, age, gender, preferences, interests and favorites" (Microsoft, 2007). Greater specificity strengthens the policy but may put a damper on the company's ability to act with flexibility (Microsoft, 2007).

Microsoft also takes a customer-driven approach to privacy, placing part of the burden of accuracy largely on the consumer or the source of the information in question (Microsoft, 2007). This being said, accuracy and completeness is a collective effort requiring both the consumer and the company to review records. Microsoft also identifies the purposes for which it collects information. Information is collected and used to "create a Microsoft billing account", to "offer you a more consistent and personalized experience in your interactions with Microsoft", and to provide "more effective customer service" (Microsoft, 2007). Opt-out consent, meaning that consent is assumed, is used for parts of the privacy policy placing the burden on the consumer to indicate that their information should not be used (Microsoft, 2007). Opt-in consent, which is used less frequently on the Internet given the logistical difficulty in obtaining this form of consent, is generally believed to create a stronger privacy policy given that the consumer must acknowledge and agree to the collection and use of the information. Further, the company reveals the limits of the use and disclosure of the information it collects, identifying the subsidiaries and business functions that have access to the information. The company also identifies the safety precautions, both technological and procedural, that it takes to protect personal data (Microsoft, 2007). Safeguards such as "unique ID" numbers, "encryption, such as the Secure Socket Layer (SSL) Protocol", and others are identified (Microsoft, 2007). Microsoft offers its online users and customers with options for pursuing concerns and complaints (i.e. challenging compliance), directing the consumer to the TrustE website & dispute resolution procedure (i.e. accountability) and a contact point at Microsoft (Microsoft, 2007). Further, the website also indicates the company's participation in the US Safe Harbor Agreement (with the EU in accordance with EU Directive 95/46/EC) (Microsoft, 2007). Lastly, Microsoft identifies means by which the consumer can access his or her personal information. Information that is not immediately available can be requested by contacting the company (Microsoft, 2007).

Reinforcing a solid privacy policy, such as the one available on the Microsoft website, with procedures, practices, and technologies that adequately meet the firm's commitments will go a long way in ensuring compliance with privacy laws. Further, having such a policy in place makes sense given the importance of privacy issues to consumers and the company's legal obligation to protect the consumer's privacy interests. Microsoft's policy exemplifies the universality of the privacy principles used in the Canadian PIPED Act and reflected in the OECD privacy principles and the EU Directive. Creating and applying policies that are consistent with these principles will be critical for companies that wish to retain customers and avoid the embarrassment of a serious privacy breach such as the one experienced by Winners.

## FUTURE TRENDS

A suitable privacy policy alone, however, is not sufficient for businesses that wish to go beyond simply satisfying the customer's privacy needs and abiding by the law. Companies that wish to both meet the demands of customers and legislators for better privacy standards while using privacy to improve client-company relations must view privacy as a tool that the customer can control. Frederick Newell, in his book *Why CRM Doesn't Work,* argues for increased customer influence when it comes to managing the client-company relationship (Newell, 2003, p. 5). This becomes particularly important for marketing professionals as better customer relations often means a better bottom line. More specifically, future trends would seem to indicate that businesses will compete with greater intensity to provide the customer with control over areas such as product offerings, services provided, and account management. Privacy standards, being an important part of the customer-company relationship, will be one of the grounds upon which businesses compete to provide greater customer control. In other words, companies that can empower customers to have control over their personal information will be able to develop better relationships with them.

In the future, this may represent an important basis for competition and could make the development and implementation of customer friendly technologies critical. It is therefore no wonder why most e-businesses, from facebook to ebay, enable customers to modify and alter their personal profiles and other information that could compromise privacy. The movement of this trend from the online sphere to all forms of electronic commerce will continue, thereby better enabling customers to protect themselves from electronic intruders and manage their personal data. According to Newell, "customers, not companies, control the purchasing process today by having access to more information, and having it in real time…the Internet has given them unprecedented research tools" (Newell, 2003, p. 6). Innovative software that allows customers to better manage their private data will accelerate this process and give customers greater control. In this light, future research on the impact that "customer management of relationships" has on electronic intrusion and the profitability of customer-company business relations is merited (Newell, 2003, p. 167).

## CONCLUSION

*Big Brother is Watching You!*

(Orwell, 1949)

In George Orwell's classic novel Nineteen Eighty-Four, the author portrays life in the modern era as defined by constant surveillance and scarce privacy. Eerily, the spirit of Orwell's novel may be more relevant today than ever before given advances in technology and our increasing willingness to share information. Indeed, today more than ever before, legislators need to address issues surrounding privacy, as personal information has become a tool that can be both used to undertake criminal acts and better meet consumer needs. In this light, privacy legislation in Canada, Europe and the United States will play a particularly important role in the electronic era. Demarcating how technology can be employed to collect, use, manage and disclose information will be a critical first step in ensuring that consumers are capable of protecting themselves. This being said, new privacy laws have implications for the business community and will lead to increased bureaucracy and create potential legal liability for those that fail to comply. By understanding the spirit of the privacy principles and undertaking to meet the consumers' need for control over personal data businesses can avoid privacy breaches and foster healthy relationships with customers. Marketers, and business people more generally, can benefit from practices and policies that live out the objectives of the privacy principles. Collection limitation, accuracy and completeness, identifying purposes, consent, limiting disclosure/use/retention, safeguards, openness, challenging compliance, accountability and access represent the key pieces of the privacy puzzle that must be implemented collectively in order to meet the legal standards enshrined in privacy laws internationally and gain the trust of consumers. Implementing a privacy policy, like the one used by Microsoft, that incorporates the privacy principles will help to protect vulnerable consumers from electronic intrusions, such as the event at Winners, while having a mixed impact on the marketing profession. Better relationships with consumers may also mean more costly marketing practices and increased investments in customer privacy. Considering the risks posed by electronic privacy breaches, ranging from identity theft to financial liability, it is more imperative than ever before that governments, companies and individuals act to protect the private citizen's "right to be let alone" (Warren & Brandeis, 1890).

## REFERENCES

*Privacy guru joins IBM.* (November 30, 2001). Retrieved March 10, 2004, from http://www.crm-forum.com

B. M. P. Global Distribution Inc. v. Bank of Nova Scotia (c.o.b. Scotiabank), B.C.J. No. 1662.

Warren, S., & Brandeis, L. (1890). The right to privacy. *Harvard Law Review*, *i*(5).

Canadian Charter of Rights and Freedoms, Part I of the Constitution Act, 1982, being, Schedule B to the Canada Act 1982 (U.K.), 1982, c.11 s. 7.

Canadian Standards Association. (November 19, 2007). *CSA Model Code for Privacy Protection.* Retrieved November 20, 2007, from http://www.csa.ca/standards/privacy/code/Default.asp?articleID=5286&language=English

Direct Marketing Association. (November 19, 2007). *Survey: 1 in 4 Credit Reports Contain Errors.* Retrieved November 19, 2007, from http://www.thedma.org/cgi/dispnewsstand?article=2440

*Eastmond v. Canadian Pacific Railway.* [2004]. F.C.J. No. 1043.

EC Directive 95/46/EC of the European Parliament and of the Council of 24 October 1995.

Prescott, E. C. (2002). *Reputation and technological knowledge sharing among R&D scientists in the multidivisional, multinational firm.* Montreal: Univeristy of Montreal, Unpublished Dissertation.

Government of the United States. (2004). *US Safe Harbor Agreement.* Retrieved November 19, 2007, from http://www.export.gov/safeharbor/SHPRINCIPLESFINAL.htm

Knight, S., Buffett, S., & Hung, Patrick C.K. (2007). Guest Editors' Introduction. *International Journal of Information*, *6*(5), 285-286.

Kutais, B. G. (Ed.) (2007). *Spam and Internet Privacy.* New York: Nova Science Publishers.

Lauer, T. W., & Xiaodong, D. (2007). Building online trust through privacy practices. *International Journal of Information Security*, *6*(5), 323-331.

Microsoft. (2008). Retrieved November 19, 2007, from http://privacy.microsoft.com/en-us/fullnotice.aspx

Newell, F. (2003). *Why CRM Doesn't Work: How to win by letting customers manage the relationship.* Princeton, NJ: Bloomberg Press.

OECD. (2002). *Guidelines on the Protection of Privacy and Transborder Flows of Personal Data.* Retrieved November 19, 2007, from http://www1.oecd.org/publications/e-book/930201le.pdf

Office of the Privacy Commissioner of Canada. (2007). *Report of an Investigation into the Security, Collection and Retention of Personal Information: TJX Companies Inc./Winners Merchant International L.P.* Retrieved November 19, 2007, from http://www.privcom.gc.ca/cf-dc/2007/TJX_rep_070925_e.asp

Orwell, G. (1949). *Nineteen Eighty-Four.* London: Martin Secker and Warburg.

*Personal Information and Electronics Document Act*, R.S.C. 2000, c.6.

Politis, D. & Gogos, K. (2001). Data mining of Personal Information: Perspectives and Legal Barriers. Proceedings of the *5th wses/IEEE World Multiconference on Circuits, Systems, Communications & Computers. CSCC 2001*, Rethymnon, Crete, 8-15 July 2001, (pp. 258-267).

Robinson, N., & Large, D. (2004, December). PIPEDA: Impact on CRM and public-private sector interaction. *Optimum Online: The Journal of Public Sector Management*, *34*(4), 47-60.

Roseman, E. (2007). How retailers can protect customer privacy. *The Toronto Star* (7 October 2007).

*Rousseau v. Wyndowe*, [2006] F.C.J. No. 1631.

Sophos Research. (2007). *The Dirty Dozen.* Retrieved November 11, 2007, from http://www.sophos.com/pressoffice/news/articles/2004/02/sa_dirtydozen.html

Stinchcombe, K. (September 25, 2006). Facebook privacy. *The Stanford Daily* (25 September 2006). Retrieved November 18, 2007, from http://daily.stanford.edu/article/2006/9/25/facebookPrivacy

Tacit, C. (2003). Complying with private sector privacy legislation (Unpublished Work).

*Thomas v. Robinson*, [2001] O.J. No. 4373.

Trott, B., & Jones, J. (April 2, 2001). Industry tows the privacy-CRM line. *InfoWorld.* Retrieved March 11, 2004, from www.infoworld.com

TrustE. (2008). Retrieved January 6, 2008, from http://www.truste.org/about/index.php

*Turner v. Telus Communications*, [2005] F.C.J. No. 1981.

*US Computer Fraud and Abuse Act* (CFAA), 18 USC ss 1030.

*Vanderbeke v. Royal Bank of Canada*, [2006] F.C.J. No. 871.

Warren, S., & Brandeis, L. (1890). The Right to Privacy. *Harvard Law Review*, 4(5).

## ADDITIONAL READING

Alderman, E., & Kennedy, C. (1997). *The Right to Privacy.* New York: Vintage.

Papazoglou, M., & Ribbers, P. (2006). *E-Business – Organizational and Technical Foundations.* West Sussex, UK: Wiley.

Solove, D. J., Rotenberg, M., & Schwartz, P. M. (2006). *Information Privacy Law.* New York: Aspen Publishers.

## KEY TERMS

**Customer Relationship Management ("CRM"):** Management practices that aim to better satisfy customer needs by seeking to understand those customer needs and build a lasting relationship with the consumer. Personal information, and therefore privacy issues, is critical to any CRM plan.

**Data Mining:** The arbitrary and often indiscriminate collection of personal data for the purposes of improving marketing efforts and sometimes criminality. Data Mining most often utilizes the Internet and other electronic means but can include more traditional methods of collecting information.

**Electronic Intrusion:** The invasion of Internet privacy through spy ware, hacking, Spam, and other electronic technologies. Electronic intrusion is a serious concern for internet-users and privacy commissions alike which have increasingly begun to look at legislative solutions to this pressing threat to consumer privacy.

**PIPEDA or PIPED Act:** The "Personal Information Protection and Electronic Documents Act" is a recent piece of Canadian privacy legislation that aims to empower Canadian consumers in protecting their privacy. PIPEDA, a law inspired by the CSA and OECD principles and various EU Directives, requires all Canadian businesses to follow strict privacy practices in regards to all personal data.

**Privacy Policy:** The collection of technological, commercial, and legal issues surrounding the protection of the right to privacy. Privacy policy encompasses and affects many different interconnected policy areas and hinges on the question of the extend to which the individual has a right to be free from outside interference.

**Privacy Principles:** These principles (developed by the CSA) are intended to guide organizations in developing practices that are respectful of privacy rights. They include (1) limiting collection, (2) accuracy and completeness, (3) identifying purposes, (4) consent, (5) limiting use retention and disclosure, (6) safeguards, (7) openness, (8) challenging compliance, (9) access, and (10) accountability. The Canadian Standards Association developed these principles and they are an important part of the PIPED Act.

# Chapter VII
# Navigating in Internet:
## Privacy and the "Transparent" Individual

**Christina Akrivopoulou**
*Aristotle University of Thessaloniki, Greece*

**Aris Stylianou**
*Aristotle University of Thessaloniki, Greece*

## ABSTRACT

*The chapter faces a series of questions that the digital era raises as far as the protection of privacy is concerned. Technology and specifically internet, apart from posing innovative, complex threats to the autonomy and privacy of the individual constructs a new frame for approaching privacy. The technological texture of the internet calls for a new conception of privacy that can be adopted in those circumstances, such as anonymity. The chapter argues that though anonymity cannot be identified with the right to privacy, represents in fact one of its key functions, its ability as a negative freedom to shield the autonomy of the individual against all kind of threats. Thus, anonymity can foster communication, speech and political expression in the internet. Nevertheless, the cost of protecting privacy as anonymity is substantial since its neutral character can function as a veil for sinister actions such as libel, hate-speech and stalking in cyberspace. The need for 'reconceptualizing' privacy in the internet, for the writers confirms the evolving, developing character of the right, whose substantial content is not given or static but is closely connected and constructed via societal change. The chapter explores the technological threats that the right to privacy confronts in the internet, such as "cookies", "spam messages", the dangers they pose to the freedom and autonomy of the individual as well as the positive dimensions of the internet, especially its role in democratic accountability and political dialogue. Concluding the writers present three architectures for the protection of privacy in the internet: (a) a model based on informational law, (b) a market based solution, where privacy is understood in contractual terms and (c) a model based on the participation of the users in the uses of their personal information as well as to the enforcement of the accountability of the internet actors, e.g. corporations, advertising agencies.*

## INTRODUCTION

### Why is Internet an Unfriendly Place for Privacy?

Privacy in the internet seems to be a myth for the ordinary user, for four distinct and yet interconnected reasons. First, it's the open character of the internet. The fact that we can log in our mail at any time, from anywhere, raises serious doubts about the confidentiality of our communication. The open character of the internet suggests that anyone can retrieve information from our personal page, our curriculum vitae, or even our photographs and use them for purposes different from those an individual had originally intended to. Secondly, it's the interactive nature of internet. Internet for the most is a part of everyday life; we use it to communicate with our friends, for professional reasons, to be entertained, to be informed or to acquire products, leaving behind us, our traces. With our ability to deny or give our consent, in limiting our privacy, as our only shield, interaction in the internet can pose serious threats to our freedoms. The third reason, for contesting privacy in the internet, is its global dimension. National legislation protecting our personal data seems ineffective since internet has no borders or limitation. In the end, the unique speed, the flow rate of the internet, as well as its ability to process information in a small amount of time, presents new challenges for the protection of our informational privacy, mainly because it enables the formation of our personal profile, by the bits and pieces of information that we are leaving behind as we are websurfing.

This chapter, is attempting to analyze this ambiguous relation between internet and the right to privacy, by posing and approaching a series of questions. In the first part of the chapter, we are facing the problematic of the way that information threatens privacy by examining, (a) the technological texture of the threats that the internet is posing to privacy, (b) the way those threats are affecting the autonomy and freedom of the individual, through judicial paradigms of Greek courts, as well as of the European Court of Human Rights, (c) the conflict between transparency of information, as a clash augmented by the use of internet and the protection of privacy. In the second part of the chapter, we examine the way a right to privacy can be conceptualized and protected in the internet by examining, (a) the right of privacy as a right constructed by the technological evolution, (b) a concept that privacy adopts in the frame of the internet, as anonymity and (c) the ways privacy can be protected in the frame of internet, through information privacy law, a market based solution, or a balanced architecture which enables control over data internet practices of institutions as well as the participation of the individual in the uses of their information.

## THE TECHNOLOGICAL DEVELOPMENT AS A WISH AND AS A CURSE: INFORMATION VS PRIVACY

### Internet and Privacy: Old Threats in New Clothes

Internet and the threats that pose to privacy are often dealt as something, emerging as utterly new. Whereas this statement is not completely untrue is quite misleading, since in reality, the threats that internet poses to privacy, are actually familiar: **loss of control over personal information, disclosure of private facts and surveillance of an individual**. All of them are threats connected with the rise of the information age, the first one identified to the use of computer data-bases and the other two to the application of monitoring devices, such as cameras. Nevertheless, these threats are merely intensified and augmented by the use of internet. Internet is threatening privacy as a completely new of course and highly atypical form of data-base (Katsch 1995). It threatens privacy because it can extract information; since its main function is being the metaphorical space where people can meet, a forum and market that people, exchange their personal information, consume or being entertained leaving behind them their trails, revealing consciously or not personal information and data. It endangers privacy with its ability to accumulate an unlimited amount of information, which are transparent and can be accessed and processed literally by millions of individuals. At the same time, internet poses yet another threat, since it can be used in order to monitor private communication, activities, preferences or habits of its users. This monitoring is not a neutral one, since that information is processed in order personalize the individual and used for targeted advertising or to manipulate his consuming preferences, posing thus a serious threat to his autonomy (Solove, 2002).

These threats though old and familiar, are differentiated and filtered through the special nature of internet, acquiring even its language, a technological vocabulary of risks and threats against the privacy of the individual. The most old-fashioned danger against privacy is consisting by the creation of **'mailing lists'**. These lists are built via the systematic monitoring of our internet purchases and buys and they are aiming to facilitate advertising, by categorizing demographically and psychographically our personal data (Solove, 2004). Thus, by the use of questionnaires, that numerous websites request in order to log us in, by purchasing certain commodities combined with the ability to maintain the 'history' of our consuming choices, we are enlisted in 'mailing lists' and categorized by our profile data, for example as persons that love classical music or pets. Those profile information can be indifferent, such as our preferences in books or music, or they may be more revealing about more personal or sensitive information, concerning for example certain diseases, age, marital or family status, income or the sexual life of an individual. Those 'mailing lists' afterwards are serving for targeted advertisement of products (Solove, 2004), by sending email with products based on my specific preferences, or adapted to my psychographic profile. Beyond this scope, this enlisting can be used as a mean to manipulate our choices, or even as a mean to expose in public or even publicize personal information. Ultimately it can serve as means for discrimination or labeling people or group of people, identifying them based on their personal data.

Another way of monitoring our personal preferences and data via internet, is by the trail we leave, when we navigate form website to website, better known as **'clickstream data'**. Thus, websites can track secretly and record our data as we are websurfing. To be specific, each website we are visiting has the ability to record data about our ISP, our computer hardware and software, the website we used in order to link, what parts of it we have visited and for how long. This is called leaving a trail and it enables the websites to measure the popularity of certain features, as well as to interact, measure the impact or the attention of the users in a way that other forms of public interaction such as television, or the press are unable to do. Through this trail, a database is gradually created by the website, where our preferences are stored. To connect this information with a certain user, the website either requires the user to log in, or it places a tag which makes him recognizable each time he returns. This latter way of identifying a user is called a **'cookie'**. A 'cookie' works as a high tech-bag. It is placed when we download web-pages, as a form of a small text file of codes (Solove & Rotenberg, 2003, Froomkin, 2002). These codes are unique and their attached to the user's hard drive. When the user logs in again, is recognizable and automatically connected with the information that has been gathered in his prior visit. Nonetheless, a 'cookie' cannot be combined with 'cookies' placed in other websites, it can only identify a computer and is unable to reveal the whole identity or profile of an individual, thus having a limited impacted in tracing its preferences.

Those limitations are surpassed by a newest strategy of monitoring and gathering information, based on the idea of sharing data between different websites. One of them is performed by a firm called **'double Click'**. When an individual logs in a website, takes a detour to 'double Click'. 'Double Click' accesses its cookie, and by the users profile determines the kind of advertisement that the website he is visiting must download. With a few words, when a website is connected with 'double click' two persons that are visiting the same website, will eventually receive totally different advertisements. 'Double Click' illustrates the most eminent threat against privacy, which consists, not in gathering personal information, but in combining them. Realistically, the problem of privacy in the internet us not that we give away, trivial information about ourselves, but the totality of information about a person and the manner it is used that inflicts the most serious threats against privacy.

Another device for collecting information in the internet is the "web bug", which can be implanted in an email message or into a web page. The web bag can also gather personal information, and it is often used alongside with spam messages in order to report when a user is opening a spam message (Kozyris, 2004). "Web bags" can also gather our personal information as we explore websites, or in some cases even enter our personal computer files. Another upcoming threat are technologies of "Digital Rights Management" (DRM), which are used to collect information about our intellectual preferences, such as our preference in music, books or even theater and cinema (Cohen, 2003, Lindsay & Ricketson, 2006). An upcoming threatening for privacy technology are 'bots', shorthand for robots, an internet 'scout' who is prowling the network, tracing and gathering personal information.

All this overwhelming technology signals a swift in the way we understand our privacy, our private life, even our identity. It refers in a new person, a digital, transparent person, whose life, personal preferences, hobbies, inclinations, needs and want are open to the public eye. It refers in a person, a transparent one, whom cannot pose limits to the intrusions upon its privacy and private life. A person who is archived, whose data are stored and use without baring any control about the way they are processed or for the purposes their accumulation fulfils. The raise of such technology rings a strong bell. We often have the feeling that surfing in the internet, is ephemeral that we can log in and out quickly without any traces or consequences. We often feel while flooding in the internet ocean that we can pass as invisible or as unseen. The truth is that we are ilussionating since, "... little in the Internet disappears or is forgotten, even when we delete or change information. The amount of personal information archived will only escalate as our lives are increasingly digitized into the electric world of cyberspace" (Solove, 2004).

## Internet and the Risks to the Autonomy and Freedom of the Individual

Loss of control over our personal information, surveillance, and disclosure of our private facts are disruptions and infringements to the privacy of the individuals, invoked by the swift to an information era (Lyon, 1994). Though at most times we focus mainly on the risks that such threats impose to the private life, actually they endanger much more, the general freedom of action of the individual, meaning its autonomy (Branscomb, 1995), whilst they potentially alter even the democratic foundations of a society itself. Protection of privacy is of chief importance for the preservation of democracy, as the powerful Orwellian, yet not legal metaphor enshrines. A society based on constant surveillance, is a society where an individual cannot exist either as private or public person, where he fades in total uniformity, looses his personality and his authenticity. Such a society is based not in democracy but in totalitarianism in the dehumanization of the concrete individual. It is emphatic that Orwell's Big Brother has gained not only the total control over the personal information of his people, but also the ability to penetrate and use their mind and soul.

Surveillance and disclosure of private facts or personal information threaten the freedom and the autonomy of the individuals, their right to be self defined to preserve their personal integrity. Constant observation, monitoring of an individual restrains him from thinking and expressing freely, subtly reshaping his behavior and reshaping his identity. The exposure of the individual generates uniformity and results in the loss of his autonomy: the loss of control over the use of his personal information. Thus the individual loses his self-determination and becomes unable to choose based on his free will. In internet the constant exposure of the individual devalues his dignity, since it reduces him to an object, rather than a subject, to a sum of digitalized information, to a profile made by "bits and pieces" (Cohen, 2000). The impact of surveillance and disclosure, over autonomy, freedom, dignity and privacy of the individual, is acknowledged by the European Court of Human Rights. In several cases such as Peck *vs United Kingdom*, Rotaru *vs Romania* and Amann *vs Switzerland*, the Strasburg Court has underlined that surveillance of the indivuals, especially the use of cameras in public spaces, poses serious threats for the freedom of the individuals. Thus the Court has focused on the fear, the anxiety and the suppression and the infringement that such a practice imposes on the privacy and dignity of the individual.

From a similar point of view the Greek Legal order, the constitutional amendment of 2001 added in Article 19(3) a norm stating that: '[U]se of evidence acquired in violation of this Article and of Articles 9 and 9A is prohibited' (Tsatsos & Kontiadis, 2001). This norm is addressed to the courts, putting them under a binding obligation to exclude from consideration any evidence, obtained by the unlawful use of electronic means such as listening devices (eg. bugs) or recording devices (eg. video cameras). It is apparent in this provision, the intention to protect the individual effectively against the threats imposed by the electronic era, as well as to confront the risk of eventually becoming a Big Brother Society. As the Greek Supreme Court has stated, influenced by this norm, in its most eminent decision 1/2001 (Akrivopoulou, 2007), surveillance and monitoring by electronic means, poses not only specific dangers to an individual, but also to society in general since if everyone would live 'with the suppressing feeling that every thoughtless or superlative expression of his could be later used against him" (Akrivopoulou, 2007). What the Greek Supreme underscores, encapsulates the greatest threat that the internet poses to the privacy and autonomy of the individual. The fact that our personal information not only can be accumulated or diffused via the internet, not only can be processed or transferred but can also be used against our will, for purposes not only undesirable or unknown but also hostile to our very existence. That way, information becomes a means not only to manipulate, fear and suppress but also to dominate the individual.

## Transparency of Information vs. Protection of Privacy

As we have underscored the internet poses serious threats to the freedom, the privacy and the autonomy of the individuals. Nonetheless, there is also another side of the coin, a positive one. Internet can foster information and knowledge and facilitate the freedom of communication, political interaction, expression and exchange of ideas. In reality, the unique features of the internet, if interpreted under this positive score, acquire a quite different value. Thus the open character of the internet, its speed, the easy access combined with the free flow of information, facilitates not only freedom of communication but mainly transparency of information, in a unique globalized sense. Transparent and available to all equally, information in internet adopts the character of a "common good", functioning as a solid basis for political and societal dialogue, debate and criticism. In that sense, internet by guaranteeing transparency and access to information is guaranteeing the presuppositions of a democratic society (Alivizatos, 2001, Bannier, 2001, Simitis, 1987).

Transparency of information is in fact a basic element of a democratic society serving two distinctive, major purposes, (a) accountability of public officials and their political actions especially of the manner they exercise their public duties, (b) democratic control over all government activities. The transparency of information sheds light in the way that the government function provides open access to public procedures, such as court trials, safeguarding that they are fairly and legitimately conducted. Transparency functions as a presupposition for the exposure of the pubic officials in cases of corruption, scandals or abuse of power, facilitating their accountability. Thus internet, by promoting through its open character transparency and diffuse of information serves as a very effective "watchdog" for society, informing and thus enabling the citizens to criticize and control public authorities.

Though transparency is a key element of a democratic society, it often clashes with the protection of the privacy, personality and dignity of individuals (Reidenberg, 2000). In such cases, transparency and privacy should be balanced, contextually, given the specific circumstances that created their conflict. Nonetheless, in cases of politics or public figures the protection of transparency prevails. In the Greek legal paradigm, characteristic of the clash between privacy and transparency is a case concerning an ex-wife of a former prime minister and currently mother of the leader of the parliamentary opposition. The dispute initiated by a breach of confidentiality of her email address by a hacker, who exposed her correspondence to a weekly Greek magazine. Her correspondence was addressed mainly to her son -leader of the parliamentary opposition- and contained political advice and criticism over political facts and figures. The letters were publicized in the magazine along with comments. The court ruled for the protection of transparency, underling that though she clearly was not a "genuine" political figure, the content of her communication, was of political interest and thus the public had the right to be informed, as well as to hold her accountable for it.

That information is a two sided coin, with both negative and positive dimensions, is the reason that not only the privacy protection but also the protection of informational freedom is augmented. Thus in the 2001 revision of the Greek Constitution (Alivizatos & Eleutheriadis, 2002), two new rights concerning freedom of information, the right to be informed (Art. 5A (1)) and the right to participate in an informational society (Art. 5A (2)) were acknowledged (Tsatsos & Kontiadis, 2001). These rights signify a new trend, a new swift, a transition to an informational era in which internet bares the greatest part. For some this swift has lead even to the death of privacy, a loss counterbalanced by the birth of a transparent society, where the free flow of information enables all equally to all, the "panoptic" state and also the citizens who have gained the ability to watch the watchers. This radical account belong to David Brin, who in his book "The Transparent Society" (1998) argues for a totally transparent society, underlying that a truly transparent society would control all those who violate our privacy and monitor our private lives. For Brin (1998), "light is going to shine into every corner of our lives".

Though such a prospective is quite encouraging for the future of our surveillance societies, it is true that a society of total transparency can not really reinforce the rights of the individual. Information still is a more effective tool when is used by a powerful state bureaucracy or by a competent private organization, which has the power not only to access, as the ordinary user can but also to gather, filter and process information. So, if it is not transparency that should rightfully conquer all, then what is the key, the answer to the tension between transparency and privacy, between democracy and individualism? The theory and judicial practice seem to be searching the solution in the way of selective protection of privacy. Such a solution though, is much easier to be enforced in public or private records than in the internet, since the latter is difficult to be regulated legislatively. According to this line, privacy is not considered to be an absolute right, and in some cases its protection can be sacrificed in order to preserve informational freedom. Implementing such a compromise in internet means that certain personal information should be accessed for specific reasons only; their commercial use should be limited as well as their combination with other information, their acquisition or distribution.

## SEARCHING FOR A NEW CONCEPT OF PRIVACY IN THE INTERNET

### The 'Right to Privacy', as a Right Constructed by the Technological Evolution

Beyond every normative, theoretical, conceptual or philosophical analysis of a right -and the right to privacy is not an exception- always lays the same question: what is the basis or causes of its genesis. For the positivists, this reason is identified with the legal recognition of a right. In a few words, the right is a creation of the law and it does not encompass any prior existence. For the liberals, a right is a product of a 'natural' understanding of our personal existence. Thus the liberal paradigm divides the world in two, public and private, and ultimately the person in two, individual and citizen. Under this division, the genesis of the rights of the individual is revolved around the individual itself and its 'natural' existence, retaining this way a distinct distance of any interplay between the individual and society, or the political realm. A third trend supports a quite different idea, concerning the genesis of rights. According to the constructivists, rights cannot simply be found out there, or emerge out of the text of law. Rights are constructed, as a product, of not only legal but also, societal and political change (Cohen, 2004). Under this thread of argument, a right is to develop and finally emerge *via* concrete social practices, which gradually are adopting characteristics that justify their legal protection (Rössler, 2005). Thus for example, social practices that serve purposes essential for the realization of the liberty or the autonomy of the individual.

Under the constructivist approach, a preeminent cause for the genesis of the right to privacy, among others, is the technological change. Based on a mainly pragmatist argument, one could underscore that between privacy and the technological evolution, exists in reality, a geometrical analogy. To be more specific, the technological developments create more and more serious threats against the privacy, the private life and sphere of the individuals. These threats relate to the development and legal recognition of the right to privacy, as the causes initially of its genesis and afterwards of its evolving constitutional and legal protection. The American example characteristically confirms this argument. It is the raising of the press at the end of 19$^{th}$ century, its ability to maintain and diffuse massively personal and private information, that initiates the genesis of the American right to privacy, as Warren and Brandeis, in their famous article "The right to privacy [the implicit made explicit]" (1984), underlined. The same trend is elaborated also, on the other side of the sea, in the European talk of the privacy of 'public figures' against the indiscrete press, as it is captured in the 1907 German law, concerning the protection of intellectual property (Spachmüller, 2007). The interplay between the protection of the right to privacy and the raise of technology is even more evident in the way they are both evolving in time. It is evident that the constitutional and legal protection of privacy is escalating, following the technological change. The acknowledgment of the right to privacy as a fundamental right, the introduction of a new right to informational privacy, along with the emerging legal regulation concerning the use of personal data, are the most obvious examples, that the legal paradigm of the protection of privacy, is growing due to and because of the sifting technological development.

Beyond the merely pragmatic approach, privacy is conceptually altered by the rise of technology. For example, one of the most traditional understandings of privacy, as a space, a physical, material sphere that protects the individual against intrusion and indiscretion, is obsolete, in internet where the meaning of physical space is futile (Byford, 1998). In the same path, any conceptual analysis of the right to privacy as property is difficult to be supported in internet, where any sense of materiality or possession seems fictionate, or is overwhelmed by the total absence of boundaries and frontiers in internet. Moreover, realistically speaking, the speed with which internet permits an information to be simultaneously accumulated by millions, does not permit, the traditional understanding of privacy as 'control' over our personal information, since such control is simply impossible to be preserved.

From another point of view the internet changes any traditional understanding of our sense of public and private, since it combines both private and public functions, whilst merely is an expression of a third intermediate sphere the social one. Thus, internet facilitates our private communication, via e-mail, serves as a space of political expression, a place where we read our newschapters and where we interact as political individuals. All the same, the internet is not a place, neither by nature private nor public but rather it lays in the edge, in a third intermediate sphere, the social one. This is because internet functions mainly as a marketplace, metaphorically and virtually. A marketplace for people to chat, meet or interact as newest trends 'facebook' or 'my space' explicitly illustrate. Also a marketplace in order to consume massively. In this understanding not only the way we conceptualize but also the way we wish to protect privacy is altered. Firstly because the source of its endangerment is differentiated, the right is no longer threatened by the state but in the social interplay, by the interpersonal relations of the individual, or by the power that the market sustains over him. Those unique trends ultimately, alter the way we understand the right to privacy, underlining that the protection of a right, is indeed not an abstract but a specific procedure, developing always in given and particular frames and circumstances.

## The Costs and the Benefits of Conceptualizing Privacy as Anonymity in the Internet

The protection of anonymity is originated in the protection of political speech, as pseudonimity is traced in the protection of literature. They represent two forms of protection of the circulation of ideas, both closely connected with the freedom of expression, speech, communication and thus with the very idea of democracy. A characteristic example of the protection that anonymity, is its function as a shield for the political participation of the individual, e.g. participation in a street demonstration, where the individual enjoys the anonymity in order to retain the ability for political expression (Lessig, 1995). As the American Supreme Court has recognized in McIntyre v. *Ohio Elections Commission*, "Anonymity is a shield from the tyranny of the majority...to protect unpopular individuals from retaliation –and their ideas from suppression- at the hand of an intolerant society...". In the Greek legal order anonymity has entered the theoretical dialogue as the limit, for the surveillance and monitoring by cameras in public places, especially public demonstrations or public assemblies.

Anonymity cannot be identified to privacy, since its substantial value, cannot be connected with basic privacy purposes, such as intimacy or emotional self realization. It represents though one of privacy chief aspects. Privacy beyond its distinct, substantial content bares a negative quality; it can safeguard and protect autonomy in a negative way, as a negative freedom from something, in order to shelter and protect a variety of purposes (Ruiz, 1998). This is a basic facet of privacy, to work as a shield, fostering purposes, instances of individual autonomy. Anonymity as a concept demonstrates exactly this instance of privacy, since it functions as a protective a barrier that the individual poses against others in order to protect a variety of purposes, unconnected with privacy itself, mainly communication, expression, circulation and demonstration of ideas. Working as a veil, anonymity, gives the individual the necessary distance and protection to carry out undisturbed goals connected with his private or political autonomy (Slobogin, 2002). In a few words we could describe anonymity as the necessary precondition for the realization of the purposes of the individual's autonomy.

The question is how and why and anonymity is functioning as privacy in the internet? In order to preserve their anonymity the individuals can resort to certain technological devices such as an 'anonymous remailer', which is a computer service that enables people to send e-mail anonymously. The remailer, when a message is send, removes the real name of the user, as well as its e-mail address, substituting it with a pseudonym, and sends it on its way (Froomkin, 2006). An 'anonymous remailer' belongs to 'Privacy Enhancing Technologies', well known as PETs, along with 'encryption'. Encryption is a way to protect the confidentiality and security of communications (Kerr, 2001). Encryption systems are methods of translating a communication into a code which is translated back to the original message by the intended recipient. Encryption manages to keep data (personal, financial information) secure from unauthorized viewers, enabling people to communicate without the fear that their messages will be monitored. Encryption also enables verification and authentication. Anonymizing technology can also be used to prevent web-sites from being able to trace their visitors, enable the users to surf the internet without leaving traces of who they are.

There are merely three reasons why anonymity is functioning as privacy in the internet. Firstly because it represents a method of self-regulation, of self-protection which is quite adopted to the open and difficult to regulate legislatively internet realm. In a second view, one can say that only technological panoply could protect the individual against technological threats in an effective manner. Though this is a true statement, we must underline that protective technology as well as self-regulation and self-protection can not substitute the legal regulation, but can only reserve a complementary role. It is the law that must create a protective architecture of the individual in the internet, and lay down the legal principles, that bind the internet interaction and communication. The third and most important reason is that anonymity, as we have emphasized functions as a protective precondition for a series of goals and instances of an individual. It is a concept general and neutral enough to protect consecutively our professional communication, our intimate communication and our political ideas and expression.

Nevertheless we must underscore that anonymity is a highly empowering technology. It renders the users the power to do a series of things without being identified. Thus it protects both valuable and harmful objectives. Thus anonymous communication can be used as a tool for evading disclosure of illegal or immoral activity. An anonymous communication can function as a means of 'protecting' electronic hate-mail or speech, libel; it can favour electronic stalking or the disclosure of valuable intellectual property (Froomkin, 2005). This is one of the main criticisms opposed to the protection of privacy, in general. As Postner (1981) argues, "... [People] want to manipulate the world around them by selective disclosure of facts about themselves...". Another strong argument against anonymity is that anonymous communication, interaction and expression makes extremely difficult to identify the self-interest and the motives behind it. That way the credibility of information or of opinion may be compromised. Anonymous communication can enforce problems for libel and intellectual property. The open character of the internet, its ability to diffuse information worldwide maximizes the impact of harmful libel, since it can be spread world-wide, and may be reproduced and stored, in countless and untraceable numbers of computers. The same maximizing impact can be invoked by the disclosure of a trade secret, a valuable piece of intellectual property (Cohen, 1996). As far as political speech or exchanging of ideas is concerned the main counterfeit seems to be the lack of accountability, basic element of a society based on democratic values. In the end the two most serious consequences of anonymity is that neutralizes communication and interaction and eventually produces a society of strangers. Under this thread of argument, one could suggest, that instead of protecting, it is in reality a threat, to the very substance and value of a right to privacy, which is intimacy and trust between individuals.

Apart from the counterfeits of protecting anonymity in internet, its protection seems to bare also a series of advantages. Firstly as we have underlined, it functions as a means for the self-regulation of the individual's privacy protection. The privacy of the individual in the internet is threatened by 'technological giants' such powerful advertising agencies, corporations and even the state. Against this power, anonymity seems to be the last line of defence for the privacy of the individual. Under a different view, anonymity is invaluable as far as freedom of expression is concerned. It enables as a precondition and encourages criticism and functions as a means against repression. Anonymity gives the opportunity to express ideas without the fear of retaliation or suppression. In the same thread of argument anonymity, enables our expression about matters that concern our privacy and our intimacy, for example to ask for advice for our disease, or for an issue concerning our sexuality. Moreover, in that way anonymity can even act as a liberating force for an individual enabling him to adopt a digital persona, different of the roles that le is playing in his real life and neutral as far as his specific qualities, such as race, religion, sex, national origin or social status are.

## Do We Have to Protect Privacy in Internet?

The reason for protecting privacy in the internet can be reduced in a sentence: the internet can not exist as public and social realm without the protection of privacy (Weintraub, 1997). As the Orwellian metaphor has underscored, the public and the social realm cannot exist without protecting individuality, privacy and freedom, and these qualities cannot survive in a world of perfect and total transparency, in space where a person can not 'hide' or retain its secrecy and anonymity. In internet terms, and because internet is not the whole but only a part, or even better an aspect of the public and social realm, that means that internet itself cannot exist without the protection of the privacy of its users. Insisting in the total transparency of the information exchanged in the internet eventually will result to its fall as a public market, a public realm and a social space. Thus, the protection of privacy in the internet, is not a question of why but mainly of how can be realized. The answer to this question is explored through three different models, or even better three architectures for protecting privacy in the internet. First an architecture based in the construction of a web of rights and legislation, a model of information privacy law, second a market architecture based on the ideas of privacy as property and its contractual protection and a third one that is trying to balance between establishing controls over the data networking practices of institutions (eg. corporations) and the participation of individuals in the uses of their information.

The first architecture is the most common one, and it is based in the adoption of a legislative and constitutional protection of the individual's privacy. Such architecture has the form of the protection of informational privacy, thus of the protection of a person's personal data. Characteristic is the Greek paradigm, where the protection of personal data is protected both in the Constitution, with the recognition of a specific right (Art. 9A), by specific legislation (2472/1997) which is enforced by an Independent Agency (Data Protection Authority). Characteristic is also the paradigm of the European Union (Sicilianos, 2001), where privacy is protected by directives which enforce data protection as well as the protection of privacy in the electronic communications (Data Protection Directive 95/46/EC, Privacy and Electronic Communication Directive 2002/58/EC).

That policy of protecting privacy is very important because it underlines two very significant points: the way that the right to privacy is evolving in time, due to societal change, as well as the need for new tools and a new language for its protection. Nevertheless, although those developments are quite promising, they lack in effectiveness. The reason is that this kind of legislation still harbors the traditional conception about privacy and its insults, conceptions not adopting with the realities of the information age. For example, the most characteristic feature of these legislative endeavors is that they protect against privacy threat, as forms of harm or libel, by providing remedies or preventing future harms. These policies overlook one fact: what endanger privacy the most in the internet are not the isolated infringements, but the systematic and diffuse ones, which cannot be traced to a single penetrator, but in most cases to a combination of actors, who may or not have the intention to infringe our privacy.

The second architecture is concerning privacy as property, via the notion of privacy as "control over our personal information" (Parker, 1974). Privacy, if conceptualized as 'control' tends to adopt a contractual character. This architecture is closely interconnected with the former one since a basic element of information privacy law, is the consent of the individual in the 'loss', 'infringement' or 'processing' of his personal information. Approaching privacy in internet, as property, is a market based solution, based on the self-regulation of our privacy. As Daniel Solove (2004), underlines, "Market proponents...argue that people should be free to contract as they see fit. If people want to give up their privacy, the government shouldn't paternalistically say that it knows best". Such architecture is based in the making of contractual agreements about privacy at the outset of forming an interaction in internet. The breach of the confidentiality, of privacy in such cases, is considered to be a breach of contractual obligation, leading the individual to legal remedies. The misgivings of a market-based solution though are quite a few. First are the limitations of its contractual character. A contract is bonding only for the contracting parties and not for third ones. In internet, due to its open character, is extremely difficult to prevent privacy invasions by third parties. In a second view, a market based-solution neglects the inequality of power between a simple user of the internet and the corporations, which usually initiate such contracts. In most cases, terms and conditions of such contracts are non-negotiable and obligatory for the individual. Moreover, this solution overlooks the fact that in most cases our 'control' over our personal information, in the form of property is almost impossible to maintain, due to the speed, flow and openness of the internet. In the end in most cases contractual regulation of privacy protection cannot protect the individual from future uses of his personal information, which are after all the most important danger to his autonomy.

A different approach is proposed by Daniel Solove. It is a radical-democratic argument about an architecture of privacy protection in the internet. It is based on two basic elements: a new concept of accountability for the network institutions as well as affording the users right to participate in the use of their information (Schwarz, 1995). Under this approach our relationship with the corporations and institutions using our personal information in internet should be considered as a fiduciary one. Thus this relationship should be based on the mutual trust and confidentiality that the law obliges to lawyers, doctors, stockbrokers etc. Redefining the relationship between users and institutions as a fiduciary one creates not only a contractual but a substantial bond between parties which grants the users with certain rights, such as: the right of the user to know what personal data an institution has obtained or used and for what purposes, the right of the user to prevent obtaining and using of his personal information, the obligation of the institutions not to keep secret data-bases as well as to protect the information they gather form third parties. Forging a radical architecture for the protection of privacy in the internet also includes participation, mainly in the collection and use of their personal information. Such participation can be facilitated by extending the obligation for consent of the user for processing their personal data, and through the recognition of their right to access such personal information freely.

## CONCLUDING REMARKS

Undoubtedly internet has marked a significant swift to the information era. It has invaded our everyday life it has altered our means of communication and expression, it has even altered the way we understand our privacy. From many aspects internet is a remedy. It enables people to create, 'digital intimacies', it facilitates knowledge, it enhances information, transparency and accountability, exchange of ideas, articulation of political speech. From another side, it's a curse. A globalized 'Big Brother' who may become in the future the stepping stone for societies of surveillance. We can argue that internet is a hostile place for our privacy and at the same time that it fosters our intimacy, our communication with our friends, our lovers, our family and dear ones. What this chapter has tried to capture, is that between internet and privacy, technology and privacy exists a much more complex relation. The rise of technology lies on the birth of the right to privacy, posing threats that not only enhance the need for protecting privacy but also nourish it protection and reshape its value. In many ways we owe to the rise of technology, and to internet, a lot about the way we understand and cherish our privacy in the modern societies. At the same time internet, the cyberspace is also 'genetically' interconnected with privacy. For one, internet cannot function as a public space, as a public market without preserving at least some amount of privacy. It is privacy, the dream of intimacy, of private 'chat' and communications that makes cyberspace so alluring to its users. In order to maintain its self-preservation, the internet must fulfill those private needs. Moreover, it is privacy that retains its credibility as a market where people everyday, buy and sell commodities and products. Security of our personal data (eg. our credit card number) is in fact an essential presupposition, for the safety of 'digital commerce'. On those terms, one is certain. Technology and privacy will coexist in the days to come and they will continue to evolve side by side. Our task, a difficult is to lay down the rules and principles of this multifaceted coexistence.

## REFERENCES

Akrivopoulou, Ch. (2007). Taking private law seriously in the application of Constitutional Rights. In D. Oliver & J. Fedtke (Eds.), *Human Rights and the Private Sphere* (pp.157-179). London & New York: Routledge.

Alivizatos, N. (2001). Privacy and Transparency: a difficult conciliation. In L.–A. Sicilianos & M. Gavouneli (Eds.), *Scientific and Technological developments & Human Rights*, (pp. 117-122). Athens: Ant. N. Sakkoulas Publishers.

Alivizatos, N., & Eleutheriadis, P. (2002). The Greek Constitutional Amendments of 2001, *South European Society & Politics, 7*(1), 63-71.

Bannier, C. (2001). Privacy or Publicity –Who drives the Wheel? *CFS Working Chapter Archive, No 2003/29.* Retrieved from: www.ifk-cfs.de/chapters/03_21_revised.pdf

Brin D. (1999). *The transparent society: Will technology force us to choose between privacy and freedom?* Cambridge & Massachusetts: Perseus Publishing.

Cohen, J. (2003). *Regulating Intimacy: A new legal paradigm.* Prineceton: Princeton University Press.

Cohen, J. (1996). The right to read anonymously: a closer look at copyright management. In Cyberspace, *Connecticut Law Review, 28*(3), 981-1039.

Cohen, J. (2000). Examined lives: informational privacy and the subject as object. *Stanford Law Review, 52(5),* 1373-1438.

Cohen, J. (2003). DRM and Privacy, *Berkely Technology Law Journal, 18*(2), 575-617.

Froomkin, M. (1995). Anonymity and its enmities, *Journal of Online Law, 1*(art. 4). Retrieved from: http://articles.umlawnet/froomkin/Anonymity-Enmities.html

Froomkin, M. (1996). Flood control on the internet ocean: living with anonymity, digital cash, and distributed databases. *University of Pittsburg Journal of Law and Commerce, 15*(2), 395-453.

Froomkin, M. (2000). The death of privacy? *Stanford Law Review, 52*(5), 1461-1543.

Katsh, E. M. (1995). Rights, camera, action: cyberspatial settings and the first amendment. *The Yale Law Journal, 104*(7), 1681-1717.

Kerr, O. (2001). The Fourth Amendment in Cyberspace: can Encryption create a 'reasonable expectation' of Privacy? *Connecticut Law Review, 33*(2), 503-545.

Kozyris, P. (2004). Freedom from Information: limiting advertising intrusion on the internet (spam) and on television. *Hellenic Review of European Law*, 1, 17-42.

Lessig, L. (1995). The path of Cyberlaw. *The Yale Law Journal, 104* (5), 1743-1755.

Lindsay, D., & Ricketson, S (2006). Copyright, privacy and digital rights management. In A. Kenyon, & M. Richardson (Eds.), *New Dimensions in Privacy Law, International and Comparative Prospectives,* (pp. 121-153) Cambridge: Cambridge University Press.

Lyon, D. (1994). *The electronic eye: the rise of Surveillance Society.* Cambridge: Polity Press.

Lyon, D. (2001). *Surveillance Society: monitoring everyday life.* Buckingham & Philadelphia: Open University Press.

Parker, R. (1974). A definition of Privacy. *Rutgers Law Review, 27*(1), 275– 296.

Posner, R. (1981). *The economics of justice.* Cambridge & Massachusetts: Harvard University Press.

Rössler, B. (2005). *The value of privacy.* Oxford: Blackwell Publishing.

Ruiz, B. (1998). *The Right to Privacy: a discourse-theoretical approach. Ratio Juris, 11*(1), 155-167.

Schatz-Byford, K. (1998). Privacy in Cyberspace: constructing a model of privacy for the electronic communication environment. *Rutgers Computer & Technology Law Journal, 24*(1), 1-74.

Sicilianos, L. –A. (2001). International protection of personal data: Privacy, Freedom of Information or both? In L. –A. Sicilianos, & M. Gavouneli, (Eds.), *Scientific and Technological Developments & Human Rights* (pp. 123-142), Athens: Ant. N. Sakkoulas Publishers.

Simitis, S. (1987). Reviewing Privacy in an Information Society. *University of Pennsylvania Law Review, 135*(2), 707-746.

Slobogin, C. (2002). Public Privacy: camera surveillance of public places and the right to anonymity. *Mississippi Law Journal, 72*(1), 213-299.

Solove, D. (2002). Conceptualizing privacy. *California Law Review, 90*(3), 1087-1156.

Reidenberg, R. (2000). Resolving conflicting International Data Privacy Rules in Cyberspace, *Stanford Law Review, 52*(5), 1315-1371.

Solove, D., & Rotenberg, M. (2003). *Information Privacy Law*. NY: Aspen Publishers.

Solove, D. (2004). *The digital person, Technology and privacy in the information age*. NY: New York University Press.

Spachmüller, D. (2007). Balancing freedom of press against the right to privacy –are the Germans still so much better? *Freiburg Law Students Journal, 3*(1), 1-24.

Tsatsos, D., & Kontiadis, X. (2001). *The Constitution of Greece*. Athens: Ant. N. Sakkoulas.

Weintraub, J. (1997). The theory and politics of public-private distinction. In J. Weintraub, & K. Kumar (Eds.), *Public and Private in thought and practice: perspectives on a grand dichotomy* (pp. 1-42), Chicago: University of Chicago Press.

Wells-Branscomb, A. (1995). Anonymity, Autonomy and Accountability: challenges to the First Amendment in Cyberspace. *The Yale Law Journal, 104*(5), 1639-1679.

# Chapter VIII
# Controlling Electronic Intrusion by Unsolicited Unwanted Bulk Spam:
## Privacy vs. Freedom of Communication

**Phaedon John Kozyris**
*Aristotle University of Thessaloniki, Greece & Ohio State University, USA*

## ABSTRACT

*The ordinary and uncomplicated Spam menace is made possible by technological advances which enable the sender to dispatch millions if not billions of commercial messages without significant monetary cost and without wasting time. The present review will focus on fundamentals, exploring what has already been done and suggesting avenues of improvement. The chapter promotes basic approaches of handling Spam depending on the actions and choices of the receiver. The anti-Spam campaign needs effective enforcement powers and should be able to use all available technological know-how. As the vagaries of enforcement are presented, the role of the Internet Service Providers and advertisers is envisaged.*

## INTRODUCTION

The Internet is vulnerable to a great variety of serious intrusive devices and practices involving mostly theft and fraud and the efforts at regulation focus mostly and justifiedly on them as discussed elsewhere in this collective volume. My topic will be pure SPAM, i.e. unsolicited, unwanted, bulk messages on line, which currently constitutes most of e-mail, containing advertising or otherwise proposing a commercial transaction but not connected with any other wrongdoing,. For my purpose, and in order to test the outer limits of the key concept of privacy, I will assume that the target address was obtained lawfully and that the message is not fraudulent.

In the United States, since the famous article of S. Warren and L.Brandeis (1890), *The Right of Privacy*, the notion of privacy has emerged as a key one needing legal protection against intrusion from many directions. The most offensive intrusion, which will not concern us here, is obtaining and/or publicizing confidential information about people without permission and without good cause. Prying is included in that. Our target instead will be Spam on the Internet which is forced on us by entering our space without invitation This kind of "privacy", which protects our personality as well as our property, needs added safeguards in the omnivorous world of the Internet, which safeguards, however, must be carefully drafted not to impinge upon the rival right of expression, even of the commercial kind, which is often constitutionally protected. Comparable intrusion is taking place through telephone calls, faxes and even regular mail as well as billboard and poster advertising in public places although the burden of avoidance and the nature of regulation differs depending on the medium. Some years ago, I published a lengthy article suggesting that even advertising on television and the print media, which are visited voluntarily by the public and not forced on them, should be controlled by a "rule of separation" invigorating the power of avoidance (Kozyris, 1973).

The ordinary and uncomplicated SPAM menace is made possible by the technology which enables the sender to dispatch millions if not billions of commercial messages without significant monetary cost and without wasting time. Even a minute response rewards the effort. The main harm of such SPAM is caused by flooding, first of the transmission lines of the Internet Service Providers and second of the computers of ordinary users whose address has been somehow harvested by the sender. The costs born by the victims of (a) filtering, with only partial success, and (b) finally separating and deleting the flood, are collectively enormous[1] while the resulting benefits to the quasi "free riders" are close to nil by comparison. In addition, the use of Spam often involves also unfair competition toward other forms of legitimate advertising. Finally, in the attempt to separate and delete Spam many legitimate messages are misread and misdirected. Thus, there no doubt whatsoever that Spamming causes a lot of harm to many for the minute benefit of a few, i.e. the practice is seriously harmful socially. Where and to what extent should the rights of privacy of the many here yield to the interests of intrusive commercial expression of the few? As reliance on the Internet for communication and information retrieval grows and spreads globally so does the harm of Spam .In this piece, it will be assumed that it cannot be seriously argued that Spam as such, unsolicited unwanted commercial bulk e-mail, excluding e.g. political or religious etc messages or custom-made personal e-mail, deserves any legal protection as against unwilling targets Thus, and quite important, the emphasis will be placed on the practices and techniques, legal and technological, for controlling it, with all the difficulties that this would entail.

The present review will focus on fundamentals, exploring what has already been done and suggesting avenues of improvement. For a recent, global eye-view of these issues, see Phaedon John Kozyris, General Report to the XVIIth Congress of the International Academy of Comparative Law, Regulating Internet Abuses: Invasion of Privacy (Phaedon John Kozyris, ed., Wolters Kluwer 2007) (hereinafter "General Report") reproduced, as modified, in Abusive Advertising on the Internet Through Spam: Problems and Solutions, General Reports to the XVIIth Congress of the International Academy of Comparative Law 587-601 (K.Boele-Woelki & S.Van Erp.eds, Bruylant 2007). See, also, Phaedon J. Kozyris, Freedom from Information: Limiting Advertising Intrusion on the Internet (Spam) and on Television, 2004 Hellenic Review of European Law 17-41 (hereinafter "Freedom").

## THE BASIC RULES: SOLICITED OR WANTED E-MAIL IS LEGITIMATE AND NOT SPAM

### Silence Allows Only for Some Limited Contact: "No-Spam" Directories Must be Respected

It makes sense to start with some basic approaches of handling Spam depending on the actions and choices of the receiver.

On the one hand, it goes without saying that all commercial communication between willing persons should be free and unhampered by controls. Since, however, it is rare that the receiver of Spam has expressly agreed to it, it is proper and legitimate to look for and validate any forms of possible implied consent. These could include not only seeking information or placing an order but also visiting sites where some promotion is clearly taking place. In such contexts, consent may be implied for Spam-type messages for similar products or services at least until countermanded. But, otherwise, the general rule should be that mere visitation of a site does not imply interest in receiving back commercial information (Kozyris, 2007)[2].

At the other end, it is perfectly clear that a receiver who has adequately expressed his unwillingness to receive all or any special kinds of Spam should be fully protected. It is possible that an appropriate authority within a state be entrusted with setting up and operating a No-Spam Directory where all those who want to be excluded can register and it should be easy for all prospective senders to consult it and not contact those who want to be left out. The objection that such a Directory will be exploited by violators who will abuse the information that it contains is not determinative.

Silence is more difficult to handle and more detailed treatment is indicated. In principle, a sender should have the opportunity to ask a silent e-mail address holder at least once whether he may send commercial messages and be bound by any response.

Failure to respond should be interpreted as refusal. The burden of responding to all such bulk messages is great, and the freedom of expression-communication does not go as far as requiring an unwilling-uncommunicative receiver to be subjected to future messages. To facilitate an intelligent and free choice of the receiver, various identification requirements (e.g. labeling the message ADV, including a true name and street and electronic address of the sender etc.) is essential and failure to abide them reinforces the qualification of silence as rejection.[3]

## THE VAGARIES OF ENFORCEMENT: BY WHOM, WHERE AND HOW?

The anti-Spam campaign needs effective enforcement powers and should be able to use all available technological know-how. However, the global dimension of the Internet and the absence of a world-wide authority to impose and enforce a regulatory regime make the control of Spam very difficult. For the present, we have to live with it and our proposals for enforcement will assume that it will take place at the national level and at the federal or union-type levels as in the United States or the European Community. Further, there is no question that some international cooperation for enforcement should be expected at least up to a point.

### The Role of the Internet Service Providers

Since the Internet Service Providers (ISPs) are the gate-keepers of the Internet and it is basically only through them that material, including Spam, may find its way on the communication channels, they constitute the first line of defense against illegal or objectionable content, including

Spam, as they are in the best position to exercise preventive control. However, any plan to regulate what is placed on these channels should take into consideration the fact that the ISPs are many, that they are located everywhere around the globe, that there is no central organ or authority that may take action binding on all of them and that they typically operate as private enterprises.

First, the prevailing view is, and this makes economic sense, that the ISPs, those who set up and share in the network and connect its users, should not be required to fully police the use of their facilities, even to regularly monitor all that is being sent over them. Not only would such an obligation involve high expense but also, and crucially, it would impinge upon the confidentiality of communications of the users and in itself constitute an invasion of privacy. Further, they are often required by law to provide access to all those who request it without discrimination and without imposing any unreasonable conditions. In a sense, the ISPs resemble the "common carriers" who pave and open the highway on which the general public travels. However, in 2005 they have been reclassified by the FCC in a manner that reduces their neutrality obligations and allows practices of network management which include the exclusion of Spam (Zhu, 2007; Rupert, 2008)[4].

Second, the authority to manage their network suggests that the ISPs cannot wash their hands of all incidence of impropriety and illegality that goes on over their channels. Indeed, it is generally recognized that they have both the power and the obligation of intervention over what they carry over their channels. For example, recently in the United States the major ISPs entered into an agreement not to provide access to sites that carry child pornography such as Newsgroups and the other are pressured to join[5]. Further, there are instances where ISPs have been required to help control violation of intellectual property rights occurring on their channels. Since the sending of Spam to unwilling targets in most jurisdictions is treated as illegal or at least objectionable and since, in any event, most of Spam violates other rules such as labeling as ADV and clearly identifying the sender under the US CAN-SPAM Act, reasonable anti-spam measures by the ISPs are obviously proper and indicated.

A major way in which ISPs could help in controlling Spam is to require, as a condition of getting access, that the applicants provide credible identification on their name and address and that they use a password before entering. This would help by enabling the authorities and the victims to know who and under what style someone is using their facilities to send Spam For many years, the telephone companies did exactly that, they gave a phone number only to persons who fully identified themselves and indeed they were even listed in their public catalogues. An electronic address and the related access should not be available anonymously but only upon subscription, providing full identity information. Public places like Internet Cafes, where people get access to the Internet, should not make their services available to any body who turns the machine on and does not provide password and user name. In sum, only a subscriber should have access to the service and only through a user name and password. However, ISPs appear to object to this kind of requirement and claim that anyway it will not work because currently ISPs from anywhere in the world may get interconnected on the network on a global basis. Thus, those established in unregulated regions would defeat the requirement. The complying providers would be enormously burdened if they had to check and control what is placed on the web by the customers of the bad guys. The simple answer is that since most ISPs are located in the West and are willing to help in the anti-spam fight, they could exclude from their facilities messages coming from suspect ISPs who do not effectively agree to abide by these rules.

In a related vein, it has been suggested that ISPs (a) use separate servers for original and separate servers for forwarded (where most Spam rides) e-mail and that (b) block channel 25 (used mostly by botnets, networks of pirated computers) where over 90% of Spam originates (*BBC News*, 2008). In Australia, one of the leading anti-spam nations, a recently adopted Code of Practice has imposed the following strict requirements on ISPs: (a) scan all traffic for open relays and botnets (b) restrict inbound connections to any service that allows forwarding of e-mail provided by third parties and (c) include clauses in their contracts that allow them to disconnect spammers[6] Under United Nations auspices, two World Summits on the Information Society have been organized addressing extensively the problem of Spam[7].

Another idea for help from the ISPs might be to require them to engage in preliminary review of all incoming mail that has characteristics that clearly trumpet "Spam!", for example comes in bulk instantly or originates in senders identified as likely spammers, and reject it. It is interesting that e.g. in the United States Virginia punishes with a jail sentence of up to five years spammers who send over 10,000 messages in a 24-hour period (Webcentric, 2008)[8]. Another effective but perhaps too limiting method is for the ISP, like Earthlink, to match all incoming e-mail against the recipients address book and not forward automatically the unknown one unless the intended receiver so asks (Webcentric, 2008).[9] Further, there is no question that the ISPs are best positioned to develop and make available to their subscribers the best filtering and related equipment or software which enables them to avoid or at least reduce the Spam messages without having to check them one by one. True, the spammers will try to by-pass such defenses through technological innovation, trying to be a step ahead, but some relief could still be available.

Finally, there is a fully effective but debatable measure that could stamp out all Spam by striking at the factor that makes it economically possible: the ability of the spammer to send out billions of messages within a short period of time at minimal cost. We could impose a minimal so-called "stamp" obligation on the sending of all messages, while proving substantial exemptions for the number of messages sent by most users, e.g. one thousand per day (Kozyris, 2004; Kozyris, 2007)[10]. It is considered too burdensome both to impose and enforce and involving overkill but one wonders whether the time has not come to take more drastic, even if annoying, measures after all.

It is important to remember that ISPs are rather easily subject to regulation and to the jurisdiction and the laws not only of the states where they are principally located, indeed they often need and get a license there, but also everywhere where they engage in business, indeed even at the location of the target to whom Spam is addressed, where the harm is felt. Thus, while the ISPs cannot do the whole job by themselves, obligations imposed on or assumed by them constitute the main line of defense against Spam[11]. In addition, ISPs have standing under both traditional law and many anti-spam statutes to take legal action, both criminal and civil, against spammer-violators, including remedies for breach of contract where the spammer has accepted conditions of proper practices in his subscription agreement.

## How about the Advertisers?

There is no question that just about every commercial bulk Spam either advertises the sale of a product or service or at least contains information leading to a commercial transaction Indeed, it is these merchants that are the cause and the beneficiaries of Spam To be effective, such information need identify the promoter even indirectly and even if located at the end of the world. However, since such promoter's message reaches the target at his home or place of business, there is both regulatory authority and civil and criminal jurisdiction in the courts and under the laws of the target's state. Such state may impose controls or even outlaw such Spam as advertising method even where the information is accurate and the transaction is not fraudulent In aide of enforcement, the payment aspects, especially the use of a bank credit card can sometimes help in obtaining information helpful to going after the advertisers themselves. Let us always keep in mind that without the advertisers there would be no Spam. Therefore, bringing them under some control is part of the solution (Kozyris, 2007)[12].

## Targets vs. Spammers?

There is no question that the targets should be advised to do their technological best in self-help to fend-off Spam. But this is not enough and we must seek regulatory and legislative assistance in this noble fight for privacy.

First, the law already contains rules that may be conscripted in the fight against Spam. Flooding your equipment and software with unwanted bulk commercial messages resembles littering, even of trespassing upon and damaging personal property. This falls then within the realm of torts and some lawsuits in the regular courts seeking damages and injunctions there have been brought successfully by the targets[13] However, it is normally quite difficult and expensive in time and money for an ordinary citizen first to discover who is his spammer and then hire legal help to locate an appropriate forum to bring suit and finally to prove the amount of his damages. Things improve considerably in states which have adopted legislation aimed specifically at the Spam menace, especially where, as e.g. in Virginia, the target can automatically be awarded $500 from the spammer for each instance of certain kinds of Spam. The device of the class action, where available, may also enable the targets to join forces and recover an amount worth the effort. Seeking a remedy through the criminal justice system is even more problematical.

Further, the fact that both judicial and legislative jurisdiction does exist at the destination of spamming, i.e. the target's home, does not mean that any remedy or judgment will be easily enforceable. Indeed, spammers typically pretend to be located in remote and unfriendly states and, in addition, frequently move around so that getting final satisfaction is likely to be quite frustrating (Kozyris, 2007)[14]. District attorneys perhaps can be more effective in seeking convictions on the basis of particular anti-spamming provisions in the law, especially those that are aimed at Spam that does not follow the identification and style requirements[15].

## CONCLUSION

The growing menace of Spam, the flood of junk e-mail invading our privacy, seriously burdens and misdirects our use of the Internet, which has now become the main means of communication and research worldwide. The fact that it is often also connected to fraud, trespass and other illegal activities explains why there is a general consensus that it must be drastically combated. While many nations and states have adopted legislation and taken other measures against Spam, such action cannot be made effective without the cooperation of the Internet Service Providers, who first receive and then dispatch such e-mail to their subscribers. In this piece, we did explain why, even absent a general obligation on the ISPs to monitor all they carry and transmit, they have the authority and they may be required to take reasonable action to identify and exclude Spam that is sent without the consent, express or implied, of the recipient. In addition, the advertisers, indirect but major beneficiaries of Spam, may be brought to justice for any violation of the rules by Spam that promotes their products or services. Last, but not least, the targets themselves may rely on property law or on specific anti-spam legislation to impose civil obligations and criminal penalties against violators.

To be sure, the global and anonymous nature of the Internet makes all enforcement difficult. However, there is no doubt about the availability of legislative and judicial civil, criminal and administrative jurisdiction not only where Spam originates but also where it travels and where it hits, and further that the ISPs are clearly more accessible to enforcement, True, catching the spammers themselves to enforce any judgments, orders or penalties may be arduous given their anonymity, move from location to location and misleading traces, but there is a lot of room for cooperative action by the ISPs themselves to exclude from their flow unreliable carriers and channels and to put into operation some reasonable identification requirements. International cooperation and coordination, hopefully even an international treaty and global authority, can play a significant role. After all, we have no alternative but to do our best to cut down Spam to an insignificant flow.

## REFERENCES

*BBC News*. (2008, June 27). Spam fighters lay down gauntlet. *BBC News*. Retrieved http://news.bbc.co.uk/1/hi/technology/7477899.stm

Brandeis, L, Warren S. (1890). The Right to Privacy. *Harvard Law Review*, 4, 193-220.

Kozyris, P. J. (1973). Advertising Intrusion: Assault on the Senses, Trespass on the Mind – A Remedy Through Separation. *Ohio State Law Journal*, *36*, 299-347.

Kozyris, P. J. (2004). Freedom from information: Limiting advertising intrusion on the internet (spam) and on television. *Hellenic Review of European Law*, *2004*, 17-41.

Kozyris, P. J. (2007). General Report. In P. J. Kozyris (ed.), *Regulating Internet Abuses: Invasion of Privacy* (1-26). Alphen aan den Rijn: Kluwer Law International.

Rupert, B. (2008). The 110th Congress and Network Neutrality – S 215 – The Information Freedom Preservation Act. *DePaul Journal of Art, Technology & Intellectual Property Law*, *18*, 325.

Webcentric Hosting Review. (2008). *Consumers, legislators, and internet service and hosting providers wage war on spam*. Retrieved from http://webcentric-hosting.com/articles/consumers.legislators.and.html

Zhu, K. (2007). Bringing Neutrality to Network Neutrality. *Berkeley Tech Law Journal*, *22*, 615.

## ENDNOTES

1 For the frequency of Spam and the harm caused by it, see General Report at 2-3. See, also, Dionysios Politis, George Fakas & Konstantinos Theodoridis, Spam, Spim and Advertisement: Proposing a Model for Charging Privacy Intrusion and Harassment 1-4 (Proceedings of 2006 Information Resources Management Association [IRMA]-International Conference, Track: Managing Electronic Communication, Washington, D.C., USA, May 21-24, 2006). Spim is Spam using telephone instant messaging which imposes some added costs both to the sender and the receiver and is so far less prevalent. The Radicati Group estimates that in 2006, 183 billion Spam messages were sent everyday worldwide and that 59% of them landed in the in-boxes of the targets. Further, for 2007, the cost in dollars of seeking to avoid Spam is estimated at $198 billion. Other estimates of current worldwide Spam range between 74 and 90%.

2 At 3-5.

3 Both the U.S. CAN-SPAM ACT, 117 Stat. 2699 (2003) and Directive 2002/58/EC of the European Community, included in part in the Appendix, infra, follow this route. Further, Directive 2000/31/EC on Electronic

Commerce recognizes that Spam may be undesirable and it must not be sent without the recipient's consent. (Recital 30). In Article 7, the requirement of its clear labeling is imposed and the ISPs are required to set up registers for the targets that do not wish to receive it. For a comparison of the two approaches, see Wolfgang Fritzmeyer & Andrew Law, The CAN-SPAM Act Analyzed from a European Perspective, Comp. & Telecomm. Law Rev. 2005 11(3) 81-90.

4 In the United States of America, the ISPs had been indeed classified by the FCC as "telecommunications services" which imposed on them serious neutrality obligations in favor of all comers. However, this classification changed in 2005 and they are now considered only as "information services" not subject to those rules in all their strictness This has been upheld by the U.S. Supreme Court in National Cable & Telecommunications Association v. Brand X Internet Services, 545 U.S. 967, 985-1000 (2005). At least four recent major federal legislative efforts to impose on them a "network neutrality" requirement have failed and currently are considered dead. By the way, the fuss about neutrality really revolved around two poles, a first-come-first-served obligation (no prioritizing) and no differential charging . In any event, in all these efforts the authority of the ISPs to reject or exclude Spam is preserved. See Kai Zhu, Bringing Neutrality to Network Neutrality, 22 Berkeley Tech. L.J. 615 (2007) and Benjamin Rupert, The 110th Congress and Network Neutrality – S 215 –The Information Freedom Preservation Act, 18 DePaul J. Art, Tech. & Intell. Prop. Law 325 (2008). Even the most ardent proponents of neutrality, Lawrence Lessig and Tim Wu would allow the exclusion of "publicly detrimental" material which would include Spam. K. Zhu, supra, at n. 76. .

5 The authority of ISPs to block inappropriate content is recognized in Title 15 U.S.C. Section 7707 (c) of the U.S. CAN-SPAM Act and has been upheld, under the Communications Decency Act, 47 U.S.C. Section 230 (c), e.g. in Zango v. Kasparsky Labs, F.Supp 3rd (W.D. Wah. Aug. 28, 2007). Indeed, in the United States there has not been a single case where the blocking action of an ISP has been challenged in court. See K.Zhu, supra note 6, at 625. For the range of proper and indicated action by the ISPs to block Spam, see also, General Report at 8-12.In the European Union, while Article 15 of Directive 2000/31/EC on Electronic Commerce provides that ISPs are under no general obligation to monitor the content of the messages they carry, even to check whether it is related to illegal activities, Recital 46 clarifies that if they are aware of it, they must exclude it or disable access. But we should not further forget that the same Directive has established the consent requirement for the receipt of Spam (see note 5, supra) and that the undesirability of Spam has been reinforced by the requirements of subsequent Directive 2002/58/EC, cited infra.

6 Available at <http://www.silicon.com/>

7 These Summits not only identify the harm caused by Spam and provide methods of combating it, especially by ISP action , but also propose international cooperation to address the problems of enforcement. For a detailed discussion, see Meyer Potashman, International Spam Regulation and Enforcement Recommendations Following the World Summit on the Information Society, 29 B.C. Int'l & Comp.L.Rev. 323 (2006), especially at 323-342. This article also contains quite useful references to anti-spam legislation and related measures around the globe as also does the General Report.

8 The Supreme Court of Virginia upheld the conviction to a long jail sentence of a notorious spammer under such statute, holding that such material is not protected by the First Amendment. See http://jurist.law.pitt.edu/printable.php.

9 Ibid.

10 See Politis et all. General Report at 9-14

11 It is to be noted that.while under Article 3 of Regulation 2000/31/EC On Electronic Commerce the ISPs are subject to regulation only in the state of their establishment, the Annex provides for an exception in so far as Spam is concerned.

12 At 12-13.

13 See Greg Lastowka, Cyberproperty in the United States: Trespass to Chattels and New Technology, supra at . See, also, Michael Carrier & Greg Lastowska, Against Cyperproperty, 22 Berkeley Tech.L.J. 1483 (2007). While this authors are not persuaded that the property, especially the real property, analogy is apt here, they do recognize that such a view has wide following both in the courts and in the literature. For a strong support of using property law concepts and techniques to combat Spam, see P.Wagner, On Software Regulation, 78 S.Cal.L.Rev. 457 (2006)

14 At 13-14.

15 Such as those of the U.S. CAN SPAM Act.

## APPENDIX

## (A) The United States CAN_SPAM ACT of 2003 (in outline)

The CAN-SPAM Act of 2003 (Public Law No. 108-187, was S.877 of the 108th Congress), signed into law by President Bush on December 16, 2003, establishes the United States' first national standards for the sending of commercial e-mail and requires the Federal Trade Commission (FTC) to enforce its provisions. The bill's full name is an acronym: **C**ontrolling the **A**ssault of **N**on- **S**olicited **P**ornography **a**nd **M**arketing Act of 2003.

It also requires the FTC to promulgate rules to shield consumers from unwanted mobile service commercial messages.

CAN-SPAM defines spam as "any electronic mail message the primary purpose of which is the commercial advertisement or promotion of a commercial product or service (including content on an Internet website operated for a commercial purpose)." It exempts "transactional or relationship messages." The FTC has yet to clarify what "primary purpose" means; it has already delayed rule-making for this terminology. Previous state laws had used bulk (a number threshold), content (commercial), or unsolicited to define spam.

The bill permits e-mail marketers to send unsolicited commercial e-mail as long as it contains all of the following:

- An opt-out mechanism
- A valid subject line and header (routing) information
- The legitimate physical address of the mailer
- A label if the content is adult

If a user opts out, a sender has ten days to remove the address. The legislation also prohibits the sale or other transfer of an e-mail address after an opt-out request. Use of automated means to register for multiple e-mail accounts from which to send spam compound other violations. It prohibits sending sexually-oriented spam without the label later determined by the FTC of SEXUALLY-EXPLICIT. This label replaced the similar state labeling requirements of ADV:ADLT or ADLT. Labeling regulations for general spam will be commented on by the FTC this summer.

CAN-SPAM pre-empts existing state anti-spam laws that do not deal with fraud. It makes it a misdemeanor to send spam with falsified header information. A host of other common spamming practices can make a CAN-SPAM violation an "aggravated offense," including harvesting, dictionary attacks, Internet protocol spoofing, hijacking computers through Trojan horses or worms, or using open mail relays for the purpose of sending spam.

CAN-SPAM allows the FTC to implement a national do-not-email list similar to the FTC's popular do-not-call registry, or to report back to Congress why the creation of such a list is not currently feasible. The FTC soundly rejected this proposal, and such a list will not be implemented. The FTC concluded that the lack of authentication of email would undermine the list, and it could raise security concerns.

The legislation does not allow e-mail recipients to sue spammers or class-action lawsuits, but allows enforcement by the FTC, State Attorneys General, Internet service provider s, and other federal agencies for special categories of spammers (such as banks). An individual could still sue as an ISP if (s)he ran a mail server, but this would likely be cost-prohibitive. Individuals can also sue using state laws about fraud, such as Virginia's which gives standing based on actual damages, in effect limiting enforcement to ISPs.

Senator John McCain is responsible for a last-minute amendment which makes businesses promoted in spam subject to FTC penalties and enforcement remedies, regardless of whether the FTC is able to identify the specific spammer who initiated the e-mail.

Representative Lofgren introduced an amendment to allow bounties for some informants. The FTC has limited these bounties to individuals with inside information. The bounties are expected to be over $100,000, but none have been awarded yet.

## (B) Directive 2002/58/EC on Privacy and Electronic Communications

Recital (17). For the purposes of this Directive, consent of a user or subscriber, regardless of whether the latter is a natural or a legal person, should have the same meaning as the data subject's consent as defined and further specified in Directive 95/46/EC. Consent may be given by any appropriate method enabling a freely given specific and informed indication of the user's wishes, including by ticking a box when visiting an Internet website.

Recital (40) Safeguards should be provided for subscribers against intrusion of their privacy by unsolicited communications for direct marketing purposes in particular by means of automated calling machines, telefaxes, and e-mails, including SMS messages. These forms of unsolicited commercial communications may on the one hand be relatively easy and cheap to send and on the other may impose a burden and/or cost on the recipient. Moreover, in some cases their volume may also cause difficulties for electronic communications networks and terminal equipment. For such forms of unsolicited communications for direct marketing, it is justified to require that prior explicit consent of the recipients is obtained before such communications are addressed to them. The single market requires a harmonised approach to ensure simple, Community-wide rules for businesses and users.

Article 13
Unsolicited communications

1. The use of automated calling systems without human intervention (automatic calling machines), facsimile machines (fax) or electronic mail for the purposes of direct marketing may only be allowed in respect of subscribers who have given their prior consent.
2. Notwithstanding paragraph 1, where a natural or legal person obtains from its customers their electronic contact details for electronic mail, in the context of the sale of a product or a service, in accordance with Directive 95/46/EC, the same natural or legal person may use these electronic contact details for direct marketing of its own similar products or services provided that customers clearly and distinctly are given the opportunity to object, free of charge and in an easy manner, to such use of electronic contact details when they are collected and on the occasion of each message in case the customer has not initially refused such use.
3. Member States shall take appropriate measures to ensure that, free of charge, unsolicited communications for purposes of direct marketing, in cases other than those referred to in paragraphs 1 and 2, are not allowed either without the consent of the subscribers concerned or in respect of

subscribers who do not wish to receive these communications, the choice between these options to be determined by national legislation.

4. In any event, the practice of sending electronic mail for purposes of direct marketing disguising or concealing the identity of the sender on whose behalf the communication is made, or without a valid address to which the recipient may send a request that such communications cease, shall be prohibited.
5. Paragraphs 1 and 3 shall apply to subscribers who are natural persons. Member States shall also ensure, in the framework of Community law and applicable national legislation, that the legitimate interests of subscribers other than natural persons with regard to unsolicited communications are sufficiently protected.

# Section II

# Electronic Intrusion:

## Technologies, Strategies and Methodologies

# Chapter IX
# Cyberproperty in the United States:
## Trespass to Chattels & New Technology

**Greg Lastowska**
*Rutgers School of Law, USA*

## ABSTRACT

*During the past three decades, the growing importance of computing technology to modern society has led to regular calls in the United States for new and stronger forms of legal protection for computer equipment. Legal reforms in the United States have included the passage of laws targeting unauthorized access to computer systems, laws regulating online advertising, new criminal provisions related to identity theft, and copyright reforms protecting private interests in digital files. One of the most interesting and controversial legal developments, however, has been the acceptance by some courts of a new modification to an old common law property interest. Under the theory of cyberproperty, the owners of computer chattels have been granted the right to prohibit non-damaging contact with their systems. Essentially, cyberproperty amounts to a right to exclude others from network-connected resources (Wagner, 2005). The right is analogized to a right to exclude others from real property. Many legal scholars in the United States have supported the creation of a cyberproperty right, arguing in law review articles that this development is justified (Bellia, 2004; Epstein, 2003; Epstein, 2005; Fairfield, 2005; Hardy, 1996; McGowan, 2003; McGowan, 2005; Wagner, 2005; Warner, 2002). Other scholars, including myself, have argued against cyberproperty doctrine, claiming that it is dangerously overbroad and ill-suited to the nature of the networked environment (Burk, 2000; Carrier & Lastowka, 2007; Hunter, 2003; Lemley, 2003; Madison, 2003; O'Rourke, 2001; Quilter, 2002; Winn, 2004). This chapter has two parts. The first part explains the doctrinal evolution of cyberproperty in the United States. In the first part of this chapter,*

*I provide an overview of the seminal cases that led up to the California Supreme Court's decision in Intel v. Hamidi (2003). Though the Hamidi case was a landmark decision for trespass to chattels on the internet, the issue of cyberproperty in the United States remains largely an open question. In the second part of this chapter, I examine and criticize what I see as the theoretical foundations of cyberproperty. Cyberproperty grows out of two confusions. First, it is based on the strange belief that exclusion of a party from access to a computer can be easily analogized to the exclusion of a person from access to land. Second, many proponents of cyberproperty have confused the operation of computer code with the power of the law. This reasoning is based on Professor Lawrence Lessig's claim that "code is law." Both of these foundations of cyberproperty theory are suspect. Computer chattels are very much unlike land. Even if we apply standard law and economic principles to computer networks, we find that private interests in computer systems are unlike standard property interests. Also, code is unlike law in many ways. In fact, almost all cyberlaw scholars who reference the "code is law" equation do so in order to criticize the equation of code and law, not endorse it. Thus, the theoretical foundations of cyberproperty doctrine in the United States seem to be both easily identified and easily criticized. Despite this, as stated earlier, it is possible that cyberproperty doctrine will continue to develop in the United States and elsewhere.*

## THE DOCTRINE OF CYBERPROPERTY

This first part considers the historical evolution of cyberproperty doctrine in the United States. Cyberproperty doctrine arose from judicial efforts to remedy new forms of technological harm with the ancient doctrine of trespass to chattels. Thus, debates over cyberproperty have not been primarily policy debates over the creation of new law, but have also included disputes over the proper interpretation of existing legal doctrine as applied to evolving technology.

The first cyberproperty case that arose in the United States was *Thrifty-Tel, Inc. v. Bezenek* (1996). *Thrifty-Tel* involved two teenage boys who attempted to obtain "free" long distance service by attempting to discover account codes. Over a seven-hour period, the boys made 1,300 calls to a telephone network. This action resulted in the denial of telephone access to paying customers. The trial court found that the boys had converted the value of the phone network and awarded the phone company $50,000 in damages and fees, in part based on the phone company's own tariff fees.

The Bezenek parents appealed the decision to the California Court of Appeals, pointing out a doctrinal problem with the conversion claim raised by the phone company. The problem was that, under California property law, intangibles (such as phone service) were not subject to conversion. Though some state courts have been less formal about the tangibility requirement for the tort of conversion, the court in *Thrifty-Tel* respected this limitation. However, in order to preserve the victory of the phone company, the court found that the plaintiffs had demonstrated (although they had not pleaded it!) a cause of action for trespass to chattels.

In common law, trespass to chattels is not a tort of spatial intrusion, but simply an intentional action which causes harm to the personal property of another. A trespass to chattels lies where a defendant has, without privilege to do so, intermeddled with or disposed of the personal property of another. In practice, the trespass to chattels tort has been largely eclipsed by the tort of conversion. However, trespass to chattels recognizes a potentially more subtle form of injury. (VerSteeg, 1994).

To illustrate this, consider a tortfeasor who damages a car. In a claim of conversion, a successful plaintiff obtains as a remedy what is essentially a forced sale of the chattel to the tortfeasor (along with additional consequential damages). So if a car were stolen or destroyed by a tortfeasor, a claim of conversion would be fully appropriate. The tortfeasor should be forced to pay the owner the full value of the car. On the other hand, a claim of trespass to chattels awards the plaintiff only those damages caused by the interference. So if a car were merely scratched, the forced sale of the car would provide an unwarranted windfall. In such a case, trespass to chattels, the "little brother of conversion" (as courts often call it), provides the appropriate remedy.

Historically, at least in the United States, trespass to chattels has required that plaintiffs demonstrate some actual damage or dispossession of the chattel in order to bring a claim. So while intentionally tapping on the hood of another person's car may not be polite, it is not a trespass. The owner of the car is, of course, free to prevent others from touching the car through self-help, but the state will not become involved if those efforts fail. (It should be noted that English and Australian common law may diverge from the American rule in this case (Epstein, 2003)).

Traditionally, American common law has made an important distinction between trespass to land and trespass to chattels. In a claim of trespass to real property, an injunction can be awarded in the absence of damages to the land. *Jacque v. Steenberg Homes* (1997). Indeed, in leading scholarly literature in the United States, the very notion of "property" rules relies on the notion that a property owner need not demonstrate evidence of damage in order to obtain a legal remedy (Calabresi & Melamed, 1972). Yet the case is different with chattels. As the Prosser & Keeton treatise explains, "the dignitary interest in the inviolability of chattels, unlike that as to land, is not sufficiently important to require any greater defense than the privilege of using reasonable force when necessary to protect them." (Keeton, 1984, p. 87).

Perhaps the most compelling justification for this distinction is the conservation of judicial resources. If there has been no harm to personal property, it is hard to see why the state should expand judicial resources investigating whether there has been an improper, non-damaging contact made with cars, umbrellas, or dogs. Affronts to a property owner's dignity may be keenly felt, but they would rarely justify resort to judicial process. (Rose, 1998).

The *Thrifty-Tel* case, however, broke with the traditional American rule governing trespass to chattel. It did so in one rather confusing footnote. Footnote six stated that that the *means* of trespass in the case was intangible. The need for this footnote was unclear. The exact means by which a chattel is tortiously damaged should not be a relevant consideration. If one intentionally destroys a car with a hammer or burns it with an intangible laser, there can be damage to the car in either case. The means of the hammer should not be generally relevant.

Yet the means of trespass would have been quite relevant if the case had involved a trespass to real property. In common law, a trespass to real property actions is *not* available when a non-damaging intrusion is made by an intangible thing (*e.g.*, noise, smoke, or light). Yet, as explained above, a non-damaging intrusion by a tangible item (*e.g.* a rock) is sufficient to state a claim. Thus, the *means* by which a trespass is made can be quite relevant in a case of trespass to real property. Though the court in *Thrifty-Tel* was considering a trespass to chattel, not a trespass to real property, it placed these two different forms of "trespass" in close proximity by stating:

*[T]he California Supreme Court has intimated migrating intangibles (e.g. sound waves) may result in trespass, provided they do not simply impede an owner's use or enjoyment of property, but cause damage. In our view, the electronic*

*signals generated by the Bezenek boys' activities were sufficiently tangible to support a trespass cause of action.*

Thus, the court referenced trespass to real property cases in holding that a trespass to chattels claim was supported when contact was made by electronic means. Although this footnote specifically requires the establishment of damage in order to state a claim, it was not long before courts began to read this footnote as a justification for a near-absolute right to enjoin any form of electronic contact with computer equipment. As many commentators have noted, United States courts, citing to *Thrifty-Tel*, soon began to apply real property trespass rules to claims about electronic intrusion (O'Rourke, 2001; Mossoff, 2004).

Professor Dan Burk summarized these ensuing developments in 1999. Burk stated that "the *Thrifty-Tel* version of trespass follows the form of trespass to chattels, and yet has the substance of trespass to land." (Burk, 1999, p. 38). He noted how *Thrifty-Tel* "essentially reversed several hundred years of legal evolution, collapsing the separate doctrines of trespass to land and trespass to chattels back into their single common law progenitor, the action for trespass."

A string of cases were soon built upon the decision of *Thrifty-Tel*, many of which involved injunctions against the transmission of mass commercial email messages. In other words, cyberproperty doctrine was first used as a newly found tool for combating the growing problem of "spam." These cases included *CompuServe, Inc. v. Cyber Promotions* (1997), *Cyber Promotions v. America Online* (1996), *America Online v. National Health Care Discounters* (2000), *America Online v. LCGM* (1998), *America Online v. IMS* (1998) and *Hotmail v. Van$ Money Pie* (1998). In these cases, United States courts sought to address complaints about spam through the doctrine of trespass to chattels.

By 2000, cyberproperty case law had moved beyond commercial spam cases to a more general notion of a right to exclude others from interacting with networked computing equipment. Three important cyberproperty cases involved plaintiffs seeking injunctions against unauthorized access to websites: *eBay v. Bidder's Edge* (2000), *Register.com v. Verio* (2000), and *Ticketmaster.com v. Tickets.com* (2000). Two of these cases, *eBay* and *Ticketmaster.com*, were litigated in California district courts, and thus applied the same California common law precedents that animated the decision in *Thrifty-Tel*. The *eBay v. Bidder's Edge* case is the most well-known of these three early decisions.

In the *eBay* case, the well-known plaintiff was awarded an injunction against a smaller auction site that had routinely accessed the eBay website without permission. Though the defendant was enjoined from obtaining further access to the eBay website, the language of the court's decision was ambiguous. It was not clear whether the court had determined that eBay had an unqualified right to exclude the defendants from its system. Many commentators still disagree about exactly what precedent *eBay* established and what portion of the opinion might be regarded as dicta (Bellia, 2004; Lemley, 2003).

According to one later court, *eBay* stood for a full recognition of cyberproperty rights. In the case of *Oyster Software, Inc v. Forms Processing, Inc.* (2001), the plaintiff claimed that the defendant had committed trespass to chattels simply by accessing its publicly available website without permission. The court agreed, stating that, in California, the "defendant's conduct was sufficient to establish a cause of action for trespass... simply because the defendant's conduct amounted to 'use' of Plaintiff's computer." In other words, according to the court in *Oyster Software*, damage was no longer an element required to state a claim of trespass to chattels—a mere lack of authorization was sufficient.

California law on this issue was significantly changed, however, by the most well-known cyberproperty case to date: *Intel v. Hamidi,* which was decided by the California Supreme Court in 2003. In a way, the case was similar to commercial "spam" cases, in that it involved unwanted email—yet the defendant in this case was not a commercial advertiser. Ken Hamidi was a former employee of the Intel Corporation. Over the course of two years, Hamidi sent six short emails to over 30,000 Intel employees on behalf of an organization named FACE-Intel ("Former and Current Employees of Intel").

According to the California Supreme Court:

*The messages criticized Intel's employment practices, warned employees of the dangers those practices posed to their careers, suggested employees consider moving to other companies, solicited employees' participation in FACE-Intel, and urged employees to inform themselves further by visiting FACE-Intel's Web site.*

Intel had instructed its employees not to reply to Hamidi's messages and had attempted to delete messages before they reached Intel employees. Hamidi successfully evaded Intel's attempts by simply sending new mass emails from new email accounts. Because Intel had not applied filters to these accounts, the messages passed through its system. In March 1998, after Hamidi's fifth mass email message, Intel wrote to Hamidi and demanded that he cease sending his mass emails to Intel employees. Hamidi stated, in reply, that he had a First Amendment right to communicate with Intel's employees at their place of work and would continue to do so. Several months later, he sent a sixth mailing to his list of employees. Intel then brought suit against him, proceeding on a cyberproperty theory of trespass to chattels.

Relying expressly on cyberproperty theory, Intel conceded that there was no damage to its system created by Hamidi's email messages. The only damages claimed were the costs of Intel's own attempts to block the messages from getting to employees and the time lost by employees who had been less productive due to Hamidi's communications. Yet this type of damage was deemed sufficient by the trial court. A permanent injunction was entered prohibiting Hamidi from sending unsolicited e-mail to addresses on Intel's computer systems.

Hamidi appealed and the California Court of Appeals affirmed. Citing footnote six of *Thrifty-Tel,* the majority explicitly indicated that it would modify trespass to chattels doctrine to create a cyberproperty right, noting how "[t]he common law adapts to human endeavor" and how "the [trespass to chattels] tort has reemerged as an important rule of cyberspace." The language of the majority's opinion was especially interesting because it seemed to embrace real property metaphors not just at a doctrinal level, but at a deeper conceptual level, likening Intel's mail system to a type of real property in the "place" of cyberspace (Hunter, 2003).

Hamidi had argued that any injunction issued would violate his free speech rights under the United States and California constitutions. These claims were rejected. The majority stated that free speech protections did not apply because "Hamidi was enjoined from trespassing onto Intel's private property." By analogizing non-damaging trespass to chattels to a physical entry "onto" Intel's property, the appellate court made clear that the cyberproperty interest it endorsed took precedence over constitutionally protected speech interests.

Hamidi petitioned to the California Supreme Court for review. In a close (4-3) decision, the California Supreme Court reversed the appellate court. The Court re-affirmed the common law rule established prior to *Thrifty-Tel* that some damage or impairment to the chattel in question was required to bring an action for trespass to chattels. Intel had relied on the case law that had evolved from *Thrifty-Tel* and this precedent that was not binding on the California Supreme Court.

Notably, though, the majority of the California Supreme Court did *not* overrule prior cyberproperty cases, but instead explained how they fit with prior trespass to chattel doctrine. The many cases involving bulk commercial email were distinguished on the basis that the transmissions in those cases "both overburdened the ISP's own computers and made the entire computer system harder to use for recipients." Strain on computer systems was thus seen as evidence of "damage" to proper functioning of the chattel. However, the California Supreme Court rejected the concept of cyberproperty, stating that it "would not be a correct statement of California or general American law on this point." Thus, pursuant to California common law, trespass to chattel today continues to require a demonstration of damage by a plaintiff (Epstein, 2003; Cohen & Hiller, 2003).

In another part of its opinion, which was clearly *obiter dicta*, the California Supreme Court rejected the notion that property rights might conclusively trump free speech rights in cyberspace. It stated that, had it decided the issue, it would have found free speech protections were raised with regard to Hamidi's actions. It explicitly rejected the spatial and metaphorical readings of cyberspace by stressing the lack of a spatial intrusion:

*Hamidi himself had no tangible presence on Intel property, instead speaking from his own home through his computer. He no more invaded Intel's property than does a protester holding a sign or shouting through a bullhorn outside corporate headquarters, posting a letter through the mail, or telephoning to complain of a corporate practice.*

While California is obviously a prominent jurisdiction for matters concerning new property rights on the Internet, there are forty-nine other state jurisdictions in the United States. Other United States courts have seemed less concerned about the traditional boundaries of trespass to chattels law.

For instance, in the New York case of *Sherwood 48 Associates v. Sony Corporation of America* (2002), Sony Entertainment had used digital images of certain buildings in Times Squares in order to create the 2002 summer blockbuster *Spider Man* (Brown, 2003). However, the film company had altered the appearance of the buildings owned by the plaintiffs to replace existing advertisements with those of Sony's partners. They claimed that Sony had committed a trespass to chattels by taking measurements of their properties with lasers, even though the buildings had not been damaged by the electromagnetic contact.

The federal district court seemed perplexed: "trespass?—bouncing a laser beam off a building to create a digital photograph? Light beams bounce off plaintiffs' three buildings day and night in the city that never sleeps." Yet the Federal Court of Appeals for the Second Circuit reversed the district court's dismissal of the trespass to chattels claim. The Second Circuit, citing to *Hamidi*, stated: "This case presents an unsettled question of New York state law, to wit, whether a trespass is committed under New York law when a party's physical contact with another party's personal property diminishes the value of that property without damaging that property.... A New York court should determine whether physical damage to the Buildings in this case is a prerequisite to a trespass claim."

Another case that sustained a trespass to chattels claim post-*Hamidi* was *Sotelo v. DirectRevenue* (2005). In this class action case, the defendant was alleged to have installed spyware on the computers of the class members. The class claimed that the unauthorized interference with its computers amounted to a trespass to chattels. The court rejected a motion to dismiss, allowing the trespass to chattels claim to go forward. The plaintiff in *Sotelo*, however, alleged that the spyware at issue damaged his personal property by over-burdening their resources and diminishing their functioning. Thus, *Sotelo* may raise the question of exactly how much a computer must be affected by unauthorized activity for the interference to amount to "diminished functioning."

Arguably, the *Hamidi* decision effectively *preserved* more of cyberproperty theory than it rejected. Though Hamidi ruled out claims where plaintiffs admitted there was no damage to the computer equipment, almost all forms of electronic interaction with a computer system use *some* resources. In light of this, what burden to a system is too great and what diminishment in functioning is legally insubstantial? The *Hamidi* opinion does not settle this question at all. Instead, it essentially invites lower courts to consider these issues on a case-by-case basis.

Cyberproperty doctrine in the United States may therefore be headed toward several possible futures (Winn, 2004). Given this, it is important to consider the theory underlying cyberproperty doctrine as future courts in the United States struggle to cabin the concept of cyberproperty.

## CYBERPROPERTY THEORY

The prior section provided an overview of the United States case law on cyberproperty. This section explains the theoretical arguments that have been made in support of cyberproperty. The question of whether these theoretical justifications are persuasive is hotly contested by legal scholars in the United States. As mentioned earlier, several prominent commentators have argued that cyberproperty doctrine is a misguided development (Hunter, 2003; Lessig, 2001).

I count myself among these opponents of cyberproperty. In a recently co-authored short article, Professor Michael Carrier and I make a direct attack against cyberproperty doctrine (Carrier & Lastowka, 2007). As Professor Carrier and I explain in that article, cyberproperty lacks the theoretical justifications that are typically found to support property rights. There are no convincing utilitarian or natural rights theories that would justify the creation of this new right. Additionally, the cyberproperty right is not conditioned by traditional mitigating doctrines that could operate to blunt its sharp edges. Also, as we explain, in the years since the early cyberproperty cases were decided, the Congress of the United States has enacted several statutes that target, much more carefully and cautiously, the specific harms that cyberproperty doctrine was attempting to remedy. For all these reasons, we conclude that cyberproperty rights are unjustified and that the doctrine should be abandoned by United States courts.

Yet if we are right about this, what is the reason for the continuing appeal of the doctrine to some jurists and scholars in the United States? Many courts have supported cyberproperty theory and several prominent law professors have also endorsed the doctrine of cyberproperty. In this section, I will attempt to explain what I see as the theoretical foundations on which arguments in favor of cyberproperty doctrine rest.

As will be readily apparent, I am setting up these justifications primarily with the intention to knock them down. Nevertheless, I think it is worthwhile to decode the logic of cyberproperty. If we understand how jurists and scholars in the United States have misunderstood the path of the law with respect to electronic networks, we may ultimately avoid similar mistakes as the law continues to evolve. Understanding the confusion that led to cyberproperty can be helpful both in the United States and in other jurisdictions considering how the law should be modified in light of new technological changes.

### Confusion about Land and Economics

The first confusion that we can find among cyberproperty supporters concerns the relation between cyberproperty and the economics of private ownership of land. It may seem strange to legally equate computing equipment with land, but this has been a common theme in cyberproperty theory in the United States.

Proponents of cyberproperty, both judicial and scholarly, have historically appealed to rights in land to support claims for new cyberproperty rights. Even before *Thrifty-Tel*, there seemed to be a common belief among many commentators that interaction with a computer could be analogized to a spatial invasion of real property. (Epstein, 2005; Madison, 2003; Mosoff, 2004). In an amicus brief submitted to the California Supreme Court in *Hamidi*, Professor Richard Epstein of the University of Chicago argued that common rhetorics used to describe digital environments supported the doctrine of cyberproperty (Epstein, 2003). He claimed that because cyberspace was understood as being like a place, it should be legally treated as a place. The *Hamidi* majority opinion, however, explicitly rejected this argument:

*Professor Epstein suggests that a company's server should be its castle, upon which any unauthorized intrusion, however harmless, is a trespass. Epstein's argument derives, in part, from the familiar metaphor of the Internet as a physical space, reflected in much of the language that has been used to describe it: "cyberspace," "the information superhighway," e-mail "addresses," and the like. Of course, the Internet is also frequently called simply the "Net," a term, Hamidi points out, "evoking a fisherman's chattel." A major component of the Internet is the World Wide "Web," a descriptive term suggesting neither personal nor real property... Metaphor is a two-edged sword.*

Yet Professor Epstein continues to argue in favor of "the extension of trespass to land rules to the Internet." (Epstein, 2005, p. 163). He believes it is sound to conflate the interoperations of software with personal entries onto real property, and has strongly criticized the Hamidi majority for failing to accept this conflation. As Dan Hunter and Mark Lemley have noted with concern, some courts have been willing to accept this conflation (Hunter, 2003; Lemley, 2003).

Most cyberproperty proponents, however, do not simply rest their claims for cyberproperty on the conflation of cyberspace with land. Even Professor Epstein counts this argument as just one arrow in his quiver. The more common course of argument is related to the conflation of land and computing equipment, but proceeds at a more abstract level. Cyberproperty proponents often argue that private property rights are more effective at achieving the efficient use of resources. These claims are based on so-called "Chicago school" understandings that strong private property rights are highly effective in creating efficient and socially beneficial market transactions.

These theories have roots in writings about the benefits that are obtained from the private ownership of land. The American economist Harold Demsetz famously argued that land held in common would tend to be used inefficiently by rationally selfish individuals engaged in overgrazing and under-cultivating (Demsetz, 1967). He argued that legal privatization solved these problems and promoted more efficient and productive uses. Many cyberproperty advocates, relying on the theories of Demsetz, have been comfortable applying these same land-based theories to networked computers.

The emergence of new private property rights on the Internet was often hailed as a beneficial development by jurists with neoliberal tendencies. Judge Frank Easterbrook, who teaches at the University of Chicago of the Federal Court of Appeals of the Seventh Circuit, was one of the first judicial proponents of new online property rights. In an early address to scholars of Internet law, Judge Easterbrook advised that judges looking at new Internet cases should "create property rights, where now there are none... to make bargains possible." (Easterbrook, 1996, pp. 212-213). Easterbrook looked forward to the creation of new forms of property online, anticipating that cyberproperty rights would lead to new markets that would efficiently distribute new resources.

Other members of the federal judiciary of the United States have also endorsed forms of "new property" online (Rose, 2003). For instance, in the case of *Kremen v. Cohen* (2003), a plaintiff alleged that a defendant had stolen his domain name ("sex.com") by filing a fraudulent transfer document with the appointed registrar. Deciding the case on appeal, Judge Alex Kozinski permitted the cause of action for conversion to proceed by equating the domain name with a personal property interest. The doctrinal problem with intangibility and conversion—which was responsible, in part, for the decision in *Thrifty-Tel*—was brushed aside. The United States Congress endorsed this equation of domain names with property by passing the Anti-Cybersquatting Consumer Protection Act ("ACPA") in 1999. ACPA permits plaintiffs to proceed with actions "in rem" to recover ownership of domain names (Chander, 2003).

In this regard, however, it is worth noting that online property rights are not necessarily cyberproperty rights. Rights in domain names and cyberproperty rights are importantly different. Joshua Fairfield explores this difference in his recent work on "virtual property." (Fairfield, 2005). Using a classic Demsetzian analysis, Fairfield argues that when computer code functions in ways that mimic the functioning of traditional land and chattel property, new virtual property concepts should step in where current property protections fail to reach. Fairfield's arguments map well to the legal result in *Kremen* and seem consistent with the exhortations of Judge Easterbrook.

Yet domain names are a property right not connected with any particular private rights in computer chattels. Indeed, the domain name system is properly understood as a cross-cutting right. It effectively intrudes upon the freedoms that certain chattel owners have with regard to the way bits and bytes are arranged on their computers. The divergence between theories of cyberproperty and virtual property is based upon the disaggregation, in a virtual property scheme, of property rights from rights of chattel ownership. Fairfield is properly understood as an advocate for virtual property (the title of his article) rather than as an advocate for cyberproperty. Cyberproperty rights are based on strengthened rights of ownership in networked chattels.

So even when one stands firmly within a traditional Demsetzian framework, as Fairfield does, there are reasons to accept the *Hamidi* court's rejection of cyberproperty. There may well be a place for new property-like rights "in cyberspace" generally, but insisting that such rights should be in the hands of chattel owners is potentially a mistake.

A broader critique could be made, of course, of the Demsetizan commitment to private property in cyberspace. Oddly enough, one can find this kind of criticism within the four walls of the Chicago School. Saul Levmore, the current dean of the Chicago Law School, has asked whether the entire Demsetzian story of private property might be skeptically described as an apologia for the capture of the legislature by well-organized private interests. In reference to question of rights in intangible value, Levmore calls "appealing" the claim that non-proprietary software development is a more efficient model of production that has been responsible for "sustained and impressive innovation." (Levmore, 2003, p. 185).

If thoughts like these can be found so close to the heartland of the law and economics movement, there is surely no reason for abstract confidence in cyberproperty doctrine as a solution to some looming tragedy of the networked commons. This is especially true when the prospect of such a tragedy seems to have been illusory. As Professor David Post has observed, claims that the Internet would be a cyber-wasteland in the absence of strong property rights were made often and early by cyber-economists, yet have turned out to be completely mistaken (Post, 2001). In the absence of strong property protections, the Internet has flourished with new content and useful functions.

As Post said years ago in a statement that seems equally true today: "Cyberspace keeps growing and growing; more and more stuff keeps appearing in new guises and new shapes; there are more and more people trying to give me information to place in my computer than I have room for." The tragedy of the commons turned out to be a comedy of the commons, disproving the conventional Demsetzian story (Rose, 1986b).

## Confusion about Code and Law

Two leading proponents of cyberproperty are Professors Polk Wagner of the University of Pennsylvania and Patricia Bellia of Notre Dame. Unlike other cyberproperty proponents, Wagner and Bellia concede that a general state of "open access" to network resources produces desirable outcomes. (Bellia, 2004; Wagner, 2005). Yet both argue that a mandatory open access rule is not desirable. Bellia and Wagner see cyberproperty not as an attempt to radically transform the fundamental nature of the Internet, but instead as a tool to address problems at the margins.

Most importantly for our purposes, Bellia and Wagner argue for cyberproperty in part on the basis of the claim that "code is law." They state that whatever the law might do with regard to cyberproperty rights, private technologies already effectively restrict access to information. Code-based exclusionary measures, such as passwords systems, firewalls, encryption, etc., are generally effective in prevent unwelcome "trespass" to networked chattel. Hence, according to Bellia and Wagner, the proper question is not whether private parties should have the *ability* to exclude others from access to networked chattels. Instead, the question is whether the ability to exclude will be rooted in law, technology, or both.

Both Bellia and Wagner claim to be influenced by the arguments of Professor Lawrence Lessig that "code is law." Lessig used this phrase as a theme of his 1999 book *Code and Other Laws of Cyberspace*. However, as Lessig acknowledges in *Code*, the original idea was found in another book, *City of Bits,* which was written in 1995 by MIT dean and architect William Mitchell. In *City of Bits*, Mitchell suggested that "on the electronic frontier, code is the law." (Mitchell, 1994, p. 111). *City of Bits* was an influential text in the cyberlaw community—legal scholars including Lessig, Ethan Katsch, Joel Reindenberg, and Jamie Boyle were soon grappling with the implications of code replacing law (Reidenberg, 1996; Lessig, 1996; Katsh, 1996; Boyle, 1997; Reidenberg, 1998). However, it was Lessig's 1999 book that provided the most thorough and popular investigation of the concept. Lessig brought the equation of code and law to wide prominence.

According to some commentators, the notion that "code is law" is the "most significant principle to emerge from the academic study of law on the Internet." (Wagner, 2005.) Oddly, though, when commentators explain what is meant by "code is law," they generally claim that code is *not* law. Scholars working out Lessig's "code is law" concepts today, like Polk Wagner, Tim Wu, and James Grimmelmann, have uniformly been interested in moving beyond it (Grimmelmann, 2005; Kerr, 2003; Wu, 2003; Sommer, 2000.) And, as James Grimmelmann has explained, this is actually consistent with what Lessig has argued.

When laying out his theory of code as a form of social regulation, Lessig associated code with a mode of "architecture" that does the work of law—not with law per se. "Code is law," as one professor notes, should really be understood as "code is not law":

*As Lawrence Lessig informs us, markets, architecture, and social norms can regulate behavior, sometimes as well as or better than law.* (Chander, 2003)

In a later summary of his intent with the phrase, Lessig explains that he meant it as a metaphor and states:

*[C]ode controls behavior as law might control behavior: You can't easily rip the contents of my DVD because the code locks it tight. The code functions as a law might function: Telling the user what she can and cannot do.* (Lessig, 2000)

But are locks laws? No one would claim this, although locks certainly control the behaviors of others in much the same manner that encryption code controls the contents of a DVD. Why would we want to equate a lock with a law?

In short, Lessig wanted people to take software more seriously. His "code is law" rhetoric was a sort of call to arms directed at the legislature and judiciary. "Code is law" was an attempt to get one group of regulators (law-makers) to pay more attention to the power of another group of regulators (code-makers) (Lessig, 2003). Lessig described how the increasing place of code in society ceded regulatory powers to companies like Microsoft and America Online. His hope was that government would be more proactive and that constitutional values could be recreated in the software "architecture" of cyberspace (Lessig, 1996).

This has occurred in the intervening decade, at least to some extent. And it is hardly surprising. Many great and socially transformative inventions have been the source of new law, both common and statutory. Justice Cardozo remarked, in an earlier day, about how the steamship, the telegraph, and the telephone had all changed both society and the law. (Cardozo, 1921, p. 61). Sometimes new technologies create both bodies of law and administrative agency. For instance, the technology of the airplane eventually led to the creation of the United States Federal Aviation Administration. While notions of striated airspace, licensing, and mandatory technologies may seem normal today, the policy of airplanes evolved through a process that demanded considerable legal creativity. As property scholar John Cribbet has noted, regulating air travel has required "a wholly new concept to respond to developing technology." (Cribbet, 1986, p. 1).

Understanding that code, like the airplane, is a new and socially disruptive technology explains why the Internet has generated calls for greater regulatory involvement. Yet, viewing code as inherently either "law" or "anti-law" pushes legal theory in strange directions.

For instance, Bellia and Wagner fault critics of cyberproperty for allowing individuals absolute freedom to employ access blocking technologies, but denying these same individuals the ability to petition the state to aid them in block access to their systems. Bellia and Wagner state that forcing the owners of hardware to rely on technology is a suboptimal state of affairs. Technological power, they say, lacks the subtlety of law. Additionally, reliance on "blunt" technologies of exclusion may lead to the over-protection of information. If individuals can use legal as well as technological mechanisms, Bellia and Wagner say, they may allow access to much information that is excluded. In other words, Bellia and Wagner are suggesting that the absence of cyberproperty rights will not maximize information access, but many instead simply lead to the popularity of overbroad technological blocking measures.

This is a sophisticated argument, but I believe it ultimately rests on a confusion between the power of technology and the power of law. Both Wagner and Bellia seem comfortable taking the position that because technological *blocking* is effective, we should consider endorsing property-based *exclusion* as an alternative to technological power.

Yet why should this be so? Technological powers enable us to do many things. Yet, in most cases, these abilities do not create any property entitlements. The ownership of a car, for instance, gives the owner the technological ability to drive fast and endanger the lives of others. The speed limit does not endorse this ability, but instead curbs technological power by forbidding its unregulated use. Privately held handguns enable their owners to commit more effective and powerful acts of violence than the human body normally can accomplish, but the law responds to this technological power by punishing violent acts committed with handguns more severely, and by requiring handguns to be licensed. The notion that new technological powers might be backed up by corresponding new property rights (mirroring the new power) therefore seems a bit strange. Cars and guns are not law—they are the things that law must wrestle with. Code may be similar.

To their credit, Bellia and Wagner both recognize that the law's relation to technology might not just encompass laws that mirror technological power, but laws that check these new powers as well. Both suggest that perhaps computer owners should be prevented, in certain situations, from employing technologies of exclusion. Bellia cautiously advocates for "technology-displacing" laws—laws that would, in other words, prohibit the free use of technologies of exclusion. Wagner calls for the consideration of "legal preemption," which he explains is the "direct [legal] control of software-regulatory effects." (Wagner, 2005, p. 463).

But one gets the sense that both Bellia and Wagner are not quite as enthusiastic or confident about these vaguely theorized inversions of cyberproperty doctrine as they are about the exclusionary rights commonly associated with cyberproperty. And there is good reason for this—pursuant to the cases cited in the above discussions of cyberproperty doctrine, convincing a court to deny a cyberproperty "owner" the ability to block what has been conceptualized as an invasion of a private interest seems rather farfetched. How, in the fairly simple logic of judicial decisions protecting cyberproperty rights, would notions of "technology-displacing law" and "legal preemption" be introduced, especially given that courts have generally seemed unaware of academic suggestions that "code is law"?

As described above, many cyberproperty proponents have a strong faith in the social utility of strong private property rights. As a dissenting judge in *Intel v. Hamidi* suggested, prohibition against technological exclusion would probably seem to, as one jurist put it: "license a form of trespass." Cyberproperty doctrine is, at its core, an expression of confidence in the wisdom of excluding access to something believed to be private property. "Code is law" operates as a gloss on what is, in essence, an assumption about the desirability of strong private property rights in the context of digital networks.

Lessig's own consideration of "trespass law in cyberspace" was presented in his book *Code*. Though in his later work, Lessig ultimately sided with Dan Burk's criticisms of cyberproperty (Lessig, 2001, p. 170), his earlier reaction was more favorable. He recounts in *Code* that a former research assistant of his claimed that "'owners' of space in cyberspace" should have "no legal protection against invasion." Lessig says that he found this idea "a bit nutty" and "in the end, I think, wrong." (Lessig, 1999, p. 122).

Lessig analogized the question of trespass in cyberspace to the problem of finding the proper balance between private fences and laws in protecting a farmer's interest in land. According to Lessig, and consistent with the driving theme of *Code*, the correct solution would be one that would not depend wholly upon technology, but that would mix some degree of private fencing and some degree of reliance upon trespass rules. "From a social perspective," said Lessig, "we would want the mix that provides the optimal protection at the lowest cost."

The point to see here is that Lessig's analogy is premised on an underlying private property right that may or may not exist in the online context. The fence (which is analogized to code) is not the key here—it is the land that makes the claim about balancing law and technology persuasive. If a farmer's fence were placed somewhere else—say, in the middle of a highway, floating in the ocean, or on someone else's land—it would seem ludicrous to state that the farmer's fence should be mirrored by a legal right to exclude others from those spaces.

Thus, it seems that "code is law" arguments are essentially restating the confusion discussed in the prior section between interests in land and interests in rights of exclusion from access to networked resources. The central question should not be whether code or law is the best means to exclude access to resources—it should be whether granting new private property rights to owners of networked resources is a desirable objective. As explained above, there is no reason to be confident that this is so—and there are many reasons to be opposed to cyberproperty.

## CONCLUSION

In this chapter, I have recounted the history of cyberproperty doctrine as it evolved from trespass to chattels doctrine in United States law. I have also explained what I believe are two of the theoretical foundations that have supported the growth of cyberproperty doctrine in United States law. First, courts have often conflated computer networks with land. Second, legal commentators have often conflated legal regulation with software regulation. Both of these ideas are misguided, yet both seem to be behind calls for the recognition of cyberproperty.

It seems inevitable that the increasing amounts of investment and reliance on digital networks will lead to new law and new forms of online property. Yet it is hardly clear that cyberproperty doctrine, based on trespass to chattels and rooted in interests in personal property, will continue to play an important role in the United States or in other common law jurisdictions. While it is possible that courts in the United States or elsewhere will continue to develop the contours of cyberproperty doctrine through new decisions, we might hope that cyberproperty will soon be an historical footnote eclipsed by superior statutory enactments and more nuanced approaches.

## REFERENCES

*America Online, Inc. v. IMS*, 24 F. Supp. 2d 548 (E.D. Va. 1998)

*America Online, Inc. v. LCGM, Inc.*, 46 F. Supp. 2d 444 (E.D. Va. 1998)

*America Online, Inc. v. Nat'l Health Care Disc., Inc.*, 121 F. Supp. 2d 1255 (N.D. Iowa 2000)

Bellia, P. L. (2004). Defending Cyberproperty. *New York University Law Review,* (79), 2164.

Boyle, J. (1997). Foucault in Cyberspace: Sur veillance, Sovereignty, and Hardwired Censors. *University of Cincinnati Law Review,* (66), 177.

Burk, D. L. (2000). The Trouble with Trespass. *Journal of Small & Emerging Business Law,* (4), 27.

Calabresi, G., & Melamed, A. D. (1972). Property Rules, Liability Rules, and Inalienability: One View of the Cathedral. *Harvard Law Review,* (85), 1089.

Cardozo, B. (1921). *The Nature of The Judicial Process.* New Haven, CT: Yale University Press.

Carrier, M., & Lastowka, G. (2007). Against Cyberproperty. *Berkeley Technology Law Journal,* (22), 1483.

Chander, A (2003). The New, New Property. *Texas Law Review,* (81), 715.

Cohen, R., & Hiller, J. S. (2003). Towards a Theory of Cyberplace: A Proposal for a New Legal Framework. *Richmond Journal of Law & Technology,* (10), 2.

*CompuServe, Inc. v. Cyber Promotions, Inc.*, 962 F. Supp. 1015 (S.D. Ohio 1997);

Cribbet, J. E. (1986). Concepts in Transition: The Search for a New Definition of Property. *University of Illinois Law Review,* (1986), 1.

*Cyber Promotions, Inc. v. America Online, Inc.*, 948 F. Supp. 436 (E.D. Pa. 1996);

Demsetz, H. (1967). Toward a Theory of Property Rights. *American Economic Review* (57), 347.

Easterbrook, F. H. (1996). Cyberspace and the Law of the Horse. *University of Chicago Legal Forum,* (1996), 207.

*eBay, Inc. v. Bidder's Edge, Inc.*, 100 F. Supp. 2d 1058 (N.D. Cal. 2000).

Epstein, R. A. (2003). Cybertrespass. *University of Chicago Law Review* (70), 73.

Epstein, R. A. (2005). Intel v. Hamidi: The Role of Self-Help in Cyberspace. *Journal of Law, Economics & Policy,* (1), 147.

Fairfield, J. A. T. (2005). Virtual Property. *Boston University Law Review,* (85), 1047.

Grimmelmann, J. (2005). Regulation by Software. *Yale Law Journal,* (114), 1719

Hardy, I. T. (1996). The Ancient Doctrine of Trespass to Web Sites. *Journal of Online Law, 7.*

*Hotmail Corp. v. Van$ Money Pie Inc.*, 47 U.S.P.Q.2d (BNA) 1020 (N.D. Cal. 1998).

Hunter, D (2003). Cyberspace as Place and the Tragedy of the Digital Anticommons. *California Law Review,* (91), 439.

*Intel v. Hamidi*, 30 Cal. 4th 1342 (2003).

*Intel v. Hamidi*, 94 Cal.App.4th 325 (2001).

*Jacque v. Steenberg Homes*, 563 N.W.2d 154 (Wisc. 1997).

Kam, S. (2004). Intel Corp. v. Hamidi: Trespass to Chattels and a Doctrine of Cyber-Nuisance. *Berkeley Technology Law Journal,* (19), 427.

Katsh, M.E. (1996). Software Worlds and the First Amendment: Virtual Doorkeepers in Cyberspace. *University of Chicago Legal Forum,* (1996), 335.

Keeton, W. P., Dobbs D. B., Keeton. R. E., et al. (1984). *Prosser and Keeton on Torts, 5th Edition.* St Paul, MN: West Publishing.

Kerr, O.S. (2003). The Problem of Perspective in Internet Law. *Georgetown Law Journal,* (91), 357.

*Kremen v. Cohen*, 337 F.3d 1024 (9th Cir. 2003)

Lastowka, G. (2007). Decoding Cyberproperty. *Indiana Law Review,* (40), 23.

Lemley, M. A. (2003). Place and Cyberspace. *California Law Review,* (91), 521.

Lessig, L. (1996). Reading the Constitution in Cyberspace. *Emory Law Journal,* (45), 869.

Lessig, L. (1999). *Code And Other Laws Of Cyberspace*. New York, NY: Basic Books.

Lessig, L. (2000). Cyberspace and Privacy: A New Legal Paradigm? *Stanford Law Review,* (52), 987.

Lessig, L. (2001). *The Future of Ideas.* New York, NY: Random House.

Lessig, L. (2003). Law Regulating Code Regulating Law. *Loyola University of Chicago Law Journal,* (35), 1.

Levmore, S. (2003). Property's Uneasy Path and Expanding Future. *University of Chicago Law Review,* (70), 181.

Madison, M. J. (2003). Rights of Access and the Shape of the Internet. *Boston College Law Review,* (44), 433.

McGowan, D. (2003). Website Access: The Case for Consent. *Loyola University of Chicago Law Journal,* (35), 341.

McGowan, D. (2005). The Trespass Trouble and the Metaphor Muddle. *Journal of Law, Economics & Policy,* (1), 109.

Mitchell, W. (1994). *City Of Bits*. Cambridge, MA: MIT Press.

Mossoff, A. (2004). Spam -- Oy, What A Nuisance!. *Berkeley Technology Law Journal, 19*, 625.

O'Rourke, M. A. (2001). Property Rights and Competition on the Internet: In Search of an Appropriate Analogy. *Berkeley Technology Law Journal,* (16), 561.

*Oyster Software, Inc v. Forms Processing, Inc.*, 2001 US Dist LEXIS 22520 (N.D. Cal. Dec. 6, 2001).

Post, D. J. (2001). His Napster's Voice. *Temple Environmental Law & Technology Journal* (20), 35.

*Pruneyard Shopping Center v. Robins*, 447 U.S. 74 (1980);

*Register.com, Inc. v. Verio, Inc.*, 126 F. Supp. 2d 238 (S.D.N.Y. 2000).

Reidenberg, J. R. (1996). Governing Networks and Rule-Making in Cyberspace. *Emory Law Journal,* (45), 911.

Reidenberg, J. R. (1998). Lex Informatica: The Formulation of Information Policy Rules Through Technology. *Texas Law Review,* (76), 553.

Rose, C. M. (1998). The Several Futures of Property: Of Cyberspace and Folk Tales, Emission Trades and Ecosystems. *Minnesota Law Review,* (83), 129.

Rose, C. M. (1998b). Canons of Property Talk, or, Blackstone's Anxiety. *Yale Law Journal* (108), 601.

*Sherwood 48 Assocs. v. Sony Corp. of Am.*, Civ. No. 02-9100, 2003 U.S. App. LEXIS 20106 (2d Cir. Sept. 29, 2003).

Sommer, J. H. (2000). Against Cyberlaw. *Berkeley Technology Law Journal,* (15), 1145.

*Sotelo v. DirectRevenue*, 384 F. Supp. 2d 1219 (N.D. Ill. 2005).

*Thrifty-Tel, Inc. v. Bezenek*, 46 Cal. App. 4th 1559 (1996)

*Ticketmaster Corp. v. Tickets.com, Inc.*, 2000 U.S. Dist. LEXIS 12987 (C.D. Cal. Mar. 7, 2000).

VerSteeg, R. (1994). Law in Ancient Egyptian Fiction. *Georgia Journal of International and Comparative Law,* (24), 37.

Wagner, R. P. (2005). On Software Regulation. *Southern California Law, Review* (78), 457.

Warner, R (2002). Border Disputes: Trespass to Chattels on the Internet. *Villanova Law Review,* (47), 117.

Winn, J. K. (2004). Crafting a License to Know from a Privilege to Access. *Washington Law Review,* (79), 285.

Wu, T. (2003). When Code Isn't Law. *Virginia Law Review,* (89), 679.

# Chapter X
# Digital Forensics and the Chain of Custody to Counter Cybercrime

**Andreas Mitrakas**
*European Network and Information Security Agency (ENISA), UK*

**Damián Zaitch**
*Erasmus University, The Netherlands*

## ABSTRACT

*Targeting information technology resources has marked a growing trend for all sorts of reasons that include, profit making, causing damage, carrying out espionage, exploiting human beings etc. Although information security is used to protect information assets, electronic crime remains firmly on the rise. Computer forensics is the analysis of data processing equipment such as a data carrier, a network etc. to determine whether that equipment has been used for illegal or unauthorised purposes. Establishing the chain of custody through appropriate policy frameworks can be used in order to assess the quality of the collected data. Policy for forensics may address the practices of forensics agents and labs in investigating cybercrime. This chapter concludes that full-scale harmonisation of policies on criminal law and legal processes is likely to only happen at regional level (e.g. the EU) rather than at a global scale. Along with the assumption that safe havens where criminals operate from are not likely to be suppressed any time soon, leads to the conclusion that cyber-crime is here to stay for the long run in spite of the good efforts made to trail digital suspects through digital forensics.*

## INTRODUCTION

The growing dependence on information technology to carry out daily transactions has led to the steep rise of crime perpetrated by using Information and Communication Technologies (ICTs). Targeting information technology resources has also seen a growing trend for all sorts of reasons that potentially include, profit making, causing damage, carrying out espionage, exploiting human beings etc. Although information security is used to protect information asset electronic crime is on the rise. The opportunity to access vast interconnected information resources through open electronic networks increases the risk for users and potential benefit that criminals can reap if successful in attacking information systems. Regulating cybercrime has been challenging due to discrepancies across the board when it comes to cross border cybercrime definition and enforcement. Forensic investigation of cybercrime emerges as a necessary link between the hard evidence that can be leveraged upon from a crime scene and its potential use in criminal proceedings. Forensic investigations aim at following on the criminals' footsteps to reconstruct a crime scene and closely describe the various elements discovered with a view to obtaining an exact view of the crime scene at the time of the act. Forensics is essential in combating cybercrime.

The emerging legal framework and the voluntary frameworks for handling, retaining and archiving systems and data require some degree of preparation in order to ease up the collection and exploitation of data collected at a crime scene. Methods and practices to conduct digital investigations are of particular importance especially in areas where rights might be at stake or sensitive information is risking disclosure. The approach to accessing and managing information is also critical for the admissibility of that information as evidence in a trial or other proceedings. Information security practices safeguard the quality and reliability of collected information mostly in terms of integrity and authentication.

This chapter provides a typology of cybercrime from a criminological perspective that brings in the social and behavioural elements that are critical in assessing criminal acts. Thereafter this chapter reviews some pertinent procedural and legal aspects as well as the methodological framework to investigate cybercrime.

## FRAMING THE DEBATE

Forensics or forensic science is the application of science to questions, which are of interest to the legal system. Computer forensics is the analysis of data processing equipment such as a data carrier, a network etc. to determine whether that equipment has been used for illegal or unauthorised purposes. Linking the equipment with its user can provide breakthroughs in the investigation process of an illegal act or a crime.

In spite of the criminological debate regarding concept and scope, most authors and policy makers interchangeably use concepts such as high-tech crime, digital crime, e-crime, computer-facilitated crime, cybercrime or computer-related crime as mere synonyms. In this chapter the term cybercrime is used to describe computer assisted crime. Additionally this chapter addresses aspects of illegal acts that do not necessarily have an interest from a penal law or a criminology point of view, they consist, nevertheless breaches that have to be dealt with.

Cybercrime involves attacking information systems or data for malicious purposes that often include a wide variety of crimes against persons, property or public interest. In these instances information systems are used to facilitate criminal activity. In other cases cyber criminals might directly target such information systems for the purpose of making profit, stealing secrets or damaging the interest of third parties. Cyber attacks have received substantial attention in view of the growing variety of means to carry them out. Various forms of attacks may target individual users (e.g. identity theft), groups of users (e.g. e-government systems, e-banking systems etc.), industrial interests (e.g. IPR theft), general malicious behaviour (e.g. spamming, spreading viruses or malware) etc. While in general property is the main target of cybercrime in the various ways that it can be accomplished, other crimes can be accomplished too such as the accessing and exchange of child pornography etc [Pfleeger, 2000].

To respond to cybercrime, law enforcement has devised methods to collect electronic evidence through forensics, which is deemed to be necessary to investigate crimes and to assure that appropriate support is afforded to evidence that is introduced in criminal or other legal proceedings. Digital forensics investigation involves examining electronic evidence, using information technology to carry out forensic investigations as well as collecting, archiving and managing digital evidence in a way that renders it admissible in legal proceedings.

The response of law enforcement to electronic crime requires that officers, investigators, forensic examiners, and managers get involved in recognising, collecting, preserving, transporting, and archiving electronic evidence according to reliable, documented and traceable methods. Digital forensics is the focus of law enforcement professionals who counter cybercrime while executing their day-to-day duties, investigators who collect electronic evidence and forensic examiners who provide assistance at crime scenes and examinations of evidence. Additionally parties implicated include system administrators, internal investigators, support staff that are all often required to produce evidence in support of investigations. The acts of the implicated law enforcement and support parties seek to ensure collect and preserve volatile electronic evidence according to established principles and procedures. While evidence must be carefully treated when collected and sorted, the courts closely scrutinize actions that allow altering, damaging, or destroying evidence in order for it to become admissible.

In recent years, digital forensics have gained in importance due to the growth of cybercrime that threatens the legal safety and security of electronic transactions to the detriment of the legitimate interests of the end users. Enabling law enforcement agencies to access data by using standard police processes and without resorting to potentially extreme measures is a matter than can be given further attention. User cooperation in terms of witness support is necessary in this regard much like provisions in law are that can render such an option viable. Consideration also merits the disclosure of evidence under certain circumstances and especially with regard to the delivery of dependable forensic recovery output and examination of digital evidence.

## ON CYBERCRIME

While cybercriminal activity threatens economic interests at large recent research carried out by an IT security firm highlights that 72% of European personal computer users shop online, while 69% use the Internet for banking and 55% for paying bills.[1] The analysis follows claims made by the European Network Information Security Agency (ENISA) that online crime can threaten the economy of Europe. Of those surveyed, 22% suggested that they had experienced some form of electronic crime.[2]

Typically, prudent users of technology take security measures in order to protect the confidentiality, integrity and availability of their assets. This is particularly true for specific high value systems in such areas as banking, eGovernment, etc. As criminals tend to stand one step ahead though, attacks might occur in all sorts of ways. While typical cyber threats include for example, identity theft, spreading viruses, etc., physical abuse and breach of systems is not unheard of.

For example, when banks became smart in securing their ATMs, criminals started ripping them physically off the wall by using bulldozers. In this analysis, however, physical threats are not necessarily taken into consideration, in spite of the obvious connection that can be made between an attack and its effect.

Cybercrime can be seen as computer-mediated activity either illegal or considered illicit by certain parties and which is conducted through global electronic networks [Thomas and Loader, 2000]. To address digital forensics, a first general distinction is made between computers as targets of crime and computer-facilitated crime. While the former refers to crimes targeting computers or other electronic channels as such and include acts like unauthorized entry into computer systems, vandalism, virus attacks or warfare offensives, so called computer-facilitated crimes are in fact "traditional crimes that can be or have been committed by using other means of perpetration which are now carried out through an Internet based computer-related venue (e.g. e-mail, newsgroups, other networks) or other technological computing advancement"; or to put in other words crimes that use the computer as a medium to commit crimes [Transcrime Research Center, 2002]. The distinction is however not nearly as clear as it first appears, for example in cases of theft, computer cracking or espionage.

Computer-facilitated crime can be more systematically classified under three main traditional categories of crime: against persons, against property and against public order and public interest. With the explosion in electronic or computer facilitated communications it is highly unlikely that even traditional forms of crime do not leave some sort of digital trace behind. Again, criminal schemes often include acts belonging to more than one of the above-mentioned categories. Computer crime against persons includes:

- Breach of privacy (spamming, use of cookies, customer profiling, database trade, but also stalking or harassment)
- Identity theft (creation, marketing and selling of high quality false identification, link capture or site cloning for copying personal data)
- Hate crime (racial hatred, xenophobia, anti-Semitism, homophobia)
- Defamation (by email, message boards or websites)
- Blackmail (e.g. threatening to publish photos)
- Cyberstalking (e.g. via chat rooms)
- Prostitution (actually cyber-pimping, sexual exploitation and pornography, since prostitution as such is not a crime in many countries)
- Human, and especially women trafficking (recruitment, arranged marriages, advertisement of fake employment opportunities)
- Child exploitation (luring, pornography)

The most common forms of computer-facilitated crime against property are:

- Violation of intellectual property (piracy, downloading of films, music or other work, plagiarism, publishing work without author's permission)
- Violation of patent and trademark (copyrights and design rights, copying, distributing or selling of unlicensed computer software, trade secrets)
- Fraud (business or financial institution fraud such as credit card fraud or e-payment systems fraud, investment fraud, customer fraud such as online auction fraud, forgery and counterfeiting, etc.)
- Economic espionage
- Theft and embezzlement

Finally, a growing number of criminal violations committed through or facilitated by computers and the Internet can be regarded as crime against public order and public interest:

- Trafficking of a variety of illicit or protected goods, including: illicit drugs (all levels from import-export to retail), weapons, human organs, firework, protected animal species, stolen art, prescription drugs, etc.
- Gambling (internet casinos, game-boys)
- Money laundering (false documents, placement, layering, integration)
- Government espionage (theft of national defence information or data)
- Terrorism (recruiting, organization, virus attacks, *info wars*, bomb making instructions, money transfers, etc.)

It is clear that this vast range of illicit or unethical acts cannot be explained by one type of factors, causes or offender's individual motivations. '*Hacktivists*' for example, hackers pursuing in their intrusions a political aim or statement, are rather different than fraudsters misusing credit cards or paedophile networks distributing child pornography. Background and profile of cyber offenders differ a great deal among each other, as their offences do in terms of aims and skills involved. In cases of criminal acts or traditional offences that merely happen to involve the use of computers (for example in some forms of fraud or hate crime), cybercriminals may not differ much from those using other means to commit the offences [Thomas and Loader, 2000].

Most cybercrimes can be explained by the conjunction of three factors: motivation, opportunity and the lack of capable guardianship or formal control [Grabosky and Smith, 1998] [Grabosky, 2000]. Motivation can be individual of collective and can range from greed, lust, revenge, political commitment, respect seeking, challenge or adventure. For example, hackers and phreaks (telephone hackers) often use ICTs for the purpose of information, exploration or curiosity, but do not seek any financial profit. In contrast, so called 'information merchants and mercenaries' [Thomas and Loader, 2000] exploit ICTs for illegal financial gain, for example engaging in identity theft, illegal transfers of funds, or the illegal trade in information. Still, other offenders would use ICTs for illegal political or social activities including information warfare, political terrorism or the distribution or consumption of child pornography.

Criminal opportunities rapidly grow at the speed of change and innovation in technology arising from the convergence of communications and information technology. Enhancing the conditions that nurture crime, ICT has become available globally and at a high speed because under certain conditions it can ensure anonymity at technical and legal level; it is prevalently inexpensive and is easy to use if compared with other technologies that seek to achieve similar goals [Savona and Mignone, 2004]. Net users can remain anonymous, invent entirely new identities, disclose there aspects of their identities that would normally be kept hidden, and engage in activities or enter worlds previously unknown and far removed from their own immediate contexts [Jawkes, 2003: 15].

Several factors account for a weak control from private, national or international agencies on cybercrimes. Firstly, victims themselves whether corporate or individual are often incapable or unwilling to react due to a lack of technical resources and know-out, vested interests or unclear codes of conduct. Although market and technological solutions, self-help prevention, self-regulation and compliance are pivotal in effectively tackling computer crime, they often involve a degree of awareness and commitment that is not always present. Secondly, the global reach and multi-jurisdictional nature of computer-related crime poses great challenges to detect, investigate and prosecute cyber offenders by law enforcement agencies. Essential questions about which law applies, for which acts, by whom and how to do it, are all still open in the field of computer crime. As Grabosky aptly notes, the policing of computer crime often has prohibitive costs, it requires concerted international co-operation, which only exists infrequently (beyond issues such as child pornography or serious fraud) and has to cope with problems such as corruption, lack of resources and lack of expertise [Grabosky, 2000]. Traditional forms of policing and law enforcement strategies deployed for real-world crimes might be even ineffective against cybercrime [Brenner, 2006: 13]. Moreover, some of the reluctance to fully engage (or invest) in policing and regulating anti-social activities on the Internet (including preventive measures, data interception, or hacking offender's computers) is probably connected with fears about privacy and civil liberties violations, and with the further erosion of traditional notions of citizenship and sovereignty.

## SHIFTING TO FORENSICS

Electronic evidence is information and data that has investigative value and that is stored in electronic devices. Quite often such data is also transmitted by electronic means putting network neatly into the scope of cybercrime investigators. Evidence is acquired when data or physical items are collected and stored in order to be examined later (Rathmell and Valeri, 2002).

A forensics investigation means using disciplined investigative techniques to discover and analyse shreds of evidence left at a crime scene (DOJ 2001). Forensics investigation seeks to determine the source and full extent of a breach [Casey, 2004; Portesi, 2008]. Starting from an on-site investigation, the existing network, application infrastructure and flows of pertinent information are analysed to discover where the breach occurred or originated from [Ward, 2003; Caelli et al., 1991]. Forensics is closely related with electronic evidence, which in return is essential to resolve case of cybercrime. In digital forensics it is necessary to associate common information security objectives with the acts at hand and strive to associate evidence in the field with the implementation of the following information security principles [eEurope, 2002]:

- Confidentiality ensuring that information is accessible only to those authorized to have access, according to the International Standards Organization (ISO). Confidentiality is typically ensured through encryption.
- Integrity is the condition that exists when data is unchanged from its source and has not been modified, altered, or destroyed at any operation according to an expectation of data quality.
- Availability of data is the degree to which a system is operable and in a committable state at the start of an assignment.
- Accountability of parties involved for acts performed being held to account, scrutinised, and being required to give an account. Especially in white-collar crime, accountability is often associated with governance.

As the above-mentioned principles might only be observed within highly organized environments that operate on the basis of audited security policies and practices (e.g. in white collar crime investigated in a corporation) more mundane methods have to be employed to ensure that odd data is equally retrieved and exploited for the purpose of gaining access to critical information for the crime under investigation. Furthermore, in recent years a clear trend can be identified with regard to enhancing the information security preparedness of enterprises of all sizes. Additional methods to employ include the setting up of the social context of the data environment by conducting interviews with key personnel that can additionally offer a more wholesome understanding of the facts of the case at hand and to identify sources of forensics data. In this regard it is necessary to focus on specific frameworks and methods that allow investigators better filter the scores of data left behind by social networkers. Perhaps the opposite is the case when sparse data is left behind by savvy cyber criminals [ENISA, 2005; OECD, 2003]. Data becomes more valuable once the operational framework is established. On-site investigation is followed by a comprehensive analysis of case evidence. Data and facts collected can be stored in a secure and controlled manner, meeting stringent chain-of-custody requirements. Incident response and forensics investigation teams are capable of providing subject matter expert testimony to assist with prosecution or litigation support requirements. Digital evidence life cycle includes four phases being collection itself, examination, reporting and analysis. Below follows a brief presentation of these elements.

The collection phase requires the search for, recognition, collection, and documentation of electronic evidence. The collection phase addresses aspects of real-time information that may be lost unless precautions are taken early enough in the investigation process. Additionally, archived information is also critical, especially if there is risk of it being perished or deteriorating due to circumstances or poor storage conditions. The examination process allows presenting evidence, determining its provenance and designating its significance with reference to the specific crime under investigation, as it might be necessary. The examination process comprises of the following:

- Documenting the content and state of the evidence in order to allow all parties discover what is contained therein and it also includes searching for information that may be hidden or otherwise obscured.
- Analysing the product of investigation for its significance and evidential value to the case.
- Examining from a technical viewpoint through a forensic practitioner and an investigative team that may need to testify the conduct of the examination, the validity of the procedure and qualifications to carry out an examination.

When dealing with electronic evidence, general forensic and procedural principles are applied:

- Actions are taken to secure and collect electronic evidence in a way that cannot be changed.
- Examiners of electronic evidence are appropriately trained for the purpose.
- Activities relating to the seizure, examination, storage, or transfer of electronic evidence are fully documented, preserved, and made available for review.

Digital forensics methodologies recognize that digital media examinations do not resemble one another and although a generic process model may be recommended the situation on the ground will ultimately determine the quality of the collected results. Circumstances might significantly influence the outcome and examiners may sometimes need to adjust to evolving conditions on the ground.

Digital investigations usually involve actors across a number of countries that render cross-border and international cooperation inevitable. Multiple agencies across several jurisdictions might have to be involved in order to investigate and analyse suspicious activities. The various procedures implemented by each implicated agency have to be somehow reconciled in terms of formal as well as substantive features they have to allow for the seamless cooperation of the parties involved. Digital devices and media can be used as evidence much like any other piece of evidence can be used in support of a case. Documentation and evidence handling is, therefore, important in collecting, handling and temporarily storing these items. A computer system for example must be physically examined and an inventory of hardware components be compiled. Supporting documentation should include a physical description and detailed notation of features of the components in question.

In forensics investigations it is critical to gain sufficient understanding of the level of sophistication of the suspect and possibly of its behavioural pattern. Suspects need to be considered experts and they should be presumed to have installed countermeasures against eavesdropping or forensic techniques aiming at intercepting their communications or attacking their systems. Forensic penetration drills must remain quite indistinguishable from any other activity in and around the system under investigation. The risk in this case is associated with the capability of a suspect to render otherwise valuable data unusable by destroying evidence, e.g. by modifying drives, deleting files etc.

When examining a computer system, time information should be collected, preferably from the BIOS set-up while effort must be made to cross check time with other dependable sources (e.g. timestamps or other remote computers that might have been accessed). The date and time should be compared to a reliable time source and any differences be noted as appropriate. It is desirable that for critical applications time stamping or time marking be used to differentiate high reliance requirements from generic application environments. If networked, the computers under examination can be checked for log traces that might have been left on remote machines to piece their activity together. Examination of media should be conducted in a sound examination environment according to a prescribed methodology. Admittedly a critical element of media that relates to volatile memory is still missing. This is quite important due to the variety of personal identifiable information or other critical information that may be stored in volatile memory. In terms of process, examining original evidence media should be avoided and examinations of copies should be conducted instead. Special care must be reserved for special compartments that are hidden or encrypted. The use of strong encryption on data under scrutiny might significantly slow down forensic investigation and require the breaking of encryption keys prior to accessing recovered data.

In some cases the forensic process can be greatly facilitated through the use of intelligent agents. Intelligent agents are software elements that work without the assistance of physical users by making choices independently from them Choices are based on rules that have been identified and built into the software system that controls the agents [Luck et al., 2003]. Operational frameworks can be set up to ensure adherence to prevailing rules by autonomous agents. Basic duty of care must also be exercised to observe accountability. Intelligent agents can be used to carry out various tasks like for example automated tasks for the user through user agents e.g. sorting out emails according to the user's order of preference, assemble customized news reports etc. In forensics, user agents can be exploited to reveal habits and patterns of behaviour in investigating criminal acts. Predictive agents are used to carry out monitoring and surveillance tasks like observing and reporting on information systems. Such agents contribute to tracking company inventory; observing directories for e.g. competitor prices, follow patterns of behaviour for stock manipulation by insider trading and rumours, etc. Data mining agents use information technology to find trends and patterns in a heap of information that originates from several sources. Data mining agents detect market conditions and changes and relay them back to the decision maker. Launching intelligent agents for the purpose of collecting forensic evidence from on line sites can reduce significantly the repetitive manual tasks that are usually associated with forensic investigations. Limitations in the use of intelligent agents include their relative incapacity to investigate data held in encrypted or otherwise stealth form.

With a view to combating serious crimes like financial crime, money laundering, and terrorism, investigations have gained in importance especially when dealing with known individuals, who may be suspects. In the first instance as comprehensive a financial profile as possible is built. Such profile is then projected as far back in the past as it is possible, seeking traces of information in connected databases, the accounts of other individuals etc. Additional input is leveraged through connecting communication records to also validate a sequence of events and possibly set up a chronology. Raw data might include bank account details, credit card transactions, dialled numbers, network addresses, corporate registries, charity records, as well as data from electoral rolls and police records. The goal of such an investigation is to reconstruct the social context of the alleged criminals and reveal the spider's web of connections between the perpetrators and their financiers, trainers and supporters.

Forensic data recovery aims at addressing the needs of private individuals and organizations that have an enhanced need to prove what has really happened in the context of a breach or crime investigation associated with their computer systems. In case of a usual drive crash a mere home user or business needs but data backup services. Forensic data recovery is required when the user needs data recovered from a drive, or if you need to find out if a drive has been illegitimately tampered with, through a recovery process that can be used in a court of law. Without a full chain of custody report, and expert witnesses testifying, a case might be deemed weak. For example if a disgruntled business associate starts stealing company info the information owner could monitor the situation and come up with reporting that would eventually be debatable with regard to its admissibility and value before a Court. It can certainly help if forensic data recovery is employed to prove that a business associate acted purposely in a way that allows information assuming a legally usable form.

In spite of good efforts to systematically classify new and older forms of cybercrime, technology proves that such targets still remain elusive. Web 2.0 technologies, have shifted efforts from the application level to an environment or platform level that relies on a collaborative model of usage. Additionally collaborative environments in spite of the alleged benefits they pose with regard to productivity and managing of contact networks, they have been taking their toll in terms of breaches of privacy, personal data, identity fraud etc. In cybercrime chasing one single perpetrator might not be the case any longer as data propagates trough various loosely coupled environments sometimes leaving traces behind, while offering new opportunities for crime.

A recent addition to the digital forensics set up is called browser application forensics (BRAP forensics), that makes reference to browsers and applications data that is left behind when the application is already closed after a session with the user. Computer activity mining can lead to information associated with logs, timeline, keystrokes, imaging etc. Log analysis for example is the lynchpin of digital forensics that allows systems administrators to reverse engineer attacks and digital forensics investigators to reconstruct the sequence of events that led to or during the attack. BRAP forensics allows the accessing stored data as well as information regarding user behaviour that is based on the analysis of e.g. cookies as well as other information that is left behind by the browser. In spite of the obvious benefits of a behavioural analysis in case of investigating serious crime, the side effects on privacy deserve attention due to the absence of automated deletion of private data left behind by browsers once a session has ended [Berghel, 2008].

While digital evidence is any information of probative value that is either stored or transmitted in a binary form it includes computers as well as digital audio and video that uses digital data for the purpose of carrying out criminal acts by using digital means [SWGDE, 2000]. Forensics investigations depend on investigators that specialize on hardware, software, processes, security aspects, applications etc. Investigation entails the ability to uncover evidence from a computer as well as to follow proper methodology when collecting and handling evidence in a way that such evidence can be used in Court. It is necessary to underline the importance of sound preparation of the operational environment that is subjected to a forensics investigation. An organized environment is the responsibility of the administrators of systems in question. Good housekeeping helps out in this respect to obtain the desirable results and facilitate an investigation. Beyond housekeeping, auditable operational environments that function within the boundaries of measurable policies definitely give assurance and facilitate the work of forensic investigators [Mitrakas 2005a; Mitrakas 2005b].

Evidence collected during investigations needs to be successfully presented and withstand challenges by opponents. The forensic investigator should be able to defend himself and avert possible legal action against him by opponents who challenge the legality of the methods employed to collect and document forensic evidence. A critical consideration in this regard might associate with breaches of privacy of the party under investigation. Breaching the right to privacy might be a secondary concern for law enforcement agents however private investigators actually run significantly more risks that make them and the product of their investigations vulnerable.

From a corporate policy point of view there are a few considerations that need to be taken into account in order to prepare for and respond to possible forensic investigations. A privacy policy is an instrument that designates the limits of private sphere respected by the organization in question. Private sphere is a term that might invariably refer to employees, associates, customers or event the general public. Determining the limits of privacy respected by the organization at hand serves the duty to inform beforehand, ahead of possible investigations carried out. Other policies that are deemed to be relevant include Acceptable Use Policy that typically sets the limits of acceptable use of systems, applications and equipment. As employees or systems' users are informed beforehand they cannot claim that they were unaware of limitations to their actions and omissions pursuant to an investigation. An incident reporting policy is also useful to ensure that when incidents are detected they are properly reported to the appropriate entity within the organization.

## CHAIN OF CUSTODY

Appropriate documentation must describe procedures employed and processes followed as well as detailed notation of any known variations thereof [Ford and Baum, 2001]. Additionally, establishing the chain of custody through appropriate policy frameworks can be used in order to assess the quality of the collected data. Chain of custody investigations may also help in establishing the hierarchical structure that prevailed at the time that the acts under investigation were committed. Policy for forensics may address the practices of forensics agents and labs in investigating cybercrime.

Chain of custody entails the clear identification of each person that has handled evidence during investigations. Each of those persons may have to testify in order to corroborate evidence that they came across for the purpose of ensuring that evidence has not been altered since it was collected. By limiting the number of persons that come in contact with evidence, the overall exposure of the evidence to tampering and foul play is limited [Casey 2004]. In many ways the concept of chain of custody in a digital environment is not substantially different from what applies in a crime scene of the real world. An officer that collects a gun at the crime scene typically places it in plastic wrapping (bag, container etc.) and hands it over to a specialised forensics expert. At the lab the forensics expert tries to connect the gun with the specific crime scene and the victim in specific. All operations carried out on the gun are duly documented along with the names of all parties that come in contact with evidence. Rarely is the purpose of the forensics investigator to come up with the smoking gun. The mail goal is to ensure that no stone has been left unturned and that the crime scene has been investigated from all possible angles. As an investigator intervenes well after a crime has taken place meticulous search is a task that prevails over catching the actor on the act when it comes to forensics investigation.

In an electronic environment, physical evidence, such as a computer's hard drive has to be documented just like any other piece of hard evidence found in a crime scene. Differently than with the case of Greater risks apply when accessing the content of the resource under investigation, e.g. a hard disk drive, because in a digital environment evidence is easier to manipulate and eventually discredit evidence. All parties that access the content of the resource should be documented. The first action when the forensics expert accesses a resource is to register the findings in order to use as leads later.

Chain of custody is documented in terms of reports that identify all parties that have come across evidence from the moment it arrives at a forensic data recovery lab. And even before if this is the case. It is also necessary to ensure that forensic experts working on data recovery and investigation are bound by confidentiality and non conflict of interest duties that disallows them spreading the word on any specific case. Records associated with chain of custody are maintained to ensure the integrity of evidence. Additionally the authenticity of evidenced should be analyzed and presented in a dedicated document. Procedures for accepting, storing and retrieving documents may also help in case investigators are summoned to testify in order to corroborate evidence or claims based thereupon. In a chain of custody environment it is required that data be kept properly copied, transported and stored. Additionally information should be kept in the same form that it was found without any additions, changes or deletions. Media should be secured throughout the lifecycle of evidence. The list below presents elements that can contribute to producing sound chains of custody:

- Documentation regarding method selected and planning.
- Inventory of medial collected for investigation.
- Audit logs, documenting searches by authorized party.

Roles and responsibilities in digital forensics include a forensics expert who can support the investigation and appropriate build up and presentation of a case. The tasks of a forensics expert include the following:

- Ascertaining whether the media seized may contain information that is interesting for the investigation at hand.
- Supporting and/or carrying out interviews with parties involved.
- Retrieving information by using forensics methods.
- Drafting briefs for the attorney and the Court.
- Acting as expert witness as it might be necessary.

Process wise, a forensics expert needs to create a mirror image of the drive at hand, in order to ensure that no alterations take place after the device has been seized and put in custody. A mirror image serves the purpose of preserving data as a large number of alterations occur when a computer is turned on that may influence the evidential outcome with regard to critical dates and activity related to the allegations under investigation. The forensics expert may use hash codes in order to enhance chain of custody. The investigator computes the hash value and the result is associated to data under investigation. Hashing is a one-way function that results in all changes made to the original data being detected. Hashing is used in several application areas including public key encryption.

When it comes to recordable media retrieval is possible through the allocation management used. When deleting a file the user does not see the file itself anymore and the file space is marked as free or unallocated space. The space remains like this until another file is overwritten in this very space. Advanced forensic techniques can be used to retrieve files whose space has been re-allocated or re-written several times. Even shreds of files can be leveraged upon to draw conclusions in a case in spite of the fact that space ahs been re-written several times. These are all clues that can be used by forensics expert to produce evidence in a case under investigation in spite of the fact that files have been apparently deleted. With proper forensics tools unallocated space as well as hidden pockets of data and can be accessed and data can be recovered by the forensic investigator. Hidden information concerns details about the activity on the computer on a network such as cookies and document files that have been accessed, using the computer under investigation. File metadata routinely stored on a file made in an application such as a word processor for example can also reveal pertinent data that can be deemed useful by an investigator.

Labeling physical objects collected such as cables, plugs, peripherals, computers, monitors, disks, and wireless access points makes good organizational sense. If a site has to be torn and reassembled in a lab, labels and associated lists make sure that connectivity is appropriate to re-construct the computer image required. Having a witness for every recorded activity is good practice with regard to specific activities carried out on the evidence collected. Labels, photos and data that are signed digitally or physically by an additional expert add to the credibility of the examination. An indisputable chain of custody requires that all evidence collected is uniquely identified within its own context by using e.g. bar codes alongside lists and descriptions. Chain of custody practice also requires keeping physical evidence behind lock and key. Electronic evidence can also be secured by using hashing algorithms that ensure the integrity of data collected and classified by the investigator.

## LEGAL CONSIDERATIONS

In Europe, there are still important gaps across the EU member state laws that address cyber-crime. While some countries have preferred to reform criminal codes, others have decided to pass specific laws on computer related crime, which were eventually included in the criminal code. Still some other countries do not have any legal provisions regarding cybercrime whatsoever [Savona and Mignone, 2004]. At European level, efforts have aimed at regulating the most press-ing and critical issues in sight. The Council of Europe Convention on Cybercrime (2001) and the Council Framework Decision on Attacks against Information Systems (2003) are both attempts to categorize and regulate the problem and they are closely connected and their definitions overlap, offences being defined as follows: illegal access, illegal interception, data interference, system interference, and misuse of devices.

Article 15 the Convention on Cybercrime of the Council of Europe stipulates that investigative powers and procedures are subject to conditions and safeguards provided for under domestic law in a way that provides for adequate protection of human rights and liberties. The protection afforded to citizens must be commensurate with the procedure or power concerned. Currently, this Convention is non-binding pending ratifica-tion by member states' parliaments [CoE 2001b; CoE 2001b]. However this Convention makes significant steps towards defining crimes related to computer systems.

The EU has also launched a number of initia-tives to tackle computer-related crime including the EU Action Plan for eEurope 2005 (2002) the

Communication Network and Information Security: Proposal for a European Policy Approach, COM (2001) 298 of 6 June 2001, and Creating a Safer Information Society by improving the Security of Information Infrastructures and combating computer-related crime, COM (2000) 890 of 22 January 2001 [Mitrakas 2006a; Mitrakas 2007]. Next to the output of the Council of Europe and the European Commission, legislation originating from the OECD can also be highlighted [OECD 1997; OECD 2002]. This legislative activity in the form of Action Plans and communications aim at preventing the exploitation of children on the Internet (child pornography), attacks against computers, economic crimes related to unauthorized access such as sabotage, intellectual property offences and privacy offences, computed-related fraud, and to a lesser extent cover issues such as racist acts and computer-related forgery. Cybercrime law protects certain rights and assets such as privacy by rendering illegal the interception and unauthorized access thereto. To investigate cybercrime and crimes carried out with the help or by information technology, law enforcement agencies seek access to the content of communications, data in transit, stored data and authentication data.

With regard to digital evidence it is important to highlight the purpose of the collection, which is to render it admissible in Court, as it might be required. The admissibility of electronic evidence greatly depends on the meticulousness of and the documentation surrounding the collection of that material. Sensitive information must also be subject to additional safeguards in terms of handling and storing it due to repercussions on third parties that might unintentionally be tangled. In the past concerns associated with the admissibility of electronic evidence have been instigated by ambiguities on the admission of electronic documents as evidence. The form that evidence assumes is essential to its admissibility. Law has developed criteria on the admission of electronic evidence that can reinforce the position of digital evidence collected in a crime scene.

When errors occur, evidence presented might be put in doubt. Case law stipulates that computer records can generally be admitted as private documents that make up business records if they were maintained according to a routine procedure for objectives they seek to assure accuracy about. In a case in the US (United States v. Salgado, 250 F3d 438, 6th Circuit, 2001) telephone records presented by prosecution, were challenged by the defendant who required the error rate of the telephone company whose telephone lines had been tapped. As the Court held that the prosecutor only had to provide evidence that the telephone company's records were sufficiently accurate, the actual computer programmer did not have to testify to authenticate computer records. Gradually case law has shifted from a single minded approach towards computer records and it has accepted the fact that there varying types thereof. Computer records that contain text can be computer-generated records or computer-stored, like it has been adjudicated in a case in the US (People v. Holowko, 486 N.E.2d 877, 878-79, Ill. 1985). Computer-stored records have been generated by natural person and they are stored in electronic form, like emails for example. In Common Law countries, such records would have to comply with the hearsay rule just like any testimony or documentary piece of evidence containing human statements must do. The trustworthiness of the record must be corroborated by a statement of a witness, as well as other technical means such as electronic signatures for example [Mitrakas 2006a]. By contrast computer-generated, such as system logs, automated receipts and notices and such like, do not contain statements of any natural person in specific. They are the output of a computer program that processes input according to a specific pattern or algorithm. Since it is a computer rather than a natural person that creates the record the interest of the Court rests with the good functioning of the computer at the time the record was generated. This requirement calls for ensuring the authenticity mechanisms that concern electronic records [Mitrakas and Polemi, 2007].

Evidence assumes two major components, the formal requirements and the material requirements. The formal requirements are drawn up in the civil procedure legislation and they refer to the means of evidence that are admissible. The material requirements concern the credibility of evidence submitted in a case. Security measures can be used to safeguard and evaluate the evidential value of electronic messages in open eCommerce [Poullet and Vanderberghe, 1998]. With respect to the admissibility of electronic documents as evidence is of paramount importance to invoke the credibility of electronic evidence methods. Admissibility requirements must relate to network and information security requirements and address also third parties such as insurers, the administration, customs, etc. are not necessarily part of the crime under investigation, which may, however, provide appropriate evidence in support of an investigation. Continental European legal systems generally require that all means of evidence, irrespectively of the form they assume, can be admitted in legal proceedings. A general framework has been drawn up which can accommodate all means, unless it is deemed otherwise. The Court may assess the value in each case of the produced piece of evidence. Within this context any kind of computer-generated evidence can be admissible, provided that specific requirements with regard to collection constraints are respected. These constraints are individually introduced in each member state under question [Poullet and Vanderberghe, 1988]. Few countries in Europe lists the acceptable means of evidence (e.g. Greek Civil Procedure); however even in those limited cases a clear trend has been marked towards the conditional acceptance of electronic evidence in court, which is carried out through appropriate interpretation of the Statute.

## FUTURE DIRECTIONS

Digital forensics requires additional attention from a research and implementation viewpoint. Accelerating cybercrime investigation will result in a speedier turnover of cases while broadening the success rate of successfully arresting and prosecuting cyber criminals. Future priorities in digital forensics may include measures such as the ones presented below. In this regard forensic methodologies can be developed in such a way as to provide a holistic answer to digital forensics. Currently available methodologies suffer from a compartmentalised approach that addresses specific, high priority areas; however special attention must be paid to a generic model that addresses all aspects of the problem.

It is necessary to enhance the ability to pin point the origin of cyber attacks regardless of the form they assume (e.g. a virus outbreak, serious crime etc.). This might require enhancing the ability of law enforcement agencies to manage and process encrypted data as well as to rely on data stored by service providers. Putting the service provider in the position of the safe keeper of collected data until such time as it might become necessary to process might also be a valuable extension of the legal framework such as the requirements emanating from Directive 00/31/EC on electronic commerce. Additionally, enhancing the ability to collect evidence in volatile environments and tracing stolen information (e.g. identity theft) emerges as an important requirement in collaborative Web 2.0 as well as in cases where identity is instrumental in carrying out an illegal act. Identity management systems can be of help by storing and safekeeping information for longer periods of time. Additionally the ability to gain access to damaged memory chips including smart cards is an additional requirement. Collecting data in unfriendly or otherwise uncooperative environments especially to investigate cases of cyberterrorism or other serious crimes is an additional matter of concern. Data retention has become a requirement for service providers as a result of Directive 2006/24/EC on the retention of data processed in connection with the provision of public electronic communication services and amending Directive 2002/58/EC. The scope of this Directive has been to harmonise provisions concerning the obligations of the providers of publicly available electronic communications services or of public communications networks with respect to the retention of certain data which are generated or processed by them, in order to ensure that the data are available for the purpose of the investigation, detection and prosecution of serious crimes.

A step further in this direction is the reporting of security incidents that would provide authorities with a coherent view regarding common vulnerabilities and risks associated with specific cases under investigation. In spite of the obvious difficulty to promulgate legislation in this regard, in other areas of interest such as port security, for example, legislation has made it mandatory to report incidents, as per Directive 2005/65/EC on enhancing port security. In spite of the practical problems caused by storing large amounts of data, that often includes scores of spam, data retention as well as reporting of security incidents can enhance the ability of authorities to act and react when faced with cybercriminal activity [ENISA, 2006]. Rendering obligatory the reporting of security breaches is a good step that could enhance public confidence and improve the analysis of data associated with attacks as collected by appropriate organisations (e.g. Computer Emergency Response Teams). Such material can be further linked with the results of digital forensics investigations in order to corroborate electronic evidence. The risk, in case of fraud, is that the spiralling influence of cybercrime will erode public trust on electronic communications and compromise the use of electronic communication means as a valid way to carry out dependable communications, as it has been vividly illustrated by experts in the US [PITAC, 2005]. The effectiveness of these measures can be further boosted through greater cross-border cooperation would also enhance the ability of law enforcement agencies to gain access to records kept beyond their jurisdiction as well as structured cooperation among various services that monitor, received reports, analyse and investigate incidents for the purpose of trailing digital suspects [Mitrakas and Zaitch, 2006c].

The harmonisation of penalties and legislation with regard to specific cybercrimes, like e.g. denial of service, hacking, etc. across EU member states may help but is just a part of a larger picture. As economic crime and terrorism mark the trend for the crime to combat in the future legislation might result in the bending of civil liberties and guaranties afforded to citizens. The selective application of such rights might erode the confidence of citizens to the ability of law enforcement agency to appropriately safeguard their rights and carry out the anti-crime fight effectively, that both can have a significant content as well as a symbolic component for the society. The fight against cybercrime must take into account the effective protection of civil liberties and forensic processes must also reflect this assertion when a suspected crime is under investigation.

Finally connecting forensic investigation with technology might additionally yield good results in supporting the application of law and assisting the operations of law enforcement agencies. Especially the areas of identity management, privacy enhancing technologies etc., can help linking actions to specific actors for the purpose of crime investigation especially in view of emerging technologies and collaborative environments such as Web 2.0.

## CONCLUSION

Cybercrime poses new challenges for law enforcement agencies, investigators, forensic examiners and managers. The complexities of policing the Net are connected with many issues, including the great variety in offences, types offenders and their motivations, technological opportunities and innovations, legal frameworks, expertise, resources and the concerns about privacy and liberty issues. To respond to cybercrime, technical and organizational measures are necessary in an effort to support the legal framework in force. More effective co-operation of law enforcement agencies across jurisdictional boundaries as well as greater involvement of service providers are two possible measures. While such requirements can be compounded under a policy framework that is followed across borders full-scale harmonisation of policies on criminal law and legal processes is likely to only take place at a regional level (e.g. the EU) rather than at a global scale. Along with the assumption that safe havens where criminals could operate from are not likely to be contained any time soon, leads to the not-so-optimistic-conclusion that cyber-crime is here to stay and it is likely to remain of the rise. The trend to shift the burden of crime fighting directly to businesses operating on the Internet is a way forward since these are the major beneficiaries of Internet as a medium for electronic transactions. However the greater public interest should also be defended in view of consumers, citizens and less technology savvy users accessing the internet increasingly more to carry out day-to-day transactions. Most importantly the application of civil liberties should not be put under question because of the advent of forensic investigations as mechanism to respond to cybercrime. Cross-border investigations can, however, be greatly facilitated by initiatives aiming at effective mutual assistance arrangements, which have to go beyond the EU, since crime does not stop at the outer EU boundaries. It is difficult to think of effective prevention strategies without more cooperation among national authorities and between them and industry players.

Cross platform investigations in collaborative Web 2.0 environments are an emerging challenge especially with regard to identity theft and privacy breaches. The ability to snatch, store and use personal data in a social networking environment poses new challenges to law enforcement that requires the collaboration of the service providers. Additionally, forensics can become sensitive to lateral requirements in information technology including identity management techniques and privacy enhancing technologies that can help linking actions to specific actors for the purpose of crime investigation. Evidence can be gathered to support one's own defence in case of litigation. Additionally evidence can be used as a way to invoke better corporate procedures and accountability while deterring insider threat. Forensic readiness that complements the security set-up of an organisation can improve security posture and provide coverage from cybercrime.

## NOTE

This article represents the authors' personal views and not those of any organization whatsoever including the authors' employers. The authors would like to thank Mrs. Isabella Santa and Dr. Silvia Portesi for their valuable input in the preparation of this chapter.

## REFERENCES

Basel (2001). Basel Committee on Banking Supervision. *Overview of The New Basel Capital Accord.* Bank of International Settlements.

Berghel, H. (2008). BRAP Forensics. *Communications of the ACM, 51*(6), 15-20.

Brenner, S. (2006). Cybercrime: re-thinking crime control strategies. In Y. Jewkes (Ed.), *Crime Online, Committing, Policing and Regulating Cybercrime*. Devon: Willan Publishing.

Caelli, W., Longley, D., & Shain, M. (1991). *Information Security Handbook*. Macmillan.

Casey, E. (2004). *Digital evidence and computer crime* (second edition). Amsterdam: Elsevier.

CEC (2001). Communication From The Commission to the Council, the European Parliament, the European Economic and Social Committee and the Committee of the Regions, *Network And Information Security: Proposal For A European Policy Approach.*

CoE (2001a). Council of Europe. *Explanatory Report to the Convention on Cybercrime.*

CoE (2001b). Council of Europe, *Convention on Cybercrime and explanatory memorandum,* Strasbourg, France: European Committee on Crime Problems.

DOJ (2001). *Electronic Crime Scene Investigation: A Guide for first responders.* Washington, DC: United States Department of Justice.

eEurope (2002). *Identification and Authentication in eGovernment.* eEurope Smart Card Charter TB2, A policy report.

ENISA (2006). *Mapping the regulatory NIS activities of Europe: ENISA publishing inventory & assessment report on EU regulatory activity in NIS.* Heraklion, Crete: ENISA.

ENISA (2005). *Raising Awareness in Information Security - Insight and Guidance for Member States.* Heraklion, Crete: ENISA.

Ford, W., & Baum, M. (2001). *Secure Electronic Commerce* (2nd edition). Prentice-Hall.

Grabosky, P. (2000). Computer Crime: A Criminological Overview. Paper for the *Tenth United Nations Congress on the Prevention of Crime and the Treatment of Offenders.* Vienna, Austrian Institute of Criminology.

Grabosky, P., & Smith, R. (1998). *Crime in the Digital Age: Controlling Telecommunications and Cyberspace Illegalities.* Sydney: The Federation Press.

ISO (2000). ISO/IEC 17799:2000 *Information technology: Code of practice for information security management.* URL: hhtp://www.iso17799.net

Jawkes, Y. (2003). Policing the Net: crime, regulation and surveillance in cyberspace. In Y. Jewkes, (Ed.), *Dot.cons. Crime, deviance and identity on the Internet.* Devon: Willan Publishing.

Luck, A., Macburney, P., & Preist C. (2003). *Agent technology: enabling next generation computing.* Agentlink.

Mitrakas, A. (2005a). Policy Frameworks for Secure Electronic Business. In M. Khosrow-Pour (Ed.), *Encyclopedia of Information Science and Technology,* Volume I-V. Hershey: IGI Publishing.

Mitrakas, A. (2005b). Soft Law constraints in eGovernment. In *Proceedings of BILETA 2005* (British Irish Law Education & Technology Association), Belfast, 7 April 2005.

Mitrakas, A. (2006a). Information security and Law in Europe: Risks checked? *Information and Communication Technology Law,* Carfax.

Mitrakas, A., & van Eecke, P. (2006b). Commentary on Directive 1999/93 on a Community framework for electronic signatures. In A. Buellesbach, Y. Poullet, & C. Prins (Eds.) *Concise European IT Law.* Alphen aan de Rijn: Kluwer Law International.

Mitrakas, A., & Zaitch, D. (2006c). Law, cybercrime and digital forensics: trailing digital suspects. In Kanellis, P., Kiountouzis, E., Kolokotronis, N., Martakos, D., *Digital Crime and Forensic Science in Cyberspace.* Hershey: IGI Publishing.

Mitrakas, A. (2007). Annex II, Legal and policy aspects of Network Information Security. In C. Douligeris, & D. Seripanos, *Network Information Security.* Wiley (IEEE Publication).

Mitrakas, A., & Polemi, D. (2007). Trustworthy eInvoice Services. In J. Malkolm, & G. Orthofer, *eTaxation: State & Perspectives*, Johannes-Kepler Universitaet Linz: Trauner Verlag.

OECD (1997). *Recommendation of the Council concerning guidelines for cryptography policy*, ver. 27 March 1997, Paris 1997.

OECD (2002). *Guidelines for the Security of Information Systems and Networks: Towards a Culture of Security*, Paris, 2002.

OECD (2003). *Guidelines for Protecting Consumers from Fraudulent and Deceptive Commercial Practices Across Borders*, Paris, 2003.

PITAC (2005). President's Information Technology Advisory Committee, *Cyber Security: A crisis in prioritisation*, COITRD, Arlington (2005).

Pfleeger, C. (2000). *Security in Computing*, Prentice Hall.

Portesi, S. (2008). *The challenges faced by police forces in searching and seizing in situ computer evidence during criminal investigations*, Ph.D. Thesis, Univestity of Trento.

Poullet, Y., & Vanderberghe, G.P.V. (Eds.) (1998). *Telebanking, Teleshopping and the Law.* Deventer: Kluwer.

Rathmell, A., & Valeri, L. (2002). *Handbook of Legislative Procedures of Computer and Network Misuse in EU Countries*, Study for the European Commission Directorate-General Information Society, Rand Europe.

Reed, C. (2000). *Internet Law: Text and Materials.* London: Butterworths.

Savona, E., & Mignone, M. (2004). The Fox and the Hunters: How IC Technologies Change the Crime Race, *European Journal on Criminal Policy and Research, 10*, 3-26Kluwer Academic Publishers.

Scholz, P. (2003). *Datenschutz beim Internet Einkauf*, Nomos.

Scientific Working Group on Digital Evidence (SWGDE) (2000). International Organization on Digital Evidence (IOCE), Digital Evidence: Standards and Principles 1999, in *Forensic Science Communications*, April 2000, 2(2). URL: http://www.fbi.gov/hq/lab/fsc/backissu/april2000/swgde.htm

Thomas, D., & Loader, B. (2000). Introduction - Cybercrime: law enforcement, security and surveillance in the information age. In D. Thomas & B. Loader (Eds.) *Cybercrime: law enforcement, security and surveillance in the information age.* London: Routlege.

Transcrime Research Centre (2002). University of Trento *Transatlantic Agenda EU/US Co-operation for Preventing Computer Related Crime – Final Report.*

Ward, J. (2003). *Towards a Culture of Security*, Information Security Bulletin, February 2003.

## ADDITIONAL READING

Jones, K.J., Bejtlich, R., & Rose, C.W. (2005). *Digital Forensics: Computer Security and Incident Response.* Addison Wesley Professional.

FIDIS. (2006). *Forensic Implications of identity Management Systems.* URL: http://www.fidis.net

Middleton, B. (2004). *Cyber Crime Investigator's Field Guide*, Second Edition. Boca Raton, FL: Auerbach Publications.

Politis, D., Papasteriadou, N., & Gallardo, M. A. (2003). The Impact of New Technologies on Forensic Engineering and Expert Witnessing in Courts of Law. In D. Politis & N. Papasteriadou (Eds.), *Recent Advances in Court Computerisation and*

*Legal Databases – First steps towards e-Justice*. Athens: Ant. N. Sakkoulas Publishers.

## KEY TERMS

**E-Banking:** Automated delivery of new and traditional banking products and services directly to customers through electronic, interactive communication channels. Customers may access e-banking services using intelligent electronic devices: networked personal computers (PCs), handheld devices like personal digital assistants (PDAs), automated teller machines (ATMs), kiosks, or Touch Tone telephones.

**E-Business:** The application of Information and Communication Technologies (ICTs) to conducting business.

**Identity Theft:** The situation where someone unlawfully uses another person's personal information to obtain credit or services, make purchases, cash checks, or apply and receive loans.

**IPR Theft:** Abbreviation for Intellectual Property Rights theft, eroding the market for genuine goods and services. It has to do with the importation and sale of counterfeit goods, and the infringement of copyrights, trademarks, and patents, caused by insufficient protection of trade secrets and other intellectual property.

**Malware:** Neologism meaning "malicious software". It refers to software programs designed to damage or commit other unwanted actions on a computer system.

## ENDNOTES

1. http://www.sans.org/newsletters/newsbites/newsbites.php?vol=10&issue=48, on study by AVG Technologies and IPSOS.
2. For a presentation of current and future threats: http://www.enisa.europa.eu/rmra/er_current_risks_01.html, last visited on 6 July 2008.

# Chapter XI
# An Analysis of Privacy and Security in the Zachman and Federal Enterprise Architecture Frameworks

**Richard V. McCarthy**
*Quinnipiac University, Hamden, Greece*

## ABSTRACT

*Enterprise architecture has had a resurgence of interest in the IT community in the past ten year; in part because of a mandate for federal agencies of the United States government and in part because of the complexity of managing today's information systems environments. It has become a critical component of an overall IT governance program to provide structure and documentation to describe the business processes, information flows, technical infrastructure and organizational management of an information technology organization. Many different enterprise architecture frameworks have emerged over the past ten years. Two of the most widely used enterprise architecture frameworks (the Zachman Framework and the Federal enterprise architecture framework) are described and their ability to meet the security and privacy needs of an organization is discussed. These frameworks represent a contrast of industry and government perspectives in addressing issues of key importance to senior IT leadership.*

## INTRODUCTION

Information technology management has become increasingly complex over the past fifteen to twenty years. Technical infrastructure has grown from a single mainframe environment to a complex hybrid of mainframes, client-server and web architectures. Software development is continuously evolving as the demand for new IT services in many organizations is ever increasing. end-user expectations of IT services continue to rise. Change is constant; for many organizations it has become the business norm. Companies seek to reinvent themselves or must prove that they can adapt to remain competitive. The ability to react quickly is a critical component of many companies' business strategy. As a result, the need for organizations' information technology to be defined in a standardized structure has become critical. Over the past ten years there has been a greater emphasis on standardization of information technology services to enable organizations to better manage their technology resources as well as their portfolio of requests for changes of those IT resources. Standardization provides greater opportunities for reuse; a key concept of the emergent service oriented architecture. Several enterprise architecture frameworks have been widely adopted to help organizations document, describe and manage their information technology environment and its relationship to the business that it supports. Several of these have been consolidated and have emerged as the *frameworks of choice* amongst many organizations.

Information technology governance has heightened the growing need to ensure that technology resources are secure and to adequately protect the privacy of the vast amounts of information that they contain. In the United States, the Sarbanes-Oxley Act of 2002 caused a frenzy of information systems change as organizations raced to ensure that their information systems controls were in compliance.

The Zachman Framework and the Federal Enterprise Architecture Framework are two widely adopted enterprise architecture frameworks. These frameworks are evaluated to analyze the extent to which they provide guidance to meet the privacy and security needs of organizations.

Several other frameworks exist. Some are highly specialized and others are designed to be adaptable. Some, such as the Department of Defense Architecture Framework (DoDAF) specifically identify privacy and security guidelines and standards that must be adhered to; others, such as The Open Group Architecture Framework (TOGAF) provide a general set of guidelines to deal with privacy and security issues.

This chapter begins by providing a definition of enterprise architecture. It then describes the Zachman and Federal Enterprise Architecture Frameworks. These were chosen because they are two of the most widely adopted enterprise architecture frameworks and because they have a sharp contrast in their approach. The chapter then concludes with a critical analysis of how well each framework meets the privacy and security needs of their users.

## ENTERPRISE ARCHITECTURE

Bernard (2004) defines enterprise architecture as a management program and a documentation method that is combined to perform an actionable and coordinated view of the enterprise strategy, business processes, and resource utilization and information flow.

Schekkerman (2005) defines enterprise architecture as "a complete expression of the enterprise; a master plan which 'acts as a collaboration force' between aspects of business planning such as goals, visions, strategies and governance principles, aspects of business operations such as business terms, organization structures, processes and data, aspects of automation such as information systems and databases; and the enabling technological infrastructure of the business such as computers, operating systems and networks."

Rico (2006, p.1) defines enterprise architecture as "a comprehensive framework or taxonomy of systems analysis models for aligning organizational strategy with information technology. Strategies are plans to satisfy organizational goals and objectives by competing, based upon size, cost, variety, speed, quality, uniqueness or innovation. Information technology refers to the computers, software and networks used for safely storing, processing, retrieving, and transmitting data and information. There is an expectation that organizations can satisfy their goals and objectives by aligning their strategy with their information technology. Enterprise architecture consists of defining an organization's (a) scope, (b) business model, (c) system model, (d) technology model, and (e) components."

The Federal Enterprise Architecture Framework (FEAF) (CIO Council, 2001) describes enterprise architecture as "a strategic information asset base, which defines the mission, the information necessary to perform the mission and the technologies necessary to perform the mission, and the transitional processes for implementing new technologies in response to the changing mission needs. Enterprise architecture includes the baseline architecture, target architecture, and a sequencing plan."

While enterprise architecture has been defined in many different ways each definition incorporates several common characteristics: they are holistic in scope, they include an integrated view of information technology processes, and they provide a description of the current technological environment, the desired technological state that an organization seeks to achieve and a plan to get from the current state to the desired state.

Enterprise architecture provides a view of the organization from four perspectives: (1) business, (2) technological, (3) information and (4) application. The business perspective outlines the key business functions, defining what is done, by whom and where within the organization the process takes place. The technological perspective describes the current information technology architecture and the desired technological architecture. Technological architectures vary by organization. A well defined enterprise architecture takes into account the varied needs caused by different environments. The information perspective provides a description of the current information architecture, the future needs and a map to achieve those needs. The application perspective provides a view to move the organizations current systems applications to their desired state. For example, El Sawy, Malhotra, Gosain and Young (1999) point out that enterprise architecture is an integral part of competing in an electronic economy.

Schekkerman (2005) surveyed 79 companies that are interested in enterprise architecture. Several reasons for the use of enterprise architecture frameworks were identified, each of which suggests that the overarching rationale for enterprise architecture implementation is the support of strategic information technology issues and decision making within an organization. Specific reasons for enterprise architecture use included using it as a road map for change, utilizing it to help manage the IT portfolio or support budget prioritization, helping support mergers and acquisitions, delivering new insights into the business and supporting decision making.

Enterprise architecture is comprehensive in its scope. It provides a guide for organizations to manage complex technology environments and to be able to provide a road map to help organizations achieve their business objectives.

## Enterprise Architecture Framework Core Components

Enterprise architecture frameworks have five core components that must be supported. These include:

1. **Alignment:** Providing a framework to improve alignment of business and information technology objectives. This should also serve as a communication tool to assist in aligning business and information technology objectives.
2. **Integration:** Establishing an infrastructure that enables business rules to be consistently applied across the organization, documents data flows, uses and interfaces.
3. **Value creation:** The economic value of information technology is better measured in an environment where there is a higher

potential for reusable hardware and software assets.

4. **Change management:** Establishing a consistent infrastructure and formalizing the management of the infrastructure and information assets better enables an organization-wide change management process to be established to handle information technology changes.
5. **Compliance:** Enterprise architecture provides the artifacts necessary to ensure legal and regulatory compliance for the technical infrastructure and environment.

These critical elements are accomplished by looking at how information technology supports an organization from four principle perspectives:

1. **Business architecture:** This is a result of defining the information technologies and strategies required to support the strategic goals and objectives of an organization. This generally assumes that the critical business processes within an organization are well defined and well understood.
2. **Information architecture:** The information architecture identifies the business information required to support both the current and future business architecture. A key component of enterprise architecture is to define the current and future state of an information technology organization so that plans can be developed to bridge that gap.
3. **Application architecture:** This identifies the application infrastructure required to support the strategic goals and objectives of the organization. It supports the efficient use of organization resources to support those goals and objectives. It provides a description of the interactions and interdependencies of the suite of organizational systems
4. **Technical architecture:** This identifies the current technical infrastructure as well as the target platform needed to support the target business architecture (Shupe and ehling, 2006).

Weill and Ross (2005) demonstrated that enterprise architecture is a critical component of an IT governance program and that effective governance aligns IT investments with business priorities. In a survey of 300 companies worldwide they concluded that a correlation between superior governance and superior financial results was achieved when the enterprise architecture was one of the critical strategic drivers in place within an information technology organization.

Enterprise architecture is comprehensive in scope. To effectively meet the needs of an organization it must also provide a framework that ensures that the security and privacy needs are included to secure organizational assets.

## Security and Enterprise Architecture Frameworks

Security infrastructure has become a critical component of the enterprise architecture of an organization. Organizations much secure their information from numerous internal and external threats.

Shupe and Behling (2006) identify information security elements to include:

1. *Security policies* that identify what areas employees should avoid or consider dangerous in the use of the organizations information technology. It must be updated regularly.
2. *Firewalls* to control legitimate and illegitimate access to the technical infrastructure of an organization.
3. *Authentication* is needed to provide a balance between the strong password protection policies and reasonable system access.
4. *Encryption* is required to secure the information infrastructure of an organization.

Information assets have become a target security threat

5. *Patching and change management* is essential to enable the technical infrastructure to remain current with all available hardware and software intrusion prevention capabilities.
6. *Intrusion detection and network monitoring* is vital to ensure that ongoing monitoring takes places to vigorous safeguard the organizational technical infrastructure against continuous security threats.

## ZACHMAN FRAMEWORK

The most widely used of the formal enterprise architecture framework models is the Zachman Framework. Developed in 1987, it defines a logical construct to control the interfaces and components of an information systems environment and provides a standardized method for considering all aspects of an information technology infrastructure. The framework utilizes a series of cells to describe the information, business and technical flows. These are organized by data, function, network, people, time and motivation that are principally driven by the business requirements of an organization. The framework successfully combines people, data and technology to show a comprehensive view of the inter-relationships within an information technology organization. It is principally driven by business requirements and although some standardized documentation is prescribed (e.g., data dictionary), it does not contain the formalized documentation structure of the Federal Enterprise Architecture Framework or the Department of Defense Architecture Framework models. It does however; present a formal picture of an entire enterprise from the perspectives of owner, designer and builder. This permits analysis of the information technology environment on the basis of WHO, WHAT, WHEN and WHERE information is used (see Figure 1) (Zachman, 1987). Neaga and Harding (2005) have further described the Zachman Framework as a conceptual methodology that describes how all

*Figure 1. The Zachmane enterprise architecture framework*

| The Zachman Framework | Data (What) | Function (How) | Network (Where) | People (Who) | Time (When) | Motivation (Why) |
|---|---|---|---|---|---|---|
| Scope (Planner) | Define What is Important to the Organization | Identify Key Business Processes | List Locations Where the Business Operates | Identify Organizations Important to the Business | List Key Business Events | Define Strategies and Goals |
| Enterprise Model (Owner) | Semantic Model | Business Process Model | Business Logistics Model | Workflow Model | Master Schedule | Business Plan |
| System Model (Logical Designer) | Logical Model (E/R D) | Application Architecture | System Architecture | Human-Computer Interface | Processing Schedule | Business Rule Model |
| Technological Model (Builder) | Physical Data Model | System Design | Technology Architecture | Presentation Architecture | Control Structure | Business Rule Design |
| Detailed Representations (Sub-Contractor) | Data Definition | Program | Network Architecture | Security Architecture | Timing Definition | Rule Strategy |
| Functioning Enterprise | Enterprise Data Model | Application Program Library | Physical Network | Comprehensive Business Organization | Business Schedule | Comprehensive Business Strategy |

specific architectures could be integrated into a single comprehensive enterprise architecture.

"Enterprise Architecture is about understanding the enterprise through the different artifacts, and the interrelations between these artifacts, and communicating with numerous people, that make up the enterprise" (Holcman, 2008). The Zachman Framework was designed to provide a structure to understand and communicate these artifacts.

The Zachman Framework is a very detailed and visual description of the functional, physical and personnel aspects of an enterprise. The framework consists of a matrix that provides a visual representation that includes the perspective of developers and end users.

The Planner perspective provides a high level contextual understanding of the architecture. The Business Personnel (Owner) perspective provides and understanding of the business and the direction that its strategic objectives are heading towards. The Logical Designer perspective provides a logical understanding of the business and its interrelationship to the technical infrastructure. The Builder perspective provides a physical understanding of the technology. The Implementation perspectives (Sub-contractor and functioning enterprise) provides detailed understandings of specific solutions.

More recently the Open Group has also developed another flexible enterprise architecture framework (TOGAF) to provide organizations with a blueprint for control of their IT resources.

The Zachman Framework describes an information architecture model that begins by developing a semantic model of the information needs of an organization (see Figure 2). It further prescribes the process that is to be used to transform data needs into secure information assets. This consists of ensuring that access requirements are documented and described during the transformation process from logical design to physical design. Also, business rule definition should clearly define any restrictions upon access and use of information.

*Figure 2. Privacy and security components of the Zachman enterprise architecture framework*

Privacy Needs Addressed Through

| The Zachman Framework | Data (What) | Function (How) | Network (Where) | People (Who) | Time (When) | Motivation (Why) |
|---|---|---|---|---|---|---|
| Scope (Planner) | Define What is Important to the | Identify Key Business Processes | List Locations Where the Business Operates | Identify Organizations Important to the Business | List Key Business Events | Define Strategies and Goals |
| Enterprise Model (Owner) | Semantic Model | Business ocess Model | Business Logistics Model | Workflow Model | Master Schedule | Business Plan |
| System Mod (Logical Designer) | Logical Model (E/R D) | App rch | ys it | han ute face | ng e | Business Rule Model |
| Technologic Model (Builder) | Physical Data Model | stem Design | Technology Architecture | Presentation Architecture | Control Structure | Business Rule Design |
| Detailed Representati (Sub-Contractor | Data Definition | Program | Network Architecture | Security Architecture | Timing Definition | Rule Strategy |
| Functionin Enterprise | Enterprise Data Model | pplication gram Library | Physical Network | Business Organization | Business Schedule | Comprehensive Business Strategy |

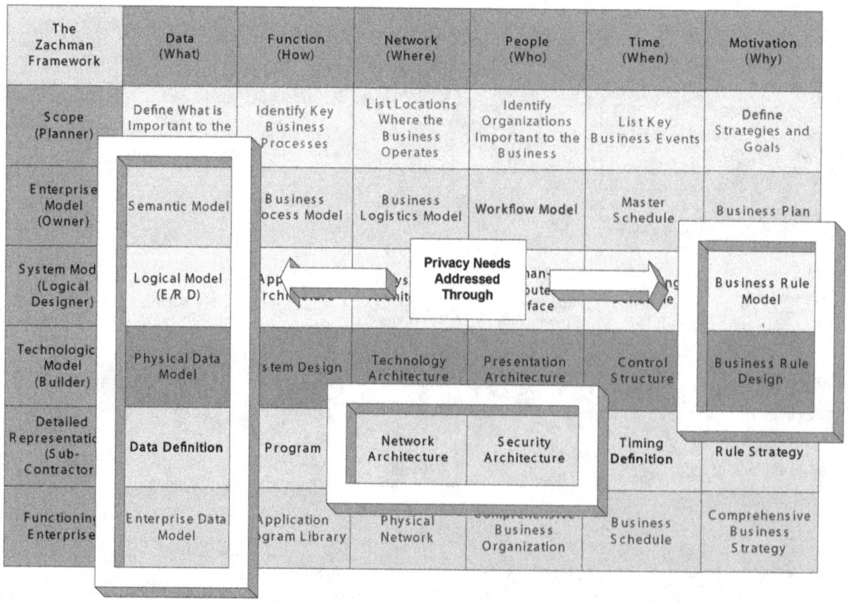

Privacy needs are addressed indirectly through the logical definition of information needs. As information requirements are defined it is the responsibility of the designer to ensure that through the definition of business rules, the privacy needs of an organization are met. The privacy needs begin first by defining the business processes and uses of information within an organization; then the business process is further defined to specifically identify how those needs are to be met. It is the responsibility of the designer to ensure that privacy needs are considered; the framework does not provide explicit guidelines to identify what should be considered or how they are to be implemented.

Unlike privacy needs, security needs are specifically addressed by the Zachman framework. At the detailed representation step, the framework addresses both the technical security needs and the need to incorporate strong procedures within an organization to ensure that security policies are upheld.

## PUBLIC SECTOR ENTERPRISE ARCHITECTURE

In 1996 the Clingler-Cohen Act directed each branch of the U.S. Federal Government to develop and maintain an enterprise architecture framework for its information technology assets to maximize the benefits of these assets for the future. As a result of this act, the CIO Council created the Federal Enterprise Architecture Framework (FEAF). The purpose of the Framework is to provide a means to coordinate and control high priority inter-agency information technology issues in a controllable manner by permitting them to be built upon a common business platform. The FEAF was developed and subsequently expanded upon from the five-layer National Institute of Standards and Technology (NIST) framework. The NIST Framework consists of interconnected layers:

1. Business architecture
2. Information architecture
3. Information systems architecture
4. Data architecture
5. Delivery systems architecture, supported by hardware, software and communications

In 2005, The Federal Enterprise Architecture Program Management Office adopted three core principles to guide its strategic direction. These principles include:

1. The FEAF is most useful when it is business driven; this includes sources such as presidential directives and agency strategic objectives.
2. Adoption of the FEAF will be achieved by proactive collaboration across agencies.
3. The government information technology resources will be improved and be more efficiently utilized by the adoption of the Federal Enterprise Architecture (CIO Council, 2005).

The CIO Council (1999) envisions that it "will serve as a reference point to facilitate the efficient and effective coordination of common business processes, information flows, systems and investments among Federal Agencies and other Governmental entities. In time, Government business processes and systems will operate seamlessly in an enterprise architecture that provides models and standards that identify and define the information services used throughout the government."

The FEAF provides a means to link federal agencies' architecture activities for the purpose of developing interoperability standards to more effectively share information resources. It provides a current and future state architecture that is defined in terms of business processes, information services, technology and security.

According to the CIO Council (1999), FEAF was developed to:

- Organize Federal information on a Federal-wide scale.
- Promote information sharing among Federal organizations.
- Help Federal organizations develop their architectures.
- Help Federal organizations quickly develop their IT investment processes.
- Serve customer needs better, faster and cost effectively.

Eight components were analyzed to develop the first level of the FEAF. They consist of:

1. **Architecture drivers:** Business drivers that consist of administrative initiatives or legislative requirements. Design drivers including new or enhanced hardware or software.
2. **Strategic direction:** Consisting of the goals and vision of the organization to set the vision for the new target architecture.
3. **Current architecture:** Defines the enterprise architecture as it currently exists.
4. **Target architecture:** Defines the enterprise architecture that should be built to support the business processes that are part of the strategic IT direction.
5. **Transitional processes:** Provides support for the migration from the current architecture to the target architecture.
6. **Architectural segments:** This represents focused subsets of the entire enterprise architecture that represent a portion of the target architecture.
7. **Architectural models:** Define the business and design models that support the enterprise architecture.
8. **Standards:** Defines the best practices and methods for achieving the target architecture.

Level II of the FEAF provides greater detail for how the design and architecture components are related together in a push/pull relationship. The business pushes the design (consisting of data, architecture, standards and technology) which in turn pulls the business by achieving new levels of service delivery (CIO Council, 1999). Level III of the Federal Enterprise Architecture Framework refines the level of detail further by providing three design architecture views (data, applications and technology). Level IV of the Federal Enterprise Architecture Framework identifies the specific models that define the three architecture views and the models that describe the business design. These models are used to provide a baseline for the current architecture and support the development of plans to move to the target Federal Architecture. This level also defines the enterprise architectures plan.

## Federal Enterprise Architecture Framework

The vision of the Federal Enterprise Architecture program, as defined by the Federal CIO Council is to "develop, maintain, and facilitate the implementation of the top-level enterprise architecture for the Federal Enterprise. This architecture will serve as a reference point to facilitate the efficient and effective coordination of common business process, information flows, systems and investments among Federal Agencies. In time, Government business processes and systems will operate seamlessly in an enterprise architecture that provides models and standards that identify and define the information services used throughout the Government." (CIO Council, 1999).

The FEAF consists of five reference models. These include the performance reference model, the business reference model, the service component reference model, the technical reference model and the data reference model.

The performance reference model permits agencies to better manage IT investments by providing metrics that are incorporated into the enterprise architecture. This is accomplished by providing a common language that describes the measures and outputs used to achieve program and agency objectives. This enables cross agency comparison of measures and can be used to facilitate more efficient cross-agency resource allocation. The performance reference model has three primary objectives:

1. Improve strategic and operational decision-making by enhancing performance information.
2. Create a "clear line of sight" of inputs to outputs to better understand the contribution of each input.
3. Identify boundary spanning performance improvement opportunities (CIO Council, 2005).

The business reference model provides a mechanism to enable a functional view of business processes rather than their historical organizational view. The purpose is to encourage greater cross agency collaboration and sharing of resources.

The service component reference model seeks to provide a classification of service components across functional organizations to better enable cross sharing of resources and to reduce redundant services. It is intended to be both horizontal and vertical in its scope supporting both inter and intra agency resource sharing.

The technical reference model establishes the technical standards required to enable the delivery of service components. It provides the architectural basis for object reuse across agencies, thus helping to achieve economies of scale and cost savings through object reuse.

The data reference model promotes enterprise wide data standards by standardizing data context, data identification and data use. It is intended to promote improved data sharing capabilities across agencies by providing an enterprise wide information platform. This is an evolving process and the current data reference model is being updated (CIO Council, 2005).

The FEAF establishes four views of information technology architecture that utilize the first three columns of the Zachman Framework and the Spewak EA Planning Methodology (also referred to as E2AF) (CIO Council, 2001). The architecture includes business, data, applications and technology domains that serve as a reference point to guide the efficient flow of information, common business processes and technology across federal agencies of the U.S. government. Documentation standards have been developed for each systems domain within the architecture framework (see Table 1) that addresses four perspectives (also consistent with the Zachman Framework). These provide a standardized approach to documenting and describing the business, information and technical flows of the complete application portfolio.

The Federal Enterprise Architecture Security and Privacy Profile, a scalable subsection of the Federal Enterprise Architecture Framework (version 2) supports the framework by:

1. Promoting an understanding of an organizations security and privacy requirements, the risks the organization faces and its capability to meet those requirements.
2. Helping to select the best solutions for meeting requirements and improving current processes.
3. Providing a structure to enable agencies to select security solutions that are linked to meeting the enterprise needs. (FEA Security and Privacy Profile, 2006).

The framework seeks to achieve a balance between the need for effective data management (recognizing the increasingly sensitive nature of data that it collects about individuals), the need to maintain a secure environment and the need to achieve business objectives (Hite, 2004).

*Table 1. Federal enterprise architecture framework architecture matrix*

| | Data Architecture | Applications Architecture | Technology Architecture |
|---|---|---|---|
| **Planner Perspective** | List of Business Objects | List of Business Processes | List of Business Locations |
| **Owner Perspective** | Semantic Model | Business Process Model | Business Logistics System |
| **Designer Perspective** | Logical Data Model | Application Architecture | System Geographic Deployment Architecture |
| **Builder Perspective** | Physical Data Model | Systems Design | Technology Architecture |
| **Subcontractor Perspective** | Data Dictionary | Programs | Network Architecture |

## Privacy and Security in the Federal Model

The FEAF is a prescriptive model that provides a detailed description for many of the components needed for an information technology organization to define and manage its technical and application infrastructure. The Federal model is intended to provide a single methodology for all branches of the U.S. federal government to utilize to meet all of their information technology needs, to standards those supports and to maximize their potential for reusable object development. The Federal model does not specifically dictate the format and content of the security and privacy procedures, rules or management guidelines needed to effectively administer them within an information systems application. It is assumed that privacy and security needs will be addressed during other components of the design process; but standards are lacking.

The Federal Enterprise Architecture Security and Privacy Profile provides a three stage process for the establishment of security requirements. The first stage, Identification, outlines how an organizations needs and capabilities fit into its respective agency within the federal government. Stage two, Analysis, introduces the idea of capital planning by supporting an organization leveraging currently deployed agency solutions to meet organizational objectives. The third stage, Selection provides an enterprise approach to ensure that security and privacy features are coordinated and budgeted across the entire organization. The three stage approach seeks to capture system security-level activities and use them to support enterprise wide security decisions.

The Privacy Act of 1974 is the foundational legislation that defines the privacy framework that the federal government of the United States must adhere to. Additional guidance describing the privacy of information about individuals is described in the E-Government Act of 2002. As a result of these acts (and other OMB guiding requirements), the Federal Security and Privacy Profile outlines 17 privacy control families that each agency must adhere to. Collectively, these describe in detail the notice, collection, acceptable use and rights and responsibilities for the management of personal data that each agency collects and maintains. Detail guidelines are included in the FEAF framework to ensure that each agency protects the privacy rights of individuals (FEA Security and Privacy Profile, 2006).

## CONCLUSION

Security management has become a cornerstone of information technology architecture. One of the key responsibilities of the IT organization is to ensure that data and information systems are secure. The consequences for security breaches can have severe economic impact on a firm.

Enterprise architecture frameworks have become an integral part of an organization's information technology planning process. Numerous frameworks have emerged, each of which attempt to provide a definitive approach to assessing the current technology of an organization, its desired goals and the plan to achieve those goals. Enterprise architecture frameworks are comprehensive in scope and include all aspects of information technology. However, there are significant differences in the enterprise architecture frameworks that exist today. Additionally, these frameworks should be considered as an evolving process, with no framework that is completely comprehensive in its scope.

Differences exist in the frameworks in how they address the privacy and security needs of an organization. The Federal Enterprise Architecture Framework, which is utilized by all branches of the U.S. federal government that are not part of the Department of Defense, does not specifically address how privacy and security goals should be achieved. There is a gap in the framework that should be addressed in subsequent updates to ensure that these critical issues are consistently addressed by federal agencies and not left to the design considerations of each individual agency. This will support the goals of improving integration and data sharing.

The Zachman framework is the oldest and best known of the enterprise architecture frameworks. Originally designed as a mainframe enterprise architecture it has been extended to address all technology infrastructures. The Zachman framework specifically addresses security needs of an organization and prescribes a method for defining what should be included as well as how security should be managed within an information technology organization. The Zachman framework, like the Federal Enterprise Architecture Framework, is deficient in its treatment of support to address the privacy concerns of most organizations. The framework needs to be updated to specifically provide provisions for an organization to define and implement their privacy needs in a consistent manner across an organization.

## REFERENCES


Bernard, S. (2004). *An Introduction to Enterprise Architecture*. Bloomington, IN: AuthorHouse.

Burk, R., (2005). *Enabling citizen-centered electronic government: 2005-2006 FEA PMO action plan*. White paper, Office of E-Government and Technology.

CIO Council (1999, September). *Federal Enterprise Architecture Framework Version 1.1.* White paper.

CIO Council, (2001, February). *A Practical Guide to Federal Enterprise Architecture*, Version 1.0, Federal Chief Information Officers Council.

CIO Council (2005). *FY07 Budget Formulation FEA Consolidated Reference Model*. White paper.

El Sawy, O., Malhotra, A., Gosain, S., & Young, K. (1999). IT Intensive value innovation in the electronic economy: Insights from Marshall Industries. *MIS Quarterly*, *23*(3), 305-335.

Hite, R. (2004). *The federal enterprise architecture and agencies architectures are still maturing*, White paper, GAO. Federal Enterprise Architecture Security and Privacy Profile, Version 2.0, White paper published by the CIO Council of the U.S. government.

Holcman, S. (2008). *What is Enterprise Architecture*. White paper, Pinnacle Business Group, Inc.

Lankhorst, M. (2004). Enterprise architecture modeling- the issue of integration. *Advanced Engineering Informatics*, 18, 205-216.

McCarthy, R., & Barrett, D. (2005). The impact of the Sarbanes-Oxley Act on information technology: Two perspectives. In *Proceedings of the International Association of Computer Information Systems Pacific conference*, Taipei, Taiwan, May 19-21, 2005, 437-442.

Neaga , E., & Harding, J. (2005, March). An enterprise modeling and integration framework based on knowledge discovery and data mining. *International Journal of Production Research, 43*(6), 1089-1108.

Richardson, G., Jackson, B., & Dickson, G. (1990, Dec.). A principles-based enterprise architecture: Lessons from Texaco and Star Enterprise. *MIS Quarterly,14*(4), 385-403.

Rico, D. (2006, April). A framework for measuring ROI of enterprise architecture. *Journal of Organizational and End-User Computing, 18*(2), 1-12.

Schekkerman, J. (2004). *How to survive in the jungle of Enterprise Architecture Frameworks.* Victoria, BC: Trafford.

Schekkerman, J. (2005). *Trends in Enterprise Architecture, Institute for Enterprise Architecture Development.* White paper.

Shupe, C., & Behling, R. (2006, July). Developing and implementing a strategy for technology development. *Information Management Journal, 40*(4), 52-57.

Weill, P., & Ross, J. (2005, Winter). A matrixed approach to designing IT governance. *MIT Sloan Management Review, 46*(2), 26-34.

Zachman, J.A., (1987). A framework for information systems architecture. *IBM Systems Journal, 26*(3) 276-292.

## KEY TERMS

**E-Business:** The application of Information and Communication Technologies (ICTs) to conducting business.

**E-Government:** A generic term that refers to any government functions or processes that are carried out in digital form over the Internet or similar communication channels. The term also refers to the standard processes that different government agencies use in order to communicate with each other and streamline processes.

**Electronic Economy:** Due to digital technology advances and Internet penetration, many services and intangible products, such as distance education, legal services, health services, banking, insurance, and many copyrighted works, can be provided directly on line. As a result, industry's products change from atoms to bits.

**Enterprise Architecture:** The practice of documenting the elements of business strategy, business case, business model and supporting technologies, policies and infrastructures that make up an enterprise.

# Chapter XII
# Surveillance in the 21st Century: Integration of Law and Technology

**Pieter Kleve**
*Erasmus University, The Netherlands*

**Richard V. De Mulder**
*Erasmus University, The Netherlands*

**Kees van Noortwijk**
*Erasmus University, The Netherlands*

## ABSTRACT

*In this chapter, some current technologies for monitoring and surveillance as well as some legal considerations regarding the application of these technologies will be discussed. The application of monitoring technology has developed from the monitoring of mere technical processes and environmental processes to the monitoring of physiological "processes" and now even of everyday human behaviour. Before discussing legal considerations, an explanation of this development is given and it is placed within a broader social perspective. This leads to an examination of the development of technology that made it possible for monitoring technologies to evolve as they did, and an analysis of norms and values resulting in a conceptual model for evaluating law in the "information society". An overview of technologies for monitoring and surveillance will be presented. From this overview it will become clear that the use of this type of technology is growing fast. At the same time, questions arise regarding its permissibility in the light of legal and constitutions rights, such as the right to privacy. These questions are then addressed in the context of the wider social developments. Finally, it is concluded that with the increasing importance and use of surveillance technology, "monitoring the surveillors" will become essential as well.*

## INTRODUCTION

Technology for surveillance and monitoring has, in today's society, become commonplace. In the Netherlands, for example, certain so-called 'sniffing poles' have been installed. These measure the level of air pollution and when a certain limit is reached a warning system is activated. As a consequence of the disastrous tsunami in December 2004, a tsunami warning system has been installed in the Indian Ocean. Hospitals use technology to monitor the state of the human body and our financial obligations are monitored by computers that send us reminders and final demands if the payment has not been made on time.

Monitoring technology is used to supervise both social and physical processes, and to monitor individual behaviour. This technology is constantly being refined. For example, speeding, as an offence that forms a risk to public health, has for some time been dealt with by technology. The standard approach has been to have a camera that takes a photograph of the car once a certain maximum speed has been exceeded. Having established the level of the speeding, a fine is then sent to the car owner. However, in this set up the camera can only register the offence if it takes place where the camera is located; speeding either before or after the location of the camera cannot be registered. To remedy that deficiency, a new form of surveillance has made its appearance: it is now possible to follow the car along a section of the road. A camera located at one place on the road registers the speed of the car at that point and a camera placed a number of miles farther down the road registers the speed there. A computer then calculates the average speed of the car along that stretch of road between the two cameras. If the average speed is too high, a fine will be sent. For the road user, this development means that it is pointless just to slow down at the location of the first camera; speed must be kept down for the whole stretch of road between the two cameras. (It should perhaps be pointed out that this technology will not catch the driver who only speeds for a very short time on that section of road.)

In the above example, there are legitimate legal grounds for the use of surveillance technology; the law has already laid down what constitutes the maximum speed and the carrying out of the procedure is the responsibility of the state. This surveillance technology has led to a certain conditioning of driving behaviour. However, even though we have become familiar with the use of road cameras, that does not mean that their existence is accepted by all road users. It could be that we consider that driving above the speed limit on that particular road, or section of the road, is not dangerous, or that we have a good excuse for speeding. When the check-points were manned by police officers, a sympathetic officer might have been prepared to accept a good story; a camera is not.

Road cameras have stimulated some drivers to find means of evasion. One such technique is the radar detection device, which warns of the vicinity of radar controlled speed measurement equipment. That has led some authorities to demand that such detection devices be made illegal (and consequently some manufacturers have developed detection devices that do not fall within the category of 'illegal radar detection devices'). What this shows is that a rule of law does not, of itself, produce compliancy. Individuals will act in their own self-interest, as they see it (cf. Jensen & Meckling (1994) pp. 4-19). This action/ reaction phenomenon draws attention to the relationship between a rule of law and the enforcement of that rule of law. The enforcement of a rule of law is of great importance. The use of technology may promote compliance with the law, although that is not always necessarily the case.

Surveillance by camera is, of course, not confined to traffic situations. The use of camera surveillance is common in shopping centres, petrol stations and industrial areas, to name just a few examples. Moreover, camera surveillance is on the increase. If you wish to visit a company, instead of signing in using the traditional guest register, visitors may have to be prepared to undergo a video registration by complying with the friendly request to look in the camera and give their name.

Although camera surveillance is an obvious example of making people feel that they are 'being watched', it is by no means the only form of surveillance. It is already the case that foreigners who wish to enter the USA must provide fingerprints of both index fingers and a passport photograph. The charter company provides other personal data. Nor is Internet as anonymous as its users have long presumed. Surfing on the net leaves countless tracks, which can be picked up by businesses that chart users' Internet behaviour. Given the state's monopoly on coercion, it is not difficult for the state to obtain access to these 'tracks'. There was considerable consternation when the press revealed the existence of the Echelon program of the American National Security Agency (NSA). This controversial program could monitor (or tap) data exchange on the Internet, and thus in effect worldwide. However, the question must also be raised as to whether the consternation would have been greater if it had appeared that the NSA did not carry out such monitoring (cf. Kerr 2003).

A relatively new phenomenon is the use of mobile phone traffic data to find out where people are. In the Netherlands, this has recently been used in the following way. After a football match in Rotterdam, serious rioting occurred. To find witnesses of what exactly had happened, approximately 17,000 mobile phone users who, according to the transmitter data of the telephone provider, had been in the vicinity of the football stadium in Rotterdam on the day of the riots were sent an SMS message by the Rotterdam police force. In this message, all those with any knowledge of the riots were urged to come forward and help the police with their inquiries. Such use of technology as an instrument of surveillance has not been without criticism, in particular with respect to infringing the right to personal privacy and creating a 'big brother' atmosphere (cf. Solove 2001).

## THE WORLD HAS CHANGED

Information technology is fundamentally changing society as we know it. A new era has arrived: the information age. This is the most obviously apparent in communications. Events from all over the world can be relayed by the mass media within the shortest time. It has deeply affected economics: markets have become global. Indeed it would not be an exaggeration to describe the world as one market place. These changes appear to have brought economic progress to the western world. Even former communist countries have converted to market economies. Exchanging goods and services via the market mechanisms instead of by controlling policies has been shown to be more advantageous. Some commentators are so convinced of the triumph of the liberal democratic state that the "end of history" has been announced (Fukuyama 1992).

The exchange of information is a characteristic of the market. If this information exchange becomes easier and cheaper, then the markets will function even better and become 'global'. Information directs the processes. However, information is more than this: it has also become a primary product. In societies saturated with material goods, the information industry has begun to have a huge influence on our behaviour. The same tendency, however, can be seen in less materially affluent lands.

At the same time, 'marketing thinking' has made huge headway. Business administration has gone through a process of becoming more scientific and technologically advanced. The successful businessman is therefore a rational and well-informed decision-maker. When a manager consults a lawyer, he can hardly be expected to be happy if the lawyer answers "it might not pose any problems" or "we might win the lawsuit".

Lawyers can expect their clients to become more critical. If a client has to decide whether to start an action, he needs certain information. For example, a client expects to be a € 100,000 richer if he wins the action. Before he decides to sue he will want to know what the legal or other procedural costs are (lets say € 70,000) as well as the chances of winning the suit. There is no point in proceeding unless the probability of success is at least 70%. The manager will require a sufficiently reliable estimation of this probability before deciding to take the case to court.

In the modern economy, marketing, production management and finance are influenced by rational decision-making. Modern managers talk in terms of expenditure and profit, and of the probability of occurrences taking place. Decisions are made on the basis of knowledge of these variables in the past and the expectations about them in the future.

## CHANGING NORMS AND CONCEPTS

Technology has increased mobility and thereby accelerated the process of globalisation. Not only can people travel more quickly from place to place, but communication has become much easier and faster with the advent of Internet and the mobile phone. The world order as we have known it is changing and that makes directing, controlling, enforcing traditional norms or obtaining an overview of society in general more difficult. Change brings uncertainties with it.

In studying how people behave, an initial analysis reveals that rationality plays a role here too. In this respect, a revolution has taken place over the last ten to twenty years. We are referring here to the paradigm (according to Kuhn 1962) that can be used to study human behaviour, and to try to explain, predict and direct it. Many social scientists base their research on a sociological model of man. This model states that people will behave in a way consistent with the norms of the group to which they belong. However, modern economists usually use a different model of man, the homo economicus or the REMP - the resourceful, evaluating, maximising person (Jensen & Meckling (1994) pp. 4-19). Processes are studied from the perspective of methodological individualism, in other words described, explained and predicted on the basis of the behaviour of individuals. The REMP is an individual who tries to maximise his own utility in all his decision-making. Ideologically, that may sound undesirable. However, in practice it is often the case that individuals see their own interests are served by taking others into account and by interacting with the outside world in a creative and anticipatory way. Negotiation is natural for the REMP.

The REMP is a relatively new concept. The rational model of man appears to have become the dominant way of thinking. Emotions, norms and values, even irrational elements, seem to be subject to radical changes. For example, the ideas about privacy appear to have changed. In the recent past, it would be unacceptable for many people to show their naked bodies, or naked emotions for that matter, to other people. At the same time it would be immoral or at least 'not done' to observe these things other than under specific circumstances, such as in a doctor-patient situation, or as a form of art. These days, people show their emotions and bodies to mass audiences and seem to feel perfectly happy with it. A related concept, anonymity, is also subject to different norms and values. Some people claim that they have a *right* to anonymity as well as a right to take on a different identity, for example while surfing the internet and chatting with others.

This shift in norms is evident in various situations. Freedom of information and intellectual property are clearly seen in a different way from in the past. The Internet has made it very easy to infringe the intellectual rights of others and at the same time many of those who would have been seen as criminals in the past, are now claiming their 'freedom of information'. The availability of information allows the reliability of accountants and firms, for example, to be challenged, as well as the enormous salaries and option plans for some managers in businesses and even in 'privatized' state bodies. On a perhaps somewhat cynical note, although war is nothing new, it now seems to be acceptable, to some at least, that thousands of civilians are killed during military operations to 'bring democracy' to other nations.

## NEW LEGAL QUESTIONS IN THE 'INFORMATION SOCIETY'

Information technology has, without doubt, made an impact on society. In the graph below the idea is expressed that the actual impact of technology on society is far greater than perceived by most people. Furthermore, the discrepancy between actual and perceived impact is growing (see Figure 1).

Technology has also affected people at an individual level. That there are more and more options open to people, and more and more information, makes it necessary for people to approach decision-making *rationally*. Increasing wealth and economic independence have prompted a process of individualisation. Traditional social structures have become less a matter of course, indeed they are sometimes experienced as obstacles in the way of reaching individual goals. The rational model of man is arguably now the best predictor of human behaviour (Jensen & Meckling (1994) pp. 4-19).

The question that arises is whether the information society is simply a modern term meaning nothing more than an increase in information together with an increase in global distribution and access possibilities, or whether a more fundamental change is taking place. This question is important because fundamental changes demand creative and, in particular, unorthodox approaches to new social issues.

Four stages can be pinpointed in the development of technology (Verhoeff (1980); also De Mulder (1984) p. 95; Kleve (2004) p. 55 and 361):

- The first stage is characterised by the ability to influence spatial structures, for example building a hut or a house.
- The second stage consists of the possibilities for changing spatial structures, for example the wheel or hinged doors.
- The third stage gives the possibility to control the powers that are necessary to bring things into motion. The invention of the steam engine announced the age of the 'Industrial Revolution'.
- The fourth stage offers the possibility of using the energy stored in an artefact to allow the artefact to start or stop itself etc.

*Figure 1.*

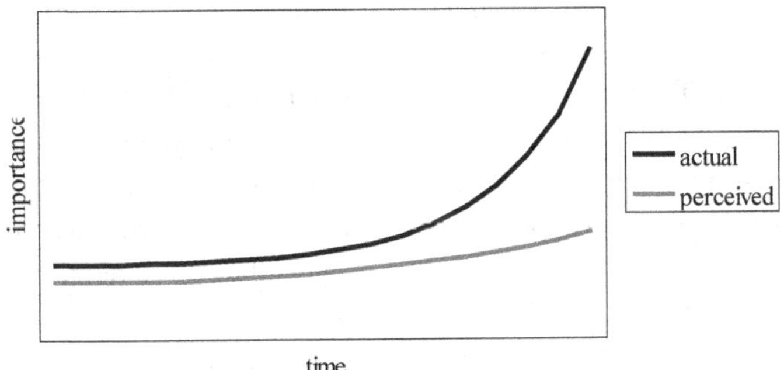

The information age can be associated with the fourth stage in the development of technology. It is characterised by the ability of machines to process information – something that formerly only people (and animals) could do – just as the third stage was characterised by the ability of machines to perform labour. The computer is to information processing what the steam engine was to the use of energy in artefacts. For this reason, this age is referred to as the 'Information Revolution'. It should be clear, that the answer to our question is that the information society is essentially new because nowadays not only animals and humans but also machines can interpret data.

The information society has brought with it many new questions, which arise in various areas. These questions range from those on intellectual property, such as the legal protection of software, chips and data, to so-called 'e-business', with its implications for commercial and contract law, into criminal law, with concerns for enforcement and cross border issues, to questions concerning privacy and to questions regarding the use of monitoring technologies, which is the subject of this chapter.

Although, given the nature of the technology, these questions may be new, not all of them raise new legal issues. It is, therefore, not the case that all the new questions which arise from the information society need to be dealt with by new laws. It should not be an automatic reflex for lawyers to resort to legislation when confronted with new questions. A balanced approach would first dictate an examination of which legal domain would be the most appropriate to look for a solution. Then existing legal rules could be consulted. The next step would be to examine the applicability of these legal rules by making use of existing doctrinal interpretation. Only then, if the conclusion is reached that an interpretational method would fail to secure a responsible and desirable application of the rule, should the issue of new legislation be raised. If, as a last resort, a decision is made to amend the law, another issue should be examined. Does the desirability of a new law stem from the incompatibility of principles or terminology in the existing law with the new factual situation, or does it arise from social developments themselves and a shifting, or even a transformation, of the norms and values behind those principles and terminology? With respect to the latter option, this is not so often the case although the chance of such a shift is greater where the paradigm has altered and where there have been radical technological developments. That is, however, the position at present.

If this approach to legislative initiative is taken into account, then it is rather surprising that in the last few decennia so many new laws have come into force as a consequence of information technology. Examples of laws that would not have survived the first stage would be the software, chips and database laws. These new laws have not achieved anything that the application of existing laws to the new questions could not have achieved. Take the law on electronic signatures, for example, where the presumption was made that the terminology of the old law was incompatible with the new factual situation. However, had existing doctrinal interpretation been applied (an 'electronic signature' is still a signature), these new laws would simply have been superfluous. Examples of the shifting of norms can be found in software and database laws and in file sharing and spam. With respect to software and database laws, when intellectual property laws were declared applicable to software and database, in the slipstream an implicit shifting of norms was implemented. In the case of software, this has taken the form of a clause forbidding decompilation, and for databases a de facto extension of the exploitation rights with a use right (Kleve, De Mulder & Van Noortwijk 2006). These are actually examples of a shifting of norms where it is not clear if this had been sufficiently realized. As to file sharing, this is an example of a social development that inevitably has to lead to a shift in norms in the form of an exception to copyright rules in order to allow copying (in the broad sense of reproduction and transformation) for private use (Kleve & Kolff 1999).

The answer to spam is, of course, 'white listing' not legislation. By white listing is meant that people may use the technology to decide for themselves who has access to their communications. The increase in spam will make white listing, *allowing* access to 'known senders', more attractive than the nowadays frequently used option of black listing, the method of *blocking* 'undesired senders'. Why is white listing the obvious answer to spam? That has to do with the fundamental characteristic of the information society, namely that in the fourth stage of the development of technology machines can also interpret data. Until the advent of this fourth phase, white listing was simply not an option because this could not be achieved effectively. The information society has made a fundamentally new problem solving system possible, one that we are discovering the possibilities of step by step.

The consecutive dependence relationships between technology, social developments and law are represented in Figure 2.

The model consists of three concentric circles. The basis for this model is positivism, in other words that one reality exists and that that reality can be known. The outer circle encircles 'can', the technology. The middle circle covers that which people 'want', within the limits of what is possible, using the REMP as the model for describing, predicting, explaining and steering human behaviour. As a multidisciplinary science, business administration offers a structure to obtain insight into (individual) utility considerations. Finally, the inner circle is the domain of law, of 'may' (and 'must') of demands and authorisations, of norms and facilitation. Law is an artefact for the facilitating of human interactions, for example in the form of 'property', 'majority', 'marriage', 'purchase'. Through fixing norms and sanctions it delineates the external boundaries of human

*Figure 2.*

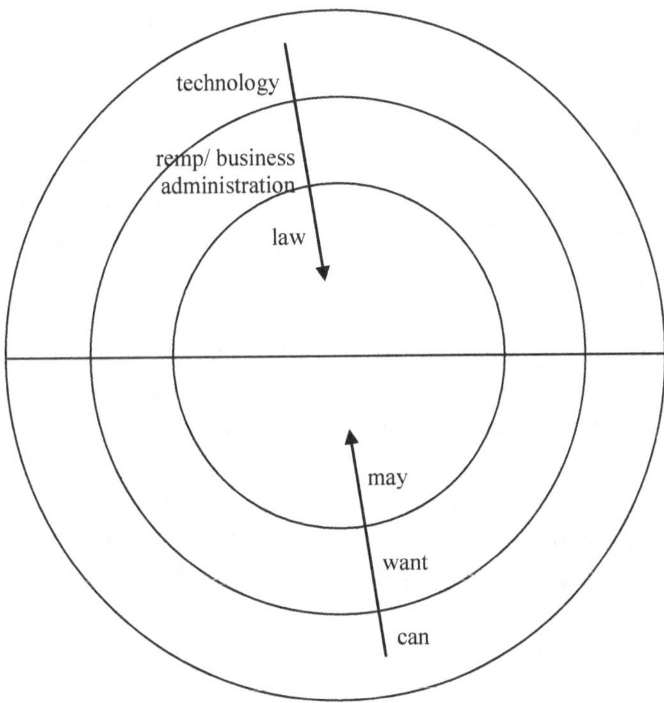

'want'. Law can steer 'want', but is not decisive, and is itself limited by 'can'.

## SURVEILLANCE WITH THE HELP OF TECHNOLOGICAL MEANS

From the introductory examples, it is clear that technology plays an important, and in some cases even an essential, role in surveillance. For that reason, attention will now be paid to a number of possibilities for surveillance that can be realized by using technology. Surveillance is not exclusively aimed at conformity with certain legal requirements. Surveillance by the authorities is often the starting point of a process that leads to tracking down offenders and prosecution. IT (information technology) has become a major means for implementing all the stages in that process.

### Camera Surveillance in Public and Non-Public Places

The use of audio-visual equipment (cameras) is closely connected to surveillance. Cameras allow real time surveillance as well as retroactive surveillance. It has been argued recently that it is the real time surveillance that makes cameras in public places particularly effective, as action can be taken directly once a situation appears on camera.

With respect to surveillance in real time, the role of IT in the process may not be immediately apparent: in principle what is involved here is a screen that must be monitored by a human supervisor. However, these days the video signal is often not recorded and broadcast in an analogue form but directly in a digital form. That opens up various new possibilities. These video images can be relayed more easily to differing locations. That is particularly the case if the camera has a network connection and can communicate via the Internet protocol. These images could then, in principle, be accessed via any computer connected to the Internet.

The traditional way of looking at the images allows the supervisor to call upon the signals from various cameras or to project the images from those cameras next to each other on a screen. Digital image processing, however, is now also a possibility, allowing the computer to analyse and process the material at various levels. The following examples illustrate this technique (ranked, more or less, according to the complexity of the operations):

- Motion detection or similar techniques that make sure that only the recordings in which something has happened are shown or stored (for example, where there has been movement or sound).
- Increasing the sharpness and contrast of a recording, so that it is possible to zoom in on details (such as a number plate or a person's face).
- Facial recognition: identifying a person by recording that person's face. Great steps forward have now been made in the application and processing of this form of biometric information (this is dealt with in more detail below). The Dutch Committee on Criminality and Technology considered this application to be one of the 'most promising' techniques dealt with in its report. With this technique, it is already possible to identify someone in a crowd (although the person's face must, at a certain moment, be visible). The technique has not encountered much resistance, probably because recording someone's face is seen as less threatening and less intrusive than, for example, an iris scan. Experiments are already underway to use this technology for controlling entrances to offices, hospitals and even swimming pools (sometimes in combination with other techniques such as fingerprint scanning).

- Where cameras are positioned at more than one location, it becomes possible to track and trace people for a certain distance and over a certain period of time on the basis of facial recognition. This technology means it is possible to make a detailed analysis of where a given person is at any given time in the area covered by the cameras.
- Object pattern analysis: this system makes it possible to look at images where something out of the ordinary is considered to be taking place. This system makes it possible to track deviant behaviour, for example, where someone remains motionless at a particular location for a much longer period than average. The technique also makes it possible to isolate deviant patterns, for example cars or lorries that exhibit an unusual route pattern.
- The use of images from special satellites which have advanced cameras and sensory equipment making it possible to localize, identify and follow people or goods.

It is clear from the above examples that the 'traditional' form of camera surveillance, whereby analogue imaging is relayed via specific, separate infrastructure to a location where the pictures can be seen or recorded, has been overtaken by new forms of technology. In particular, the fact that digital cameras, based on Internet technology, do not need separate infrastructure or cables is a great advantage. It is, therefore, expected that this technique will supersede the analogue version in the years to come.

## Surveillance of Telecommunication

As well as extensive camera surveillance, the monitoring of all forms of telecommunication has also become large-scale. That monitoring applies not just to telephone and fax messages, but also, and increasingly, to data traffic on the Internet.

From a technical viewpoint, in most cases it no longer matters what sort of communication is involved; even speech can often be directly digitalized and then transmitted. This is, for example, the case with respect to mobile telecommunication via GSM (mobile phones) and via VOIP, 'Voice Over IP'. This implies that there is little point in monitoring or tapping data on the basis of which type of communication is going to be the subject of the surveillance. It is usually not possible to distinguish these types before the data has been received and decoded. The decoding establishes, inter alia, what type of data is involved (digitalized speech or computer data etc). However, it is also quite likely that the sender of the data has sent them in an encrypted form. This is, in principle, very easy where digital data are involved. Trying to decrypt without the right key can be extremely difficult and time consuming, in particular when a so-called strong form of encryption has been used. Even the use of technology does not mean this problem can be easily solved. This is why authorities have considered placing encryption under legal regulation. In the Netherlands, an attempt was made to make the users of encryption provide the data for decryption where a criminal investigation was concerned. This provision never became law. Nor did the rule that encryption keys had to be deposited with 'Trusted Third Parties' (TTPs).

A specific form of surveillance, entailing the surveillance of people rather than of telephone or data traffic, allows people to be located, based on their mobile phone data. This information can be derived from one or more transmitters for mobile phones. It makes it possible to determine who was where (in the vicinity of one of these transmitters) at a certain time, at least if the mobile phone was on. This technique is now used regularly to follow a suspect. However, the use made of this data by the Rotterdam police to sent SMS messages to all those who had been in the vicinity of the football stadium at a certain time, was new, at least for the Netherlands. Of interest here is that the data of bystanders was used for the purposes of a criminal investigation, not just the data of those suspected of a criminal offence.

A similar, but even more complicated challenge is the location of stationary computer equipment (and with it, its user) that is connected to the internet. Research to improve this form of 'geolocation' has been increasingly successful in the past few years. State of the art techniques in this field are based on the measurement of response delays of a certain target computer, when messages are sent to it from several host computers with known location. The results from such measurements can be improved further when combined with information about the network topology in the respective area (see Katz-Bassett, John, Krishnamurthy, Wetherall, Anderson & Chawathe 2006).

For this sort of location data, as well as data traffic itself, it is obvious that the registration and storage of such data can be of great important for retrospective monitoring. European law has already been introduced to make this possible. Nonetheless, its introduction has met resistance from providers and Internet user organisations, such as 'Bits of Freedom'.

## Entry Control: Determining the Identification of Persons and Goods

The time that entry would be granted to a person based on no more than an identification card, specifying the carrier's name and photograph, is drawing to an end. The traditional identification papers are simply too easy to copy. It is, therefore, not surprising that measures have been taken to make passports, driving licences and similar forms of identification more difficult to forge. The newest weapon against forgery is the use of digitalized biometric information as a means of identification.

Biometrics (literally 'measuring life') has quite a long history. The use of the finger and handprint for identification was known in China in the 14th century. In Europe, fingerprints have been used as a means of identification since the end of the 19th century, based on a system developed by Richard Edward Henry of Scotland Yard (See Jain, Hong, Pankanti & Bolle 1997). Fingers are not the only parts of the body, however, that can be used for identification purposes: hands, eyes (the iris and retina), the face, the voice and the DNA itself can be used. However, they all require specific technology. The certainty of identification they provide may vary. DNA is generally regarded as being the most accurate and reliable biometrical method. Because of this, the technique has become extremely important for the investigation of crimes. The rules to use DNA for this purpose have been liberalized in some respects during the past few years in the Netherlands. Since 2003 it is allowed, for instance, to use DNA samples to establish the race and the gender of a suspected offender.

The disadvantage of using DNA for identification is that the process requires considerable time and cost, whereas an iris scan, a face scan or a fingerprint can be carried out quickly and cheaply. It is for these reasons, that the latter techniques are the ones used at entry points.

IT plays an important role in the use of biometric techniques. For example, the characteristics of a fingerprint are normally stored in the form of a so-called template. The accuracy with which that process takes place determines the dimensions of the template and also its reliability. The template can be stored in a memory chip which, for example, can be used in an identity card.

Not only persons, but also goods can be identified and traced. One traditional form is the traditional metal detector, for example a screening doorway at airports, which makes use of a magnetic field. Other techniques that are increasingly being used include MRI scans, microwave radar registration and microwave dielectrometrics, each of which are capable of detecting specific types of objects, for example in baggage. Explosives can be detected by, inter alia, 'Explosives Trace Detection' (ETD), a relatively cheap system in which traces of explosive materials are traced by way of samples, and by 'Explosive Detection Systems', which uses expensive automated scanners with x-ray capacity in order to analyse the content of packages and suitcases. Similar techniques are available to detect other materials, for instance chemicals or biological substances that can be used as weapons and also drugs. X-ray scans at airports can be used to detect drugs that have been ingested by the smugglers (usually in the form of small 'eggs' that are swallowed). In the Netherlands, it has become common practice to scan *all* the passengers from certain 'risk flights', for instance those coming from the Netherlands Antilles.

These techniques have in common that they make use of the existing characteristics of persons or goods. It is, however, possible to track a person or goods by means of a tagging system. With respect to goods, a good example of this form of tagging is the security barcode label that is now found on many products, which triggers an alarm once the exit has been passed. A similar application can be found in cars and scooters, enabling stolen items to be returned to their rightful owners. One technique that is of much interest at the moment is RFID, 'Radio Frequency Identification'. It functions in the same way as the security bar code, but it is so cheap and so small that it can be inserted during the manufacturing process of virtually any product. This technique could replace the barcodes as an effective means of preventing shoplifting. The privacy aspect of this development, as it is, in principle, possible to collect information unobtrusively about what products a person has, has led to much discussion with respect to privacy. (See GAO (2005) for technical as well as for privacy aspects of RFID).

Finally, mention must be made of the GPS, the 'Global Positioning System'. Apart from being used for navigational purposes, this system can also detect the precise location of persons or goods. If this information is then passed on to the police, for example via a GSM connection, it makes it much simpler to track down stolen goods. When this system is applied to persons in the form of an ankle tag, new possibilities for electronic house arrest arise.

## Surveillance Techniques for Detection and Prosecution of Crimes

Many of the techniques described above are suitable not just for the purposes of crime prevention, but also for detection and prosecution when a crime has been committed. For example, cameras can be used for face recognition, data from data exchanges and location data can be stored by computer and biometric methods can be used. Such techniques affect criminal procedure; evidence obtained through the use of highly advanced technology must comply to the same standards of validity and reliability as evidence obtained in a more traditional way, for example by witness statements. (See Budowle, Carmody, Chakraborty, & Monson (2000) for background information on the use of DNA profiles). The use of new technology can cause problems for judges, whose lack of familiarity with the technology involved means they have to rely heavily upon the expert opinions of those behind the technology. It is of great importance to deal with this problem because the probability is that the use of evidence obtained by technology will increase rather than decrease.

## Conclusions Regarding Surveillance Technology

In the future, surveillance technology will make use of various techniques. Information in a digital form makes it possible to use techniques that were unknown only a short time ago. Equipment can be used not only for (passive) registration, but also for analysis and interpretation. One example of the combination of techniques can already be found in American airports: video cameras utilising image recognition software used in combination with pre-existing information. This method is also used to deal with hooligans at football matches, rather than checking their individual club cards. Surveillance technology also includes fingerprint and DNA techniques. These methods are not only used for active control, for example to gain access to restricted areas, but also retroactively to reconstruct a given situation. Digital technology is also responsible for the increasing use of biometric techniques.

Surveillance technology has, without doubt, made an impact on society. Technological advances, in general, have been considerable over the last 150 years. It is a period that has seen the Industrial Revolution superseded by the Information Revolution. Technological applications are numerous and various, and have become integral to the society we know today. That technology should be used for surveillance is, in this context, not extraordinary. Indeed, its application is rather obvious given that the techniques are easily applied to surveillance and that society as a whole has acquired a more technically orientated character.

What perhaps is less obvious, is that technology offers diverse possibilities with respect to complex relations. Management is of vital importance in carrying out tasks, whether those tasks are related to business or public sector organisations. Technology can assist in planning, control and communication.

## LEGAL CONSIDERATIONS

The legal considerations in this chapter will focus on five problem areas with respect to monitoring and surveillance technology. These areas include the invasion of personal privacy, the use of surveillance technology by the authorities in the enforcement of criminal law, surveillance technology as a means of social control, whether surveillance technology leads to a better use of resources, and the principles of proportionality and subsidiarity.

### Privacy vs. Safety?

The influence of technology on safety is twofold. On the one hand, social safety is increasingly threatened by technology, in particular the use of weapon technology (chemical, biological and nuclear), and the use of computers and communication systems (Muller, Spaaij & Ruitenberg (2003) p. 87) is often said to be dangerously monopolized by state authorities and large corporations. On the other hand, technology can be deployed precisely to promote social safety. As we have seen, a whole range of technological applications to enhance safety is already available: security systems (such as camera supervision), the identification of both goods and persons (the tagging of products and people as well as tracking and tracing methods based on GMS or GPS or DNA), information processing (image processing, biometrics, sensor fusion and data mining), communication and process support (group decision systems, virtual reality, coordination systems) and, finally, in law enforcement and criminal investigation (shared reporting systems, camera supervision systems and the 'information pistol').

One opinion that is often voiced is that people find it unpleasant to be spied on and to know that their movements can be checked out later. However, when members of the public are asked if they would like to see more uniformed policemen on the street, the vast majority answers in the affirmative; most people apparently find a police presence on the streets reassuring. Is it, then, a question of finding the right balance: yes to surveillance in itself but no to surveillance in an extreme form? If that is the case, it implies a remarkable conclusion; that we actually *want* a certain level of uncertainty. Research has shown that the public judges risk not just in terms of the chance of something happening or the effect of that something happening. That other considerations play a role comes to the fore where behaviour in traffic or smoking habits are concerned.

With respect to the relationship between privacy and safety, the question seems to be how much of their privacy are people prepared to surrender in order to increase their safety. These two basic rights, the right to privacy and the right to protection, seem to be uneasy partners. However, the question itself is not as straightforward as it may seem. Why is it that most of us are perfectly prepared to have our baggage examined in airports but resent our past being looked into? Privacy is not a clear concept; the term includes various aspects of private life. It may encompass various dimensions, such as the spatial dimension. This spatial dimension is concerned with our freedom of movement: if there were no controls at airports would we feel freer or less free to go as we pleased? And if our past is looked into, would the examination of our baggage no longer be necessary? Privacy and safety do not have to be opposites, but the one can affect the other. It would be hard to think of something that is a greater infringement of a person's privacy than having to undergo a body search, or having personal belongings searched, or even the threat of it.

Constitutional rights have a special place in the relationship between the authorities and members of the public. Rights and freedoms are formulated that are intended to protect citizens against the arbitrary use of power by the authorities. In the course of time, the concept of the horizontal working of constitutional rights has developed. The right to respect for personal privacy is not just between the authorities and the public, but also between members of the public themselves. In former times, it was necessary to protect citizens from the arbitrary behaviour of the authorities (or the monarch). Today, in the developed democratic states of the West, it would seem that the 'danger' emanates not so much from the authorities, which are open to public review, but from those who reject authority. Fear restricts the movements of citizens, either because they are not sure if it is safe to take an airplane or the local metro, or to voice a possibly controversial opinion. It would now appear that it is the authorities that have become the champion of constitutional rights, rather than the body that could be guilty of flouting them. The question now before us is which aspects of privacy must weigh heavier in a given situation? The means used will depend upon how that question is answered.

Another question that comes to the fore in determining whether someone's privacy has been infringed, is what criteria should be used. Where there is a choice or where there is an advantage to the person concerned, it is less likely that an infringement of privacy will be considered as unacceptable. In order to respect personal privacy it would seem more important to formulate these criteria rather than paying attention to actual forms of behaviour, as this does not sufficiently take into account the personal character of privacy.

However, the choice for applying surveillance technology, or being placed under such surveillance, is often not one made at an individual level. This runs counter to the present day tendency whereby the individual plays a central role. That is because the protection of privacy is not just an issue for individuals; it must also take collective needs into account. Paradoxically, it would seem that the 'protection' of constitutional rights justifies a certain selective infringement of those rights. This can be explained in terms of the relative utility of the application. To the extent that it affects individuals, legislators must be careful not to make unwarranted generalizations, as this could result in the public rejecting the use of technology. This would be a pity as research into such matters as the registration of DNA and the use of extensive databanks holding sensitive information, has shown that many people attach more importance to safety than to privacy.

## Suspects and Non-Suspects

When it is contended that surveillance technology infringes personal privacy, one aspect that is brought to the fore is that surveillance technology does not differentiate between people; the surveillance entails the monitoring of both suspects and non-suspects. This infringes the legal principle that coercive measures should only be used against those for whom there are reasonable grounds to suspect them of criminal activity.

Modern technology means that an innocent person's privacy can be infringed as a side effect of tracking a suspected person's movements. It is this, rather than the use of technology against the suspects themselves, that causes problems; those who are not considered to be suspects must also accept that they too are subjected to the coercive measures made possible by the application of this technology. This would seem contrary to the usual principle of criminal procedure that a person's status as 'suspect' must first be established (for example, that reasons for suspicion are first presented to a judge in order to obtain a search warrant before the premises of a suspect may be searched).

In the first place, it is not the case that the authorities, including the police and the judiciary, may only do what has been laid down in detail. To a certain extent they may, just like ordinary citizens, ask people questions, telephone people and send sms messages. These activities cannot be categorized as coercive measures, for citizens are free in deciding whether to answer or not, nor are such activities limited to 'suspects'. That people do not like to be spoken to by the police, that they could feel intimidated, means that the police must be careful in the way they approach the public, but there is no reason, and indeed it would not be desirable, to fetter their capacity to ask questions. This applies even where if a person refuses to answer the question, he could become a suspect, and as such the subject of coercive measures.

Nor does receiving an SMS message from the police mean that the recipient must be considered to be a suspect. During an investigation, the police needs to contact people as potential witnesses. In the case of the SMS messages sent after the football riots in Rotterdam, these messages were sent to ask whether anyone had seen anything of interest to the investigation. The police could have achieved the same result by carrying out a house to house check or by questioning all those attending the next football match in Rotterdam. The choice to send an SMS message would seem more attractive: only those people who were in the vicinity of the football stadium at the time of the riots were 'bothered' by the police, it is much less labour intensive to send a message than to send out police officers, a message saves time and the costs of it are relatively low. An SMS message is also probably less intimidating than a personal encounter with the police.

Nor is it the case that the authorities may only exercise coercion against someone who is suspected of an offence. In many cases, the law lays down a general competence for a certain activity. For example, returning an income tax form is compulsory and surveillance cameras may be used to detect speeding. Checking that drivers do not exceed the maximum speed limit does not make all road users 'suspect'. And a possible automation of the surveillance of income tax forms, which could include coupling this with data from other sources, is, in principle, not an extension of tax control. Making data available – coupling files – should take place in accordance with existing legal regulations. However, because computers have made it easier to compare data, this area might be subject to further legal regulation.

## Technology and Social Control

The use of surveillance technology, as illustrated by the above example of tax supervision, does not always entail an extension of an existing competence. It is more often a means by which that existing competence becomes more effective and efficient. The simple fact that something is useful, or more useful than it used to be, leads in itself to a certain shift in norms. It is, however, important that it is borne in mind that technology itself is primarily a 'means'; it is a means to make possible those things people find useful. Surveillance technology is, in this sense, a tool to enforce norms, in the same way as the law itself is a tool to enforce norms.

When people go on holiday, they often ask their neighbours to keep an eye on the house. If someone hangs around the deserted house, the neighbours might ask whether they can 'be of help'. That a police car would drive past the house more often while they were gone would also be welcome. In former times, it was far more common for people to keep an eye on the behaviour of others. There are various reasons why that is less the case today. One reason is the tendency noted above for increased mobility and individualization. People are also aware that an intervention may not be without risk.

The social control and cohesion typical of society several decades ago no longer exist, at least not in that form. It is generally recognized that social control and social cohesion have a useful function. The gap left by the lack of social control can be filled by the use of technology; it can give social control and social cohesion form once again. In any evaluation of surveillance technology, factors to be taken into account are not only the costs and disadvantages, but also what it contributes and its social advantages.

## Technology and Solidarity

Whether a decision is made to use surveillance technology seems to be largely a matter of efficiency. Efficiency is a norm more often associated with the private sector, yet this consideration is relevant with respect to the public sector as well. Although it would seem that efficiency as a norm has achieved greater acceptance in the private sector than the public sector, it is not the case that the aim of efficiency is without criticism in the private sector, for example with respect to commercial profit at the cost of service. When this criticism is analysed, it would appear that the services sacrificed are those that were not sufficiently profitable or provided at a loss. What the private and public sectors share is that those individuals who are affected want a result that suits them, even if it is disadvantageous for others, although they are not personally willing to contribute more. This leads to a conservative approach. Efficiency as a criterion is nevertheless an important guarantee of solidarity. The use of technology can promote efficiency.

An important question is to what extent people will be prepared to contribute financially to an expensive system of redistribution, in which not all those who are intended to benefit from the redistribution do so, and some of those who do benefit were not intended to do so. Many of the organizations charged with the task of redistribution are founded on the principle of solidarity. This solidarity could be in the form of unemployment benefits, insurance, housing or social security benefits, contribution to church funds, or charitable organizations. An important factor here is the tendency pointed out above; the increasing complexity of society, increased mobility and individualization. As a consequence, it has become more difficult to reach those who have the right to such assistance, and more difficult to prevent fraud by those who do not have the right to this assistance. This puts solidarity under pressure and makes it crumble away. Surveillance and control could be made more efficient by using technology, for example to prevent the fraudulent use of social security systems, and indeed its use could be demanded.

In practice, it is no longer possible to implement complex legal projects without the use of technology. Technology has, in turn, influenced the content of these legal rules, as the automation process itself may impose certain requirements and restrictions. Creating and keeping consensus depends on correct implementation, certainly in the long term. Using technology as a means of control or as a means to support the enforcement of control, could give those involved a greater feeling of certainty. It is because we have computers that we can refine general rules, so that relevant individual circumstances can be taken into account. It is this very ability to distinguish between cases that makes it possible to uphold the principle of equality. In this way, technology could contribute to a feeling of solidarity.

## Subsidiarity and Proportionality

The use of surveillance technology cannot, in general, be seen as irreconcilable with the right to the protection of personal privacy. Safety is not in opposition to privacy, but an aspect of it. Furthermore, it could be argued that the right to personal privacy is not an absolute right; other factors can, and sometimes must, be taken into account. Thirdly, it has already been pointed out that the scope of the concept of privacy, and its interpretation, must be seen against a background of technical and social developments.

Similarly, it has been argued that a general application of surveillance technology does not have to be contrary to the principle of criminal procedure that there should be reasonable grounds to see the subject as a suspect. That is because surveillance technology is not in itself a coercive measure. Surveillance technology is a means that is not confined to use for the purposes of criminal procedure. A person may cooperate, for example at a checkpoint, without having first to be identified as a suspect. There are also positive effects, such as the use of technology to increase the usefulness of services to the public and to respect the enforcement of basic rights.

It is often not necessary to change the law in order to implement surveillance technology. Technology can already be implemented within the existing legal context. However, the use of technology, either in general or for particular forms of surveillance, can lead to shifts in norms.

With respect to surveillance technology, just as with other means, attention should be paid to the legal issues that may arise from one situation to another. The boundaries for legal application are usually determined by the principles of subsidiarity and proportionality. In the example of the SMS messages sent by the Rotterdam police, it can be argued, without trivializing the potential threat this could form, that this application stayed within accepted limits. Another example is the experiment with camera surveillance last year in the centre of Groningen, a city in the north of the Netherlands. These cameras did not operate continuously, but were triggered when the microphones that were attached to the cameras picked up sound. Although it could be said that the surveillance was continual, nonetheless the system was only activated if there was a reason: the sound registered by the microphones. This is a good example of proportionality; modern technology has made it possible to limit the infringement of privacy.

In setting down legal conditions for use, it should be realized that a too conservative approach could unfairly favour criminals. While acknowledging that there should be reasonable grounds before someone is considered to be a suspect, it should also be borne in mind that it is increasingly the case that the threat could come from an unknown source, as is often the case with terrorist threats. What should be taken into account is that surveillance technology does not only have to be seen as a means of repression: it is also a means of prevention. It gives a high quality service and is cost effective (for consumer and tax payer). It is possible to organise the surveillance in such a way that not all the information need be made known. It is sometimes sufficient that it can be made known. To use the example of the Rotterdam police once again, it would seem that no names or addresses were made available but only the telephone numbers. Much work is taking place in the field of so-called privacy enhancing technology (PET) and techniques to ensure anonymity. It is, of course, necessary to consider safety precautions, any loss of data and possible claims by those affected by a loss of data, misuse of data or use that causes damage. In general, it would seem wise to make the legal framework known on the introduction of the technology.

## Conclusions, Legal Considerations

In part, the objections to surveillance technology arise when people become the objects of that surveillance. Nonetheless, the public appears to benefit from surveillance by the authorities, as well as by private companies. Most of the criticism emanates from lawyers and institutions, such as the national Data Protection Authorities. Given the rational model of man, it is quite easy to explain why the objections come from this direction: it is in the self-interest of these groups to protest (which is not the same as saying that their interest is a selfish one).

Furthermore, it would seem that resistance is a characteristic of the assimilation process of new technology. It is resistance to technology and resistance to change. Not knowing whether there is surveillance, what the scope of that surveillance is, who is carrying out the surveillance and what will be done with the data can make people feel uncomfortable. It is rather like the situation of 'I can't see you, but you can see me'. Without transparency with respect to these issues, it is quite possible that people feel more vulnerable rather than less. That would inhibit the assimilation process, which would be a pity given how important it is that the usefulness of information technology is acknowledged; one conclusion that is rarely seen in legal literature is that technology, also surveillance technology, actually makes it easier to respect and protect basic rights.

A good example of how the authorities can use new technology is the questioning of potential witnesses on the basis of their locations revealed by their mobile phones. Another example of how authorities can use technology to deal with new, and partly unknown, threats is to keep data from networks for a certain period with the help of Internet or telephone providers. These examples show how new technology can be used for the more effective enforcement of existing norms. However, there is a clear possibility of the infringement of rights such as the right to privacy. That the norms will adjust is a logical consequence of the technological developments. An important criterion for people to change their ideas about norms and values with respect to the application of new technology is whether the technology 'works"; whether the effectiveness of it has been established.

Five points to be taken into account were presented above. The points were 'privacy and safety', the importance of the presence of a 'suspect', 'technology and social control', 'technology and solidarity' and 'cost effectiveness'. The conclusion has to be that surveillance technology leads to a new consideration of values and interests.

The right to privacy – and other rights that have come into existence as a consequence of technological developments, such as copyright – are ripe for review. The automatic reaction of support for these rights is no longer adequate. The right to privacy is no longer just under pressure with respect to the concerns for safety, but also in its relationship with other rights, such as the freedom of information and there are even conflicts within the right to privacy itself. Often the privacy of one person means the infringement of the privacy of another person.

There is a steady, and growing, market for gossip publications; apparently people are quite happy to read privacy sensitive stories about others. Perhaps an even more important consideration than the dichotomy of privacy and safety is the tension between privacy and the right to information. Where more weight is given to privacy than the right to information, the current trend for weblogs could be made impossible. Similarly, where the number of people who have changed their gender or have tried to change their age is increasing so fast, their right to keep this information private could be weakening.

Limiting constitutional rights, or reassessing them, means that it is desirable to put into place an effective control on the power of the authorities. Those who object to surveillance technology not only point out the dangers to individual rights and the costs, but in particular the danger of misuse by the authorities. Traditionally, this misuse of power should be prevented by the 'system of checks and balances", the separation of powers, or "Trias Politica".

## FROM TRIAS TO TETRAS POLITICA

Information technology and in particular surveillance technology will produce fundamental changes in the way in which the state operates. There can be positive effects on legal administration. Modern legislators in liberal, democratic states should take it upon themselves to enter all legislation that is in force into an information system that would be accessible to everyone. In this way, everybody could monitor the state's legislative activities.

However, the use of technology could alter the current balance of power with respect to the executive and judicial powers. Furthermore, it will provide the executive (or 'administration') with new means to increase its control of society. Is it possible to avoid or reduce the risks that may arise for citizens?

A critical assessment of the trias politica is required (De Mulder 1998). It traditionally consists of the following powers:

- Judicial power
- Legislative power
- Executive power

In order to analyse the characteristics and differences between the powers, the method used is the analysis of the dimensions of concepts. It is beyond the scope of this article to give a detailed description of the methodology here, but put briefly the analysis often start with a tri-part division. The tri-part division used by Weber (1968) for the legitimation of state power serves here as an example. 'Authority', according to a well-known sociological definition, is the acceptance of power. ('Power' is the ability to influence the behavioural alternatives of others). 'Power' is accepted by people if they consider it to be 'legitimate'. Weber distinguishes three elements of authority:

- Charismatic
- Traditional
- Rational

Charismatic leaders or authority figures acquire their authority from 'impulses', from the emotions of those who ascribe authority to them. Traditional authority is power, either that of an individual or of a group of people, which is accepted because the ruler or the group to which the man in power belongs has 'always had the power'. Authority can also be rational: it can be accepted because people consider the power to be useful. An analysis of this brief outline of the tri-part division allows the conclusion to be drawn that at least two different aspects (dimensions) can be distinguished, namely:

- The level of consciousness (having thought about the acceptance of power).
- The level of flexibility (being prepared to accept another authority figure than the current one).

Weber also used a four-part division to explain statements on legitimacy: he returned to his categorisation of types and aspects of social activities. Social activities, according to Weber, can be determined as follows:

- **Goal-rational:** From 'contemplation', 'calculation'
- **Value-rational:** From 'conviction', 'principle'

*Table 1. The legitimacy of power*

| | *not conscious* | *conscious* |
|---|---|---|
| *not flexible* | traditional | rational (?) |
| *flexible* | charismatic | rational (?) |

*Table 2. "Double Dichotomy"*

| | *supervising and correcting* | *initiating and acting* |
|---|---|---|
| *not suitable for large-scale exertion of power* | judicial power | legislative power |
| *suitable for large-scale exertion of power* | ? | executive power |

- **Affective:** From 'impulse', 'emotion'
- **Traditional:** 'Durch eingelebte Gewohnheit'

This double dichotomy can, with a certain creativity, be applied to other situations. For example, political parties allow themselves to be distinguished according to their attitude towards the power of state organisations. In their political programmes, terms such as 'traditional', 'principle' and even 'pragmatic' often appear.

Having set out the methodology for analysing concepts, it will also be used for the analysis of the referred powers of the trias politica:

- Judicial power
- Legislative power
- Executive power
- Other?

Legislative and executive powers are both concerned with initiating and acting, whereas the judicial power is mainly concerned with supervising and correcting. The executive power is associated with the large-scale exertion of state power. This is illustrated by the 'double dichotomy' shown in Table 2.

In the cell, marked with '?', there is space for a fourth power that is supervising and correcting as well as associated with the large-scale exertion of power. Such a power could be called the 'monitoring power'. Institutions like the government audit office and the ombudsman are probably the first signs of the new power.

*Table 3. The Tetras politica*

| The **Tetras** politica | |
|---|---|
| Judicial power | Legislative power |
| Monitoring power | Executive power |

The monitoring power would not be concerned with individual cases - those would stay within the realm of the judiciary - but with systematic, empirical investigation into the functioning of the other powers, including the judiciary. All the formal powers needed would be the competence to access all the information that the other powers have access to, as well as the competence to interrogate the members of the other powers.

The work of the new power is not limited to monitoring the other powers solely on the basis of conformity to the existing legal rules. The monitoring power will evaluate and criticise the other powers in a more general and comprehensive way. Not only legitimacy, but also effectiveness and efficiency would be investigated. Citizens are better off with the ombudsman than with a court for certain complaints. The ombudsman could carry out empirical research into the way civil servants have acted in general and suggestions for improvement could be made. On the basis of these investigations, the citizen could put his case to a judge if that would still be required. Furthermore, for the evidence to be produced with respect to certain complaints, for example in discrimination cases, statistical data are necessary. The victims in such cases would usually not have the means to produce these data themselves. Finally, for all citizens it would seem to be an attractive prospect if the judiciary - as well as the other powers - would be systematically monitored by an organisation that has the relevant powers and the skills for such monitoring.

## CONCLUSION: THE MONITORING POWER

It would seem that the advent of the information society has had an effect on traditional priorities. More information is available than ever before and the easy access to information has transformed the way in which people deal with and value information. The dichotomy between personal privacy and free access to information, which has come increasingly to the fore with the advance of information technology, justifies a reconsideration of these traditional values and interests.

A pre-requisite to prevent the abuse of surveillance technology is that its use has to be transparent. Those involved then have the opportunity to know how the information about them is used, and may take appropriate action. As surveillance technology is used by government agencies as well as by private parties, it is increasingly important that the monitoring of this use is organized in an independent way. Openness and transparency – as well as proper monitoring - are more important in this respect than restrictions and limitations to the access and to the processing of information.

The most important factor in the implementation of new technology is the expected level of efficiency and effectiveness. The use of technology depends on what it can achieve and how much it costs. Less obvious perhaps is that it is also responsible for a shift in norms. Technology has made things possible that were once not possible; this ranges from copying films from the Internet at home to interactive television to in vitro fertilisation. New technology has made existing norms less self-evident; indeed some norms seem to change with the times. A person who would not dream of going to a cinema without paying for a ticket, could easily be prepared to download a new film at home.

Technology not only makes surveillance a more practical matter, in a more complex way it leads to a new organization of state power. This is possibly the most important point of discussion with respect to legal and social change as a response to technological progress. It has been argued that a new fourth power is inevitable; just as the appearance of an executive power was inevitable once the law could not only be written but also printed. That development led to the large-scale bureaucracies we see today. The technical possibilities offered by computers and the Internet will not be less far-reaching. The appearance of a new power, a monitoring power, would seem likely. We have already witnessed this development in the form of such institutions as the Ombudsman, the National Audit Office and the National Competition Authority.

This new power, the result of social change, will have far-reaching consequences for the law, and for the functioning of the state of law and the legal profession. The growth of the executive power led to large-scale bureaucracies. Bureaucracies may be of use, but can easily lead to excesses. The systematic monitoring of those in charge of the use of surveillance technology in a democratic state is a necessity. In a globalizing and increasingly technological world democracies will need monitoring powers to supervise the use of surveillance techniques.

## REFERENCES

American Government Accountability Office (GAO) (2005). *Information Security, Radio*

*Frequency Identification Technology in the Federal Government*. From http://www.gao.gov/new.items/d05551.pdf

Budowle, B., Carmody, G., Chakraborty, R., & Monson, K. L. (2000). Source attribution of a forensic DNA profile. In *Forensic Science Communications, 2*(3), FBI Laboratory. From http://www.fbi.gov/hq/lab/fsc/backissu/july2000/source.htm

Fukuyama, F. (1992). *The end of history and the last man*. New York, New York: Avon Books.

Jain, A. K., Hong, L., Pankanti, S., & Bolle R. (1997). An identity authentication system using fingerprints. In *Proceedings of the IEEE, 85*(9), (pp. 1365-1388).

Jensen, M. C., & Meckling, W. H. (1994). The Nature of Man. *Journal of Applied Corporate Finance,* (2), 4-19.

Katz-Bassett, E., John, J. P., Krishnamurthy, A., Wetherall, D., Anderson T., & Chawathe, Y. (2006). Towards IP geolocation using delay and topology measurements. In *IMC '06: Proceedings of the 6th ACM SIGCOMM conference on Internet measurement* (pp. 71-84). Rio de Janeiro: ACM.

Kerr, O. S. (2003). Internet Surveillance Law After the USA Patriot Act: The Big Brother That Isn't'. *Northwestern University Law Review*, (97). From http://ssrn.com/abstract=317501

Kleve, P., & Kolff, F. (1999). MP3: The End Of Copyright As We Know It? *Proceedings of the IASTED International Conference Law and Technology (LawTech'99)*. Honolulu, Hawaii: IASTED.

Kleve, P. (2004). *Juridische iconen in het informatietijdperk* (Legal Icons in the Information Age, with summary in English) (diss.) Rotterdam/Deventer, Holland: Sanders/Kluwer.

Kleve, P. Mulder, R. V. De, & Noortwijk, C. van (2006). The Amazing Diversity Framework of the Intellectual Property Rights Harmonisation. In Brockdorff et al., (Eds.), *Globalisation and Harmonisation in Technology Law, proceedings 21th Bileta conference 06-04-2006*. Malta: Bileta.

Kuhn, T. S. (1962). *The structure of scientific revolutions*. Chicago, Illinois: University of Chicago Press.

Mulder, R. V. De (1984). *Een model voor juridische informatica (A Model for Legal Computer Science, with summary in English)* (diss.), Lelystad, Holland: Vermande.

Mulder, R. V. De (1998). The Digital Revolution: From Trias to Tetras Politica. In I. Th. M. Snellen & W. B. H. J. van de Donk (Eds.), *Public Administration in an Information Age. A Handbook* (pp. 47-56). Amsterdam, Holland: IOS Press.

Muller, E. R., Spaaij, R. F., & Ruitenberg, A. G. W. (2003). *Trends in terrorisme*. Alphen aan den Rijn, Holland: Kluwer.

Solove, D. J. (2001). Privacy and Power: Computer Databases and Metaphors for Information Privacy. *Stanford Law Review*, (53). From http://docs.law.gwu.edu/facweb/dsolove/Privacy-Power.pdf

Verhoeff, J. (1980). Is de chip in de hand te houden? (Can we keep a grip on the chip?). In *Spectrum Yearbook 1980*. Utrecht, Holland: Het Spectrum.

Weber, M. (1968). *Economy and Society. An Outline of Interpretive Sociology*, New York, New York: Bedminster Press.

# Chapter XIII
# Designing Light Weight Intrusion Detection Systems:
## Non-Negative Matrix Factorization Approach

**Václav Snášel**
*VSB—Technical University of Ostrava, Czech Republic*

**Jan Platoš**
*VSB—Technical University of Ostrava, Czech Republic*

**Pavel Krömer**
*VSB—Technical University of Ostrava, Czech Republic*

**Ajith Abraham**
*Norwegian University of Science and Technology, Norway*

## ABSTRACT

*Recently cyber security has emerged as an established discipline for computer systems and infrastructures with a focus on protection of valuable information stored on those systems from adversaries who want to obtain, corrupt, damage, destroy or prohibit access to it. An Intrusion Detection System (IDS) is a program that analyzes what happens or has happened during an execution and tries to find indications that the computer has been misused. This chapter presents some of the challenges in designing efficient ad light weight intrusion detection systems, which could provide high accuracy, low false alarm rate and reduced number of features. Finally, the authors present the Non-negative matrix factorization method for detecting real attacks and the performance comparison with other computational intelligence techniques.*

## INTRODUCTION TO INTRUSION DETECTION SYSTEMS

Intrusion detection system were proposed to complement prevention-based security measures. An intrusion is defined to be a violation of the security policy of the system; intrusion detection thus refers to the mechanisms that are developed to detect violations of system security policy. Intrusion detection is based on the assumption that intrusive activities are noticeably different from normal system activities and thus detectable. Intrusion detection is not introduced to replace prevention-based techniques such as authentication and access control; instead, it is intended to complement existing security measures and detect actions that bypass the security monitoring and control component of the system. Intrusion detection is therefore considered as a second line of defense for computer and network systems. Generally, an intrusion would cause loss of integrity, confidentiality, denial of resources, or unauthorized use of resources. Some specific examples of intrusions that concern system administrators include (Bishop, 2003):

- Unauthorized modifications of system files so as to facilitate illegal access to either system or user information.
- Unauthorized access or modification of user files or information.
- Unauthorized modifications of tables or other system information in network components (e.g. modifications of router tables in an internet to deny use of the network).
- Unauthorized use of computing resources (perhaps through the creation of unauthorized accounts or perhaps through the unauthorized use of existing accounts).

Some of the important features an intrusion detection system should possess include:

- Be fault tolerant and run continually with minimal human supervision. The IDS must be able to recover from system crashes, either accidental or caused by malicious activity.
- Possess the ability to resist subversion so that an attacker cannot disable or modify the IDS easily. Furthermore, the IDS must be able to detect any modifications forced on the IDS by an attacker
- Impose minimal overhead on the system to avoid interfering with the normal operation of the system.
- Be configurable so as to accurately implement the security policies of the systems that are being monitored. The IDS must be adaptable to changes in system and user behavior over time.
- Be easy to deploy: This can be achieved through portability to different architectures and operating systems, through simple installation mechanisms, and by being easy to use by the operator.
- Be general enough to detect different types of attacks and must not recognize any legitimate activity as an attack (false positives). At the same time, the IDS must not fail to recognize any real attacks (false negatives).

An IDS maybe be a combination of software and hardware. Most IDSs try to perform their task in real time. However, there are also IDSs that do not operate in real time, either because of the nature of the analysis they perform or because they are meant for forensic analysis (analysis of what happened in the past to a system). There are some intrusion detection systems that try to react when they detect an unauthorized action. This reaction usually includes trying to limit the damage, for example by terminating a network connection.

Since the amount of audit data that an IDS needs to be examined is very large even for a small network, analysis is difficult even with computer assistance because extraneous features can make it harder to detect suspicious behavior patterns (Lee et al., 1999). Audit data captures various features of the connections. For example, the audit data would show the source and destination bytes of a TCP connection, or the number of failed login attempts or duration of a connection. Complex relationships exist between the features, which are difficult for humans to discover. An IDS must therefore reduce the amount of data to be processed. This is very important if real-time detection is desired. Some data may not be useful to the IDS and thus can be eliminated before processing. In complex classification domains, features may contain false correlations, which hinder the process of detecting intrusions. Further, some features may be redundant since the information they add is contained in other features. Extra features can increase computation time, and can have an impact on the accuracy of the IDS. Feature selection improves classification by searching for the subset of features, which best classifies the training data (Sung and Mukkamala, 2003).

In the literature several machine learning paradigms, fuzzy inference systems and expert systems, have been used to develop IDSs (Lee et al, 1999; Luo and Bridges, 2000). Sung and Mukkamala (2003) have demonstrated that a large number of features are unimportant and may be eliminated, without significantly lowering the performance of the IDS. The literature indicates very little scientific efforts aimed at modeling efficient IDS feature selection. The task of an IDS is often modeled as a classification problem in a machine-learning context.

In this chapter, we provide an overview of the different data mining techniques for selecting a subset of significant features from a feature set for network data. We then introduce the matrix factorization approach for feature reduction and detection.

Rest of the chapter is organized as follows: In Section 2 the aims and objectives of different intrusion detection methods are presented. The different types of intrusion detection systems are described in Section 3. In Section 4, we review modern data mining approaches for intrusion detection. Our proposed data mining paradigms for intrusion detection, namely, for feature selection and classification based on Non-Negative Matrix Factorization (NMF) reduction dimension method are presented in Sections 5 and 6. Experimental results are reported in Section 7 followed by conclusions.

## INTRUSION DETECTION METHODS

The signatures of some attacks are known, whereas other attacks only reflect some deviation from normal patterns. Consequently, two main approaches have been devised to detect intruders.

### Anomaly Detection

Anomaly detection assumes that an intrusion will always reflect some deviations from normal patterns. Anomaly detection may be divided into static and dynamic anomaly detection. A static anomaly detector is based on the assumption that there is a portion of the system being monitored that does not change. Usually, static detectors only address the software portion of a system and are based on the assumption that the hardware need not be checked. The static portion of a system is the code for the system and the constant portion of data upon which the correct functioning of the system depends. For example, the operating systems software and data to bootstrap a computer never change. If the static portion of the system ever deviates from its original form, an error has occurred or an intruder has altered the static portion of the system. Therefore Static anomaly detectors focus on integrity checking (Kim and Spafford, 1995; Forrest et al., 1994). Dynamic anomaly detection typically operate on audit records or on monitored networked traffic data. Audit records of operating systems do not record all events; they only record events of interest. Therefore only behavior that results in an event that is recorded in the audit will be observed and these events may occur in a sequence. In distributed systems, partial ordering of events is sufficient for detection. In other cases, the order is not directly represented; only cumulative information, such as cumulative processor resource used during a time interval, is maintained. In this case, thresholds are defined to separate normal resource consumption from anomalous resource consumption.

## Misuse Detection

Misuse detection is based on the knowledge of system vulnerabilities and known attack patterns. Misuse detection is concerned with finding intruders who are attempting to break into a system by exploiting some known vulnerability. Ideally, a system security administrator should be aware of all the known vulnerabilities and eliminate them. The term intrusion scenario is used as a description of a known kind of intrusion; it is a sequence of events that would result in an intrusion without some outside preventive intervention. An intrusion detection system continually compares recent activity to known intrusion scenarios to ensure that one or more attackers are not attempting to exploit known vulnerabilities. To perform this, each intrusion scenario must be described or modeled. The main difference between the misuse techniques is in how they describe or model the behavior that constitutes an intrusion. The original misuse detection systems used rules to describe events indicative of intrusive actions that a security administrator looked for within the system. Large numbers of rules can be difficult to interpret. *If-then* rules are not grouped by intrusion scenarios and therefore making modifications to the rule set can be difficult as the affected rules are spread out across the rule set. To overcome these difficulties, new rule organizational techniques include model-based rule organization and state transition diagrams. Misuse detection systems use the rules to look for events that possibly fit an intrusion scenario. The events may be monitored live by monitoring system calls or later using audit records.

## Advantages and Disadvantages of Anomaly Detection and Misuse Detection

The main disadvantage of misuse detection approaches is that they will detect only the attacks for which they are trained to detect. Novel attacks or unknown attacks or even variants of common attacks often go undetected. At a time when new security vulnerabilities in software are discovered and exploited every day, the reactive approach embodied by misuse detection methods is not feasible for defeating malicious attacks. The main advantage of anomaly detection approaches is the ability to detect novel attacks or unknown attacks against software systems, variants of known attacks, and deviations of normal usage of programs regardless of whether the source is a privileged internal user or an unauthorized external user. The disadvantage of the anomaly detection approach is that well-known attacks may not be detected, particularly if they fit the established profile of the user. Once detected, it is often difficult to characterize the nature of the attack for forensic purposes. Another drawback of many anomaly detection approaches is that a malicious user who knows that he or she is being profiled can change the profile slowly over time to essentially train the anomaly detection system to learn the attacker's malicious behavior as normal. Finally a high false positive rate may result for a narrowly trained detection algorithm, or conversely, a high false negative rate may result for a broadly trained anomaly detection approach.

## TYPES OF INTRUSION DETECTION SYSTEMS

There are two types of intrusion detection systems that employ one or both of the intrusion detection methods outlined above. Host-based systems base their decisions on information obtained from a single host (usually audit trails), while network-based intrusion detection systems obtain data by monitoring the traffic in the network to which the hosts are connected.

### Host-Based Intrusion Detection

A generic intrusion detection model proposed by Denning (1987) is a rule-based pattern matching system in which the intrusion detection tasks are conducted by checking the similarity between the current audit record and the corresponding profiles. If the current audit record deviates from the normal patterns, it will be considered an anomaly. Several IDSs were developed using profile and rule-based approaches to identify intrusive activity (Lunt et al., 1988).

### Network-Based Intrusion Detection

With the proliferation of computer networks, more and more individual hosts are connected into local area networks and/or wide area networks. However, the hosts, as well as the networks, are exposed to intrusions due to the vulnerabilities of network devices and network protocols. The TCP/IP protocol can be also exploited by network intrusions such as IP spoofing, port scanning, and so on. Therefore, network-based intrusion detection has become important and is designed to protect a computer network as well as all of its hosts. The installation of a network-based intrusion detection system can also decrease the burden of the intrusion detection task on every individual host.

## DATA MINING APPROACHES TOWARD INTRUSION DETECTION

Data mining approaches are new methods in intrusion detection systems. Data mining is defined as the semi-automatic discovery of patterns, associations, changes, anomalies, rules, and statistically significant structures and events in data (Hand et al., 2001). Data mining attempts to extract knowledge in the form of models from data, which may not be seen easily with the naked eye. There exist many different types of data mining algorithms including classification, regression, clustering, association rule abduction, deviation analysis, sequence analysis etc.

Various data mining techniques have been applied to intrusion detection because it has the advantage of discovering useful knowledge that describes a user's or program's behavior from large audit data sets. Data mining has been used for anomaly detection (Lee and Stolfo, 1998; Lunt et al., 1992). Statistics (Debar et al., 1992; Anderson et al., 1995), Artificial Neural Network (ANN) (Lippmann and Cunningham, 2000; Cho and Park, 2003) and Hidden Markov Model (HMM) (Cohen, 1995), Rule Learning (Lazarevic et al., 2003), Outlier Detection scheme (Han and Cho, 2003), Support Vector Machines (Abraham, 2001a), Neuro-Fuzzy (NF) computing (Mukkamala et al., 2003), Multivariate Adaptive Regression Splines (Banzhaf et al, 1998) and Linear Genetic Programming (Mukkamala et al., 2004b) are the main data mining techniques widely used for anomaly and misuse detections.

Statistics is the most widely used technique, which defines normal behavior by collecting data relating to the behavior of legitimate users over a period of time (Anderson et al., 1995). NIDES (Next-generation Intrusion Detection Expert Systems) is the representative IDS based on statistics that measures the similarity between a subject's long-term behavior and short term behavior for intrusion detection (Debar et al., 1992). The detection rate is high because it can use various types of audit data and detect intrusion based on the previous experimental data. In NIDES known attacks and intrusion scenarios are encoded in a rule-base. It is therefore not sensitive to some behaviors and detectable types of intrusions are limited. Hyperview is a representative IDS using neural networks (Lippmann and Cunningham, 2000). It consists of 2 modules: a neural network and an expert system. R. Lippmann et al. have applied neural networks to a keyword-based detection system (Cho and Park, 2003). While the artificial neural network has some similarity to statistical techniques, it has the advantage of easier representation of nonlinear relationships between input and output. Even if the data is incomplete or distorted, a neural network would be capable of analyzing the data from a network. Another advantage of neural networks is its inherent computational speed. The defects of neural networks are that its computational load is very heavy and it is difficult to interpret the relationship between inputs and outputs. An HMM is a useful tool to model the sequence of observed symbols of which the construction mechanism cannot be known (Cohen, 1995). While HMM produces better performance in modeling system call events compared to other methods, it requires a very long time for modeling normal behaviors. Using this model, raw data is first converted into ASCII network packet information, which in turn is converted into connection level information using Mining Audit Data for Automated Models for Intrusion Detection (MADAMID - Lee et al., 1999). RIPPER (Lazarevic et al., 2003), a rule learning tool, is then applied to the data generated by MADAMID. RIPPER automatically mines the patterns of intrusion. Although it is a good tool for discovering known patterns, an anomaly detection technique is required for the detection of novel intrusions. Another data mining technique, the outlier detection scheme attempts to identify a data point that is very different from the rest of the data. A. Lazarevic et al. have applied it to anomaly detection (Han and Cho, 2003). Support Vector Machines (SVM) are learning machines that plot training vectors in high dimensional feature space, labeling each vector by its class. SVMs have proven to be a good candidate for intrusion detection because of its speed and scalability (Mukkamala et al., 2003).

In Neuro-Fuzzy (NF) computing (Abraham, 2001a), if we have knowledge expressed in the form of linguistic rules, we can build a Fuzzy Inference System (FIS), and if we have data, then we can use ANNs. While the learning capability is an advantage from the viewpoint of FIS, the formation of a linguistic rule base will be advantageous from the viewpoint of ANN. An Adaptive neuro-fuzzy IDS is proposed by Shah et al. (2004). Multivariate Adaptive Regression Splines (MARS) is an innovative approach that automates the building of accurate predictive models for continuous and binary dependent variables. It excels at finding optimal variable transformations and interactions, and the complex data structure that often hides in high-dimensional data (Abraham and Steinberg, 2001; Banzhaf et al, 1998). An IDS based on MARS is proposed in (Abraham and Steinberg, 2001). In Linear Genetic Programming (LGP) (as opposed to tree-based Genetic Programming (GP) - Sequeira and Zaki, 2002) computer programs are evolved at the machine code level, using lower level representations for the individuals. This can tremendously hasten up the evolution process. LGP based IDS is presented in (Mukkamala et al., 2004a). To overcome the drawbacks of single-measure detectors, a multiple measure intrusion detection method is proposed by Jolliffe (1986). In this approach hidden Markov model, statistical method and rule-base method are integrated with a rule-based approach. In (Chebrolu et al., 2004) the authors have proposed an ensemble IDS that combines the strengths of Bayesian Networks and Classification and Regression Trees for intrusion detection.

None of the above works have proposed a rigorous and scientific approach for increasing and improving the efficiency of intrusion detection. The next section outlines our proposed data mining approach for faster and more effective intrusion detection.

## THE DATA MINING PROCESS OF BUILDING INTRUSION DETECTION MODELS

Raw (binary) audit data is first processed into ASCII network packet information (or host event data), which is in turn summarized into connection records (or host session records) containing a number of within-connection features, e.g., service, duration, flag etc. (indicating the normal or error status according to the protocols). Data mining programs are then applied to the connection records to compute the frequent patterns i.e. association rules and frequent episodes, which are in turn analyzed to construct additional features for the connection records. Classification algorithms are then used to inductively learn the detection model. This process is of course iterative. For example, poor performance of the classification models often indicates that more pattern mining and feature construction is needed.

### Importance of Data Reduction for Intrusion Detection Systems

IDSs have become important and widely used tools for ensuring network security. Since the amount of audit data that an IDS needs to be examined is very large even for a small network, manual classification is impossible. Analysis is difficult even with computer assistance because extraneous features can make it harder to detect suspicious behavior patterns. Complex relationships exist between the features, which are practically impossible for humans to discover. An IDS must therefore reduce the amount of data to be processed. This is extremely important if real-time detection is desired. Reduction can occur in one of several ways. Data that is not considered useful can be filtered, leaving only the potentially interesting data. Data can be grouped or clustered to reveal hidden patterns. By storing the characteristics of the clusters instead of the individual data, overhead can be significantly reduced. Finally, some data sources can be eliminated using feature selection.

### Data Filtering

The purpose of data filtering is to reduce the amount of data directly processed by the IDS. Some data may not be useful to the IDS and thus can be eliminated before processing. This has the advantage of decreasing storage requirements, reducing processing time and improving the detection rate (as data irrelevant to intrusion detection is discarded). However, filtering may throw out useful data, and so must be done carefully.

### Feature Selection

In complex classification domains, some data may hinder the classification process. Features may contain false correlations, which hinder the process of detecting intrusions. Further, some features may be redundant since the information they add is contained in other features. Extra features can increase computation time, and can impact the accuracy of IDS. Feature selection improves classification by searching for the subset of features, which best classifies the training data. The features under consideration depend on the type of IDS, for example, a network based IDS will analyze network related information such as packet destination IP address, logged in time of a user, type of protocol, duration of connection etc. It is not known which of these features are redundant or irrelevant for IDS and which ones are relevant or essential for IDS. There does not exist any model or function that captures the relationship between different features or between the different attacks and features. If such a model did exist, the intrusion detection process would be simple and straightforward. In this paper we use data mining techniques for feather selection. The subset of selected features is then used to detect intrusions.

### Data Clustering

Clustering can be performed to find hidden patterns in data and significant features for use in detection. Clustering can also be used as a reduction technique by storing the characteristics of the clusters instead of the individual data. In previous work a number of experiments have been performed to measure the performance of different machine learning paradigms as mentioned in Section 3.3. Classifications were performed on the binary (normal/attack) as well as five-class classifications (normal, and four classes of attacks). It has been demonstrated that a large number of the (41) input features are unimportant and may be eliminated, without significantly lowering the performance of the IDS (Sung and Mukkamala, 2003). In terms of the five-class classification, Sung and Mukkamala (2003) have found that by using only 19 of the most important features, instead of the entire 41 feature set, the change in accuracy of intrusion detection was statistically insignificant. Sung and Mukkamala applied the technique of deleting one feature at time. Each reduced feature set was then tested on Support Vector Machines and Neural Networks to rank the importance of input features. The reduced feature set that yielded the best detection rate in the experiments was considered to be the set of important features. Unlike the work reported by Sung and Mukkamala (2003), which employed a trial-and-error based approach, we investigate feature reduction using data mining techniques. Our work correspondingly focuses on approaches that will improve the performance of IDSs by providing real-time intrusion detection. This is achieved by reducing the data space and then classifying intrusions based on the reduced feature space.

## FEATURE SELECTION AND CLASSIFICATION

Data reduction is a critical problem for intrusion detection; there are large collections of documents that must be analyzed and processed, raising issues related to performance, lossless reduction etc. Matrix factorization or factor analysis is an important task helpful in the analysis of high dimensional real world data. There are several well known methods and algorithms for factorization of real data but many application areas including information retrieval, pattern recognition and data mining require processing of binary rather than real data see (Moravec and Snášel, 2006; Húsek et al., 2007; Snášel et al., 2007). Non-negative matrix factorization is really a class of decompositions whose members are not necessarily closely related to each other (Elden, 2007; Skillicorn, 2007). They share the property that are designed for datasets in which attribute values are never negative – and its does not make sense for the decomposition matrices to contain negative values either. A side-effect of this non-negativity property is that the mixing of components that we have seen is one way to understand decompositions can only be additive. With the standard vector space model a set of data S can be expressed as a $m \times n$ matrix V, where m is the number of attributes and n is the number of documents in S. Each column $V_j$ of V is an encoding of a document in S and each entry $v_{ij}$ of vector $V_j$ is the value of i-th term with regard to the semantics of $V_j$, where i ranges across attributes. The NMF problem is defined as finding an approximation of V in terms of some metric (e.g., the norm) by factoring V into the product WH of two reduced-dimensional matrices W and H. Each column of W is a basis vector. It contains an encoding of a semantic space or concept from V and each column of H contains an encoding of the linear combination of the basis vectors that approximates the corresponding column of V. Dimensions of W and H are $m \times k$ and $k \times n$, where k is the reduced rank. Usually k is chosen to be much smaller than n. Finding the appropriate value of k depends on the application and is also influenced by the nature of the collection itself.

Common approaches to NMF obtain an approximation of V by computing a (W, H) pair to minimize the Frobenius norm of the difference V-WH. The matrices W and H are not unique. Usually H is initialized to zero and W to a randomly generated matrix where each $W_{ij} > 0$ and these initial values are improved with iterations of the algorithm.

**Algorithm**

1. Initialize W and H with nonnegative values, and scale the columns of W to unit norm.
2. Iterate until convergence or after l iterations:
   a. $W_{ic} \leftarrow W_{ic} \frac{(VH^T)_{ic}}{(WHH^T)_{ic}+\varepsilon}$, for c and i [$\varepsilon=10^{-9}$]
   b. Rescale the columns of W to unit norm
   c. Solve the constrained least squares problem $\min_{H_j} \{\| V_j - WH_j \|_2^2 + \lambda \| H_j \|_2^2 \}$, where the subscript j denotes the j-th column, for j = 1,..,m. Any negative values in Hj are set to zero. The parameter k is a regularization value that is used to balance the reduction of the metric $\| V_j - WH_j \|_2^2$ with the enforcement of smoothness and sparsity in H.

For any given matrix V, matrix W has k columns or basis vectors that represent k clusters, matrix H has n columns that represent n documents. A column vector in H has k components, each of which denotes the contribution of the corresponding basis vector to that column or document. The clustering of documents is then performed based on the index of the highest value of k for each document. For document i (i = 1,…,n), if the maximum value is the j-th entry (j = 1,…,k), document i is assigned to cluster j. Thus, NMF can be used to organize data collections into partitioned structures or clusters directly derived from the nonnegative factors. Potential applications include the monitoring, tracking and clustering of semantic features (topics) and can be used for intrusion detection.

## EXPERIMENTAL RESULTS

The data for our experiments was prepared by the 1998 DARPA intrusion detection evaluation program by MIT Lincoln Labs (MIT Lincoln Laboratory). The original data contains 744 MB data with 4,940,000 records. The data set has 41 attributes for each connection record plus one class label. Some features are derived features, which are useful in distinguishing normal connection from attacks. These features are either nominal or numeric. Some features examine only the connections in the past two seconds that have the same destination host as the current connection, and calculate statistics related to protocol behavior, service, etc. These are called same host features. Some features examine only the connections in the past two seconds that have the same service as the current connection and are called same service features. Some other connection records were also sorted by destination host, and features were constructed using a window of 100 connections to the same host instead of a time window. These are called host-based traffic features.

Our experiments have three phases namely data reduction, a training phase and a testing phase. In the data reduction phase, important variables for real-time intrusion detection are selected by feature selection. In the training phase, the matrix factorization method is used construct a model using the training data to give maximum generalization accuracy on the unseen data. The test data is then passed through the saved trained model to detect intrusions in the testing phase. The data set for our experiments contains randomly generated 11982 records having 41 features (KDD cup, 1999). The labels of the 41 features and their

*Table 1. Network data feature labels*

| Label | Network Data Feature | Label | Network Data Feature | Label | Network Data Feature | Label | Network Data Feature |
|---|---|---|---|---|---|---|---|
| *A* | *duration* | *L* | *logged_in* | *W* | *count* | *AH* | *dst_host_ same_srv_rate* |
| *B* | *protocol-type* | *M* | *num_compromised* | *X* | *srv_count* | *AI* | *dst_host_diff_srv_rate* |
| *C* | *service* | *N* | *root_shell* | *Y* | *serror_rate* | *AJ* | *dst_host_same_ src_port_rate* |
| *D* | *flag* | *O* | *su_attempted* | *Z* | *srv_serror_rate* | *AK* | *dst_host_srv_ diff_host_rate* |
| *E* | *src_bytes* | *P* | *num_root* | *AA* | *rerror_rate* | *AL* | *dst_host_serror_rate* |
| *F* | *dst_bytes* | *Q* | *num_file_creations* | *AB* | *srv_rerror_rate* | *AM* | *dst_host_srv_ serror_rate* |
| *G* | *land* | *R* | *num_shells* | *AC* | *same_srv_rate* | *AN* | *dst_host_rerror_rate* |
| *H* | *wrong_fragment* | *S* | *num_access_files* | *AD* | *diff_srv_rate* | AO | *dst_host_srv_rerror_rate* |
| *I* | *urgent* | *T* | *num_outbound_ cmds* | *AE* | *srv_diff_host_rate* | | |
| *J* | *hot* | *U* | *is_host_login* | *AF* | *dst_host_count* | | |
| *K* | *num_falied_ logins* | *V* | *is_guest_login* | *AG* | *dst_host_srv_ count* | | |

*Table 2. Performance using non-negative matrix factorization (NMF) approach*

| Attack Class | 41 variable data set | | | 12 variable reduced data set | | |
|---|---|---|---|---|---|---|
| | Train (sec) | Test (sec) | Accuracy (%) | Train (sec) | Test (sec) | Accuracy (%) |
| **Normal** | 23.36 | 27.39 | **77.68** | 5.17 | 9.64 | 77.42 |
| **Probe** | 23.51 | 32.48 | 89.87 | 5.00 | 6.31 | **95.09** |
| **DOS** | 23.37 | 34.95 | 78.13 | 4.82 | 7.61 | **81.04** |
| **U2R** | 23.23 | 29.90 | **97.45** | 5.29 | 8.84 | 92.50 |
| **R2L** | 22.78 | 30.00 | 98.55 | 5.53 | 9.29 | **98.59** |

corresponding network data features are shown in Table 1.

The training and test comprises of 5092 and 6890 records respectively. We focus on User to Root (U2R) attack category and a binary classification method was used. Performance of the Non-negative matrix factorization (NMF) approach using the complete dataset and the reduced data set is depicted in Table 2. A comparison of NMF approach with other computational intelligence approaches is depicted in Table 3. Comparison results presented in Table 3 are adapted from Abraham et al. (2005).

## CONCLUSION

In this chapter, we illustrated the basic taxonomy of intrusion detection systems with a focus on data mining approach for system design. We

*Table 3. Classification accuracies for U2R attack category using complete data set*

| Computational intelligence technique | Classification Accuracy (%) |
|---|---|
| Artificial neural network | 48.00 |
| Bayesian neural network | 64.00 |
| Support vector machine | 40.00 |
| Decision trees | 68.00 |
| Linear genetic programming | 64.00 |
| Multi expression programming | 99.75 |
| Multi-variate adaptive regression trees | 99.71 |
| Ant-colony clustering | 64.00 |
| Flexible neural trees | 99.70 |
| Non-negative matrix factorization | 97.45 |

explored a detection model based on clustering using NMF dimension reduction method. We have also demonstrated performance comparisons using reduced data sets for the U2R attack category. From the empirical results, it is evident that data mining approach offers a promising tool for real time intrusion detection system design.

## REFERENCES


Abraham, A. (2001). Neuro-Fuzzy Systems: State-of-the-Art Modeling Techniques, Connectionist Models of Neurons, Learning Processes, and Artificial Intelligence. *Lecture Notes in Computer Science Volume 2084*, J. Mira and A. Prieto (Eds.), Granada, Spain. Germany: Springer-Verlag, (pp. 269-276).

Abraham, A., Grosan, C., & Chen, Y. (2005). Cyber Security and the Evolution in Intrusion Detection Systems. *Journal of Engineering and Technology, ISSN 0973-2632, I-Manager Publications, 1*(1), 74-81.

Anderson, D., Lunt, T. F., Javits, H., Tamaru, A., & Valdes, A. (1995). Detecting unusual program behavior using the statistical components of NIDES. *NIDES Technical Report*, SRI International, May 1995.

Banzhaf, W., Nordin, P., Keller. E. R., & Francone F. D. (1998). *Genetic Programming: An Introduction on The Automatic Evolution of Computer Programs and its Applications*. Morgan Kaufmann Publishers, Inc.

Bishop, M. (2003). *Computer Security – Art and Science*. Addison Wesley.

Chebrolu, S., Abraham, A., & Thomas, J. P. (2004). Hybrid Feature Selection for Modeling Intrusion Detection Systems. *11th International Conference on Neural Information Processing.*

Cho, S.-B., & Park, H.-J. (2003). Efficient anomaly detection by modeling privilege flows with hidden Markov model. *Computers & Security, 22*(1), 45-55.

Cohen, W. W. (1995). Fast effective rule induction. *Proceedings of the 12th International Conference on Machine Learning,* (pp. 115-123), July 1995.

Debar, H., Becker, M., & Siboni, D. (1992). A neural network component for an intrusion detection system. *Proceedings of 1992 IEEE Computer Society Symposium on Research in*

*Security and Privacy*, Oakland, CA, May 1992, (pp. 240-250).

Denning, D. E. (1987). An Intrusion-Detection Model. *IEEE Transactions on Software Engineering, SE-13*(2), 222-232.

Elden, L. (2007). Matrix Methods in Data Mining and Pattern Recognition. *SIAM 2007.*

Forrest, S., Perelson, A. S., Allen, L., & Cherukuri, R. (1994). Self-Nonself Discrimination in a Computer. *Proceedings of the 1994 IEEE Symposium on Research in Security and Privacy.* Los Alamitos, CA: IEEE Computer Society Press.

Han, S.-J., & S.-B. Cho, S.-B. (2003). Detecting intrusion with rule-based integration of multiple models. *Computers & Security, 22*(7), 613-623.

Hand, D. J., Mannila, H., & Smyth, P. (2001). *Principles of Data Mining (Adaptive Computation and Machine Learning).* Bradford Books.

Húsek, D., Moravec, P., Snásel, V., Frolov, A. A., Rezanková, H., & Polyakov, P. (2007).*Comparison of Neural Network Boolean Factor Analysis Method with Some Other Dimension Reduction Methods on Bars Problem.* Springer, LNCS 4815, PReMI 2007: (pp. 235-243).

Jolliffe, I.T. (1986). *Principal Component Analysis.* Germany: Springer-Verlag.

KDD cup 99. *Intrusion detection data set.* http://kdd.ics.uci.edu/databases/kddcup99/kddcup.data_10_percent.gz

Kim, G. H., & Spafford, E. H. (1995). *Experiences with Tripwire: Using Integrity Checkers for Intrusion Detection.* http://citeseer.ist.psu.edu/kim95experiences.html

Lazarevic, A., Ertoz, L., Kumar, V., Ozgur, A., & Srivastava, J. (2003). A comparative study of anomaly detection schemes in network intrusion detection. *Proceedings of Third SIAM Conference on Data Mining*, May 2003.

Lee, W., & Stolfo, S. (1998). Data Mining Approaches for Intrusion Detection. *Proc. of the 7th USENIX Security Symposium*, San Antonio, Texas, January 26-29.

Lee, W., Stolfo, S., & Mok, K. (1999). A Data Mining Framework for Building Intrusion Detection Models. *Proceedings of the IEEE Symposium on Security and Privacy.*

Lippmann, R., & Cunningham, S. (2000). Improving intrusion detection performance using keyword selection and neural networks. *Computer Networks, 34*(4), 594- 603.

Luo, J., & Bridges, S. M. (2000). Mining Fuzzy Association Rules and Fuzzy Frequency Episodes for Intrusion Detection. *International Journal of Intelligent Systems, 15*(8), 687-704. John Wiley & Sons

Lunt, T. F., Jagannathan, R., Lee, R., Listgarten, S., Edwards, D. L. , Javitz, H. S., & Valdes, A. (1988). IDES: The Enhanced Prototype - A Real-Time Intrusion-Detection Expert System. *Number SRI-CSL-88-12. Computer Science Laboratory, SRI International, Menlo Park, CA.*

Lunt, T. F., Tamaru, A., Gilham, F., Jagannathan, R., Jalali, C., & Neuman, P.G. (1992). A real-time intrusion-detection expert system (IDES). *Technical Report Project 6784*, CSL, SRI International, Computer Science Laboratory, SRI International, February 1992.

*MIT Lincoln Laboratory.* http://www.ll.mit.edu/IST/ideval/

Moravec, P., & Snášel, V. (2006). Dimension Reduction Methods for Image Retrieval. In *Proceedings of the Conference on Intelligent Systems Design and Applications* (ISDA2006), Jinan, Shandong, China, October 2006. USA: IEEE Press.

Mukkamala, S., Sung, A. H., & Abraham, A. (2003). Intrusion Detection Using Ensemble of Soft Computing Paradigms. 3[rd] *International*

*Conference on Intelligent Systems Design and Applications, Intelligent Systems Design and Applications, Advances in Soft Computing.* Germany: Springer Verlag, (pp. 239-248).

Mukkamala, S., Sung, A. H., & Abraham, A. (2004a). Modeling Intrusion Detection Systems Using Linear Genetic Programming Approach. *The 17th International Conference on Industrial & Engineering Applications of Artificial Intelligence and Expert Systems,* Innovations in Applied Artificial Intelligence, R. Orchard, C. Yang, M. Ali (Eds.), LNCS 3029. Germany: Springer Verlag, (pp. 633-642).

Mukkamala, S., Sung, A. H., Abraham, A., & Ramos, V. (2004b). Intrusion Detection Systems Using Adaptive Regression Splines. In I. Seruca, J. Filipe, S. Hammoudi, & J. Cordeiro (Eds.), *6th International Conference on Enterprise Information Systems, ICEIS'04, 3,* 26-33. Portugal, ISBN 972-8865-00-7.

Shah, K., Dave, N., Sampada, C., Mukherjee, S., Abraham, A., & Sanyal, S. (2004). Adaptive Neuro-Fuzzy Intrusion Detection System. *IEEE International Conference on Information Technology: Coding and Computing (ITCC'04), 1,* 70-74. USA: IEEE Computer Society.

Skillicorn, D. (2007). *Understanding Complex Datasets: Data Mining with Matrix Decomposition.* Chapman & Hall.

Snášel, V., Húsek, D., Frolov, A. A., Řezanková,H., Moravec, P., & Polyakov, P. (2007). Bars Problem Solving - New Neural Network Method and Comparison. *Lecture Notes in Computer Science 4827, MICAI 2007*: (pp. 671-682).

Sung, A. H., & Mukkamala, S. (2003). Identifying Important Features for Intrusion Detection Using Support Vector Machines and Neural Networks. *Proceedings of International Symposium on Applications and the Internet (SAINT 2003),* (pp. 209-217).

Sequeira, K., & Zaki, M. (2002). ADMIT: Anomaly based Data Mining for Intrusions. *SIGKDD 2002,* Edmonton, Alberta, Canada.

## ADDITIONAL READING

Brieman, L., Friedman, J., Olshen, R., & Stone, C. (1984). *Classification of Regression Trees.* Wadsworth Inc.

Cheng, J., Greiner, R., Kelly, J., Bell, D. A., & Liu, W. (2002). Learning Bayesian Networks from Data: an Information-Theory Based Approach. *The Artificial Intelligence Journal, 137,* 43-90.

Dzeroski, S., & Zenko, B. (2002). Is Combining Classifiers Better than Selecting the Best One? *ICML 2002,* 123-130.

Hyvärinen, A., Karhunen, J., & Oja, E. (2001). *Independent Component Analysis.* John Wiley & Sons.

Ji, C., & Ma, S. (1997). Combinations of weak classifiers. *IEEE Transaction on Neural Networks, 8*(1), 32–42.

Neapolitan, R.E. (1990). *Probabilistic reasoning in expert systems: theory and algorithms.* John Wiley and Sons.

Tsamardinos, I., Aliferis, C.F., & Statnikov, A. (2003). Time and Sample Efficient Discovery of Markov Blankets and Direct Causal Relations. *9th ACM SIGKDD International Conference on Knowledge Discovery and Data Mining.* USA: ACM Press, (pp. 673-678).

## KEY TERMS

**Artificial Intelligence (AI):** The science of making intelligent machines, especially intelligent computer programs, that can engage on behaviors that humans consider "intelligent".

**Data Mining:** Techniques and processes used for searching, analyzing and filtering large amounts of data to find relationships, patterns, or any significant statistical correlations. With the advent of computers and especially the Internet, enormous databases, containing billions and even trillions of pieces of data can be systematically analyzed aiming to extract useful information.

**Expert System:** Software that performs a task that would otherwise be performed by a human expert. Some expert systems are designed to take the place of human experts, while others are designed to aid them. In both cases they are "experts" in some narrow problem area, and more or less embody a true human expert's knowledge, experience and problem-solving strategies.

**Fuzzy Logic:** Fuzzy logic is a superset of conventional (Boolean) logic that has been extended to a powerful problem-solving methodology with a numerous applications in embedded control and information processing. It handles the concept of partial truth - truth values between "completely true" and "completely false", resembling in a way the human decision making process which can yield precise solutions from approximate data.

**Neural Networks:** A broad term including diverse models and approaches of *artificial intelligence*, somewhat analogous to the human brain functioning. They capture, represent and process complex input/output relationships. They perform "intelligent" tasks by acquiring knowledge through "learning". They store "knowledge" within inter-neuron connection strengths known as synaptic weights.

# Chapter XIV
# Data Mining of Personal Information:
## A Taste of the Intrusion Legacy with a Sprinkling of Semantic Web

**Dionysios Politis**
*Aristotle University of Thessaloniki, Greece*

## ABSTRACT

*In this chapter data-mining techniques are presented that can be used to create data-profiles of individuals from anonymous data that can be found freely and abundantly in open environments, such as the Internet. Although such information takes in most cases the form of an approximation and not of a factual and solid representation of concrete personal data, nevertheless it takes advantage of the vast increase in the amount of data recorded by database management systems as well as by a number of archiving applications and repositories of multimedia files.*

## INTRODUCTION

It is a common secret that personal data that should be handled cautiously are "leaking" intentionally or unintentionally due to "mistakes", mismatches in Information Systems handshaking, or hacking. The last threat is the most difficult to cope with since the guardians in the inner circle have to supervise not only the hierarchical administrative structure that maintains and accesses the data, but also to watch carefully the Information and Communication Technologies advances that provide alternative routes to sensitive data for a variable number of support personnel.

However, technological innovations and multimedia gadgets of various forms have shaped another way to form personal data repositories. Indeed, in recent years there has been a vast increase in the amount of data recorded by database management systems as well as by a number of archiving applications. This explosion in the amount of electronically stored data was accelerated by the success of the relational model for storing data and the development and maturing of data retrieval and manipulation technologies. Apart from the large corporate databases which have been implemented, new forms of spreading information and storing data have emerged; the most notable of them are the World Wide Web (WWW) and the various multimedia databases formed out of diverse multimedia applications and presentations. The conjunction of hypertext languages and multimedia data such as images, video and audio, shape an immense network of information. It could be said that the WWW virtually is the largest database ever built.

While technology for storing the data has developed fast to keep up with the demand, little emphasis was paid to developing software for analyzing the data. It can be readily shown in Example 1 that the conventional Data Manipulating Language (DML) interfaces are insufficient or cumbersome in extracting statistical information.

Until recently, it was difficult not only to process but even to correlate information merging from diverse fields of data warehouses. The huge amounts of stored or tracked data contain knowledge that can be deduced, covering many aspects of the activities recorded as "raw" data. Database Management Systems in use at present manage these data sets allowing the user to access only information explicitly present in the databases.

**EXAMPLE 1.**

The following relation describes the students of a University with many departments according to the relational model. For each student a grade is recorded marking his overall performance.

```
STUDENT (SN(integer[6])PRIMARY KEY, NAME(string[20]), SEX (character),
MARK(integer[3]), DEPARTMENT(string[15], ADDRESS(string[40]), GRADUATION
(date))
```

Following this definition, sample tuple values for table `STUDENT` look like:

| SN | NAME | SEX | MARK | DEPARTMENT | ADDRESS | GRADUATION |
|---|---|---|---|---|---|---|
| 4567 | BABOULI | F | 74 | LAW | THESSALONIKI | 20-OCT-2003 |
| 7501 | KINTS | M | 85 | RURAL ENGINEERING | VEROIA | 15-JUN-2007 |
| ... | ... | ... | ... | ... | ... | ... |

If we want a histogram on student performance deduced out of database records, we will have difficulty in **grouping by** student marks from 0 to 9, 10 to 19, 20 to 29, …, 90 to 100 using the standard Structured Query Language (SQL). Consequently, extensions to the SQL syntax have been proposed to simplify the task. For instance, the *N_tile* (Siberschatz et al, 1997) function supported by some database systems divides values into percentiles:

```
SELECT PERCENTILE, AVG(MARK)
FROM STUDENT
GROUPBY N_TILE (MARK, 10) AS PERCENTILE;
```

*N_TILE*(`MARK, 10`) divides attribute MARK values into 10 consecutive ranges, with an equal number of values in each range; duplicates are not eliminated.

The actual data stored in a database is only a fraction of the knowledge base that can be extracted from it. The term *knowledge* practically is defined as some kind of *declarative* language in the form of *rules*. This extraction of knowledge from large data sets is called Data Mining or Knowledge Discovery in Databases and is defined as the non-trivial extraction of **implicit, previously unknown** and **potentially useful information** from data (Frawley et al, 1991). However, the exhaustively mined data set does not contain only implicit information about a number of aspects of the underlying database. It also contains latent data links that can be harnessed and recorded out of free and full text retrieval data sets. The obvious benefits of Data Mining have resulted in a lot of resources being directed towards its development.

## DATA MINING TECHNIQUES AND PRACTICES

Large databases are searched for relationships, patterns, and trends, which prior to the search were not known to exist or were not visible. Sometimes these relationships might be assumed by knowledge engineers but need to be proven or refined. The result of data mining is new information or knowledge that will allow the user community to ameliorate its performance.

The profound difficulty with data mining is that very large databases need to be processed for what is often just a few related facts. The search criteria, once used to gain insight into some particular pattern or trend, will tend to be modified before the next execution, and the data that is being examined tends to cover years of details or terabytes of storage.

In simpler terms, data mining is asking a processing engine to give answers to questions which we can not express explicitly. Instead of forming the query "find all the students who live in region XXX and have received a mark better than 80%" in normal DML terms to the relational database of Example 1, it can ask the processing mechanism to "find related performance patterns" and the outcome is a response "If a student is proficient in operating computers and other high technology machinery, he is bound to move into region XXX with probability x% within the next 2 years after his graduation" (Bischof and Alexander, 1997).

It is obvious that the former, the DML relation, is a projection of selected tuples out of the STUDENT table:

$$\Pi_{\text{NAME, MARK}} (\sigma_{\text{MARK BETWEEN 80 AND 100}} (\text{STUDENT}))$$

while the latter is an association rule based approach applied on the knowledge base frame (deduced or explicitly stated) of the database:

```
IF (a set of conditions are satisfied)
THEN (a set of consequences can be inferred)
```

When setting queries for specific relationships, more important relationships might be missed. Asking to find relationships that we do not know that exist will yield more meaningful data or knowledge. However, not all rules are of the same strength. We can use two rather *fuzzy* terms, ***support*** and ***confidence*** in order to measure the strength and interestingness of association rules (Tsoukalas and Uhrig, 1997; Agrawal and Sikant, 1994).

If an association rule is of the form:

$$E_1 \rightarrow E_2 \text{ [support, confidence]}$$

then the pair of elements $E_1$, $E_2$ are related to a degree described by the factors of ***support*** s = $P(E_1 \cup E_2)$ and ***confidence*** c = $P(E_2 \mid E_1)$. The former relation describes the possibility to have event $E_1$ OR $E_2$ OR both. In this sense it a measure of affinity between events $E_1$, $E_2$. The latter relation is a probabilistic measurement of certainty whether event $E_2$ will take place after event $E_1$ has occurred. With these measures, we are able to select the "***strong*** rules of high ***confidence***" that yield accurate predictions of associations (KianSing et al, 1998).

Before proceeding to an example illustrating the degree of association, it is important to clarify the universe of discourse (Tsoukalas and Uhrig, 1997) for the data sets that are used as predicates in rules.

## Full Text Retrieval Databases

Although vast information about people is stored explicitly according to the relational model described in Example 1, the majority of documents that exist are the outcome of procedures like Electronic Document Management (EDM), Electronic Document Interchange (EDI) and they are text oriented (van der Meer and Uijlenbroek, 1996). While the ASCII text format is the simplest form in which the documents exist and the other storage forms add formatting information to the text, usually with some multimedia enhancements, in the semantics axiological system the motion is reversed and all the storage forms converge in their simple text equivalent.

As seen in Figure 1, nearly all documents are stored either in some widely spread proprietary formats that act as industry standards, or in image, video and audio formats from which a relevant text can be extracted depicting the content in natural language. After collecting the various text files, the content of them can be transformed to a uniform format. In such documents that have been formed and stored, retrieval techniques can be applied on them.

At this point how "Free Text" differs from "Full Text" will be described (Gethin, 1987).

Free text retrieval involves finding information in text; the text itself however does not have to be very extensive. The term "free" is used because the information does not have to conform to a rigorous pattern or size but is in free format.

Although free text retrieval can be used for a number of applications (library catalogues, per-

*Figure 1. The process of forming full or free text retrieval systems*

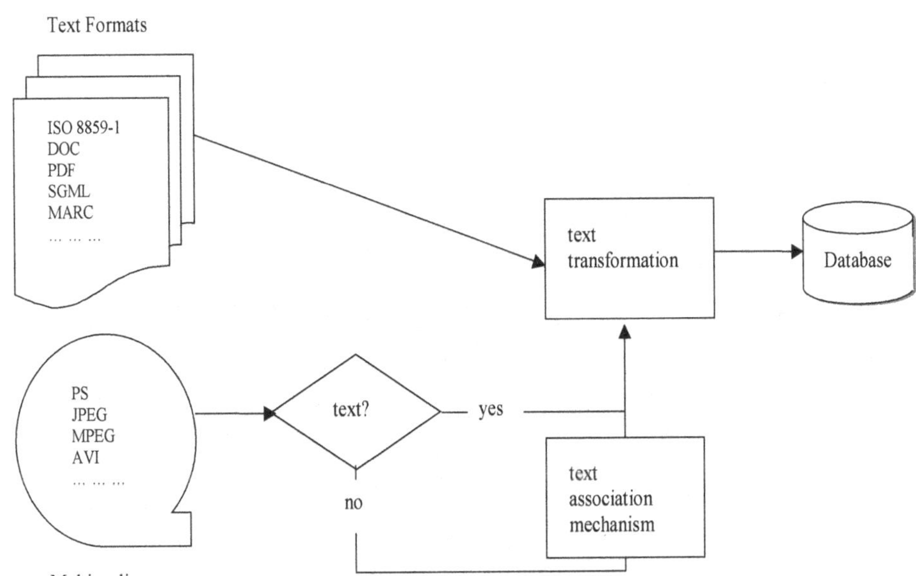

sonnel references, parts catalogues, bibliographic references) it has severe limitations.

By Full Text Retrieval free text capabilities are extended. A Full Text Retrieval system can be used to find information in huge archives like Legal documents, Encyclopaedias, Medical Textbooks, Newspaper Archives.

In a Full Text Retrieval system an effective index structure is important for the efficient processing of queries. Such systems can locate documents that contain a specified target keyword using an *inverted index*, which maps each keyword $L_i$ to the set $S_i$ of identifiers of the documents that contain $L_i$. To support relevance ranking based on proximity of keywords, such an index may provide not just identifiers of documents, but also a list of locations in the document where the keyword appears.

Each keyword may be contained in a large number of documents; hence, a compact representation is critical to keep space usage of index low. Thus, the sets of documents for a keyword are maintained in a compressed form.

A pictorial definition of the entity document can be seen in Figure 2 and a description of the dictionary indexing mechanism in Figure 3.

As seen in Figure 3, when seeking a specific word in the database, the dictionary of the database is searched for the pattern using usually a B-Tree indexing scheme. Once the target word $L_i$ is found, then it is recorded in the dictionary in how many documents the target appears and how many occurrences of it exist. From the dictionary the search engine locates the exact position of each occurrence using as coordinates the document number, the paragraph and the sentence in which it has been positioned.

Once the lemma has been found, the whole document or a part of it can be retrieved.

When the full text retrieval system is filled in with documents, the search engine is in position to retrieve documents by forming the queries over the dictionary index. A valid search statement can range in complexity from a single word (or "term") to a series of words connected by "operators". Operators are either Boolean (AND, OR, NOT), Relational (<, >,=) or Positional (SAME, WITH, NEAR, ADJACENT) for words of the same sentence or paragraph. Special features (pattern matching, paragraph qualification, and statistical operations) can also be employed within search

*Figure 2. Full text retrieval document entities*

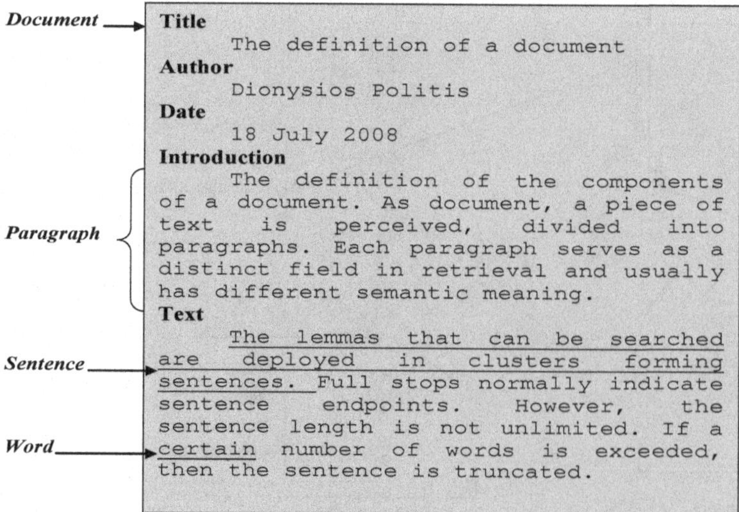


**Title**

The definition of a document

**Author**

Dionysios Politis

**Date**

18 July 2008

**Introduction**

The definition of the components of a document. As document, a piece of text is perceived, divided into paragraphs. Each paragraph serves as a distinct field in retrieval and usually has different semantic meaning.

**Text**

The lemmas that can be searched are deployed in clusters forming sentences. Full stops normally indicate sentence endpoints. However, the sentence length is not unlimited. If a certain number of words is exceeded, then the sentence is truncated.

*Figure 3. Full text retrieval indexing mechanism*

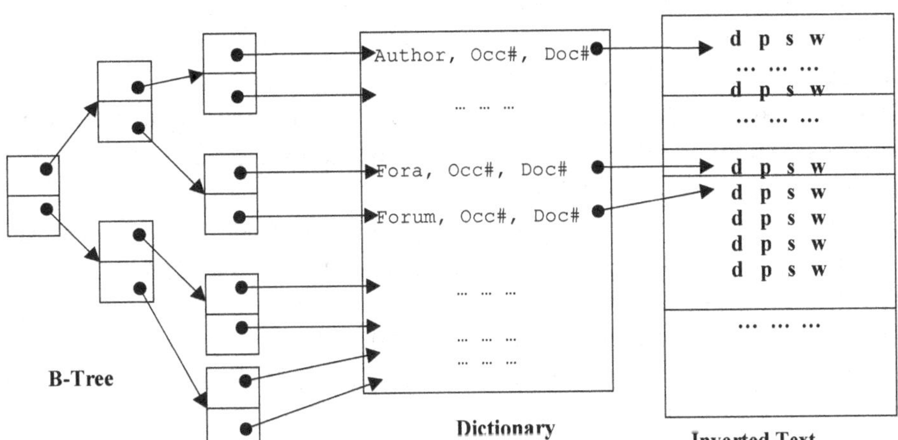


statements. Also, semantic relations can be given in order to search the dictionary.

The retrieving power of such searching engines is remarkable. For instance, the AND operation finds documents that contain all of a specified set of keywords $L_1, L_2, ..., L_n$. We implement the AND operator by first retrieving the sets of document identifiers $S_1, S_2, ..., S_n$ of all the documents that contain the respective keywords. The intersection, $S_1 \cap S_2 \cap ... \cap S_n$ of the sets gives the document identifiers of the desired set of documents. The OR operation gives the set of all documents that contain at least on of the keywords $L_1, L_2, ..., L_n$. We implement the OR operation by computing the union $S_1 \cup S_2 \cup ... \cup S_n$ of the sets. The NOT operation finds documents of a specific keyword $L_i$ by taking the difference $S - S_i$, where $S_i$ is the set of identifiers of documents that contain the keyword $L_i$.

Two metrics are used to measure how well an information-retrieval system is able to answer queries. The first, *precision*, measures what percentage of the retrieved documents are actually relevant to the query. The second, *recall,* measures what percentage of the documents relevant to the query where retrieved. Apart from these two rather quantitative measures of retrieval performance, there is another set of more qualitative ones: noise and silence.

By noise we define the number of documents retrieved that lexicographically contain one or more of the targeted keywords $L_1, L_2, ..., L_n$ but do not contain much information about what actually was requested. Usually noise can be reduced by query optimisation techniques that refine the search conditions using mainly positional operators.

By silence we describe the absence of response of the search engine not due to *false drops* but due to inability to express the query properly.

The term *false drop* refers to the fact that when quering the system, the index is sometimes stored in such a way that the retrieval is approximate; a few relevant documents may not be retrieved (called a *false drop*), or a few irrelevant documents may be retrieved (called *false positive*). A good index structure will not have any *false drops*, but may permit a few false positives.

## World Wide Web Accessible Data Mining

Perhaps the most radical example of the diversity of convergence in the global communications area is the Internet. It is a vehicle for the delivery to users of both existing services (electronic mail, video, audio, voice telephones) and completely new services (like electronic commerce transactions via the World Wide Web or Geographical Information Systems positioning). In this context it is interesting to note that the Internet is doubling its number of users each year without having reached yet a saturation point.

The Internet has developed differently from traditional broadcasting and the telecommunications services. It has essentially been user-driven. The decentralized nature of the Internet is seen by many as the single main reason for its success. Its convergence of separate communication systems is exemplified in its broadcast content, which is traditionally regulated, and private communication, which is traditionally unregulated. These different traditions constitute one of the main challenges of the Internet regulation.

In the World Wide Web domain two are the main sources of information: the various Internet sites that contain information in text format, covering a wide range of subjects, and secondly, the "traces" that are left when a user visits a certain site or when an electronic message is broadcast. In both cases the volume of the exchanged data is immense and it is rather impossible to store all the transactions that take place.

However, all the information that circulates in the Internet, apart from the transactions that are intended to be private or secure, forms a huge database of data that is *public domain*. Examples demonstrating the potential of retrieval methods are the various *search engines* of the WWW that can locate persons, data and multimedia enhancements by storing in huge repositories text documents collected from almost all the web sites of the Internet. In order to collect data, these engines scan uninterruptedly and perpetually all the sites they can locate and store in their full text retrieval systems keywords and abstracts referring to the full documents. The full documents are not stored, since that would demand a database size greater than that of the WWW volume; instead, they use URL links to index the location of the related HTML file.

## The MP3 Paradigm and the Non-Linearity of Geographical Space

One of the latest technological assets that has apparent legal implications is that of the compression standard "MPEG 1, Audio Layer 3" for audio signals, amply known as MP3 (McCandless, 1999). Although the MP3 issue has to do more with intellectual property matters, it has two views that are connected with the circulation of personal data. The first is the hysteresis in the digital memory of the MP3 propagation mechanism, and the second is the non-linearity of the propagation mechanism that gives new content to the definition of neighbouring country or third country.

Virtually all forms of speech and musical information can be recorded in digital audio formats. In this terrain MP3 serves as a vehicle for redundant music and audio propagation, as it combines small size with unharmed fidelity. For example, a CD ROM disk that contains a few dozens of songs in normal audio coding can host a few hundreds of MP3 compressed songs. Unfortunately, although MP3s help artists and consumers, they also facilitate the piracy of copyrighted material. One can create an MP3 version of a CD he owns or he can download it from a circumstantial Internet site. It is questionable whether this MP3 file is legally freely distributed via a Web site; however, the significant point in digital reproduction is that the distributed file is an exact copy of the original without any loss in quality, as it happens in the case of analog recordings.

Even if legal action is undertaken to prevent free distribution, the copies of the original that have been already distributed form a hysteresis residue that is difficult to eliminate and that can serve as proliferation material for a future distribution. It is very difficult in such cases to eliminate digital memory completely. The traces left behind can be easily assembled and web based search can enhance access turning the whole procedure to a virtual broadcast. In the same sense, the articles posted to newsgroups, the e-mails and the surfing traces of each individual user can be tracked and form an unbiased data repository that can bring up to surface refined threads of information (Keen and Dally, 1997).

The second point has to do with the impact of digital technology on Geography: it results in a non-linear distribution space in correlation with the actual geographical space. For instance, distribution between two neighboring European countries in terms of Internet architecture may be more cumbersome, more slow, more "distant" than it is between the originating country and the "central hub" of the web, the USA.

Consequently, what has been reported for the MP3 paradigm could be repeated to a certain degree for personal data proliferation.

Recently, an emphatically pronounced parallelism of the above paradigm has been reported. It has to do with compressed video spots of all kinds dispersed and posted in various formats through gateways like YouTube[1]. Whether they are copyrighted or not, whether they are promotional or defamatory, whether they enclose personal data or they provide multiple, amateur views of public events, they all have a common characteristic: they constitute a huge repository of audiovisual information that has never before existed.

## THE SEMANTIC WEB PARADIGM

The Web gives users access to a vast array of documents that are connected to each other by means of hypertext or hypermedia links—i.e., hyperlinks, electronic connections that link related pieces of information in order to allow a user easy access to them. Hypertext allows the user to select a word from text and thereby access other documents that contain additional information pertaining to that word; hypermedia documents feature links to images, sounds, animations, and movies. Additionally, *metadata*, i.e. data about data are used to describe what the actual data refer to. Imagine the mechanism of Figure 1 extended to the Web, cueing information about the multimedia and textual entries that exist worldwide!

The *Semantic Web* is a way of using metadata to give added layers of meaning to Web content. The current Web is a powerful tool for both research and education, but its use is hindered by the inability of the user to navigate easily the multitude of links for the exact information that he requires (see Figure 4a).

*Figure 4. The Web. (a) Current picture. (b) The vision.*

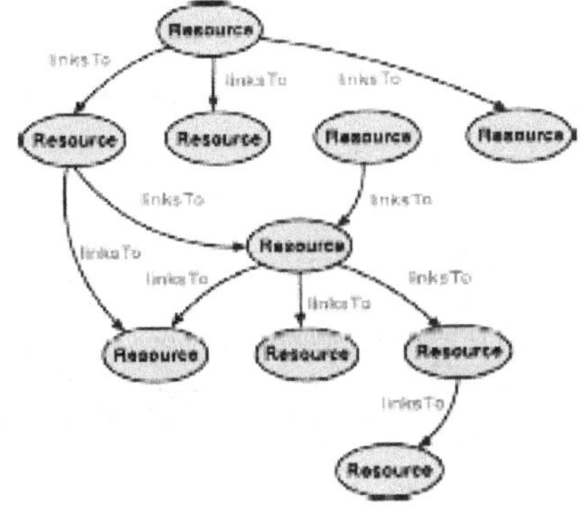


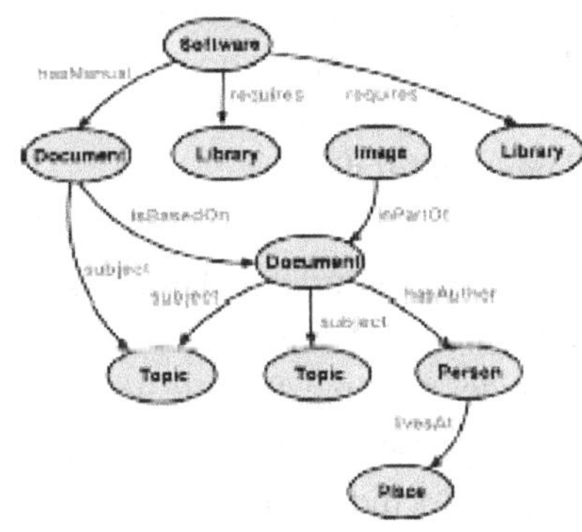

The Semantic Web envisages a solution to this problem. It is proposed that the new Web architecture will support not only information content but also associated formal semantics.

The idea is that the Web content and accompanying semantics (or metadata) will be accessed not only by humans, but also by Web software "agents", allowing these agents to reason about the content and produce intelligent answers to users' queries. Not only that, but a semantic network representation is formed within the Web (Figure 4b).

The current Web content is defined by HTML. HTML stands for HyperText Markup Language, a form of posting a hypertext document with its corresponding text, multimedia material and hyperlinks. This cluster is assigned an online address called a Uniform Resource Locator (URL).

Under the new vision HTML has now been upgraded to XHTML –eXtensible HTML. The existing language for is thus enriched with XML. XML stands for eXtended Markup Language.

Unfortunately, the saying "no pain, no gain" applies to the Semantic Web, which deploys over the existing infrastructure a much more complex (but worth it) schema.

The Semantic Web comprises a layered framework:

- An XML layer for expressing the Web page form
- A Resource Description Framework (RDF) layer for representing the semantics of the content
- An *ontology* layer for describing the vocabulary of an application domain
- A logic layer to enable intelligent reasoning with meaningful data

This layered frameworks architecture can be seen in Figure 5.

XML provides a simple, flexible way of transporting structured documents across the Web. With XML, "tags" or hidden labels may be created - such as <module> or <section> - that annotate Web pages or sections of text within a page. XML is machine-readable, i.e. programs can read and understand it, but the program developer has to know what each XML tag represents.

In other words, XML allows users to add arbitrary structure to their documents but says nothing about what the structures mean.

The semantics of document content is expressed with RDF - this is simply a data model and format that allows the creation of machine-readable data.

It comprises a sets of triples that may be used to describe any possible relationship existing between the data – subject, predicate and object.

Thus, all data stored in the system is easily readable and processable. It is important to note that RDF provides the syntax, but not the actual meaning of the properties we ascribe to the data. For example, it does not define what data properties such as Module or Sub-Section or Related-To mean.

Properties like these are not standalone; they are part of the vocabulary of the application domain, whether it be Computer Science, Law or whatever. Thus, for every domain, there is a need for a specific ontology to describe the vocabularies and to make sure they are compatible.

Ontologies in the context of the Semantic Web are specifications of the conceptualization

*Figure 5. The Semantic Web architecture*

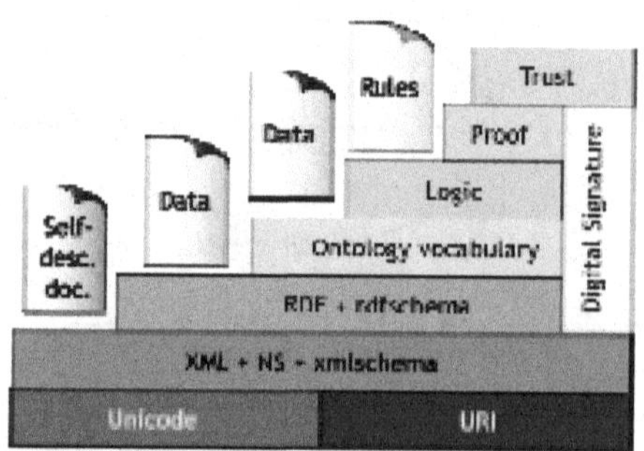

and corresponding vocabulary used to describe a domain. Any semantic on the Web is based on an explicitly specified ontology, so different Semantic Web applications can communicate by exchanging their ontologies.

Several representation schemes have been defined for the ontology layer. One of the most popular is the Ontology Interchange Language (OIL), combined with the DARPA Agent Markup Language (DAML), DAML+OIL, provides a rich set of language structures with which to create ontologies and to markup information so that it is machine understandable.

As a result OWL – the Web Ontology Language – has been derived from DAML+OIL, and is currently the favored approach. The logic layer part of the Semantic Web is not fully developed yet. Its implementation will allow the user to state any logical principles and permit the computer to infer new knowledge by applying these principles to the existing data.

Since there are many different inference systems on the Web that are not completely interoperable, the vision is to develop a universal logic language for representing proofs – systems will then be able to export these proofs into the Semantic Web

## PERSONAL DATA TRACES AND DEDUCTIVE DATA BASES

Our every day transactions, being normally habitual, reveal a lot about our personality and our biases. Considering that most transactions of ordinary people are committed under virtually non-existing privacy conditions, it is plausible to state that insecure electronic mails can be intercepted, Internet logs monitored and audio-visual communications scanned. Of course, these actions are illegal and the outcome of such activity is not public domain information. Still, there are many other activities, which are sufficient to build databases that can record personal profiles.

Key factors that can be found in public domain Internet transactions and can render the portrait of an identifiable person are: the present and former employment and occupation, the educational

**EXAMPLE 2.**

User X uses Internet services frequently at work (where he is provided with a static IP connection) and at home where he uses an Internet Service Provider using dynamic IP connection. After office hours, when connected with the Internet at home, he surfs to certain commercial sites, occasionally he visits sites of political content and from time to time he posts articles to certain newsgroups expressing his opinion mainly for business matters.
He is provided with two e-mail addresses,
x@y.com at work and
x@z.country_code from his Internet service provider.

Although the texts in most newsgroups or blogspots are not kept for long and disappear after some time, X's texts can be scanned for certain keywords revealing political content. The ones who comply with the criteria set are stored in a full text retrieval system and they are indexed.
More exhaustive search can be performed on them using the full text retrieval operators and some patterns of behavior can be spotted. Although user X rarely reveals his true identity, his e-mail address can be associated with his true name, the company for which he works, his home address, if it is recorded or was ever recorded in white pages telephone guides, etc.
It can be said that his personal profile can be reverse engineered.

background, the asserted qualifications and skills, economic and financial information, property data, tax position, behavioral data, movement monitoring and places frequented, drug abuse, previous convictions, medical records, etc.

Such data are already recorded by many institutes, organizations and companies regarding their employees or customers with their prior consent, usually in relational data bases. These data sets should not be broadcast, according to directive 95/46/EEC. However, even though if not malpractice is used, Internet public domain transactions are by themselves revealing and **new** personal data can be formed, as explained in Example 2.

The knowledge extracted from Internet transactions and public domain information is not always structured and information is not extracted readily. But it can be retrieved and under some pre-conditions it can **render** personal profiles.

The reverse engineering of personal data can be based on certain attributes rendered from public domain texts. The co-relation between these factors is described in Table 1.

Although the reverse engineering of personal data is a quite fuzzy procedure, it can lead in cases of strong confidence to an explicit profile of an identifiable person.

## DATA MINING AND THE PROTECTION OF PERSONAL DATA

The storage and processing of information relating to natural persons is regulated in the European Union by the common Directive 95/46/EEC of the European Council and the European Parliament. Basic aim of the Directive is to harmonize existing national legislature relating to personal data and to achieve an equivalent level of protection of privacy rights in the member states; the considerations of the Directive emphasize particularly the need to ensure the protection of privacy, civil rights and liberties (Kilian, 1996). From an economic point of view, the final objective of the Directive is to achieve within the European Union a free flow of information, which will not be inhibited on

*Table 1. Tracing threads of personal data attributes correlated with confidence and support*

| Personal Data Attributes | Support/ Confidence | Possible source of identification |
|---|---|---|
| Present employment and occupation | + | Electronic mail<br>IP address & domain name |
| Former employment and occupation | +/- | Electronic mail<br>IP address & domain name |
| Education (school/university/professional) | - | Electronic mail<br>Scientific on-line publications |
| Skills and other fields of knowledge (language/ other) | - | Message contents<br>Scientific on-line publications<br>References |
| Lifestyle | + | Internet Surfing<br>Videos or photos (from places like YouTube or similar) |
| Movements<br>Places frequented | + | WWW sites visited<br>Internet surfing |
| Sexual information | +/- | Internet surfing, message content |
| Political Information | +/- | Internet surfing, message content |

*(ratings: - : weak confidence, +/- : plausible, + : strong confidence)*

grounds relating to the protection of rights and freedoms of individuals (Schild, 1996)[2].

The framework set by Directive 95/46 generally associates processing personal information with the knowledge and permission of the concerned individuals. The Directive distinguishes between "ordinary" personal data and personal data of sensitive nature, belonging to special categories. "Ordinary" personal data enjoys the protection granted by article 7 of the Directive, that allows processing of such information if the concerned individuals have given their consent. In the absence of consent, processing of personal data is permitted, if one of the special reasons described in article 7 of the Directive renders it necessary. Article 8 of the Directive provides enhanced protection to personal information belonging to special categories that concern intimate aspects of life, such as ethnic or racial origin, politics, sexual behaviour, physical or mental health, financial situation etc. Such "sensitive" personal data may not be archived or processed, unless the subjects give their consent or one of the specific conditions set in article 8 of the Directive are met[3]. The member states are however free to ban completely the processing of sensitive personal data, even if the consent of the concerned individuals has been granted. In any case, the subject of personal data enjoys the right to be informed about the processing of his/her data (article 10), the right to access this data (article 12) and to object to its further processing (article 14).

In any case, the Directive applies only to the processing of "personal data". Article 2a of the Directive defines personal data as any information relating to an identified or identifiable natural person (article 2a), whereas an identifiable person is defined as "*one who can be identified, directly or indirectly, in particular by reference to an identification number or to one or more factors specific to his physical, physiological, mental, economic, cultural or social identity*". The Directive does not apply to the processing of anonymous data, that is information that does not allow the identification of the person(s) it refers to. Thus, the Directive does not rule out the creation of statistical studies or the processing of summarized personal data of three or more persons in an anonymous profile (Schild, 1996). Article 6 (e) of the Directive makes obvious that the Directive regards the processing of anonymous personal information as harmless for the privacy rights of individuals: According to that provision, the member states must ensure that personal data may only be "*kept in a form which permits identification of data subjects for no longer than is necessary for the purposes for which the data were collected or for which they are further processed*"; processing the same data for a longer period is allowed, if the data is kept in a form that does not permit the identification of its subjects.

The Directive 95/46 applies according to article 2(b) to "*any operation or set of operations, which is performed upon personal data*". As a result of that wide definition, which has sometimes been the object of critical remarks (Bergfeld, 1996), all new types of data processing fall under the rules of the Directive (Schild, 1996; Louveaux et al., 2001), including data-mining and data-extracting operations. However, as it was mentioned above, the Directive does not apply to operations of any kind used for processing anonymous, "bulk", data that can be found scattered in various public domain environments, as the Internet[4]. When used in that environment, data-mining can be a method of creating detailed profiles of individuals and thus transforming anonymous information into personal data, that is information referring to an identified or an identifiable person(Pearce and Platten, 1998); in other words, data-mining may be used to extract the subject of otherwise anonymous data. If that is the case, the processing of the ensuing personal data is subject to the rules set by the Directive.

The Directive applies to data that belongs to an identifiable person, but it does not specify who and to what extent must be able to identify the subject of that data. Information that is anonymous for one person, can be easily deciphered by somebody else in order to achieve identification od the data subject: A simple telephone number cannot by itself be used for identification purposes by normal individuals, but a telephone company can easily find out the name of its holder.

To give an example, many providers collect personal information when one registers to use on-line services or to access services, to find partners, to enter promotional sites or sweepstakes. These providers may combine information about their clients and combine it with information obtained from business partners or other companies.

The pieces of information used when one registers may be name, email address, birth date, gender, ZIP code, occupation, industry, and personal interests. For some financial products and services a user may be queried for his address, Social Security number, and information about his assets.

This kind of personal profile is maintained with the user's active participation and consent. However, for many other purposes "anonymous" data may be gathered. In such a case a provider collects automatically and records information from one's computer and browser, including his IP address (denoting at a first glance the country of origin or the language used), cookie information, software and hardware attributes, and the page he requests. In the latter case the provider uses information for the following general purposes: to customize the advertising and content his client visits, to estimate statistically and fulfill requests for products and services, to improve his services, to conduct research, and provide anonymous reporting for internal and external clients.

For security reasons access to personal information about clients is limited to the employees of carriers or providers. Also physical, electronic, and procedural safeguards are imposed that comply with federal regulations (in the case of USA) or local laws that protect personal information about the users of a service provider.

However, a provider may give this kind of information to trusted partners who work on behalf of or with him under confidentiality agreements. These companies may use personal information or may possess simply "anonymous like" data. Usually these companies do not have any independent right to share this information, but it is evident that a propagation mechanism is set with unpredictable some times results. This is especially true for the transfer of information when a company is acquired by or merged with another company. Even worse, these kind of files seem to follow uncontrolled trajectories when a company ceases to exist.

Although at a first approach this seems to be indifferent, interestingly, the use of data-mining techniques appears to transform the identification of the data subjects into a process with quantifiable results: The outcome of data-mining may of course be the positive identification or the complete inability to identify the subject of data, but besides those extreme cases exists the possibility of a probable identification, that is the probability (e.g. expressed in a percentage) that a person is the subject of the relevant data. For example: The processor has in his hands a telephone number with 8 digits in a country where only three cities have telephone numbers with that number of digits and would like to identify the owner of that number. The processor does not have the area code assigned to the number and is allowed to use a search engine that enables him to look up the names of telephone subscribers by entering the telephone number and specifying the relative area. By using this search method the processor will end up with three (at minimum) possible owners of the given telephone number, that is he will be able to identify the subject of the data with a probability ratio (at maximum) of 33,3%.

Article 2a of the Directive does not specify the degree of probability that is necessary for the data subject to be qualified as identifiable. However it should be clear that even probable identification presents the same dangers to individual privacy rights, at least after a certain threshold of probability. It is almost certain that the processor will regard data as referring to a specific person, if the probability of identification exceeds 90%. In general, it is extremely difficult to set the threshold of "identifiability" and every proposed solution will be more or less arbitrary.

Besides the Internet, data-mining may also take place inside the restricted environment of a data filing system, in such a way as to extract further information from existing and legitimately collected personal data . Even if these data-mining and data-extracting techniques are implemented in a regulated environment, where the rights of data subjects in relation to personal data that was previously gathered have been respected, they also present specific dangers to data subjects: data-mining in this context does not only imply storing and processing existing information, but also creates *new* personal data. Personal data processed by conventional methods remains in principle information either granted by the individual or from a third party with the knowledge of the data subject, who may exercise his right to object; with conventional methods the external form of information may change, new connections may appear, but the individual generally remains in control, as he finally decides over the handling of his information. Data-mining on the contrary renders individual consent for processing of personal data meaningless, as the individual cannot possibly know what further data, even with a certain amount of errors, could be deduced about his person from existing information. As data mining techniques reduce the value of individual knowledge and consent, they are to be considered as highly dangerous for personal liberties. In the words of the first annual report (1997) of the Data Protection Working Party, that was set up by the Directive 95/46, "*increasing amounts of personal information can be processed in a very sophisticated fashion with techniques such as 'data-warehousing' and 'data-mining' which are potentially more intrusive to individual's privacy than traditional processing techniques*".

Two factors enhance even farther the potential dangers arising out of the use of such techniques: First of all, the individual is exposed to dangers presented not only by the new data itself, but also by noise-factors and errors contained in the new data. As data-mining frequently operates on the basis of assumptions, the results it provides will often be probable and not definite. The citizen is not only endangered because third parties will know *more* things about him, than he has allowed them to; he is also in danger because some of the new information concerning his person might be *false* or *inaccurate*. This is especially true in cases where data are collected from newspapers. Since many things written there may be rumors or speculation, it is possible to deduce false statements. Personal profiles extracted from existing information will frequently contain data regarding intimate aspects of individual life; in fact, one of the major motives for using such techniques will probably be gaining access to sensitive data that would not be otherwise available.

## CONCLUSION

Data-mining techniques can be used to create data-profiles of individuals from anonymous data that is to be found freely in open environments, such as the Internet. Such information takes in most cases the form of an approximation and not of a factual and solid representation of concrete data. Also information may be gathered from carriers in order to investigate, prevent, or take action regarding illegal activities, suspected fraud, situations involving potential threats to the physical safety of any person, etc. This information may be rather "anonymous", but when applied within the closed environment of data filing system, data-mining techniques pose increased risks to the privacy of data subjects and should therefore be the object of prior administrative checks.

## REFERENCES

Agrawal, R., & Sikant, R. (1994). Fast Algorithms for Mining Association rules in Large Databases. Proceedings of the *20th VLDB Conference,* Santiago, Chile. (pp. 487-499).

Bergfeld, J. P. (1996). EC Data Protection Directive, impact on Dutch Data Protection Law. *The Journal of Information, Law and Technology (JILT), 1.* http://elj.warwick.ac.uk/elj/jilt/dp/1dutch/

Bischof, J., & Alexander, T. (1997). *Data Warehouse.* New York: Prentice Hall. (pp 310-313).

Frawley, W., Piatevsky-Shapiro, G., & Matheus, C. J. (1991). An Overview of Knowledge Discovery in Databases. *Knowledge Discovery in Databases.* AAAI/MIT Press. (pp. 1-27).

Gethin, P. (1987). Text Retrieval. *BRS/SIRSI Training Notes.* BRS Corp.

Keen, J., & Dally, W. (1997). Extended Ephemeral Logging: Log Storage Management for Applications with Long-Lived Transactions. *ACM Transactions on Database Systems, 22*(1), 1-42.

KianSing, Ng, Huan, L., & HweeBong Kwah. (1998). A Data Mining Application: Customer Retention at the Port of Singapore Authority. Proceedings of the *ACM-SIGMOD International Conference on Management of Data*, Seattle. (pp. 522-25).

Kilian, W. (1996). *Europäisches Wirtschaftsrecht.* München:Beck.

Louveaux, S., Poullet, Y., & Salaün, A. (2001). User protection in the cyberspace: some recommendations. *Electronic Commerce – Der Abschluss von Verträgen im Internet*, 196, 103-111.

McCandless, M. (1999). The MP3 revolution. *IEEE Intelligent Systems, 3*, 8-9.

Pearce, G., & Platten, N. (1988). Achieving Personal Data Protection in the European Union. *Journal of Common Market Studies.*

Schild, H. (1996). *Die EG-Datenschutz-Richtlinie.* Europäische Zeitschrift für Wirtschaftsrecht.

Silberschatz, A., Korth, H., & Sudarshan, S. (1997). *Database System Concepts.* New York: McGraw-Hill.

Tsoukalas, L., & Uhrig, R. (1997). *Fuzzy and Neural Approaches in Engineering.* New York: John Wiley & Sons.

van der Meer, K., & Uijlenbroek, J. (1996). The possibilities of electronic document management for supporting *ad hoc* processes: A case study. *DLM-Forum on Electronic Records.* Brussels. (pp. 249-259).

## ENDNOTES

1 YouTube is a video sharing website where users can upload, view and share video clips.

2 Grounds 8 and 9 of the Directive.

3 Processing of sensitive personal data is permitted if (a) the data subject has given his explicit consent to the processing of those data, except where the laws of the Member State provide that the prohibition referred to in paragraph 1 may not be lifted by the data subject's giving his consent; or (b) processing is necessary for the purposes of carrying out the obligations and specific rights of the controller in the field of employment law in so far as it is authorized by national law providing for adequate safeguards; or (c) processing is necessary to protect the vital interests of the data subject or of another person where the data subject is physically or legally incapable of givfooing his consent; or (d) processing is carried out in the course

of its legitimate activities with appropriate guarantees by a foundation, association or any other non-profit-seeking body with a political, philosophical, religious or trade-union aim and on condition that the processing relates solely to the members of the body or to persons who have regular contact with it in connection with its purposes and that the data are not disclosed to a third party without the consent of the data subjects; or (e) the processing relates to data which are manifestly made public by the data subject or is necessary for the establishment, exercise or defence of legal claims. Similarly, processing sensitive data is allowed if required for the purposes of preventive medicine, medical diagnosis, the provision of care or treatment or the management of health-care services, and where those data are processed by a health professional subject under national law or rules established by national competent bodies to the obligation of professional secrecy or by another person also subject to an equivalent obligation of secrecy.

4 See consideration 26 of the Directive.

# Chapter XV
# Surveillance of Employees' Electronic Communications in the Workplace:
## An Employers' Right to Spy or an Invasion to Privacy?

**Ioannis Iglezakis**
*Aristotle University of Thessaloniki, Greece*

## ABSTRACT

*The use of Information and Communication Technologies in the workplace is constantly increasing, but also the use of surveillance technology. Electronic monitoring of employees becomes an integral part of information systems in the workplace. The specific software which is used for monitoring electronic communications is, however, intrusive and infringes upon the employees' right to privacy. The issue of surveillance of employees' electronic communications is subject to different approaches in various jurisdictions. The most comprehensive protection to employees is afforded in the EU, however, there are still ambiguities concerning the balancing of interests between employers and employees.*

## INTRODUCTION

The penetration of Internet technology in the workplace is constantly increasing, as almost every office today is equipped with computer systems and Internet connections. The low cost and high efficacy of computers and electronic communications are important factors that make the use of Information and Communication Technologies (ICTs) in the workplace unavoidable (Kierkegaard, 2005, p. 226). However, this ever growing trend has also its drawbacks, due to the fact that it raises privacy risks for employees, since employers are taking advantage of surveillance technology in order to monitor employees' e-mail and internet usage. In addition, monitoring of electronic communications increases working stress and generates discomfort amongst employees.

The monitoring of workers in the workplace is not a new phenomenon. Employers have used various methods to control the performance of employees and their behavior at work on the past and they continue to do so. Yet, there were limits to the amount of information that could be collected and used for monitoring purposes with traditional means (Fraser, 2005, p. 227).

Nowadays, new technologies provide more advanced possibilities for monitoring of employees and in more particular, of their surfing activities and the electronic communications that they use, such as e-mail, instant messaging, etc. Other aspects of workplace monitoring include drug testing, closed-circuit video monitoring, phone monitoring, location monitoring, personality and psychological testing and keystroke logging.

The particular subject which will be addressed in this chapter concerns workplace monitoring in relation to employees' electronic communications. This issue constitutes a specific aspect of the more general topic of electronic workplace surveillance, i.e. the use of information technology to monitor the activities and work performance of workers (Godfrey, 2001). Our attention will be drawn at the surveillance of electronic communications at work, that is, the use of monitoring devices in order to gain access to employees' e-mail communications and to data revealing their online activities.

The use of electronic communications by employees and of the Internet in big businesses is very high, while in medium and small-sized businesses it is also constantly rising. Besides the benefits of the wide use of e-mails, this brings about serious issues for companies, such as the dissemination of illegal or offensive material and the leak of trade secrets by disappointed employees to third parties (Mitrou & Karyda, 2006). Additionally, a great number of employees are wasting their working time surfing on the Net and sending private e-mails (so-called "cyberslacking"), whereas this may give rise to termination of employment contracts.

For those reasons employers consider as their right to control the online activities of their employees. Certainly, employers have a legitimate interest in monitoring the behavior of their employees in order to secure the acceptable performance of employees and maximize productive use of their computer systems, to prevent the leak of sensitive company information, to prevent or even detect unauthorized use of said systems for criminal activities and ensure security of computer systems, to avoid sexual harassment in the workplace and discrimination, and monitor employees' compliance with employment workplace policies related to use of ICT (EPIC; Lasprogata et al., 2004, pp. 2-3). However, such monitoring may have as a consequence the intrusion into the private life of employees and an infringement of their rights to respect of privacy and confidentiality of communications.

## MONITORING METHODS OF ELECTRONIC COMMUNICATIONS AND MONITORING DEVICES

New technologies not only provide unlimited access to information, which becomes available to employees, but also effective means for their surveillance. Specific software applications exist, which facilitate the interception of communications and real time surveillance of surfing behavior. Such applications provide central control over software on individual PCs, meaning that programs can be remotely modified or suspended, while e-mail traffic and surfing activities can be read and analyzed (Davies). Companies are making extensively use of such software, which is affordable and widely available. In a survey carried out by the American Management Association and the ePolicy Institute in 2007, it was determined that employers were concerned over inappropriate use of the Internet in a great extent and as a result, they proceeded into monitoring of e-mail and Internet activities. Pursuant to the survey, 66% of employers monitor Internet connections and 65% block connections to unauthorized Internet sites (Survey, 2007).

In particular, according to this survey, intrusion into employee's communications takes the following forms:

- 45% of employers track content, keystrokes, and time spent at the keyboard.
- 43% store and review computer files.
- 12% monitor the blogosphere to see what is being written about the company.
- 10% monitor social networking sites.

Another interesting finding of the survey is that of the 43% of companies that monitor e-mail, 73% use technology tools to automatically monitor e-mail and 40% assign an individual to manually read and review e-mail. Furthermore, blocking access to the Internet concerned adult sites, games sites, social networking sites, shopping/auctions sites, sport sites and external blogs.

E-mail and Internet misuse resulted into termination of employment relationship. A 28% of employers fired workers for e-mail misuse and 30% for Internet misuse. The reasons cited by employers were violation of company police, inappropriate or offensive language, excessive personal use and breach of confidentiality for e-mail related termination, whereas Internet related termination relied upon viewing, downloading or uploading of inappropriate or offensive content, violation of company police and excessive personal use.

Other workplace surveillance methods include monitoring of telephone and voice mail, whereas 45% of companies monitored time spent and numbers called, 16% recorded phone conversations and 9% monitored employees' voicemail message. In accordance with the survey, 48% of the companies surveyed used video monitoring to address theft, violence and sabotage, and a small percentage used global satellite positioning technology for employee surveillance.

Monitoring of employees' electronic communications is assisted by specific software, for which there is a vast market, since companies install such software in their computer systems that they appreciate as very useful in the modern work environment. Software packages monitoring e-mail offer varying services, ranging from full e-mail monitoring to programs that only record the employee name, the date and the time at which the employees pick up their e-mails (Ciocchetti, 2001, p. 26).

There exists also software that intercepts e-mail messages, on the basis of keywords which the employer specify that constitute offensive language, and block web pages, which are off-limits for employees. Other computer programs intercept emails of a private nature, in order to discover possible leakage of company information. Monitoring software allows in a great extent covert interception of emails and control of web pages visited by employees, which are exceedingly intrusive (Kierkegaard, 2005, p. 229). Such practices raise, therefore, risks for employees' rights, as it has been mentioned above, particularly, in the modern information society where the boundaries between professional and private life are blurred.

## THE LEGAL FRAMEWORK

### Constitutional Protection of the Right to Privacy

Intrusions into the private life of workers may infringe their right to privacy and in more particular, their right to information privacy.[1] The latter concerns a specific aspect of the more general right to privacy, i.e. the protection of the personal information with regard to their processing. It should be noted that, in our understanding, privacy is more than the right "to be let alone", as it is traditionally defined by Warren and Brandeis (Warren & Brandeis, 1890). Information privacy is conceived as the freedom of the individual to determine whether one's personal information is communicated to other member of society (Westin, 1967; Gormley, 1992).

Privacy is recognized as a fundamental right in most jurisdictions, with the exception of U.S.A. It is enshrined in international law treaties such as the Universal Declaration of Human Rights, which states in Article 12 that "no one shall be subjected to arbitrary interference with his privacy, family, home or correspondence, nor to attacks upon his honour and reputation. Everyone has the right to the protection of the law against such interference or attacks". With the same formulation it is also included in the International Covenant on Civil and Political Rights, in Article 17.

However, there are convergences concerning the approach followed as regards the constitutional status of privacy worldwide. In the U.S. privacy is not explicitly derived by the Constitution, but has been developed by jurisprudence[2], which recognized a right to privacy, but a limited one. The right to privacy, in particular, applies only against government intrusion and where the individual has a reasonable expectation of privacy (Kesan, 2002, p. 294).

In Europe, privacy is elevated at the status of a fundamental right, which stems from the principle of human dignity and is either enshrined as a specific right (e.g., Belgium, Spain, Portugal, Greece) or as a right deriving from other constitutional principles (e.g., Germany). The European Convention for the Protection of Human Rights and Fundamental Freedoms (ECHR), laid down by the Council of Europe, establishes the right to privacy in Article 8[3]. The Charter of Fundamental Rights of the European Union also includes this right[4] and a more specific right for data protection[5], but this legal text does not have a binding nature.

The right to privacy, however, is not an absolute right and it may be subject to restrictions that are based on other rights or the interests of others or the society. Such restrictions are provided for in Article 8 ECHR, stating that no public authority should interfere with the exercise of the right to privacy except such as is in accordance with the law and is necessary in a democratic society in the interests of national security, public safety or the economic well-being of the country, for the prevention of disorder or crime, for the protection of health or morals, or for the protection of the rights and freedoms of others. It is evident that in the case concerning workplace monitoring, the right to information privacy has to be balanced against the legitimate interests of the employers. It has to be examined, therefore, whether the law provides for salient solutions, taking into account the need to respect of employees' privacy and the interests of employers.

## International Regulations

On international level, a notable instrument concerning data protection of employees is the "Code of Practice on the Protection of Workers' Personal Data" from 1997. The Code purports to providing guidance on the protection of workers' personal data. It does not have binding force, but rather contains principles, which can be used in the development of legislation, regulations, collective agreements, work rules, policies and practical measures at enterprise level.

The Code contains general principles, such as that personal data should be processed lawfully and fairly, and only for reasons directly relevant to the employment of the worker (Section 5.1); also, it states that personal data collected in connection with technical or organizational measures to ensure the security and proper operation of automated information systems should not be used to control the behaviour of workers (Section 5.4) and further, that personal data collected by electronic monitoring should not be the only factors in evaluating worker performance (Section 5.6).

It also contains provisions on collection, storage, use and communication of personal data, and on individual and collective rights. Concerning monitoring it provides the following in Section 6.14:

*(1) If workers are monitored they should be informed in advance of the reasons for monitoring, the time schedule, the methods and techniques used and the data to be collected, and the employer must minimize the intrusion on the privacy of workers.*
*(2) Secret monitoring should be permitted only: (a) if it is in conformity with national legislation; or (b) if there is suspicion on reasonable grounds of criminal activity or other serious wrongdoing.*
*(3) Continuous monitoring should be permitted only if required for health and safety or the protection of property.*

Furthermore, in section 12.2 it is provided that:

*The workers' representatives, where they exist, and in conformity with national law and practice, should be informed and consulted:*

*(a) concerning the introduction or modification of automated systems that process worker's personal data;*
*(b) before the introduction of any electronic monitoring of workers' behaviour in the workplace; (...)*

Apparently, monitoring of employees is not prohibited, but underlies specific requirements. Particularly, secret monitoring is permitted exceptionally where there are reasonable grounds of criminal activity or if national legislation so permits. In addition, it is provided for collective protection, since representatives of workers should be informed and consulted before the introduction of electronic monitoring systems.

Furthermore, the Council of Europe issued a Recommendation on the Protection of Personal Data used for Employment Purposes[6]. This recommendation does not include provisions regulating the legitimacy of monitoring, but address this issue only with regard to information and collective protection of workers. In Section 3.1. it is stated that:

*In accordance with domestic law or practice and, where appropriate, in accordance with relevant collective agreements, employers should, in advance, fully inform or consult their employees or the representatives of the latter about the introduction or adaptation of automated systems for the collection and use of personal data of employees. This principle also applies to the introduction or adaptation of technical devices designed to monitor the movements or productivity of employees.*

A legal obligation to introduce monitoring practices in the workplace is foreseen in the Cybercrime Convention of Council of Europe, which lays down in Article 12 that criminal liability may be inflicted upon corporations, if they allow the commission of illegal acts through lack of supervision or control. In particular, it is stated that:

*1) Each Party shall adopt such legislative and other measures as may be necessary to ensure that legal persons can be held liable for a criminal offence established in accordance with this Convention, committed for their benefit by any natural person, acting either individually or as part of an organ of the legal person, who has a leading position within it, based on: a) a power of representation of the legal person; b) an authority to take decisions on behalf of the legal person; c) an authority to exercise control within the legal person. 2) In addition to the cases already provided for in paragraph 1 of this article, each Party shall take the measures necessary to ensure that a legal person can be held liable where the lack of supervision or control by a natural person referred to in paragraph 1 has made possible the commission of a criminal offence established in accordance with this Convention for the benefit of that legal person by a natural person acting under its authority.*

This provision might be interpreted so as to encourage businesses to introduce electronic surveillance measures in order to make sure that their employees do not commit illegal acts and more precisely, any activities which constitute cybercrimes or other offences such as copyright infringement, pornography, etc (Kierkegaard, p. 232).

In the EU, besides the General Data Protection Directive, there is no specific legal instrument regulating privacy of employees. The EU Data Protection Working Party has set down general principles applying to email and internet monitoring in the Working Document on the surveillance of electronic communications in the workplace (WP 55, 2002), which is complementary to Opinion 8/2001[7]. The Working Party lays down general principles and rules that implement the EU Privacy Directive in the specific circumstances of the employment relationships.

The EU also contemplates the adoption of a Directive on the protection of workers' personal data. The European Commission's document for the second stage consultation of the social partners on workers' personal data covers specific issues related to data protection at the workplace, including treatment of sensitive information, such as health data, drug testing and genetic testing data, and monitoring of workers' e-mails and internet use. Concerning electronic monitoring it provides the following:

- The workers' representatives should be informed and consulted before the introduction, modification or evaluation of any system likely to be used for monitoring/ surveillance of workers.
- Prior check by a national Data Protection supervisory authority should be considered.
- Continuous monitoring should be permitted only if necessary for health, safety, security or the protection of property.
- Secret monitoring should be permitted only in conformity with the safeguards laid down by national legislation or if there is reasonable suspicion of criminal activity or other serious wrongdoing.
- Personal data collected in order to ensure the security, the control or the proper operation of processing systems should not be processed to control the behaviour of individual workers except where the latter is linked to the operation of these systems.
- Personal data collected by electronic monitoring should not be the only factors in evaluating workers' performance and taking decisions in their regard.
- Notwithstanding particular cases, such as automated monitoring for purposes of security and proper operation of the system (e.g. viruses), routine monitoring of each individual worker's e-mail or Internet use should be prohibited. Individual monitoring may be carried out where there is reasonable suspicion of criminal activity or serious wrongdoing or misconduct, provided that there are no other less intrusive means to achieve the desired purpose (e.g. objective monitoring of traffic data rather than of the content of e-mails; preventive use of technology etc.)
- Prohibition in principle imposed on the employer as regards opening private e-mail and/or other private files, notably those explicitly indicated as such, irrespective of whether use of the work tools for private purposes was allowed or not by the employer. In particular, private e-mails/files should be treated as private correspondence; secrecy of correspondence should not be able to be waived with a general consent of the worker, in particular upon conclusion of the contract of employment.
- Communication to occupational health professionals and representatives of workers should receive particular protection.

The proposal for Community action in this field is taking into account the existing international regulations and goes even further. However, no specific proposal for a legal instrument has been submitted until now and it is doubtful whether it would be submitted in the future.

## Review of the Legality of Employees' Electronic Communications Monitoring

In USA and in Europe there are different approaches concerning the issue at stake, i.e. the surveillance of employees' electronic communications. Generally speaking, US law and jurisprudence afford minimal protection to employees, whereas in Europe the principles for a balanced approach have been elaborated. However, there is no straightforward answer to the question whether surveillance of private e-mails could be permitted and to which extend, also in Europe.

Privacy of electronic communication under federal US law is afforded by the Electronic Communications Privacy Act, which prohibits unauthorized access to communications in electronic storage. Although this act applies to workplace surveillance of electronic communications, it includes many exceptions, which result in excluding employee protection (Kesan; Lasprogata). The jurisprudence also adopts a restrictive stance, taking into account the public nature of the workplace, which leads to denial of employee privacy. Courts in the USA apply the "tort of intrusion upon seclusion" (Restatement of Torts § 652B, 1976)[8] and upheld that monitoring of employees' Internet use is not an invasion of privacy, since employees have no reasonable expectation of privacy for communications voluntarily transmitted on an employer's network, and that, even if there were such an expectation, the intrusion upon seclusion is not highly offensive (Fazekas, 2004, p. 15).

In *Smyth v. Pillsbury Co.*[9], the court held that an employee has no reasonable expectation of privacy, although the employee had been assured that the content of monitored emails would remain confidential and would not be used against employees for termination or reprimand. In this case the employee was terminated for abusing the email privilege by sending too many emails, which were reviewed by the employer and it was found that they contained offensive material about the employer. The court applied the tort of intrusion upon seclusion and it held that the plaintiff - employees' right to privacy was not infringed because "once plaintiff communicated the alleged unprofessional comments to a second person over an e-mail system which was apparently utilized by the entire company, any reasonably expectation of privacy was lost".

In *McLaren v. Microsoft Corp.*[10], McLaren accused Microsoft of privacy invasion, for it accessed and distributed the email stored in his personal folder on his computer. McLaren had been suspended pending an investigation following accusations of sexual harassment and "inventory questions". McLaren's email messages in his personal folder were read by Microsoft, which fired him based on their contents. In this case the court held that the employee did not have a reasonable expectation of privacy, since the e-mails were transmitted over the company's network and were at some point accessible to a third-party. It was stressed that although the plaintiff used a password to access his messages and he stored them in his personal folder, the messages were not McLaren's personal property, but were merely an inherent part of the office environment. The court cited Smyth v. Pillsbury and it came to the conclusion that the employers' "interest in preventing inappropriate and unprofessional comments, or even illegal activity, over its e-mail system would outweigh McLarens's claimed privacy interest in those communications" (Desrochers & Roussos, 2001).

In Europe, a different approach is adopted, as already mentioned. Namely, it is recognized that employees have a legitimate expectation of privacy in the workplace, but this right has to be balanced with other legitimate rights and interests of the employer, who is the owner of the facilities in his business and, in principle, can decide whether to allow employees private use of Internet and e-mail or not. The employee has the right to manage his business efficiently and to protect himself from the liability or harm caused by employees' actions (WP 55, p. 4).

The differences in the expectations of privacy in USA and in Europe are primarily reflected in the jurisprudence of courts, particularly in those of the European Court of Human Rights (ECtHR). The ECtHR ruled in *Niemitz v. Germany* that no distinction can be made between private life and professional life regarding the protection of the right to privacy. This case concerned the search by a government authority of the law office of the complainant. The latter alleged, inter alia, that the search had violated his right to respect for his home and correspondence, guaranteed by Article 8 of the Convention. The argument of the government was that Article 8 did not afford protection against the search of someone's office, since "the Convention drew a clear distinction between private life and home, on the one hand, and professional and business life and premises, on the other".

The Court rejected this argument and pointed out that it would be too restrictive to limit the notion of "private life" – enshrined in Article 8 ECHR – to an "inner circle", in which the individual would live his own personal life as he chooses and to exclude therefrom entirely the outside world. On the contrary, it held that respect for private life must also comprise to a certain degree the right to establish and develop relationships with other human beings. Accordingly, it found that there is no reason to exclude activities of a professional or business nature from the notion of private life, particularly because the majority of people have a significant, if not the greatest, opportunity of developing relationships with the outside world in the course of their working lives. This argument is also supported by the view that it is not always possible to distinguish clearly which of an individual's activities form part of his professional or business life and which do not.

The ECtHR dealt with the monitoring of telephone and e-mail communications more precisely in two cases. In the case of *Halford v. the United Kingdom* the Court decided that interception of employees' phone calls at work constituted a violation of Article 8 ECHR. In more particular, the complainant, Ms Halford was provided with her own office two telephones, one of which was for private use, and these telephones were part of the police internal telephone network. The complainant alleged that calls made from her home and her office telephones were intercepted and this interception amounted to unjustifiable interferences with her rights to respect for her private life and freedom of expression, etc. The Government was of the opinion that telephones made by Ms Halford from her workplace fell outside the protection of Article 8, because she could have no reasonable expectation of privacy in relation to them. The Court, however, found that "telephone calls made from business premises as well as from the home may be covered by the notions of "private life" and "correspondence" within the meaning of Article 8 paragraph 1". It also noted that "there is no evidence of any warning having been given to Ms Halford, as a user of the internal telecommunication system that calls made on that system would be liable to interception. She would, the Court considers, have had a reasonable expectation of privacy for such calls..."

In the case of *Copland v. the United Kingdom*, the ECtHR found that a College that monitored an employee's e-mail, Internet usage and telephone calls infringed her right to privacy. This monitoring took place in order to ascertain whether the applicant was making excessive use of College facilities for personal purposes. The Government alleged that there has been no monitoring of content data, but that only an analysis of automatically generated information, i.e. of traffic data. Therefore, this case differed from the case of *Halford v. the United Kingdom*, where the applicant's telephone calls were intercepted. The Court held that e-mails sent from work and information derived from the monitoring of personal Internet usage is protected under Article 8, likewise as telephone calls. As the applicant had been given no warning that her communications were subject to monitoring, she held a reasonable expectation as to the privacy of calls made from her work telephone and to her e-mail and Internet usage. The Court also held that "the collection and storage of personal information relating to the applicant's telephone, as well as to her e-mails and Internet usage, without her knowledge, amounted to an interference with her right to respect for her private life and correspondence without the meaning of Article 8." Thus, it was irrelevant that the data held by the college were not disclosed or used against the applicant in disciplinary proceedings.

The jurisprudence of the ECtHR in the case of *Niemitz v. Germany* and in other cases did have a considerable impact upon the jurisprudence of national courts in Europe. In *Onof v. Nikon France*, the French Supreme Court held that an employee enjoyed the right to respect for his private life under Article 8 of the Convention in the workplace, and this right extended to private e-mails received at work, although the employer had prohibited the professional use of the computer facilities. The Court noted that an employer cannot read personal e-mail messages of an employee without violating the right of privacy and the right to respect of confidentiality of communications.

It is notable that the EU Data Protection Working Party attaches great significance upon the jurisprudence of the ECtHR and that, although they concern government action, the findings of the Court, as well as Article 8 of the Convention apply in a private action, also. This view is supported by the fact that in Europe under the concept of *Drittwirkung*, fundamental rights can be directly applied against private bodies by the courts[12]. The Working Party states three principles, which derive from the jurisprudence in relation to Article 8 ECHR:

a. Workers have a legitimate expectation of privacy at the workplace, which is not overridden by the fact that workers use communication devices or any other business facilities of the employer. However the provision of proper information by the employer to the worker may reduce the workers legitimate expectation of privacy.
b. The general principle of secrecy of correspondence covers communications at the workplace. This is likely to include electronic mail and related files attached thereto.
c. Respect for private life also includes to a certain degree the right to establish and develop relationships with other human beings. The fact that such relationships, to a great extent, take place at the workplace puts limits to employer's legitimate need for surveillance measures.

More specific criteria for assessing when monitoring of employees' communications may be lawful could be derived from the data protection legislation and in more particular, from the EU Data Protection Directive[13]. The legitimacy of monitoring can be based on Article 7 (f) of the Directive; accordingly, a monitoring activity should be necessary for the purposes of the legitimate interests pursued by the controller and it must not infringe upon the interests for fundamental rights and freedoms of employees, including the secrecy of communications.

Another legal basis for the legitimacy of monitoring could be the employee's consent. However, this stumbles upon the fact that e-mails contain personal data of both the sender and the recipient, and therefore, with the exception of inter-staff correspondence, this possibility is very limited (WP 55, p. 21). Besides that, due to the nature of employment relationship, in which there is an inherent asymmetry of power, employees would not have the possibility to make a free choice for monitoring (Mitrou & Karyda). The Working Party has stressed out in this particular regard that "reliance on consent should be confined to cases where the worker has a genuine free choice and is subsequently able to withdraw the consent without detriment." (WP 2001, p. 23)

In case, however, the rules for monitoring of e-mail and Internet use are agreed between the employer and the employees' works council, this would amount to consent, pursuant to Article 7 (a) of the Directive.

General principles derived by the Directive also apply to e-mail and Internet monitoring. These are the principles of necessity, finality, transparency, proportionality and accuracy and limited storage of data (WP 55, p. 13). In accordance with the principle of necessity, the employer must check if monitoring is absolutely necessary for a specified purpose before introducing any such activity. Under the principle of finality, data must be collected for a specified, explicit and legitimate purpose and not further processed in a way incompatible with those purposes.

Furthermore, the principle of transparency means that an employer must be clear and open about his activities. Hence, covert e-mail monitoring would not be allowed, except in those cases where it is necessary for the investigation, detection of criminal offences, committed by employees, or for the protection of the rights and freedom of others and in particular, where sensitive company information should be protected[14]. Thus, there should be suspicion on reasonable grounds of criminal activity and monitoring should be permitted if it is in conformity with national legislation (ILO, 1997). Moreover, the principle of transparency necessitates the obligation to provide information to the data subject and this entails the need to establish an e-mail/ Internet policy within the policy, and an obligation to notify supervisory authorities.

The principle of proportionality means that personal data must be adequate, relevant and not excessive in relation to the purposes for which they are collected and/or further processed. As the Working Party points out (WP 55, p. 17), the application of this principle would prohibit blanket monitoring of individual e-mails and Internet use of all staff other than where necessary for the purpose of ensuring the security of the system. This also implies that monitoring of e-mail should be limited to traffic data and not extend to the content of communications.

The principle of accuracy and limited storage of data obliges employers to store only data from employees' e-mail accounts or concerning use of the Internet, which are accurate and kept up to date and not kept for longer than necessary.

## CONCLUSION

In accordance with the general principles and rules which derive from the Data Protection Directive and the jurisprudence of the ECtHR, final conclusions which are arrived at, are the following.

Concerning e-mail monitoring, a distinction should be made between monitoring of company e-mails and private ones (Däubler, 2002, p. 100-101). This distinction derives from the fact that employees offered private e-mail accounts by the employer have a higher privacy expectation than those employees which use company e-mail. Consequently, monitoring of company e-mails would be permitted basically without restrictions, but where an e-mail address has a personal character, particularly where it is composed of the employee's name (e.g. employee@company.com), the principles of necessity, finality, transparency, proportionality and accuracy and limited storage of data should be applied.

Where private use of the Internet is permitted and private e-mail accounts are provided to employees, monitoring of private e-mails would be permitted only in limited cases. This would be the case, for example, where it is necessary for the purposes of the legitimate interest pursued by the controller or by the third party or parties to whom the data are disclosed (Article 7 (f) of the Directive). This requirement would not be applied for monitoring the work performance of employees, since in this case the employee's right to privacy would be overridden. Furthermore, where sensitive personal data are concerned, monitoring of electronic communications would not be permitted, since Article 8 of the Directive does not provide for an equivalent with Article 7 (f) provision.

Concerning monitoring of Internet access, it should be underlined that allowing the personal use of the Internet lies at the discretion of the employer. However, a ban on the use of Internet for private purposes seems unrealistic in our information society. Thus, a reasonable use of the Internet appears to be more suitable (Bouchet. 2002). Monitoring of Internet use may also be regarded lawful in restricted cases and for security reasons or for access control. Such control may be exercised through filtering mechanisms and it would be less intrusive. It would also be less intrusive to exercise a posteriori control of Internet use of more general nature and not an individualized, personal control of accessed sites, which may reveal users preferences pertaining to sensitive data, such as political opinions, etc (Bouchet, op. cit.).

In relation with monitoring of e-mail and Internet access, employees should be informed about monitoring. It is recommended to draft a company policy defining the rules for the use of the Internet and the standards to e-mail monitoring (WP 55, p. 25; Bouchet, p. 15). In addition, it is recommended to inform and consult workers' representatives before introducing monitoring systems (Council of Europe,).[15]

## REFERENCES

Article 29 Data Protection Working Party, *Opinion 8/2001.*

Article 29 Data Protection Working Party, *Working document on the surveillance of electronic communications in the workplace*, adopted on 29 May 2002, 5401/01/EN/Final, WP 55.

Bouchet, H. (2002). *Cyber-Surveillance in the Workplace*, report adopted by the CNIL, 2002, p. 11, online available at: http://www.cnil.fr/fileadmin/documents/uk/CNIL-cybersurveillance-feb2002-VA.pdf

Ciocchetti, C. A. (2001). Monitoring Employee e-mail: Efficient Workplaces vs. Employee Privacy. *Duke Law & Technology Review.*

Däubler, W. (2002). *Gläserne Belegschaften? Datenschutz in Betrieb und Dienststelle, 4.* Aufl., 2002.

Davies, S. (n.d.). *New Techniques and Technologies of Surveillance in the Workplace.* Online available at: http://www.amicustheunion.org/pdf/surveillencetechniques.pdf

Desrochers, S., & Roussos, A. (2001). The Jurisprudence of Surveillance: a Critical Look at the Laws of Intimacy. *Lex Electronica, 6*(2). Online available at: http://www.lex-electronica.org/articles/v6-2/desroussos.htm

*Electronic Monitoring & Surveillance Survey, 2007.* http://www.amanet.org/movingahead/editorial.cfm?Ed=697

EPIC. *Workplace Privacy*, online available at: http://epic.org/privacy/workplace

Fazekas, C. P. (2004). 1984 is still fiction: Electronic Monitoring in the Workplace and U.S. Privacy Law. *Duke Law & Technology Review* 2004, *15.* Online available at: http://www.law.duke.edu/journals/dltr/articles/pdf/2004dltr0015.pdf

Fraser, J. (2005). Telecommunications (Lawful Business Practice) (Interception of Communications) Regulations 2000 Workplace Surveillance, Privacy and New Technologies. In L. Edwards (Ed.), *The New Legal Framework for E-Commerce in Europe*, (pp. 277-291).

Godfrey, B. (2001). Electronic Work Monitorung: An Ethical Model. In J. Weckert (Ed.), *Proc. Selected papers from the 2nd Australian Institute of Computer Ethics Conference (AICE2000)*, Canberra: ACS.

Gormley, K. (1992). One Hundred Years of Privacy. *Wisconsin Law Review*, (pp. 1335-1441).

International Labour Organization (ILO) (n.d.). *Protection of workers' personal data.* An ILO code of practice.

Kesan, J. P. (2002). Cyber-Woring or Cyber-Shrinking?: A First Principles Examination of Electronic Privacy in the Workplace. *Florida Law Review 2002*(54).

Kierkegaard, S. (2005). Privacy in electronic communication. Watch your e-mail: Your boss is snooping! *CLSR* 2005, (pp. 226-236).

Lasprogata, G., King, N. J., & Pillay, S. (2004). Regulation of Electronic Employee Monitoring: Identifying Fundamental Principles of Employee Privacy through a Comparative Study of Data Privacy Legislation in the European Union, United States and Canada. *Stanford Technology Law Review 2004*(4).

Mitrou, L., & Karyda, M. (2006). Employees' privacy vs. employers' security: Can they be balanced? *Telematics and Informatics, 23*(3), 164-178.

Warren, S., & Brandeis, L. (1890). The right to privacy. *Harvard Law Review,* (4), 193-220.

Westin, A. (1967). *Privacy and Freedom.*

## ADDITIONAL READING

Theoharidou, M., Kokolakis, S., Karyda, M., & Kiountouzis, E. (2005). The insider threat to Information Systems and the effectiveness of ISO 17799. *Computers and Security Journal, 24*(6), 472-484.

Moukiou, Ch. (2003). The European Legal Frame and its Effectiveness in Greek Reality – The Special Issue of Digital Signature. In D. Politis, N. Papasteriadou (Eds.), *Recent Advances in Court Computerisation and Legal Databases – First Steps towards e-Justice.* Athens: A. N. Sakkoulas Publications.

Mitrou, E., & Karyda, M. (2006). Employees' Privacy vs. Employers' Security: Can they be balanced? *Telematics and Informatics Journal,* 23(3), 2006, 164 – 178.

Delbar, C., Mormont, M., Schots, M. (2003). *New technology and respect for privacy at the workplace. MSF Information Professionals' Association,* London School of Economics, London. Available from: http://www.eiro.eurofund.eu.int/print/2003/07/study/TN0307101S.html

Schwartz, P., & Reidenberg, J. (1996). *Data Privacy Law.* Charlottesville.

Simitis, S. (1999). Reconsidering the Premises of Labour Law: Prolegomena to an EU Regulation on the Protection of Employees'Personal Data. *European Law Journal, 5,* 1/1999, 45-62.

Simitis, S. (1987). Reviewing Privacy in an Information Society. *University of Pennsylvania Law Review, 135*(1987), 707 ff.

Watson, G. (n.d.). E-mail surveillance in the UK workplace – a management consulting case study. *In Aslib Proceedings, MCB UP Ltd. 54*(1), 23-40.

## KEY TERMS

**Informational Privacy:** The protection of the personal information with regard to collection and processing of data relating to an individual.

**Lawful Interception:** The interception of electronic communications by law enforcement agencies and other government services, in accordance with national legislation and after following due process and receiving proper authorization from competent authorities.

**Right to Private Life:** The right of the individual to continue its life privately, without government interference, respecting the rights of other people.

**Secrecy of Communications:** The right to protection of the secrecy of communications, which derives from the classic right to secrecy of correspondence. It protects the content of the communication, but also the information on when and to whom any messages (if any) have been sent.

**Workplace Surveillance:** The use of information technology by businesses in the course of employees' communications and work in order to monitor their activities. This includes, inter alia, telephone, PC monitoring and also, e-mail and Internet surfing monitoring.

## ENDNOTES

1 The right to privacy includes many aspects; the most important ones are i) information privacy, i.e. the right of protection of private information, ii) physical privacy, which refers to respect of a person and the surrounding environment and iii) decisional privacy, referring to respect of one's personal decisions; see Lasprogata et al., op. cit., p. 4.

2 See, e.g., Griswold v. Connecticut, 381 U.S. 479 (1965); Olmstedt v. United States, 277 U.S. 438 (1928).

3 "Everyone has the right to respect for his private and family life, his home and correspondence".

4 Article 7 (Respect for private and family life): "Everyone has the right to respect for his or her private and family life, home and communications".

5 Article 8 (Protection of personal data): "1. Everyone has the right to the protection of personal data concerning him or her. 2. Such data must be processed fairly for specified purposes and on the basis of the consent of the person concerned or some other legitimate basis laid down by law. Everyone has the right of access to data which has been collected concerning him or her, and the right to have it rectified. 3. Compliance with these rules shall be subject to control by an independent authority."

6 Recommendation No R (89) 2, 1989.

7 Article 29 Data Protection Working Party, Opinion 8/2001 on the processing of personal data in the employment sector, adopted on 13 September 2001, 5062/01/EN/Final, WP 48.

8 "One who intentionally intrudes, physically or otherwise, upon the solitude or seclusion of another or his private affairs or concerns, is subject to liability to the other for invasion of his privacy, if the intrusion would be highly offensive to a reasonable person."

9 C. P. Fazekas, "1984 is still fiction: Electronic Monitoring in the Workplace and U.S. Privacy Law", *Duke Law & Technology Review* 2004, 15, online available at: http://www.law.duke.edu/journals/dltr/articles/pdf/2004dltr0015.pdf

10 No 05-97-00824-CV.

11 See: www.courdecassation.fr

12 The European Court of Human Rights recognized this concept in the case of *X and Y v. the Netherlands.*

13 Directive 95/46/EEC of the European Parliament and of the Council of 24 October 1995 on the protection of individuals with regard to the processing of personal data and on the free movement of such data, L 281/31, 23.11.1995.

14 The EU Data Protection Working Party refers to Article 13 of the Directive, which states that: "Member States may adopt legislative measures to restrict the scope of the obligations and rights provided for in Articles 6 (1), 10, 11 (1), 12 and 21 when such a restriction constitutes a necessary measures to safeguard: (a) national security; (b) defence; (c) public security; (d) the prevention, investigation, detection and prosecution of criminal offences, or of breaches of ethics for regulated professions; (e) an important economic or financial interest of a Member State of the European Union, including monetary, budgetary and taxation matters; (f) a monitoring, inspection or regulatory function connected, even occasionally, with the exercise of official authority in cases referred to in (c), (d) and (e); (g) the protection of the data subject or of the rights and freedoms of others."

15 See Council of Europe, Recommendation No R(89)2, Article 3.1; ILO, Code of Practice on the protection of workers' personal data, Sections 5.8, 12.2, 5.11.

# Section III
# The Forensic Challenges for Intrusion

# Chapter XVI
# Forensic Watermarking for Secure Multimedia Distribution

**Farook Sattar**
*Nanyang Technological University, Singapore*

**Dan Yu**
*Hewlett-Packard, Shanghai, China*

## ABSTRACT

*This chapter discusses on forensic tracking through digital watermarking for secure multimedia distribution. The existing watermarking schemes are elaborated and their assumptions as well as limitations for tracking are discussed. Especially, an Independent Component Analysis (ICA) based watermarking scheme is presented, which overcomes the problems of the existing watermarking schemes. Multiple watermarking techniques are used where one watermark is used for ownership verification and the other one is used to identify the legal user of the distributed content. In the absence of a priori information, i.e. the original data, original watermark, embedding locations as well as the strength, our ICA technique provides efficient watermark extraction scheme with the help of side information. The robustness against common signal processing attacks is presented. Lastly, the challenges in the forensic tracking through digital watermarking techniques are discussed.*

## INTRODUCTION

In recent years, there has been enormous growth in multimedia technologies and computer network. Thus, the distribution of digital multimedia such as audio, image, video, text have become quite easy through various communications media e.g. *Internet.* It has a world-wide broadcasting capability, a mechanism for information distribution, and a medium for collaboration and interaction between individuals and their computers irrespective to geographic location. This allows researches and professionals to share the relevant data, information with each other.

As image, audio, video and other works become available in digital form, it may be ease for some one to make perfect copies of the multimedia data. The widespread use of *Internet* have added substantially an astonishing abundance of information in digital form, as well as offering unprecedented ease of access to it. Creating, publishing, distributing, using, and reusing information have become much easier and faster in the past decade. The good news is the enrichment that this explosive growth in information brings to society as a whole. The bad news is the enrichment that it can also bring to those who take advantage of the properties of digital information and the Web to copy, distribute, and use information illegally. The Web is an information resource of extraordinary size and depth, yet it is also an information reproduction and dissemination facility of great demand and capability. Therefore, there has been currently significant amount of research in intellectual property protection issues involving the multimedia content distribution through *Internet.*

Thus the aim of this chapter is to present the forensic tracking through digital watermarking. An Efficient Independent Component Analysis (ICA) based watermarking technique is applied for watermark extraction in order to verify the authorized user of the distributed content, and hence to do the forensic tracking of the multimedia data to be protected.

## MULTIMEDIA DISTRIBUTION STRATEGY THROUGH DIGITAL WATERMARKING

The rapid growth of networked multimedia systems has increased the need for the protection and enforcement of intellectual property (IP) rights of digital media. The IP protection for multimedia distribution in the *Internet* can be elaborated as follows:

- **Ownership identification:** The owner of the original Work must be able to provide the trustful proof that he/she is the rightful owner of the content.
- **Transaction tracking:** The owner must be able to track the distributions of the Work, so that he/she is able to find the person who should be responsible for the illegal replication and re-distribution.
- **Content authentication:** The owner should be able to detect any illegal attempts to alter the Work.

This chapter concentrates on the task of forensic tracking for multimedia distribution applications. Let consider the scenario when an owner would like to sell or distribute the Work for the registered users only. To enforce the IP rights, two primary problems are to be solved. First of all, the owner needs to prove that he/she is the legal owner of the distributed content. Secondly, if the data have been subsequently copied and redistributed illegally, how it is possible for the owner to find the person who is responsible for the illegal copying and redistribution of the data (see Figure 1).

The first technology adopted to enforce protection of IP rights is the cryptography. The cryptographic technology (Schneier, 1995) provides an effective tool to secure the distribution process and control the legal uses of the contents that have been received by an user. The content to be delivered in the Internet is encrypted, and only the legal users who hold the decryption key are able to use the encrypted data whereas the data stream would be useless to a pirate without the appropriate decryption key. However, for the error-free transmission through a network, the contents after the decryption in the cryptography will be exactly the same as the original data. The data contents can be replicated perfectly as many times and the user can also manipulate the contents.

Researchers and scientists are then turned to search for other technologies to counter copyright piracy on the global networks that are not

*Figure 1. A multimedia distribution system, where the digital content could be illegally redistributed to an illegal user.*

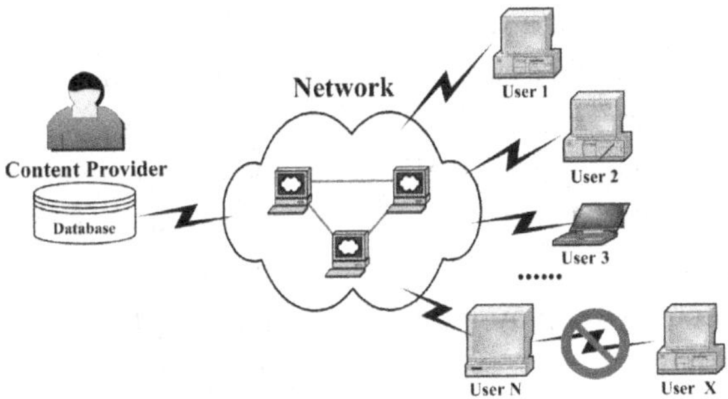


*Figure 2. The multimedia distribution framework by inserting an owner's watermark to identify the ownership of the Work and a unique user's watermark to identify each unique legal user.*

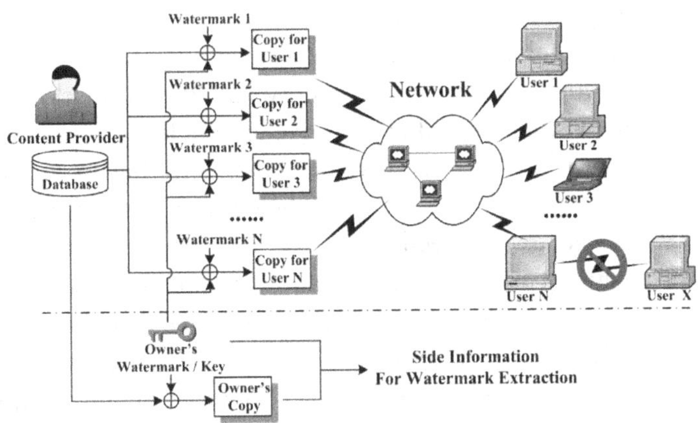


solvable by the cryptography. In this context, recently *digital watermarking* technology (Cox, & Bloom, 2002) has been drawn a lots of attentions. In the digital watermarking the information is transparently embedded into the Work, rather than a specific media format, such as the header of a file that could be lost during transmission or file format transformation. Digital watermarking technique thus provides an efficient means for transaction tracking for the illegal copying as well as distribution of the multimedia information. For a typical transaction tracking application, the watermark identifies the first legal recipient of the Work. If it is subsequently discovered that the Work has been illegally redistributed, the watermark can then help to identify the person who is responsible for it.

Figure 2 presents a multimedia distribution framework to enforce the IP rights through technique of multiple watermarking. Multiple watermarking (Lu, & Mark, 2001; Mintzer, & Braudaway, 1999; Sheppard), as suggested by the name, refers to embed different types of watermarks into single multimedia content to accomplish different purposes. For example, one of the watermarks could be used to verify the ownership, the second one is to identify the recipient, and the third one is to authenticate the content integrity.

For the Internet distribution application, the users firstly send request to the content provider whenever they are interested for the multimedia contents. Then the owner can always distribute the Work by signing a watermark to a registered user to uniquely identify the recipient of the Work, as shown in Figure 2. All the data sent to a registered user are embedded with an assigned watermark as well as an owner's watermark, while maintaining a good perceptual visual quality of the marked content. In this presented framework, the IP rights of the distributed Works are enforced from the two following aspects by employing a multiple watermarking technique:

- Every copy of the Work contains the owner's watermark to identify the rightful ownership of the Work.
- The owner or an authorized representative can uniquely identify the recipient or the legal user of a particular copy of the multimedia content according to the embedded user's unique watermark.

Consider the case when the owner needs to prove the rightful ownership of the content. The owner can present its original data (without any marks) of the Work as well as the owner's watermark as evidences. The two embedded watermarks including one owner's watermark and one user's watermark are, therefore, able to extract by a simple subtraction method (Cox, & Bloom, 2002; Cox, Leighton, & Shamoon, 1997). One extracted watermark, that is the owner's watermark, is matched with the previously presented owner's watermark. The rightful ownership of the content is thus verified. It is an essentially important pre-requisite for IP protection to embed the owner's watermark into every copy of the Work to be distributed in the Internet. The more difficult and challenging task as discussed in this chapter is to identify the legal users efficiently in the absence of the original data, and hence to trace the transactions of a particular copy of the multimedia content. For the security purpose in multimedia, the original data are always kept in secret and should not be known to the public during watermark extraction. In some real applications, the owner need the authorize representatives, or service providers to perform the transaction tracking tasks. For security reason, the owner also cannot provide the original data to those representatives. Therefore, there arises a challenging issue as how to extract the user's watermark in the absence of original data. This is the main problem in transaction tracking through digital watermarking, which has been discussed in this chapter.

## BACKGROUND

Assumptions as well as limitations for most of the existing watermarking schemes are summarized in the following that can cause difficulties and ineffectiveness to apply those watermarking schemes in forensic tracking:

a. In some watermarking algorithms, the watermark detection and extraction requires the presence of the original content. This is not a desirable solution, since the original data should always keep in secret and should not be shown to the public, or sometimes the original data is even not available immediately. Therefore, *blind* watermarking techniques are of great interests and concerns nowadays.
b. Most of the existing watermarking schemes (Cox, & Bloom, 2002; Cox, Leighton, & Shamoon, 1997; Katzenbeisser, & Petitcolas, 2000) are based on some assumptions for watermark detection and extraction, such as the previous knowledge of watermark location, strength or some threshold. However, in order to ensure the robustness and invisibility of the watermark, the optimum embedding locations as well as the embedding strength are generally different for different images. For a large image database, it could be a dis-

advantage if it requires watermark location and strength information for the detection and extraction of the watermark. As a result, a large amount of side information is needed to be stored.

c. As explained above, Figure 2 shows a framework to prevent illegal redistribution of the data by a legal user. In such scenario, the current watermark detection and extraction algorithms requiring information of the watermark location and strength, or even the original watermark could fail, because no one knows which watermark exists in the received copy of the Work.
d. Moreover, the general watermark detection algorithm is based on a match filter finding the maximum correlation of the recovered watermark with the stored watermarks in the database containing the watermarks used to identify all the possible users. It is rather a time consuming and inefficient process, especially when a large database is needed for distribution among a large number of users.

In this chapter, an Independent Component Analysis (ICA) based technique is proposed for watermark extraction (Yu, Sattar, & Ma, 2002). The proposed ICA-based blind watermarking scheme (Yu, & Sattar, 2003), can overcome the existing problems of the current watermarking scheme for multimedia tracking as mentioned above. No *a priori* knowledge such as watermark locations, strengths, threshold setting, or the original watermark is required for watermark extraction. This presented watermarking algorithm is found very effective in the application of legal data tracking compared to other watermarking algorithms. Therefore, by adopting this ICA-based watermarking approach, an efficient multimedia distribution framework for copyright protection can be accomplished.

## A NEW ICA-BASED WATERMARKING SCHEME FOR FORENSIC TRACKING

This section presents an ICA-based wavelet-domain watermarking scheme. Two watermarks are to be embedded into two selected wavelet transform sub-bands of the original image, respectively. One is the owner's watermark (or the key of the watermarking system), and the other is a unique watermark assigned for a unique legal user. ICA technique is applied for extraction of the user's watermark with the help of side information. The proposed scheme is described in the context of watermarking in grayscale images, but this technique can be extended to color images, and other digital media such as audio and video.

### Proposed Watermark Embedding Scheme

Figure 3 shows a second level wavelet decomposition of the Lena image into four bands -- low frequency band (LL), high frequency band (HH), low-high frequency band (LH), and high-low frequency band (HL). Sub-bands LL and HH are not suitable for watermark embedding among these four sub-band components. The image quality can be degraded if the watermark is embedding in LL sub-band, since it contains the most important information of an image. Sub-band HH is insignificant compared to LH and HL sub-bands, and watermark embedding in such sub-band is difficult to survive attacks, such as, lossy JPEG compression. Watermark embedding in the two sub-bands (e.g. LH2, HL2 of the second level wavelet decomposition) consisting the middle frequency pair is to be demonstrated.

Some digital signature/pattern or company logo (**S**), for example, a text image in Figure 4(b), can be used to generate the watermark (**W**) to be embedded. This type of recognizable image pattern is more intuitive and unique than the random

Figure 3. Second level wavelet decomposition of the Lena image.

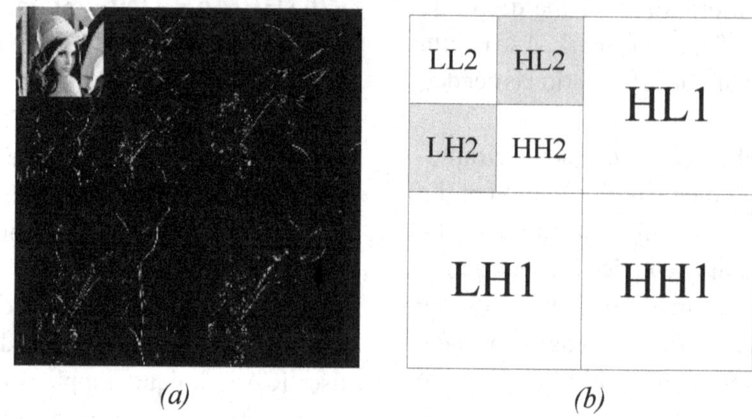


(a) (b)

Figure 4. (a) A NVF masking function, (b) a text signature (64×64), (c) modified text watermark based on the visual mask in (a), (d) an owner's watermark or key of watermarking system, (e) modified key based on (a), (f) original Lena image (256×256), and (g) a watermarked Lena image (PSNR = 45.50dB).

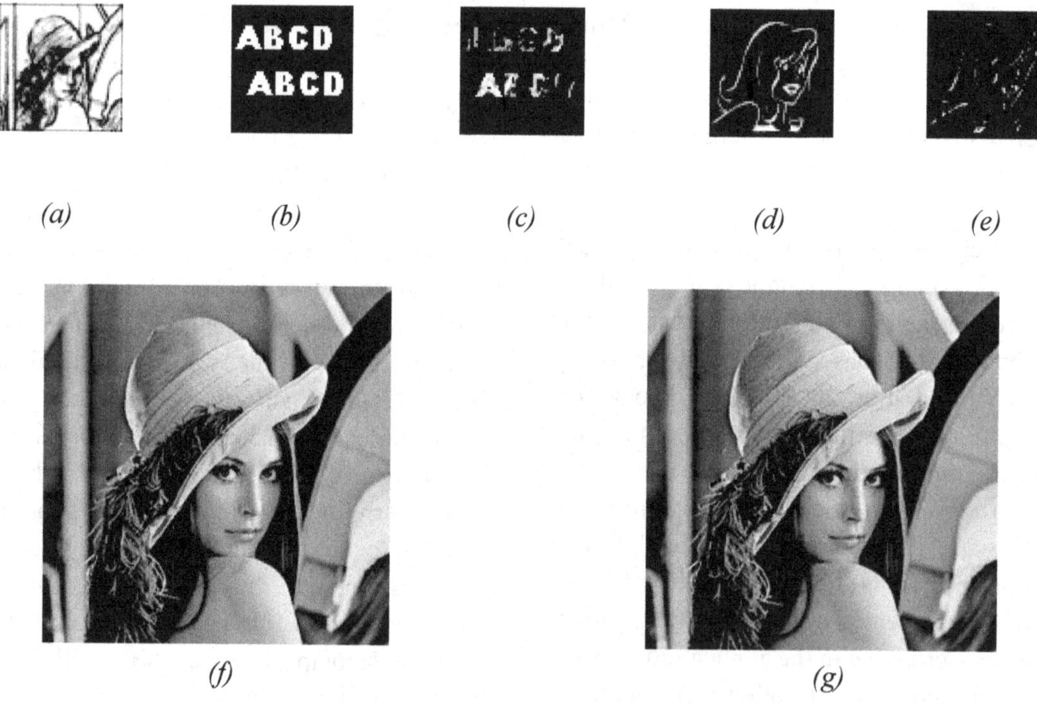


(a) (b) (c) (d) (e)

(f) (g)

sequence to identify the ownership of the Work. By using grayscale watermark, our method is found to be more robust against various attacks, because the grayscale images can always preserve a certain level of structural information, which are meaningful and recognizable and also can be much easy to be verified by human eyes rather than some objective similarity measurements. A masking function -- Noise Visibility Function (NVF)(Voloshynovskiy, Herrigel, Baumgaertner, & Pun, 1999) -- is applied to characterize the local image properties, identifying the textured and edge regions where the information can be more strongly embedded. Such high activity regions are generally highly insensitive to distortion. With the visual mask, the watermark strength can be reasonably increased without visually degrading the image quality.

In the next, the watermark generation and the detailed embedding algorithm are demonstrated, followed by the generation of side information for watermark extraction.

## Watermark Embedding Algorithm

Figure 5 illustrates the watermark embedding procedure using second level decomposed middle frequency pair (LH2 and HL2).

- **Step 1:** Perform the second level discrete wavelet decomposition of the original image **I**. Sub-bands LH2 and HL2 are selected for the watermark insertion.
- **Step 2:** The NVF masking function (Voloshynovskiy, Herrigel, Baumgaertner, & Pun, 1999), **M**, of the original image is generated. Figure 4(a) shows a NVF mask for the Lena image. For the homogeneous region, NVF approaches 1 (white color), and the strength of the embedded watermark approaches to zero. The watermark should embed in highly textured regions containing edges instead of homogeneous regions. The original signature image **S**, is modified according to the generated NVF masking function to assure the imperceptibility of the watermark embedded. The final watermark is quantized into [0-7] gray levels. The expression for watermark generation is given as:

$$\mathbf{W} = \mathbf{Q}_8 [ ( 1 - \mathbf{M} ) . \mathbf{S} ] \quad (1)$$

where $\mathbf{Q}_8$ denotes the quantization operator with 8 gray levels. Figure 4(c) shows a text watermark generated using the NVF masking function shown in Figure 4(a).

*Figure 5. The proposed watermark embedding algorithm (for the second level wavelet decomposition).*

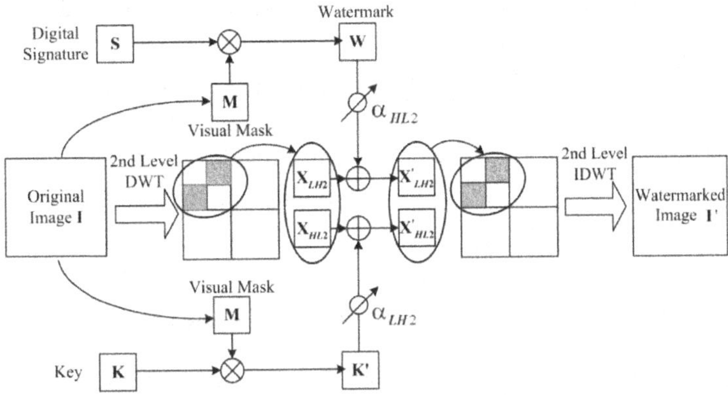

- **Step 3:** The key **K** that is also the owner's watermark, is pre-processed by multiplying the same visual mask **M** as:

$$\mathbf{K}' = \mathbf{Q}_8 [ ( 1 - \mathbf{M} ) . \mathbf{K} ] \qquad (2)$$

where $\mathbf{Q}_8$ denotes the quantization operator with 8 gray levels. Figure 4(d) gives a key image for ownership authentication. Figure 4(e) shows the modified key after pre-processing by using the NVF masking function in Figure 4(a).

- **Step 4:** The watermark **W** and the modified key **K′** are inserted into the LH2 and HL2 sub-band, respectively, in the following way:

$$\mathbf{X}'_{LH2} = \mathbf{X}_{LH2} + \alpha_{LH2} \cdot \mathbf{W} = \mathbf{X}_{LH2} + \alpha_{\mathbf{X}} \cdot \mu(|\mathbf{X}_{LH2}|) \cdot \mathbf{W}$$

$$\mathbf{X}'_{HL2} = \mathbf{X}_{HL2} + \alpha_{HL2} \cdot \mathbf{K}' = \mathbf{X}_{HL2} + \alpha_{\mathbf{X}} \cdot \mu(|\mathbf{X}_{HL2}|) \cdot \mathbf{K}' \qquad (3)$$

where **X** and **X′** are the wavelet transform coefficients of the original and the watermarked image, respectively. In Equation 3, $\alpha_{LH2}$ and $\alpha_{HL2}$ denote the weighting coefficients of the watermark embedding in sub-bands LH2 and HL2, respectively, while $\mu(|\cdot|)$ denotes the operation of mean of the absolute value. A common control parameter $\alpha_{\mathbf{X}}$ in Equation 3 is used to adjust the watermark embedding strength to preserve a satisfactory quality of the final watermarked image (Peter, 2001).

- **Step 5:** The watermarked image, **I′**, is obtained by the inverse discrete wavelet transform.
- **Step 6:** The Steps 4 and 5 are repeated until the quality of the final watermarked image is satisfied, for instant, the PSNR (*Peak-Signal-to-Noise-Ratio*) measure is within the range of 40-50dB. Particularly the parameter $\alpha_{\mathbf{X}}$ is tuned to adjust the watermark strength to obtain the desired embedding result. Decreasing the magnitude of $\alpha_{\mathbf{X}}$ results a better quality of final marked image and vice versa. Figure 4(e) gives a watermarked Lena image with PSNR 45.50dB. Table 1 shows the quality of watermarked image (in dB) with respect to the control parameter $\alpha_{\mathbf{X}}$.

## Side Information for Watermark Extraction

As discussed earlier, the original data may be unavailable in many real applications for the security purpose. In order to identify the legal users, some side information is required for user's watermark extraction in the absence of the original data. The method used in the proposed scheme to solve the problem is that the user can keep a copy of the dataset embedding with only owner's watermark following the same procedure shown in Figure 5. The owner's watermark is also known as the *key* of the watermarking system, which is used for watermark extraction. Using only the owner's copy, $\mathbf{I}'_0$, and the key, **K**, the owner is able to identify the recipient of any distributed image by ICA methods. This will be elaborated in next sub-section in detail.

Figure 6 is an owner's copy of the Lena image, embedded with an owner's watermark shown in Figure 4(d). The owner's copy is obtained similarly by embedding the modified key **K′** in the wavelet domain using the following equations:

*Table 1. PSNR (in dB) of the watermarked image with respect to $\alpha_{\mathbf{X}}$*

| $\alpha_{\mathbf{X}}$ | 0.01 | 0.05 | 0.10 | 0.15 | 0.20 | 0.25 | 0.30 |
|---|---|---|---|---|---|---|---|
| PSNR (dB) | 67.50 | 53.52 | 47.50 | 43.98 | 41.48 | 39.54 | 37.96 |

$$\mathbf{X}'_{0LH2} = \mathbf{X}_{LH2} + \alpha_{LH2} \cdot \mathbf{K}' = \mathbf{X}_{LH2} + \alpha_{X0} \cdot \mu(|\mathbf{X}_{0LH2}|) \cdot \mathbf{K}'$$

$$\mathbf{X}'_{0HL2} = \mathbf{X}_{HL2} + \alpha_{HL2} \cdot \mathbf{K}' = \mathbf{X}_{HL2} + \alpha_{X0} \cdot \mu(|\mathbf{X}_{0HL2}|) \cdot \mathbf{K}' \quad (4)$$

where $\mathbf{X}_0$ and $\mathbf{X}'_0$ are respectively the wavelet transform coefficients of the original image and the watermarked channel, $\alpha_{X0}$ is a control parameter for the visual quality of the watermarked image $\mathbf{I}'_0$.

Suppose an owner wants to authorize a third party named as *appointed representative* to do the tracing task. In such case, the owner should also assign a unique watermark for the appointed representative. This representative's watermark would then replace the owner's watermark embedded in the HL2 wavelet sub-band. It would also be used as the key during watermark extraction. However, at the same time, for ownership verification, the owner's watermark is still required to be embedded in the selected wavelet sub-band other than LH2 and HL2.

## Proposed Watermark Extraction Scheme Using ICA Method

In this section, the concept of ICA is firstly introduced briefly. A blind watermark extraction scheme is then proposed, where ICA is employed for watermark extraction successfully without knowing the original image and any prior knowledge on which watermark is hidden and what the embedding strength and location are.

*Figure 6. The owner's copy of Lena image (256×256 and PSNR = 46.72dB).*

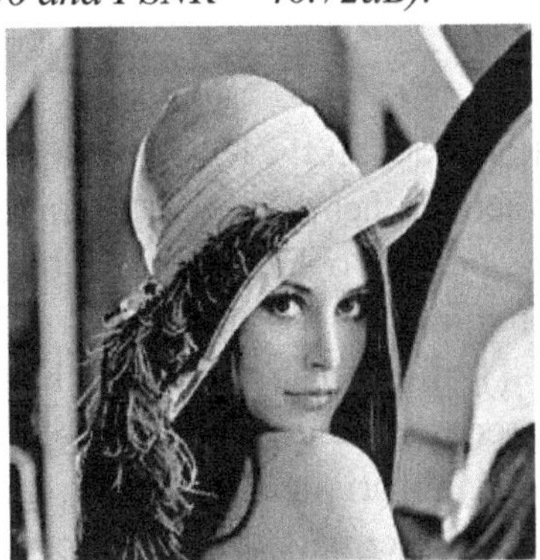

## Independent Component Analysis

Independent Component Analysis (ICA) is one of the most widely used methods for performing Blind Source Separation (BSS). It is a very general-purpose statistical technique to recover the independent sources given only sensor observations that are linear mixtures of independent source signals (Hyvärinen, 1999a; Hyvärinen, & Oja, 1999; Lee, 1998). ICA has widely applied in many areas such as audio processing, biomedical signal processing and telecommunications. In this paper, ICA is further applied in watermarking for the blind watermark extraction.

ICA model consists of two parts: the mixing process and unmixing process. In the mixing process (Hyvärinen, 1999a; Hyvärinen, & Oja, 1999; Lee, 1998), the observed linear mixtures $x_1, \ldots, x_m$ of $n$ number of independent components are defined as:

$$x_j = a_{j1}s_1 + a_{j2}s_2 + \ldots + a_{jn}s_n;\ 1 \le j \le m \quad (5)$$

where $\{s_k, k = 1, \ldots, n\}$ denote the source variables, i.e., the independent components, and $\{a_{jk}, j = 1, \ldots, m; k = 1, \ldots, n\}$ are the mixing coefficients. In vector-matrix form, the above mixing model can be expressed as:

$$\mathbf{x} = \mathbf{A}\mathbf{s} \quad (6)$$

where

$$\mathbf{A} = \begin{pmatrix} a_{11} & a_{12} & \cdots & a_{1n} \\ a_{21} & a_{22} & \cdots & a_{2n} \\ \vdots & \vdots & \ddots & \vdots \\ a_{m1} & a_{m2} & \cdots & a_{mn} \end{pmatrix}$$

is the mixing matrix (Hyvärinen, 1999a; Hyvärinen, & Oja, 1999; Lee, 1998), $\mathbf{x} = [x_1\ x_2\ \ldots\ x_m]^T$, $\mathbf{s} = [s_1\ s_2\ \ldots\ s_n]^T$, and $T$ is the transpose operator. For unmixing process (Hyvärinen, 1999a; Hyvärinen, & Oja, 1999; Lee, 1998), after estimating the matrix **A**, one can compute its inverse -- the unmixing matrix, **B**, and the independent components are obtained as:

$$\mathbf{s} = \mathbf{B}\mathbf{x} \qquad (7)$$

To assure the identifiability of the ICA model, following fundamental restrictions are imposed (Hyvärinen, 1999a; Hyvärinen, & Oja, 1999):

- The source signals in the mixing process should be principally statistically independent.
- All the independent components $\mathbf{s}_k$, with the possible exception of one component, must be non-Gaussian.
- The number of observed linear mixtures $m$ must be at least as large as the number of independent components $n$, i.e., $m \geq n$.
- The matrix **A** must be of full column rank.
- There are many various ICA algorithms that have been proposed recently. Some popular ICA methods include Bell and Sejnowski's Infomax (1995), Hyvärinen and Oja's FastICA (1999b), Cichocki and Barro's RICA (Robust batch ICA) (1999) and Cardoso's JADE (Joint Approximate Diagonalization of Eigen-matrices) (1999) and so on.

From the stability issue, it is more appropriate to choose RICA or JADE algorithms, rather than Infomax and FastICA algorithms, for our watermark extraction process. Both Infomax algorithm and FastICA algorithm require that the values of the mixing coefficients for the sources cannot be very close (Bell, & Sejnowski, 1995; Hyvärinen, 1999b). However, both the watermark and the key are embedded by multiplication with small weighting coefficients to make them invisible. Therefore, the extraction of such weak watermark signals would be failed by using Infomax or FastICA algorithm. The extraction results using FastICA algorithm also very much depend on the initial guess of the weighting coefficients (Hyvärinen, 1999b).

Cichocki and Barro's RICA algorithm is an effective blind separation approach particularly for the temporally correlated sources, since it models the signal as an autoregressive (AR) process (Cichocki, & Barros, 1999). This RICA algorithm thus can achieve the best extraction results when both the embedding and extraction are performed in the spatial domain. This is because, generally speaking, the natural images are spatially correlated, and can be effectively modeled as temporally correlated sequences. However, for the proposed watermarking scheme described in this chapter, the watermark is embedded in the wavelet domain instead of the spatial domain. The experimental results show that the JADE algorithm (Cardoso, 1999) outperforms the other ICA algorithms for watermark extraction in our proposed watermarking scheme. This could be due to the use of higher-order statistical parameters in the JADE algorithm, such as fourth order cumulant, which can model the statistical behavior of the wavelet coefficients more effectively. Therefore, the JADE algorithm is employed to elaborate the watermark extraction process in our proposed watermarking scheme to be described next.

## Proposed Blind Watermark Extraction Scheme

This section proposes the ICA-based blind watermark extraction scheme. Instead of using the original image, only an owner's copy of the original image is required for watermark extraction. The new useful feature of the proposed scheme is that the proposed method does not require the previous knowledge of original watermark, embedding locations and watermark strength information for

*Figure 7. The proposed blind watermark extraction scheme (using the second level decomposed images).*

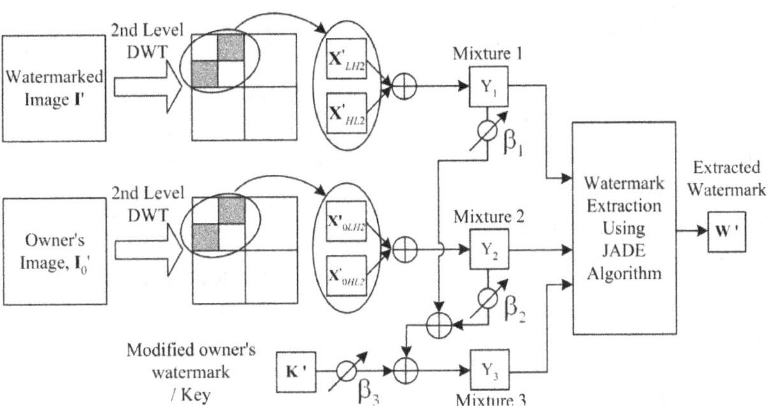


extraction. The main idea is to consider two sub-bands ($\mathbf{X}'_{\mathbf{R}}$) of the watermarked image to have a mixture image of the wavelet transformed image ($\mathbf{X}_{\mathbf{R}}$) of the original image (**I**), the watermark image (**W**), and the modified key (**K'**). Figure 7 shows the proposed blind watermark extraction scheme. Let denotes the received watermarked image as $\tilde{\mathbf{I}}'$. The symbol (~) is to indicate that the received data may or may not be the same as its original watermarked data due to transmission errors or possibly pirate attacks. This symbol (~) is removed in the following for simplicity.

- **Step 1:** Perform the second level discrete wavelet decomposition of the watermarked image **I'** in order to obtain the wavelet coefficients, $\mathbf{X}'_{LH2}$ and $\mathbf{X}'_{HL2}$ for the two selected sub-bands of LH2 and HL2.
- **Step 2:** The first mixture signal, $\mathbf{Y}_1$, is obtained by:

$$\mathbf{Y}_1 = \mathbf{X}'_{LH2} + \mathbf{X}'_{HL2} \quad (8)$$

From Equation 3, $\mathbf{X}'_{\mathbf{R}}$ ($\mathbf{R} \in [LH2, HL2]$) are the mixture observations of the wavelet transform of the original image ($\mathbf{X}_{\mathbf{R}}$), the watermark (**W**) and the modified key (**K'**), therefore, Equation 8 can be rewritten as:

$$\mathbf{Y}_1 = \mathbf{X} + \alpha_1 \mathbf{W} + \alpha_2 \mathbf{K}' \quad (9)$$

where $\mathbf{X} = \mathbf{X}_{LH2} + \mathbf{X}_{HL2}$, $\alpha_1 = \alpha_{\mathbf{X}} \cdot \mu(|\mathbf{X}_{LH2}|)$ and $\alpha_2 = \alpha_{\mathbf{X}} \cdot \mu(|\mathbf{X}_{HL2}|)$. It is found that the first mixture signal is a linear mixture of the three independent sources, i.e., **X**, **W** and **K'**.

- **Step 3:** Repeat the same procedure in Steps 1 and 2 for the owner's image $\mathbf{I}'_0$. The second mixture, $\mathbf{Y}_2$, is obtained by:

$$\mathbf{Y}_2 = \mathbf{X}'_{0LH2} + \mathbf{X}'_{0HL2} \quad (10)$$

Similarly $\mathbf{Y}_2$ is also a linear mixture of the wavelet transform of the original image ($\mathbf{X}_{\mathbf{R}}$, $\mathbf{R} \in [LH2, HL2]$) and the key/owner's watermark (**K**). It can be written as:

$$\mathbf{Y}_2 = \mathbf{X} + \alpha_3 \mathbf{K}' \quad (11)$$

where $\alpha_3 = \alpha_{\mathbf{X}0} \cdot [\mu(|\mathbf{X}_{0LH2}|) + \mu(|\mathbf{X}_{0HL2}|)]$.

- **Step 4:** From Equations 8 and 10, two mixture images can be obtained containing three sources or independent components in the observations -- **X**, the modified key **K'** and the watermark **W**. As pointed out earlier, to exploit ICA methods for watermark extraction, it is required that the number of observed linear mixture inputs is at least equal to or larger than the number of independent sources, in order to assure the identifiability of ICA model (Hyvärinen, 1999a; Hyvärinen, & Oja, 1999; Lee, 1998). Therefore, another linear mixture of the three independent sources is needed. The third mixture $\mathbf{Y}_3$ can then be generated by linear superposition of $\mathbf{Y}_1$, $\mathbf{Y}_2$ and $\mathbf{K}'$:

$$\mathbf{Y}_3 = \beta_1 \mathbf{Y}_1 + \beta_2 \mathbf{Y}_2 + \beta_3 \mathbf{K}' \quad (12)$$

where $\beta_1$ and $\beta_2$ are arbitrary real numbers, and $\beta_3$ is a non-zero arbitrary real number. Either $\beta_1$ or $\beta_2$ can be set to zero to efficiently reduce the computational load of ICA. Note that the modified key $\mathbf{K}'$ can be easily obtained by re-generating the NVF visual mask and multiplying to the original owner's watermark $\mathbf{K}$.

- **Step 5:** The three mixtures input into the JADE ICA algorithm (Cardoso, 1999), and the watermark image, $\mathbf{W}'$, is extracted. The user of the particular image copy is verified directly from the extracted signature. Figure 8 shows the extracted watermark from the watermarked image shown in Figure 4(g).

## PERFORMANCE EVALUATION

The robustness results of the proposed watermarking scheme are shown in this section using the Lena image of size (256 × 256) when the simulations are performed in the MATLAB 6.5 software environment. A watermarked image (PSNR = 45.50 dB) in Figure 4(g) is generated by setting the watermark strength control parameter $\alpha_X$ as 0.15. In the experiments of watermark extraction, the parameters $\beta_1$, $\beta_2$ and $\beta_3$ are set as 0, 1, 1, respectively, to simplify the computational load of ICA; Daubechies-1 (Haar) orthogonal filters are employed for wavelet decomposition. In order to investigate the robustness of the watermark, the watermarked image is attacked by various signal processing techniques, such as JPEG and JPEG2000 compression, color quantization, cropping and geometric distortions. The watermark extraction is performed for the distorted watermarked image and compared the extracted watermark with its original one.

*Figure 8. The extracted user's watermark image using JADE ICA method (normalized correlation coefficient, r = 0.9790).*

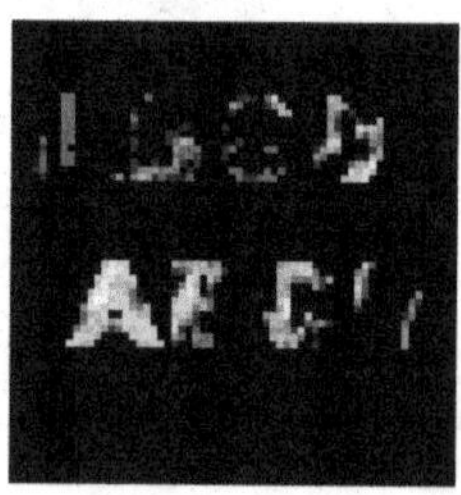

### The Performance Index

The performance of the blind watermark extraction result is evaluated in term of *normalized correlation coefficient*, *r*, of the extracted watermark $\mathbf{W}'$ and the original watermark $\mathbf{W}$ as:

$$r = \frac{W \cdot W'}{\sqrt{W^2 \cdot W'^2}} \quad (13)$$

The magnitude range of *r* is [-1, 1], and the unity holds if the extracted image perfectly matches its original image.

### Robustness against Compression and Quantization Attacks

In the following, the robustness of the proposed watermarking scheme is compared with some other blind wavelet-domain watermarking schemes (Peter, 2001) in terms of *normalized correlation coefficient r* as shown by Equation 13. These techniques include Wang's algorithm (1998), Inoue's blind algorithm (based on manipulating insignificant coefficients) (1998), Dugad's algorithm (1998), Kundur's algorithm (1998) and Xie's algorithm (1998).

Wang, Su, and Kuo (1998) proposed an adaptive watermarking method to embed watermarks into selected significant sub-band wavelet coefficients. A blind watermark retrieval technique was proposed by truncating selected significant coefficients to some specific value. Inoue, Miyazaki, Yamamoto, and Katsura (1998) classified wavelet coefficients as insignificant and significant by zerotree that is defined in the embedded zerotree wavelet (EZW) algorithm. Information data embedding algorithms in the locations of significant and insignificant coefficients have been developed. Information data are detected using the position of the zerotree's root and the threshold value after decomposition of the watermarked image. Dugad, Ratakonda, and Ahuja (1998) added the watermark in selected coefficients with significant image energy in the transform domain in order to ensure non-erasability of the watermark. During watermark detection, all the high pass coefficients above the threshold are chosen and correlated with the original copy of the watermark. Kundur, and Hatzinakos (1998) presented a novel technique for the digital watermarking of still images based on the concept of multiresolution wavelet fusion, which is robust to a variety of signal distortions. Xie, and Arce (1998) developed a blind watermarking digital signature for the purpose of authentication. The signature algorithm is first implemented in wavelet transform domain and is coupled within the SPIHT (Set Partitioning in Hierarchical Trees) compression algorithm.

Figure 9 shows the comparison results in terms of performance index against JPEG compression. For the proposed scheme, the extracted watermark's correlation decreases gradually as with the compression quality factor. The image quality (in PSNR) has degraded significantly to 27 dB when the compression quality becomes quite low to 10%. In this difficult case, the watermark can be still extracted with the value of $r$ equal to 0.2553 for watermark embedding in second level wavelet decomposition. According to Figure 9, the presented scheme performs better than Wang's and Kundur's methods, and much better than Inoue's method in terms of robustness against JPEG compression attack when the compression quality factor is very low.

Figure 10 is the extraction comparison against the JPEG2000 compression attacks. The robustness of the proposed scheme is demonstrated up to the compression factor 0.05 or compression rate 0.4 bpp (bit per pixel). The proposed scheme has better result than Kundur's method, and comparable result to Wang's method. The extraction

*Figure 9. Comparisons of results against JPEG compression attacks*

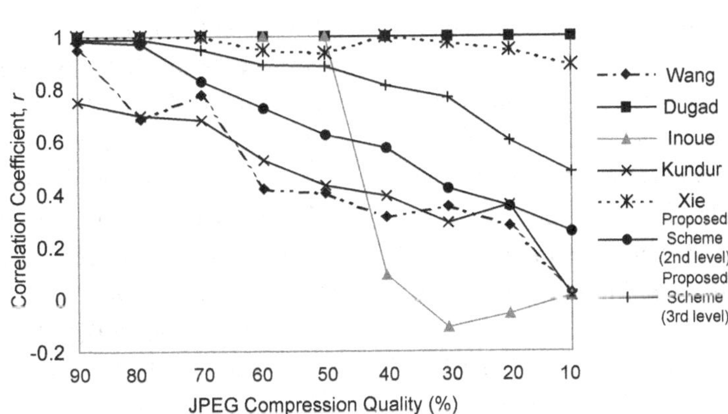

*Figure 10. Comparisons of results against JPEG2000 compression attacks*

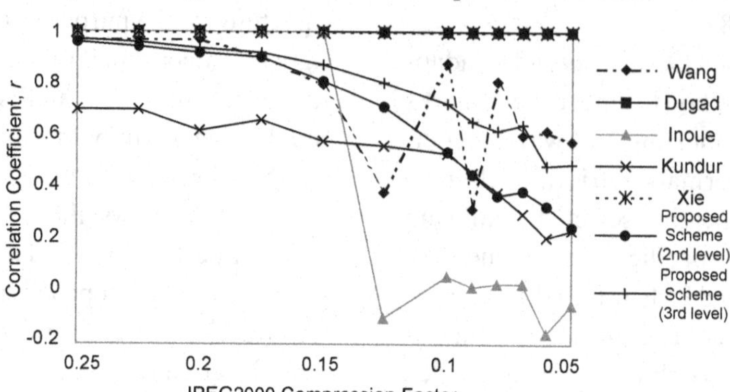

*Figure 11. Comparisons of results against color quantization*

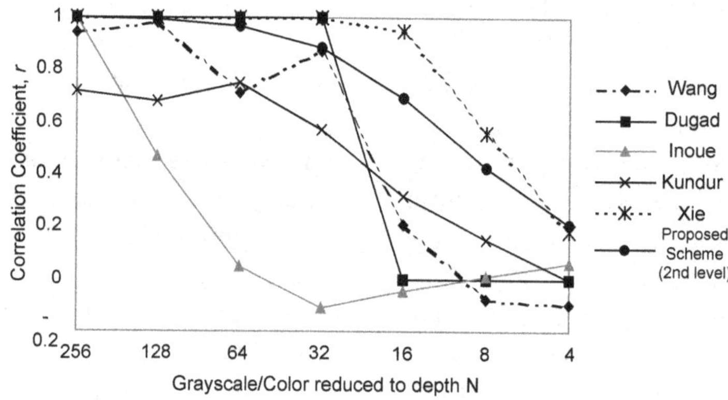


performance of Inoue's method drops sharply when the JPEG2000 compression factor goes to 0.125. Embedding in the sub-bands of higher-level wavelet decomposition (see curves for extraction performance of third level decomposition in Figure 9 and 10), can improve significantly the robustness of the proposed scheme against compression attacks.

Figure 11 shows extraction results against color quantization from gray level 256 to 4 per pixel. The proposed scheme has very good robustness result against color quantization. The performance of the proposed scheme can be comparable to that of the Xie's method, and much better than the other methods.

From Figures 9 and 10, it is found that Xie's and Dugad's methods have excellent robustness against JPEG and JPEG2000 compression. In Xie's algorithm, the watermark is embedded solely in the approximation image (LL sub-band) of the host image (Xie, & Arce, 1998). Although LL sub-band embedding is robust against compression attacks, the image quality could be degraded visually because the coefficients of this portion always contain the most important information of an image (Peter, 2001). It is claimed that the robustness of Xie's method much depends on the number of decomposition steps. Very good robustness result can be obtained by employing a five-level wavelet decomposition using Daubechies-7/9 bi-orthogonal filters (Xie, & Arce, 1998; Peter, 2001). Dugad's method embeds the watermark in the significant coefficients of all the detail sub-bands (Dugad, Ratakonda, &

Ahuja, 1998), therefore, it is more resistant to compression. During the watermark detection using Dugad's method, the original watermark is required to compute the correlation for the high pass coefficients with the values above a threshold (Dugad, Ratakonda, & Ahuja, 1998). The presence of the watermark is determined by comparing this correlation with a threshold setting. It is not as general as our proposed scheme where the original watermark and the threshold are not required for extraction.

The experimental results show that the proposed scheme has good robustness against the most prominent attacks -- JPEG and JPEG2000 compression, color quantization, and can be comparable to the existing blind wavelet-domain watermarking schemes. Experiments also show that the type of wavelet transform used is not critical for the robustness of the proposed watermarking scheme (the corresponding results are not included), which is crucial for Xie's method from robustness point of view (Xie, & Arce, 1998; Peter, 2001).

## Robustness against Cropping and Geometric Distortions

Many watermarking techniques cannot survive geometric transformations such as rotation, scaling and translation (RST) and sometimes cropping attack as well due to the loss of the synchronization of the watermark detector. A solution to such geometric attacks is a resynchronization process in either a blind or non-blind way before watermark extraction. Non-blind solution requires the presence of the original data or at least some knowledge of the image features (Dugelay, & Petitcolas, 2000). Davoine, Bas, Hébert, and Chassery (1999) proposed a non-blind solution by splitting the original picture into a set of triangular patches. This mesh serves as reference mesh and is kept in memory for synchronization pre-processing. This proposed method, however, is only efficient in case of involving minor deformations. Johnson, Duric, and Jajodia (1999) proposed a method to invert affine transformations by estimating the difference in the least square sense between the salient image feature points in the original and transformed images. Kutter (1998) proposed alternative methods to retrieve the watermark from geometric distorted image without using the original data. The first method is to pre-set part of the watermark to known values and to use them for spatial resynchronization. This approach decreases the hiding capacity for the useful information, and is also computationally very expensive. The second method proposed by Kutter (1998) is to use self-reference systems that embed the watermark several times at shifted locations.

Generally speaking, the tuning process is easier, more accurate and requires less computational load when the original data or reference feature points are available, though it may need extra memory to store those reference data. In our proposed watermarking scheme, original data is not available during extraction, however, an owner's or a representative's copy of the data is available. This image copy would be very close to the original data, thus it is convenient to use it directly as a reference for synchronization of geometric distorted or cropped data. By simple comparisons, the tampered data can be adjusted back to original size and position rapidly and accurately. In the following, the watermark extraction results against attacks of cropping and RST are shown. The effectiveness of employing synchronization pre-processing is demonstrated by showing the significant improvements of extraction results with and without synchronization.

As shown in Figure 12(a), the face portion of a marked Lena image is cropped. By comparison with the owner's Lena image copy, it can be easily detected that the pixels within a square area, with row index from 121 to 180 and column index from 121 to 180, is corrupted. The absence of the watermark information in this corrupted region (by considering both rows and columns from 31

($\lceil 121/4 \rceil$) to 45 ($\lceil 180/4 \rceil$) results in an undesired over brightness effect for the extracted watermark due to its high values in the corrupted region. This makes both the subjective and the objective verification measurements quite poor (see Figure 12(b)). One simple solution is to discard the corresponding undesired high valued pixels from the extracted watermark and replace them with zero valued pixels. In this way, according to Figure 12(c), the extracted watermark can be recovered mostly with some information loss in the corrupted region. Therefore, the normalized correlation coefficient *r* is found to increase from 0.2706 to 0.9036 showing the recovery of the low contrast watermark (compare Figures 12(b) and 12(c)).

The watermark extraction of the geometric distorted image may fail due to the loss of synchronization. A resynchronization pre-processing of the received data is necessary to tune it back to the right positions or sizes before further input to watermark decoder. However, the side information in the proposed watermarking scheme—the owner's or the representative's copy of the original image —provides a good reference to assist the synchronization process. The watermark extraction performance is consequently improved. Figures 13(d), 13(e) and 13(f) show the extraction results under attacks of rotation, scaling and translation respectively, with the use of synchronization operations. The extracted watermarks are of satisfactory qualities in both subjective visualization and objective similarity measurement.

## Discussions

The proposed ICA-based watermarking scheme shows its main advantage in terms of generality. Unlike other methods, no *a priori* information about the original watermark, embedding location, strength as well as threshold, is needed for our blind watermark extraction scheme. Therefore, it is possible to extract the watermark from

*Figure 12. (a) A cropped Lena image, (b) the extracted watermark (r = 0.2706) and (c) the extracted watermark after improving the contrast of (b) (r = 0.9036).*

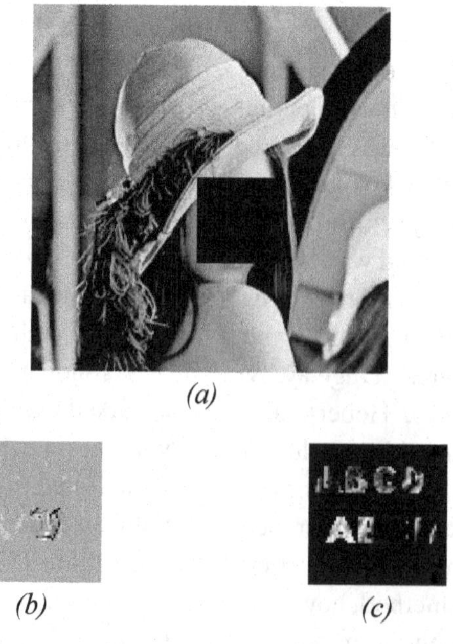

any copy of the watermarked image, where the embedded watermark is previously unknown. The other advantage of the proposed ICA-based method is that without using a pre-defined threshold, the extracted watermark could simply be verified from visual inspection instead of using the correlation based matching technique with a threshold setting. This is possible because the embedded watermark used in our scheme is a readable digital signature image or a logo image. The generality of the proposed scheme implicates this method to be a quite useful tool for the transaction tracking in the application of Internet distribution. The only disadvantage to achieve the generality using ICA-based technique could be the complexity of the ICA itself. In this chapter, this has been compromised by the use of JADE algorithm, which is simple and computationally efficient. Furthermore, there are only three mixing sources (i.e., the original data, the key and the watermark) all together involving in the presented watermarking scheme, which enables our ICA based extraction processing to be fast.

In future, more experiments would be carried out in order to evaluate the resilience of this scheme against other types of attacks. For example, the collusion attacks and the possible counterattack methods in multimedia distribution systems are to be investigated to improve the robustness of the system. The issue on the generation of a better perceptual mask, used to simulate the human visual system, will also be studied to improve the visual quality of the watermarked data.

*Figure 13. (a) A Lena image rotated by 10°, (b) its corresponding extracted watermark (r = 0.5847); (c) a Lena image down-sized by reducing the number of rows and columns by 1/4, and (d) its corresponding extracted watermark (r = 0.4970); (e) a Lena image translated to the left and downwards by 10 and 36 lines, respectively, and (f) its corresponding extracted watermark (r = 0.5356).*

## SUMMARY

This chapter studies the forensic transaction tracking by means of digital watermarking terminology. One feasible solution by an ICA-based watermarking technique is proposed for ownership verification and traitor tracking in the multimedia distribution application for the *Internet*. Two watermarks consisting of an owner's watermark for ownership identification and a user's watermark for unique recipient identification, are embedded. Watermark is obtained by modifying the signature image with a visual mask to prevent perceptual quality degradation of the watermarked image. The watermarks are inserted in the two middle frequency sub-band pair for the higher wavelet decomposition level (say second/third decomposition level) of the original image. Without requiring any information such as original watermark, embedding location and strength, our proposed scheme can extract the user's watermark with the help of an owner's copy of the image and the owner's watermark/key. Experimental results show that the proposed watermarking scheme can provide good resilience under attacks of image compression, color quantization, cropping and geometric transformations.

It has been elaborated in this chapter that the ICA-based watermarking scheme can be employed as an efficient tool to trace the recipient of the distributed content. From a wider point of view, the challenging issues of digital watermarking in the applications of forensic tracking for the *Internet* distribution include:

- The original data is not available during extraction of the recipient's watermark. Thus the watermarking technique should be *blind.*
- No prior information about the embedded watermark and the corresponding locations is available for watermark extraction.
- In order to present as trustful evidence in court to litigate the pirate, a highly robust watermarking scheme against common signal possessing attacks as well as collusion attacks is needed.
- For some applications, for example, searching for pirated watermarked image using Web crawlers, it is required that the watermarking scheme is able to extract the watermark easily and with a low complexity.

There is no doubt that transaction tracking is a more difficult task than copyright protection by means of digital watermarking. More general watermarking techniques are urged such that no original data and prior watermark information is required for embedding while providing the methods are reliable, robust and computationally efficient.

Another requirement to enforce the IP rights of the distributed Work could be that the owner should be able to detect any illegal attempts to alter the content. The authentication watermark should be then very sensitive to various attacks and able to locate the possible modifications. In such scenario, three watermarks would be hidden in the Work in order to verify the owner, to identify the user and to authenticate the content, respectively. Since the information hiding capacity of the cover media is limited, we could have further challenges to investigate, e.g., how to compromise the three demands including the information hiding capacity, the imperceptibility and the robustness of the hidden watermark.

## REFERENCES

Bell, A., & Sejnowski, T. (1995). An information-maximization approach to blind separation and blind deconvolution. *Neural Comput., 7*, 1129-1159.

Cardoso, J.-F. (1999). High-order contrasts for independent component analysis. *Neural Comput., 11*, 157-192.

Cichocki, A., & Barros, A. K. (1999). Robust batch algorithm for sequential blind extraction of noisy biomedical signals. *Proc. ISSPA'99, 1*, 363-366.

Cox, I. J., Leighton, F. T., & Shamoon T. (1997). Secure spread spectrum watermarking for multimedia. *IEEE Trans. on Image Processing, 6*, 1673-1687.

Cox, I. J., Miller, M. L., & Bloom, J. A. (2002). *Digital Watermarking*. Morgan Kaufmann Publishers.

Davoine, F., Bas, P., Hébert, P.-A., & Chassery, J.-M. (1999). Watermarking et résistance aux déformations géométriques. *Cinquièmes journées d'études et d'échanges sur la compression et la représentation des signaux audiovisuels (CORESA'99)*, Sophia-Antiplis, France.

Dugad, R., Ratakonda, K., & Ahuja, N. (1998). A new wavelet-based scheme for watermarking images. *Proc. of IEEE ICIP*.

Dugelay, J.-L., & Petitcolas, F. A. P. (2000). Possible counter-attacks against random geometric distortions. *Proc. SPIE Security and Watermarking of Multimedia Contents II, 3971*, California, USA.

Hyvärinen, A. (1999a). Survey on independent component analysis. *Neural Computing Surveys, 2*, 94-128.

Hyvärinen, A. (1999b). Fast and robust fixed-point algorithms for independent component analysis. *IEEE Trans. Neural Networks, 10*, 626-634.

Hyvärinen, A., & Oja, E. (1999). *Independent component analysis: a tutorial*. [On-line]. Available: http://www.cis.hut.fi/projects/ica/

Inoue, H., Miyazaki, A., Yamamoto, A., & Katsura, T. (1998). A digital watermark based on the wavelet transform and its robustness on image compression. *Proc. of IEEE ICIP*.

Johnson, N. F., Duric, Z., & Jajodia, S. (1999). Recovery of watermarks from distorted images. *Preliminary Proc. of the Third Int. Information Hiding Workshop*, Dresden, Germany, (pp. 361-375).

Katzenbeisser, S., & Petitcolas, F. A. P. (2000). *Information Hiding Techniques for Steganography and Digital Watermarking*. Boston: Artech House.

Kundur, D., & Hatzinakos, D. (1998). Digital watermarking using multiresolution wavelet decomposition. *Proc. of IEEE ICASSP, 5*, 2969-2972.

Kutter, M. (1998). Watermarking resisting to translation, rotation and scaling. *Proc. of SPIE Int. Symposium on Voice, Video, and Data Communications - Multimedia Systems and Applications, 3528*, Boston, Massachusetts, U.S.A., (pp. 423-431).

Lee, T.-W. (1998). *Independent Component Analysis: Theory and Applications*. Kluwer Academic Publishers.

Lu, C.-S., & Mark, Liao H.-Y. (2001). Multipurpose watermarking for image authentication and protection. *IEEE Transaction on Image Procssing, 10*.

Mintzer, F. & Braudaway, G. (1999). If one watermark is good, are more better? *Proc. of the International Conference on Acoustics, Speech, and Signal Processing, 4*.

Peter, P. (2001). *Digital image watermarking in the wavelet transform domain*. Master's Thesis.

Schneier, B. (1995). *Applied Cryptography* (2nd ed.). John Wiley and Sons Inc.

Sheppard, N. Paul, Safavi-Naini R., & Ogunbona, P. (2001). On multiple watermarking. *Proc. of ACM Multimedia 2001*.

Voloshynovskiy, S., Herrigel, A., Baumgaertner, N., & Pun, T. (1999). A stochastic approach to content adaptive digital image watermarking. *Proc. of IWIH*, Dresden, Germany.

Wang, H.-J. M., Su, P.-C., & Kuo, C.-C. J. (1998). Wavelet-based digital image watermarking. *Optics Express, 3*(12), 491-496.

Xie, L., & Arce, G. R. (1998). Joint wavelet compression and authentication watermarking. *Proc. of IEEE ICIP.*

Yu, D., Sattar, F., & Ma, K.-K. (2002). Watermark detection and extraction using independent component analysis method. *EURASIP Journal on Applied Signal Processing -- Special Issue on Nonlinear Signal and Image Processing (Part II).*

Yu, D., & Sattar, F. (2003). A new blind image watermarking technique based on independent component analysis. *Springer-Verlag Lecture Notes in Computer Science, 2613*, 51-63.

# Chapter XVII
# Spam and Advertisement:
## Proposing a Model for Charging Intrusion

**Dionysios Politis**
*Aristotle University of Thessaloniki, Greece*

## ABSTRACT

*A significant problem of our times, accelerated by the advances in technology, is the plethora of commercial Internet messages usually defined as spam, while the equivalent in classic television emission is the frequent and uncontrollable advertisement. Advertisement, perceived as an expression and factor of the economy, is legitimate and desirable. However, abusive advertising practices cause multiple damage: invasion in our private communication space, homogenisation of morals and customs leading to globalized overconsumption. Variations and cloning of spam and advertisement include spim, distributed instant messaging using bulk SMS's over mobile telephone networks or the web, wireless attacks and penetration, targeted unsolicited online harassment and others.*

## DEFINITIONS AND PROVISIONS

Spam is usually defined as "unsolicited bulk e-mail". This is generally done for financial reasons, but the motive for spamming may be social or political. Unsolicited means that the recipient has not granted verifiable permission for the message to be sent. Bulk means that the message is sent as part of a larger collection of messages, all having substantively identical content (Cheng, 2004).

Rough estimates conclude that e-mails like "Buy this product" or "Participate in this campaign" are more than 60% of what is the normal daily load. Generally, the longer an email address has been in use, the more spam it will receive. Moreover, any email address listed on a website or mentioned in newsgroups postings will be spammed disproportionally. Mailing lists are also a good target (Loia, Senatore, Sessa, 2004).

Recent figures show a dramatic increase of spam trafficking (Jung, Sit, 2004). Although not easily verifiable[1], they are indicative of the extent:

- Spam trafficking has increased the last couple of years about 1.000 % in comparison to previous years.
- The average user now gets 6 spams per day, or over 2.000 per year. Of these, 24% of spam accounts for scams and fraud, 23% for product advertising, 14-19% for pornography -91% of users find these the most annoying- 11% for health remedies, 1% for politics.
- Up to 8% of internet users have purchased spam promoted goods and services.
- Up to 28% of internet users have replied to spam mail at some stage.
- Costs of spamming are so low that even a few replies in a million make the spammers' efforts profitable.

Although spam is readily conceived, confusion reigns over its phenotype (Robinson, 2003). More than the two thirds of e-mail account holders think that they can determine an e-mail message when they see it, while 9% have to open the message to ascertain the infringement. The extent of intrusion is also variably conceived. 70% of e-mailers believe that spam has made being online "unpleasant or annoying". 27% think spam is a "big problem" for them. However, a 14% thinks its impact is negligible (Grimes, Hough, Signorella, 2005; Fetterly, Manasse, Najork, 2004).

Spam has a rigorous impact on lost productivity. Many hours are lost daily on deleting unwanted email, reporting spammers or researching about companies that send spam (European Union, 2001)[2].

The evolution of the phenomenon is presented in Figure 1.

A variation of spam is spim. It is defined as unsolicited commercial messaging produced via an instant messaging (IM) system.

Marketers have never seen a medium they didn't want to exploit. So it is that spam has evolved to IM yielding spim. It's been around for a few years, but only in the past few months has it reached the threshold of disruption.

Most spim is generated by using "bots" according to IM providers and industry watchers. These automated programs simulate IM users and

*Figure 1. The increase of spam trafficking. Bottom line: spam sent to reference accounts. Top line: Spam sent to all accounts*

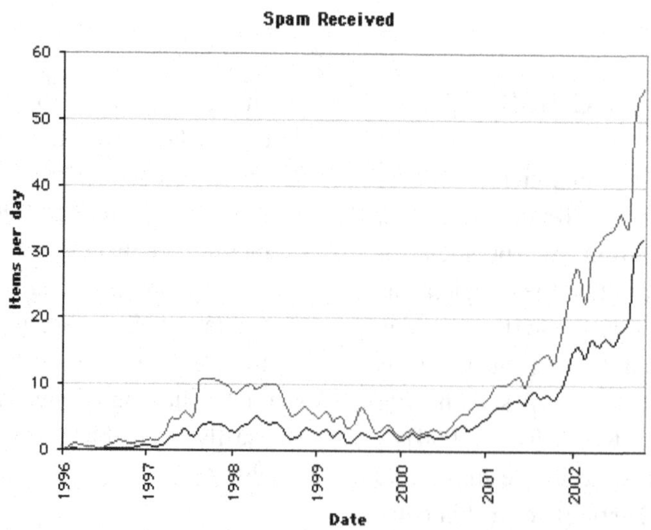

send spam messages to a pre-determined set of screen names, which are generated randomly or are harvested off the Internet.

## LEGAL ASPECTS OF SPAM

### Spam and the Protection of Personal Data

Apart from the fact that spam is a nuisance, there is definitely the aspect of violation in the sphere of personal communications. Data Protection Authorities are involved in the spam issue as far as:

- Legal gathering of personal data definitely involves the prior consent of the subject.
- By "harvesting", a file is created containing personal data that have not been legally accumulated. No prior consent of the subject has been given in collecting his data. As a result, electronic addresses and communication numbers are associated with specific persons. It should be noted that data, originating from lists addressed to the general public or publicly accessible sources, such as trade exhibitions directories, web sites etc., do not fall into this constraint[3].
- The exploitation of personal data files is unacceptable, especially when illegally gathered or formed e-mail address directories are used. In any case, even when a file of personal data is formed legally, it should not be transferred, sold, or elsewhere marketed.

In this sense, for a third party, keeping a file with personal data like a directory of mobile telephone numbers and recipient data is illegal, if the controller has not given his prior consent. However, the use of an algorithm to find valid mobile telephone numbers and to send them a promotional e-mail en masse does not violate legislation.

### Anti-Spam Legislation in the USA and the EU

The increasing intensity of the spam phenomenon caused the timely reaction of the legislator, who is exceedingly often asked to regulate the internet behaviour. This act involves by necessary implication, the balancing of the interests of user protection, on the one hand, and the guarantee of fundamental freedoms of citizens and mostly of netizens, on the other.

#### USA

USA is not only the cradle of Internet but also a basic spam source (almost 90% of the spam received in Europe is sent from USA)[4]. Since 1996 many cases[5] between Internet Service Providers (ISPs) and spammers found their way to the court; however the problem has always remained the same: lack of specific legal regulation, which led to objectionable decisions[6]. The need for an ad hoc federal law was obvious and after many rejected drafts, on 01.01.2004, the "CAN SPAM Act 2003"[7] was finally put into force. This Act includes a variety of measures (Clarke, Zugelder, Flaherty, 2005) for the prevention and the restriction of the problem and provides serious penalties for the spammers. More specifically, among others:

- Spammers face penalties of imprisonment up to 5 years and/or high fines.
- The falsification of the sender identity or header information, the harvesting of electronic addresses and the unauthorized manipulation of computers and servers is penalized (Sec. 4).
- Advertisers are obliged to include an "Opt-out" option in each advertising e-mail (Sec. 5).

- E-mail advertisements must be labelled as such, with the addition of the abbreviation "ADV" in the line of subject (Sec. 11).
- The formation of a " Do-Not-E-Mail registry" is foreseen (Sec. 9), where the internet users can register themselves in order to avoid receiving advertising e-mails. Advertisers owe, theoretically, to consult this list before launching a mass electronic advertising campaign.

According to the "CAN SPAM Act", the ISPs are granted the right of legal action against spammers (Sec. 7 (g)) and did not waste any time in putting it in use[8]. However, anti-spam activist organisations[9] criticise consistently the lack of a clause enabling individual users to take spammers to court.

## EU

The European Union demonstrated its prompt reflex as far as the protection of European consumers is concerned, by publishing the Directive 1997/7/EC "on the protection of consumers in respect of distance" and preventing the use of certain means of distance communication (telephone, fax), without the prior consent of the consumer (Art. 10). Later on, the Directive 2000/31/EC "on electronic commerce" focused further on the unsolicited commercial electronic communication prescribing the formation of opt-out registers (Art. 7). Finally the Directive 2002/58/EC "on privacy and electronic communication"[10], replacing the Directive 1997/66/EC, is providing a powerful legal tool against spamming. According to article 13 of the new Directive:

- The communication for the purpose of direct marketing via telephone, fax or e-mail requires the prior consent of the consumer-user (opt-in) or is acceptable in the context of the sale of a product or a service (soft opt-in).
- Each advertising e-mail must incorporate an easy and costless "opt-out" opportunity for the recipient in order to object to such use of electronic contact details.
- Disguising or concealing the sender identity and providing an invalid reply address for the opt-out, shall be prohibited

A careful reading of the Directive 2002/58/EC, reveals a stricter anti-spam protection compared to the "CAN SPAM Act". Selecting the "Opt-in" (or at least "Soft Opt-in") method, the EU Directive prevents a priori all the advertising e-mails, without the prior consent of the user, while the "CAN SPAM Act" permits the first sending of spam and tries to restrict it ex post using the "Opt-out" way. However it depends on the will of the national legislator, to adjust the content of the Directive to the internal legislation of each member-state. For example, the Netherlands have already adjusted the national legislation and have established regulatory authorities like OPTA (LeClaire, 2005; Leavitt, 2004)[11], that has issued its first fines[12].

It should be noted that litigation on spam is some times problematic; laws are uneven over jurisdictions, and it is often hard to find the spammer. It is estimated that 70% of spam is sent via hijacked computers. Currently, the number one spam mail recipient is USA, followed by China (Yeh, 2004; Chua, Wareham, 2004) and the EU on the whole. However, the uniform application of national measures, i.e. the degree of harmonisation, is questionable (Khong, 2001).

## ADVERTISEMENT: THE SOCIAL AND ECONOMIC BACKGROUND OF SPAM

On the socio-economic part, the advent of spam has caused deregulation both in financial terms as in terms of internet trafficking. Although, as we will see, spam does not have only evil aspects, it is an insidious malady over the backdoors of the internet, afflicting the economies of the networked industries. Internet advertising is a recent phenomenon. It remains the dominant business model for business-to-consumer e-commerce: apart from promoting products via the Internet, advertisements are placed on or near them. The charges of Web-based advertising space are dependent on the "relevance" and the "popularity" of the surrounding Web content.

In order to explore and estimate the socio-economic impacts of spam on advertising, it is essential to define spam as an advertising technique. As with many new services, this is not a simple matter, as definitions given by various sources differ significantly. Even the ones used thus far in this paper, classify spam more as a phenomenon than as an explicit procedure. If the equivalent of TV hidden advertisement is conceived for spam, then for instance we may have problems in characterising as spam a newsletter e-mail with implied promotional orientation.

Spam as a social phenomenon arises from an on-line social situation that technology created. First, it costs no more to send a million e-mail messages than to send one. Second, hits are percentage of transmissions, so sending more spam means expecting more profit (B. Whitworth, E. Whitworth, 2004). So, from the advertising point of view, the important characteristic of spam is that it is practically with no charge. It is not the best e-mail communication technique, it is not the most efficient but it attracts people because of its free ride.

To date, having in mind that spam responses are less than 1%, it is obvious that spam is a resource-consuming means[13]. It has been estimated that if the 1‰ of Internet users decided to spam sending a moderate rate of 100 000 spams per day, than every other user would be receiving more than 100 spams per day.

This is exactly the social-economic impact of spam: how can we compare two advertising techniques, from and advertisers point of view, when one may be more appealing but expensive, while the other is un-orthodox but free?

## CHARGING SPAM

### Estimations and Projections

In order to propose a model for charging spam, the authors of this article conducted a survey on spam. The graphical outputs of the survey can be seen in Figure 2.[14] For 8 months the 16.478 active e-mail accounts where monitored, not of course on their content, but on their reaction to spam as far as an anti-spam filter was concerned, applied at the e-mail server's level.[15] For legal reasons having to do with the protection of personal data, it was not possible to estimate the filtering strength of the software devices that end users deploy themselves at their e-mail clients.

Although only a fraction of the e-mail users takes advantage of the filtering mechanism at server level, the size of the sample space is adequately large to track spam penetration in real world scenarios using statistical methods. The statistical processing was carried out using SPSS.

### Charging Spam: A Calculus Analysis

Suppose that there are n potential spammers, indexed by i = 1, ..., n. Each of them transmits qi packets to the Internet, so the aggragate number of transmitted packets in a given period is $Q \stackrel{def}{=} \sum_{i=1}^{n} q_i$. The network is supposed to have a limited capacity, denoted by $\bar{Q}$, which is measured not in communication terms, since the present Gigabit Ethernet does not seem to congest from text messages, but from user dysphoria, caused by imponderable and excessive spam.

Consumers gain utility by communicating via the net, with e-mails, and gain disutility most of their communication is spam, i.e. noise, intrusion or harassment.

*Figure 2. Spam trafficking at AUTh (Aristotle University of Thessaloniki). Top line: the e-mail messages that AUTh's 16.478 active users received. Middle line: the number of e-mails diagnosed as spam by the Spamassasin® software. Bottom line: the percentage of active users deploying the Spamassasin spam filtering mechanism.*

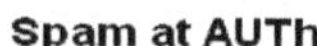


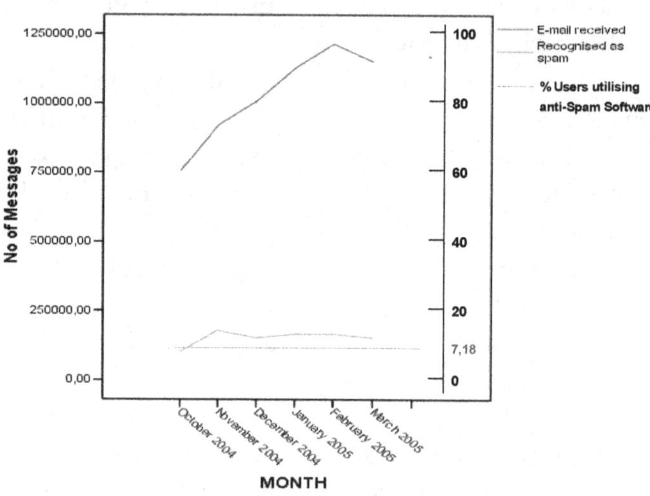


In this case, there is a price p per transmitted packet, whether this is charged a-priori, as a preventive measure, or afterwards, as and ad-hoc fine[16].

Therefore, the utility function of each consumer is defined as follows (Shy, 2001):

$$U_i \stackrel{def}{=} \sqrt{q_i} - \delta \frac{Q}{\bar{Q}} - pq_i = \sqrt{q_i} - \delta \frac{\sum_{j=1}^{n} q_j}{\bar{Q}} - pq_i \tag{1}$$

where δ>0 measures the intensity of disutility caused by spamming. The "latency" caused by the spam effect is measured by $Q/\bar{Q}$ which is the ratio of actual, non infected by spam, e-mail communication capacity. If $Q < \bar{Q}$ the network is not congested by spam. If, however, $Q > \bar{Q}$, the network bristles with spam and user discontent increases.

Since each consumer participates as a peer in this communication, (s)he takes the network usage by other consumers and chooses his/her usage qi that solves:

$$\max_{q_i} U_i = \sqrt{q_i} - \delta \frac{q_i + \sum_{j \neq 1} q_j}{\bar{Q}} - pq_i \tag{2}$$

yielding that the first and second order derivatives, regarding the transmitted packets $q_i$ for maximum conditions are given by:

$$0 = \frac{\partial U_i}{\partial q_i} = \frac{1}{2\sqrt{q_i}} - \frac{\delta}{\bar{Q}} - p \quad \text{and}$$

$$\frac{\partial^2 U_i}{\partial (q_i)^2} = \frac{-1}{4\sqrt{(q_i)^3}} < 0 \tag{3}$$

Hence, the individual and aggregate packet transmission levels are:

$$q_i = \frac{\bar{Q}^2}{4(\delta^2 + p^2 \bar{Q}^2 + 2\delta\, p\bar{Q})} \qquad (4)$$

## Proposition

Provided that a charge p is assigned to each spam attempt, as shown by equation 4, the levels $q_i$ of spam messages per attempt will be reduced dramatically, as inversely proportional to *p*. In the case of a non charging network, i.e. virtually the current situation in the Internet, eq. 4 becomes

$$q_i = \left(\frac{\bar{Q}}{2\delta}\right)^2 \qquad (5)$$

meaning that the only way to reduce spam effect is to increase the e-mail capacity of the network. This was the situation before the exaltation off the spam effect, when spam email was negligible. This can be achieved again if software tools prove successful in preventing spam trafficking.

If this does not take place, then only legal action and fines, in the sense of eq. 4 can be to only means to combat spam.

## Example

Suppose that a spammer sends spam messages to the 16.478 active e-mail users of the Aristotle University of Thessaloniki (AUTh) – a message per day, for one month. It has been estimated for theses users that they accept on average 1.064.573,286 messages per month (see Figure 2), therefore the distribution of messages per user for one month interval is 1.064.573,286 / 16.478 ≈ 65 messages.

The e-mail capacity of the server is not limited however to only 1.000.000 e-mail messages per month. AUTh hosts about 50.000 students, researchers and employees. The average world user is considered to send and receive about 200 messages per month. So, the system would be saturated if all 50.000 users were sending and receiving e-mails, i.e.:

$$\bar{Q} = 200 \text{ x } 50.000 = 10.000.000 \qquad (6)$$

Hence, solving equation (5) we have that:

$$\delta = \frac{\bar{Q}}{2\sqrt{q_i}} = \frac{10.000.000}{2\sqrt{64,61}} = 622.042,6 \qquad (7)$$

Solving equation (4) for *p* yields $p = 0,001$ € per every spam message sent.

Accordingly, we deduce that if detected and litigated, the spammer should be charged with $p = 0,001$ € per spam message, that he would be charged for 16.478 x 30=494.340 illegally sent messages. These sum up for 494. 340 x 0,001 = 494,34 €.

This amount is roughly equivalent with the cost of advertising for a month to the campus with any other method, like say, distributing leaflets, having in mind of course that statistically only 1% of the spam recipients correspond to the advertiser, i.e. 1% x 16.478 = 16 individuals!

# EPILOGUE AND CONCLUSION

The combined action of substantial legal countermeasures and advanced techniques of content filtering have limited the exaltation of spam. Recent statistics asses spam prevalence to 67% of daily e-mail communication, in a world scale.

The spam issue is part of a more complex phenomenon concerning the governance of the Internet, the economics of networked industries, technological advances and software development.

In the prospect of new technological initiatives like the launch of digital television, the convergence of the Internet with broadcasting networks, it has importance on major e-commerce practices like advertisement.

The spam issue does not merely threaten the future of a self governed Internet; it tests the tolerances of many factors for the networked economies.

## REFERENCES


Cheng, T. (2004). Recent international attempts to can spam. *Computer Law & Security Report, 20*(6), 472-479.

Chua, C. E. H., & Wareham, J. (2004). Fighting Internet Auction Fraud: An Assessment and Proposal. *IEEE Computer, 37*(10), 31-37.

Clarke, I., Zugelder, M. T., & Flaherty, T. B. (2005). The CAN-SPAM Act: New rules for sending commercial e-mail messages and implications for the sales force. *Industrial Marketing Management, 34*(4), 399-405.

Doyle, E. (2004 November/December). Spam rules – and there's nothing you can do. *Elsevier Infosecurity Today*, (pp. 24-28).

European Union. (2001). *Data protection: "Junk" e-mail costs internet users 10 billion a year worldwide* (EU Reference Number IP/01/154). Brussels: European Commission Study.

Fetterly, D., Manasse M., & Najork, M. (2004). *Proceedings from 7th International Workshop on the Web and Databases*. Paris, France.

Grimes, G. A., Hough, M. G., & Signorella, M. L. (2007). E-mail end users and spam: relations of gender and age group to attitudes and actions. *Computers in Human Behavior, 23*(1), 318-332.

Jung, J., & Sit, E. (2004). *Proceedings from IMC '04: Internet Measurement Conference*. Taormina, Italy.

Kaprzycki, D. (2004). Trends in regulating unsolicited commercial communication. *CRi, 3*, 77.

Khong, W. (2001). Spam law for the internet. *The Journal of Information, Law and Technology – JILT*, 2001(3).

Leavitt, N. (2005). Mobile phones: the next frontier for hackers? *IEEE Computer, 38*(4), 20-23.

LeClaire, J. (12/29/2004). Netherlands issues its first fines against spammers. *e-Commerce Times*.

Loia, V., Senatore S., & Sessa, M. I. (2004). Combining agent technology and similarity-based reasoning for targeted E-mail services. *Fuzzy Sets and Systems, 145*(1), 29–56.

Robinson, G. (2003). Statistical approach to the spam problem-using Bayesian statistics to detect an e-mail's spamminess. *ACM Linux Journal*.

Shy, O. (2001). *The Economics of Network Industries*. New York: Cambridge University Press.

Whitworth, B., & Whitworth, E. (2004). Spam and the Social-Technical Gap. *IEEE Computer, 37*(10), 38-45.

Yeh, A. (2004). China Now World's Number Two Spam Recipient, After United States. *Privacy and Security Law Report, 3*(13), 361.


## ENDNOTES

1. Figures are taken from various sources, mainly from anti-spam or a-virus Internet on-line sites and have some variance, depending on the source and the date they were cropped.
2. See also the research of University of Maryland in http://www.smith.umd.edu/ntrs.
3. E.g. see Data Protection Authority, Greece, Decision No. 050/20.01.2000, Terms for the lawful processing of personal data as regards the purposes of direct marketing/advertising and the ascertainment of creditworthiness, in http://www.dpa.gr.

4 See http://www.spamhaus.org/statistics.lasso.

5 E.g. America Online Inc. v. Cyber Promotions Inc. (E.D. Pa. 1996), CompuServe Inc. v. Cyber Promotions Inc. (S.D. Ohio 1997), Hotmail Corp. v. Van$ Money Pie Inc. (N.D. Cal. 1998), America Online Inc. v. LCGM Inc. (E.D. Va. 1998).

6 Kasprzycki D., Trends in regulating Unsolicited Commercial Communication, CRi 3/2004, p. 77.

7 Controlling the Assault of Non-Solicited Pornography and Marketing Act of 2003, 15 U.S.C.A. § 7701-7713.

8 See http://www.macworld.co.uk/news/index.cfm?newsid=8137&page=1&pagepos=2.

9 About anti-spam organisations, see: Watel J., Le problème du Spamming ou comment guérir le cancer de l' Internet, JurPC Web-Dok. 163/2001, Abs. 12; criticism in http://spamcon.org and http://www.wired.com/news/business/0,1367,62020,00.html?tw=wn _story_related.

10 Directive 2002/58/EC of the European Parliament and of the Council of 12 July 2002 concerning the processing of personal data and the protection of privacy in the electronic communications sector (Directive on privacy and electronic communications). OJ L 201, 31.7.2002, pp. 37-47.

11 OPTA, Netherland's Independent Post and Telecommunications Authority. http://www.opta.nl.

12 E.g. US$ 61.000 against an individual, who was involved in four spam campaigns, US$ 34.000 against a company spamming about financial software, $27.000 against a company sending spam text messages on mobile phones.

13 See supra note 16, p. 6.

14 Statistical data from a survey conducted at the Network Operations Center (NOC) of the Aristotle University of Thessaloniki (AUTh) from 1.10.2004 till 30.4.2005.

15 The award winner Spamassasin software package was used. It is a mail filter, written in Perl, to identify spam using a wide range of heuristic tests on mail headers and body text. It is a free software package, of open source origin. For more information, visit the site http://www.spamassasin.org.

16 See supra note no. 3.

# Chapter XVIII
# European E-Signatures Solutions on the Basis of PKI Authentication Technology

**Ioannis P. Chochliouros**
*Hellenic Telecommunications Organization S.A. (OTE), Greece*

**Anastasia S. Spiliopoulou**
*Athens Bar Association, Greece*

**Stergios P. Chochliouros**
*Independent Consultant, Greece*

**Konstantinos N. Voudouris**
*Technological Educational Institute of Athens, Greece*

## ABSTRACT

*This chapter presents systems of certification authorities and registration authorities and other supporting servers and agents that perform certificate management, archive management, key management, and token management functions. These activities that support security policy by monitoring and controlling security services, elements and mechanisms, distributing security information, and reporting security events are examined with the main focus on PKI authentication technology.*

## INTRODUCTION

After a period of rapid growth in 1998-2000, the electronic communications sector is now undergoing a complete "re-adjustment" process, with targeted investments focused on specific technological sectors, able to satisfy a variety of customer-oriented requirements in global and competitive markets. However its implications and possible outcomes raise extremely important issues for the future and for economic growth, worldwide (European Commission, 2003). In particular, the importance of the electronic communications sector lies in its impact on all other sectors of the economy: It offers the potential and the dynamism for organisations to make best use of their investment in Information Society Technology (IST) and to realise productivity gains, improvements in quality and opportunities for greater social inclusion (Chochliouros & Spiliopoulou, 2003a).

New communication technologies, new media, the Internet and devices carrying modern functionalities are expected to meet consumers' demand for seamless, simple and user-friendly digital tools providing access to an extended range of services and content (i2010 High Level Group, 2006).

In particular, electronic communication networks and information systems have been developed exponentially in recent years and are now an essential part of the daily lives of citizens in various environments worldwide, also comprising the sector of Europe. Such information systems and network infrastructures constitute fundamental "tools" to the success of the broader European economy in the international scenery (European Commission, 2002).

Despite the multiple and obvious benefits due to the modern (and converged) electronic communications development, this evolutionary process has also brought with it the worrying threat of intentional attacks against relevant systems and networks. As cyberspace gets more and more complex and its components increasingly sophisticated, especially due to the fast development and evolution of (broadband) Internet-based platforms, new and unforeseen vulnerabilities may emerge and affect further progress (Organization for Economic Coordination and Development, 2004). Moreover, as Internet becomes ubiquitous for all business and personal communications, the sensitivity and economic value of the content of information transmitted is highly increasing (Shoniregun, Chochliouros, Laperche, Logvynoskiy & Spiliopoulou, 2004).

Thus, the rollout of innovative technologies (such as broadband and 3G) together with the development of new content, applications and/or (public and private) services (European Commission, 2004), results to new and severe security challenges (Kaufman, 2002). Addressing security issues is also crucial to stimulating demand for new electronic communications services and to develop, further, the digital worldwide economy (Chochliouros & Spiliopoulou, 2005). Networks and information systems are now supporting services and carrying data of great value, which can be vital to other forms of applications. Increased protection of infrastructures is therefore necessary against various types of attacks on their availability, authenticity, integrity and confidentiality. In the relevant scene of the current European marketplace, the use of encryption technologies and electronic signatures towards providing enhanced security, are becoming indispensable (European Parliament and Council of the European Union, 1999; Brands, 2000), while an increasing variety of authentication mechanisms is required to meet different needs in wider converged environments (European Commission, 2002).

Within such a generalized context, Public Key Infrastructure (PKI) can perform a central part of securing today networked world. PKI can provide a focal point for many aspects of security management while, *at the same time*, can serve as a "enabler" for a growing number of various security applications both in private and public organizations (International Organization for Standardization, 2005). Most standard protocols for secure e-mail, web access, virtual private networks (VPNs) and single-sign-on user authentication systems make use of some form of "public key" certificates and for that reason require some specific form of PKI. The security of transactions and data has become essential for the supply of electronic services, including e-Commerce and online public services, and low confidence in security could slow down the widespread introduction of such services. Given the rapid evolution of today computer and network technology, the present work examines the impact of this evolution to the notion of PKI and the supporting business and legal framework in the context of relevant policies, mainly promoted through the European Union (EU).

## BACKGROUND: PKI FUNDAMENTAL TECHNOLOGIES AND BASIC INFRASTRUCTURES

In general, a PKI is a combination of hardware and software products, policies and procedures which offers enhanced security, required to carry out e-Commerce activities in order that various users can communicate securely through a "chain of trust". Among its basis are digital identifications known as "digital certificates" (Brands, 2000). These act like an "electronic passport" and bind the user's "digital signature" to his public key. In the following clauses we discuss some basic notations relevant to public key cryptography processes, and afterward we analyze some essential features of PKI. In fact, PKI is an authentication technology or a technical means for identifying entities within an environment.

### Public Key Cryptography

Public key cryptography is used (Feghhi, Williams & Feghhi, 1998) in conjunction with the following options to create a technology for "identifying" entities: (i) A mechanism for establishing trust according to a (pre-)defined trust model; (ii) a mechanism for uniquely naming entities, and; (iii) a mechanism for distributing information regarding the validity of the binding between a particular *"key pair"* and a *"name"*. Under appropriate conditions (Kaufman, 2002), the use of public key cryptography can be considered as a modern technological basis for securing electronic business processes. Security requirements such as data integrity, non-repudiation of signing, data authentication, confidentiality, and authentication for access control can be implemented by using cryptographic tools, providing digital signature and encryption facilities.

Public key cryptography was initially invented in 1976 (Diffie & Hellmann, 1976). Unlike symmetric cryptography (such as, *for example*, the Data Encryption Standard-DES), in which the same cryptographic key is shared between all parties (i.e. senders and receivers), pairs of corresponding public and private keys for each party allow the realization of the necessary cryptographic operations (Coppersmith, 1994). The process of public key cryptography involves creating a public and private key simultaneously, using the same algorithm provided by an appropriate *"Certificate Authority"*. The private key is given only to the requesting party, while the public key is made publicly available in a directory that can be accessed by all potential parties, aiming to realize electronic transactions. The private key is kept secret by the appropriate Authority, it is never given to anyone other that the original requester and is never sent across the Internet. The private key is then used to decrypt data that has been encrypted by a third entity, by using the corresponding public key.

Public key cryptography is a critically important technology, since it realizes the concept of the *"digital certificate"*. The idea of the "key-pair" (one private, one publicly available) enables a variety of different services and protocols, including confidentiality, data integrity, secure (pseudo-) random generation and zero-knowledge proofs of knowledge.

The concepts of public key cryptography (with various implementation algorithms) have, nowadays, reached a state of high maturity, in a broader context. However, in order to create conditions for further expansion to end-users (either corporate or private) it should be necessary to make the related technologies available to an extensive variety of applications and environments, in a uniform way, to guarantee immediate and reliable applicability.

## Public Key Infrastructures: Functional Operations

Public Key Infrastructure assumes the use of public key cryptography, which is a common method on the Internet for authenticating a message sender or encrypting (and/or decrypting) a message. Thus, PKI allows users to exchange data securely over any kind of network. It involves the use of a public and private cryptographic key pair, which is obtained through a *trusted authority*. PKI provides for digital certificates (Feghhi, Williams, & Feghhi, 1998) that can identify individuals or organisations and directory services that can store and revoke them, if necessary.

A "*Digital Signature*" is a digital code that can be attached to an electronically transmitted message that uniquely identifies the sender (Aalberts & Van der Hof, 1999). Digital signatures are based on public key technology and can also be used to ensure that the contents of a received message have remained unchanged while in transit. Digital signatures can be used with encrypted (or decrypted) messages, allowing the receiver to decide about the claimed "nature" of the sender, and to ensure that a message arrives in its "original" format. A digital signature is also encapsulated within a digital certificate to identify the authority responsible for issuing the certificate. Additional benefits to its use are that it is straightforwardly transportable, cannot easily be repudiated, cannot be imitated by another party, and can be automatically time-stamped. (Time-stamping is the mechanism to provide the existence of a time source that the population of the PKI environment users will trust).

The seed idea is to consider PKI as the basis of a security infrastructure capable to provide services implemented and delivered by using public key concepts and related techniques (Adams & Lloyd, 2002). On its own, public key technology only supports asymmetric, mathematical operation on data (such as encrypting or "signing" a message), while it does not provide a connection to application (or environments) such as email, e-Business, or e-Government. A fully functional PKI, as the basis of the security infrastructure, to provide such a connection, encompasses several additional components and services (Housley, Ford, Polk & Solo, 1999).

As already mentioned, in order to verify the sender's on-line identity, it is necessary to create a separate entity, known as the "*Certification Authority (CA)*". The latter acts as a "trusted party" by a large population for the function of binding a cryptographic key pair to an entity, verifying the sender's identity and issuing both public and private keys. A CA certifies the binding by digitally signing a data structure (which is called "*public-key certificate*") that contains some representation of the identity and the correspondent public key, for a specific time period. In addition, a "Certificate Repository" is the particular location where any entity can retrieve an issued public key certificate. The private key is forwarded securely to the sender and the CA signs the latter's public key with its own private key, known as the "*Root Key*". The combination of these two keys composes the sender's *digital certificate*. The root key is seen as a "*watermark*" that validates the sender's certificate and proves that the sender is indeed who claims to be (Brands, 2000).

In the meantime, various functions can occasionally take place, like, for example: (i) the *key update*, which is the (ideally automatic) mechanism to force the expiration of a given certificate and the replacement with a new certificate prior to its lifetime-end, or; (ii) the *key back-up and recovery* which is a specific function that, when properly implemented, offers the possibility to avoid the loss of encrypted data protected by inaccessible private cryptographic keys, ideally without the user knowledge.

In general, the following steps must be followed to incorporate PKI as an appropriate method of purchasing goods electronically:

- A trusted third party (i.e. the CA) issues a private key to an individual user, and a validated public key, accessible to the wider public.
- A customer expresses his wish to purchase an item from a vendor's web-site. The vendor requests that the customer proves his identity to ensure the purchase order is genuine.
- The customer "signs" the order with the private key, earlier issued by the CA.
- PKI software uses the private key and a complex mathematical formula to generate a digital signature that is unique to the purchase order.
- The encrypted signed purchase order is forwarded to the vendor.
- The vendor uses the customer's public key, which must be validated by the CA, to decrypt the purchase order and validate the relevant "signature".
- The PKI software uses the public key to run a similar mathematical formula upon the order to generate a matching computation.
- If the original and subsequent computations match, then customer's identity is confirmed and the order is processed normally.

The method conducts a public and private key exchange, with the backing of a trusted CA. It provides a secure way of conducting business across public and private networks. PKI technology means that business transactions (such as credit card transactions) can be performed with the knowledge that the details: (i) are sent by the right sender; (ii) can be read only by the intended recipient, and; (iii) arrive at their destination in the form originally intended by the sender.

Under appropriate terms public key cryptography (and the PKI) can become a preferred approach on the Internet, as they can offer significant guarantee to avoid unwanted decryption and/or malicious changes of informative data transferred over modern networks, especially when keys are discovered (or intercepted) by unauthorized parties.

## PKI BASIC SERVICES: SECURITY REQUIREMENTS

The deployment of PKI technology has a substantial impact on business entities, in a way that not only the technical aspects, but also the organisational and legal ones have to be taken into account. The management of a PKI depends on a detailed control framework for certificate issuance and for the use of certificates (Adams & Lloyd, 2002). There is a range of services/applications to be exploited that can bring excellent new business opportunities for telecommunication operators (and/or other market players as well). In the near future, digital certificates are able to become a widely used means/facility for purposes of user authentication; inevitably, they can play a crucial role for providing services over a variety of network infrastructures.

A great variety of key applications can benefit from an effective PKI integration (Eurescom GmbH, 2000). These can comprise, for example, document exchange (Electronic Document Interchange-EDI, eXtensible Markup Language (XML), secure e-mail, registered mail, secure workflow), e-Commerce, mobile commerce, home banking, health-care services, single sign-on services, ISP (Internet Service Provider) roaming, distance learning, secure networking (virtual private networking) and remote work. A PKI is generally considered to be associated with three main security requirements, which in turn, can be considered as the essential (core) services such an environment offers. These are: Authentication, integrity and confidentiality.

***Authentication*** is the assurance provided to an entity that a second one is really "who" claims to be. Authentication finds application in two primary contexts: Entity identification and data origin identification (Boyd & Mathuria, 2003). Rapid technological development and the global character of the Internet necessitate particular approaches, open to various technologies and services capable of authenticating data electronically. In electronic communications, the concept of digital signatures is linked to the use of a kind of "electronic seal", affixed to the data and allowing the recipient to verify the data origin or, *more accurately*, to the use of a key assigned to a certain sender. However, authentication of the data source does not necessarily prove the identity of the key-owner. The recipient of the message cannot be sure whether the sender is really the "original" one, as the "public" key may be published under another name. A method for the recipient to obtain reliable information on the identity of the sender is confirmation by a third party, i.e. a person (or institution) mutually trusted by both parties.

***Integrity*** is the assurance offered to an entity that data (either in transit or in storage) has not been altered (with or without intention) between two communication points or a given time gap (Merkle, 1978). The challenge for ensuring communications' integrity is a very important one (especially when realizing several electronic commerce activities), and proper technical solutions have to be applied (European Commission, 2002). The response to this problem again lies in the use of a digital signature, involving not encryption of the "message text" itself but solely encryption of the signature, which is attached to the normal readable "text" (or information) and so enables the receiver to check whether the data has been changed. As previously mentioned, from the technical point of view, the most effective digital signatures have been proved to consist of two keys: a published "public key" and a confidential "private key". The relevant public key is used to check whether the signature has, in fact, been created using the private key. The recipient can also use it to check whether data has been changed, thus enabling him to check whether the sender's public and private keys form a complementary pair and whether data has been remained unchanged during transmission. A certification authority need not be involved at this stage.

***Confidentiality*** is the assurance given to an entity that nobody can "read" a particular piece of data, except the recipient properly intended (Treasury Board of Canada Secretariat, 1999). PKI support is an important component for key-agreement procedures in confidentiality services, where public key algorithms (and certificates) are used to securely negotiate/establish symmetric encryption keys. Obviously, electronic commerce and many other innovative applications will only develop if confidentiality can be guaranteed in a user-friendly and cost-efficient way.

It is evident that when consumers use services such as teleshopping or telebanking, they have to be sure that personal data (such as credit card numbers) remain secret. In commercial contacts performed on open networks, firms have to be able to protect themselves against industrial espionage relating to their business plans, invitations to tender and/or research results. On the other hand, law enforcement authorities and national security agencies fear that more widespread use of encrypted communication may hinder them in the fight against crime. It is remarkable to point out that any economic burden imposed by illegal actions on public bodies, companies and individuals is of considerable validity. As a consequence, all the previous aspects challenge entities to "prove" their identities, to be assured that important data has not been altered in any way, and to be convinced that data sent to another recipient can be understood only by the latter one.

In order to realize the provision of the above fundamental features, various implementation mechanisms (Adams & Lloyd, 2002) can be taken into account:

A PKI service of authentication (as opposed to the non-PKI operation to the authentication in a local environment, which may include single or multi-factor authentication also providing password or biometric devices) employs the cryptographic technique of a digital signature. The signature may be computed over the hash value of one of the following three factors: (1) Data to be authenticated; (2) submission of a request for data to be sent to a remote server and; (3) creation of a "*random*" challenge, issued by a remote party. The first issue supports the PKI service of data origin authentication, while the other two support the PKI services of entity authentication.

The PKI service of integrity may employ one of two specific techniques: The first technique is a *digital signature*. Although it serves the purpose of authentication, it simultaneously provides integrity over the signed data, due to the necessary property of the related (hash and signature) algorithms. Consequently, any possible change in the input data may lead to a large unpredictable change in the output data. The second technique that can be deployed is the *Message Authentication Code*. It uses a symmetric block cipher (or a hash function). Although these two alternatives are symmetric solutions, it is important to indicate that both are "*keyed mechanisms*", as they strongly depend on a "key", which has to be shared between the sender and receiver. The shared key can be derived if considering the key establishing functions of a PKI.

The PKI service for confidentiality uses a mechanism similar to one of the alternatives of the integrity.

## CURRENT EUROPEAN REGULATORY ISSUES

### The European Policy Approach

In the light of the increasingly important role played by electronic services in (both the European and the global) economy, the security of networks and services is of growing public interest (European Commission, 2001). In particular, there is a increasing potential for information security issues in Europe, which is a direct result of the rapid development of the Internet, electronic commerce and business-to-business (B2B) transactions (Chochliouros & Spiliopoulou, 2003a). Consequently, the security of network infrastructures has been improved significantly and can continue to improve in the next few years. This has increased the demand for a variety of applicable PKI solutions.

It is a prerequisite for individuals, businesses, administrations, and other organisations to protect their own data and information by deploying effective security technologies, where appropriate and to the extent possible. In particular, market players acting in a competitive market environment (and through their capacity to innovate) have to provide a variety of solutions, all adapted to genuine market needs.

More and more European companies (also including a growing number of small and medium-sized enterprises (SMEs)) now think in terms of a Europe-wide market. This implies that, at a time when those companies increasingly rely on electronic communications to carry out their day-to-day business, incompatible national solutions in the field of cryptography create impediments that lessen the benefits of the internal market.

In the European context, there are legal requirements imposed on providers of telecommunications services to take appropriate technical and organisational measures to safeguard security of their services. To this aim, the "core" principles (European Commission, 2001; 2003; 2004) are about: (1) Ensuring the availability of services and data; (2) preventing the disruption and unauthorised interception of communications; (3) providing appropriate confirmation that data which has been sent, received or stored are complete and unchanged; (4) securing the confidentiality of data; (5) protecting information systems against unauthorised access (and against malicious attacks), and; (6) securing dependable authentication.

In order to fully support implementation of PKI concept, the European Union has addressed the above issues in a pragmatic way, establishing an explicit distinction between authentication and confidentiality, even though they both rely on the same cryptographic technologies. For authentication, a European Directive has been enabled dealing with the matter of *Electronic Signatures*, to secure the internal EU market for certificates and certification services (European Parliament and Council of the European Union, 1999). However, things get more sensitive when they refer to the perspective of confidentiality. The scrambling of electronic communications has lead to some legitimate public security concerns, for which various research projects have been developed (especially in the field of cryptography).

The most challenging short-term goal is to bring existing security and privacy solutions into the large-scale mass market, for the benefit of the end-user. Research results and prototypes for most technologies leading to a substantial increase of end-user security and privacy already exist. Since these are exploited by offering products, the major short-term goal is to increase the market demand for security and privacy-enhancing technologies. This can lead to an increased supply and, as a consequence, to increased security and privacy for the end user.

Modern electronic communication and commerce necessitate electronic signatures and related services able to allow data authentication, under appropriate (and if possible "common") practices. Divergent rules with respect to legal recognition of electronic signatures and the accreditation of certification-service providers in the European Member States may create significant barriers to the use of these electronic facilities (including electronic communications and electronic commerce). On the other hand, a clear European framework regarding the conditions applying to electronic signatures can strengthen confidence in, and general acceptance of, the new technologies.

Actual legislation in the EU does not hinder the free movement of goods and services in the internal market, and enables certification-service-providers to develop their cross-border activities with a view to increasing their competitiveness, and so to offer consumers and businesses new opportunities to exchange information and trade electronically, in a secure way, regardless of frontiers. However, it is always important to strike a balance between consumer and business needs (Ford & Baum, 2001).

At the European level, a variety of legislative action (Chochliouros & Spiliopoulou, 2003b; Weber, 2002) has mainly taken the form of measures especially in the fields of the protection of the fundamental right to privacy and data protection, together with electronic commerce (and other relevant electronic services) and electronic signatures (Kamal, 2005).

The *e-Signatures Directive* has established a set of detailed criteria with the purpose to form the appropriate "basis" for an effective legal recognition of electronic signatures on the basis of the PKI context and to create an open environment for secure transactions, while simultaneously promoting interoperability between related products and similar facilities. Its purpose was to facilitate the use of electronic signatures and to contribute to their legal recognition among EU Member States. Global electronic communication and commerce are dependent upon the progressive adaptation of international and domestic laws to the rapidly evolving technological infrastructure.

The proposed regulatory measure intended to create a harmonized framework for e-Signatures and certain certification-related services, in order to ensure the proper functioning of the European marketplace (thus avoiding divergent national laws in the area). The Directive has also identified requirements (or obligations) that need to be met by service providers. These obligations have to be supported by detailed technical standards and open specifications which also meet the requirements of European business, so that related products and services can be known to provide legally valid signatures - thus furthering the competitiveness of European business in the international market arena.

The Directive establishes a legal framework for certain certification services made available to the public. It focuses particularly on certification services and sets up common requirements for Certification Service Providers (CSP) and certificates to ensure the cross-border recognition of signatures and certificates within the European Community. It follows a technology neutral approach by covering a broad spectrum of "signatures". It is based on a dual concept: CSP are in general free to offer their services without prior authorization. In parallel, Member States are allowed to introduce voluntary accreditation schemes based on common requirements and aimed at a higher level of security. To support the trust-building process for both consumers and business that rely on the certificates the work introduces liability rules for CSP. Co-operation mechanisms with third countries are also embodied, in order to contribute to the global recognition of certificates.

In particular, the Directive aims at harmonizing national provisions, which safeguard public interest objectives such as the protection of the right to privacy and personal data in the specific context of electronic signatures. Furthermore, it provides the necessary tool (certificates indicating a pseudonym instead of the signatory's name) permitting consumers to remain anonymous in on-line transactions.

Thus, electronic signatures can be used in a large variety of circumstances and applications, resulting in a wide range of innovative service offerings and products related to or using e-Signatures. The definition of such products and services should not be limited to the issuance and management of certificates, but should also encompass any other service and product using, or ancillary to, electronic signatures, such as registration services, time-stamping services, directory services, computing services or even related consultancy services.

A reliable system of electronic signatures that work across intra-EU borders is vital for safe electronic commerce and efficient electronic delivery of public services to businesses and citizens (Commission of the European Communities, 2006).

(Further information about the current status of the implementation of the *e-Signatures Directive* at national level, the existing regulatory framework and exact depiction of all appropriate progress for each separate Member State can be found in: http://ec.europa.eu/information_society/eeurope/2005/all_about/security/esignatures/index_en.htm).

## Adopting the Solutions in the Marketplace

The deployment and use of authentication products (and services) is currently in progress, at various levels. Up to the present date several systems exist which all make use of authentication for commerce, administration and public services; however, it is necessary to develop and to approve a full "set" of internationally accepted industry standards (and/or related technical specifications) for their proper adoption or usage in the marketplace. Without such standards it is not possible to provide a common level of security, recognized as "valid for use" at national/regional level, even less at international level (Dempsey, 2003).

In particular, it is of major importance for the EU not only to develop practices (and/or methods) for a successful adoption of digital signatures, but also to realize progress in the field of standardization and so to become able to offer products which are interoperable with other (similar) international ones (or at least to possess a common interface with them). Thus, the principal aim is to provide support to all sectors of society (and particularly the European industry), to design, develop and endorse commonly accepted standards not only at national level but also at international level (bearing in mind the importance of ensuring that such standards comply with best practice and the state-of-the-art) (Dumortier, Kelm, Nillson, Skouma & Van Eecke, 2003).

The work of the European Committee for Standardization/Information Society Standardization System (CEN/ISSS) and the European Telecommunications Standards Institute (ETSI) in providing technical specifications and guidance material for their implementation and market adoption was "decisive" to the future of e-Commerce, to make available timely standards allowing full and efficient implementation of a commonly adopted framework. These two authorized standardization bodies work in close co-operation with each other and with other standardization organizations around the world, as appropriate, by applying certain fundamental principles (mainly including openness, transparency, consensus and effectiveness and relevance). In January 1999 therefore, to coordinate the necessary standardization effort, a new initiative was launched (i.e. the European Electronic Signature Standardization Initiative (EESSI)), bringing together industry, market players, public authorities, and legal and technical experts (http://www.ict.etsi.org/EESSI_home.htm). Its essential task was to develop the standardization activities required to enable electronic signatures in a coherent manner (particularly in the business environment) and to monitor the implementation of a suitable work program to meet this need and to harmonize specifications at the international level to maximize market take-up (Nilsson, Van Eecke, Madina, Pinkas & Pope, 1999).

EESSI's deliverables have been developed mostly on the basis of PKI and related certificate techniques, as PKI technology is known by the industry as a "*reference tool*" for digital signature since several years (Chochliouros, Chochliouros, Spiliopoulou & Lampadari, 2007). It is however clear that, other technologies are relevant and consideration is already being given to these. EESSI has put all its effort to the definition of operating procedures and security environment assisting users and trust service providers in the implementation of electronic signature applications. The produced deliverables have so contributed to fundamental objectives of the European strategic framework as: *On the one hand*, they propose to providers trust products and service solutions for compliance with the critical requirements of the basic Directive in the area, thus contributing to a harmonized implementation of electronic signatures in the EU (in respect of the free movement of goods and services in the internal market); *on the other hand*, they contribute to the creation of an open, market-led environment for the availability of interoperable products and services, thus enabling the development of cross-border trust services with a view to increasing competitiveness and favoring exploitation of services in the internal market for the benefits of the whole user community. EESSI's activities have been well publicized outside Europe and appropriate links have been set with various fora and consortia world-wide. With the detailed publication of a full set of standards, EESSI has fulfilled its mandate and consequently has terminated its work in October 2004.

However, standardization work in the area is still ongoing and carried out by various European bodies, mainly on the basis of the results performed by the previous effort (Lacroix, Delos, Van Eecke, Custers & Janin, 2007). A great part of the relevant work has been considered as the basis for solutions already applied in several national legislative regimes (i.e. in Italy and in Germany).

Nevertheless, the lack of mutual recognition of electronic signatures (and certificates) among the European Member States has been recognised as one of the barriers in conducting business at the European level. Under the current circumstances practical guidance and technical specifications are necessary to help the private sector and the public authorities to put into practice the legal EU framework in a clear, efficient and cost effective manner. The e-Signatures Directive is, *by defini-*

*tion*, "technology neutral". Standards, however, are not. There is a strong (market-led) requirement for technical interoperability standards of electronic signature functions, working within an open and competitive marketplace, to achieve interoperability between products and services. Thus, standards and applied solutions have to be structured upon specific business models that are considered to be as relevant. Simultaneously, security aspects must be fully respected to give legal recognition to any suggested electronic signatures and to conform to specific national conditions. Taking these requirements together, suggested standards must be adequately open and internationally agreed; they have to be satisfactorily flexible to cover different business models and to provide quite secure solutions (Van Eecke, Pinto & Egyedi, 2007).

According to the current European legislation, the responsibility for the recognition of electronic signatures remains with the national authorities, whether common standards exist or not. This may occasionally lead to conflicts (and case law) about various kinds of e-Signatures, while national laws can be enacted, *in several instances,* with various security requirements with regards to authentication issues, etc. So legislation ranges from a "minimalist" approach that simply authorizes the use of e-Signatures in very limited circumstances, to legislation that establishes some evidentiary presumptions and default provisions that parties can contract out of, to a very formal and highly regulatory approach governing the manner in which digital signatures may be used and certification authorities may operate (IDABC, 2007).

The relevant EU initiatives addressed two major aspects of openness: one was to support fast and easy establishment of trust between parties who desired to do business online; the other was to take care of the technical compatibility of services and components. Such a context can support new business relationships, while it "minimizes" risks involved with investments by corporations and/or by private users. An open environment is favorable for public services to the citizen and for all kinds of business activity.

## CONCLUSION

As Internet has created a borderless space for information exchange the keyword for the deployment of corresponding applications in most sectors of the worldwide economy is trust. Rapid technological development and the global character of all underlying platforms (and infrastructures) impose the requirement/necessity for an effective approach, adequately "open" to various technologies and services and capable of authenticating data electronically (Kamal, 2005; Shoniregun et *al.*, 2004).

Since the early introduction of asymmetric key algorithms, with the further development of high-speed digital electronic communications (Chochliouros & Spiliopoulou, 2005), a need became evident for ways in which users could securely communicate with each other and, *as a consequence of that,* for ways in which users could be sure with whom they were actually interacting. The idea of cryptographically protected certificates binding user identities to public keys was eagerly developed. With the deployment of the World Wide Web and its rapid spread, the need for authentication and secure communication became still more acute. The result was the effective creation of a PKI structure for Web users/sites wishing secure (or more secure) communications. The deployment of PKI technology had a substantial impact on multiple business entities.

The use of PKI is having, and will continue to have, a huge impact on the European (and the global) telecommunications business. For example, corporate and personal electronic banking (e-Banking) is an important application for PKI, while other applications (such as the e-Government) are expected to develop in the future, especially in the context of recent business initiatives (Lalopoulos, Chochliouros & Spiliopoulou, 2004). Trusted third party services generate different kinds of business opportunities. One large class is generic PKI services, providing public key certificates and their management. However, an application-independent service area is the support of electronic signatures, where the provision of time-stamps constitutes a fundamental component. While certificates are issued once and can be used many times, time-stamps are to be invoked for every transaction, in some cases (as in contract negotiations) repeatedly, during the process. This is generally valid for all non-repudiation services. In the area of PKI-based electronic signatures, it is estimated, in the future, to see more products based on recent technological developments (such as mobile signatures and signature servers). It is of great importance therefore, that supervision bodies, regulators, the industry sector and of course all market players involved in the development of PKI-integration, look at these technologies with an "open mind", to promote appropriate and applicable solutions, enhancing network security.

Technological methods and specifications used for authentication are often based on cryptographic techniques. The prevailing technique at the present technology situation is the use of public key infrastructures. PKI technology is known by the industry as a "reference tool" for digital/electronic signatures. The latter open up opportunities to exploit the (broadband) Internet for several aspects, such as secure document exchange, purchase requisitions, contracts and invoice applications. Electronic signatures can be used in the public sector within national and European administrations and in communications between such administrations and with citizens and economic operators, for example in the public procurement, taxation, social security, health and justice systems.

From a European perspective, national legislation with differing requirements risks holding back the effective establishment of the internal market especially in areas which depended on e-Signature related products and services. Avoiding disruption of the internal market, via the effective promotion and adoption of technical standards and related solutions is "critical" to the future of electronic transactions in the European economy.

Electronic signatures mostly rely on PKI and this seems to last in time, certainly for the next decade(s). PKI technology is indeed now a 30 years-old mature technology that other potential emerging technologies are not ready to replace. Even more, 30 years after its creation, we can affirm that the emergence of new tools such as mobile and wireless or centralised signing facilities tends to complement the usage of PKI and furthermore reinforce its presence in our day to day life.

## ACKNOWLEDGMENT

All authors would like to dedicate the present work to the memory of Panagiotis Chochliouros, who was, and will always be, an active inspiration.

## REFERENCES

Aalberts, B., & Van der Hof, S. (1999). *Digital Signature Blindness - Analysis of legislative approaches toward electronic authentication.* Tilburg, The Netherlands: Tilburg University. [Retrieved on October 28, 2007 from http://www.buscalegis.ufsc.br/busca.php?acao=abrir&id=15433]

Adams, C., & Lloyd, S., (2002). *Understanding PKI: Concepts, Standards, and Deployment Considerations. 2nd Edition.* Addison-Wesley Professional, USA.

Boyd, C., & Mathuria, A. (2003). *Protocols for Key Establishment and Authentication*, Springer-Verlag, Berlin and Heidelberg GmbH & Co., Germany.

Brands, S.A. (2000). *Rethinking Public Key Infrastructures and Digital Certificates: Building in Privacy.* MIT Press, USA.

Chochliouros, I. P., & Spiliopoulou, A. S. (2003a). Perspectives for Achieving Competition and Development in the European Information and Communications Technologies (ICT) Markets, *The Journal of the Communications Network, 2(3)*, 42-50.

Chochliouros, I. P., & Spiliopoulou, A.S. (2003b). Innovative Horizons for Europe: The New European Telecom Framework for the Development of Modern Electronic Networks and Services. *The Journal of The Communications Network,* 2(4), 53-62.

Chochliouros, I. P., & Spiliopoulou, A. S. (2005). Broadband Access in the European Union: An Enabler for Technical Progress, Business Renewal and Social Development, *The International Journal of Infonomics (IJI), vol.1, January 2005,* 05-21.

Chochliouros, I. P., Chochliouros, S. P., Spiliopoulou, A. S., & Lampadari, E. (2007). Public Key Infrastructures (PKI): A Means for Increasing Network Security. In L. J. Janczewski & A. M. Colarik (Eds.), *Cyber Warfare and Cyber Terrorism,* (pp. 281-290). Hershey-PA: Information Science Reference.

Commission of the European Communities (2006). *Report on the operation of Directive 1999/93/EC on a Community framework for electronic signatures [COM(2006) 120 final, 15.03.2006].* Brussels, Belgium: Commission of the European Communities.

Coppersmith, D. (1994). The data encryption standard (DES) and its strength against attacks, *IBM Journal of Research and Development,* 38(3), 243-250.

Dempsey, J. X. (2003). *Creating the Legal Framework for ICT Development: The Example of E-Signature Legislation in Emerging Market Economies.* Washington, DC: Center for Democracy and Technology. *Information Technologies and International Development (ITID), 1*(2), 39-52. [Retrieved on September 17, 2007, from www.internetpolicy.net/e-commerce/20030900esignature.pdf]

Diffie, W., & Hellman, M. (1976). New Directions in Cryptography, *IEEE Transactions on Information Theory, IT-22*(6), 644-654.

Dumortier, J., Kelm, S., Nillson, H., Skouma, G., & Van Eecke, P. (2003). *The Legal and Market Aspects of Electronic Signatures. Study for the European Commission - DG Information Society (Service Contract Nr. C28.400).* Brussels, Belgium: The Interdisciplinary Centre for Law & Information Technology & Katholieke Universiteit Leuven. [Retrieved on February 24, 2006, from europa.eu.int/information_society/eeurope/2005/all_about/security/electronic_sig_report.pdf]

European Commission (2001). *Communication on Network and Information Security: Proposal for a European Policy Approach, [COM (2001) 298 final, 06.06.2001].* Brussels, Belgium: European Commission.

European Commission (2002). *Communication on eEurope 2005: An information society for all - An Action Plan, [COM(2002) 263 final, 28.05.2002].* Brussels, Belgium: European Commission.

European Commission (2003). *Communication on Electronic Communications: the Road to the Knowledge Economy, [COM(2003) 65 final, 11.02.2003].* Brussels, Belgium: European Commission.

European Commission (2004). *Communication on Connecting Europe at high speed: recent developments in the sector of electronic communications, [COM(2004) 61 final, 03.02.2004].* Brussels, Belgium: European Commission.

Eurescom (European Institute for Research and Strategic Studies in Telecommunications) GmbH (2000). *EURESCOM Project P944: Impact of PKI on the European Telecommunications Business. Deliverable 1, Main Report, January 2000.* Heidelberg, Germany: Eurescom GmbH.

European Parliament and Council of the European Union (1999). *Directive 1999/93/EC of 13 December 1999, on a Community framework for electronic signatures, (Official Journal (OJ) L13, 19.01.2000, pp.12-20).* Brussels, Belgium: European Parliament and Council of the European Union.

Feghhi, J., Williams, P., and Feghhi J. (1998). *Digital Certificates: Applied Internet Security.* Addison-Wesley, MA, USA.

Ford, W., & Baum, M. (2001). *Secure Electronic Commerce (2nd edition).* Prentice-Hall, Upper River Saddle.

Housley, R., Ford, W., Polk, W., & Solo, D. (1999). *Internet X.509 Public Key Infrastructure. Certificate and CRL Profile, Request for Comments (RFC) 2459.* Sterling, VA, USA: IETF.

i2010 High Level Group (2006). *The Challenges of Convergence - Discussion Paper, Dec.12, 2006.* Brussels, Belgium: European Commission. [Retrieved on December 22, 2007 from http://ec.europa.eu/information_society/eeurope/i2010/docs/i2010_high_level_group/i2010_hlg_convergence_paper_final.pdf]

IDABC (2007). *Preliminary Study on Mutual Recognition of eSignatures for eGovernment applications. (Contract No. 1, Framework contract ENTR/05/58-SECURITY, Specific contract N°1).* Brussels, Belgium: European Communities. [Retrieved on June 16, 2008 from http://europa.eu.int/idabc/]

International Organization for Standardization (ISO) (2005). *ISO/IEC 17799: Information technology - Security Techniques - Code of practice for information security management.* Geneva, Switzerland: ISO.

Kamal, A. (2005). *The Law of Cyber-Space.* Geneva Switzerland: United Nations Institute of Training and Research (UNITAR).

Kaufman, C. (2002). *Network Security: Private Communication in a Public World, Second Edition.* Prentice Hall, USA.

Lacroix, S., Delos, O., Van Eecke, P., Custers, M., & Janin, W. (2007). *Study on the Standardization Aspect of eSignature. (Final Report, 22.11.2007 for the European Commission, DG Information Society and Media).* Tounai, Belgium: SEALED sprl.

Lalopoulos, G. K., Chochliouros, I. P., & Spiliopoulou, A. S. (2004). Challenges and Perspectives for Web-based Applications in Organizations. In M. Pagani (Ed.), *The Encyclopedia of Multimedia Technology and Networking,* (pp. 82-88). Hershey, PA, USA: IRM Press, Idea Group Inc.

Merkle, R. C. (1978). Secure Communications over Insecure Channels, *Communications of the ACM, 21*(4), 294-299.

Nilsson, H., Van Eecke, P., Medina, M., Pinkas, D., & Pope, N. (1999). *Final Report of the EESSI Expert Team, 20th July 1999.* European Electronic Signature Standardization Initiative (EESSI). [Retrieved on October 16, 2005, from http://www.ictsb.org/EESSI_home.htm]

Organization for Economic Coordination and Development (OECD) (2004). *Digital Delivery of Business Services (JT00162724).* Paris, France: OECD.

Shoniregun, C. A., Chochliouros, I. P., Laperche, B., Logvynovskiy, Ol., & Spiliopoulou, A. S. (2004). *Questioning the Boundary Issues of Internet Security.* London, United Kingdom: e-Centre for Infonomics.

Treasury Board of Canada Secretariat (1999). *Digital Signature and Confidentiality - Certificate*

*Policies for the Government of Canada Public Key Infrastructure. Government of Canada (GOC), PKI Certificate Policies version 3.02.*

Van Eecke, P., Pinto, P., & Egyedi, T. (2007). *EU Study on the specific policy needs for ICT standardisation. Final Report. Brussels, July 2007. (Ref. ENTR/05/059).* Brussels, Belgium; DG Enterprise, European Commission. [Retrieved on October 21, 2007, from http://www.ictstandardisation.eu/]

Weber, R. (2002). *Regulatory Models for the Online World.* Zurich, Switzerland: Schulthess Juristische Medien.

## KEY TERMS

**Authentication:** A process of verifying an identity claimed by or for a system entity. An authentication process consists of two steps: (i) Identification step: Presenting an identifier to the security system; (ii) Verification step: Presenting or generating authentication information that corroborates the binding between the entity and the identifier.

**Certification:** This is the process in which a CA issues a certificate for a user's public key, and returns that certificate to the user's client system and/or posts that certificate in a repository.

**Certification Authority (CA):** An entity that issues digital certificates (especially X.509 certificates) and vouches for the binding between the data items in a certificate. Consequently, it is an authority trusted by one or more users to create, assign and manage certificates. Optionally, the CA may create the user's keys. As certificate users depend on the validity of information provided, a CA usually holds an official position created and granted power by a government, a corporation, or some other organization.

**Cryptographic Key:** A parameter (e.g., a secret 64-bit number for Data Encryption system-DES) used by a cryptographic process that makes the process completely defined and usable only by those having that key.

**Encryption:** The process of transforming data to an unintelligible form in such a way that the original data either cannot be obtained (one-way encryption) or cannot be obtained without using the inverse decryption process (two-way encryption). It is a cryptographic transformation of data (called "plaintext") into a form (called "ciphertext") that conceals the data's original meaning to prevent it from being known or used.

**Public-Key Infrastructure (PKI):** A system of certification authorities (and, optionally, registration authorities and other supporting servers and agents) that perform some set of certificate management, archive management, key management, and token management functions for a community of users in an application of asymmetric cryptography.

**Security Management:** System activities that support security policy by monitoring and controlling security services, elements and mechanisms, distributing security information, and reporting security events. The associated functions comprise: (1) Controlling (granting or restricting) access to system resources; (2) Retrieving (gathering) and archiving (storing) security information, and; (3) Managing and controlling the encryption process.

# Chapter XIX
# Security of Alternative Delivery Channels in Banking:
## Issues and Countermeasures

**Manish Gupta**
*State University of New York, USA*

**H. Raghav Rao**
*State University of New York, USA*

**Shambhu Upadhyaya**
*State University of New York, USA*

## ABSTRACT

*To sustain competitive advantages, financial institutions continuously strive to innovate and offer new banking channels to their customers as technology creates new dimensions to their banking systems. One of the most popular such diversification of channel is electronic banking (e-banking). Information assurance is a key component in e-banking services. This chapter investigates the information assurance issues and tenets of e-banking security that would be needed for design, development and assessment of an adequate electronic security infrastructure. The technology terminology and frameworks presented in the chapter are with the view to equip the reader with a glimpse of the state-of-art technologies that may help towards learned and better decisions regarding electronic security.*

## INTRODUCTION

The Internet has emerged as the dominant medium in enabling banking transactions. Adoption of e-Banking has witnessed an unprecedented increase over the last few years. Twenty per cent of Internet users now access online banking services, a total that will reach 33 per cent by 2006, according to

The Online Banking Report. By 2010, over 55 million US households will use online banking and e-Payments services, which are tipped as "growth areas". The popularity of online banking is projected to grow from 22 million households in 2002 to 34 million in 2005, according to Financial Insite, publisher of the Online Banking Report newsletter. Developing alternative channels for retaining customers as well as for attracting new ones is very important to financial institutions (Kimball & Gregor, 1995; Thornton & White, 2001). For this reason, financial institutions offer new banking channels to their customers, as the technology adds new dimensions to the classic banking systems (Eriksson & Nilsson, 2007). For example, over the last few years, self-service technologies have replaced the need for face-to-face interaction between banks and customers (Eriksson & Nilsson, 2007).

Electronic banking uses computer and electronic technology as a substitute for checks and other paper transactions. E-Banking is initiated through devices such as cards or codes to gain access to an account. Many financial institutions use an automated teller machine (ATM) card and a personal identification number (PIN) for this purpose. Others use home banking, which involves installing a thick client on a home PC and using a secure dial-up network to access account information and still others allow banking via the Internet. In industrialized countries, the use of electronic channels to manage one's wealth has increased. From the customers' perspective, electronic payments instruments and channels have made money impersonal and virtual (Singh, 2004). In a survey of e-banking customers, 76% persons without disability with a household income above $50,000 said they used Internet banking (Singh et al, 2009).

This chapter will discuss the information assurance issues (Maconachy, et.al , 2002) that are associated with e-banking infrastructure. We hope that the chapter will allow IT managers to understand information assurance issues in e-banking in a holistic manner, and help them make recommendations and actions to ensure security of e-banking components.

## INTERNET/WEB BANKING

A customer links to the Internet from his PC. The Internet connection is made through a public Web server. When the customer brings up the desired bank's Web page, he goes through the front-end interface to the bank's Web server, which in turn interfaces with the legacy systems to pull data out for the customer's request. Pulling legacy data is the most difficult part of Web banking. While connection to a Direct Dial Access (DDA) system is fairly straightforward, doing wire transfer transactions or loan applications requires much more sophisticated functionality. A separate e-mail server may be used for customer service requests and other e-mail correspondence. There are also other middleware products that provide security to ensure that the customer's account information is secured, as well as products that convert information into an HTML format. In addition, many of the Internet banking vendors provide consulting services to assist the banks with Web site design and overall architecture. Some systems store financial information and records on client PCs, but use the Internet connections to transmit information from the bank to the customer's PC. For example, the Internet version of Intuit's BankNOW runs offline at the client and connects to the bank via the Internet only to transmit account and transaction information (Walsh, 1999). Although the banking industry has a large capital invested in ATMs, banks are failing to get the desired results (Colonia-Willner, 2004). E-banking services allow customers to remotely, via Internet, manage their bank accounts and transactions (Weir, Anderson, & Jack, 2006). Nowadays, banks provide a complete range of financial services through their Internet banking channels because they are more cost-effective than other customer-contact channels (Gopalakrisnan, Wischnevsky, & Dmanpour, 2003; Polatoglu & Ekin, 2001). Internet-based channels typically require lesser staff and fewer physical branch requirements (Cheng, Lam, & Yeung, 2006). Yakhlef (2001) indicates that the average transaction cost at a full-service bank is $1.08, whereas on the Internet the cost is 13 cents or less.

In this section, we discuss some of the key nodal points in Internet banking. These points that are the foundations and principal aspects of e-banking: web site and service hosting, possibly through providers; application software that includes middleware; regulations surrounding e-banking and standards that allow inter-organizational and cross platform communication over the Internet.

## Web Site and Banking Service Hosting

Banks have the option of hosting Web sites in-house or outsourcing to either service bureaus or core processing vendors with expertise in Internet Banking. Whether outsourced or packaged, Internet Banking architectures generally consist of the following components: Web Servers; Transaction Servers; Application Servers; Data storage and access servers. Vendors such as Online Resources (http://www.orcc.com/) offer a package of Web banking services that include the design and hosting of a financial institution's Web site and the implementation of a transactional Web site. Online's connection makes use of the bank's underlying ATM network for transactions and real-time bill payment. In addition, optional modules are generally available for Bill Payment, Bill Presentment, Brokerage, Loan Application/ Approval, Small Business, and Credit Cards. The fact that multiple options of web hosting exist also brings with them issues in security and privacy – a topic that is considered in a later section.

The components that form a typical Internet banking initiative (see Figure 1) are as follows (Starita, 1999):

- **Internet banking front-end:** The front-end is often the Client-side browser access to the bank's Web server. Client-side thin-client access to the bank's Web server: This model allows the customer to download a thin-client software product from the bank's Web site and may allow storing financial data locally. Client-side thick-client access to the bank's Web server: This is the model used when supporting personal financial management packages as tools to access account data and execute transactions. It is important to note that these models are not mutually exclusive of each other (Starita, 1999).
- **Internetbanking transaction platforms:** The Internet banking transaction platform is the technology component that supports transactional processes and interfaces between the front-end user interface and the back-end core processors for functions

*Figure 1. Architectural pieces of Internet banking*

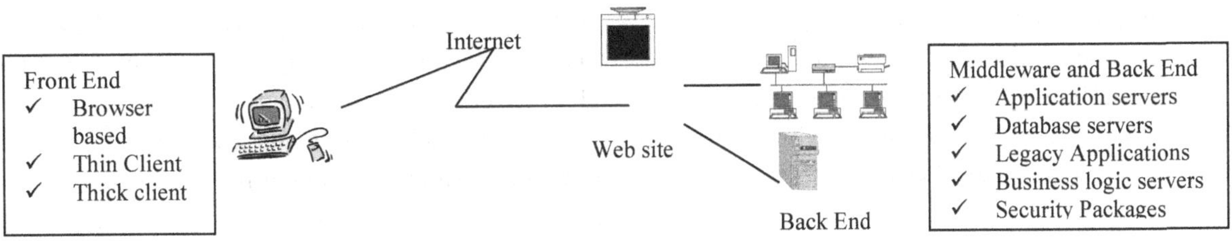

like account information retrieval, account update etc. In general, the transactional platform defines two main things: 1) the functional capabilities of the Internet banking offering (e.g., whether it offers bill payment or credit card access) and 2) the method of access or interface between the front-end and back-end legacy processors (Starita, 1999).

## Internet Banking Platforms and Applications

Most of the Internet plumbing to present data onto web interfaces from data sources is offered by Internet Banking Application Software vendors who link legacy systems to allow access to account data and transaction execution. Most players position themselves as end-to-end solution providers by including a proprietary front-end software product, integration with other front-end software, or Web design services.

Some of the solutions are middleware platforms with plug-in applications to provide bill payment, bill presentment, brokerage, loan, small business, and/or credit card functionality. Most vendors use Open Financial Exchange standard (OFX) to connect to different delivery channels such as Interactive Voice Response (IVRs), Personal Finance Managers (PFMs), and the Internet. Middleware tools are designed to handle Internet-delivered core banking and bill payment transaction (Walsh, 2002). Middleware platforms provide a link between financial institutions' legacy host systems and customers using browser-based HTML interfaces and OFX-enabled personal financial management software (Walsh, 2002).

Middleware is designed for financial institutions that require a platform that translates messages between collections of separate processing systems that house core processing functions. Core processing systems include bill payment, credit card, brokerage, loans and insurance. Electronic bill payment and presentment is widely believed to be the compelling application that brings large volumes of customers to the Internet channel to handle their finances. There are two kinds of websites: non-transactional and transactional. The non-transactional sites, commonly known as promotional websites, publish content with information about bank products and allow customers to investigate targeted areas such as college loans or retirement planning. These sites give basic information on bank products and do not allow any transactions. Banks can collect information to start to develop customer profiles by recording where a customer visits on the Web site and comparing it with demographic information to develop personalized marketing strategies.

Transactional sites link to back-end processing systems and include basic functionality such as the ability to view recent transactions and account histories, download information into PFM software, and transfer funds between existing accounts. As banks become more sophisticated with transactional capabilities, such things as electronic bill payment or moving of funds outside of the bank become possible. Integrating with a third-party processor such as Checkfree or Travelers Express most often does this. Bill presentment is also part of transactional capability; however, it is being done on a limited basis through a small number of pilots. Some banks allow customers to apply for loans, mortgages, and other products online, although much of the back-end process is still done manually. In transactional Web sites, every page must be dynamically composed and offer continual updates on products and pricing.

## Standards Compliance

Standards play a vital role in seamless flow and integration of information across channels and help in reducing risk emanating from diverse platforms and standards. In addition to the challenge of integrating Internet banking products into the banks own IT environment; many Internet banking functions involve third-party participation. This poses a significant integration question: What is the best way to combine separate technology systems with third parties in a cost-effective way to enable each participant to maintain control over its data, and maintain autonomy from other participants? The response from the technology marketplace has been to establish Internet banking standards to define interactions and the transfer of information between multiple parties (Bohle, 2001). The premise of a standard is that everyone would use it in the same consistent fashion; unfortunately, that is not the scenario in the current Internet banking environment. One of the problems for the lackluster performance of e-banking arguably is the industry's failure to attend to the payments infrastructure (Orr, 2002). One initiative that does show promise is by the National Institute of Standards and Technology that has developed a proposed standard, "Security Requirements for Cryptographic Modules," that will require role based authentication and authorization (FIPS, 1992). Some of the standards pervasive in current e-banking models are the ADMS standard, the GOLD standard, the OFX standard.

## INFORMATION ASSURANCE

The financial services industry, confronts cyber and physical threats from a great variety of sources ranging from potentially catastrophic attacks launched by terrorist groups or other national interest groups to the more commonly experienced and met several extremely targeted attacks perpetrated by hackers and other malicious entities such as insiders (Gupta et al., 2008). Financial organizations have traditionally been at the forefront of security, and they should maintain this posture in the Internet era (Slewe and Hoogenboom, 2004). Web banking sites include Financial Calculators, e-mail addresses/Customer Service Information, New Account Applications, Transactions such as account balance checks, transfers, and bill payment, bill presentment/payment, cash management, loan applications, small business, credit card, etc. The modes by which they can be accessed include Online Service Provider or Portal Site, Direct-Dial PC Banking Program, Internet-bank Web sites, WebTV and Personal Financial Manager. Depending on the functionality of the web sites different information assurance requirements are found.

*Table 1. Standards in e-banking models*

| | |
|---|---|
| **The ADMS Standard** | Access Device Messaging System (ADMS) is a proprietary standard developed and supported by Visa Interactive. From September 1998, this standard has been made obsolete for GOLD standard. |
| **The GOLD Standard** | The GOLD standard is an electronic banking standard developed and supported by Integrion[1] to facilitate the exchange of information between participants in electronic banking transactions. |
| **The OFX Standard** | Open Financial Exchange (OFX) is a standard developed cooperatively by Microsoft, Intuit and Checkfree. Recently, Microsoft launched its OFX version 2.0 without the involvement of its partners, Checkfree and Intuit. OFX v.2.0 is developed with XML to enable OFX to be used for bill presentment. Though OFX can be considered, as a much better solution for inter-operability needs of banks, it imposes problems of incompatibility between older OFX versions. |
| **The IFX Standard** | Interactive Financial exchange (IFX) initiative was launched in early 1998 by BITS (the Banking Industry Technology Secretariat) in order to ensure convergence between OFX and another proposed specification, GOLD, propounded by Integrion Financial Network. According to the IFX forum, IFX specification provides a robust and scalable framework for the exchange of financial data and instructions independent of a particular network technology or computing platform. |
| **XML as standard** | XML language is often perceived as a solution to the problem of standards incompatibility. XML appears as an ideal tool for multi-banking, multi-service Internet banking applications. |

Some examples of exploitation of Information Assurance issues in the web-banking arena include:

- Many ATMs of Bank of America were made unavailable in January 2003 by the SQL Slammer worm, which also affected other financial services like Washington Mutual[2,3].
- Barclays suffered an embarrassing incident when it was discovered that after logging out of its online service, an account could be immediately re-accessed using the "back" button on a Web browser. If a customer accessed their Barclays account on a public terminal, the next user could thereby view banking details of the previous customer. According to the bank, when customers join the online banking service they are given a booklet that tells them to clear the cache to prevent this from happening. However, this procedure shifts the responsibility for security to the end user[4].

## Security and Privacy Issues

In their annual joint study in April 2002, the FBI and the Computer Security Institute, noted that the combined financial losses for 223 of 503 companies that responded to their survey (*Computer Crime and Security Survey)* was $455 million for year 2002 (Junnarkar, 2002). Security and integrity of online transactions are the most important technical issues that a bank offering web services will need to tackle. The Internet bank web sites handle security in different ways. They can choose either public or private networks. The Integrion consortium, for example, uses the private IBM/AT&T Global Network for all Internet network traffic (Walsh, 1999)]. Server security is another important issue, usually accomplished by server certificates and SSL authentication. Banks must look at three kinds of security (Walsh, 1999)]: Communications Security; Systems Security—from the Applications/Authorization Server; Information Security. According to Furnell (2004), customers have a tendency to be confidential about their accounts and are concerned with the security of banking transactions, which impacts adoption of Internet banking services (Aladwani, 2001). There are many studies published on Internet banking related with Internet banking adoption and acceptance, security and risks of online banking system and interface designs (Bauer & Hein, 2006; Cheng et al., 2006; Claessens et al., 2002; Lai & Li, 2004; Luarn & Lin, 2005; Suh & Han, 2002; Weir et al., 2006).

From a user's perspective, security must accomplish privacy, integrity authentication, access control, and non-repudiation. Issues with end user's security need to be seen as part of a wider range of user-facing initiatives, including awareness-raising and education, so that users properly appreciate their need for security and the threats that they may face (Furnell, 2008). Security becomes an even more important issue when dealing with international banks, since only up to 128K encryption is licensed for export. Currently, most Internet bank web sites use a combination of encryption, firewalls, and communications lines to ensure security. The basic level of security starts with a SSL-compliant browser. The SSL protocol provides data security between a Web browser and the Web server, and is based on public key cryptography licensed from Security Systems. Security has been one of the biggest roadblocks that have kept consumers from fully embracing Internet banking. Even after the advent of highly secure sites with the aid of 128K encryption, a virtually invulnerable encryption technology, the perception among some consumers is that Internet banking is unsafe. They apprehend privacy violations, as the bank keeps track of all transactions, and they are unsure of who has access to privileged data about their personal net worth. The basic security concerns that face financial institutions offering banking services and products through the Internet are summarized in Figure 2 and are discussed next.

## Authentication

Authentication relates to assurance of identity of person or originator of data. Reliable customer authentication is imperative for financial institutions engaging in any form of electronic banking or commerce. Strong customer authentication practices are necessary to enforce anti-money laundering measures and help financial institutions detect and reduce identity theft. Customer interaction with financial institutions is migrating from physical recognition and paper-based documentation to remote electronic access and transaction initiation. The risks of doing business with unauthorized or masquerading individuals in an electronic banking environment could be devastating resulting in financial loss and intangible losses like reputation damage, disclosure of confidential information, corruption of data or unenforceable agreements. Any Internet banking system must solve the issues of authentication, confidentiality, integrity, and non-repudiation, which means it must ensure that only qualified people can access an Internet banking account, that the information viewed remains private and can't be modified by third parties, and that any transactions made are traceable and verifiable (Hiltgen et al., 2006).

There is a gamut of authentication tools and methodologies that financial institutions use to authenticate customers. These include the use of passwords and personal identification numbers (PINs), digital certificates using a public key infrastructure (PKI), physical devices such as smart cards or other types of "tokens," database comparisons, and bio-metric identifiers. The level of risk protection afforded by each of these tools varies and is evolving as technology changes. Multi-factor authentication methods are more difficult to compromise than single factor systems. Properly designed and implemented multi-factor authentication methods are more reliable indica-

*Figure 2. E-banking security infrastructure*

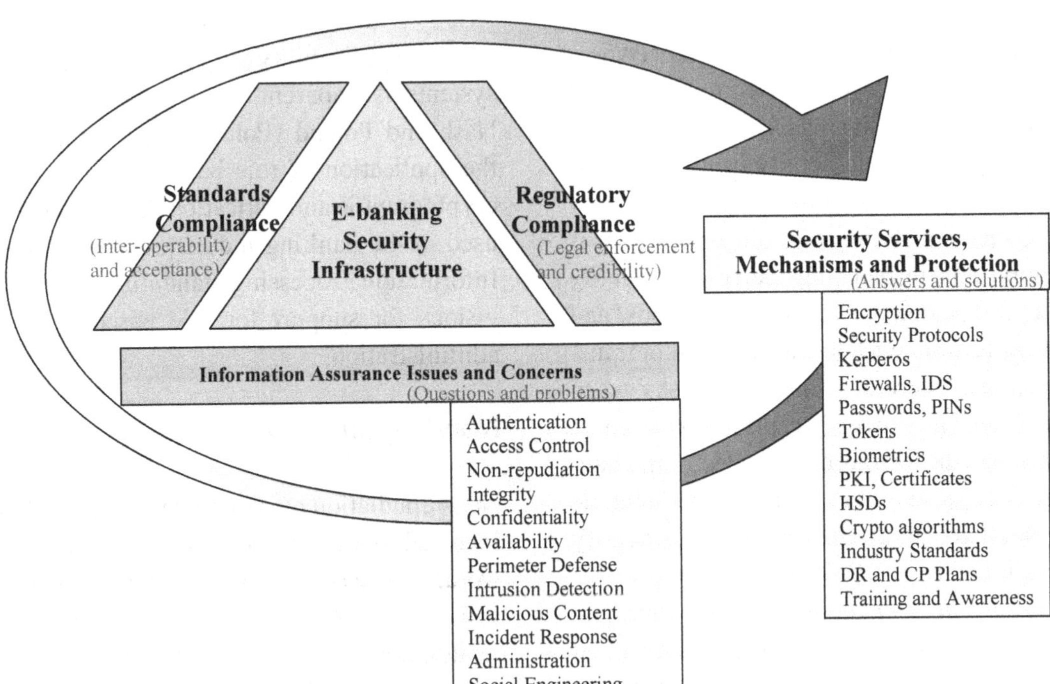

tors of authentication and stronger fraud deterrents. Broadly the authentication methodologies can be classified based on: what a user knows (password, PINs); what a user has (smart card, magnetic card); and what a user is (fingerprint, retina, voiceprint, signature). Recently, in US, FFIEC guidelines for authentication in e-banking has been published that will aid banks understand how to devise and implement strategies and technologies for their own e-banking offerings. Ultimately, the choice of authentication solutions will also be different for each bank, depending on its assets, the risks the organization considers acceptable, and the costs of the (considered) security measures (Gupta and Rao, 2007).

The issues that face banks using the Internet as a channel are the risks and risk management controls of a number of existing and emerging authentication tools necessary to initially *verify* the identity of new customers and *authenticate* existing customers that access electronic banking services. Besides, effective authentication framework and implementation provides banks with a foundation to enforce electronic transactions and agreements:

- *Account Origination and Customer Verification:* With the growth in electronic banking and commerce, financial institutions need to deploy reliable methods of originating new customer accounts online. Customer identity verification during account origination is important in reducing the risk of identity theft, fraudulent account applications, and unenforceable account agreements or transactions. There are significant risks when financial institution accepts new customers through the Internet or other electronic channels because of the absence of the tangible cues that banks traditionally use to identify individuals (FDIC, 2001).
- *Monitoring and Reporting* Monitoring systems play vital role in detecting unauthorized access to computer systems and customer accounts. A sound authentication system should include audit features that can assist in the detection of fraud, unusual activities (e.g., money laundering), compromised passwords or other unauthorized activities[5] (FDIC, 2001).

## Access Control

Access Control refers to the regulating of access to critical business assets. Access Control provides a policy-based control of who can access specific systems, what they can do within them, and when and from where they are allowed access. One of the primary modes of access control is based on roles. A role can be thought of as a set of transactions that a user or set of users can perform within the context of an organization. For example, the roles in a bank include teller, loan officer, and accountant each of whom can perform different functions. Role based access control (RBAC) policy bases access control decisions on the functions that a user is allowed to perform within an organization. In many applications, RBAC is concerned more with access to functions and information than strictly with access to information.

The applicability of RBAC to commercial systems is apparent from its widespread use. Nash and Poland (Poland, et.al, 1990) discuss the application of role based access control to cryptographic authentication devices commonly used in the banking industry. Even the Federal Information Processing Standard (FIPS) has provisions for support for role based access and administration.

## Non-Repudiation

Non-repudiation refers to the need for each party involved in a transaction to not go back on their word, i.e. break the electronic contract (Pfleeger, 1997). Authentication forms the basis for non-repudiation. It requires strong and substantial evidence of the identity of the signer of a message and of message integrity, sufficient to prevent a party from successfully denying the origin, submission or delivery of the message and the integrity of its contents. This is important for an e-banking environment where, in all electronic transactions, including ATMs (cash machines), all parties to a transaction must be confident that the transaction is secure; that the parties are who they say they are (authentication), and that the transaction is verified as final. Essentially banks must have mechanisms that must ensure that a party cannot subsequently repudiate (reject) a transaction. There are several ways to ensure non-repudiation which includes digital signatures, which not only validates the sender, but also 'time stamps' the transaction, so it cannot be claimed subsequently that the transaction was not authorized or not valid.

## Integrity

Ensuring integrity means maintaining data consistency and protecting from unauthorized data alteration (Pfleeger, 1997). Integrity is very critical for Internet banking applications as transactions have information that is consumer and business sensitive. To achieve integrity, data integrity mechanisms can be used. These typically involve the use of secret-key or public-key based algorithms that allow the recipient of a piece of protected data to verify that the data has not been modified in transit,. The mechanisms are further presented in the Section "Security Services, Mechanisms and Security Protection."

## Confidentiality and Privacy

Privacy and security concerns are not unique to banking systems. Privacy and confidentiality are related but are distinct concepts. Protection of personally identifiable information like banking records must be ensured before consumers. Information Privacy (NIIAC, 1995) is the ability of an individual to control the use and dissemination of information that relates to him/her. *Confidentiality* (NIIAC, 1995) is a tool for protecting privacy. Sensitive information is accorded a confidential status that mandates specific controls, including strict limitations on access and disclosure. Those handling the information must adhere to these controls. Information confidentiality refers to ensuring that customer information is secured and hidden as it is transported through the Internet environment. Information must not only be protected wherever it is stored (E.g., on computer disks, backup tape and printed form), but also in transit through the Internet.

## Availability

Availability in our context means that legitimate users have access when they need it. With Internet banking, one of the strongest selling propositions is 24x7 availability, therefore it becomes even more critical for e-banks. Availability applies to both data and to services. Expectations of availability include presence of a service in usable form, capacity to meet service needs, timeliness of service, fair allocation, fault tolerance, controlled concurrency and deadlock management. One example where availability is compromised is the Denial of Service attack. On the Internet, a denial of service (DoS) attack is an incident in which a user or organization is deprived of the services of a resource they would normally expect to have. When there are enormous transactions on the Internet bank's web site, the losses that may arise owing to unavailability are severe, in terms of financial losses and reputation losses. Typically, the loss of service is the inability of a particular network service, such as e-mail, to be available or the temporary loss of all network connectivity and services. services It becomes imperative and crucial for IT managers in the Internet banking world to better understand the kind of denial of attacks possible Some of the common and well-known types of denial of service attacks (IESAC, 2003) are:

- **SYN attack:** It floods the server with open SYN connections, without completing the TCP handshake.
- **Teardrop attack:** It exploits the way that the Internet Protocol (IP) requires a packet that is too large for the next router to handle be divided into fragments. Here, the attacker's IP puts a confusing offset value in the second or later fragment of the packet. It can cause the system to crash.
- **Smurf attack:** In this attack, the perpetrator spoofs the source IP address and broadcasts ping requests to multitude of machines to overwhelm the victim.

## Perimeter Defense

Perimeter defense refers to the separation of an organization's computer systems from the outside world (IETF, 2000). This must allow free sharing of certain information with clients, partners, suppliers and so on, while also protecting critical data from them. A security bulwark around network and information assets of any bank can be achieved, to a certain extent, by implementing firewalls and correctly performing tuning and configuration of firewalls.

Today, with the kind of traffic generated towards web-banking sites for all kind of purposes, from balance enquiries to Inter-bank fund transfers, implementation of screening routers to ensure incoming and outgoing traffic would add another layer of security. In this age of systems being hijacked for cyber-attacks, it is also important that screen routers detect and prevent outgoing traffic that attempt to gain entry to systems like spoofing IP addresses. Further the periphery of the corporate computer infrastructure can be bolstered by implement VPN solutions to ensure privacy of data flowing through the firewall into the public domain.

Probes and scans are often used techniques that are exploited to learn about exposures and vulnerabilities on the network systems. A probe is characterized by unusual attempts to gain access to a system or to discover information about the system. Probes are sometimes followed by a more serious security event, but they are often the result of curiosity or confusion. A scan is simply a large number of probes done using an automated tool. Scans can sometimes be the result of a misconfiguration or other error, but they are often a prelude to a more directed attack on systems that the intruder has found to be vulnerable.

## Intrusion Detection

Intrusion Detection refers to the ability to identify an attempt to access systems and networks in a fashion that breaches security policies. The Internet banking scenario where most of business these days is carried out over public domain Internet and where a banking web site becomes a single point interface for information as well as transactions, gives hackers enough motivation to intrude into Internet banks' systems. To safeguard from such unwanted activities, organizations need to be able to recognize and distinguish, at a *minimum,* the following (Gartner, 1999): internal & external intrusion attempts; human vs. automated attacks; unauthorized hosts connecting to the network from inside and outside the perimeter; unauthorized software being loaded on systems; and all access points into the corporate network.

Intrusion detection systems (IDS) allow organizations to protect their systems from the threats that come with increasing network connectivity and reliance on information systems. Given the level and nature of modern network security threats, the question for security professionals should not be whether to use intrusion detection, but which intrusion detection features and capabilities to use. IDSs have gained acceptance as a necessary addition to every organization's security infrastructure. IDS products can provide worthwhile indications of malicious activity and spotlight security vulnerabilities, thus providing an additional layer of protection. Without them, network administrators have little chance of knowing about, much less assessing and responding to, malicious and invalid activity. Properly configured, IDSs are especially useful for monitoring the network perimeter for attacks originating from outside and for monitoring host systems for unacceptable insider activity.

## Security Event Detection

Security Event Detection refers to the use of logs and other audit mechanisms to capture information about system and application access, types of access, network events, intrusion attempts, viruses, etc.

Logging is an important link in analysis of attack and real time alerts of any kind of suspicious activity on the Internet bank web site. For proper tracking of unusual events and attempts of intrusion the following logs should be collected: basic security logs, network event logging, log authentication failures, log access violations, log attempts to implant viruses and other malicious code, and log "abnormal" activity. This strongly implies that the technical department that is analyzing logs to identify "unusual behavior" must be aware of business initiatives. Besides, it has to be ensured that audit logs are retained long enough to satisfy legal requirements. Also, at a minimum, investigation of security breaches should be allowed for up to 14 days after any given attack (IETF, 2000). Today, data mining techniques can interpret millions of items of log data and reveal any unobserved attempts to breach an e-bank's web site. For this it has to be ensured that logs do not overwrite themselves causing loss of data. For analysis of events at a site, documentation of automated systems that identify what the logs mean should be maintained. Understanding the nature of attempts such as whether an attack was from within organization or from outside or whether it was just a false alarm is critical to security.

## Malicious Content

Malicious Content refers to programs of any type that are introduced into a system to cause damage or steal information. Malicious Content includes viruses, Trojans, hacker tools, and network sniffers. While common in multiple domains this is as important in the e-banking world as well. Malicious code brings with it the potential to create serious technical and economic impact by crashing e-mail servers and networks, causing millions of dollars of damage in lost productivity.

Some of the common forms of malicious contents are:

- **Virus:** A *virus* is a computer program that runs on a system without being asked to do so, created to "infect" other computer programs with copies of itself. Pioneer virus researcher Fred Cohen[6] has defined a *virus* as *"a program that can* 'infect' other programs by modifying them to include a, possibly evolved, copy of it."
- **Worm:** A *worm* has the ability to spread over a network and, thus, can take advantage of the Internet to do its work. Worms reside in memory and duplicate themselves throughout the network without user intervention.
- **Trojan Horse:** *Trojan horse* is the name applied to malicious computer program disguised as a seemingly innocent activity such as initiating a screen saver, accessing an e-mail attachment, or downloading executable files from an untrusted Web site. Some of the widely manifested malicious codes are Stoned, Yankee, Michelangelo, Joshi, Lehigh, Jerusalem, MBDF (for Macintosh), Melissa, Concept, LoveBug (ILOVEYOU), ShapeShift, Fusion, Accessiv, Emporer, Sircam, Nimda, Badtrans.

Protection against malicious codes like viruses, worms, Trojan horses, etc could be effectively dealt with installing security protection software that thwarts and mitigates the effects of codes.

However, such software provides only a level of defense and is not by itself sufficient. Recommendations for e-banking IT infrastructure include (Noakes, 2001):

- Install detection and protection solutions for all forms of malicious code, not just an Anti-Virus solution.
- Ensure that all users are aware of and follow safe behavior practices – don't open attachments that haven't been scanned, don't visit untrusted websites, etc.
- Ensure that users are aware of how easy data may be stolen automatically just by visiting a web site. Install an effective solution. Keep it current with the latest signatures as new forms of malicious code are identified.
- Use anti-spammers, harden operating systems, configure stricter firewall rules, etc.

## Security Services, Mechanisms and Security Protection

Security risks are unlike privacy risks; they originate outside the Financial Service Provider (FSP) and change rapidly with advances in technology (DeLotto, 1999). In December 2000, IATF released guidelines that require all covered institutions to secure their clients' personal information against any "reasonably foreseeable" internal or external threats to their security, confidentiality and integrity. By 1 July 2001, FSPs were expected to develop customer information security programs that: ensured the security and confidentiality of customer information, protected against any anticipated threats or hazards to the security or integrity of customer information; and protected against unauthorized access to or use of customer information that could result in substantial harm or inconvenience to customers.

The services and mechanisms that are prevalent in e-banking environment are presented below in order to provide an understanding of key issues and terms involved.

### Encryption

Encryption is the process of using a key to scramble readable text into unreadable cyphertext. Encryption on the Internet in general, and e-banking, in particular, has many uses, from the securing transmission of credit card numbers via the Web to protecting the privacy of personal email messages. Authentication also uses encryption, by using a key or key pair to verify the integrity of a document and its origin. The data encryption standard (DES) has been endorsed by the National Institute of Standards and Technology (NIST) since 1975 and is the most readily available encryption standard. Rivest, Shamir, and Adleman (RSA) encryption is a public-key encryption system, is patented technology in the United States, and thus is not available without a license. RSA encryption is growing in popularity and is considered quite secure from brute force attacks. Another encryption mechanism is pretty good privacy (PGP), which allows users to encrypt information stored on their system as well as to send and receive encrypted e-mail. Encryption mechanisms rely on keys or passwords. The longer the password, the more difficult the encryption is to break. VPNs employ encryption to provide secure transmissions over public networks such as the Internet.

### Security Protocol Services

The Internet is viewed as an insecure place. Many of the protocols used in the Internet do not provide any security. Today's businesses, particularly the banking sector, must integrate security protocols into their eCommerce infrastructure to protect customer information and privacy. Some of the most common protocols are briefly discussed in Appendix A.

## Firewalls and Intrusion Detection Systems

A firewall[7] is a collection of hardware and software designed to examine a stream of network traffic and service requests. Its purpose is to eliminate from the stream those packets or requests that fail to meet the security criteria established by the organization. A simple firewall may consist of a filtering router, configured to discard packets that arrive from unauthorized addresses or that represent attempts to connect to unauthorized service ports. Firewalls can filter packets based on their source and destination addresses and port numbers. This is known as address filtering. Firewalls can also filter specific types of network traffic. This is also known as protocol filtering because the decision to forward or reject traffic is dependant upon the protocol used, for example HTTP, ftp or telnet. Firewalls can also filter traffic by packet attribute or state. But a firewall cannot prevent individual users with modems from dialing into or out of the network, bypassing the firewall altogether (Odyssey, 2001). In this age of systems being hijacked, it is also important that firewalls and screen routers detect and prevent outgoing traffic that attempt to compromise the integrity of the systems.

A network intrusion detection system (NIDS) analyzes network traffic for attacks. It examines individual packets within the data stream to identify threats from authorized users, backdoor attacks and hackers who have thwarted the control systems to exploited network connections and access valuable data. NIDS add a new level of visibility into the nature and characteristics of the network. They provide information about the use and usage of the network. Host Based IDS / Event Log Viewers are a kind of IDS that monitor event logs from multiple sources for suspicious activity. Host IDS are best placed to detect computer misuse from trusted insiders and those who have infiltrated the network.

The technology and logical schemes used by these systems are often based on *Knowledge-Based Misuse Detection* (Allan, 2002) . Knowledge-based detection methods use information about known security policy, known vulnerabilities, and known attacks on the systems they monitor. This approach compares network activity or system audit data to a database of known *attack signatures* or other misuse indicators, and pattern matches produce alarms of various sorts. Behavior-based detection (Allan, 2002) methods use information about repetitive and usual behavior on the systems they monitor. Also called *anomaly detection*, this approach notes events that diverge from expected (based on repetitive and usual) usage patterns. One technique is *threshold detection* (Allan, 2002), in which certain attributes of user and system behavior are expressed in terms of counts, with some level established as permissible. Another technique is to perform *statistical analysis* (Allan, 2002) on the information, build statistical models of the environment, and look for patterns of anomalous activity.

## Passwords and Personal Identification Numbers (PINs)

The most common authentication method for existing customers requesting access to electronic banking systems is the entry of a user name or ID and a secret string of characters such as a password or PIN. User IDs combined with passwords or PINs are considered a single-factor authentication technique. There are three aspects of passwords that contribute to the security they provide: secrecy, length and composition, and system controls. In the present Internet banking scenario, there are policies, for both customers as well as employees, set by banks for passwords, to ensure effective authentication, like prohibiting using public email ids as user IDs, ensure that there are no user IDs with no password, ensure that policies exist and can be automatically enforced concerning minimum password length, password format (which characters make up a valid password), expiration and renewal of passwords, uniqueness of passwords, not allowing the use of "real" words for passwords, etc.

## Tokens

The use of a token represents authentication using "something the customer possesses." Typically, a token is part of a two-factor authentication process, complemented by a password as the other factor. There are many benefits to the use of tokens. The authentication process cannot be completed unless the device is present. Static passwords or biometric identifiers used to activate the token may be authenticated locally by the device itself. This process avoids the transmission of shared secrets over an open network such as the Internet.

## Digital Certificates and Public Key Infrastructure (PKI)

A financial institution may use a PKI system to authenticate customers to its own electronic banking product. Institutions may also use the infrastructure to provide authentication services to customers who wish to transact business over the Internet with other entities or to identify employees and commercial partners seeking access to the business's internal systems. A properly implemented and maintained PKI may provide a strong means of customer identification over open networks such as the Internet. By combining a variety of hardware components, system software, policies, practices, and standards, PKI can provide for authentication, data integrity, and defenses against customer repudiation, and confidentiality (Odyssey, 2001). The *certificate authority* (CA), which may be the financial institution or its service provider, plays a key role by attesting with a *digital certificate* that a particular public key and the corresponding private key belongs to a specific individual or system. It is important when issuing a digital certificate that the registration process for initially verifying the identity of customers is adequately controlled. The CA attests to the individual's identity by signing the digital certificate with its own private key, known as the *root key*. Each time the customer establishes a communication link with the financial institution, a digital signature is transmitted with a digital certificate. These electronic credentials enable the institution to determine that the digital certificate is valid, identify the individual as a customer, and confirm that transactions entered into the institution's computer system were performed by that customer. PKI, as the most reliable model for Security and Trust on the Internet offers a comprehensive e-Security solution for Internet banking. Unlike the other security models, PKI is standards compliant, most credible Trust framework, highly scalable and modular. PKI comprehensively satisfies the security requirements of e-Banking (Odyssey, 2001).

A brief discussion on the processes and mechanisms used in PKI to address common security concerns follows:

- **Authentication:** The customer requests the Registration Authority (RA) for a certificate. The Registration Authority validates the customer's credentials. After valid credentials are ensured, the RA passes the certificate request to the Certification Authority (CA). CA, then, issues the certificates A Digital Certificate can be stored on the Browser on the Users Computer, on a floppy disk, on a Smart Card or on other Hardware Tokens.
- **Confidentiality:** The customer generates a random session key at his end. The session key is sent to the bank, encrypting it with the bank's public key. The bank decrypts the encrypted session key with its private key. The session key is employed for further transactions.
- **Integrity:** The message is passed through a suitable hashing algorithm to obtain a message digest or hash. The hash, encrypted

with the sender's private key is appended to the message. The receiver on receiving the message passes it through the same hashing algorithm. The digest he obtains is compared with the received and decrypted digest. If the digests are same, it implies that the data has not been tampered with, in transit.

- **Non-repudiation:** The hash is encrypted with the sender's private key to yield the sender's digital signature. Since the hash is encrypted with the sender's private key (which is accessible only to him), it provides an indisputable means of non-repudiation.
- The use of Digital Signatures and Certificates in Internet Banking has provided the Trust and Security needed to carry out banking transactions across open networks like the Internet. PKI, being a universally accepted standards compliant security model provides for the establishment of a **global Trust chain** (Odyssey, 2001).

## Biometrics

A biometric identifier measures an individual's unique physical characteristic or behavior and compares it to a stored digital template to authenticate that individual. A biometric identifier representing "something the user is" can be created from sources such as a customer's voice, fingerprints, hand or face geometry, the iris or retina in an eye, or the way a customer signs a document or enters keyboard strokes (FDIC, 2001). The success of a biometric identifier rests on the ability of the digitally stored characteristic to relate typically to only one individual in a defined population. Although not yet in widespread use by financial institutions for authenticating existing customers, biometric identifiers are being used in some cases for physical access control.

Banks could use a biometric identifier for a single or multi-factor authentication process. ATMs that implement biometrics like iris-scan technologies are examples of the use of a biometric identifier to authenticate users. The biometric identifier may be used for authentication, instead of the PIN. A customer can use a PIN or password to supplement the biometric identifier, making it part of a more secure two-factor authentication process. Financial institutions may also use biometric identifiers for automating existing processes. Another application would be a financial institution that allows customer to reset a password over the telephone with voice-recognition software that authenticates the customer. An authentication process that relies on a single biometric identifier may not work for everyone in a financial institution's customer base. Introducing a biometric method of authentication requires physical contact with each customer to initially capture the physical identifier, which further buttresses the initial customer verification process. But this process may increase the deployment costs.

## Hardware Security Devices (HSDs)

This mechanism is an extension to usage of tokens for authentication. Using hardware devices for authentication provide "hacker-resistant" and "snooping-proof" two-factor authentication, resulting in easy-to-use and effective user identification (Grand, 2001). To access protected resources, the user simply combines his secret PIN (something he knows) with the code generated by his token (something he has). The result is a unique, one-time-use code that is used to positively identify, or authenticate the user (Grand, 2001). Some central server validates the code. Goal: provide acceleration, secure key management. A Hardware Security Module is a hardware-based security device that generates stores and protects cryptographic keys.

There are universal criteria for rating these devices. The criteria are documented in a Federal Information Processing Standard (FIPS) called FIPS 140-1 to 140-4 – Security for Cryptographic Modules. Such hardware devices generate tokens that are dynamic one-time passwords, through the use of a mathematical function. Passwords generated by tokens are different each time the user requests one, so an intercepted password is useless as it will never be used again. Acceptance and credibility of the devices is reflected in the increasing number of devices in use.

### Industry Standards and Frameworks

Industry standards for financial transactions over the Internet are an absolute necessity for ensuring various security aspects of business as well as consumer confidence. There has been a constant search and development of standards for e-banking infrastructural tenets like authentication, access control, non-repudiation, etc. Some of the standards developed and advocated by different industry players and their proponents are briefly discussed in Appendix B for overall understanding of the evolution and prevalence of some of the standards.

## User and E-Banking Focus on the Security Issues

To summarize, Table 2 presents issues that user has direct control on or involvement with and issues that are commonly left for the systems to handle.

## CONCLUSION

It should be noted that the discussion of e-banking information assurance (IA) issues has also included several generic IA issues. To illustrate this, Table 3 briefly categorizes e-banking specific information assurance issues and generic issues separately. Some issues may be more significant than in other areas. We have made an attempt to comprehensively discuss all the areas in the chapter.

Financial services institutions' use of technology in selling to and serving customers has grown at an unprecedented pace. At the same time, at

*Table 2. End user involvement with the security issues*

| Security issues with direct user focus | User-focused mechanisms that are available | User-transparent mechanisms/ technology |
|---|---|---|
| Authentication | Passwords, PINs tokens, HSDs, Biometrics | Radius, TACACS, PKI, ISAKMP |
| Access Control | Roles, User Discretion, Hard-coded systems | |
| Confidentiality | Training | Encryption |
| Integrity | Encryption (hashing) | |
| Malicious Content | Training | Mail/Spam filters, anti-virus |
| Non-repudiation | Use of PKI, and authentication mechanisms | |
| Incident Response | Training | |
| Social Engineering | Training | |
| **Security Issues with system-only focus** | | |
| Availability | IDSs, Firewall, redundancy, fault-tolerance, application-level security rules | |
| Security Event, Intrusion Detection | IDSs, probes, firewalls | |
| Perimeter Defense | Firewalls, IDSs, | |
| Administration | Depends on the system policies as well as administrators. | |

*Table 3. IA issues*

| E-banking Specific Issues | Generic Issues (in E-banking) |
|---|---|
| E-banking related regulations, Banking and E-banking standards and frameworks, banking-specific protocol services. | Authentication, Access Control, Integrity, Availability, Perimeter Defense, Security Event Detection, Malicious Content, Incident Response, Social Engineering, Administration. |

the rate at which current technology is evolving, it is constantly bringing new dimensions to offer newer services. E-banking systems strive to provide us with easy, reliable and secure access to banking services, while also improving the service levels. The interaction between user and bank has been substantially improved by deploying ATMs, phone banking, Internet banking, and more recently, mobile banking. This chapter discusses the different information assurance issues and countermeasures in today's electronic banking systems. We also, throughout the chapter, also present the best practices for banks. Security for financial transactions is of vital importance to financial institutions providing or planning to provide service delivery to customers over the public Internet, as well as to suppliers of products, services, and solutions for Internet-based E-commerce. The actual and perceived threats to Internet-based banking define the need for a set of interrelated security services to provide protection to all parties that can benefit from Web banking in a secure environment. Such services may be specific to counter particular threats or may be pervasive throughout an Internet based environment to provide the levels of protection needed.

There are also requirements that the entire E-commerce environment be constructed from components that recognize the need for security services and provide means for overall security integration, administration, and management. These services that offer the security from infrastructure standpoint, are found throughout the E-commerce network and computing infrastructure. Financial institutions should carry out, as a matter of corporate security policy, identification of likely targets which should include all systems that are open to the public network, such as routers, firewalls, and Web servers, modem banks web sites, internal unsecured systems such as desktops. They should regularly revise and update their policies on auditing, risk assessment, standards, and key management. Vulnerability assessment and identification of likely targets and the recognition of systems most vulnerable to attack is critical in the e-banking arena. Accurate identification of vulnerable and attractive systems will contribute to prioritization when addressing problem areas.

## REFERENCES


Aladwani, A. M. (2001). Online banking: A field study of drivers, development challenges, and expectations. *Internal Journal of Information Management, 21*(3), 213–225.

Allan, A. (2002). *[Technology Overview] Intrusion Detection Systems (IDSs): Perspective.* Gartner Research Report (DPRO-95367).

Basel Committee (2001). Risk management principles for electronic banking. *Basel Committee publications No. 82.*

Bauer, K., & Hein, S. E. (2006). The effect of heterogeneous risk on the early adoption of Internet banking technologies. *Journal of Banking and Finance, 30*, 1713–1725.

Bohle, K. (2001). *Integration of Internet Payment Systems – What's the Problem?* ePSO (E-payments systems Observatory) –Newsletter. (Retrieved on 3/1/3 from http://epso.jrc.es/newsletter/vol11/5.html)

Burt, S. (2002). *Online Banking: Striving for Compliance in Cyberspace*. Bankers Systems Inc. article. (Retrieved on 9/5/02 from http://www.bankerssystems.com/compliance/article13.html)

Cheng, T. C. E., Lam, D. Y. C., & Yeung, A. C. L. (2006). Adoption of Internet banking: An empirical study in Hong Kong. *Decision Support Systems, 42*(3), 1558–1572.

Claessens, J., Dem, V., De Cock, D., Preneel, B., & Vandewalle, J. (2002). On the security of today's online electronic banking systems. *Computers and Security, 21*(3), 257–269.

Colonia-Willner, R. (2004). Self-service systems: New methodology reveals customer real-time actions during merger. *Computers in Human Behavior, 20*, 243–267.

DeLotto, R. (1999). *Competitive Intelligence for the E-Financial Service Provider.* Gartner Group Research Report.

Dittrich, D. (1999). *Incident Response Steps.* Lecture series at University of Washington.

Eriksson, K., & Nilsson, D. (2007). Determinants of the continued use of self-service technology: The case of Internet banking. *Technovation, 27*, 159–167.

FDIC (Federal Deposit Insurance Corporation) (2001). Authentication in Electronic Banking. *Financial Institution Letters.*

FIPS (Federal Information Processing Standard) (1992). *Security Requirements for Cryptographic Modules*. Federal Information Processing Standard 140-1. National Institute of Standards and Technology.

Furnell, S. (2004). E-commerce security: A question of trust. *Computer Fraud and Security, 10*, 10–14.

Furnell, S. (2008). Security usability challenges for end-users. In M. Gupta & R. Sharman (Eds.), *Social and Human Elements of Information Security: Emerging Trends and Countermeasures*. IGI Global Inc publishing, Hershey, PA. September 2008.

GartnerGroup RAS Services (1999). *Intrusion Detection Systems*. R-08-7031.

Glaessner, T., Kellermann, T., & McNevin, V. (2002). *Electronic Security: Risk Mitigation in Financial Transactions.* Public Policy Issues, The World Bank.

Gopalakrisnan, S., Wischnevsky, J. D., & Dmanpour, F. (2003). A multilevel analysis of factors influencing the adoption of Internet banking. *IEEE Transactions on Engineering Management, 50*(4), 413–426.

Grand, J. (2001). *Authentication Tokens: Balancing the Security Risks with Business Requirements.* @Stake, Inc., Cambridge, MA.

Gupta, M., Lee, J., & Rao, H. R. (2008). Implications of FFIEC Guidance on Authentication in Electronic Banking. In N. D. J. Gupta & S. Sharma (Eds.), *Handbook of Research on Information Security and Assurance.* IGI Publishing, Hershey, PA, April, 2008. USA. (isbn: 978-1-59904-855-0).

Gupta, M., & Rao, H. R. (2007). Financial Services Information Sharing and Analysis Center: Countering Cyber Terrorism in Financial Services Industry. In J. Janczewski & A. M. Colarik (Eds.), *Encyclopedia of Cyber Warfare and Cyber Terrorism.* Editors.

Hiltgen, A., Kramp, T., & Weigold, T. (2006). Secure Internet Banking Authentication. *IEEE Security and Privacy,* Mar/April 2006

IESAC (2003). *Transactional Security*, Institution of Engineers, Saudi Arabian Center. (Retrieved on 1/12/2003 from http://www.iepsac.org/papers/p04c04a.htm)

Internet Security Task Force (2000). *Initial Recommendations for Conducting Secure eBusiness*. (Retrieved on 1/12/03 from http://www.ca.com/ISTF/recommendations.htm)

Junnarkar, S. (2002). Online Banks: Prime targets for attacks. *e-Business ZDTech News Update*.

Kimball, R., & Gregor, W. (1995). How distribution is transforming retail banking: Changes leading banks are making. *Journal of Retail Banking Services, 17*(3), 1–9.

Lai, V. S., & Li, H. (2004). Technology acceptance model for Internet banking: An invariance analysis. *Information and Management, 42*, 373–386.

Luarn, P., & Lin, H. (2005). Toward an understanding of the behavioral intention to use mobile banking. *Computers in Human Behavior, 21*(6), 73–91.

Maconachy, W. V., Schou, C. D., Ragsdale, D., & Welch, D. (2001). A Model for Information Assurance: An Integrated Approach. *Proceedings of the 2001 IEEE, Workshop on Information Assurance and Security*, United States Military Academy, West Point, NY, 5-6 June.

Marchany, R. (1998). *Internet Security & Incident Response: Scenarios & Tactics*. September'1998. (Retrieved on 2/2/03 from https://courseware.vt.edu/marchany/InternetSecurity/Class)

NIIAC (The National Information Infrastructure Advisory Council) (1995). *Common Ground: Fundamental Principles for the National Information Infrastructure*.

Noakes, K. (2001). Virus and Malicious Code Protection Products: Perspective. *Fry Technology Overview*, Gartner Research Group, DPRO-90840.

OCC (Office of the Comptroller of the Currency) (1998). *OCC Bulletin 98-3 - Technology Risk Management. OCC Bulletin 98-38 - Technology Risk Management: PC Banking*.

OCC (Office of the Comptroller of the Currency) (2001). *AL 2001-4 - OCC Advisory Letter*.

Odyssey Technologies (2001). *PKI for Internet banking*. (Retrieved on 8.23.2002 from http://www.odysseytec.com)

Orr, B. (2002). Infrastructure, not innovation. *ABA Banking Online Journal*. (Retrieved on 8/8/02 from http://www.banking.com/aba/infrastructure.asp)

Pfleeger, C. P. (1997). *Security in Computing* (Second Edition). Upper Saddle River, NJ: Prentice Hall.

Poland, K. R., & Nash, M. J. (1990). Some Conundrums Concerning Separation of Duty. In *IEEE Symposium on Computer Security and Privacy*.

Polatoglu, V. N., & Ekin, S. (2001). An empirical investigation of the Turkish consumers' acceptance of Internet banking services. *International Journal of Bank Marketing, 19*(4), 156–165

Singh, S. (2004). Impersonalisation of electronic money: Implications for bank marketing. *The International Journal of Bank Marketing, 22*(7), 505-521.

Singh, S., Jackson, M. & Beekhuyzen, J. (2009). Privacy and Banking in Australia. In M. Gupta & R. Sharman (Eds.), *Handbook of Research on Social and Organizational Liabilities in Information Security*. IGI Global Inc publishing, Hershey, PA. Forthcoming in 2009.

Slewe, T., & Hoogenboom, M. (2004). Who Will Rob You on the Digital Highway? *Communications of the ACM, 47*(5), 56-60.

Starita, L. (1999). *Online Banking: A Strategic Perspective*. Context Overview Report (R-08-7031-Gartner).

Suh, B., & Han, I. (2002). Effect of trust on customer acceptance of Internet banking. *Electronic Commerce Research and Applications, 1*, 247–263.

The United States Senate (2002). *Financial Services Modernization Act: provisions of GLB Act.* The United States Senate publication. (Retrieved on 8/8/02 from http://www.senate.gov/~banking/conf /grmleach.htm)

Thornton, J., & White, L. (2001). Customer orientations and usage of financial distribution channels. *Journal of Services Marketing, 15*(3), 168–185.

Walsh, E. (1999). *Technology Overview: Internet Banking: Perspective.* DPRO-90293, Gartner.

Walsh, E. (2002). *Product Report: S1 Corporate Suite e-Banking Software*. DPRO-95913 (Gartner Research Group.

Weir, C. S., Anderson, J. N., & Jack, M. A. (2006). On the role of metaphor and language in design of third party payments in eBanking: Usability and quality. *International Journal of Human–Computer Studies, 64*, 770–784.

Yakhlef, A. (2001). Does the Internet compete with or complement bricks and mortar bank branches? *International Journal of Retail and Distribution Management, 29*(6), 272–281.

## ENDNOTES

1. Integrion is a PC direct-dial and Internet banking vendor developed as a consortium with 16 member banks, IBM and Visa Interactive (through acquisition) in an equal equity partnership. IBM is the technology provider for the Integrion consortium.
2. Robert Lemos, Satff Writer, CNET news.com, "Counting the cost of Slammer", Retrieved on March 31, 2003 from http://news.com.com/2100-1001-982955.html
3. Reuters, Seattle(Washington),CNN.com, Technology news, Feb 5, 2003. Retrieved on 3/8/03 from http://www.cnn.com/2003/TECH/internet/02/05/virus.spread.reut/
4. Atomic Tangarine Inc, NPV: Information Security", Retrieved on 3/21/03 from www.ttivanguard.com/risk/netpresentvalue.pdf
5. In addition, financial institutions are required to report suspicious activities to appropriate regulatory and law enforcement agencies as required by 31 CFR 103.18.
6. Fred Cohen is an early developer of some of the virus defense techniques behind antivirus software. In 1983 he coined the term "computer virus" in a research paper.
7. The term firewall comes from the earlier manifestations of routers that segmented a network into different physical sub-networks, and thus limited the exposure and damage that could spread from one subnet to another like fire-doors or firewalls.

## APPENDIX A: COMMON SECURITY PROTOCOL SERVICES

| Protocol | Description |
|---|---|
| **Secure Sockets Layer (SSL)** | Originally developed by Netscape, the SSL security protocol provides data encryption, server authentication, message integrity, and optional client authentication for a TCP/IP connection. SSL has been universally accepted on the World Wide Web for authenticated and encrypted communication between clients and servers. However, SSL consumes large amounts of the Web server's processing power due to the massive cryptographic computations that take place when a secure session is initiated. If many secure sessions are initiated simultaneously, then the Web server quickly becomes overburdened. The results are slow response times, dropped connections, and failed transactions. |
| **Secure Shell (SSH)** | SSH Secure Shell is the de facto standard for remote logins. It solves an important security problem on the Internet of password hacking. Typical applications include secure use of networked applications, remote system administration, automated file transfers, and access to corporate resources over the Internet. |
| **AS1 and AS2** | AS1 provides S/MIME encryption and security over SMTP (Simple Mail Transfer Protocol) through object signature and object encryption technology. AS2 goes a step further than AS1 by supporting S/MIME over HTTP and HTTPS. Both AS1 and AS2 provide data authentication, proving that the sender and receiver are indeed the people or company that they claim to be. |
| **Digital Certificates** | Digital certificates are used to authenticate the identity of trading partners, ensuring partners are really who they say they are. In addition to data authentication, digital signatures support non-repudiation, proving that a specific message did come from a known sender at a specific time. A digital signature is a digital code that can be sent with electronically transmitted message and it uniquely identifies the sender. It is based on digital certificates. This prevents partners from claiming that they didn't send or receive a particular message or transaction. |
| **Pretty Good Privacy (PGP)** | PGP is a freely available encryption program that uses public key cryptography to ensure privacy over FTP, HTTP and other protocols. PGP is the de-facto standard software for the encryption of e-mail and works on virtually every platform. But PGP suffers from absence of Trust management and it is not standards compliant though it could provide for integrity, authentication, non-repudiation and confidentiality. PGP also provides tools and utilities for creating, certifying, and managing keys. |
| **Secure Multipurpose Internet Mail Extension (S/MIME)** | S/MIME addresses security concerns such as privacy, integrity, authentication and non-repudiation, through the use of signed receipts. S/MIME provides a consistent way to send and receive secure MIME data. Based on the MIME standard, S/MIME provides authentication, message integrity, non-repudiation of origin (using digital signatures) and data confidentiality (using encryption) for electronic messaging applications. Since its development by RSA in 1996, S/MIME has been widely recognized and widely used standard for messaging. The technology for S/MIME is primarily built on the Public Key Cryptographic Standard, which provides cryptographic interoperability. Two key features of S/MIME are the digital signature and the digital envelope. Digital signatures ensure that a message has not been tampered with during transit. Digital signatures also provide non-repudiation so senders can't deny that they sent the message. |
| **Secure HTTP (S-HTTP)** | S-HTTP is an extension to HTTP, which provides a number of security features, including Client/Server Authentication, Spontaneous Encryption and Request/Response Non-repudiation. S-HTTP allows the secure exchange of files on the World Wide Web. Each S-HTTP file is either encrypted, contains a digital certificate, or both. For a given document, S-HTTP is an alternative to another well-known security protocol, Secure Sockets Layer (SSL). A major difference is that S-HTTP allows the client to send a certificate to authenticate the user whereas, using SSL, only the server can be authenticated. S-HTTP is more likely to be used in situations where the server represents a bank and requires authentication from the user that is more secure than a userid and password. |
| **Simple Key management for Internet Protocols (SKIP)** | It is a manifestation of IP-Level Cryptography that secures the network at the IP packet level. Any networked application gains the benefits of encryption, without requiring modification. SKIP is unique in that an Internet host can send an encrypted packet to another host without requiring a prior message exchange to set up a secure channel. SKIP is particularly well suited to IP networks, as both are stateless protocols. |
| **Encapsulating Security Payload (ESP)** | ESP is security protocol that provides data confidentiality and protection with optional authentication and replay-detection services. ESP completely encapsulates user data. ESP can be used either by itself or in conjunction with AH. ESP may be implemented with AH, as discussed in next paragraph, in a nested fashion through the use of tunnel mode. Security services can be provided between a pair of communicating hosts, between a pair of communicating security gateways, or between a security gateway and a host, depending on the implementation. ESP may be used to provide the same security services, and it also provides a confidentiality (encryption) service. Specifically, ESP does not protect any IP header fields unless those fields are encapsulated by ESP (tunnel mode). |

*continued on following page*

| | |
|---|---|
| **Authentication Header (AH)** | A security protocol that provides authentication and optional replay-detection services. AH is embedded in the data to be protected (a full IP datagram, for example). AH can be used either by itself or with Encryption Service Payload (ESP). The IP Authentication Header is used to provide connectionless integrity and data origin authentication for IP datagrams, and to provide protection against replays. AH provides authentication for as much of the IP header as possible, as well as for upper level protocol data. However, some IP header fields may change in transit and the value of these fields, when the packet arrives at the receiver, may not be predictable by the sender. The values of such fields cannot be protected by AH. Thus the protection provided to the IP header by AH is somewhat piecemeal and not complete. |

## APPENDIX B: SOME INDUSTRY STANDARDS AND FRAMEWORKS IN E-BANKING

| Standard | Description |
|---|---|
| *SET* | Secure Electronic Transaction (SET) is a system for ensuring the security of financial transactions on the Internet. It was supported initially by Mastercard, Visa, Microsoft, Netscape, and others. With SET, a user is given an *electronic wallet* (digital certificate) and a transaction is conducted and verified using a combination of digital certificates and digital signatures among the purchaser, a merchant, and the purchaser's bank in a way that ensures privacy and confidentiality. SET makes use of Netscape's Secure Sockets Layer (SSL), Microsoft's Secure Transaction Technology (STT), and Terisa System's Secure Hypertext Transfer Protocol (S-HTTP). SET uses some but not all aspects of a public key infrastructure (PKI). SET provides authentication, integrity, non-repudiation and confidentiality. |
| *HBCI* | HBCI is a specification for the communication between intelligent customer systems and the corresponding computing centers for the exchange of home banking transactions. The transmission of data is done by a net data interface, which is based on flexible delimiter syntax. |
| *EMV*[1] | Specifications by Europay, MasterCard and Visa that define a set of requirements to ensure interoperability between chip cards and terminals on a global basis, regardless of the manufacturer, the financial institution, or where the card is used. |
| *CEPS* | The Common Electronic Purse Specifications (CEPS) define requirements for all components needed by an organization to implement a globally interoperable electronic purse program, while maintaining full accountability and auditability. CEPS, which were made available in March of 1999, outline overall system security, certification and migration. CEPS have paved the way for the creation of an open, de facto, global electronic purse standard (http://www.cepsco.com/). |
| *XMLPay* | XMLPay is a standard proposed/developed by Ariba and Verisign. It defines an XML syntax for payment transaction requests, responses and receipts in a payment processing network. The intended users are Internet merchants and merchant aggregators who need to deal with multiple electronic payment mechanisms (credit/debit card, purchase card, electronic cheque and automated clearing house payment). The supported operations include funds authorization and capture, sales and repeat sales, and voiding of transactions. |
| *ECML* | The Electronic Commerce Modeling Language ECML is a specification that describes the format for data fields that need to be filled at checkout in an online transaction. The fields defined include shipping information, billing information, recipient information, payment card information and reference fields. Version 2.0 describes these fields in XML syntax. |
| *W3C standard on micropayments* | The W3C standard on micropayments has originated from IBM's standardization efforts. It covers the payment function for payment of digital goods. The Micropayment initiative specifies how to provide in a Web page all the information necessary to initialize a micropayment and transfer this information to the wallet for processing. The W3C Ecommerce/Micropayment Activity is now closed. |
| *Passport* | Microsoft Passport is an online user-authentication service. Passport's primary service is user authentication, referred to as the Passport single sign-in (SSI) service. Passport also offers two other optional services: Passport express purchase (EP), which lets users store credit card and billing/shipping address information in their optional Passport wallet profiles to expedite checkout at participating e-commerce sites, and Kids Passport (source: Microsoft Passport Technical White Paper). |
| *eWallet project of CEN/ISSS*[2] | CEN/ISSS Electronic Commerce Workshop initiated the eWallet project in mid-2001 assuming a need for standardization in the field. CEN/ISSS has chosen a flexible working definition considering an eWallet as "a collection of confidential data of a personal nature or relating to a role carried our by an individual, managed so as to facilitate completion of electronic transactions". |

*continued on following page*

| | |
|---|---|
| ***SEMPER*** | Secure Electronic Market Place for Europe (SEMPER) was produced by an EU supported project under a special program, undertaken by a 20 partner consortium led by IBM. It is a definition of an open and system independent architecture for Electronic Commerce. The project was concluded in 1999. Based on access via a browser, the architecture specifies common functions to be supported by applications which include Exchange of certificates, Exchange of signed offer/order, Fair contract signing, Fair payment for receipt, and Provision of delivery information. |
| ***IOTP*** | The Internet Open Trading Protocol (IOTP) is defined as an interoperable framework for Internet commerce. It is optimized for the case where the buyer and the merchant do not have a prior acquaintance. IOTP is payment system independent. It can encapsulate and support several of leading payment systems. |
| ***SEPP*** | Secure Electronic Payment Process is a protocol developed by MasterCard and Netscape to provide authentication, integrity and payment confidentiality. It uses DES for confidentiality and 512, 768, 1024 or 2048 bit RSA and 128 bit MD5 hashing. RSA encrypts DES key to encrypt hash of account numbers. It uses up to three public keys, one for signing, one for key exchange, one for certificate renewal. Besides, SEPP uses X.509 certificates with CMS at top of hierarchy[ 26]. |
| ***STT*** | Secure Transaction Technology was developed by Visa and Microsoft to provide authentication, integrity and confidentiality to the Internet based transactions. It is based on 64 bit DES or 64 bit RC4 (24-bit salt) for confidentiality and 512, 768, 1024 or 2048 bit RSA for encryption with 160 bit SHA hashing. It uses two public keys, one for signing, one for key exchange. It has credentials similar to certificates but with account details and higher level signatures, though they are not certificates. |
| ***JEPI*** | (Joint Electronic Payment Initiative) CommerceNet and the W3 Consortium are jointly initiating a multi-industry project to develop an Internet payment negotiation protocol. The project explores the technology required to provide negotiation over multiple payment instruments, protocols and transports. Examples of payment instruments include credit cards, debit cards, electronic cash and checks. Payment protocols include STT and SEPP (amongst others). Payment transport encompasses the message transmission mechanism: S-HTTP, SSL, SMTP, and TCP/IP are all categorized as transport technologies that can be used for payment. |

1 *The latest version of the specifications, EMV 2000 version 4.0, was published in December 2000 (http://www.emvco.com/).*

2 *CEN/ISSS was created in mid-1997 by CEN (European Committee for Standardization) and ISSS(Information Society Standardization) to provide with a comprehensive and integrated range of standardization-oriented services and products.*

# Compilation of References


Aalberts, B., & Van der Hof, S. (1999). *Digital Signature Blindness - Analysis of legislative approaches toward electronic authentication.* Tilburg, The Netherlands: Tilburg University. [Retrieved on October 28, 2007 from http://www.buscalegis.ufsc.br/busca.php?acao=abrir&id=15433]

Abraham, A. (2001). Neuro-Fuzzy Systems: State-of-the-Art Modeling Techniques, Connectionist Models of Neurons, Learning Processes, and Artificial Intelligence. *Lecture Notes in Computer Science Volume 2084,* J. Mira and A. Prieto (Eds.), Granada, Spain. Germany: Springer-Verlag, (pp. 269-276).

Abraham, A., Grosan, C., & Chen, Y. (2005). Cyber Security and the Evolution in Intrusion Detection Systems. *Journal of Engineering and Technology, ISSN 0973-2632, I-Manager Publications, 1*(1), 74-81.

Act IV of 1978 on the Criminal Code, Chapter XVII, Title I, Section 300/C, Criminal code of the Republic of Hungary, Section 300/C (2005).

Act IV of 1978 on the Criminal Code, Chapter XVII, Title I, Section 300/C, Paragraph 2a, Criminal code of the Republic of Hungary, Section 300/C, Paragraph 2a (2005).

Act IV of 1978 on the Criminal Code, Chapter XVII, Title I, Section 300/C, Criminal code of the Republic of Hungary, Section 300/E (2005).

Adams, C., & Lloyd, S., (2002). *Understanding PKI: Concepts, Standards, and Deployment Considerations. 2nd Edition.* Addison-Wesley Professional, USA.

Agrawal, R., & Sikant, R. (1994). Fast Algorithms for Mining Association rules in Large Databases. Proceedings of the *20th VLDB Conference,* Santiago, Chile. (pp. 487-499).

Akrivopoulou, Ch. (2007). Taking private law seriously in the application of Constitutional Rights. In D. Oliver & J. Fedtke (Eds.), *Human Rights and the Private Sphere* (pp.157-179). London & New York: Routledge.

Aladwani, A. M. (2001). Online banking: A field study of drivers, development challenges, and expectations. *Internal Journal of Information Management, 21*(3), 213–225.

Alderman, E., & Kennedy, C. (1997). *The Right to Privacy.* New York: Vintage.

Alivizatos, N. (2001). Privacy and Transparency: a difficult conciliation. In L.–A. Sicilianos & M. Gavouneli (Eds.), *Scientific and Technological developments & Human Rights,* (pp. 117-122). Athens: Ant. N. Sakkoulas Publishers.

Alivizatos, N., & Eleutheriadis, P. (2002). The Greek Constitutional Amendments of 2001, *South European Society & Politics, 7*(1), 63-71.

Allan, A. (2002). *[Technology Overview] Intrusion Detection Systems (IDSs): Perspective.* Gartner Research Report (DPRO-95367).

*America Online, Inc. v. IMS,* 24 F. Supp. 2d 548 (E.D. Va. 1998)

*America Online, Inc. v. LCGM, Inc.,* 46 F. Supp. 2d 444 (E.D. Va. 1998)

*America Online, Inc. v. Nat'l Health Care Disc., Inc.*, 121 F. Supp. 2d 1255 (N.D. Iowa 2000)

American Government Accountability Office (GAO) (2005). *Information Security, Radio Frequency Identification Technology in the Federal Government.* From http://www.gao.gov/new.items/d05551.pdf

Ammann, T., Lehnhard, M., Meißner, G., Stahl, S. (1989). Hacker für Moskau. Reinbek: Wunderlich Verlag.

Anderson, D., Lunt, T. F., Javits, H., Tamaru, A., & Valdes, A. (1995). Detecting unusual program behavior using the statistical components of NIDES. *NIDES Technical Report*, SRI International, May 1995.

Anti-Corruption Law 161/2003, Chapter III, Section 1, Article 42-1 Romanian Anti-Corruption Law 161/2003, Article 42-1 (2003).

Anti-Corruption Law 161/2003, Chapter III, Section 1, Article 44-1 Romanian Anti-Corruption Law 161/2003, Article 44-1 (2003).

Anti-Corruption Law 161/2003, Chapter III, Section 1, Article 45 Romanian Anti-Corruption Law 161/2003, Article 45 (2003).

Anti-Corruption Law 161/2003, Chapter III, Section 1, Article 46 Romanian Anti-Corruption Law 161/2003, Article 46 (2003).

Article 29 Data Protection Working Party, *Opinion 8/2001.*

Article 29 Data Protection Working Party, *Working document on the surveillance of electronic communications in the workplace*, adopted on 29 May 2002, 5401/01/EN/Final, WP 55.

Ayoade J. (2007). Roadmap to solving security and privacy concerns in RFID systems. *Computer Law & Security Report, 23*(2007), p. 557.

Azari, R. (2003). *Current Security Management & Ethical Issues of Information Technology.* Hershey, PA: IRM Press.

B. M. P. Global Distribution Inc. v. Bank of Nova Scotia (c.o.b. Scotiabank), B.C.J. No. 1662.

Bannier, C. (2001). Privacy or Publicity –Who drives the Wheel? *CFS Working Chapter Archive, No 2003/29.* Retrieved from: www.ifk-cfs.de/chapters/03_21_revised.pdf

Banzhaf, W., Nordin, P., Keller. E. R., & Francone F. D. (1998). *Genetic Programming: An Introduction on The Automatic Evolution of Computer Programs and its Applications.* Morgan Kaufmann Publishers, Inc.

Basel (2001). Basel Committee on Banking Supervision. *Overview of The New Basel Capital Accord.* Bank of International Settlements.

Basel Committee (2001). Risk management principles for electronic banking. *Basel Committee publications No. 82.*

Bauer, K., & Hein, S. E. (2006). The effect of heterogeneous risk on the early adoption of Internet banking technologies. *Journal of Banking and Finance, 30*, 1713–1725.

*BBC News.* (2008, June 27). Spam fighters lay down gauntlet. *BBC News.* Retrieved http://news.bbc.co.uk/1/hi/technology/7477899.stm

Bell, A., & Sejnowski, T. (1995). An information-maximization approach to blind separation and blind deconvolution. *Neural Comput., 7*, 1129-1159.

Bellia, P. L. (2004). Defending Cyberproperty. *New York University Law Review,* (79), 2164.

Bennett, C. (1992). *Regulating Privacy, Data protection and Public Policy in Europe and the United States.* Ithaca, New York: Cornell University Press, 1992.

Bergfeld, J. P. (1996). EC Data Protection Directive, impact on Dutch Data Protection Law. *The Journal of Information, Law and Technology (JILT), 1.* http://elj.warwick.ac.uk/elj/jilt/dp/1dutch/

Berghel, H. (2008). BRAP Forensics. *Communications of the ACM, 51*(6), 15-20.

Bernard, S. (2004). *An Introduction to Enterprise Architecture.* Bloomington, IN: AuthorHouse.

Beugelsdijk R. (2006). RFID, Promising or irresponsible? Contribution to the social debate about RFID. *College bescherming persoonsgegevens*. The Hague, October 2006.

Bischof, J., & Alexander, T. (1997). *Data Warehouse*. New York: Prentice Hall. (pp 310-313).

Bishop, M. (2003). *Computer Security – Art and Science*. Addison Wesley.

Bohle, K. (2001). *Integration of Internet Payment Systems – What's the Problem*? ePSO (E-payments systems Observatory)–Newsletter. (Retrieved on 3/1/3 from http://epso.jrc.es/newsletter/vol11/5.html)

Borges, G., & Schwenk, J. (2007). *Identitätsschutz: eine zentrale Herausforderung für IT und E-Commerce*. Available online at: https://www.a-i3.org/images/stories/recht/itgipfel_paper061218.pdf

Bouchet, H. (2002). *Cyber-Surveillance in the Workplace*, report adopted by the CNIL, 2002, p. 11, online available at: http://www.cnil.fr/fileadmin/documents/uk/CNIL-cybersurveillance-feb2002-VA.pdf

Bowden, C. (2002). Closed circuit television for inside your head: blanket traffic data retention and the emergency anti-terrorism legislation. *Duke Law & Technology Review, 5*.

Boyd, C., & Mathuria, A. (2003). *Protocols for Key Establishment and Authentication*, Springer-Verlag, Berlin and Heidelberg GmbH & Co., Germany.

Boyle, J. (1997). Foucault in Cyberspace: Surveillance, Sovereignty, and Hardwired Censors. *University of Cincinnati Law Review*, (66), 177.

Brandeis, L, Warren S. (1890). The Right to Privacy. *Harvard Law Review*, 4, 193-220.

Brands, S.A. (2000), *Rethinking Public Key Infrastructures and Digital Certificates: Building in Privacy*. MIT Press, USA.

Brenner, S. (2001). *Cybercrime Investigation and Prosecution: the Role of Penal and Procedural Law*. Available at http://www.murdoch.edu.au

Brenner, S. (2004). Cybercrime Metrics: Old Wine, New Bottles? *Virginia Journalof Law & Technology*, *9*(13), 3-52.

Brenner, S. (2006). Cybercrime: re-thinking crime control strategies. In Y. Jewkes (Ed.), *Crime Online, Committing, Policing and Regulating Cybercrime*. Devon: Willan Publishing.

Brieman, L., Friedman, J., Olshen, R., & Stone, C. (1984). *Classification of Regression Trees*. Wadsworth Inc.

Brin D. (1999). *The transparent society: Will technology force us to choose between privacy and freedom?* Cambridge & Massachusetts: Perseus Publishing.

Brito J. (2004). Relax Don't Do It: Why Rfid Privacy Concerns are Exaggerated and Legislation is Premature., *UCLA Journal of Law and Technology*, (5), 2.

Bruin, R. de (2002). *Consumer Trust in Electronic Commerce: Time for Best Practice*. Kluwer Law.

*BSA-ISSA Information Security Survey*. (2005). Available at http://www.issa.org

Buchholz, C. (2002). Digital Identities and Federations. *Datenschutz und Datensicherheit* (9), 527.

Budowle, B., Carmody, G., Chakraborty, R., & Monson, K. L. (2000). Source attribution of a forensic DNA profile. In *Forensic Science Communications*, *2*(3), FBI Laboratory. From http://www.fbi.gov/hq/lab/fsc/backissu/july2000/source.htm

Burk, D. L. (2000). The Trouble with Trespass. *Journal of Small & Emerging Business Law*, (4), 27.

Burk, R., (2005). *Enabling citizen-centered electronic government: 2005-2006 FEA PMO action plan*. White paper, Office of E-Government and Technology.

Burt, S. (2002). *Online Banking: Striving for Compliance in Cyberspace*. Bankers Systems Inc. article. (Retrieved on 9/5/02 from http://www.bankerssystems.com/compliance/article13.html)

C-46, Criminal Code, Invasions of Privacy, Section 183, Canadian Criminal Code, Section 183 et seq. (1985).

Caelli, W., Longley, D., & Shain, M. (1991). *Information Security Handbook*. Macmillan.

Calabresi, G., & Melamed, A. D. (1972). Property Rules, Liability Rules, and Inalienability: One View of the Cathedral. *Harvard Law Review*, (85), 1089.

Camisch, J., Hohenberger, S., Karjoth, G., Meints, M., & Wohlgemuth, S. (2007). Privacy-aware Business Process Design and Identity Management. In *FIDIS Deliverable, D13.2: Study on Privacy in Business Processes by Identity Management*, online available at: www.fidis.net

Canadian Charter of Rights and Freedoms, Part I of the Constitution Act, 1982, being, Schedule B to the Canada Act 1982 (U.K.), 1982, c.11 s. 7.

Canadian Standards Association. (November 19, 2007). *CSA Model Code for Privacy Protection*. Retrieved November 20, 2007, from http://www.csa.ca/standards/privacy/code/Default.asp?articleID=5286&language=English

Cannataci, J. A., & Mifsud-Bonnici, J. P. (2005). Data Protection Comes of Age: The Data Protection Clauses in the European Constitutional Treaty. *Information & Communications Technology Law*, *14*(1), 5-15.

Cardoso, J.-F. (1999). High-order contrasts for independent component analysis. *Neural Comput.*, *11*, 157-192.

Cardozo, B. (1921). *The Nature of The Judicial Process*. New Haven, CT: Yale University Press.

Carrier, B. (2003). Defining Digital Forensic Examination and Analysis Tools Using Abstraction Layers. *International Journal of Digital Evidence*, Winter 2003a. http://www.ijde.org.

Carrier, M., & Lastowka, G. (2007). Against Cyberproperty. *Berkeley Technology Law Journal*, (22), 1483.

Carter, D. (1995). *Computer Crime Categories: How Techno-criminals Operate*. Available at http://nsi.org/Library/Compsec/crimecom.html

Casey, E. (2004). *Digital evidence and computer crime* (second edition). Amsterdam: Elsevier.

Cavoukian, A. (1999). *Privacy and Biometrics*. online available at: http://www.pcpd.org.hk/english/infocentre/files/cakoukian-paper.doc

CDT Working Group on RFID (2006). *Best Practices for Deployment of RFID Technology of the Center for Democracy and Technology*, Interim Draft, May 1, 2006. Retrieved from http://www.cdt.org/privacy/20060501rfid-best-practices.php

CEC (2001). Communication From The Commission to the Council, the European Parliament, the European Economic and Social Committee and the Committee of the Regions, *Network And Information Security: Proposal For A European Policy Approach*.

Chander, A (2003). The New, New Property. *Texas Law Review*, (81), 715.

Chapter 9, Criminal Code, Book First, Part II, Title IX, Section 337C, Paragraph 1, Criminal Code of the Republic of Malta, Section 337C (2004).

Chapter 9, Criminal Code, Book First, Part II, Title IX, Section 337D (a), Criminal Code of the Republic of Malta, Section 337D (a) (2004).

Chapter 9, Criminal Code, Book First, Part II, Title IX, Section 337F, Paragraph 2, Criminal Code of the Republic of Malta, Section 337F (2004).

Chawki, M., & Wahab, M. S. (2006). Identity Theft in Cyberspace: Issues and Solutions. *Lex Electronica*, *11*(1), available online at: http://www.lex-electronica.org/articles/v11-1/chawki_abdel-wahab.htm

Chebrolu, S., Abraham, A., & Thomas, J. P. (2004). Hybrid Feature Selection for Modeling Intrusion Detection Systems. *11th International Conference on Neural Information Processing*.

Cheng, J., Greiner, R., Kelly, J., Bell, D. A., & Liu, W. (2002). Learning Bayesian Networks from Data: an Information-Theory Based Approach. *The Artificial Intelligence Journal*, *137*, 43-90.

Cheng, T. (2004). Recent international attempts to can spam. *Computer Law & Security Report*, *20*(6), 472-479.

Cheng, T. C. E., Lam, D. Y. C., & Yeung, A. C. L. (2006). Adoption of Internet banking: An empirical study in Hong Kong. *Decision Support Systems, 42*(3), 1558–1572.

Chia, C. C., Jiann-Min, Y., & W.-Y., Jen (2007). Determining technology and forecasts of RFID by a historical review and bibliometric analysis from 1991 to 2005. *Technovation*, Vol. 27, Issue 5, May 2007, p.p. 268-279.

Cho, S.-B., & Park, H.-J. (2003). Efficient anomaly detection by modeling privilege flows with hidden Markov model. *Computers & Security, 22*(1), 45-55.

Chochliouros, I. P., & Spiliopoulou, A. S. (2003). Perspectives for Achieving Competition and Development in the European Information and Communications technologies (ICT) Markets, *The Journal of the Communications Network, 2(3)*, 42-50.

Chochliouros, I. P., & Spiliopoulou, A. S. (2005). Broadband Access in the European Union: An Enabler for Technical Progress, Business Renewal and Social Development, *The International Journal of Infonomics (IJI), vol.1, January 2005*, 05-21.

Chochliouros, I. P., & Spiliopoulou, A.S. (2003). Innovative Horizons for Europe: The New European Telecom Framework for the Development of Modern Electronic Networks and Services. *The Journal of The Communications Network, 2*(4), 53-62.

Chochliouros, I. P., Chochliouros, S. P., Spiliopoulou, A. S., & Lambadari, E. (2007). Public Key Infrastructures (PKI): A Means for Increasing Network Security. In L. J. Janczewski & A. M. Colarik (Eds.), *Cyber Warfare and Cyber Terrorism*, (pp. 281-290). Hershey-PA: Information Science Reference.

Chua, C. E. H., & Wareham, J. (2004). Fighting Internet Auction Fraud: An Assessment and Proposal. *IEEE Computer, 37*(10), 31-37.

Cichocki, A., & Barros, A. K. (1999). Robust batch algorithm for sequential blind extraction of noisy biomedical signals. *Proc. ISSPA'99, 1*, 363-366.

CIO Council (1999, September). *Federal Enterprise Architecture Framework Version 1.1.* White paper.

CIO Council (2005). *FY07 Budget Formulation FEA Consolidated Reference Model.* White paper.

CIO Council, (2001, February). *A Practical Guide to Federal Enterprise Architecture*, Version 1.0, Federal Chief Information Officers Council.

Ciocchetti, C. A. (2001). Monitoring Employee e-mail: Efficient Workplaces vs. Employee Privacy. *Duke law & Technology Review.*

Claessens, J., Dem, V., De Cock, D., Preneel, B., & Vandewalle, J. (2002). On the security of today's online electronic banking systems. *Computers and Security, 21*(3), 257 269.

Clarke, I., Zugelder, M. T., & Flaherty, T. B. (2005). The CAN-SPAM Act: New rules for sending commercial e-mail messages and implications for the sales force. *Industrial Marketing Management, 34*(4), 399-405.

Code Penal, Book II, Title IX, Chapter II, Section VII, Article 509-1. Penal Code of the Grand Duche of Luxembourg, Article 509-1 (1993).

Code Penal, Book II, Title IX, Chapter II, Section VII, Article 509-4. Penal Code of the Grand Duche of Luxembourg, Article 509-4 (1993).

Code Penal, Book II, Title IX, Chapter II, Section VII, Article 509-7. Penal Code of the Grand Duche of Luxembourg, Article 509-7 (1993).

Code Penal, Book II, Title IXbis, Article 550bis, Belgian Penal Code, Article 550bis (2007).

Code Penal, Book III, Title II, Chapter III, Article 323-1, Criminal Code of the French Republic, Article 323-1 (2002).

Code Penal, Book III, Title II, Chapter III, Article 323-2, Criminal Code of the French Republic, Article 323-2 (2002).

Code Penal, Book III, Title II, Chapter III, Article 323-3-1, Criminal Code of the French Republic, Article 323-3-1 (2002).

Code Penal, Book III, Title II, Chapter III, Article 323-4, Criminal Code of the French Republic, Article 323-4 (2002).

Codice Penale, Libro II, Titolo XII, Capo II, Sezione IV, Artt 615 quinquis, Italian Penal Code, Arti 615 quinquies (1999).

Codice Penale, Libro II, Titolo XII, Capo III, Sezione IV, Artt 615 ter, Italian Penal Code, Artt 615 ter (1999).

Codice Penale, Libro II, Titolo XII, Capo III, Sezione V, Artt 617 bis and 623 bis, Italian Penal Code, Artt 617 bis and 623 bis (1999).

CoE (2001). Council of Europe. *Explanatory Report to the Convention on Cybercrime.*

CoE (2001). Council of Europe, *Convention on Cybercrime and explanatory memorandum*, Strasbourg, France: European Committee on Crime Problems.

Cohen, J. (1996). The right to read anonymously: a closer look at copyright management. In Cyberspace, *Connecticut Law Review, 28*(3), 981-1039.

Cohen, J. (2000). Examined lives: informational privacy and the subject as object. *Stanford Law Review, 52(5),* 1373-1438.

Cohen, J. (2003). DRM and Privacy, *Berkely Technology Law Journal, 18*(2), 575-617.

Cohen, J. (2003). *Regulating Intimacy: A new legal paradigm.* Prineceton: Princeton University Press.

Cohen, R., & Hiller, J. S. (2003). Towards a Theory of Cyberplace: A Proposal for a New Legal Framework. *Richmond Journal of Law & Technology,* (10), 2.

Cohen, W. W. (1995). Fast effective rule induction. *Proceedings of the 12th International Conference on Machine Learning,* (pp. 115-123), July 1995.

Collins, J. M. (2006). *Investigating Identity Theft: A Guide for Businesses, Law Enforcement, and Victims.* New Jersey: Wiley.

Colonia-Willner, R. (2004). Self-service systems: New methodology reveals customer real-time actions during merger. *Computers in Human Behavior, 20,* 243–267.

Commission nationale de l'informatique et des libertés. Séance du 30 octobre 2003. Communication de M. Philippe Lemoine relative à la Radio-Identification (Radio-Tags ou RFIDs), p. 1. Retrieved from http://www.cnil.fr

Commission of the European Communities (2006). *Report on the operation of Directive 1999/93/EC on a Community framework for electronic signatures [COM(2006) 120final, 15.03.2006].* Brussels, Belgium: Commission of the European Communities.

Communication from the Commission to the Council, the European Parliament, The Economic and Social Committee and the Committee of the Regions. (2001). *Creating a Safer Information Society by Improving the Security of Information Infrastructures and Combating Computer-related Crime.* Brussels, 26.1.2001. Available at http://europa.eu.int/ISPO/eif/InternetPoliciesSite/Crime/CrimeCommEN.html

*CompuServe, Inc. v. Cyber Promotions, Inc.*, 962 F. Supp. 1015 (S.D. Ohio 1997);

Computer Misuse Act 1990, Chapter 18, Article 1, Section 1a (1990).

Cooley T. M. (1888). *Law of Torts*, 2d ed. Chicago: Callaghan.

Coppersmith, D. (1994). The data encryption standard (DES) and its strength against attacks, *IBM Journal of Research and Development, 38*(3), 243-250.

*Council of Europe Convention for the Protection of Individuals with Regard to Automatic Processing of Personal Data* (1981). Retrieved on November 23, 2008 from http://conventions.coe.int/Treaty/en/Treaties/Html/108.htm

Council of Europe, *Convention on Cybercrime*, Budapest 2001.

Cox, I. J., Leighton, F. T., & Shamoon T. (1997). Secure spread spectrum watermarking for multimedia. *IEEE Trans. on Image Processing, 6*, 1673-1687.

Cox, I. J., Miller, M. L., & Bloom, J. A. (2002). *Digital Watermarking.* Morgan Kaufmann Publishers.

Cribbet, J. E. (1986). Concepts in Transition: The Search for a New Definition of Property. *University of Illinois Law Review,* (1986), 1.

Criminal Code of the Republic of Albania, Special Part, Chapter II, Section VIII, Article 122, Criminal Code of the Republic of Albania, Article 122 (2001).

Criminal Code of the Republic of Albania, Special Part, Chapter III, Section VII, Article 192/b, Criminal Code of the Republic of Albania, Article 192/b (2001).

Criminal Code, Chapter 27, Article 298, Criminal Code of the Republic of Serbia, Article 298 (2006).

Criminal Code, Chapter 27, Article 299, Criminal Code of the Republic of Serbia, Article 299 (2006).

Criminal Code, Chapter 27, Article 300, Criminal Code of the Republic of Serbia, Article 300 (2006).

Criminal Code, Chapter 27, Article 302, Paragraph 1, Criminal Code of the Republic of Serbia, Article 302, Paragraph 1 (2006).

Criminal Code, Chapter 27, Article 302, Paragraph 3, Criminal Code of the Republic of Serbia, Article 302, Paragraph 3 (2006).

Criminal Code, Part 2, Special Section, Title 4, Section 246, Criminal Code of the Slovak Republic, Section 246 (2005).

Criminal Code, Part 2, Special Section, Title 4, Section 247, Paragraph 1b, Criminal Code of the Slovak Republic, Section 247, Paragraph 1b (2005).

Criminal Code, Part 2, Special Section, Title 4, Section 247, Paragraph 1c-d, Criminal Code of the Slovak Republic, Section 247, Paragraph 1c-d (2005).

Criminal Code, Part 2, Special Section, Title 4, Section 247, Paragraph 2a, Criminal Code of the Slovak Republic, Section 247, Paragraph 2a (2005).

Criminal Code, Part 2, Special Section, Title 9, Section 257, Criminal Code of the Czech Republic, Section 257 (2006).

Criminal Code, Second Volume, Third Chapter, Tenth Section, Article 243, Paragraph 1, Criminal Code of the Republic of Turkey, Article 243 (2004).

Criminal Code, Second Volume, Third Chapter, Tenth Section, Article 244, Paragraph 4, Criminal Code of the Republic of Turkey, Article 244 (2004).

Criminal Code, Special Part, Chapter 17, Section 223-1, Croatian Criminal Code, Section 223-1 (2003).

Criminal Code, Special Part, Chapter 17, Section 223-3, Croatian Criminal Code, Section 223-3 (2003).

Criminal Code, Special Part, Chapter 17, Section 223-4, Croatian Criminal Code, Section 223-4 (2003).

Criminal Code, Special Part, Chapter 17, Section 223-5, Croatian Criminal Code, Section 223-5 (2003).

Criminal Code, Special Part, Chapter 17, Section 223-6,7, Croatian Criminal Code, Section 223-6,7 (2003).

Criminal Code, Special Part, Chapter 23, Section 251-1, Criminal code of the former Yugoslav Republic of Macedonia, Section 251-1 (2004).

Criminal Code, Special Part, Chapter 23, Section 251-3 to 251-5, Criminal code of the former Yugoslav Republic of Macedonia, Section 251-3 to 251-5 (2004).

Criminal Code, Special Part, Chapter 23, Section 251-6, Criminal code of the former Yugoslav Republic of Macedonia, Section 251-6 (2004).

Criminal Code, Special Part, Chapter 23, Section 251a-1,3, Criminal code of the former Yugoslav Republic of Macedonia, Section 251a-1,3 (2004).

Criminal Code, Title 4, Chapter 15, Section 201, German Criminal Code, Section 201 (2008).

Criminal Code, Title 4, Chapter 15, Section 202a, German Criminal Code, Section 202a (1998).

Criminal Code, Title 4, Chapter 15, Section 202c, German Criminal Code, Section 202c (2008).

Criminal Code, Title 4, Chapter 27, Section 303a, German Criminal Code, Section 303a (2008).

Criminal Code, Title 4, Chapter 27, Section 303b, German Criminal Code, Section 303b (2008).

CSI. (2007). *The 12th Annual Computer Crime and Security Survey.*

*Cyber Promotions, Inc. v. America Online, Inc.*, 948 F. Supp. 436 (E.D. Pa. 1996);

Däubler, W. (2002). *Gläserne Belegschaften? Datenschutz in Betrieb und Dienststelle, 4.* Aufl., 2002.

Davies, S. (n.d.). *New Techniques and Technologies of Surveillance in the Workplace.* Online available at: http://www.amicustheunion.org/pdf/surveillencetechniques.pdf

Davoine, F., Bas, P., Hébert, P.-A., & Chassery, J.-M. (1999). Watermarking et résistance aux déformations géométriques. *Cinquièmes journées d'études et d'échanges sur la compression et la représentation des signaux audiovisuels (CORESA'99)*, Sophia-Antiplis, France.

Debar, H., Becker, M., & Siboni, D. (1992). A neural network component for an intrusion detection system. *Proceedings of 1992 IEEE Computer Society Symposium on Research in Security and Privacy*, Oakland, CA, May 1992, (pp. 240-250).

Delaitre, S. (2005). Identity schemas in ubiquitous (and mobile computing). In: *FIDIS, D2.3: Models.*

Delbar, C., Mormont, M., Schots, M. (2003). *New technology and respect for privacy at the workplace. MSF Information Professionals' Association*, London School of Economics, London. Available from: http://www.eiro.eurofund.eu.int/print/2003/07/study/TN0307101S.html

DeLotto, R. (1999). *Competitive Intelligence for the E-Financial Service Provider.* Gartner Group Research Report.

Dempsey, J. X. (2003). *Creating the Legal Framework for ICT Development: The Example of E-Signature Legislation in Emerging Market Economies.* Washington, DC: Center for Democracy and Technology. *Information Technologies and International Development (ITID), 1*(2), 39-52. [Retrieved on September 17, 2007, from www.internetpolicy.net/e-commerce/20030900esignature.pdf]

Demsetz, H. (1967). Toward a Theory of Property Rights. *American Economic Review* (57), 347.

Denning, D. E. (1987). An Intrusion-Detection Model. *IEEE Transactions on Software Engineering, SE-13*(2), 222-232.

Department of Trade and Industry (DTI). (2006). *Information Security Breaches Survey (ISBS)*, Technical Report. Available at http://www.dti.gov.uk/

Desrochers, S., & Roussos, A. (2001). The Jurisprudence of Surveillance: a Critical Look at the Laws of Intimacy. *Lex Electronica, 6*(2). Online available at: http://www.lex-electronica.org/articles/v6-2/desroussos.htm

Diary of the Republic, Series 1, Law 109/91, Chapter 2, Article 7, Paragraph 1, Portuguese Criminal Law, Article 7, Paragraph 1 (1991).

Diffie, W., & Hellman, M. (1976). New Directions in Cryptography, *IEEE Transactions on Information Theory, IT-22*(6), 644-654.

Direct Marketing Association. (November 19, 2007). *Survey: 1 in 4 Credit Reports Contain Errors.* Retrieved November 19, 2007, from http://www.thedma.org/cgi/dispnewsstand?article=2440

Directive 2002/58/EC of the European Parliament and of the Council of 12 July 2002 concerning the processing of personal data and the protection of privacy in the electronic communications sector (Directive on privacy and electronic communications), *Official Journal of the European Communities*, 31.7.2002, L 201/37.

Directive 95/46/EC of the European Parliament and of the Council of 24 October 1995 on the protection of individuals with regard to the processing of personal data and on the free movement of such data, *Official journal of the European Communities*, 23. 11. 95, n. L 281/31.

Dittrich, D. (1999). *Incident Response Steps.* Lecture series at University of Washington.

DOJ (2001). *Electronic Crime Scene Investigation: A Guide for first responders.* Washington, DC: United States Department of Justice.

Doyle, E. (2004 November/December). Spam rules – and there's nothing you can do. *Elsevier Infosecurity Today*, (pp. 24-28).

Dugad, R., Ratakonda, K., & Ahuja, N. (1998). A new wavelet-based scheme for watermarking images. *Proc. of IEEE ICIP.*

Dugelay, J.-L., & Petitcolas, F. A. P. (2000). Possible counter-attacks against random geometric distortions. *Proc. SPIE Security and Watermarking of Multimedia Contents II, 3971*, California, USA.

Dumortier, J., & Goemans, C. (2004). Legal Challenges for Privacy Protection and Identity Management. In *Proceedings of the NATO/NASTEC Workshop on Advanced Security Technologies in Networking*, Bled (Slovenia) 15-18 September 2003, pp. 191-212.

Dumortier, J., Kelm, S., Nillson, H., Skouma, G., & Van Eecke, P. (2003). *The Legal and Market Aspects of Electronic Signatures. Study for the European Commission - DG Information Society (Service Contract Nr. C28.400).* Brussels, Belgium: The Interdisciplinary Centre for Law & Information Technology & Katholieke Universiteit Leuven. [Retrieved on February 24, 2006, from europa.eu.int/information_society/eeurope/2005/all_about/security/electronic_sig_report.pdf]

Dzeroski, S., & Zenko, B. (2002). Is Combining Classifiers Better than Selecting the Best One? *ICML 2002*, 123-130.

Easterbrook, F. H. (1996). Cyberspace and the Law of the Horse. *University of Chicago Legal Forum,* (1996), 207.

*Eastmond v. Canadian Pacific Railway.* [2004]. F.C.J. No. 1043.

*eBay, Inc. v. Bidder's Edge, Inc.*, 100 F. Supp. 2d 1058 (N.D. Cal. 2000).

EC Directive 95/46/EC of the European Parliament and of the Council of 24 October 1995.

ECPA Pub. L. 99-508, Oct. 21, 1986, 100 Stat. 1848, 18 U.S.C. § 2510.

*E-Crime Watch Survey*, 2006.

*E-Crime Watch Survey*, 2007.

eEurope (2002). *Identification and Authentication in eGovernment.* eEurope Smart Card Charter TB2, A policy report.

El Sawy, O., Malhotra, A., Gosain, S., & Young, K. (1999). IT Intensive value innovation in the electronic economy: Insights from Marshall Industries. *MIS Quarterly, 23*(3), 305-335.

Elden, L. (2007). Matrix Methods in Data Mining and Pattern Recognition. *SIAM 2007.*

*Electronic Monitoring & Surveillance Survey, 2007.* http://www.amanet.org/movingahead/editorial.cfm?Ed=697

ENISA (2005). *Raising Awareness in Information Security - Insight and Guidance for Member States.* Heraklion, Crete: ENISA.

ENISA (2006). *Mapping the regulatory NIS activities of Europe: ENISA publishing inventory & assessment report on EU regulatory activity in NIS.* Heraklion, Crete: ENISA.

EPIC, Electronic Privacy Information Center (2004). *EPIC questions to RFID industry, Summary of Manufacturers and Retailers' Answers.* Retrieved from http://www.epic.org/privacy/rfid/survey.html

EPIC. *Workplace Privacy*, online available at: http://epic.org/privacy/workplace

Epstein, R. A. (2003). Cybertrespass. *University of Chicago Law Review* (70), 73.

Epstein, R. A. (2005). Intel v. Hamidi: The Role of Self-Help in Cyberspace. *Journal of Law, Economics & Policy,* (1), 147.

Eriksson, K., & Nilsson, D. (2007). Determinants of the continued use of self-service technology: The case of Internet banking. *Technovation, 27,* 159–167.

Eschet, G. (2004). FIPs and PETs for RFID: protecting privacy on the web of radio frequency identification. *Jurimetrics, The Journal of Law, Science and Technology, 45*, 44.

Eurescom (European Institute for Research and Strategic Studies in Telecommunications) GmbH (2000).

*EURESCOM Project P944: Impact of PKI on the European Telecommunications Business. Deliverable 1, Main Report, January 2000.* Heidelberg, Germany: Eurescom GmbH.

European Commission (2001). *Communication on Network and Information Security: Proposal for a European Policy Approach, [COM (2001) 298 final, 06.06.2001].* Brussels, Belgium: European Commission.

European Commission (2002). *Communication on eEurope 2005: An information society for all - An Action Plan, [COM(2002) 263 final, 28.05.2002].* Brussels, Belgium: European Commission.

European Commission (2003). *Communication on Electronic Communications: the Road to the Knowledge Economy, [COM(2003) 65 final, 11.02.2003].* Brussels, Belgium: European Commission.

European Commission (2004). *Communication on Connecting Europe at high speed: recent developments in the sector of electronic communications, [COM(2004) 61 final, 03.02.2004].* Brussels, Belgium: European Commission.

European Parliament and Council of the European Union (1999). *Directive 1999/93/EC of 13 December 1999, on a Community framework for electronic signatures, (Official Journal (OJ) L13, 19.01.2000, pp.12-20).* Brussels, Belgium: European Parliament and Council of the European Union.

European Union. (2001). *Data protection: "Junk" e-mail costs internet users 10 billion a year worldwide* (EU Reference Number IP/01/154). Brussels: European Commission Study.

Fairfield, J. A. T. (2005). Virtual Property. *Boston University Law Review,* (85), 1047.

Fazekas, C. P. (2004). 1984 is still fiction: Electronic Monitoring in the Workplace and U.S. Privacy Law. *Duke Law & Technology Review* 2004, *15*. Online available at: http://www.law.duke.edu/journals/dltr/articles/pdf/2004dltr0015.pdf

FDIC (Federal Deposit Insurance Corporation) (2001). Authentication in Electronic Banking. *Financial Institution Letters.*

Federal Privacy Commissioner (Australia) (2001). *Privacy and Public Key Infrastructure: Guidelines for Agencies using PKI to communicate or transact with individuals*, online available at: http://www.privacy.gov.au/government/guidelines/#a

Federal Privacy Commissioner (Australia), (2001). *Privacy Issues in the Use of Public Key Infrastructure for Individuals and Possible Guidelines for Handling Privacy Issues in the Use of PKI for Individuals by Commonwealth agencies*, online available at: http://www.privacy.org.au/Papers/PCPKIGs0107.doc.

Federal Trade Commission (2003). *Identity Theft Survey Report*, online available at: http://www.ftc.gov/os/2003/09/synovatereport.pdf

Federal Trade Commission (2006). *Identity Theft Survey Report*, available at: http://www.ftc.gov/os/2007/11/SynovateFinalReportIDTheft2006.pdf

Feghhi, J., Williams, P., and Feghhi J. (1998). *Digital Certificates: Applied Internet Security.* Addison-Wesley, MA, USA.

Fetterly, D., Manasse M., & Najork, M. (2004). *Proceedings from 7th International Workshop on the Web and Databases.* Paris, France.

*FIDIS Deliverable D2.3: 'Models'*; available online at: http://www.fidis.net/resources/deliverables/identity-of-identity/int-d2300/

*FIDIS, 'D 2.1: Inventory of topics and cluster'*, p. 27 et seq., available online at: http://www.fidis.net

FIDIS. (2006). *Forensic Implications of identity Management Systems.* URL: http://www.fidis.net

FIPS (Federal Information Processing Standard) (1992). *Security Requirements for Cryptographic Modules.* Federal Information Processing Standard 140-1. National Institute of Standards and Technology.

Firesmith, D. G. (2003). Engineering security requirements. *Journal of Object Technology, 2*(1), 53-68.

Flegel, U. (2007). Privacy-Respecting Intrusion Detection. *Series: Advances in Information Security, 35.* Springer: New York.

Flint, D. (2006). RFID tags, security and the individual. *Computer Law & Security Report* (22 ), 165-168.

Ford, W., & Baum, M. (2001). *Secure Electronic Commerce (2nd edition).* Prentice-Hall, Upper River Saddle.

Ford, W., & Baum, M. (2001). *Secure Electronic Commerce* (2nd edition). Prentice-Hall.

Forrest, S., Perelson, A. S., Allen, L., & Cherukuri, R. (1994). Self-Nonself Discrimination in a Computer. *Proceedings of the 1994 IEEE Symposium on Research in Security and Privacy.* Los Alamitos, CA: IEEE Computer Society Press.

Fraser, J. (2005). Telecommunications (Lawful Business Practice) (Interception of Communications) Regulations 2000 Workplace Surveillance, Privacy and New Technologies. In L. Edwards (Ed.), *The New Legal Framework for E-Commerce in Europe*, (pp. 277-291).

Frawley, W., Piatevsky-Shapiro, G., & Matheus, C. J. (1991). An Overview of Knowledge Discovery in Databases. *Knowledge Discovery in Databases.* AAAI/MIT Press. (pp. 1-27).

Frayssinet J. (2001). La protection des données personnelles. In Lucas, Deveze & Fraussinet, *Droit de l'informatique et de l'Internet,* Thémis, Droit privé, PUF, Paris, 2001, p. 1.

Fried, C. (1968). Privacy. *Yale Law Review, 77,* 475-493.

Froomkin, M. (1995). Anonymity and its enmities, *Journal of Online Law, 1*(art. 4). Retrieved from: http://articles.umlawnet/froomkin/AnonymityEnmities.html

Froomkin, M. (1996). Flood control on the internet ocean: living with anonymity, digital cash, and distributed databases. *University of Pittsburg Journal of Law and Commerce, 15*(2), 395-453.

Froomkin, M. (2000). The death of privacy? *Stanford Law Review, 52*(5), 1461-1543.

Fukuyama, F. (1992). *The end of history and the last man.* New York, New York: Avon Books.

Furnell, S. (2004). E-commerce security: A question of trust. *Computer Fraud and Security, 10,* 10–14.

Furnell, S. (2007). Identity impairment: The problems facing victims of identity fraud. *Computer Fraud & Security,* (12), 6-11.

Furnell, S. (2007). An Assessment of website password practices. *Computer Law & Security Report* (7-8), 445-451.

Furnell, S. (2008). Security usability challenges for end-users. In M. Gupta & R. Sharman (Eds.), *Social and Human Elements of Information Security: Emerging Trends and Countermeasures.* IGI Global Inc publishing, Hershey, PA. September 2008.

Gajek, S., Schwenk, J., & Wegener, C. (2005) Identitätsmissbrauch im Onlinebanking. *Datenschutz und Datensicherheit,* (11), 639-642.

Ganley, P. (2002). Access to the Individual: Digital Rights Management Systems and the Intersection of Informational and Decisional Privacy Interests. *International Journal of Law and Information Technology,* (pp. 241-293).

GartnerGroup RAS Services (1999). *Intrusion Detection Systems.* R-08-7031.

Gavison, R. (1980). Privacy. *Yale Law Journal, 89,* 421-471.

General Penal Code No. 19, Chapter XXIV Offenses against personal freedom, Article 228, Paragraph 1, Icelandic General Penal Code, Article 228 (1998).

General Penal Code, Chapter 13 Felonies against the general order and peace, Article 145, Paragraph 1, Criminal Code of the Kingdom of Norway, Article 145 (1994).

General Penal Code, Chapter 13 Felonies against the general order and peace, Article 145b, Paragraph 1,

Criminal Code of the Kingdom of Norway, Article 145b (1994).

General Penal Code, Chapter 14 Felonies against public safety, Article 151a, Criminal Code of the Kingdom of Norway, Article 151a (1994).

General Penal Code, Chapter 14 Felonies against public safety, Article 151b, Criminal Code of the Kingdom of Norway, Article 151b (1994).

Gethin, P. (1987). Text Retrieval. *BRS/SIRSI Training Notes*. BRS Corp.

Glaessner, T., Kellermann, T., & McNevin, V. (2002). *Electronic Security: Risk Mitigation in Financial Transactions*. Public Policy Issues, The World Bank.

Godfrey, B. (2001). Electronic Work Monitorung: An Ethical Model. In J. Weckert (Ed.), *Proc. Selected papers from the 2nd Australian Institute of Computer Ethics Conference (AICE2000),* Canberra: ACS.

Gopalakrisnan, S., Wischnevsky, J. D., & Dmanpour, F. (2003). A multilevel analysis of factors influencing the adoption of Internet banking. *IEEE Transactions on Engineering Management, 50*(4), 413–426.

Gormley, K. (1992). One Hundred Years of Privacy. *Wisconsin Law Review*, (pp. 1335-1441).

Government of the United States. (2004). *US Safe Harbor Agreement*. Retrieved November 19, 2007, from http://www.export.gov/safeharbor/SHPRINCIPLESFINAL.htm

Grabosky, P. (2000). Computer Crime: A Criminological Overview. Paper for the *Tenth United Nations Congress on the Prevention of Crime and the Treatment of Offenders*. Vienna, Austrian Institute of Criminology.

Grabosky, P. (2000). Cyber Crime and Information Warfare. *Transnational Crime Conference*, Canberra, 9-10 March 2000.

Grabosky, P., & Smith, R. (1998). *Crime in the Digital Age: Controlling Telecommunications and Cyberspace Illegalities*. Sydney: The Federation Press.

Grand, J. (2001). *Authentication Tokens: Balancing the Security Risks with Business Requirements.* @Stake, Inc., Cambridge, MA.

Grijpink, J. (2004). Identity fraud as a challenge to the constitutional state. *Computer Law & Security Report,* (1), 29.

Grimes, G. A., Hough, M. G., & Signorella, M. L. (2007). E-mail end users and spam: relations of gender and age group to attitudes and actions. *Computers in Human Behavior, 23*(1), 318-332.

Grimmelmann, J. (2005). Regulation by Software. *Yale Law Journal,* (114), 1719

Gupta, M., & Rao, H. R. (2007). Financial Services Information Sharing and Analysis Center: Countering Cyber Terrorism in Financial Services Industry. In J. Janczewski & A. M. Colarik (Eds.), *Encyclopedia of Cyber Warfare and Cyber Terrorism*. Editors.

Gupta, M., Lee, J., & Rao, H. R. (2008). Implications of FFIEC Guidance on Authentication in Electronic Banking. In N. D. J. Gupta & S. Sharma (Eds.), *Handbook of Research on Information Security and Assurance*. IGI Publishing, Hershey, PA, April, 2008. USA. (isbn: 978-1-59904-855-0).

Hafner, K., Markoff, J. (1991). CYBERPUNK: Outlaws and hackers on the computer frontier. Simon & Schuster.

Halperin, R. (2006). Identity as an Emerging Field of Study. *Datenschutz und Datensicherheit,* (9), 533-537.

Han, S.-J., & S.-B. Cho, S.-B. (2003). Detecting intrusion with rule-based integration of multiple models. *Computers & Security, 22*(7), 613-623.

Hand, D. J., Mannila, H., & Smyth, P. (2001). *Principles of Data Mining (Adaptive Computation and Machine Learning)*. Bradford Books.

Hansen, M., & Meints, M. (2006). Digitale Identitäten – Überblick und aktuelle Trends. *Datenschutz und Datensicherheit,* (9), 543-547.

Hardy, I. T. (1996). The Ancient Doctrine of Trespass to Web Sites. *Journal of Online Law, 7.*

Henkin, L. (1974). Privacy and Autonomy. *Columbia Law Review, 74*, 1410-25.

Hildebrandt, M. (2006). Privacy and Identity. In E. Claes, A. Duff, & S. Gutwirth (Eds.), *Privacy and the criminal law*, (pp. 43-57).

Hildebrandt, M., Gutwirth, S., & Hert, P. De (2005). *Implications of profiling on democracy and the rule of law, FIDIS (Deliverable 7.4)*, available online at: http://www.fidis.net/resources/deliverables/profiling/int-d74000/

Hilley, S. (2007). Biometrics: the right to identity or privacy invasion? *Computer Fraud and Security*, (1), 6-7.

Hiltgen, A., Kramp, T., & Weigold, T. (2006). Secure Internet Banking Authentication. *IEEE Security and Privacy*, Mar/April 2006

Hite, R. (2004). *The federal enterprise architecture and agencies architectures are still maturing*, White paper, GAO. Federal Enterprise Architecture Security and Privacy Profile, Version 2.0, White paper published by the CIO Council of the U.S. government.

Hjorth, Th. (2004). *Supporting privacy in RFID systems*. IMM, DTU, Lyngby, Denmark, December 14, 2004.

Holcman, S. (2008). *What is Enterprise Architecture*. White paper, Pinnacle Business Group, Inc.

Home Office Consultation Paper (2007). *The initial transposition of Directive 2006/24/EC on the retention of data generated or processed in connection with the provision of publicly available electronic communications services or of public communications networks and amending Directive 2002/58/EC*, 27 March 2007. Retrieved on November 23, 2008 from http://www.homeoffice.gov.uk/documents/euro-directive-retention-data/cons-eur-dir-comm.pdf?view=Binary

Home Office Consultation Paper (2008). *Transposition of Directive 2006/24/EC*. August 2008. Retrieved on November 23, 2008 from http://www.homeoffice.gov.uk/documents/cons-2008-transposition?view=Binary

Home Office Working Document (2007). *The Initial Transposition of Directive 2006/24/EC: Government Responses to the Consultation*, June 2007. Retrieved on November 23, 2008 from http://www.homeoffice.gov.uk/documents/euro-directive-retention-data/cons-responses-07-euro-directive?view=Binary

Hornung, G. (2004). Biometric Identity Cards: Technical, Legal, and Policy Issues. In S. Paulus, N. Pohlman, & H. Reiner (Eds.), *Securing Electronic Business Processes*, (pp. 47-57).

Hornung, G. (2007). The European Regulation on Biometric Passports: Legislative Procedures, Political Interactions, Legal Framework and Technical Safeguards. *Script-ed* (3), 246- 262.

*Hotmail Corp. v. Van$ Money Pie Inc.*, 47 U.S.P.Q.2d (BNA) 1020 (N.D. Cal. 1998).

Housley, R., Ford, W., Polk, W., & Solo, D. (1999). *Internet X.509 Public Key Infrastructure. Certificate and CRL Profile, Request for Comments (RFC) 2459*. Sterling, VA, USA: IETF.

Hunter, D (2003). Cyberspace as Place and the Tragedy of the Digital Anticommons. *California Law Review*, (91), 439.

Húsek, D., Moravec, P., Snásel, V., Frolov, A. A., Rezanková, H., & Polyakov, P. (2007).*Comparison of Neural Network Boolean Factor Analysis Method with Some Other Dimension Reduction Methods on Bars Problem*. Springer, LNCS 4815, PReMI 2007: (pp. 235-243).

Hyvärinen, A. (1999). Survey on independent component analysis. *Neural Computing Surveys, 2*, 94-128.

Hyvärinen, A. (1999). Fast and robust fixed-point algorithms for independent component analysis. *IEEE Trans. Neural Networks, 10*, 626-634.

Hyvärinen, A., & Oja, E. (1999). *Independent component analysis: a tutorial*. [On-line]. Available: http://www.cis.hut.fi/projects/ica/

Hyvärinen, A., Karhunen, J., & Oja, E. (2001). *Independent Component Analysis*. John Wiley & Sons.

i2010 High Level Group (2006). *The Challenges of Convergence - Discussion Paper, Dec.12, 2006*. Brussels, Belgium: European Commission. [Retrieved on December 22, 2007 from http://ec.europa.eu/information_society/eeurope/i2010/docs/i2010_high_level_group/i2010_hlg_convergence_paper_final.pdf]

IDABC (2007). *Preliminary Study on Mutual Recognition of eSignatures for eGovernment applications. (Contract No. 1, Framework contract ENTR/05/58-SECURITY, Specific contract N°1).* Brussels, Belgium: European Communities. [Retrieved on June 16, 2008 from http://europa.eu.int/idabc/]

IESAC (2003). *Transactional Security*, Institution of Engineers, Saudi Arabian Center. (Retrieved on 1/12/2003 from http://www.iepsac.org/papers/p04c04a.htm)

Inoue, H., Miyazaki, A., Yamamoto, A., & Katsura, T. (1998). A digital watermark based on the wavelet transform and its robustness on image compression. *Proc. of IEEE ICIP.*

*Intel v. Hamidi*, 30 Cal. 4th 1342 (2003).

*Intel v. Hamidi*, 94 Cal.App.4th 325 (2001).

International AntiCounterfeiting Coalition (IACC). (2003). Facts on Fakes. Retrieved from: http://www.iacc.org/resources/Facts_on_fakes.pdf

International Labour Organization (ILO) (n.d.). *Protection of workers' personal data.* An ILO code of practice.

International Organization for Standardization (ISO) (2005). *ISO/IEC 17799: Information technology - Security Techniques - Code of practice for information security management.* Geneva, Switzerland: ISO.

International Working Group on Data Protection in Telecommunications (2001). *Working Paper on Data protection aspects of digital certificates and public-key infrastructures.*

Internet Security Task Force (2000). *Initial Recommendations for Conducting Secure eBusiness.* (Retrieved on 1/12/03 from http://www.ca.com/ISTF/recommendations.htm)

ISO (2000). ISO/IEC 17799:2000 *Information technology: Code of practice for information security management.* URL: hhtp://www.iso17799.net

ISSA/UCD Irish Cybercrime Survey. (2006). *The Impact of Cybercrime on Irish Organisations.* Available at http//www.issaireland.org

*Jacque v. Steenberg Homes*, 563 N.W.2d 154 (Wisc. 1997).

Jain, A. K., Hong, L., Pankanti, S., & Bolle R. (1997). An identity authentication system using fingerprints. In *Proceedings of the IEEE, 85*(9), (pp. 1365-1388).

Jawkes, Y. (2003). Policing the Net: crime, regulation and surveillance in cyberspace. In Y. Jewkes, (Ed.), *Dot.cons. Crime, deviance and identity on the Internet.* Devon: Willan Publishing.

Jensen, M. C., & Meckling, W. H. (1994). The Nature of Man. *Journal of Applied Corporate Finance,* (2), 4-19.

Jervis, C. (2005). Chips with everything: Is RFID ready for healthcare? *British Journal of Healthcare Computing and Information Management, 22*(2). Retrieved from http://www.kineticconsulting.co.uk/

Ji, C., & Ma, S. (1997). Combinations of weak classifiers. *IEEE Transaction on Neural Networks, 8*(1), 32–42.

Johnson, N. F., Duric, Z., & Jajodia, S. (1999). Recovery of watermarks from distorted images. *Preliminary Proc. of the Third Int. Information Hiding Workshop*, Dresden, Germany, (pp. 361-375).

Jolliffe, I.T. (1986). *Principal Component Analysis.* Germany: Springer-Verlag.

Jones, K., Bejtlich, R., & Rose, C. (2005). *Real Digital Forensics: Computer Security and Incident Response.* London: Addison-Wesley Professional.

Juels, A. (2006). RFID Security and Privacy: A Research Survey. *IEEE Journal on selected areas in communications, 24*(2), February 2006, p. 381-394.

Jung, J., & Sit, E. (2004). *Proceedings from IMC '04: Internet Measurement Conference.* Taormina, Italy.

Junnarkar, S. (2002). Online Banks: Prime targets for attacks. *e-Business ZDTech News Update.*

Kam, S. (2004). Intel Corp. v. Hamidi: Trespass to Chattels and a Doctrine of Cyber-Nuisance. *Berkeley Technology Law Journal,* (19), 427.

Kamal, A. (2005). *The Law of Cyber-Space.* Geneva Switzerland: United Nations Institute of Training and Research (UNITAR).

Kaprzycki, D. (2004). Trends in regulating unsolicited commercial communication. *CRi, 3,* 77.

Karyda, M., & Kokolakis, S. (2007). Privacy Perceptions Among Members of Online Communities. Acquisti, A., De Capitani di Vimercati, S., Gritzalis, S., & Lambrinoudakis, C. (Eds.), *Digital Privacy: Theory, Technologies and Practices.* Auerbach Publications (Taylor and Francis Group)

Karyda, M., & Mitrou, E. (2007). Internet Forensics: Legal and Technical issues. Proceedings of the *2nd Annual Workshop on Digital Forensics and Incident Analysis* (WDFIA 2007), August 27, 2007, Samos-Greece.

Katsh, E. M. (1995). Rights, camera, action: cyberspatial settings and the first amendment. *The Yale Law Journal, 104*(7), 1681-1717.

Katsh, M.E. (1996). Software Worlds and the First Amendment: Virtual Doorkeepers in Cyberspace. *University of Chicago Legal Forum,* (1996), 335.

Katz-Bassett, E., John, J. P., Krishnamurthy, A., Wetherall, D., Anderson T., & Chawathe, Y. (2006). Towards IP geolocation using delay and topology measurements. In *IMC '06: Proceedings of the 6th ACM SIGCOMM conference on Internet measurement* (pp. 71-84). Rio de Janeiro: ACM.

Katzenbeisser, S., & Petitcolas, F. A. P. (2000). *Information Hiding Techniques for Steganography and Digital Watermarking.* Boston: Artech House.

Kaufman, C. (2002). *Network Security: Private Communication in a Public World, Second Edition*, Prentice Hall, USA.

KDD cup 99. *Intrusion detection data set.* http://kdd.ics.uci.edu/databases/kddcup99/kddcup.data_10_percent.gz

Keen, J., & Dally, W. (1997). Extended Ephemeral Logging: Log Storage Management for Applications with Long-Lived Transactions. *ACM Transactions on Database Systems, 22*(1), 1-42.

Keeton, W. P., Dobbs D. B., Keeton. R. E., et al. (1984). *Prosser and Keeton on Torts, 5th Edition.* St Paul, MN: West Publishing.

Kerr, O. (2001). The Fourth Amendment in Cyberspace: can Encryption create a 'reasonable expectation' of Privacy? *Connecticut Law Review, 33*(2), 503-545.

Kerr, O. S. (2003). Internet Surveillance Law After the USA Patriot Act: The Big Brother That Isn't. *Northwestern University Law Review*, (97). From http://ssrn.com/abstract=317501

Kerr, O.S. (2003). The Problem of Perspective in Internet Law. *Georgetown Law Journal,* (91), 357.

Kesan, J. P. (2002). Cyber-Woring or Cyber-Shrinking?: A First Principles Examination of Electronic Privacy in the Workplace. *Florida Law Review 2002*(54).

Khong, W. (2001). Spam law for the internet. *The Journal of Information, Law and Technology – JILT,* 2001(3).

KianSing, Ng, Huan, L., & HweeBong Kwah. (1998). A Data Mining Application: Customer Retention at the Port of Singapore Authority. Proceedings of the *ACM-SIGMOD International Conference on Management of Data*, Seattle. (pp. 522-25).

Kierkegaard, S. (2005). Privacy in electronic communication. Watch your e-mail: Your boss is snooping! *CLSR* 2005, (pp. 226-236).

Kilian, W. (1996). *Europäisches Wirtschaftsrecht.* München:Beck.

Kim, G. H., & Spafford, E. H. (1995). *Experiences with Tripwire: Using Integrity Checkers for Intrusion Detection.* http://citeseer.ist.psu.edu/kim95experiences.html

Kimball, R., & Gregor, W. (1995). How distribution is transforming retail banking: Changes leading banks are making. *Journal of Retail Banking Services, 17*(3), 1–9.

Kindt, E. (2007). Biometric applications and the data protection legislation. *Datenschutz und Datensicherheit*, (3), 166-170.

Kleve, P. (2004). *Juridische iconen in het informatietijdperk* (Legal Icons in the Information Age, with summary in English) (diss.) Rotterdam/Deventer, Holland: Sanders/Kluwer.

Kleve, P. Mulder, R. V. De, & Noortwijk, C. van (2006). The Amazing Diversity Framework of the Intellectual Property Rights Harmonisation. In Brockdorff et al., (Eds.), *Globalisation and Harmonisation in Technology Law, proceedings 21th Bileta conference 06-04-2006*. Malta: Bileta.

Kleve, P., & Kolff, F. (1999). MP3: The End Of Copyright As We Know It? *Proceedings of the IASTED International Conference Law and Technology (LawTech'99)*. Honolulu, Hawaii: IASTED.

Knight, S., Buffett, S., & Hung, Patrick C.K. (2007). Guest Editors' Introduction. *International Journal of Information, 6*(5), 285-286.

Koops, B. J. (2005). *A survey on legislation on ID theft in the EU and a number of other countries* (Fidis Deliverable, D. 5.1).

Koops, B.-J., & Leenes, R. (2006). Identity Theft, Identity Fraud and/or Identity-related Crime. *Datenschutz und Datensicherheit*, (9), 553-556.

Kosta, E., Zibuschka, J., Scherner, T., & Dumortier, J. (2008). Legal considerations on privacy-enhancing Location Based Services using PRIME technology. *Computer Law & Security Report 2008*(2), 139-146.

Kotschy, W (2006). Directive 95/46/EC. In Bullesbach, Poullet & Prins (ed.), *Concise European IT Law*. Kluwer Law International, the Netherlands.

Kozyris, P. J. (1973). Advertising Intrusion: Assault on the Senses, Trespass on the Mind – A Remedy Through Separation. *Ohio State Law Journal, 36*, 299-347.

Kozyris, P. J. (2004). Freedom from information: Limiting advertising intrusion on the internet (spam) and on television. *Hellenic Review of European Law, 2004*, 17-41.

Kozyris, P. J. (2007). General Report. In P. J. Kozyris (ed.), *Regulating Internet Abuses: Invasion of Privacy* (1-26). Alphen aan den Rijn: Kluwer Law International.

Krasemann, H. (2006). Selbstgesteuertes Identitätsmanagement. *Datenschutz und Datensicherheit*, (4), 211-214.

*Kremen v. Cohen*, 337 F.3d 1024 (9th Cir. 2003)

Kuhn, T. S. (1962). *The structure of scientific revolutions*. Chicago, Illinois: University of Chicago Press.

Kundur, D., & Hatzinakos, D. (1998). Digital watermarking using multiresolution wavelet decomposition. *Proc. of IEEE ICASSP, 5*, 2969-2972.

Kutais, B. G. (Ed.) (2007). *Spam and Internet Privacy*. New York: Nova Science Publishers.

Kutter, M. (1998). Watermarking resisting to translation, rotation and scaling. *Proc. of SPIE Int. Symposium on Voice, Video, and Data Communications - Multimedia Systems and Applications, 3528*, Boston, Massachusetts, U.S.A., (pp. 423-431).

Lacroix, S., Delos, O., Van Eecke, P., Custers, M., & Janin, W. (2007). *Study on the Standardization Aspect of eSignature. (Final Report, 22.11.2007 for the European Commission, DG Information Society and Media)*. Tounai, Belgium: SEALED sprl.

Lai, V. S., & Li, H. (2004). Technology acceptance model for Internet banking: An invariance analysis. *Information and Management, 42*, 373–386.

Lalopoulos, G. K., Chochliouros, I. P., & Spiliopoulou, A. S. (2004). Challenges and Perspectives for Web-based Applications in Organizations. In M. Pagani (Ed.), *The Encyclopedia of Multimedia Technology and Networking*, (pp. 82-88). Hershey, PA, USA: IRM Press, Idea Group Inc.

Lankhorst, M. (2004). Enterprise architecture modeling- the issue of integration. *Advanced Engineering Informatics*, 18, 205-216.

Lasprogata, G., King, N. J., & Pillay, S. (2004). Regulation of Electronic Employee Monitoring: Identifying

Fundamental Principles of Employee Privacy through a Comparative Study of Data Privacy Legislation in the European Union, United States and Canada. *Stanford Technology Law Review 2004*(4).

Lastowka, G. (2007). Decoding Cyberproperty. *Indiana Law Review,* (40), 23.

Lauer, T. W., & Xiaodong, D. (2007). Building online trust through privacy practices. *International Journal of Information Security,* *6*(5), 323-331.

Lazarevic, A., Ertoz, L., Kumar, V., Ozgur, A., & Srivastava, J. (2003). A comparative study of anomaly detection schemes in network intrusion detection. *Proceedings of Third SIAM Conference on Data Mining*, May 2003.

Leavitt, N. (2005). Mobile phones: the next frontier for hackers? *IEEE Computer, 38*(4), 20-23.

LeClaire, J. (12/29/2004). Netherlands issues its first fines against spammers. *e-Commerce Times.*

Lee, T.-W. (1998). *Independent Component Analysis: Theory and Applications.* Kluwer Academic Publishers.

Lee, W., & Stolfo, S. (1998). Data Mining Approaches for Intrusion Detection. *Proc. of the 7th USENIX Security Symposium*, San Antonio, Texas, January 26-29.

Lee, W., Stolfo, S., & Mok, K. (1999). A Data Mining Framework for Building Intrusion Detection Models. *Proceedings of the IEEE Symposium on Security and Privacy.*

Leenes, R. (n.nd). Introduction. In *FIDIS, ID-related Crime: Towards a Common Ground for Interdisciplinary Research* (Fidis Deliverable, D 5.2b).

Lemarteleur, X. (2004). *Traçabilité contre vie privée: les RFIDs ou l'immixtion de technologie dans la sphère personnelle.* Mémoire, DESS droit du multimédia et de l'informatique, Université Paris II, Panthéon /Assas, octobre 2004. Retrieved from Juriscom.net, 22 octobre 2004, http://www.juriscom.net

Lemley, M. A. (2003). Place and Cyberspace. *California Law Review,* (91), 521.

Lessig, L. (1995). The path of Cyberlaw. *The Yale Law Journal, 104* (5), 1743-1755.

Lessig, L. (1996). Reading the Constitution in Cyberspace. *Emory Law Journal,* (45), 869.

Lessig, L. (1999). *Code And Other Laws Of Cyberspace.* New York, NY: Basic Books.

Lessig, L. (2000). Cyberspace and Privacy: A New Legal Paradigm? *Stanford Law Review,* (52), 987.

Lessig, L. (2001). *The Future of Ideas.* New York, NY: Random House.

Lessig, L. (2003). Law Regulating Code Regulating Law. *Loyola University of Chicago Law Journal,* (35), 1.

Levmore, S. (2003). Property's Uneasy Path and Expanding Future. *University of Chicago Law Review,* (70), 181.

Liberty Alliance Project (2005). *Circles of Trust: The Implications of EU Data Protection and Privacy Law for Establishing a Legal Framework for Identity Federation.*

Lindsay, D., & Ricketson, S (2006). Copyright, privacy and digital rights management. In A. Kenyon, & M. Richardson (Eds.), *New Dimensions in Privacy Law, International and Comparative Prospectives,* (pp. 121-153) Cambridge: Cambridge University Press.

Lippmann, R., & Cunningham, S. (2000). Improving intrusion detection performance using keyword selection and neural networks. *Computer Networks, 34*(4), 594- 603.

Lockton, V., & Rosenberg, R. (2005). RFID: the next serious Threat to Privacy. *Ethics and Information Technology, 7*(4), 221.

Loia, V., Senatore S., & Sessa, M. I. (2004). Combining agent technology and similarity-based reasoning for targeted E-mail services. *Fuzzy Sets and Systems, 145*(1), 29–56.

Louveaux, S., Poullet, Y., & Salaün, A. (2001). User protection in the cyberspace: some recommendations.

*Electronic Commerce – Der Abschluss von Verträgen im Internet*, 196, 103-111.

Lu, C.-S., & Mark, Liao H.-Y. (2001). Multipurpose watermarking for image authentication and protection. *IEEE Transaction on Image Procssing, 10*.

Luarn, P., & Lin, H. (2005). Toward an understanding of the behavioral intention to use mobile banking. *Computers in Human Behavior, 21*(6), 73–91.

Luck, A., Macburney, P., & Preist C. (2003). *Agent technology: enabling next generation computing.* Agentlink.

Lunt, T. F., Jagannathan, R., Lee, R., Listgarten, S., Edwards, D. L., Javitz, H. S., & Valdes, A. (1988). IDES: The Enhanced Prototype - A Real-Time Intrusion-Detection Expert System. *Number SRI-CSL-88-12. Computer Science Laboratory, SRI International, Menlo Park, CA.*

Lunt, T. F., Tamaru, A., Gilham, F., Jagannathan, R., Jalali, C., & Neuman, P.G. (1992). A real-time intrusion-detection expert system (IDES). *Technical Report Project 6784*, CSL, SRI International, Computer Science Laboratory, SRI International, February 1992.

Luo, J., & Bridges, S. M. (2000). Mining Fuzzy Association Rules and Fuzzy Frequency Episodes for Intrusion Detection. *International Journal of Intelligent Systems, 15*(8), 687-704. John Wiley & Sons

Lyon, D. (1994). *The electronic eye: the rise of Surveillance Society.* Cambridge: Polity Press.

Lyon, D. (2001). *Surveillance Society: monitoring everyday life.* Buckingham & Philadelphia: Open University Press.

Maconachy, W. V., Schou, C. D., Ragsdale, D., & Welch, D. (2001). A Model for Information Assurance: An Integrated Approach. *Proceedings of the 2001 IEEE, Workshop on Information Assurance and Security*, United States Military Academy, West Point, NY, 5-6 June.

Madison, M. J. (2003). Rights of Access and the Shape of the Internet. *Boston College Law Review,* (44), 433.

Manny, C. H. (2003). Personal privacy – transatlantic perspectives. *Computer Law & Security Report,* (1), 4-10.

Marchany, R. (1998). *Internet Security & Incident Response: Scenarios & Tactics.* September 1998. (Retrieved on 2/2/03 from https://courseware.vt.edu/marchany/InternetSecurity/Class)

Marshall, A. M., & Tompsett, B.C. (2005). Identity theft in an online world. *Computer Law & Security Report,* (2), 128-137.

Mason, S. (2004). Validating Identity for the electronic environment. *Computer Law & Security Report,* (3), 164-170.

Mc Kenna, L. (2007). *Aldridge's Blog. California Senate fights required RFID in schools.* (April 20, 2007). Retrieved from http://rfidlawblog.mckennalong.com/archives/state-legislation-california-senate-fights-required-rfid-in-schools.html

McCandless, M. (1999). The MP3 revolution. *IEEE Intelligent Systems, 3*, 8-9.

McCarthy, R., & Barrett, D. (2005). The impact of the Sarbanes-Oxley Act on information technology: Two perspectives. In *Proceedings of the International Association of Computer Information Systems Pacific conference*, Taipei, Taiwan, May 19-21, 2005, 437-442.

McGowan, D. (2003). Website Access: The Case for Consent. *Loyola University of Chicago Law Journal,* (35), 341.

McGowan, D. (2005). The Trespass Trouble and the Metaphor Muddle. *Journal of Law, Economics & Policy,* (1), 109.

Meikle, G. (2002). *Future active: Media activism and the Internet.* Routledge.

Meints, M. (2006). Identität. *Datenschutz und Datensicherheit*, (9), 576.

Meints, M., Rost, M., Zuccato, A., Delaitre, S., & Maghiros, I. (2006). Socio-Economic aspects. In *FIDIS, ID-related Crime: Towards a Common Ground for Interdisciplinary Research*, (p. 66). et seq., available online at: www.fidis.net.

Merkle, R. C. (1978). Secure Communications over Insecure Channels, *Communications of the ACM, 21*(4), 294-299.

Microsoft. (2008). Retrieved November 19, 2007, from http://privacy.microsoft.com/en-us/fullnotice.aspx

Middleton, B. (2004). *Cyber Crime Investigator's Field Guide*, Second Edition. Boca Raton, FL: Auerbach Publications.

Millard, Ch., & Church, P. (2006). Directive 95/46/EC, article 14 (2006). In Bullesbach, Poullet & Prins (Ed.), *Concise European IT Law*. The Netherlands: Kluwer Law Internatinal.

Mintzer, F. & Braudaway, G. (1999). If one watermark is good, are more better? *Proc. of the International Conference on Acoustics, Speech, and Signal Processing, 4.*

*MIT Lincoln Laboratory*. http://www.ll.mit.edu/IST/ideval/

Mitchell, W. (1994). *City Of Bits*. Cambridge, MA: MIT Press.

Mitrakas, A. (2005). Policy Frameworks for Secure Electronic Business. In M. Khosrow-Pour (Ed.), *Encyclopedia of Information Science and Technology*, Volume I-V. Hershey: IGI Publishing.

Mitrakas, A. (2005). Soft Law constraints in eGovernment. In *Proceedings of BILETA 2005* (British Irish Law Education & Technology Association), Belfast, 7 April 2005.

Mitrakas, A. (2006). Information security and Law in Europe: Risks checked? *Information and Communication Technology Law*, Carfax.

Mitrakas, A. (2007). Annex II, Legal and policy aspects of Network Information Security. In C. Douligeris, & D. Seripanos, *Network Information Security*. Wiley (IEEE Publication).

Mitrakas, A., & Polemi, D. (2007). Trustworthy eInvoice Services. In J. Malkolm, & G. Orthofer, *eTaxation: State & Perspectives*, Johannes-Kepler Universitaet Linz: Trauner Verlag.

Mitrakas, A., & van Eecke, P. (2006). Commentary on Directive 1999/93 on a Community framework for electronic signatures. In A. Buellesbach, Y. Poullet, & C. Prins (Eds.) *Concise European IT Law*. Alphen aan de Rijn: Kluwer Law International.

Mitrakas, A., & Zaitch, D. (2006). Law, cybercrime and digital forensics: trailing digital suspects. In Kanellis, P., Kiountouzis, E., Kolokotronis, N., Martakos, D., *Digital Crime and Forensic Science in Cyberspace*. Hershey: IGI Publishing.

Mitrou, E., & Karyda, M. (2006). Employees' Privacy vs. Employers' Security: Can they be balanced? *Telematics and Informatics Journal*, 23(3), 2006, 164 – 178.

Moakes, J. (1986). Data protection in Europe – Part 1, *Journal of International Banking Law, 1*(2), 77-86.

Moravec, P., & Snášel, V. (2006). Dimension Reduction Methods for Image Retrieval. In *Proceedings of the Conference on Intelligent Systems Design and Applications* (ISDA2006), Jinan, Shandong, China, October 2006. USA: IEEE Press.

Mossoff, A. (2004). Spam -- Oy, What A Nuisance!. *Berkeley Technology Law Journal,* 19, 625.

Moukiou, Ch. (2003). The European Legal Frame and its Effectiveness in Greek Reality – The Special Issue of Digital Signature. In D. Politis, N. Papasteriadou (Eds.), *Recent Advances in Court Computerisation and Legal Databases – First Steps towards e-Justice.* Athens: A. N. Sakkoulas Publications.

Mukkamala, S., Sung, A. H., & Abraham, A. (2003). Intrusion Detection Using Ensemble of Soft Computing Paradigms. 3rd *International Conference on Intelligent Systems Design and Applications, Intelligent Systems Design and Applications, Advances in Soft Computing.* Germany: Springer Verlag, (pp. 239-248).

Mukkamala, S., Sung, A. H., & Abraham, A. (2004). Modeling Intrusion Detection Systems Using Linear Genetic Programming Approach. *The 17th International Conference on Industrial & Engineering Applications of Artificial Intelligence and Expert Systems*, Innovations in Applied Artificial Intelligence, R. Orchard, C. Yang,

M. Ali (Eds.), LNCS 3029. Germany: Springer Verlag, (pp. 633-642).

Mukkamala, S., Sung, A. H., Abraham, A., & Ramos, V. (2004). Intrusion Detection Systems Using Adaptive Regression Splines. In I. Seruca, J. Filipe, S. Hammoudi, & J. Cordeiro (Eds.), *6th International Conference on Enterprise Information Systems, ICEIS'04, 3*, 26-33. Portugal, ISBN 972-8865-00-7.

Mulder, R. V. De (1984). *Een model voor juridische informatica (A Model for Legal Computer Science, with summary in English)* (diss.), Lelystad, Holland: Vermande.

Mulder, R. V. De (1998). The Digital Revolution: From Trias to Tetras Politica. In I. Th. M. Snellen & W. B. H. J. van de Donk (Eds.), *Public Administration in an Information Age. A Handbook* (pp. 47-56). Amsterdam, Holland: IOS Press.

Muller, E. R., Spaaij, R. F., & Ruitenberg, A. G. W. (2003). *Trends in terrorisme*. Alphen aan den Rijn, Holland: Kluwer.

Nabeth, T. (2006). Identity of Identity: Building a Shared Understanding of the Concept of Identity in the FIDIS Network of Excellence. *Datenschutz und Datensicherheit*, (9), 538-542.

Natsui, T. (2004). *Traceability system using RFID and legal issues*. Retrieved from www.sics.se/privacy/wholes2004/papers/takato.pdf

Neaga, E., & Harding, J. (2005, March). An enterprise modeling and integration framework based on knowledge discovery and data mining. *International Journal of Production Research, 43*(6), 1089-1108.

Neapolitan, R.E. (1990). *Probabilistic reasoning in expert systems: theory and algorithms*. John Wiley and Sons.

Newell, F. (2003). *Why CRM Doesn't Work: How to win by letting customers manage the relationship*. Princeton, NJ: Bloomberg Press.

NIIAC (The National Information Infrastructure Advisory Council) (1995). *Common Ground: Fundamental Principles for the National Information Infrastructure.*

Nilsson, H., Van Eecke, P., Medina, M., Pinkas, D., & Pope, N. (1999). *Final Report of the EESSI Expert Team, 20th July 1999*. European Electronic Signature Standardization Initiative (EESSI). [Retrieved on October 16, 2005, from http://www.ictsb.org/EESSI_home.htm]

Noakes, K. (2001). Virus and Malicious Code Protection Products: Perspective. *Fry Technology Overview*, Gartner Research Group, DPRO-90840.

Nykodym, N., Taylor, R., & Vilela, J. (2005). Criminal profiling and insider cyber crime. *Computer Law & Security Report, 21*, 408-414.

O'Rourke, M. A. (2001). Property Rights and Competition on the Internet: In Search of an Appropriate Analogy. *Berkeley Technology Law Journal*, (16), 561.

OCC (Office of the Comptroller of the Currency) (1998). *OCC Bulletin 98-3 - Technology Risk Management. OCC Bulletin 98-38 - Technology Risk Management: PC Banking.*

OCC (Office of the Comptroller of the Currency) (2001). *AL 2001-4 - OCC Advisory Letter.*

Odyssey Technologies (2001). *PKI for Internet banking.* (Retrieved on 8.23.2002 from http://www.odysseytec.com)

OECD (1980). *OECD Guidelines on the Protection of Privacy and Transborder Flows of Personal Data.*

OECD (1997). *Recommendation of the Council concerning guidelines for cryptography policy*, ver. 27 March 1997, Paris 1997.

OECD (2002). *Guidelines for the Security of Information Systems and Networks: Towards a Culture of Security*, Paris, 2002.

OECD (2003). *Guidelines for Protecting Consumers from Fraudulent and Deceptive Commercial Practices Across Borders*, Paris, 2003.

*OECD Declaration on Transborder Data Flows* (1985). Retrieved on November 23, 2008 from http://www.oecd.org/document/32/0,3343,en_2649_34255_1888153_1_1_1_1,00.html.

*OECD Guidelines on the Protection of Privacy and Transborder Flows of Personal Data of 23 September 1980*. Retrieved November 23, 2008 from http://www.oecd.org/document/0,2340,en_2649_34255_1815186_1_1_1_1,00.html.

OECD. (2002). *Guidelines on the Protection of Privacy and Transborder Flows of Personal Data*. Retrieved November 19, 2007, from http://www1.oecd.org/publications/e-book/9302011e.pdf

Office of the Privacy Commissioner of Canada. (2007). *Report of an Investigation into the Security, Collection and Retention of Personal Information: TJX Companies Inc./Winners Merchant International L.P.* Retrieved November 19, 2007, from http://www.privcom.gc.ca/cf-dc/2007/TJX_rep_070925_e.asp

Olsen, T., & Mahler, T. (2007). Risk, responsibility and compliance in 'Circles of trust' – Part I. *Computer Law & Security Report,* (4), 342-351.

Olsen. T., & Mahler, T. (2007). Risk, responsibility and compliance in 'Circles of trust' – Part II. *Computer Law & Security Report,* (5), 415-426.

Opinion of the European Data Protection Supervisor on the communication from the Commission to the European Parliament, the Council, the European Economic and Social Committee and the Committee of the Regions on 'Radio Frequency Identification (RFID) in Europe: Steps towards a policy framework', COM(2007) 96, *Official Journal of the European Union*, 23.4.2008, C101/7.

Organization for Economic Coordination and Development (OECD) (2004). *Digital Delivery of Business Services (JT00162724)*. Paris, France: OECD.

Orr, B. (2002). Infrastructure, not innovation. *ABA Banking Online Journal*. (Retrieved on 8/8/02 from http://www.banking.com/aba/infrastructure.asp)

Orwell, G. (1949). *Nineteen Eighty-Four*. London: Martin Secker and Warburg.

*Oyster Software, Inc v. Forms Processing, Inc.*, 2001 US Dist LEXIS 22520 (N.D. Cal. Dec. 6, 2001).

Papazoglou, M., & Ribbers, P. (2006). *E-Business – Organizational and Technical Foundations*. West Sussex, UK: Wiley.

Parker, D.B. (1998). *Fighting Computer Crime: A New Framework for Protecting Information*. New York: Wiley.

Parker, R. (1974). A definition of Privacy. *Rutgers Law Review, 27*(1), 275–296.

Pearce, G., & Platten, N. (1988). Achieving Personal Data Protection in the European Union. *Journal of Common Market Studies*.

Penal Code, Particular Part, Chapter XXXIII, Article 267, Section 1, Criminal Code of the Republic of Poland, Article 267, Section 1 (1997).

Penal Code, Particular Part, Chapter XXXIII, Article 267, Section 2, Criminal Code of the Republic of Poland, Article 267, Section 2 (1997).

Penal Code, Particular Part, Chapter XXXIII, Article 268, Criminal Code of the Republic of Poland, Article 268 (1997).

Penal Code, Particular Part, Chapter XXXIII, Article 269, Section 1, Criminal Code of the Republic of Poland, Article 269, Section 1 (1997).

Penal Code, Special Part, Chapter 13, Division 1, Subdivision 2, Section 206, Paragraph 1, Criminal Code of the Republic of Estonia, Section 206, Paragraph 1 (2007).

Penal Code, Special Part, Chapter 13, Division 1, Subdivision 2, Section 208, Criminal Code of the Republic of Estonia, Section 208 (2007).

Penal Code, Special part, Chapter 3, Section V, Article 171-3, Criminal code of the Republic of Bulgaria, Article 171-3 (2002).

Penal Code, Special Part, Chapter IX "A", Section 319b, Criminal code of the Republic of Bulgaria, Section 319b (2002).

Penal Code, Special Part, Chapter IX "A", Section 319d, Criminal code of the Republic of Bulgaria, Section 319d (2002).

Penal Code, Special Part, Chapter IX, Section 319, Criminal code of the Republic of Bulgaria, Section 319 (2002).

Penal Code, Special Part, Fifth Section, Article 118, Paragraph 1, Austrian Penal Code, Article 118, Paragraph 1 (2004).

Penal Code, Special Part, Fifth Section, Article 118a, Austrian Penal Code, Article 118a (2004).

Penal Code, Special Part, Fifth Section, Article 119a, Austrian Penal Code, Article 119a (2004).

*Personal Information and Electronics Document Act*, R.S.C. 2000, c.6.

Peter, P. (2001). *Digital image watermarking in the wavelet transform domain.* Master's Thesis.

Pfitzmann, A., & Hansen, M. (2008). Anonymity. *Undetectability, Unobservability, Pseudonymity, and Identity Management – A Consolidated Proposal for Terminology.* Available online at: http://dud.inf.tu-dresden.de/Anon_Terminology.shtml

Pfitzmann, B. (2003). Privacy in Enterprise Identity Federation: Policies for Liberty Single Signon. *Proc. Workshop on Privacy Enhancing Technologies*, Springer Verlag.

Pfleeger, C. P. (1997). *Security in Computing* (Second Edition). Upper Saddle River, NJ: Prentice Hall.

Philippsohn, S. (2001). Trends in Cybercrime: An Overview of Current Financial Crimes on the Internet. *Computers & Security, 20*, 2001, 53-69.

PITAC (2005). President's Information Technology Advisory Committee, *Cyber Security: A crisis in prioritisation*, COITRD, Arlington (2005).

Poland, K. R., & Nash, M. J. (1990). Some Conundrums Concerning Separation of Duty. In *IEEE Symposium on Computer Security and Privacy.*

Polatoglu, V. N., & Ekin, S. (2001). An empirical investigation of the Turkish consumers' acceptance of Internet banking services. *International Journal of Bank Marketing, 19*(4), 156–165

Politis, D. & Gogos, K. (2001). Data mining of Personal Information: Perspectives and Legal Barriers. Proceedings of the *5th wses/IEEE World Multiconference on Circuits, Systems, Communications & Computers. CSCC 2001*, Rethymnon, Crete, 8-15 July 2001, (pp. 258-267).

Politis, D., Papasteriadou, N., & Gallardo, M. A. (2003). The Impact of New Technologies on Forensic Engineering and Expert Witnessing in Courts of Law. In D. Politis & N. Papasteriadou (Eds.), *Recent Advances in Court Computerisation and Legal Databases – First steps towards e-Justice.* Athens: Ant. N. Sakkoulas Publishers.

Portesi, S. (2008). *The challenges faced by police forces in searching and seizing in situ computer evidence during criminal investigations*, Ph.D. Thesis, Univestity of Trento.

Posner, R. (1981). *The economics of justice.* Cambridge & Massachusetts: Harvard University Press.

Post, D. J. (2001). His Napster's Voice. *Temple Environmental Law & Technology Journal* (20), 35.

Poullet, Y., & Vanderberghe, G.P.V. (Eds.) (1998). *Telebanking, Teleshopping and the Law.* Deventer: Kluwer.

Pound, R. (1915). Interests in Personality. *Harvard Law Review, 28*, 343-365

Prescott, E. C. (2002). *Reputation and technological knowledge sharing among R&D scientists in the multidivisional, multinational firm.* Montreal: Univeristy of Montreal, Unpublished Dissertation.

President's Information Technology Advisory Committee. (2005). *Report to the President, Cyber Security: A crisis of prioritization.* Washington, D.C. February 2005.

*Privacy guru joins IBM.* (November 30, 2001). Retrieved March 10, 2004, from http://www.crm-forum.com

Prosser, W. (1960). Privacy. *California Law Review, 48*, 383-423.

*Pruneyard Shopping Center v. Robins*, 447 U.S. 74 (1980);

R v. Gold and Shifreen. 2 Weekly Law Reports AC 984 (House of Lords 1988).

Radio Frequency Identification (RFID) in Europe: steps towards a policy framework (2007). *Communication from the Commission to the European Parliament, the Council, the European Economic and Social Committee and the Committee of the Regions*. COM(2007)96 final.

Rand Europe. (2003). *Benchmarking Security and Trust in the Information Society in Europe and the US, in the context of the IST-26276-SIBIS project* ("SIBIS Statistical Indicators Benchmarking the Information Society"). Available at http://www.sibis-eu.org

Rathmell, A., & Valeri, L. (2002). *Handbook of Legislative Procedures of Computer and Network Misuse in EU Countries*, Study for the European Commission Directorate-General Information Society, Rand Europe.

Rauhofer, J. (2006). History does not matter to them – Moves towards the adoption of mandatory communications data retention in the European Union. In P. Sint & E. Schweighofer (Eds.), *Knowledge Rights – Legal, Societal and Related Technological Aspects: Proceedings of an International Conference, Vienna, 16th – 17th February 2006* (pp. 203-215) Vienna: Austrian Computer Society Series, Volume 202.

Rauhofer, J. (2006). Just because you're paranoid, doesn't mean they're not after you: Legislative developments in relation to the mandatory retention of communications data in the European Union, (2006) *SCRIPTed* 3:4, 322. Retrieved on November 23, 2008 from http://www.law.ed.ac.uk/ahrc/script-ed/vol3-4/rauhofer.asp.

Reed, C. (2000). *Internet Law: Text and Materials*. London: Butterworths.

*Register.com, Inc. v. Verio, Inc.*, 126 F. Supp. 2d 238 (S.D.N.Y. 2000).

Reid A. (2007). Is society smart enough to deal with smart cards. *Computer Law & Security Report*, (23), 53-61.

Reidenberg, J. R. (1996). Governing Networks and Rule-Making in Cyberspace. *Emory Law Journal*, (45), 911.

Reidenberg, J. R. (1998). Lex Informatica: The Formulation of Information Policy Rules Through Technology. *Texas Law Review*, (76), 553.

Reidenberg, R. (2000). Resolving conflicting International Data Privacy Rules in Cyberspace, *Stanford Law Review*, *52*(5), 1315-1371.

Reisen, A. (2008). Digitale Identität im Scheckkartenformat. *Datenschutz und Datensicherheit*, (3), 164-167.

Reuven, R., Levary, et al (2005). Radio Frequency Identification: Legal Aspects. 12 *RICH. J.L. & TECH.* 6 (2005), p. 12. Retrieved from http://law.richmond.edu/jolt/v12i2/article6.pdf

Richardson, G., Jackson, B., & Dickson, G. (1990, Dec.). A principles-based enterprise architecture: Lessons from Texaco and Star Enterprise. *MIS Quarterly*, *14*(4), 385-403.

Rico, D. (2006, April). A framework for measuring ROI of enterprise architecture. *Journal of Organizational and End-User Computing*, *18*(2), 1-12.

Robinson, G. (2003). Statistical approach to the spam problem-using Bayesian statistics to detect an e-mail's spamminess. *ACM Linux Journal*.

Robinson, N., & Large, D. (2004, December). PIPEDA: Impact on CRM and public-private sector interaction. *Optimum Online: The Journal of Public Sector Management*, *34*(4), 47-60.

Rose, C. M. (1998). The Several Futures of Property: Of Cyberspace and Folk Tales, Emission Trades and Ecosystems. *Minnesota Law Review*, (83), 129.

Rose, C. M. (1998). Canons of Property Talk, or, Blackstone's Anxiety. *Yale Law Journal* (108), 601.

Roseman, E. (2007). How retailers can protect customer privacy. *The Toronto Star* (7 October 2007).

Rössler, B. (2005). *The value of privacy*. Oxford: Blackwell Publishing.

*Rousseau v. Wyndowe*, [2006] F.C.J. No. 1631.

Ruiz, B. (1998). *The Right to Privacy: a discourse-theoretical approach. Ratio Juris, 11*(1), 155-167.

Rupert, B. (2008). The 110[th] Congress and Network Neutrality – S 215 – The Information Freedom Preservation Act. *DePaul Journal of Art, Technology & Intellectual Property Law, 18*, 325.

Savage, N., & Edwards, C. (1986). Transborder Data Flows: The European Convention and United Kingdom Legislation. *The International and Comparative Law Quarterly, 35*(3), 710-717.

Savirimuthu, A., & Savirimuthu, J. (2007). Identity Theft and Systems Theory: The Fraud Act 2006 in Perspective. *SCRIPT-ed* (4), p. 439, available online at: http://www.law.ed.ac.uk/ahrc/script-ed/vol4-4/savirimuthu.asp

Savona, E. U., & Mignone, M. (2004). The Fox and the Hunters: How IC Technologies Change the Crime Race. *European Journal on Criminal Policy and Research, 10*, 3–26.

Schatz-Byford, K. (1998). Privacy in Cyberspace: constructing a model of privacy for the electronic communication environment. *Rutgers Computer & Technology Law Journal, 24*(1), 1-74.

Schekkerman, J. (2004). *How to survive in the jungle of Enterprise Architecture Frameworks*. Victoria, BC: Trafford.

Schekkerman, J. (2005). *Trends in Enterprise Architecture, Institute for Enterprise Architecture Development*. White paper.

Schild, H. (1996). *Die EG-Datenschutz-Richtlinie*. Europäische Zeitschrift für Wirtschaftsrecht.

Schneier, B. (1995). *Applied Cryptography* (2nd ed.). John Wiley and Sons Inc.

Scholz, P. (2003). *Datenschutz beim Internet Einkauf*, Nomos.

Schrijver, S. De, & Schraeyen, J. (2005). Spyware: Innocent espionage in cyberspace? *Communications Law*, (1), 17-24.

Schwartau, W. (Ed.). (1996). *Information warfare: Cyberterrorism: Protecting your personal security in the information age* (2[nd] ed.). New York: Thunder's Mouth Press.

Schwartz, P., & Reidenberg, J. (1996). *Data Privacy Law*. Charlottesville.

Scientific Working Group on Digital Evidence (SWGDE) (2000). International Organization on Digital Evidence (IOCE), Digital Evidence: Standards and Principles 1999, in *Forensic Science Communications*, April 2000, 2(2). URL: http://www.fbi.gov/hq/lab/fsc/backissu/april2000/swgde.htm

Sequeira, K., & Zaki, M. (2002). ADMIT: Anomaly based Data Mining for Intrusions. *SIGKDD 2002*, Edmonton, Alberta, Canada.

Shah, K., Dave, N., Sampada, C., Mukherjee, S., Abraham, A., & Sanyal, S. (2004). Adaptive Neuro-Fuzzy Intrusion Detection System. *IEEE International Conference on Information Technology: Coding and Computing (ITCC'04), 1*, 70-74. USA: IEEE Computer Society.

Sheppard, N. Paul, Safavi-Naini R., & Ogunbona, P. (2001). On multiple watermarking. *Proc. of ACM Multimedia 2001.*

*Sherwood 48 Assocs. v. Sony Corp. of Am.*, Civ. No. 02-9100, 2003 U.S. App. LEXIS 20106 (2d Cir. Sept. 29, 2003).

Shoniregun, C. A., Chochliouros, I. P., Laperche, B., Logvynovskiy, Ol., & Spiliopoulou, A. S. (2004). *Questioning the Boundary Issues of Internet Security*. London, United Kingdom: e-Centre for Infonomics.

Shupe, C., & Behling, R. (2006, July). Developing and implementing a strategy for technology development. *Information Management Journal, 40*(4), 52-57.

Shy, O. (2001). *The Economics of Network Industries*. New York: Cambridge University Press.

Sicilianos, L. –A. (2001). International protection of personal data: Privacy, Freedom of Information or both? In L. –A. Sicilianos, & M. Gavouneli, (Eds.), *Scientific and Technological Developments & Human Rights* (pp. 123-142), Athens: Ant. N. Sakkoulas Publishers.

Sieber, U. (1987). The International Handbook on Computer Crime. John Wiley & Sons, Inc.

Silberschatz, A., Korth, H., & Sudarshan, S. (1997). *Database System Concepts.* New York: McGraw-Hill.

Simitis, S. (1984) Die informationelle Selbstbestimmung – Grundbedingung einer verfassungskonformen Informationsordnung, *Neue Juristische Wochenschrift*, (pp. 394-405).

Simitis, S. (1987). Reviewing Privacy in an Information Society. *University of Pennsylvania Law Review, 135*(2), 707-746.

Simitis, S. (1999). Reconsidering the Premises of Labour Law: Prolegomena to an EU Regulation on the Protection of Employees'Personal Data. *European Law Journal, 5,* 1/1999, 45-62.

Singh, S. (2004). Impersonalisation of electronic money: Implications for bank marketing. *The International Journal of Bank Marketing, 22*(7), 505-521.

Singh, S., Jackson, M. & Beekhuyzen, J. (2009). Privacy and Banking in Australia. In M. Gupta & R. Sharman (Eds.), *Handbook of Research on Social and Organizational Liabilities in Information Security.* IGI Global Inc publishing, Hershey, PA. Forthcoming in 2009.

Skillicorn, D. (2007). *Understanding Complex Datasets: Data Mining with Matrix Decomposition.* Chapman & Hall.

Slemmons, S. J., & Stratford, J. (1998). *Data Protection and Privacy in the United States and Europe.* Retrieved from atalib.library.ualberta.ca/publications/iq/ iq22/ iqvol223stratford.pdf

Slewe, T., & Hoogenboom, M. (2004). Who Will Rob You on the Digital Highway? *Communications of the ACM, 47*(5), 56-60.

Slobogin, C. (2002). Public Privacy: camera surveillance of public places and the right to anonymity. *Mississippi Law Journal, 72*(1), 213-299.

Smith, R. E. (1993). The law of privacy in a nutshell. *Privacy Journal,* (6), 50-51.

Snášel, V., Húsek, D., Frolov, A. A., Řezanková,H., Moravec, P., & Polyakov, P. (2007). Bars Problem Solving - New Neural Network Method and Comparison. *Lecture Notes in Computer Science 4827, MICAI 2007*: (pp. 671-682).

Solove, D. (2002). Conceptualizing privacy. *California Law Review, 90*(3), 1087-1156.

Solove, D. (2004). *The digital person, Technology and privacy in the information age.* NY: New York University Press.

Solove, D. J. (2001). Privacy and Power: Computer Databases and Metaphors for Information Privacy. *Stanford Law Review*, (53). From http://docs.law.gwu.edu/facweb/dsolove/Privacy-Power.pdf

Solove, D. J., Rotenberg, M., & Schwartz, P. M. (2006). *Information Privacy Law.* New York: Aspen Publishers.

Sommer, J. H. (2000). Against Cyberlaw. *Berkeley Technology Law Journal,* (15), 1145.

Sophos Research. (2007). *The Dirty Dozen.* Retrieved November 11, 2007, from http://www.sophos.com/pressoffice/news/articles/2004/02/sa_dirtydozen.html

*Sotelo v. DirectRevenue*, 384 F. Supp. 2d 1219 (N.D. Ill. 2005).

Spachmüller, D. (2007). Balancing freedom of press against the right to privacy – are the Germans still so much better? *Freiburg Law Students Journal, 3*(1), 1-24.

Starita, L. (1999). *Online Banking: A Strategic Perspective.* Context Overview Report (R-08-7031-Gartner).

Statute book of criminal law, Second book indictable offenses, Title V Indictable offenses against the public safety, Article 138a, Dutch statute book of criminal law, Article 138a (1997).

Statute book of criminal law, Second book indictable offenses, Title V Indictable offenses against the public safety, Article 138b, Dutch statute book of criminal law, Article 138b (1997).

Sterling, B. (1993). *The Hacker Crackdown: Law and Disorder on the Electronic Frontier.* New York: Bantam Books.

Stinchcombe, K. (September 25, 2006). Facebook privacy. *The Stanford Daily* (25 September 2006). Retrieved November 18, 2007, from http://daily.stanford.edu/article/2006/9/25/facebookPrivacy

Stoll, C. (1989). The cuckoo's egg: Tracking a spy through the maze of computer espionage. Pocket Books.

Straffeloven, Special Part, Chapter 27, Section 263, The Danish Penal Code, Section 263 (2005).

Suh, B., & Han, I. (2002). Effect of trust on customer acceptance of Internet banking. *Electronic Commerce Research and Applications, 1*, 247–263.

Sung, A. H., & Mukkamala, S. (2003). Identifying Important Features for Intrusion Detection Using Support Vector Machines and Neural Networks. *Proceedings of International Symposium on Applications and the Internet (SAINT 2003),* (pp. 209-217).

Swiss Penal Code, Book 2, Chapter 2, Article 143 bis, Criminal Code of the Swiss Confederation, Article 143 bis (2004).

Swiss Penal Code, Book 2, Chapter 2, Article 144 bis, Criminal Code of the Swiss Confederation, Article 144 bis (2004).

Tacit, C. (2003). Complying with private sector privacy legislation (Unpublished Work).

Taylor, N. (2003). Policing, privacy and proportionality, *European Human Rights Law Review*, Supp (Special issue: privacy 2003), (pp. 86-100).

The Criminal Code of the Russian Federation, Special Part, Section IX, Chapter 28, Section 272, Paragraph 1, Criminal Code of the Russian Federation, Section 272 (1996).

The Criminal Code of the Russian Federation, Special Part, Section IX, Chapter 28, Section 273, Paragraph 1, Criminal Code of the Russian Federation, Section 273 (1996).

The Criminal Code, Special Part, Chapter 30, Article 196 to 197, Lithuanian Criminal Code, Article 196 to 197 (2000).

The Criminal Code, Special Part, Chapter 30, Article 198-2, Lithuanian Criminal Code, Article 198-2 (2000).

The Criminal Code, Special Part, Chapter 30, Article 198-3, Lithuanian Criminal Code, Article 198-3 (2000).

The Criminal Law, Special Part, Chapter XX, Section 241, Criminal Code of the Republic of Latvia, Section 241 (2006).

The Criminal Law, Special Part, Chapter XX, Section 243, Criminal Code of the Republic of Latvia, Section 243 (2006).

The Criminal Law, Special Part, Chapter XX, Section 244, Criminal Code of the Republic of Latvia, Section 244 (2006).

The Criminal Law, Special Part, Chapter XX, Section 245, Criminal Code of the Republic of Latvia, Section 245 (2006).

The Penal Code of Finland, Chapter 34, Section 9a, Finnish Penal Code, Section 9a (1999).

The Penal Code of Finland, Chapter 35, Sections 1-3, Finnish Penal Code, Sections 1-3 (1990).

The Penal Code of Finland, Chapter 38, Section 1, Finnish Penal Code, Section 1 (1995).

The Penal Code of Finland, Chapter 38, Section 8, Finnish Penal Code, Section 8 (1995).

The Penal Code, Book II, Title, XII, Chapter VI, Section III, Article 256, The Spanish Penal Code, Article 256 (2003).

The Penal Code, Part 2 On crimes, Chapter 4 On crimes against liberty and peace, Section 9c, The Penal Code of the Kingdom of Sweden, Section 9c (1998).

*The Privacy Act of 1974*, 5 U.S.C. § 552a. Available on line: http://www.usdoj.gov/

The United States Senate (2002). *Financial Services Modernization Act: provisions of GLB Act.* The United States Senate publication. (Retrieved on 8/8/02 from http://www.senate.gov/~banking/conf /grmleach.htm)

Theoharidou, M., Kokolakis, S., Karyda, M., & Kiountouzis, E. (2005). The insider threat to Information Systems and the effectiveness of ISO 17799. *Computers and Security Journal, 24*(6), 472-484.

*Thomas v. Robinson*, [2001] O.J. No. 4373.

Thomas, D., & Loader, B. (2000). Introduction - Cybercrime: law enforcement, security and surveillance in the information age. In D. Thomas & B. Loader (Eds.) *Cybercrime: law enforcement, security and surveillance in the information age*. London: Routlege.

Thornton, J., & White, L. (2001). Customer orientations and usage of financial distribution channels. *Journal of Services Marketing, 15*(3), 168–185.

*Thrifty-Tel, Inc. v. Bezenek*, 46 Cal. App. 4th 1559 (1996)

*Ticketmaster Corp. v. Tickets.com, Inc.*, 2000 U.S. Dist. LEXIS 12987 (C.D. Cal. Mar. 7, 2000).

Title 18 Crimes and Criminal Procedure § 2510-2521, U.S.C. § 2510-2521 (2007).

Title 47 Telegraphs, Telephones, and Radiotelegraphs § 605, U.S.C. § 605 (2006).

Transcrime Research Centre (2002). University of Trento *Transatlantic Agenda EU/US Co-operation for Preventing Computer Related Crime – Final Report.*

Treasury Board of Canada Secretariat (1999). *Digital Signature and Confidentiality - Certificate Policies for the Government of Canada Public Key Infrastructure. Government of Canada (GOC), PKI Certificate Policies version 3.02.*

Trott, B., & Jones, J. (April 2, 2001). Industry tows the privacy-CRM line. *InfoWorld.* Retrieved March 11, 2004, from www.infoworld.com

TrustE. (2008). Retrieved January 6, 2008, from http://www.truste.org/about/index.php

Tsamardinos, I., Aliferis, C.F., & Statnikov, A. (2003). Time and Sample Efficient Discovery of Markov Blankets and Direct Causal Relations. *9th ACM SIGKDD International Conference on Knowledge Discovery and Data Mining.* USA: ACM Press, (pp. 673-678).

Tsatsos, D., & Kontiadis, X. (2001). *The Constitution of Greece.* Athens: Ant. N. Sakkoulas.

Tsoukalas, L., & Uhrig, R. (1997). *Fuzzy and Neural Approaches in Engineering.* New York: John Wiley & Sons.

*Turner v. Telus Communications*, [2005] F.C.J. No. 1981.

*U.N. Resolution 45/95* of 14 December 1990.

UK Parliamentary Office of Science and technology (2001, November). *Biometrics & Security, 165.*

UK Presidency Paper (2005). *Liberty and Security – Striking the right balance*, Paper by the UK Presidency of the European Union. Retrieved on November 23, 2008 from http://www.edri.org/docs/UKpresidencypaper.pdf.

Union de Fabricants (2003). *Counterfeiting & organized crime.* Retrieved from: http://www.interpol.int/public/financialcrime/intellectualproperty/publications/UDF-Counterfeiting.pdf

*US Computer Fraud and Abuse Act* (CFAA), 18 USC ss 1030.

Vacca, J. R. (2005). *Computer Forensics: Computer Crime Scene Investigation.* Massachusetts: Charles River Media.

van der Meer, K., & Uijlenbroek, J. (1996). The possibilities of electronic document management for supporting *ad hoc* processes: A case study. *DLM-Forum on Electronic Records.* Brussels. (pp. 249-259).

Van Eecke, P., Pinto, P., & Egyedi, T. (2007). *EU Study on the specific policy needs for ICT standardisation. Final Report. Brussels, July 2007. (Ref. ENTR/05/059).* Brussels, Belgium; DG Enterprise, European Commission. [Retrieved on October 21, 2007, from http://www.ictstandardisation.eu/]

*Vanderbeke v. Royal Bank of Canada*, [2006] F.C.J. No. 871.

Verhoeff, J. (1980). Is de chip in de hand te houden? (Can we keep a grip on the chip?). In *Spectrum Yearbook 1980*. Utrecht, Holland: Het Spectrum.

VerSteeg, R. (1994). Law in Ancient Egyptian Fiction. *Georgia Journal of International and Comparative Law*, (24), 37.

Voloshynovskiy, S., Herrigel, A., Baumgaertner, N., & Pun, T. (1999). A stochastic approach to content adaptive digital image watermarking. *Proc. of IWIH*, Dresden, Germany.

Von Neumann, J. (1958). *The Computer and the Brain.* Yale University.

Wagner, R. P. (2005). On Software Regulation. *Southern California Law, Review* (78), 457.

Walsh, E. (1999). *Technology Overview: Internet Banking: Perspective.* DPRO-90293, Gartner.

Walsh, E. (2002). *Product Report: Sl Corporate Suite e-Banking Software*. DPRO-95913 (Gartner Research Group.

Wang, H.-J. M., Su, P.-C., & Kuo, C.-C. J. (1998). Wavelet-based digital image watermarking. *Optics Express, 3*(12), 491-496.

Ward, J. (2003). *Towards a Culture of Security*, Information Security Bulletin, February 2003.

Warner, J. (2005). The right to oblivion: Data retention from Canada to Europe in Three backward Steps. *University of Ottawa law & technology journal, 2.*

Warner, R (2002). Border Disputes: Trespass to Chattels on the Internet. *Villanova Law Review*, (47), 117.

Warren, S. D. & Brandeis, L. D. (1890). The right to privacy. *Harvard Law Review*, 4, 193-220.

Warrer, M. J. (2003). The impact of hackers. In *Proceedings of the Second European Conference on Information Warfare and Security*, University of Reading, United Kingdom, June 30 - 1 July 2003.

Watson, G. (n.d.). E-mail surveillance in the UK workplace – a management consulting case study. *In Aslib Proceedings, MCB UP Ltd. 54*(1), 23-40.

Webcentric Hosting Review. (2008). *Consumers, legislators, and internet service and hosting providers wage war on spam*. Retrieved from http://webcentric-hosting.com/articles/consumers.legislators.and.html

Weber, M. (1968). *Economy and Society. An Outline of Interpretive Sociology*, New York, New York: Bedminster Press.

Weber, R. (2002). *Regulatory Models for the Online World.* Zurich, Switzerland: Schulthess Juristische Medien.

Weihrauch. (1988). Der Morris-Wurm im Internet. *Datenschutz-Berater*, 12, 1 et seq.

Weill, P., & Ross, J. (2005, Winter). A matrixed approach to designing IT governance. *MIT Sloan Management Review, 46*(2), 26-34.

Weinberg, J. (2007). *Tracking RFID.* Retrieved from http: //www.law.wayne.edu.

Weintraub, J. (1997). The theory and politics of public-private distinction. In J. Weintraub, & K. Kumar (Eds.), *Public and Private in thought and practice: perspectives on a grand dichotomy* (pp. 1-42), Chicago: University of Chicago Press.

Weir, C. S., Anderson, J. N., & Jack, M. A. (2006). On the role of metaphor and language in design of third party payments in eBanking: Usability and quality. *International Journal of Human– Computer Studies, 64*, 770–784.

Wells-Branscomb, A. (1995). Anonymity, Autonomy and Accountability: challenges to the First Amendment in Cyberspace. *The Yale Law Journal, 104*(5), 1639-1679.

Westin, A. (1967). *Privacy and Freedom.*

Westin, A. F. (1967). *Privacy and Freedom.* New York: Atheneum.

Whitworth, B., & Whitworth, E. (2004). Spam and the Social-Technical Gap. *IEEE Computer, 37*(10), 38-45.

Wilkinson, P. (1975). *Political Terrorismn.* ew York: Halstead Press.

Wimmer, M., & Bredow, B. v. (2002). Sicherheitskonzepte fur e-Government. *Datenschutz und Datensicherheit*, (9), 536-541.

Winn, J. K. (2004). Crafting a License to Know from a Privilege to Access. *Washington Law Review*, (79), 285.

*Working document on data protection issues related to RFID technology*, January 19, 2005. Article 29 Data Protection Working Party on the protection of individuals regarding to the processing of personal data. Retrieved from http://www.europa .eu.int./comm/privacy

WP 100 (2004). Article 29 Working Party. *Opinion on More Harmonised Information Provisions*. November, 25, 2004.

WP 112 (2004). *Article 29 Working Party, Opinion on Implementing the Council Regulation (EC) No 2252/2004 of 13 December 2004 on standards for security features and biometrics in passports and travel documents issued by Member States.*

WP 68 (2003). *Article 29 Working Party, Working Document on on-line authentication services, adopted on 29 January 2003.*

WP 80 (2003). *Article 29 Data Protection Working Party, Working Document on biometrics, adopted on 1 August 2003.*

Wu, T. (2003). When Code Isn't Law. *Virginia Law Review*, (89), 679.

Xie, L., & Arce, G. R. (1998). Joint wavelet compression and authentication watermarking. *Proc. of IEEE ICIP.*

Yakhlef, A. (2001). Does the Internet compete with or complement bricks and mortar bank branches? *International Journal of Retail and Distribution Management, 29*(6), 272–281.

Yeh, A. (2004). China Now World's Number Two Spam Recipient, After United States. *Privacy and Security Law Report, 3*(13), 361.

Yu, D., & Sattar, F. (2003). A new blind image watermarking technique based on independent component analysis. *Springer-Verlag Lecture Notes in Computer Science, 2613*, 51-63.

Yu, D., Sattar, F., & Ma, K.-K. (2002). Watermark detection and extraction using independent component analysis method. *EURASIP Journal on Applied Signal Processing -- Special Issue on Nonlinear Signal and Image Processing (Part II).*

Zachman, J.A., (1987). A framework for information systems architecture. *IBM Systems Journal, 26*(3) 276-292.

Zhu, K. (2007). Bringing Neutrality to Network Neutrality. *Berkeley Tech Law Journal, 22*, 615.

# About the Contributors

**Dionysios Politis** is an assistant professor of the Multimedia Lab, in the Department of Informatics, Aristotle University of Thessaloniki. He has earned his BS in Physics (1987), MSc in Radio Engineering and Electronics (1990), and PhD in Computer Science (1998) from the same University. He is a holder of a Graduate Diploma in Computing Studies (1991) from RMIT University as a scholar of the Australian Government. He has been a collaborator of the Centre of International and European Economic Law (1992-2002) and has participated in various computer law projects, mainly focusing on the pre-accession route of South Eastern Europe countries to EU integration. His research interests focus on multimedia reconstructions and visualizations, mainly with an e-Learning orientation. He has edited, published or presented more than 60 books, chapters in books, journals, magazines, newspapers, radio-television emissions and international conferences.

**Phaedon Kozyris,** professor of law, emeritus, Universities of Thessaloniki, Greece, and Ohio State, USA. Subjects: Corporations, conflict of law, jurisprudence, international transactions, communications . Member of American Society of Comparative Law. Author of many articles in legal periodicals. Co-editor and author of two chapters in *Introduction to Greek Law* (3rd ed. Kluwer).

**Ioannis Iglezakis** is an assistant professor at the Aristotle University in Thessaloniki and attorney at law at the Thessaloniki Bar Association. He was born in Thessaloniki in 1965. He graduated from the Aristotle University in Thessaloniki in 1987 and received his PhD from the same university in 2000. He has Master's of laws from the Aristotle University in Thessaloniki (1990) and from the University of Hanover, Germany (1993). He is the author of books related to IT and public and EU law (in Greek) and has various publications in Greek, German and English legal reviews, on issues related to IT law, public, economic and EU law. He is the co-author of *Cyberlaw* (Hellas), Kluwer Law Editions.

* * *

**Ajith Abraham** is working with the Norwegian University of Science and Technology, Norway. He works in a multi-disciplinary environment involving computational intelligence, network security, sensor networks, e-commerce, Web intelligence, Web services, computational grids, data mining and applied to various real world problems. He has authored/co-authored over 400 refereed journal/conference papers and book chapters and some of the works have also won best paper awards at international conferences and also received several citations. More information at: http://www.softcomputing.net

**Christina Akrivopoulou** lives in Thessaloniki, Greece. She is attorney of law and doctor of constitutional law in the Aristotle University of Thessaloniki. Her thesis analyzes the Greek constitutional protection of privacy. She has published papers, articles and comments in English. Among them, "Taking private law seriously in the application of Constitutional Rights", in *Human Rights and the Private Sphere* (eds Oliver Dawn & Jörg Fedtke), Routledge, 2007 and "Validity and effect of Constitutional Rights in interpersonal relations" *European Review of Public Law*, Vol. 19, No 3, 2007.

**Ioannis P. Chochliouros** is a telecommunications electrical engineer, graduated from the Polytechnic School of the Aristotle University of Thessaloniki, Greece, holding also a MSc & a PhD from the University *Pierre et Marie Curie*, Paris VI, France. He possesses an extreme research and practical experience in a great variety of matters for modern electronic communications. He currently works as the head of the Research Programs Section of the Hellenic Telecommunications Organization S.A. (OTE) in Greece, where he has been involved in different national, European and international R&D projects and market-oriented activities, many of which have received international awards. He is coordinator of OTE's research activities in the scope of recent European (and national) initiatives for the promotion and the deployment of innovative services/facilities, with emphasis given on Future Internet related issues. He has published more than 125 distinct scientific and business papers and reports in the international literature (books, book chapters, journals-magazines, conferences and workshops), especially for technical, business and regulatory options arising from innovative e-Infrastructures and e-Services, in a global converged environment. He is a member of several national and international scientific committees.

**Stergios P. Chochliouros** is an independent consultant, specialist for environmental-related studies, and holding a PhD from the Dept. of Biology of the University of Patras, Greece, and a University Degree as an agriculturist. He has gained enormous experiences as an academic researcher and has been involved in various research activities, especially including options for extended use and/or applicability of modern technologies. In particular, he has participated, as an expert, in many European research projects, relevant to a variety of environmental studies. Moreover, he has gained significant experience both as educator and advisor, while he is author of various papers, studies and reports.

**Richard De Mulder** (1946) is a professor of computers and law at the Erasmus University, one of the leading universities in Europe, situated in Rotterdam, the Netherlands. He is a law graduate of the University of Amsterdam and he holds a PhD in computers and law from the Erasmus University. He also holds an MBA (with honors) from the Simon Business School at the University of Rochester in New York. His teaching and research interests are multi- and interdisciplinary, generally involving law, technology, and management. Areas of particular expertise include computer law; computer science and law (legal expert systems and conceptual legal information retrieval); jurimetrics (the empirical, quantitative study of the law); law and management; safety and security in society; and technology, leadership and innovation. Dr. De Mulder is a member of various research institutes, and he serves on the legal tools expert committee of the International Criminal Court in The Hague. Current research projects include "Eyewitmem", an interdisciplinary research initiative financed by the European Union (6th Framework) that aims to produce a means for testing the reliability of eyewitness statements. In addition to his academic work, Dr. De Mulder is the director of Andromatics.com, which produces software for information retrieval, marking assignments, and identifying plagiarism and academic fraud. He lives in Rotterdam and is married with three children.

**Prescott C. Ensign**, PhD, is an assistant professor at the Telfer School of Management, University of Ottawa, Ontario, Canada. He is a Fulbright Scholar and has been recognized for excellence in teaching and research. Ensign has written articles on the strategy and structure of enterprise, and his current work investigates innovative efforts of entrepreneurs in high-growth, technology based firms and entry strategies in emerging markets.

**Manish Gupta** is an information security professional at a Northeast US based financial institution and also a PhD candidate at State University of New York at Buffalo. He has more than ten years of experience in information systems, security policies and technologies. He has published 3 books in the area of information security, ethics and assurance. He has published more than 30 research articles in leading journals, conference proceedings and books including DSS, ACM Transactions, IEEE and JOEUC. He serves in editorial boards of six international journals. He is a member of ACM, AIS, IEEE, INFORMS, APWG, ISACA and ISC2. His research interests are in social, human and economic issues of information security.

**Maria Karyda** holds a BSc in informatics, an MSc in information systems and a PhD in information systems security management from the Athens University of Economics and Business, Greece. She is currently a lecturer with the University of the Aegean, Greece, Department of Information and Communication Systems Engineering. Her research interests include organizational aspects of information systems security management, privacy protection, computer crime and digital forensics and security culture and awareness issues. Her published work includes several referred papers in international journals and conferences, as well as six chapters in books. She has also served as a reviewer for international journals and has participated in the programme and organizing committees of several international conferences in the area of information systems and information security. She is a member of the ACM, IEEE, AIS and the Greek Computer Society.

**Pieter Kleve** (1954) started his professional career as a salesman of computers and telecommunication systems. When he finished his (evening) law study at Erasmus University Rotterdam, in 1985, he started working as a lecturer and researcher in the field of computers and law, with a special emphasis on computer law. At the same time, he started with a marketing consultancy agency, integrating law, management and information technology, which he ended in 2000 to start writing his PhD. In 2004 he published his thesis on 'legal icons in the information society', about the uselessness of the enormous amount of legislation related to information technology, for the characterisation of which he introduced the term 'phantom law'. Dr. Kleve teaches computer law at law students, students business administration and computer science students. His research interest lies particularly in the fields of innovation, the development of the information society and safety and security in society, from the multi- and interdisciplinary perspective of law, management and technology. He is specialised in intellectual property law, e-commerce, constitutional rights and computer crime.

**Pavel Krömer** has received master degree in computer science from the VSB - Technical University of Ostrava in 2006. Since then, he is graduate student at the Dept. of Computer Science, VSB - Technical

University of Ostrava. Pavel's area of interest includes computational intelligence, information retrieval, World Wide Web and data mining. His work focuses on development of innovative techniques as well as deployment of intelligent methods in different application domains. He coauthored and presented award winning papers at international computer science conferences in 2007 and 2008.

**Greg Lastowka** is an associate professor at Rutgers School of Law-Camden. He teaches courses in the laws of property, intellectual property, and the regulation of technology. His current research project is a book about law and online communities. He publishes regularly on internet law and intellectual property issues.

**Richard V. McCarthy** (MBA, Western New England College, DBA, Nova Southeastern University) is the associate dean and a professor of information systems management at the School of Business, Quinnipiac University. Prior to this, Dr. McCarthy was an associate professor of management information systems at Central Connecticut State University. He has twenty years of experience within the insurance industry and has held a charter property casualty underwriter (CPCU) designation since 1991. He has authored numerous research and pedagological information systems journal articles and contributed to the several textbooks. His current research interest is in the area of enterprise architecture.

**Andreas Mitrakas** (andreas@mitrakas.com) is head of Administration Department at the European Network and Information Security Agency (ENISA). He has previously been senior counsel at Ubizen (a Cybertrust company) and general counsel at GlobalSign, (Vodafone Group). His research interests include the legal and organisational implications of technology in business and government. He is a qualified attorney (Athens Bar) and in the past he was visiting lecturer at the University of Westminster and the Athens University for Economics and Business. He is chair of the CEN/ISSS standardisation workshop on cyber-identity for business. He has (co)authored over a hundred peer-reviewed publications including *Open EDI and law in Europe: A regulatory framework* (Kluwer, 1997). More recently he co-edited the volume *Secure eGovernment Web Services* (IGI, 2007). He holds a Doctorate in electronic commerce and the law from Erasmus University of Rotterdam, a Master's in computers and law from Queen's University of Belfast, a law degree from the University of Athens and a Diploma in project management from ParisTech (Grandes Ecoles d'Ingenieurs de Paris).

**Jan Platoš** has received bachelor degree in computer science from the VSB - Technical University of Ostrava in 2005 and Master's degree in computer science from the VSB - Technical University of Ostrava in 2006. Since then, he is graduate student at the Dept. of Computer Science, VSB - Technical University of Ostrava. Jan is interested in data compression, computational intelligence, data security and information retrieval. His work is focused on development of new and innovative methods for data compression, as well as deployment of intelligent methods in different application domains.

**H. Raghav Rao** is a professor of MIS and an adjunct professor of CSE at SUNY Buffalo.

**Judith Rauhofer** qualified as a solicitor in 1999, having previously qualified as a Rechtsanwalt in Germany. She practised as a solicitor for five years, specialising in data protection, e-commerce and general commercial law. She currently works as a research fellow for law, information and converging technologies at the University of Central Lancashire. Her research interests include data retention, data protection, privacy/social control issues arising in the context of security and anti-terrorism legislation, internet law, privacy issues arising from new technologies (biometrics, RFID, etc).

**Nicholas P. Robinson**, BComm, BCL, LLB is a graduate of the Faculty of Law of McGill University. Robinson has written a number of case studies and research papers on international management, marketing, public policy, and law. Robinson founded and ran an e-business, and worked for the online music store Puretracks. He resides in Canada, and he is affiliated with McGill University.

**Farook Sattar** is a faculty member at the Information Engineering Division of Nanyang Technological University, Singapore. He has received his Technical Licentiate and PhD degrees in signal and image processing from Lund University, Sweden. His current research interests include signal and image processing for multimedia and biomedicine. He has training in both signal and image processing, and had been involved in a number of signal and image processing related projects sponsored by Swedish National Science & Technology Board (NUTEK) and Singapore Academic Research Funding (AcRF) Scheme. His research has been published in a number of leading journals and conferences.

**Anastasia S. Spiliopoulou** is a lawyer, possessing a Post-Graduate Diploma in Internet-related studies from the Athens University Law School, where she currently exercises research activities as a PhD candidate. As a lawyer, she is member of the Athens Bar Association in Greece. During the latest years, she had a major participation in matters related to telecommunications & broadcasting policy, in Greece and abroad, within the wider framework of the information society. She has been involved in current legal, research and business activities, as a specialist for e-commerce and e-businesses, electronic signatures, e-contracts, e-procurement, e-security and other modern information society applications. She has published more than 90 scientific and business papers in the international literature (books, book chapters, journals, conferences and workshops), with specific emphasis given on regulatory, business, commercial and social aspects. She also works as lawyer-partner of the Hellenic Telecommunications Organization S.A. (OTE) in the General Directorate for Regulatory Affairs, Dept. for Regulatory Framework Issues, where she has been efficiently involved in a various regulatory issues, with impact on business and market related matters.

**Tatiana-Eleni Synodinou,** Attorney-at- law, member of the Bar Office of Thessaloniki since September 2000. Postgraduate studies in media law (DEA droit des médias, France). Doctor in Law, copyright law. Postdoctoral studies also in copyright law. Author of three books: *The Legal Protection of Databases* (2004); *The Legal Protection of Image* (2007); *Copyright Law and the New Technologies* (2008). Author of various articles in the field of intellectual property law and information law. Scientific expert in EU programs Scientific collaborator of Kluwer Law International as a case law reporter.

**Aris Stylianou**, assistant professor of political philosophy in the School of Political Sciences (Faculty of Law, Economics and Political Sciences, Aristotle University of Thessaloniki). He studied philosophy at the Aristotle University of Thessaloniki, continued his studies at the postgraduate level at the Paris-IV University and received his doctorate from Paris-I at Sorbonne. He has taught at the Schools of Journalism and Mass Media (1995-1997) and Philosophy and Pedagogy (1997-2002), and at the School of Political Sciences of the Aristotle University of Thessaloniki from 2002 onwards. His research interests include political philosophy and political theory, as well as translation. His publications include: *Histoire et* *politique chez Spinoza*, Lille, 1994; 'Spinoza et le temps historique', *Les Études Philosophiques* (1997); 'Spinoza et l'histoire antique', *Studia Spinozana* (2001); *Social Contract Theories. From Grotius to Rousseau* (Polis, Athens 2006). He has edited 'Spinoza: Towards Freedom', *Axiologika*, special issue 2 (Exantas, Athens 2002). He has translated and edited philosophical texts.

**S. Upadhyaya** is an associate professor of CSE and director of the Center of Excellence in Information Systems Assurance Research and Education at SUNY Buffalo.

**Kees (C.) van Noortwijk** studied law with a strong emphasis on information science. He started working as a researcher at Erasmus University Rotterdam in 1984. He was involved in the development of more than a dozen 'computer advice systems', which where brought onto the market in 1986 under the name 'JURICAS'. He then started to perform research on legal word use and other characteristics of legal text. This research resulted in a thesis called 'Het woordgebruik meester' (Legal Word Use - a comparison of some quantitative aspects of the word use in legal and general Dutch texts) in 1995. Dr. Van Noortwijk is now a senior lecturer and researcher at Erasmus University. He teaches subjects such as 'computers and law' and 'legal knowledge management' to law students, as well as several post-graduate courses. Research projects he has been involved in recently include the development of conceptual legal information retrieval systems and of software that can serve as an aid in correcting 'open question' exams and assignments.

**Irini E. Vassilaki** is attorney-at-law in Athens specialising in information law, media criminal law and economic criminal law and associate professor at the Faculty of Law of the University of Goettingen since 2002, where she is teaching IT-criminal law and legal informatics. She is member of several international boards, such as the legal advisory board of the EU, in committees of the Council of Europe and of UN and member of the executive board of national associations, e.g. the German Association for Law and Informatics, German Foundation for Law and Informatics and the Greek Scientific Council for the Information Society, that work on the area of law and informatics. Dr. Vassilaki is additionally member of the board of editors of scientific journals (e.g. *Computer Law and Security Report, Computer und Recht, Kommunikation und Recht, Recht der Datenverarbeitung, IT-Rechts-Berater, European Review for ICT/Law*). With an international experience of 20 years and more than 100 publications Dr. Vassilaki belongs to the groundbreaking European lawyers in the area of Information Law. The native language of Dr. Vassilaki is Greek; she also speaks German, English, French, Italian, Spanish and Dutch.

**Konstantinos N. Voudouris** is an assistant professor on wireless telecommunication systems within the Department of Electronics of the Technological Educational Institute (TEI) of Athens. His work experience is extensive in the field of telecommunications, initially, as an academic postdoctoral research fellow in the University of Kent at Canterbury, UK (1990-1993), then as a telecoms expert within the incumbent telecom operator in Greece – OTE (1996-2000). In 2000 he joined the Greek telecom regulator (EETT) and the next year he was appointed as advisor to the deputy-minister of transports and telecommunications. From Oct. 2001 to Sept. 2004 he served as embassy counsellor, within the permanent representation of Greece to the European Union in Brussels, responsible for telecommunications and information society. Furthermore, he served as member of the ENISA Board and chaired the European Council Working Party on Telecommunications & Information Society Services. Dr. Voudouris has published over 30 scientific papers in international journals and conferences in the areas of broadband wireless communications subsystems design, microstrip patch antennae, microwave measurements, and *e*Applications.

**Dan Yu** is a project manager in HP Global Delivery China Center (GDCC), in Shanghai, P. R. of China. She received her BEng (1st Class Honors) in communication engineering in 2000, and obtained her PhD degree in image processing and information security in 2005, both from Nanyang Technological University, Singapore. Then she held a one-year post-doc position in INRIA, France. She has been involved in various image processing and pattern recognition projects as researcher and developer in past several years. Her research interests include digital watermarking, texture classification and segmentation, license plate recognition, face recognition and verification.

**Damián Zaitch** (zaitch@frg.eur.nl) is lecturer and researcher at the Department of Criminology, Erasmus University Rotterdam. He has for the past 10 years researched and published on organised crime and drug policies in the Netherlands and Latin America. He obtained his PhD (2001, *cum laude*) at the Amsterdam School for Social Science Research, University of Amsterdam, with an ethnographic research on Colombians involved in the cocaine business in the Netherlands (Trafficking Cocaine (2002), Springer) for which he obtained the Willem Nagel Prize in 2003. He is currently focusing his interests on various forms of cross-border, transnational organised and corporate crime. He is founding member of CIROC, the Centre for Information and Research on Organised Crime.

# Index

## K



## L



## M



## N



## O



## P



## R



## S